MECHANICAL AND ELECTRICAL SYSTEMS

IN CONSTRUCTION AND ARCHITECTURE

Second Edition

MECHANICAL AND ELECTRICAL SYSTEMS

IN CONSTRUCTION AND ARCHITECTURE

Second Edition

Frank R. Dagostino

Registered Architect
Architectural and Construction Consultant
Instructor
Trident Technical College
Charleston, South Carolina

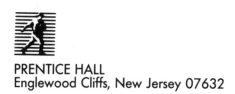

PRENTICE HALL
Englewood Cliffs, New Jersey 07632

Library of Congress Cataloging-in-Publication Data

Dagostino, Frank R.
    Mechanical and electrical systems in construction
and architecture / Frank R. Dagostino.—2nd ed.
      p. cm.
    ISBN 0-13-571308-0
    1. Buildings—Mechanical equipment. 2. Buildings
—Electric equipment. I. Title.
TH6010.D33 1991
696—dc20   89-38868
                                            CIP

National Electrical Code® and NEC® are registered
trademarks of the National Fire Protection Association,
Inc., Quincy, MA 02269.

Editorial/production supervision: *Ann L. Mohan*
Cover design: *Wanda Lubelska*
Manufacturing buyer: *Lori Bulwin*

 © 1991, 1978 by Prentice-Hall, Inc.
A Division of Simon & Schuster
Englewood Cliffs, New Jersey 07632

Printed in the United States of America
10 9 8 7 6 5 4 3 2 1

ISBN 0-13-571308-0

Prentice-Hall International (UK) Limited, *London*
Prentice-Hall of Australia Pty. Limited, *Sydney*
Prentice-Hall Canada Inc., *Toronto*
Prentice-Hall Hispanoamericana, S.A., *Mexico*
Prentice-Hall of India Private Limited, *New Delhi*
Prentice-Hall of Japan, Inc., *Tokyo*
Simon & Schuster Asia Pte. Ltd., *Singapore*
Editora Prentice-Hall do Brasil, Ltda., *Rio de Janeiro*

CONTENTS

PREFACE

This text is geared for use by the entire construction industry—from those interested in the actual design of the systems to those who realize they must know and understand the mechanical systems in order to successfully design, draw or build a building or project.

The second edition has been updated to include all of the latest code and association design revisions in each area of the text. The designer must check the code requirements in the area where the building will be constructed and use that code in designing the system.

The mechanical equipment covered in this book is an integral part of the design and construction of all buildings and projects built. Its *successful* integration into the design depends upon the close cooperation of the designer, the draftsmen, the mechanical systems designer, the general construction contractor and each of the contractors who may install a portion of the mechanicals.

To be successful, each of these people or groups of people must be familiar with the requirements of the mechanical systems. Each should at least be familiar with the basic design procedures used, flexibilities in each system, space required and the time at which such work must be done on the job so it is fully coordinated. To get an idea of the coordination, consider each step briefly.

The designer must consider whether the layout provides space for the equipment required by the heating system (ducts, pipes, radiation devices, etc.), the water supply and drainage systems and the electrical system.

The architectural (general construction) draftsman must be certain that the details allow for the inclusion of the mechanicals, that the walls are wide enough for pipes to pass through, that there is enough space for the ducts to run and that soffits are provided where required to conceal pipes.

The mechanical systems designers must work closely with all of the others. During the design stage, they must work with the designer and the owner to analyze what the requirements of the project are and to be certain that the designer incorporates the systems required in the design. Next, they must coordinate the mechanical systems designed with the draftsman who will draw the system up. This drafter may be working right with them or be in a separate part of the architectural designer's office. If this is a different drafter from those working on the general construction drawings, their efforts will have to be coordinated. Once the project is under construction, they will be involved in the coordination of the mechanical drawings, the general contractor, and the mechanical contractor.

The mechanical drafter may or may not be the same drafter doing the general construction drawings. The drafter must be careful to check against the general construction drawings to be certain that there is sufficient space for all of the mechanicals required.

The general construction contractor, and all the workers, must be certain that the mechanical contractors have adequate notice and opportunity to install their work as the project proceeds. There will be pipe sleeves in foundation walls, conduit and pipes in concrete floors, conduit and boxes in masonry walls, cable and boxes in stud walls before the wall boards are installed—and many, many other installations that require coordination.

Mechanical contractors are specialists in the field, tested and licensed by the government. Their staff will do an estimate on the mechanicals, submit bids and, if they are successful bidders, install the mechanical systems. Generally, these contractors are separated into three groups: plumbing; electrical; and heating, ventilation and air conditioning contractors. There may be separate contractors for each of these, and quite often a firm may bid plumbing and heating, ventilation and air conditioning.

Because all of these people are involved, and because the mechanicals must fit into the construction of the building, it is important that the entire construction "team" be familiar with the mechanical systems and their principles of design.

The basic format of this text is to discuss the chapter topic, describe the materials available and then show, step-by-step, how to approach a design problem. In those chapters that describe how to design a system, an actual design has been worked out.

For easy reference, the charts and tables used in the designs have been located at the end of each chapter. In addition, examples of how to use the charts and tables are contained in the chapters.

It has been the goal of this book to explain, step-by-step, the process of designing the mechanical systems, and how to accumulate and tabulate the design information. Where it is applicable, the text not only discusses how to design a system but also what to look out for, what the variables are.

In addition, this book provides a basis for all members of the construction team to be able to search through the tremendous amount of claims and counterclaims by salesmen, industry representatives, and manufacturers' representatives—and to separate fact from fiction.

Frank R. Dagostino

MECHANICAL AND ELECTRICAL SYSTEMS

IN CONSTRUCTION AND ARCHITECTURE

Second Edition

CHAPTER 1

WATER SUPPLY

1-1   WATER

Basically, water may be *potable* (suitable for human drinking) or *nonpotable* (not suitable for human drinking). While an abundant supply of water is vital to a prosperous economy, on an individual basis a supply of potable water is even more important to survival than food. This potable water must be supplied, or be available, for drinking and cooking. Nonpotable water may be used for flushing water closets (toilets), watering grass and gardens, washing cars, irrigating farms, and for any use other than drinking or cooking.

At this time potable water is commonly used for many activities that could be done with nonpotable water. As potable water becomes scarcer and as the cost of treating nonpotable water to make it potable increases, less and less potable water will be wasted by using it where nonpotable water will adequately serve. Already in some communities the cost of potable water is so high that many of the residents have shallow wells that provide them with the water to water their lawns and gardens and to wash their cars.

1

1-2 WATER SOURCES

Rain is the source of most of the water available for our use, and it is classified as *surface water* or *groundwater*. Surface water is the rain that runs off the surface of the ground into streams, rivers, and lakes. Groundwater is the water that percolates (seeps) through the soil, building the supply of water below the surface of the earth.

Surface water readily provides much of the water needed by cities, counties, large industry, and others. However, this source is dependent on rain, and during a drought, the flow of water may be significantly reduced. Most surface water will probably have to be treated to provide the potable water required. Where nonpotable water is required, such as for irrigating farms, no treatment of the water may be necessary.

Also classified as surface water is rain which may be collected in a small reservoir or tank (cistern) (Fig. 1-1) as it drains from the roof of a building. This water is then pumped into the supply line of the building for use. The need for water is so critical on certain islands that the government has covered part of the land surface (usually the side of a mountain or a hill facing the direction from which the rains usually come) with a plastic so that rain may be collected and stored for later use.

As groundwater percolates through the soil, it forms a water level below the surface of the earth. This water level, is referred to as the *water table*. The distance from the ground surface to the water table (referred to as the *depth* of the water table) varies considerably; generally the more rainfall an area gets, the higher the water table will be. During a dry spell the water table will usually go down, while during a rainy season it will probably rise.

Since the water table is formed by an accumulation of water over an impervious stratum (a layer of earth, usually rock, that the water cannot pass through), the flow of the water follows the irregular path of the stratum, sometimes moving close to the surface while dropping off nearby (Fig. 1-2). This underground supply of water flows horizontally, and if it reaches a low spot in the ground surface, it may flow as a spring

FIGURE 1-1 / Cistern

FIGURE 1-2 / Water table

or seep out creating a swampy area. Or, if the flowing underground water becomes confined between impervious strata, enough pressure may be built up in the water that if opened (by drilling through the top stratum or by a natural opening in the stratum), it will create an artesian well.

Groundwater may require treatment to provide potable water, *but* often it does not. When treatment is required, it is generally less treatment than is required when making surface water potable.

The increased use (and misuse) of our potable water supply has forced the development of additional sources of water. This need for potable water has led to the desalination (taking the salt out) of water from the oceans and the purification of waste (sewage) water to be returned to the water system for reuse. To date, these methods involve a great deal of additional cost compared with the use and treatment of surface and groundwater.

1-3   IMPURITIES

All water sources contain some impurities. It is the type and amount of these impurities which may affect the water's suitability for particular use.

As surface water runs over the ground, it may pick up various organic matter such as algae, fungi, bacteria, vegetable matter, animal decay and wastes, garbage wastes, and sewage.

As groundwater percolates down through the soil, it dissolves minerals such as calcium, iron, silica, sulphates, fluorides, and nitrates, and it may also entrap gases such as sulfide, sulphur dioxide, and carbon dioxide. It may also pick up contamination from public or private underground garbage and sewage wastes. Generally, as it percolates, it will filter out any organic matter which may have been accumulated at the surface or in the ground.

The impurities in the water may be harmful, of no importance or even beneficial to a person's health. To determine what is in the water it must be tested.

1-4   TESTS

All potable water supplies should be tested before being put in use and periodically checked during their use. It is assumed that whatever agency of a city, municipality, etc., controls the supply of water to a community regularly tests its water to be certain it is potable. Private water supplies, such as wells and streams, should always be checked before the water system is put into use and periodically thereafter.

Such tests are usually performed free of charge, or at a very low cost, by the local governmental unit in charge of public health; the governing unit (town hall, city hall, county health department) will put you in touch with the proper authorities, or it will refer you to a private testing laboratory.

The test for potable water provides a chemical analysis of the water, indicating the parts per million (ppm) of each chemical found in the water. A separate test is made for bacteriological quality of the water, providing an estimate of the density of bacteria in the water supply. Of particular concern in this test is the presence of any coliform organisms which indicate that the water supply may be contaminated with human wastes (perhaps seepage from a nearby septic tank field). Since the test reports mean little to most people, a written analysis of the test or a standardized form is included with the test results saying whether the water is potable or not.

Water may have an objectionable odor and taste, even be cloudy and slightly muddied or colored in appearance, and yet the test may show it to be potable. This may not mean you *want* to drink it, but it does mean that it is drinkable. Such problems are often overcome by use of water-conditioning equipment, such as filters. As any traveler can quickly tell you, water varies considerably from place to place, depending on the water source of the area, the chemical and bacteria contents of the water and the amount and type of treatment given the water before it is put into the system.

1-5   WATER SYSTEMS

The design of any water supply begins with a check of the water system from which the water will be obtained. Basically, water is available through systems which serve the community or through private systems.

COMMUNITY SYSTEMS

Systems which provide water to a community may be government owned, as in most cities, or privately owned, such as in a housing development where the builder or real estate developer provides and installs a central supply of water to serve the community. The water for these systems may have been obtained from any of the water sources listed in Sec. 1-2, and quite often it is drawn from more than one source. For example, part of the water may be taken from a river, and it may be supplemented by deep wells.

Before proceeding with the design of the water supply, the following information should be obtained:

1.   What is the exact location of the water main (pipe) in relation to the property being built on?

2. If the main is on the other side of the street from the property, what procedures must be followed to get permission (in writing) to cut through the street, set up barricades and patch the street? Also, what permits are required from local authorities, how much do the permits cost and who will inspect the work and when? If available, obtain the specifications (written requirements) concerning the cutting and patching of the street.

3. If the water main does not run past the property, can it be extended from its present location to the property (Fig. 1-3), and who pays for the extension?

4. Is there a charge to connect (tap) onto the community system? Many communities charge just to tap on, and the charge is often hundreds of dollars.

5. What is the pressure in the main at the property? If it is too low for a residence [less than 30 psi (pounds per square inch)], a storage tank and pump may be required to raise the pressure. Such a system is often used on commercial and industrial projects where the pressure may have to be quite high to meet the water demands. Water pressure that is too high (above 60 psi for a residence) will probably require a pressure-reducing valve in the system to cut the pressure to an acceptable level.

    Since plumbing fixtures are manufactured to operate efficiently with water pressures from about 30 to 60 psi, higher pressure may result in poor operation of the fixtures, rapid wearing out of the washers and valves and noises in the piping. Low pressure may cause certain fixtures to operate sluggishly, especially dishwashers, showers, flush valve water closets (toilets) and garden hoses. The required water pressure at various fixtures and the water pressure from the main to the fixtures are discussed in detail in Sec. 2-10 and Fig. 2-33.

6. What is the cost of the water? Typically, a water meter is installed, either out near the road or somewhere in the project, and there is a charge for the water used. After determining what the charges are, a cost analysis may show that it is

FIGURE 1-3 / Water main location

cheaper to put in a private system. Some areas do not allow private systems for potable water, but quite often it will be desirable to put in a well to provide nonpotable water for sprinkling the lawn and garden and for washing the car. Where costs for potable water are extremely high, it may be feasible to use separate potable and nonpotable water supply systems within the project (especially industrial and commercial projects).

PRIVATE SYSTEMS

Private systems may also use any of the water sources discussed in Sec. 1-2. Large industrial and commercial projects may draw all of their supply from one source, or they may draw part of their supply from one source (such as a stream) and supplement the supply with another source (such as a well). Such systems often include treatment plants, water storage towers and sometimes even lakes or reservoirs to store the water.

Small private systems, such as those used for residences, usually rely on a single source of water to supply potable water through the system. Installing a well is the most commonly used method of obtaining water, and springs may be used when one is available.

Experts, usually consulting mechanical engineers, soil engineers or water supply and treatment specialists, should be consulted early in the planning for any large project requiring its own private water system. Such specialists can make tests, interpret what the tests mean to the project and make recommendations as to the quality and amount of water available.

1-6 · WELLS

Most private water systems use wells to tap the underground water source. Wells are classified according to their depth and the method used to construct the well.

DEPTH	CONSTRUCTION METHOD
Shallow (25 ft or less)	Dug Driven Drilled
Deep (in excess of 25 ft)	Drilled Bored

The depth of the well is determined by the depth of the water table and the amount of water which can be pumped. This flow of water is considered the *yield* or capacity of the well. Once the water *demand* (the amount of water required) has been calculated (Sec. 1-9), it can be determined whether one well is enough or whether other wells will be needed to provide the required water for the project. Where the water table is high, it may not be necessary to go 25 ft deep, but it is not unusual for wells to be 100 ft deep, and in some areas well depths of several hundred feet are required to provide an adequate supply of water.

Dug wells (Fig. 1-4) should be 3 to 5 ft in diameter and not more than 20 to 25 ft deep. To minimize the chances of surface contamination, the well should have a watertight top and walls. The top should be either above the ground (Fig. 1-5) or sloped so that surface water will run away from it and not over it. The watertight walls should extend at least 10 ft down. The walls may be concrete block, poured concrete, clay tile, precast concrete tile or curved masonry units referred to as *man-hole block* (Fig. 1-6).

The water will flow into the well through the bottom of the well (and the water in the well will rise to about the level of the water table). Some wells also allow water to seep through the walls by use of porous construction near the bottom of the wall. This porous construction may be concrete block or manhole block placed without mortar (normally used to hold the blocks together and make them watertight).

The placing of washed gravel in the bottom of the well, and on the sides of the well when porous walls are used, will reduce the sand particles or discoloration in the well water. Washed gravel is gravel (stone) that has been put through a wash (water sprayed over the stone) to remove much of the sand or clay from the stone. To further protect the water from possible contamination, tightly seal around the suction line pipe where it passes through the wall. And don't take water out with a bucket or other container since it may have contamination on it, and by dipping such a container into the water, the contaminant is transferred to the water supply.

Shallow wells may also be driven. To drive a well, first attach a well point to a drive pipe and drive cap (Fig. 1-7). Then, by means of an impact loading device such as a small pile driver or even a sledge hammer for very shallow wells in soft, sandy soil, the well point is driven into the ground until it is into the water table. The well point has holes or slots in the side, allowing water to be sucked up to the surface by

FIGURE 1-4 / Dug well

FIGURE 1-5 / Dug well—top
above ground

a shallow well pump (Sec. 1-7). As the point is driven, additional lengths of pipe may be attached (usually 5-ft lengths are used) by the use of a coupling (Fig. 1-7). Driven wells will not pass through rock formations, and the maximum diameter commonly available is 2 in.

Shallow wells may have to be drilled if it is necessary to pass through rock to get to the water table.

Drilling and boring methods are used for deep wells. A well-drilling rig (Fig. 1-8) is used to form the well hole. Drilled and bored wells differ in that drilled wells have the holes formed by using rotary bits (Fig. 1-9) and spudders, while bored wells have the holes formed by using augers (Fig. 1-10). Only the drilling method is effective in passing through rock.

As the hole is formed, a casing (pipe) is lowered into the ground. This steel or wrought-iron pipe (usually 3 to 6 in. in diameter) protects the hole against cave-ins where unstable soil conditions are encountered and keeps out surface drainage and possible surface or underground contamination. To further protect against surface drainage and contamination, a concrete apron, sloping away from the well, is poured around the casing at the surface (Fig. 1-11).

Well location and construction are often controlled by governmental regulations that set minimum distances between the well and any possible ground contaminant. When certain types of construction methods are used, these regulations may even require that licensed well drillers install the well. Various authorities and governmental regulations require different minimum distances, and there is no single set of standards

FIGURE 1-6 / Manhole block

MANHOLE
BLOCK

PRECAST CONC.
TILE (PIPE)

FIGURE 1-7 / *Shallow well materials*

used. The table in Fig. 1-12 shows minimum distances required in one locale. It is important that local regulations be checked for each project.

Possible well contamination from an underground flow of contaminants through rock formations which allow free-flowing groundwater to travel long distances is always possible, especially through strata of eroded limestone. Constant testing of water quality is required wherever there is a possibility of such contamination. For the well contaminated in this manner, three methods used to eliminate the problem are water treatment, relocation of the well and elimination of the source of the contamination.

Before planning the well, local conditions should be checked to provide some background information. For example, existing local wells should be checked for depth and yield of water. This information can be obtained from local well drillers and

FIGURE 1-8 / *Well-drilling rig*

FIGURE 1-9 / Rotary bit

governmental agencies and, if possible, verified by testing existing or just completed wells.

Where insufficient information on well yields is available, and especially where large projects will require substantial water supplies, it may be necessary to have test wells made so that the yield can be checked. The well(s) should be tested by the driller to determine the yield, and a sample should be taken so that the quality of the water can be analyzed. It is important that this be done at an early stage in the design so that the size of the water storage tank can be determined (Sec. 1-9) and so that any water treatment equipment required can be designed and space allowed in the design of the project to locate the tank and equipment.

When a large supply of water is required for the continuous operation of the project, it may be necessary to put in other wells to be certain that the water yield will be sufficient to meet the projected demand (Sec. 1-9). For example, if one well

FIGURE 1-10 / Auger

FIGURE 1-11 / Drilled well

provides adequate water, it may be a good investment to have a second well put in to act as a "back-up" in case the first well should fail in some way. This is usually not done for residences, but for industries or businesses which need water to operate (such as a car wash, farm or apartment complex), it is a wise investment.

When more than one well is used, they must be spaced so that the use of one well will not lower the water table in the other well. Generally, deep wells must be 500 to 1,000 ft apart, while shallow wells must be 20 to 100 ft apart. Due to soil variables, the minimum distance between wells can be determined only by testing (usually trial and error).

Many industries and businesses which draw their water from community systems have private systems that can be put into operation in case of a water shortage due to a breakdown in the system or a prolonged drought. As an example, during a recent drought in Raleigh, N.C., a local ordinance was passed prohibiting the washing of cars. This meant that all car washes served by the community system had to close down. Imagine the relief of one owner who had a well as an alternate source of water; he was in business while all the other car washes closed. The local newspaper even carried a story on it, providing the owner with free advertising.

Type of system	Distance from well
Building sewer	50'
Septic tank	50'
Distribution box	50'
Disposal field	100'
Seepage pit	100'
Drywell	50'

FIGURE 1-12 / Well locations

1-7   PUMPS

Pumps used to bring well water to the surface are referred to as *shallow well* and *deep well,* depending on the type of well.

Shallow-well pumps are located above the ground, and a suction line extends into the well below the water table (Fig. 1-13). The pump cannot lift or pull the water up more than about 25 ft, so any well with the water table deeper than 25 ft is considered a deep well, and a deep-well pump is used. The shallow-well pumps commonly used are the shallow-well jet, rotary and reciprocating piston pumps.

The deep-well pumps most commonly used are the jet and submersible pumps. Jet pumps are located above ground, either directly over or offset from the well (Fig. 1-14). Submersible pumps have a waterproof motor and are placed in the well below the water table.

1-8   PLUMBING FIXTURES

The plumbing fixtures may be selected by the designer of the plumbing system, the architect, the owner, or a combination of these people. It is important that the designer of the plumbing system know what fixtures will be used (and even the manufacturer and model number, if possible) in order to do as accurate a job as possible in the design.

The fixtures are the only portion of the plumbing system that the owners or occupants of the building will see regularly since most of the plumbing piping is concealed in walls and floors. All fixtures should be carefully selected since they will be in use for years, perhaps for the life of the building.

The available sizes for each fixture should be carefully checked in relation to the amount of space available. Most manufacturers supply catalogs which show the dimensions of the fixtures they supply.

FIGURE 1-13 / Shallow well pump

SUCTION FROM WELL

FOR WELL LIFTS LESS THAN 25'

FIGURE 1-14 / Deep well pump

Whoever selects the fixtures should check with the local supplier to be certain that those chosen are readily available; if not, they may have to be ordered far in advance of the time they are required for installation. In addition, most of the fixtures are available in white or colors, so the color must also be selected.

Fixtures are grouped according to their use: water closets; urinals; bidets; bathtubs; showers; lavatories; kitchen sinks; and service sinks.

WATER CLOSETS

Water closets are made of solid vitrified china cast with an integral trap (Fig. 3-3 and Sec. 3-3). Water closets are available as flush tank or flush valve fixtures.

A flush tank water closet (Fig. 1-15) has a water tank as a part of the fixture. As the handle (or button) is pushed, it lifts the valve in the tank, releasing the water to

FIGURE 1-15 / Typical flush tank water closets

Two piece   One piece

"flush out" the bowl. Then, when the handle is released, the valve drops and the tank fills through a tube attached to the bottom of the tank. This type of fixture cannot be effectively flushed again until the tank is refilled. There are several types of flushing action available on water closets, as illustrated in Fig. 1-16.

Flush tank models range from those having the tank as a separate unit set on the closet bowl to those having a low tank silhouette with the tank cast as an integral part of the water closet. Generally, this low-slung appearance is preferred by clients, but it is considerably more expensive.

Flush valve water closets (Fig. 1-17) have no tank to supply water. Instead, when the handle is pushed, the water to flush the bowl comes directly from the water supply system at a high rate of flow. When used, it is important that the water supply system be designed to supply the high flow required. While most of the fixtures operate effectively at 20 psi pressure, the manufacturer's specifications should be checked, since higher pressure is often required and must be considered in the design.

Water closets may be floor or wall mounted, as shown in Figs. 1-17 and 1-18. The floor-mounted fixture is much less expensive in terms of initial cost, but the wall-mounted fixture allows easier and generally more effective cleaning of the floor. Wall-mounted fixtures are considered desirable for public use, and some codes even require their use in public places. When wall-mounted fixtures are used in wood stud walls, a 2-in. × 6-in. stud will be required instead of the 2-in. × 4-in. stud sometimes used with floor-mounted fixtures.

Washdown
Least expensive
Least efficient
Noisiest

Reverse trap
Efficient
Moderately noisy

Siphon jet
Efficient
Fairly quiet

Siphon jet
Quietest
Most expensive

FIGURE 1-16 / Types of flushing action

Floor mounted   Wall mounted

FIGURE 1-17 / Flush valve water closets

URINALS

Urinals are commonly used in public restrooms where it is desirable to reduce any possible contamination of the water closet seats. They are commonly available in vitreous china and sometimes in enameled iron. They may be flush tank or flush valve and are available in three basic styles—wall, stall, and pedestal—as shown in Fig. 1-19.

BIDETS

Bidets (Fig. 1-20) are designed to wash the perineal area after using the water closet. The bidet is used extensively in Europe and South America and is enjoying increased usage in Canada and the United States. It is designed for use by the entire family and is installed beside the water closet. The user sits on the fixture facing the wall (and the water controls) and is cleansed by a rinsing spray. It is available in vitreous china.

BATHTUBS

Bathtubs are available in enameled iron, cast iron, or fiberglass. Tubs are available in quite a variety of sizes, the most common being 30 or 32 in. wide; 12, 14, or 16 in. high; and 4 to 6 ft long.

   Enameled iron tubs (formed steel with a porcelain enamel finish) are generally available in lengths of 4½ and 5 ft, widths of 30 to 31 in., and typical depths of 15 to 15½ in.

FIGURE 1-18 / Floor- and wall-mounted water closets

Floor mounted   Wall mounted

Wallhung

Stall   Pedestal

FIGURE 1-19 / Urinals

Fiberglass bathtubs have been in widespread use since about 1968. The most commonly available length is 5 ft, and it takes 34 to 36 in. of width to install. Generally, the units are cast in a single piece which includes three walls (eliminating the need for ceramic tile around the tub). It is this single-piece feature, with no cracks or sharp corners to clean, which makes the fiberglass tub so popular with clients. The size of the unit makes it almost impossible to fit it through the standard bathroom door; it must therefore be ordered and delivered early enough to be set in place before walls and doors are finished. In wood frame buildings, these units are usually delivered to the job and put in place before the plaster or gypsum board is put on the walls or the doors installed. When selecting fiberglass tubs, be certain to specify only manufacturers who are widely known and respected, with long experience in the plumbing fixture field. Off-brands often give unsatisfactory results in that the fiberglass "gives" as it is stepped on, making a slight noise. In addition, some may be far more susceptible to scratching and damage.

FIGURE 1-20 / Bidets

Bathtub fittings may be installed on only one end of a tub, and the tub is designated by the end at which they are placed. As you face the tub, if the fittings are placed on the left, it is called a *left-handed* tub, and, if placed on the right, it is *right-handed*.

SHOWERS

Showers (Fig. 1-21) are available in units of porcelain enameled steel or fiberglass. They may be built in with a base (bottom) of tile, marble, cement, or molded compositions, and walls may be any of these finishes or porcelain enameled steel. Showers

Typical fiberglass and metal
shower shapes.

Metal shapes

Shower enclosure
may be marble,
slate, structural
glass, ceramic tile
or metal.

Base

FIGURE 1-21 / Showers   Base and enclosure

have overhead nozzles which spray water down on the bather. Shower fittings may be placed over bathtubs instead of having a separate shower space; this is commonly done in residences, apartments, and motels. However, it is important that when a shower head is used with a bathtub fixture, the walls be of an impervious material (one that will not absorb water).

Showers of tile, concrete, or marble may be built to any desired size or shape. Preformed shower stall bases are most commonly available in sizes of 30 in. × 30 in. and 30 in. × 36 in.; other sizes may be ordered. Steel showers are usually available in sizes of 30 in. × 30 in. and 30 in. × 36 in.; special sizes may also be ordered. Fiberglass showers are commonly available in sizes of 36 in. × 36 in. and 36 in. × 48 in.

Special showers available include corner units and gang head units. Gang head showers are commonly used in institutions, schools, factories where workers must shower after work, and other situations where large numbers of people must shower.

LAVATORIES

Lavatories (Fig. 1-22) are generally available in vitreous china or enameled iron, or they may be cast in plastic or a plastic compound with the basin and integral part of the countertop. They are available in a large variety of sizes, and the shapes are usually square, rectangular, round, or oval (and even shell shaped). The lavatory may be wall hung, set on legs or on a stand, or built into a cabinet (Fig. 1-22). Lavatory styles are usually classified as flush-mount, self-rimming, under-the-counter, or integral, or as units which can be wall hung or supported on legs.

Special fittings for lavatories include foot controls (often used in institutions such as hospitals and nursing homes), and self-closing faucets, which are commonly used in public facilities (especially on hot water faucets) to conserve water.

KITCHEN SINKS

Kitchen sinks are most commonly made of enameled cast iron or stainless steel. Sinks are usually available in a single- or a double-bowl arrangement; some even have a third bowl which is generally much smaller. Quite often a garbage disposal is connected to one of the sinks. Kitchen sinks are generally flush mounted into a plastic laminate (such as Formica®) or into a composition plastic counter.

SERVICE SINKS

Service sinks are made of enameled cast iron or vitreous china, and they are often called *slop sinks*. Most service sinks have high backs, and there may be two or as many as three bowl compartments. Other sinks commonly used are laundry trays, pantry sinks, bar sinks, and surgeon's sinks.

Countertop

Corner, wall
or floor mounted

Floor mounted

FIGURE 1-22 / Lavatories

MINIMUM REQUIREMENTS

The codes generally set the minimum number of fixtures that must be installed on a project according to the type of occupancy (Fig. 1-26). For example, a theatre with 300 seats must have two water closets for men (of which one may be a urinal), two water closets for women, and one lavatory in each bathroom. When designing any commercial, industrial, or institutional project, this minimum fixture chart must be checked.

1-9   WATER DEMAND

The amount of water required for the operation of the fixtures installed in a project will depend on the number and kind of fixtures installed and on the probable simultaneous use of the fixtures (for example, it would be highly unlikely that every sink, dishwasher, water closet, bathtub, shower, clothes washer and garden hose in a residence would be used at one time). The amount of water required is referred to as a *demand load*.

An apartment building with a floor plan such as that shown in Fig. 1-23 would require two risers. When there is more than one riser, it is important that the demand be subtotaled for each riser and then totaled for the building.

STEP-BY-STEP APPROACH

1. The first step in determining the demand load is to list the plumbing fixtures required on the project. Using the small apartment house shown in Appendix A, the following information is gathered:

   4-story apartment building

   3-in. service main

   Street main pressure: 50 psi

   Fixtures *per* floor:

   > 2 flush tank water closets (toilets)
   >
   > 2 tubs with shower heads
   >
   > 2 lavatories (bathroom sinks)
   >
   > 2 kitchen sinks
   >
   > 2 hose bibbs on the first floor (⅜″ supply, public)

   > It should be noted at this point that the apartment building being sized for a water system has a repetitive floor plan for each floor. This allows the entire apartment to be serviced from a single water pipe (riser) going up the building (Fig. 1-24).

2. Next, the demand for each plumbing fixture is listed. This demand is measured in *fixture units* (f.u.), and the fixture-unit ratings for various commonly used plumbing fixtures are shown in Fig. 1-27. The fixture unit provides a means of

FIGURE 1-23 / *Water riser location*

FIGURE 1-24 / Single water riser

comparing the water supply demands for the fixtures since they are "relative to each other," meaning that a private bathtub with faucet rated at 2 fixture units requires twice as much water as a private lavatory with faucet which is rated at 1 fixture unit.

As the table in Fig. 1-27 shows, the type of occupancy of the building (public or private use) has an effect on the fixture-unit value since the greater use of the fixtures in public buildings increases the amount of simultaneous use. Since the water demand supplies the water for both hot and cold requirements, use the total f.u. column in Fig. 1-27.

Now, calculate the fixture units for the entire apartment building (Appendix A):

Total fixture units per floor:

2 bathroom groups, flush tank, private	6 f.u. × 2 = 12 f.u.
2 kitchen sinks	4 f.u. × 2 = 8 f.u.
	20 f.u. per floor

Total fixture units on this riser:

$$20 \text{ f.u. (per floor)} \times 4 \text{ (floors)} = 80 \text{ f.u.}$$

Total additional fixture units:

$$2 \text{ hose bibbs (first floor)} \quad 3 \text{ f.u.} \times 2 = 6 \text{ f.u.}$$

Total fixture units on this project:

$$80 \text{ f.u. (on riser)} + 6 \text{ f.u. (hose bibbs)} = 86 \text{ f.u.}$$

3. The demand for water in gallons per minute (gpm) can now be determined by using the table in Fig. 1-28 for various fixture-unit loads (39 gpm).

1-10 WATER REUSE SYSTEM

At this time, there are experimental houses being built throughout the world in order to study and analyze the new products and technology available and to examine the possibility of preserving our natural resources by using these new materials. One such project is the Tech House, the NASA Technology Utilization House in Hampton, Virginia. One portion of the design involves the possibility of processing household waste water for reuse.

In the design of the system a typical family of four is used with typical household appliances. The water from the bathtub or shower and the washing machine is run into a collection tank instead of going into the sewer lines. From the collection tank the water is filtered and chlorinated and then reused as water to flush the toilets. A schematic illustrating the flow of the water is shown in Fig. 1-25. This water reuse system cuts water consumption by one-half. Of course, the potable water system is kept completely separate from the reuse portion of the system, and all waste from water closets goes directly into the sewer.

In another experiment all of the household water, except for that from the garbage disposal and water closets, is processed for multiple reuse in the system. This results in savings of up to 70% of overall household water consumption.

Of course, the real significance of this type of reuse system is the reduced amount of water required. The savings from such a system result in:

1. Smaller community or private sewer systems.
2. Smaller community treatment plants required to treat sewage.
3. Smaller community treatment plants required to treat supply water (when required).

QUESTIONS

1-1. What is the difference between potable and nonpotable water? For what purposes may each be used?

1-2. What sources of water supply may be available to a city? To a private individual?

1-3. Why should any source of water be tested before the water is used?

1-4. What is the basic difference between a community and a private water supply system, and what are the advantages and disadvantages of each?

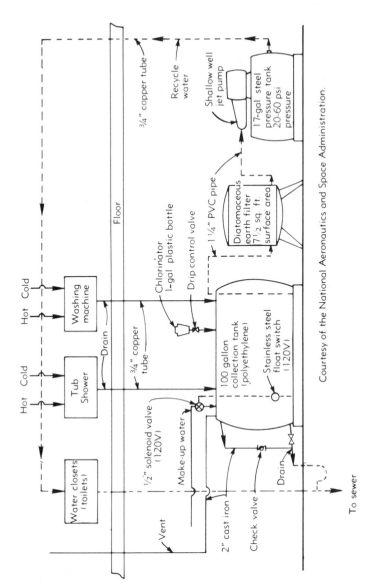

FIGURE 1-25 / Water reuse system

1-5. When a project (building) being designed is going to connect to a community water supply system, what information about the system must be obtained?

1-6. How are wells classified, and what methods of construction may be used for each type?

1-7. Show with a sketch how a well may be protected from surface water contaminants.

1-8. How are wells protected from possible underground contamination from sewage disposal fields?

1-9. What two types of pumps are used, and what are the limitations of each?

1-10. What is a water reuse system, how does it work, and why might such a system be desirable?

Design Exercise

1-11. Determine the demand load of water required for the apartment building in Appendix B.

MINIMUM NUMBER OF PLUMBING FIXTURES[1]

Use Group or Type of Bldg.	Water Closets (Urinals—See Note 4)		Lavatories	Drinking Fountains	Bathtubs or Showers	Other	Note Reference
	No. of Persons	No. of Fixtures					
I. Assembly							
A. Assembly—"Quiet" or "Brief" includes churches, auditoriums, museums, theatres, waiting rooms, visiting rooms, day rooms, libraries, and other similar uses.	1-50 51-300 each add'n 300	1 2 add 1	½ no. of water closets	1/1000 people	—	—	3, 5, 8
B. Assembly—where food and drinks are served. Includes arenas, ball parks, stadiums, passenger terminals, convention halls and other similar uses.	1-100 101-200 201-400 each add'n 300	2 3 4 add 1	½ no. of water closets	1/1000 people	—	—	2, 3, 5, 8
C. Assembly—Restaurants and nightclubs where seating is provided.	1-50 51-100 101-200 each add'n 200	2 3 4 add 1	½ no. of water closets	1/200 people	—	—	2, 3, 5, 8

Extracted from the 1988 Supplement to the *1987 National Standard Plumbing Code* with permission of PHCC.

FIGURE 1-26 / Minimum number of plumbing fixtures[1]

Type of building	Water closets		Urinals	Lavatories	Bathtubs or showers	Service sink	Drinking fountains
D. Assembly—Recreational facilities includes health spas, country clubs, public swimming pools and other similar uses.	1-40 each add'n 40	1 add 1	1/75 people	½ no. of water closets	1 shower/ 15 people Over 150 people add 1 for each 30 people	1 service sink/floor (where applicable)	3, 5, 8, 10
E. Assembly—Schools							
1. Preschool	1-15 each add'n 15	1 add 1	1/30 people	½ no. of water closets	—	1 service sink/floor	3, 5, 8, 10
2. Elementary	1-25 each add'n 25	1 add 1	1/40 people	½ no. of water closets	—	1 service sink/floor	3, 5, 8, 10
3. Secondary	1-30 each add'n 30	1 add 1	1/50 people	½ no. of water closets	—	1 service sink/floor	3, 5, 8, 10
II. Workplaces							
A. Industrial/Service when a locker room is provided and used mainly at shift change.	1-10 11-25 26-50 51-75 76-100 each add'n 50	1 2 3 4 5 add 1	1/75 people	½ no. of water closets	1 shower/ 10 people 1 shower and wash sink/floor when exposed to extreme heat or skin contamination	1 service	3, 5, 8, 10

Extracted from the 1988 Supplement to the *1987 National Standard Plumbing Code* with permission of PHCC.

FIGURE 1-26 (Continued) / Minimum number of plumbing fixtures[1]

Type							Notes
B. Multiple	—	1/unit	1/unit	—	1/unit	1 kitchen sink/unit 1 laundry tray/10 units	9
C. Dormitories, Boarding Houses.	1-20 each add'n 20	2 add 1	½ no. of water closets	1/100 people or 1/floor	1-20 people 2 fixtures, each add'n 20- add 1	1 service sink/floor 1 laundry tray/10 people	3, 9
D. Hotel/Motel	—	1/unit	1/unit	—	1/unit	1 service sink/floor	
V. Institutional							
A. Hospital-	1-8 patients each add'n 8	1 add 1	½ no. of water closets	—	1/20 patients	1 service sink/floor	
B. Hospital - Private or semi-private rooms	—	1	1	—	1	—	
C. Penal short term detention	1/cell or 1/4 inmates	—	1/cell or 1/4 inmates	—	1/6 inmates	1 service sink/floor	Water closet & lav. may be a combination fixture.
Long term correctional	1/cell or 1/8 inmates	—	1/cell or 1/8 inmates	—	1/15 inmates	1 service sink/floor	All showers and lav. in penal institutions to have thermostatic control and timing devices

Extracted from the 1988 Supplement to the *1987 National Standard Plumbing Code* with permission of PHCC.

FIGURE 1-26 (Continued) / Minimum number of plumbing fixtures[1]

MINIMUM NUMBER OF PLUMBING FIXTURES[1] Continued

Use Group or Type of Bldg.	Water Closets (Urinals—See Note 4) No. of Persons	No. of Fixtures	Lavatories	Drinking Fountains	Bathtubs or Showers	Other	Note Reference
B. Employees—all occupancies except industrial/service such as in stores, shopping centers, banks, office buildings & light industrial/service uses without locker rooms.	1-15 16-40 41-75 each add'n 60	1 2 3 add 1	½ no. of water closets	1/100 people	—	1 service sink/floor	, 5, 7, 8, 10
III. Mercantile/Business— Customers in stores, shopping centers, banks, office buildings and carry-out food establishments where seating is not provided.	1-50 51-300 each add'n 300	1 2 add 1	½ no. of water closets	1/1000 people			Requirements for fixtures for customers may be met by fixture requirements for employees. No additional fixtures are required if the employee facilities are available for customer uses. 2, 3, 5, 6, 8
IV. Dwelling Units A. Single	—	1	1	—	1	1 kitchen sink	

Extracted from the 1988 Supplement to the *1987 National Standard Plumbing Code* with permission of PHCC.

FIGURE 1-26 (Continued) / Minimum number of plumbing fixtures[1]

MINIMUM NUMBER OF PLUMBING FIXTURES[1]

NOTES:

1. This table shall be used in the absence of local building code requirements. Fire codes may also be consulted for assembly values. For handicap requirements see local, state and national ordinances. Additional fixtures may be required where environmental conditions or special activities may be encountered.

2. In food preparation areas, fixture requirements may be dictated by local health codes.

3. Whenever both sexes are present in approximately equal numbers, multiply the total census by 60% to determine the number of persons for each sex to be provided for. This regulation only applies when specific information, which would otherwise affect the fixture count, is not provided.

4. Not more than 50% of the required number of water closets may be urinals.

5. In buildings constructed with multiple floors, accessibility to the fixtures shall not exceed one vertical story.

6. Fixtures for public use as required by this section may be met by providing a centrally located facility accessible to several stores. The maximum distance from entry to any store to this facility shall not exceed 500 feet.

7. In stores with floor area of 150 square feet or less, the requirements of this section to provide facilities for use by employees may be met by providing a centrally located facility accessible to several stores. The maximum distance from entry to any store to this facility shall not exceed 300 ft.

8. Fixtures accessible only to private offices shall not be counted to determine compliance with this section.

9. Multiple dwelling units or boarding houses without public laundry rooms shall not require laundry trays.

10. Where only one water closet is required, one toilet facility with a lockable door is permitted.

Extracted from the 1988 Supplement to the *1987 National Standard Plumbing Code* with permission of PHCC.

FIGURE 1-26 (Continued) / Minimum number of plumbing fixtures[1]

LOAD VALUES ASSIGNED TO FIXTURES

Fixture	Occupancy	Type of Supply Control	Load Values, in Water Supply Fixture Units		
			Cold	Hot	Total
Water closet	Public	Flush valve	10.		10.
Water closet	Public	Flush tank	5.		5.
Urinal	Public	1″ flush valve	10.		10.
Urinal	Public	¾″ flush valve	5.		5.
Urinal	Public	Flush tank	3.		3.
Lavatory	Public	Faucet	1.5	1.5	2.
Bathtub	Public	Faucet	3.	3.	4.
Shower head	Public	Mixing valve	3.	3.	4.
Service sink	Offices, etc.	Faucet	2.25	2.25	3.
Kitchen sink	Hotel, restaurant	Faucet	3.	3.	4.
Drinking fountain	Offices, etc.	3/8″ valve	0.25		0.25
Water closet	Private	Flush valve	6.		6.
Water closet	Private	Flush tank	3.		3.0
Lavatory	Private	Faucet	0.75	0.75	1.
Bathtub	Private	Faucet	1.5	1.5	2.
Shower stall	Private	Mixing valve	1.5	1.5	2.
Kitchen sink	Private	Faucet	1.5	1.5	2.
Laundry trays (1 to 3)	Private	Faucet	2.25	2.25	3.
Combination fixture	Private	Faucet	2.25	2.25	3.
Dishwashing machine	Private	Automatic		1.	1.
Laundry machine (8 lbs.)	Private	Automatic	1.5	1.5	2.
Laundry machine (8 lbs.)	Public or General	Automatic	2.25	2.25	3.
Laundry machine (16 lbs.)	Public or General	Automatic	3.	3.	4.

NOTE: For fixtures not listed, loads should be assumed by comparing the fixture to one listed using water in similar quantities and at similar rates. The assigned loads for fixtures with both hot and cold water supplies are given for separate hot and cold water loads and for total load, the separate hot and cold water loads being three-fourths of the total load for the fixture in each case.

Extracted from the *1987 National Standard Plumbing Code* with permission of PHCC.

FIGURE 1-27 / Fixture units (water supply)

Lower   *public*

Supply Systems Predominantly For Flush Tanks *and Flushometer Tanks*		Supply Systems Predominantly For Flushometers	
Load (Water Supply Fixture Units)	Demand GPM	Load (Water Supply Fixture Units)	Demand GPM
6	5		
8	6.5		
10	8	10	27
12	9.2	12	28.6
14	10.4	14	30.2
16	11.6	16	31.8
18	12.8	18	33.4
20	14	20	35
25	17	25	38
30	20	30	41
35	22.5	35	43.8
40	24.8	40	46.5
45	27	45	49
50	29	50	51.5
60	32	60	55
70	35	70	58.5 .
80	38	80	62
90	41	90	64.8
100	43.5	100	67.5
120	48	120	72.5
140	52.5	140	77.5
160	57	160	82.5
180	61	180	87
200	65	200	91.5
225	70	225	97
250	75	250	101
275	80	275	105.5
300	85	300	110
400	105	400	126
500	125	500	142
750	170	750	178
1,000	208	1,000	208
1,250	240	1,250	240
1,500	267	1,500	267
1,750	294	1,750	294
2,000	321	2,000	321
2,250	348	2,250	348
2,500	375	2,500	375
2,750	402	2,750	402
3,000	432	3,000	432
4,000	525	4,000	525
5,000	593	5,000	593
6,000	643	6,000	643
7,000	685	7,000	685
8,000	718	8,000	718
9,000	745	9,000	745
10,000	769	10,000	769

Extracted from the 1988 Supplement to the *1987 National Standard Plumbing Code* with permission of PHCC.

FIGURE 1-28 / *Estimating demand*

CHAPTER 2
WATER SUPPLY DESIGN

2-1   INTRODUCTION

Plumbing systems are used to perform the two primary functions of water supply and waste disposal. The water supply portion of the system consists of the piping and fittings which supply hot and cold water from the building water supply to the fixtures, such as lavatories, bathtubs, water closets, dishwashers, clothes washers, and sinks, in the building or project. Only water supply is included in this chapter. The waste disposal portion of the system, which consists of the piping and fittings required to take that water supplied to the fixtures out of the building and into the sewer line or disposal field, is discussed in Chapter 3.

2-2   CODES

Building codes are the regulations which govern the private actions of those who build or modify buildings. They are for the protection of public health, safety and welfare. The codes establish certain minimum requirements for the construction and subsequent occupancy of buildings.

Plumbing codes may be a part of the general building code or, more commonly, a separate code. The code in force in any locale is determined by the municipality involved (each individual area, or governmental unit, selects its own code). The most commonly used codes are the national, regional, and state codes which may be used intact (complete) or with changes to meet the local needs and requirements. It should also be noted that the governmental unit also has a right to decide to have no code at all.

Since the code in a given locale is a law, it must be complied with in all of the buildings constructed under its jurisdiction. For this reason, it is important that all of the people involved in the planning, design, and construction phases of the project become familiar with the code in effect in the locale in which the building will be constructed.

The *National Standard Plumbing Code* has been used as a basis for this text since this is the code most often used, referred to or adapted from. But it is important for anyone using the text and learning about the construction industry to find out what code is used in your locale and to get a copy. You will probably find it very much in agreement with the *National Standard Plumbing Code* which should also be a part of your library.

In general, plumbing codes limit the types of materials and the sizes of pipe used in the system. The codes generally also form the basis for regulating installation methods.

MULTIPLE GOVERNING CODES

A proposed project may be regulated by several codes, covering the same items at the same time. This situation occurs quite often when the government, or a governmental agency, is providing some or all of the financing on a project and they have certain "rules" or "guidelines" which must be followed. This situation also sometimes occurs when doing business with large corporations. In such cases, the designers involved will have to become familiar with all of the applicable codes and regulations and, when they are in conflict, use the more stringent requirements.

ADMINISTRATION

Where codes are in force, there will probably be some form of Building Department or Department of Building in the government. The local administration and enforcement of the codes are performed by a building inspector or an engineer who usually reviews the proposed contract documents (drawings and specifications) for compliance with the codes and then checks for compliance during construction. It is important to know just what work must be inspected. Inspections should be scheduled so that work which must be inspected will not be covered before being inspected; otherwise, the inspector may require it to be uncovered so it can be checked.

Such responsibilities require qualified personnel—those who are experienced, informed and objective. Many levels of government offer courses for the inspectors to provide them with great experience and to make the latest technical information available to them.

2-3   PARTS OF THE SYSTEM

The parts of a typical water supply system are shown in Fig. 2-1. They include the building main, riser, horizontal fixture branch, fixture connection, and a meter in community systems.

Building main: Connects to the community or private source and extends into the building to the furthest riser. The building main is typically run (located) in a basement, crawl space, or below the concrete floor slab.

Riser: Extends from the building main vertically in the building to the furthest horizontal fixture branch. It is typically run vertically in the walls.

Horizontal fixture branch: Extends horizontally from the riser to the furthest fixture to be connected. It is usually run in the floor or in the wall behind the fixtures.

Fixture connection: Extends from the horizontal fixture branch to the fixture.

Meter: Required by most community water supply systems to measure and record the amount of water used. It may be placed in a meter box located in the ground, near the street or inside the building.

FIGURE 2-1 / Parts of a typical water supply system

Only piping used for water supply is included in this section. Drainage, waste, and vent piping are covered in Sec. 3-3. Piping most commonly used for water supply includes copper, wrought-iron, steel, plastic, and occasionally brass.

Copper is one of the most popular water supply pipes. The pipe types available are K, L, and M, with K having the thickest walls, then L, and finally M with the thinnest walls of this group (DWV copper tubing is used for drainage, waste, and vent piping.) The thin walls of copper pipe are usually soldered to the fittings. This allows all of the pipes and fittings to be set into place before joints must be "finished" (in this case, by soldering). This advantage generally allows faster installation of copper pipe. Compared with iron or steel pipe, copper pipe also has the advantage of not rusting and of being highly resistant to any accumulation of scale (particles) in the pipe.

Type K copper tube is available either rigid (hard temper) or flexible (soft temper). It is used primarily for underground water service in water supply systems. Soft temper tubing 1 in. and smaller is usually available in coils 60 or 100 ft long while 1¼ and 1½ in. tubing is available in 40- or 60-ft coils. Hard temper is available in 12- and 20-ft straight lengths. Type K copper tubing is color coded in green for quick visual identification.

Type L copper tube is also available in either hard or soft temper in coils and straight lengths. The soft temper tubing is often used as replacement plumbing because the flexibility of the tube allows easier installation. Hard temper tubing is often used for new installations, particularly in commercial work. Type L copper tubing is color coded blue. This type of tubing is most popular for use in water supply systems.

Type M copper tube is made in hard temper only and is available in straight lengths of 12 and 20 ft. It has the thinnest wall and is used for branch supplies where water pressure is not too great, but it is not used for risers and mains. It is also used for chilled water systems, exposed lines in hot water heating systems, and drainage piping. Type M copper tubing is color coded red.

Copper tubing has a lower friction loss per 100 ft than wrought-iron or steel, providing the designer with an additional advantage. Also, the outside dimensions of the fittings are smaller which makes a neater, better-looking job. With wrought-iron and steel pipe the bigger outside dimensions of the fittings sometimes require that wider walls be used in the building.

Red brass piping, consisting of 85% copper and 15% zinc, is also sometimes used as water supply piping. The pipe is threaded for fitting connections, but this requires thicker walls to accommodate the threading, making installation and handling more difficult than for copper. In addition, its relatively higher total cost, installed on the job, limits its usage.

Plastic pipe is also available for water supply systems. Its economy and ease of installation make it increasingly popular, especially on projects such as low-cost housing or apartments, where "cost economy" is most important. Available in 10-ft lengths, it is lighter than steel or copper and requires no special tools to install. While many plumbing subcontractors, engineers, and architects still prefer copper, the use of plastic pipe will continue to increase. It is important to check the plumbing code in force in your locale since some areas still do not allow the use of plastic pipe for water supply systems. This dates back to early concern about possible toxicity (poisoning) resulting from the use of plastic pipe; this concern has long since been proved groundless. Plastic pipe used for water supply should carry the NSF (National Sanitation Foundation) seal. However, not all plastic pipe available should be used for water supply; much of it has been manufactured for use in the drainage portion of the plumbing system. The chart in Fig. 2-2 shows plastic pipe materials and their usual use in the water supply system.

Wrought-iron pipe is available in diameters from ⅛ in. to 24 in. Lightweight wrought-iron pipe, designated standard (or schedule 40), is the type most commonly used for water supply systems. The wrought-iron pipe used is most commonly galvanized to add extra corrosion resistance. Quite often it is used as the service main from the community main to the riser. Wrought-iron pipe is threaded for connection to the fittings, and it can be identified by a red spiral stripe on the pipe. The higher cost of wrought-iron pipe limits its increased use. Wrought-iron pipe also has a higher friction loss per 100 ft than copper.

Steel pipe is available in diameters from ⅛ in. to 12 in. Plain steel pipe is usually used only when the water is not corrosive. Galvanized steel pipe is moderately corrosion resistant and suitable for mildly acid water. It is not used extensively in water supply systems; most plumbers and engineers prefer copper tubing because of its superior resistance to corrosion. Steel pipe is connected to its fittings with threaded connections. Steel pipe also has a higher friction loss per 100 ft than copper.

2-5   FITTINGS

A variety of fittings must be used to install the piping in a project and make all the pipe turns, branch lines, joinings on the straight runs, and stops at the end of the runs. Fittings for steel and wrought-iron pipe are threaded and made of malleable iron and cast iron. The fittings for plastic, copper, and brass pipe are made of the same materials

Type	Cold water	Hot water
Polyethylene (PE)	●	
Polyvinyl Chloride (PVC)	●	
Acrilylonitrile Butadiene Styrene (ABS)	●	●
Polyvinyl Dichloride (PVDC)	●	
Chlorinated Polyvinyl Chloride (CPVC)	●	●

FIGURE 2-2 / Plastic pipe use

as the pipe being connected. Typical fittings for the various materials are shown in Figs. 2-3, 2-4, and 2-5.

The 45° and 90° elbows are used to change the direction of the pipe. Unions and couplings are used to join straight runs of pipe. A clamping piece on the coupling allows it to be more easily disengaged for uncoupling of the pipes when future piping revisions are expected at a given point. Tees are used when branch lines must be made; the reducing tee allows different pipe sizes to be joined together. Adapters are used where threaded pipe is being connected to copper or plastic. Adapters have one end threaded to accommodate the steel pipe.

2-6 VALVES

Valves are used to control the flow of the water throughout the system. There are usually valves at risers (vertical pipe serving the building), branches (horizontal pipe serving the fixtures), and any pipes to individual fixtures or equipment. The proper location of valves simplifies repairs to the system, fixtures, or equipment being serviced.

The *globe valve* (Fig. 2-6) is a compression-type valve, commonly used where there is occasional or periodic use, such as lavatories (faucets) and hose connections (called hose bibbs). This type of valve usually closes the flow of water and is partially or fully opened only periodically to allow the water to flow. In reviewing Fig. 2-6, the handle is turned and a washer on the bottom of the stem is forced against the metal seat which stops the flow of water. To allow the water to flow, the handle is turned and the washer separates from the seat; the more flow desired, the more the valve is opened. The design of the globe valve is such that the water passing through is forced to make two 90° turns, which greatly increases the friction loss in this valve compared with that in a gate valve.

The *angle valve* (Fig. 2-7) is similar in operation to the globe valve, utilizing the same principle of compressing a washer against a metal seat to cut the flow of water. It is commonly used for outside hose bibbs. The angle valve has a much higher friction loss than the gate valve and about half the friction loss of the globe valve.

The *gate valve* (Fig. 2-8) has a wedge-shaped leaf which, when closed, seals tightly against two metal seats which are set at slight angles. This type of valve is usually used where the flow of the water is left either completely opened or closed for most of the time. Because the flow of water passes straight through the valve, there is very little water pressure lost to friction. The gate valve is usually used to shut off the flow of water to fixtures and equipment when repairs or replacement must be made.

FIGURE 2-3 / Copper tubing and fitting

90°
Elbow

45°
Elbow

Tee   Reducing
       tee

FIGURE 2-4 / Plastic fittings

Coupling   Reducer   Union

FIGURE 2-5 / Wrought-iron fittings

The *check valve* (Fig. 2-9) has a hinged leaf which opens to allow the flow of water in the direction desired (indicated by an arrow in the illustration). But the leaf closes if there is any flow of water in the other direction. This eliminates any possible flow of water in a direction other than that desired, or required, by the designer. The check valve works automatically so there is no need for a handle. This valve is used in such places as the water feed line to a boiler (heating unit) where the water from the boiler might pollute the system if it backed up. The inside of the valve is made accessible for repairs by removing the cover (see Fig. 2-9).

Valves referred to as *standard weight* will withstand pressures up to 125 psi; high-pressure valves are also available. Most small valves used have bronze bodies, while large valves (2 in. and larger) have iron bodies with noncorrosive moving parts and seats which may be replaced. They are available threaded or soldered to match the pipe or tubing used.

2-7   WATER SHOCK

Water pressure surges from the quick closing of water valves (faucets) may cause the water system to be noisy. This abrupt closing of the valve causes the fast-flowing water to stop quickly and make the pipes rattle. A length of pipe, installed above the water connection, will act as a cushion or shock absorber as it controls the pressure surge of

FIGURE 2-6 / Globe valve

FIGURE 2-7 / Angle valve

2 / WATER SUPPLY DESIGN

FIGURE 2-8 / Gate valve

FIGURE 2-9 / Check valve

the water (Fig. 2-10). Special shock absorbers are also available (Fig. 2-11). Oftentimes the noise in the system is referred to as *water hammer*.

2-8   EXPANSION ALLOWANCES

No matter what type of pipe is used in the water supply system, some expansion in the pipe will occur, and this expansion must be considered in the design of the system. The amount of expansion will depend on the type of piping used and the range of temperatures to which the pipe will be subjected.

The piping for hot water will have to withstand a temperature range from about 70°F, the average indoor temperature, to about 180°F, the temperature of the water. This range will vary, sometimes considerably, on projects and must be checked. Cold water piping will be subjected to a much smaller temperature range, usually with a low

FIGURE 2-10 / Air cushion

FIGURE 2-11 / Shock absorber   Water

of 40°F and a high of 75°F. This range may vary if the piping is placed very close to the hot water line, heating line or other heat source which may raise the temperature.

The amount of expansion of pipe and tubing which will occur due to temperature change is shown in Fig. 2-12. A review of the expansion figures shows that it would be minimal in the average residence, but it must be considered in large homes and commercial projects. The expansion is allowed for in the system by using one of the methods shown in Fig. 2-13.

EXAMPLE

Given: A four-story apartment building; water service (riser) height of about 40 ft.

Problem: What would the expansion be in a copper tube system if the temperature increases from 70° to 180°F?

With a temperature difference of $180° - 70° = 110°F$, Fig. 2-12 shows the following expansion figures:

$$100°F \text{ temperature difference} = 1.12 \text{ in. per 100 ft}$$
$$120°F \text{ temperature difference} = 1.35 \text{ in. per 100 ft}$$

A 110°F temperature difference will cause expansion between 1.12 and 1.35 in. per 100 ft. So, to find the value, add them together and divide by 2:

FIGURE 2-12 / Pipe and tubing expansion (elongation in

Elongation in inches per 100 ft of pipe or tube

Increase in Temperature, Deg. F	Steel pipe	Wrought iron pipe	Copper tubing
120	.91	.95	1.35
20	.15	.16	.22
40	.30	.31	.44
60	.45	.47	.67
80	.60	.63	.90
100	.76	.79	1.12

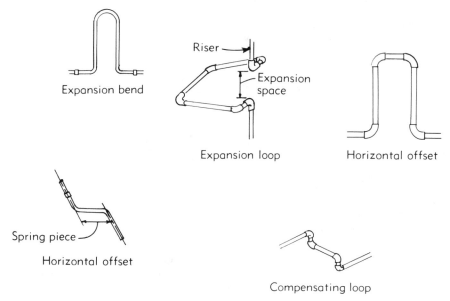

FIGURE 2-13 / Expansion allowance

$$(1.12 \text{ in.} + 1.35 \text{ in.}) \div 2 = 2.47 \text{ in.} \div 2 = 1.235 \text{ in.}$$
110°F temperature difference = 1.235 in. per 100 ft

Since there are 40 ft of riser in this problem, the answer is 40/100, 40% or 0.4 of 1.235 in.:

$$1.235 \text{ in.} \times 0.4 = 0.494 \text{ in. of expansion}$$

2-9   WATER SUPPLY SYSTEMS

The two basic types of water supply system used inside the building (or project) are the *upfeed* and the *downfeed* systems.

Since the water pressure in community mains averages about 50 to 60 psi, and this is also considered about the upper limit for private systems, this places limits on how far the water can be moved in an *upfeed* system (Fig. 2-14). The 50–60 psi pressure will be used up in friction losses as the water passes through the building main pipe, the meter and the various fittings. In addition, part of the pressure is used to overcome *static head*—the pressure required to push water up vertically (up the riser). Also, there must be sufficient pressure left at the top floor to provide proper operation of the fixtures (a shower requires 12 psi, a bathtub 5 psi, etc.).

It requires 0.434 psi to push the water up 1 ft. Pushing the water up 20 ft will require 20 × 0.434 psi = 8.68 psi. Even if the entire 50 psi were available for static

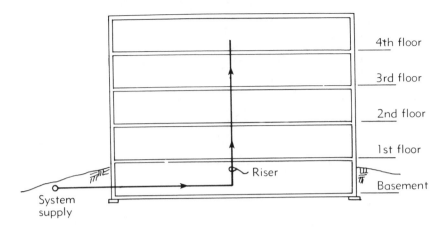

FIGURE 2-14 / Upfeed system

head, the maximum height would be 50 psi ÷ 0.434 psi per ft = 115.2 ft. (It should be noted that 0.434 psi per ft is the same as saying 1 psi can raise water 2.3 ft and 50 psi × 2.3 ft of head per psi = 115 ft.) Depending on the exact floor-to-floor height, this would raise the water 10 to 15 stories (floors) *if there were no friction loss or fixture operation to consider*. Practical limitations set about 60 ft as the usual maximum height, and 40 ft is the preferred height.

In buildings which cannot be adequately serviced to the top floor by an upfeed system, the water is pumped to elevated storage tanks in, or on, the building, and the water is fed down into the building by gravity. This gravity system, fed from the upper stories to the lower, is called a *downfeed* system (Fig. 2-15).

2-10   UPFEED SYSTEM DESIGN

Water supply pipes must be of sufficient size to provide adequate pressure to all fixtures in the system at a reasonable cost. Selection of economical sizes for the piping and the meter is based on the total demand for water (Sec. 1-9); this process must take into account the available water pressure (street main pressure), the pressure loss due to static head (pressure loss to raise the water up the pipe), the pressure loss due to friction in piping and fittings, and the pressure required to operate the fixture requiring the most pressure on the top floor.

Street main pressure must be adequate to supply:

Required fixture flow pressure

+

Static head

+

Friction in pipe and meter

FIGURE 2-15 / Downfeed system

STEP-BY-STEP APPROACH

The accumulated information to this point (using the apartment building discussed in Sec. 1-9 and shown in Appendix A) is as follows:

4-story apartment building	20 f.u. per floor
3-in. service main	86 f.u. total
Street main pressure: 50 psi	Water demand: 39 gpm
Predominately flush tank	

1. The first step in sizing the supply is to determine the pressure losses. The pressure loss due to static head is figured by multiplying 0.434 psi per ft times the vertical distance of the riser from the service main into the building to the top branch water line (Fig. 2-16).

System
supply

Vertical rise about 40'

FIGURE 2-16 / Vertical riser

Static head loss = 0.434 psi × Vertical rise of water (in ft)

From Fig. 2-16, the vertical rise in this four-story building is about 40 ft from the top of the main to the top of the riser.

Static head loss = 0.434 psi × 40 ft = 17.36 psi

2. Next, find the pressure required to operate the fixture on the top floor requiring the most pressure. The rate of water flow and the required pressure to properly operate various fixtures are shown in Fig. 2-33.

   At this time only the pressure is needed, and the maximum pressure required on the top floor is that for the water closet, 15 psi. Of course, the design should also leave some excess pressure so that more than one fixture can be operated properly at the same time.

3. The pressure loss due to friction in the main and riser pipes, the fittings and the meter must be found next. Add the static head and the pressure required for the top fixture; then subtract the total from the available street main pressure to find the pressure left, which is the maximum amount that can be lost to friction.

Street main pressure	50.00 psi
Static head + fixture pressure (17.36 + 15)	−32.36 psi
Pressure left to overcome friction	17.64 psi

4. Sizing the piping is often a matter of trial and error, even for experienced engineers; the process involves first selecting a pipe size for the building main

2 / WATER SUPPLY DESIGN

which runs from the water system to the riser(s) and then determining the friction loss for the pipe used from the charts in Figs. 2-34 through 2-36. The chart used will depend on the type of pipe used.

Since these charts have many lines and numbers, use them with care (Fig. 2-17). Before beginning the selection, review what information is on each chart. Along the left and right is the flow in gpm, and along the bottom and top is the friction loss in the pipe per *100 ft of length*. The heavy, solid lines running

FIGURE 2-17 / Use of the friction loss chart

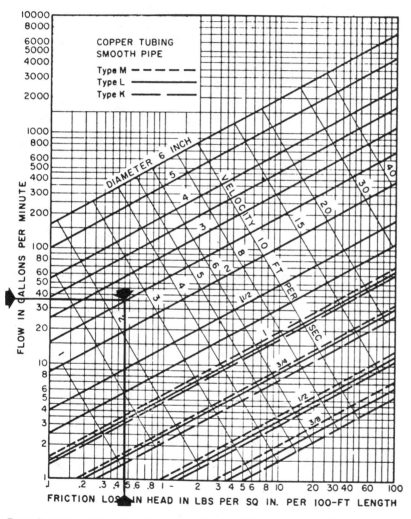

diagonally on the chart represent the diameters of pipe which may be used; the long-short-long lines going perpendicular (at a 90° angle) to the pipe diameter lines represent the velocity of the water in a pipe of a given size. Be certain that you do not confuse the diagonal lines.

To make a tentative building main pipe selection:

a. Find the flow, in gpm, along the side of the chart (in this case, 39 gpm from Sec. 1-9).

b. Follow horizontally across the chart to the first pipe diameter (solid line) and note its size.

Going from the left side toward the right, the first pipe size servicing 39 gpm is 3 in. Since this is the same size as the street main, keep moving to the right to the 2½-in. pipe. Where the horizontal line from 39 gpm touches the line representing 2½-in., draw a vertical line to the bottom (or top), and the friction loss reads about 0.45 psi per 100 ft.

Continuing to the right, the following friction readings are taken:

> 2½-in. pipe = 0.45 psi per 100 ft
> 2-in. pipe = 1.3 psi per 100 ft
> 1½-in. pipe = 5.8 psi per 100 ft
> 1¼-in. pipe = 13.0 psi per 100 ft
> 1-in. pipe = 36.0 psi per 100 ft (type L copper)

5. Since all friction losses are given per 100 ft of pipe length, the distance from the street main (or point of service, such as a storage tank) to the base of the riser must be checked on the plot plan.

Referring to Appendix A, the horizontal building main distance is estimated at 60 ft. So, for this example, the friction loss in the building main pipe will be 60/100, 3/5, 0.6 or 60% of the figures recorded.

Friction losses for 60 ft of pipe are as follows:

> 2½-in. pipe = 0.45 psi per 100 ft = 0.45 psi (0.6) = 0.27 psi
> 2-in. pipe = 1.3 psi per 100 ft = 1.3 psi (0.6) = 0.8 psi
> 1½-in. pipe = 5.8 psi per 100 ft = 5.8 psi (0.6) = 3.5 psi
> 1¼-in. pipe = 13 psi per 100 ft = 13 psi (0.6) = 7.8 psi
> 1-in. pipe = 38 psi per 100 ft = 36 psi (0.6) = 21.6 psi

By observation, the 1-in. pipe is eliminated since its friction loss is slightly greater than the pressure left in the calculations (17.64 psi).

The 1¼-in., 1½-in., 2-in., and 2½-in. pipe are all possibilities at this point.

6. The next step is to determine the pressure loss at the water passes through the meter (if one is required; if not, this step is eliminated). The chart in Fig. 2-37 gives the pressure loss for various meter sizes with the flow in gpm along the bottom and the pressure loss on the left.

    When the main size is 1½ in. or greater, the most common main-meter selection will have the meter one size smaller than the main.

    For this problem, locate the gpm along the bottom—in this case, 39 gpm—and go vertically to the first diagonal line (2-in. meter); at this point move horizontally to the pressure loss reading (1.2 psi). Referring to Fig. 2-37, the pressure loss for a 1½-in. pipe meter is about 3.1 psi.

    2-in. meter   = 1.2 psi
    1½-in. meter = 3.1 psi
    1-in. meter   = 12 psi

Totaling the pressure for main and meter:

    2½-in. pipe and 2-in. meter = 0.27 +   1.2 =   1.47 psi
    2-in. pipe and 1½-in. meter = 0.8 +   3.1 =   3.9 psi
    2-in. pipe and 1-in. meter   = 0.8 + 12   = 12.8 psi
    1½-in. pipe and 1-in. meter = 3.5 + 12   = 15.5 psi
    1¼-in. pipe and 1-in. meter = 7.8 + 12   = 29.8 psi

    Referring back in the notes, there are 17.64 psi left to overcome pressure losses due to friction in the main, meter and riser. The totals above are pressure losses for the main and meter; the riser pressure loss must still be calculated.

    Since the most economical solution involves the use of the smallest pipe sizes which will provide an adequate flow of water throughout the system, at this point a preliminary selection of 2-in. pipe and 1-in. meter is made. This means that of the 17.64 psi that are left to overcome friction, 12.8 psi will be used in the 2-in. pipe and the 1-in. meter. This leaves 4.8 psi as the maximum friction loss in the riser.

       17.64 psi available for friction loss
    − 12.8 psi friction loss in 1½-in. main and 1-in. meter
       4.8   psi available for riser friction loss

Using a 2-in. main and 1½-in. meter would leave (17.64 − 3.90) = 13.74 psi for riser friction loss. Using the 2½-in. main and 2-in. meter would leave (17.64 − 1.35) = 16.29.

7. The next step will be to select the possible pipe sizes for the riser. Using the friction-loss pipe chart (Fig. 2-34), find the 39 gpm on the left; the following friction-loss readings are then taken:

$$
\begin{array}{lll}
\text{2-in. pipe} & = & \text{1.3 psi per 100 ft} \\
\text{1½-in. pipe} & = & \text{4.7 psi per 100 ft} \\
\text{1¼-in. pipe} & = & \text{13 psi per 100 ft} \\
\text{1-in. pipe} & = & \text{36 psi per 100 ft}
\end{array}
$$

Once again, note that the friction losses are given per 100 ft of pipe length. This means that the vertical distance from the main to the highest and most remote fixture must be estimated. On some projects this may mean a meeting with the architects to be certain of how high the ceilings in the building are and of how thick the floor construction is or of what the floor-to-floor height is.

For this apartment building, with floor-to-floor heights of *about* 10 ft-0 in., the riser height will be approximately 40 ft. In such piping there is an additional friction loss for fittings (such as valves and tees). When the entire system has been designed and all pipes sized and fittings located, it is possible to determine the friction loss for the fittings. An example of how to calculate fittings is given later in this section. In reviewing Fig. 2-38 in order to determine the friction loss for fittings, the table lists the fitting across the top, the diameter required along the left and the equivalent length of pipe for each type and size. This equivalent length of pipe means that, for example, when water passes through a 2-in.-diameter standard 90° ell, the same friction loss occurs as when water passes through 2 lineal ft of 2-in. pipe. So the equivalent length of the 2-in.-diameter 90° ell is 2 ft.

Since, during this stage of the design, the fittings have not been determined, it is common practice to allow an additional 50% of the piping length to account for the friction loss in the fittings.

In this case, the pipe length is 40 ft, and, adding 50% for friction loss in the fittings, the total *equivalent feet of piping* is 40 + 20 = 60 ft.

The friction loss for riser pipes and fittings is calculated next.

Using the friction loss for various pipe sizes per 100 ft (previously taken from Fig. 2-34), convert the friction loss to the equivalent length—in this case, 60 ft or 60/100, 0.60 or 60% of the figures recorded.

$$
\begin{array}{lllll}
\text{2-in. pipe} & = & \text{1.3 psi per 100 ft} & = & \text{1.3 psi (0.60)} & = & \text{0.78 psi} \\
\text{1½-in. pipe} & = & \text{4.7 psi per 100 ft} & = & \text{4.7 psi (0.60)} & = & \text{2.82 psi} \\
\text{1¼-in. pipe} & = & \text{13 psi per 100 ft} & = & \text{13 psi (0.60)} & = & \text{7.8 psi} \\
\text{1-in. pipe} & = & \text{36 psi per 100 ft} & = & \text{36 psi (0.60)} & = & \text{21.6 psi}
\end{array}
$$

These friction losses are now compared with the preliminary main size selections, and a final selection for main and riser is made. The choices are as follows:

a. Using a 2-in. main and 1-in. meter which has 12.8 psi friction loss leaving 4.8 psi for riser friction loss, the choice is limited to 1½-in. and 2-in. riser pipe.

b. Using a 2-in. main and 1½-in. meter which has 3.90 psi friction loss, leaving 13.74 psi for riser friction loss, the riser choices are the 1¼-in., 1½-in. and 2-in. pipe. The final selection may also depend on whether there is any possibility of adding any length to the riser (by adding more stories to the building, making it taller).

The final selection would depend on other variables—in particular whether the main will serve any other building and whether there is any chance of further development on the site (perhaps another apartment building).

There is no *one* correct answer; in this case, the solution which seems most economical is:

2-in. main and 1-in. meter with 1½-in. riser

Another approach to finding riser pipe size is often used. In this approach, once a main size has been tentatively selected, the riser may be more directly selected from the chart in Fig. 2-34. Using a main size of 1½-in. with a 1-in. meter, the friction loss available for the riser is 7.14 psi. The following formula will convert the psi left for friction loss and the equivalent length of riser into the friction loss per 100 ft using a 100-ft constant, so that the chart in Fig. 2-34 may be used more easily.

$$\frac{\text{Available psi} \times 100\text{ ft}}{\text{Equivalent length}} = \text{psi loss per 100 ft}$$

In this case:

$$\frac{(4.8)(100)}{(40 + 20)} = 8\text{ psi loss per 100 ft}$$

Now the chart in Fig. 2-34 is used in a slightly different way. The gpm is found on the left, and a horizontal line is made to the right. The available friction loss per 100 ft is found along the bottom and a vertical line made. The smallest riser size which can be used is selected by finding the intersection of the horizontal and vertical lines and taking the first pipe size to the left.

For this problem, there are 39 gpm and 8 psi available for loss per 100 ft. Referring to Fig. 2-34, a horizontal line would be projected from the 39 gpm, a vertical line projected from about 8 psi, and the intersection found. The 1¼-in. pipe is slightly to the right of the intersection. Moving to the left of the intersection, the first pipe size is 1½-in. From the point that the 39 gpm crosses the 1½-in. pipe size, drop a vertical line down and the friction loss for this combination is 5.8 psi per 100 ft.

In an actual layout, the equivalent length of the fittings should be checked against the assumed length. Assuming the following fittings are in the riser, the equivalent lengths are taken from Fig. 2-38.

	Length Per Fitting
3 tees, branch, 2 in.	= 7.0 = 21.0
3 tees, run, 2 in.	= 1.0 = 3.0
1 gate valve, 2 in.	= 2.0 = 2.0

In this case the equivalent length added (20 ft) is slightly more than what is needed. This actual equivalent length will sometimes be more than allowed and sometimes less. When there is considerable difference, the riser size selected may have to be recalculated.

At this point, the information on the upfeed system should be tabulated. The required information includes the fixture units per floor, the accumulated fixture units (which are the units that the riser must serve at any given point), the demand flow and the pipe size. The tabulated information for this problem is shown in Fig. 2-18.

Now the riser for the upper floors can be sized. First, the accumulated fixture units are figured:

2nd floor . . . . . . 20 f.u. . . . . . . 60 accumulated f.u.
3rd floor . . . . . . 20 f.u. . . . . . . 40 accumulated f.u.
4th floor . . . . . . 20 f.u. . . . . . . 20 accumulated f.u.

Next, the demand load is determined for each floor by using Fig. 1-21 and the accumulated fixture units for each floor (use line 2, predominantly flush tank):

2nd floor . . . . . . 60 accumulated f.u. . . . . . . 32 gpm
3rd floor . . . . . . 40 accumulated f.u. . . . . . . 24.8 (25) gpm
4th floor . . . . . . 20 accumulated f.u. . . . . . . 14 gpm

The riser pipe sizes are now selected by using the demand load (gpm) for each floor, the pressure available for friction loss in the riser (previously calculated as 8.1 psi per 100 ft) and the chart in Fig. 2-34.

WATER SUPPLY				
UPFEED ZONE, APT. BLDG – PROJ.# 20-1				
Floor	Accumulated f.u.	Demand load (gpm)	Friction loss (psi per 100')	Pipe size
1	86	39		
2	60	32		
3	40	25		
4	20	14		

FIGURE 2-18 / Upfeed data

2nd floor . . . . . . 32 gpm . . . . . . 1½-in. pipe
3rd floor . . . . . . 25 gpm . . . . . . 1¼-in. pipe
4th floor . . . . . . 14 gpm . . . . . . 1-in. pipe

Once all of this information is tabulated as shown in Fig. 2-19, the design is complete.

FIGURE 2-19 / Upfeed data

WATER SUPPLY				
UPFEED ZONE, APT. BLDG. – PROJ.# 20-1				
	Accumulated f.u.	Demand load (gpm)	Friction loss (psi per 100')	Pipe size
1	70	36	28.1	1½"
2	48	28		1½"
3	32	21		1¼"
4	16	16		1"

2-11 DOWNFEED SYSTEM DESIGN

For all tall buildings a downfeed system will be used (Fig. 2-15).

STEP-BY-STEP APPROACH

1. The first step in the design is to list all the information about the project.

    20-story public building
    50 psi at community main

    Floors 1–18:   Floors 19 and 20:

    3 flush valve water closets   3 flush tank water closets
    2 urinals, flush valve   2 urinals, flush tank
    2 lavatories   2 lavatories
    1 service sink   1 service sink

    Floor-to-floor height: 11 ft
    Distance from community main to riser: 40 ft

2. In order to determine the main, meter, and riser sizes for the system, the next step is to determine the fixture units per floor and the total fixture units in the building.

    Floors 1–18 (Fixture units from Fig. 1-27):

3 flush valve water closets	10 f.u. each =	30
2 urinals, flush valve (¾")	5 f.u. each =	10
2 lavatories	2 f.u. each =	4
1 service sink	3 f.u. each =	3
		47 f.u. per floor

    47 f.u. (per floor) × 18 (floors) = 846 f.u. for floors 1–18

    Floors 19 and 20:

3 flush tank water closets	5 f.u. each =	15
2 urinals, flush tank	3 f.u. each =	6
2 lavatories	2 f.u. each =	4
1 service sink	3 f.u. each =	3
		28 f.u. per floor

28 f.u. (per floor) × 2 (floors) = 56 f.u. for floors 19 and 20

Total fixture units:

846 f.u. (floors 1–18)
+ 56 f.u. (floors 19 and 20)
902 f.u. total

3. The next step is to determine the demand load for water in gpm (from Fig. 1-28).

The system is predominantly flush valve, and the approximate demand load is 200 gpm.

4. In this problem, the bottom floors of the building will be serviced by upfeed zones (Fig. 2-20) and the upper floors by downfeed zones.

The first step will be to make a preliminary decision on how many floors each zone will supply and the number of zones required. The upfeed zone (refer to Sec. 2-10) is limited to a practical maximum height of about 60 ft. With a floor-to-floor height given as 11 ft, the upfeed system will serve five to six floors (stories), depending on how deep the community main is (a deep main would limit the zone to five floors).

Since on this project the main is shallow (about 4 ft below ground level), it will be possible to have an upfeed zone of six floors, if necessary.

5. Downfeed zones also have maximum heights (distances they can serve) without using special pressure reducing and control valves. First, since the water is stored in the tank, it has no pressure in the riser as it leaves the tank. As the water leaves the tank and travels down the riser, the water pressure begins to build at a rate of 0.434 psi per ft (without considering friction loss). This means that the highest fixtures, those nearest the tank, will receive the least pressure.

In this design, the flush tank water closet on the top floor requires a water pressure of 15 psi to operate (Fig. 2-33). So, if 15 psi is required and the water pressure increases 0.434 psi per foot, then 15 psi ÷ 0.434 psi = 34.6 ft of vertical distance would be required

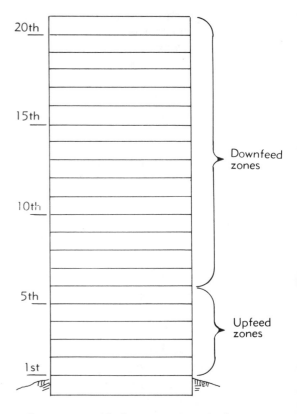

FIGURE 2-20 / Water supply zoning

20th
15th
10th
5th
1st

Downfeed zones

Upfeed zones

between the tank and the top fixture to provide the pressure required. (This distance would be even greater if flush valve water closets were used on the top floors, since they may require more pressure than the flush tank. In addition to the 34.6 ft of distance required to operate top fixture, a small additional height would be required to overcome the friction loss in the pipes and fittings (an additional 5 ft is usually sufficient unless very small risers are used).

6. The zoning for the downfeed systems is determined next. Since the water pressure is increasing as it goes down the downfeed riser, the vertical distance that a zone can service is limited to the maximum amount of pressure that can be put on the lowest fixture and still have it operate properly. This maximum pressure varies with the type and manufacturer of the fixtures being used; the allowable pressure may range from about 45 to 60 psi.

In this design, we will assume that 55 psi is the preferred maximum. This means that the downfeed zone can be 55 psi divided by 0.434 psi per foot or about 126 ft. Since there will be some pressure loss due to friction in the riser pipe, the zone may be slightly longer if required.

In review then, the upfeed portion of the system can easily service the bottom five floors. This leaves 15 floors to be serviced by the downfeed system. With a floor-to-floor height of 11 ft, this is a vertical distance of about 165 ft, which cannot be served by one downfeed zone. Two downfeed zones will easily provide the water service required to the 15 floors that the upfeed zone (Fig. 2-20) does not serve.

Note: In reviewing the schematic water supply system (Fig. 2-15), note that the house tank used to provide water for zone 2 must be placed high enough above the fixtures it is to supply that there will be sufficient pressure for the fixtures to operate efficiently. In this case, 20 psi will be required to operate the flush valve water closets, calling for a height of 20 psi ÷ 0.434 psi per ft = 46 ft, plus a short distance to overcome friction in the riser (totalling about 50 to 52 ft, depending on the final riser size selected).

7.   The accumulated information for the upfeed zone (zone 1) is now tabulated (Fig. 2-21), with each floor listed along with its fixture units, the accumulated fixture units (remember that the water at the bottom floor must service the floors above it, so the fixture units are the accumulated total of what must be serviced), the demand flow (gpm) for the accumulated fixture units and the pipe size selected.

8.   *Static head loss:* From Fig. 2-20, the vertical height of the riser from the top of the main to the top of the upfeed zone is about 55 ft.

Static head loss = 0.434 psi × 55 ft = 23.87 psi

Pressure required to operate fixture at top (5th) floor of the upfeed zone

Flush valve water closet: 20 psi

FIGURE 2-21 / Tabulated upfeed data (predominantly flush valve)

WATER SUPPLY				
UPFEED ZONE, FLOORS 1-5			PROJ. 20-2	
Floor	Accumulated f.u.	Demand load (gpm)	Friction loss (psi per 100')	Pipe size
1	235	99		
2	188	89		
3	141	78		
4	94	66		
5	47	50		

Pressure left to overcome friction:

$$55 \text{ psi} - (23.87 \text{ psi} + 20 \text{ psi}) = 55 \text{ psi} - 43.87 \text{ psi} = 11.13 \text{ psi}$$

9. At this point, the service main should be selected for 902 accumulated fixture units with a demand load of 200 gpm. Referring to Fig. 2-34, the preliminary main pipe selections are:

$$
\begin{aligned}
\text{5-in. main} &= 0.35 \text{ psi per 100 ft} \\
\text{4-in. main} &= 1.1 \text{ psi per 100 ft} \\
\text{3½-in. main} &= 2.1 \text{ psi per 100 ft} \\
\text{3-in main} &= 4.5 \text{ psi per 100 ft} \\
\text{2½-in. main} &= 11.0 \text{ psi per 100 ft}
\end{aligned}
$$

Since the main distance is given as 40 ft, the friction loss for each pipe would be:

$$
\begin{aligned}
\text{5-in. main} &= 0.35 \text{ psi per 100 ft} = 0.35 \, (0.4) = 0.14 \text{ psi} \\
\text{4-in. main} &= 1.1 \text{ psi per 100 ft} = 1.1 \, (0.4) = 0.44 \text{ psi} \\
\text{3½-in. main} &= 2.1 \text{ psi per 100 ft} = 2.1 \, (0.4) = 0.84 \text{ psi} \\
\text{3-in. main} &= 4.5 \text{ psi per 100 ft} = 4.5 \, (0.4) = 1.80 \text{ psi} \\
\text{2½-in. main} &= 10.1 \text{ psi per 100 ft} = 11.0 \, (0.4) = 4.4 \text{ psi}
\end{aligned}
$$

10. The friction loss in the meter (if required) is checked next (Fig. 2-37).

6-in. meter, 200 gpm: 1 psi
4-in. meter, 200 gpm: 4 psi
 (a 4-in. meter would be used if 5-in. pipe were used)
3-in. meter, 200 gpm: 10.5 psi
 (a 3-in. meter would be used if 4-in. pipe were used)

11. Obviously, the 3-in. main will not work, and the 4-in. and 5-in. mains are next considered. (It should be noted here that 3½-in. pipe is not readily available in many areas, and in such a situation, the 4-in. pipe would be used.)

At this time, a preliminary selection of a 5-in. main and 4-in. meter is made and tabulated.

Pressure available for friction loss	11.13 psi
Friction loss in 5-in. main and 4-in. meter (0.14 psi + 4.0 psi)	−4.14 psi
Pressure available for riser friction loss	6.99 psi

2 / WATER SUPPLY DESIGN

12. Before the riser selections can be made, the fixture units and demand load (in gpm) for this upfeed zone must be calculated and put in the tabulated form.

Fixture units, floors 1–5, were previously calculated at 48 f.u. per floor:
47 f.u. (per floor) × 5 (floors) = 235 (accumulated) f.u.
Demand load (Fig. 1-28 predominantly flush valve): 98 gpm.

13. This time the available pressure left to overcome friction loss will be converted into loss per 100 ft by using the formula (see Sec. 2-10):

$$\frac{\text{Available psi} \times 100 \text{ (ft)}}{\text{Equivalent length}} = \text{psi loss per 100 ft}$$

$$\frac{6.99 \times 100}{55 + 22.5} = \frac{699}{77.5} = 9.02 \text{ psi loss per 100 ft (maximum)}$$

14. Riser pipe selection (from Fig. 2-34).

2-in. pipe   = 8.0 psi per 100 ft
2½-in. pipe = 2.7 psi per 100 ft
3-in. pipe   = 1.3 psi per 100 ft

15. As previously discussed in regard to upfeed systems, Sec. 2-10, the size of the riser may be decreased in the upper floors, as the gpm decreases, as long as the friction loss for each segment does not increase.

While the 2-in. riser could be used, the 2½-in. pipe is selected to allow some extra pressure at the top fixtures. Now, complete the tabulations for the upfeed zone. (Later, once the design is fully laid out, the actual equivalent length would be rechecked.)

2-12   HOT WATER

By piping part of the water in the building main (Fig. 2-22) into a heating device, the hot water required on the project can be supplied. The heating device may be a direct or an indirect heater and may operate on oil, gas, electricity, or the sun (solar heat). Direct heaters (Fig. 2-23) are designed solely to provide the hot water required. Indirect heaters (Fig. 2-24) use some type of boiler (heater) to heat the hot water and also to provide heat or steam to the heating system of the project.

Direct heaters come in a variety of sizes and capacities that allow them to be located in the basement, crawl space or closet; in a cabinet under the counter; or as

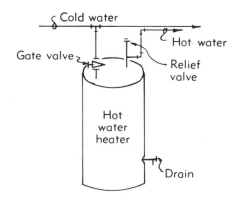

FIGURE 2-22 / Hot water heater

units which look similar to clothes washers. Many times for projects such as apartments, cold water is run to a direct heater (usually electric) in each apartment, instead of using one large hot water heating unit. This also allows for each individual apartment to be on a separate electric meter and for each resident to pay for the electricity he uses. Residences commonly use a direct heater, and in large homes two units are sometimes used (one near the kitchen–laundry and one near the bathrooms) to cut down the amount of hot water piping required and to provide the almost instant availability of hot water when a faucet is turned on. (The hot water in a pipe will cool off when not used for awhile.)

Indirect heaters use the same heating unit to provide hot water or steam to the heating system and to heat the hot water required for use at the fixtures. The same water used in the heating system is not used for the fixtures; instead, a separate compartment or coil containing the water is fed through the unit to be heated. Such units have been used in residences as well as commercial projects. This method is more commonly used in colder climates where the heating system is in operation for more months of the year. Often it is not an economical solution because during the warmer months, the heating system (boiler or furnace) will have to go on to provide hot water when no heating is required. Indirect heaters usually have tanks to store the heated water, or they may have a high-capacity coil capable of providing hot water very quickly.

Some projects use a combination of direct and indirect hot water heaters (Fig. 2-25) whereby the cold water is piped through the indirect heater and then to the direct

FIGURE 2-23 / Direct heater

2 / WATER SUPPLY DESIGN

FIGURE 2-24 / Indirect heaters

heater. When the indirect heater is being used for heating, it will provide fully or partially heated water to the direct heater. This means that at times the direct heater will have little or no additional heating to do.

The cold water supply should have a cutoff valve so that the water supply to the heater can be cut off if necessary. This allows for easier repair or replacement of the heater if required. The hot water pipe exits off the top of the tank and should have a relief valve to allow escape of any excess pressure built up in the system. Heaters which operate on oil or gas will require ventilation to the exterior, usually through a chimney, to get rid of poisonous gases. Electric and solar units do not require venting to the exterior.

2-13   HOT WATER DISTRIBUTION SYSTEMS

Hot water systems make use of upfeed zones to provide the water, under pressure, throughout the project. In taller buildings, the heaters are fed cold water from the tanks supplying water to the downfeed systems (Fig. 2-26). This allows the water from the tank to build up sufficient pressure, as it feeds down to the heater, to create an upfeed zone.

When designing hot water piping systems, the best solution is one which requires the hot water to travel as short a distance as possible from the heater to the point at which it will be used. The longer the supply pipe, the less efficient the system because as the water stays in the pipe, it quickly loses its heat to the surrounding air, even if the pipe is insulated.

For example, review the situation shown in Fig. 2-27, in which the bathroom faucet is about 75 ft from the heater. This means that if the water has had time to cool

FIGURE 2-25 / Combination
heater

in the pipe (say, during the night), when the faucet is turned on, cool water will come
from the faucet until the 75 ft of cool water has flowed through the faucet. Only at that
time will hot water come out of the faucet. Then, once the faucet has been shut off,
there is 75 ft of hot water in the pipe which begins to lose its heat. Back at the heater,
as the hot water is drawn out, cold water begins to enter and be heated, and enough
extra hot water must be heated to fill the 75-ft supply pipe again. This process is
repeated over and over, several times a day, every day.

FIGURE 2-26 / Multistory hot
water zones

2 / WATER SUPPLY DESIGN

BEDROOM #1

BEDROOM #2

LIVING - FAMILY

BATH

BEDROOM #3

ENTRY

DINING

KITCHEN

Hot water supply

GARAGE

Heater

FIGURE 2-27 / Hot water supply length

One solution to this problem, in projects such as apartment buildings, is to provide each apartment with a direct-type water heater which can be located as conveniently as possible. Typical locations include under the bathroom sink, in a kitchen cabinet and in a closet.

In large residences, it is quite common to put in two (or perhaps more) heaters to reduce the distance from heater to source of use. Quite often, one heater will be located near the kitchen with another in the bedroom area. These units are commonly located in a crawl space, basement, or closet or in a kitchen or bathroom closet.

Most plumbing installations have a noncirculating, direct supply layout, similar to that shown in Fig. 2-28 and discussed in this section. But when the rapid delivery of hot water becomes part of the design requirements and it is not practical to provide small direct heaters throughout the project, a system which circulates the hot water through the supply piping and back to the heater for reheating is used (Fig. 2-29). Circulating systems have a continuous riser going from the tank, through the project and back to the tank; the fixtures being serviced are fed by a direct branch supply off the riser. The only hot water which stays in the pipe and may cool off is that which is in the branch piping. The hot water will circulate through the system by gravity flow as the hot water rising to the top of the system forces the cooler water back toward the tank.

The circulating system may be upfeed, downfeed or a combination upfeed-and-downfeed system. A check valve keeps the water flowing in the proper direction.

FIGURE 2-28 / Noncirculating hot
water

A pump may be required for circulation of the water where the tank is not below the
lowest fixture being served.

2-14   HOT WATER SUPPLY DESIGN

STEP-BY-STEP APPROACH

1.   In sizing hot water supply piping, the first step is to determine the total demand
     in fixture units for the project. To calculate the total demand in fixture units for
     hot water, it is necessary to list the fixtures which require hot water. (The hot
     water demands for various types of buildings are shown in Fig. 2-40. Use these
     tables when the exact fixtures are not available.)

     To calculate the fixture units for the four-story apartment building,
     first list the hot water fixtures for each floor (Fig. 2-30).

FIGURE 2-29 / Circulating hot
water

APT. BLDG. PROJ. #20-1 (Appendix A)
HOT WATER FIXTURES, EACH FLOOR

                                        FU

2 BATHTUBS
2 KITCHEN SINKS
2 LAVATORIES

FIGURE 2-30 / Hot water fixtures

2. The next step is to list the equivalent fixture units from Fig. 1-27 for each fixture (Fig. 2-31). When added together, this gives the total fixture-unit demand of these fixtures for hot *and* cold water. To determine the fixture units for hot water only, the plumbing code requires that three-fourths of the listed demand be used.

APT. BLDG. PROJ., #20-1 (Appendix A)
HOT WATER FIXTURES, EACH FLOOR

	FU
2 BATHTUBS	4
2 KITCHEN SINKS	4
2 LAVATORIES	2
	10

$10 \times .75 = 7.5$ FU PER FLOOR

(From Fig. 1-27, hot water only)

7.5 FU $\times$ 4 FLOORS $= 30$ FU (Hot water)

FIGURE 2-31 / Hot water fixture units

In this case, the hot water demand would be 10 f.u. $\times$ ¾ = 7.5 f.u. per floor. So for four floors, the total hot water fixture-unit demand is 7.5 f.u. (per floor) $\times$ 4 floors = 30 f.u.

3. The hot water demand (in gallons per minute or gpm) is determined from Fig. 1-28 by finding the total hot water fixture units (in this case, 30) along the left and reading the gpm at the right (in this case, 20 gpm).

4. Next, the riser pipe size is determined. Remember that when the cold water riser was sized, the total demand in fixture units for hot *and* cold water was used. This means that the friction loss has already been calculated in the cold water supply (Sec. 2-10).

In sizing the cold water riser, a 1¼-in. riser with a friction loss of 10 psi per 100 ft and 6.0 psi for the 60 ft of riser height was used. Since the hot water demand was included in this calculation, the friction loss of 10 psi per 100 ft may be used for the hot water. From Fig. 2-33, using a gpm of 20 and a friction loss of 10 psi, the riser should be a 1-in. pipe (copper). In actual design practice, a 1¼-in. pipe would probably be used for the first two floors; then it would be reduced to a 1-in. pipe.

5. Selection of the hot water branch pipe serving each floor is based on the demand load in gpm and the permissible friction loss (using the 10 psi which included the distance in the branch).

    The gpm is based on 7.5 f.u. per floor and, taken from Fig. 1-28, is about 6.5 gpm.

    Using Fig. 2-34, the branch size selected (based on 6.5 gpm and 10 psi per 100 ft) is ¾ in.

6. The minimum size of the pipe from the branch to the fixture (called the supply pipe) is taken from Fig. 2-39. All fixture supply pipe sizes should be checked against the minimum sizes in Fig. 2-39.

2-15   TESTING THE SYSTEM

In many larger cities and municipalities, a separate plumbing permit must be taken out. Oftentimes building departments will even review the drawings to see if the design conforms to the code in force; others may simply require a brief written description of the system.

Also, depending on the locale, once the plumbing is roughed in, the municipal plumbing inspector will check all installed work, particularly the waste portion of the system, for conformance with the code. This inspection should be made before any pipes are covered, and most inspectors will not approve a system unless a complete inspection can be made. It is far better to find a leak in the system before the walls, ceilings and floor are finished than after.

Tests on a system are made to be certain that it will perform satisfactorily and not solely for inspectors or because it is required. The water supply system is checked by sealing all openings in the system, filling it with potable water and then pressurizing it (up to the normal operating pressure). Such a check of the system will show any leaks in the fittings.

There are still many areas which do not have inspectors and do not enforce the building codes. The codes are designed to protect human life and to ensure that the completed system will fulfill the function it was designed for. Tests should be made on any system whether it is inspected or not.

2-16   WATER HEATER TIMERS

Many projects (residential, institutional and commercial) use time clocks to control the operation of the water heater. Even when the needs of the facility are carefully analyzed to determine peak loading periods, there are many times when the water heater will heat the water and then the hot water will sit in the tank for hours before it is used. In the second example of hot water demand, the plant runs two shifts. In reviewing the data, the last showers are taken between 12 midnight and 12:30 A.M. The hot water is not used again until 3:30 P.M. when the first shift crew begins to shower. The heating capacity has been calculated to heat all of the hot water required in 8 hours. So during the 15 hours from 12:30 A.M. to 3:30 P.M., the heater will work to heat the water for the first 8 hours (until 8:30 A.M.) and then continue to work to keep the water hot (since there will be a heat loss through the tank) for the next 7 hours (until 3:30 P.M.). In such a situation, a timer would shut the water heater off at 12:30 A.M. and turn it on at about 7 A.M. to begin to heat the water for the 3:30 shower.

The hot water needs of a residence can also be analyzed. For example, assume that someone will be home all day and prefers to do the clothes washing and to run the dishwasher during the day. Also, assume the family arises at 6:30 A.M. and retires at about 11 P.M. Since a quick recovery water heater will restore hot water in about 45 minutes, after their 11 P.M. showers, all of the hot water will be reheated in the tank by 12 midnight, and then the heater must maintain the temperature of the water until 6:30 A.M. Energy could be saved if the timer were set to shut the water heater off from 11 P.M. until 5:30 A.M. Then at 5:30, the heater would come on and heat all the water needed before 6:30 A.M.

As people begin to organize their day to conserve energy, the hours that hot water is required will be reduced considerably. The majority of studies show that most of the hot water is required during a 1-hour time period in the morning and a 2-hour time period at night. To provide the hot water required for these periods, the heater will need to work about 3 hours a day. Generally, if it is set to turn on a half hour before rising, to operate for an hour and then to turn back on about suppertime for 2 hours, there will be sufficient hot water to meet all of a family's needs. This will work if clothes are washed in cold water during the day or in hot water in the evening, and if the dishwasher is run only during the evening hours. This type of conservation can reduce the energy used for hot water by as much as 35% to 40%, a significant savings.

2-17 SOLAR HOT WATER

Solar hot water heating systems are no longer a dream of the future. Development continues on systems which capture the heat from the sun to heat water for use in the home or project. The final chapter cannot yet be written on these systems as experimentation continues and as millions of dollars from government and private enterprise are poured into further research and development. Meanwhile, many dependable and cost-effective hot water heating systems are now available for purchase.

The most successful solar hot water heater, in the author's opinion, is the solar flat-plate absorber/collector; the principles of operation are shown in Fig. 2-32. In many areas, the solar heating unit is supplemented with an electric heating coil to provide hot water in case of prolonged cloudiness which will limit the amount of solar energy available to heat water. This is not to imply that the solar heater cannot be designed to provide all of the hot water required—just that it is most efficient costwise

Tank—This tank could be used to just hold water heated by the collector medium or it could be a direct hot water heater used to supplement the collector during times when the collector cannot provide all of the hot water required.

FIGURE 2-32 / Solar hot water system

to design the solar system to provide 85% to 95% per year. Whether it is a good investment or not depends on whether it will give a good return on the investment. The economics of the system will vary according to the geographic location, total amount of hot water required, and the current (and future) cost of hot water.

QUESTIONS

2-1. What are plumbing codes, and why are they used?

2-2. What is meant by *multiple governing codes,* and why must the designer be aware of them?

2-3. Who is most likely to enforce the plumbing code?

Fixture	Flow Pressure (a) psi	Flow rate gpm
Ordinary basin faucet	8	3.0
Self-closing basin faucet	12	2.5
Sink Faucet - 3/8 in.	10	4.5
Sink Faucet - 1/2 in.	5	4.5
Bathtub faucet	5	6.0
Laundry tub cock - 1/2 in.	5	5.0
Shower	12	5.0
Ball-cock for closet	15	3.0
Flush valve for closet	10-20	15-40 (b)
Flush valve for urinal	15	15.0
Garden hose, 50 ft. and sill cock	30	5.0

FIGURE 2-33 / Fixture flow pressure and flow

(a) Flow pressure is the pressure in the pipe at the entrance to the particular fixture considered.

(b) Wide range due to variation in design and type of flush-valve closets.

2 / WATER SUPPLY DESIGN

2-4. What materials are most commonly used for the pipes and tubing in a water supply system?

2-5. How and where are the following valves used in the system?
a. Globe c. Gate
b. Angle d. Check

2-6. What is *water shock,* and how can it be reduced in the system?

2-7. How may expansion be allowed for in the system, and what type of pipe expands the most?

2-8. What are the two basic types of water supply systems used, and what determines which will be used?

2-9. What is meant, in water supply systems, by *static head?*

2-10. What is the difference between a direct and an indirect water heater?

2-11. Why is more than one hot water heater sometimes used in larger residences?

2-12. What is the difference between circulating and noncirculating hot water systems, and when would the circulating system most likely be used?

2-13. Briefly, describe and sketch how a solar hot water heating system might work.

2-14. What factors affect whether or not it might be economical to use a solar hot water heating system?

2-15. Why are supplemental heating units often installed in solar hot water heating systems?

Design Exercises

2-16. Design an upfeed water supply system for the apartment building in Appendix B. Use copper pipe and tubing for this design problem.

2-17. Determine the hot water consumption and the equipment sizes required for the building in Appendix B. Use the information in Fig. 2-40.

2-18. Determine the hot water consumption and the equipment sizes required for a 150-room motel based on the following information:
Hot water required: 30 gal per day per person
Occupancy rate: 2.4 persons per room, 100% occupied
Storage capacity (tank): 60% of total daily use (of which 75% is usable)
Maximum hourly demand: ⅙ of total daily use
Peak demand time: 3 hr.

2-19. Design the upfeed hot water supply system required for the apartment in Appendix B. Use copper pipe and tubing.

FLOW IN GALLONS PER MINUTE

COPPER TUBING
SMOOTH PIPE

Type M − − − − −
Type L ———————
Type K ——— ———

FRICTION LOSS IN HEAD IN LBS PER SQ IN. PER 100-FT LENGTH

FIGURE 2-34 / Friction loss (smooth pipe)

FIGURE 2-35 / *Friction loss (fairly rough pipe)*

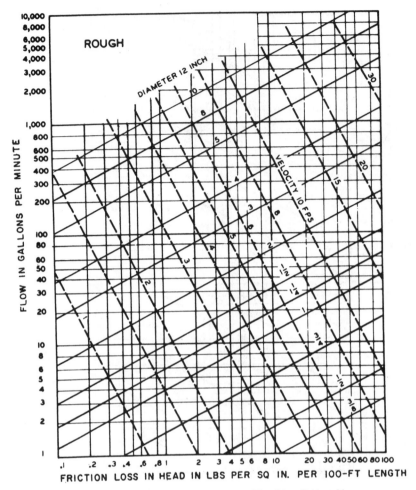

FIGURE 2-36 / Friction loss (rough pipe)

Reprinted with permission from ASHRAE, *Fundamentals Handbook*, 1989.

FIGURE 2-37 / Meter pressure loss

(*See manufacturer's data for exact value for meter used*)

ALLOWANCE IN EQUIVALENT LENGTH OF PIPE FOR FRICTION LOSS IN VALVES AND THREADED FITTINGS

Fitting or valve	Equivalent feet of pipe for various sizes							
	½ in.	¾ in.	1 in.	1¼ in.	1½ in.	2 in.	2½ in.	3 in.
45° elbow	1.2	1.5	1.8	2.4	3.0	4.0	5.0	6.0
90° elbow	2.0	2.5	3.0	4.0	5.0	7.0	8.0	10.0
Tee, run	0.6	0.8	0.9	1.2	1.5	2.0	2.5	3.0
Tee, branch	3.0	4.0	5.0	6.0	7.0	10.0	12.0	15.0
Gate valve	0.4	0.5	0.6	0.8	1.0	1.3	1.6	2.0
Balancing valve	0.8	1.1	1.5	1.9	2.2	3.0	3.7	4.5
Plug-type cock	0.8	1.1	1.5	1.9	2.2	3.0	3.7	4.5
Check valve, swing	5.6	8.4	11.2	14.0	16.8	22.4	28.0	33.6
Globe valve	15.0	20.0	25.0	35.0	45.0	55.0	65.0	80.0
Angle valve	8.0	12.0	15.0	18.0	22.0	28.0	34.0	40.0

ALLOWANCE IN EQUIVALENT LENGTH OF TUBE FOR FRICTION LOSS IN VALVES AND FITTINGS[1]
(Copper Water Tube)

Fitting or valve	Equivalent feet of tube for various sizes							
	½ in.	¾ in.	1 in.	1¼ in.	1½ in.	2 in.	2½ in.	3 in.
45° elbow (wrought)	0.5	0.5	1.0	1.0	2.0	2.0	3.0	4.0
90° elbow (wrought)	0.5	1.0	1.0	2.0	2.0	2.0	2.0	3.0
Tee, run (wrought)	0.5	0.5	0.5	0.5	1.0	1.0	2.0	-
Tee, branch (wrought)	1.0	2.0	3.0	4.0	5.0	7.0	9.0	-
45° elbow (cast)	0.5	1.0	2.0	2.0	3.0	5.0	8.0	11.0
90° elbow (cast)	1.0	2.0	4.0	5 0	8.0	11.0	14.0	18.0
Tee, run (cast)	0.5	0.5	0.5	1.0	1.0	2.0	2.0	2.0
Tee, branch (cast)	2.0	3.0	5.0	7.0	9.0	12.0	16.0	20.0
Compression Stop	13.0	21.0	30.0	-	-	-	-	-
Globe Valve	-	-	-	53.0	66.0	90.0	-	-
Gate Valve	-	-	1.0	1.0	2.0	2.0	2.0	2.0

[1]From "Copper Tube Handbook" 1965, by Copper Development Association, Inc.

Extracted from the *1987 National Standard Plumbing Code* with permission of PHCC.

FIGURE 2-38 / Equivalent lengths

Fixture or Device	Size, (in.)
Bathtub	½
Combination sink and laundry tray	½
Drinking fountain	⅜
Dishwashing machine (domestic)	½
Kitchen sink (domestic)	½
Kitchen sink (commercial)	¾
Lavatory	⅜
Laundry tray (1, 2, or 3 compartments)	½
Shower (single head)	½
Sink (service, slop)	½
Sink (flushing rim)	¾
Urinal (1″ flush valve)	1
Urinal (¾″ flush valve)	¾
Urinal (flush tank)	½
Water closet (flush tank)	⅜*
Water closet (flush valve)	1
Hose bib	½
Wall hydrant or still cock	½

*Fixtures may require larger sizes—see manufacturer's instructions.

Extracted from the *1987 National Standard Plumbing Code* with permission of PHCC.

FIGURE 2-39 / Minimum size of fixture branch piping

Table 6 Hot Water Demands and Use for Various Types of Buildings

Type of Building	Maximum Hour	Maximum Day	Average Day
Men's dormitories	3.8 gal (14.4 L)/student	22.0 gal (83.4 L)/student	13.1 gal (49.7 L)/student
Women's dormitories	5.0 gal (19 L)/student	26.5 gal (100.4 L)/student	12.3 gal (46.6 L)/student
Motels: no. of units[a]			
20 or less	6.0 gal (22.7 L)/unit	35.0 gal (132.6 L)/unit	20.0 gal (75.8 L)/unit
60	5.0 gal (19.7 L)/unit	25.0 gal (94.8 L)/unit	14.0 gal (53.1 L)/unit
100 or more	4.0 gal (15.2 L)/unit	15.0 gal (56.8 L)/unit	10.0 gal (37.9 L)/unit
Nursing homes	4.5 gal (17.1 L)/bed	30.0 (113.7 L)/bed	18.4 gal (69.7 L)/bed
Office buildings	0.4 gal (1.52 L)/person	2.0 gal (7.6 L)/person	1.0 gal (3.79 L)/person
Food service establishments:			
Type A—full meal restaurants and cafeterias	1.5 gal (5.7 L)/max meals/h	11.0 gal (41.7 L)/max meals/h	2.4 gal (9.1 L)/avg meals/day[b]
Type B—drive-ins, grilles, luncheonettes, sandwich and snack shops	0.7 gal (2.6 L)/max meals/h	6.0 gal (22.7 L)/max meals/h	0.7 gal (2.6 L)/avg meals/day[b]
Apartment houses: no. of apartments			
20 or less	12.0 gal (45.5 L)/apt.	80.0 gal (303.2 L)/apt.	42.0 gal (159.2 L)/apt.
50	10.0 gal (37.9 L)/apt.	73.0 gal (276.7 L)/apt.	40.0 gal (151.6 L)/apt.
75	8.5 gal (32.2 L)/apt.	66.0 gal (250 L)/apt.	38.0 gal (144 L)/apt.
100	7.0 gal (26.5 L)/apt.	60.0 gal (227.4 L)/apt.	37.0 gal (140.2 L)/apt.
200 or more	5.0 gal (19 L)	50.0 gal (195 L)/apt.	35.0 gal (132.7 L)/apt.
Elementary schools	0.6 gal (2.3 L)/student	1.5 gal (5.7 L)/student	0.6 gal (2.3 L)/student[b]
Junior and senior high schools	1.0 gal (3.8 L)/student	3.6 gal (13.6 L)/student	1.8 gal (6.8 L)/student[b]

[a]Interpolate for intermediate values.
[b]Per day of operation.

Reprinted with permission from ASHRAE, *HVAC Handbook*, 1987.

FIGURE 2-40 / Hot water demands and use for various types of buildings

DEMAND AT INDIVIDUAL WATER OUTLETS

Type of Outlet	Demand, (gpm)
Ordinary lavatory faucet	2.0
Self-closing lavatory faucet	2.5
Sink faucet, 3/8" or 1/2"	4.5
Sink faucet, 3/4"	6.0
Bath faucet, 1/2"	5.0
Shower head, 1/2"	5.0
Laundry faucet, 1/2"	5.0
Ballcock in water closet flush tank	3.0
1" flush valve (25 psi flow pressure)	35.0
1" flush valve (15 psi flow pressure)	27.0
3/4" flush valve (15 psi flow pressure)	15.0
Drinking fountain jet	0.75
Dishwashing machine (domestic)	4.0
Laundry machine (8 or 16 lbs.)	4.0
Aspirator (operating room or laboratory)	2.5
Hose bib or sill cock (1/2")	5.0

Extracted from the 1988 Supplement to the *1987 National Standard Plumbing Code* with permission of PHCC.

FIGURE 2-40 (Continued) / *Hot water demands and use for various types of buildings*

CHAPTER 3
PLUMBING DRAINAGE

3-1 DRAINAGE PRINCIPLES

In Chapter 2, hot and cold water supply systems were described, with pipes to provide sufficient running water to all of the fixtures throughout a building or project. Following the flow of the water through the system, the next step will be to dispose of the waste matter, both fluid and organic, which is accumulated. The wastes will come from almost all sections of the building—bathrooms, kitchens, and laundry areas, and, in commercial projects, even the equipment being serviced. Because all of the wastes tend to decompose quickly, one of the primary objectives of the plumbing system is to dispose of decaying wastes quickly, before they cause objectionable odors or become hazardous to health.

Water is used to transport the wastes into the drainage piping and to the point where they will enter a community sewer line leading either to a community sewage treatment plant or to a private sewage treatment system. The sewage from residences, apartments, motels, office buildings, and other similar types of buildings is referred to as *domestic sewage*. Special sewage from laboratories and many industrial plants requires special handling and such treatment is not discussed here. However, it is important to note that such wastes should not be put into a community sewage system without first getting approval from the community.

3-2   PLUMBING CODES

The *National Standard Plumbing Code* is used as the basis for the plumbing discussed in this text. Increasingly, all plumbing codes are being modeled after this code with only minor revisions to meet the requirements of specific geographic locations. References in this portion of the text relate to the *National Standard Plumbing Code,* and everyone who is learning about plumbing, its design and its requirements, should have a current copy available. In addition, any relevant state or local plumbing codes should be made a part of your library for future reference.

3-3   THE DRAINAGE SYSTEM

In this section the terminology and function of each of the parts of the drainage system are explained. The basic parts of the system are illustrated in Fig. 3-1.

TRAPS

A *trap* (Fig. 3-2) is a device which catches and holds a quantity of water, thus forming

FIGURE 3-1 / *Drainage system*

FIGURE 3-2 / Traps

a seal which prevents the gases resulting from sewage decomposition from entering the building through the pipe. Traps are installed at each fixture as bent pipes unless the fixture is designed with the trap as an integral part of it (as in the case of the water closet in Fig. 3-3).

Traps may be made of copper, plastic, steel, wrought iron, or brass, with brass most commonly used. Traps in water closets are made of vitreous china and are cast right into the fixture.

The trap is located as close to the fixture as possible, usually within 2 ft of it. Occasionally, more than one fixture is tied to one trap. Quite often a laundry tray and a kitchen sink, a dishwasher and a kitchen sink, or two kitchen sinks may be connected to a single trap, provided all fixtures are close to one another. There should never be more than three closely located fixtures (such as lavatories) on a single trap, or the trap may not operate properly (it may lose its *water seal,* also called *trap seal*). Since the trap may occasionally need to be cleaned, either there should be a plug in the bottom which may be removed (Fig. 3-4), or the trap should have screwed connections on each end for easy removal (Fig. 3-5).

In locations where the fixtures are infrequently used, care must be taken or the water in the traps may evaporate, and once the water seal is gone, gases may back up from the sewer and drainage pipes through the fixture and into the building. Floor drains (Fig. 3-6) which are used to take away the water after washing floors or which may be used only in case of equipment malfunctions or repairs present the most serious possibility of losing the water seal. When these floor drains are connected to the drainage system, the possibility of a serious gas problem exists. The designer of the system can avoid such a situation by *not* tying the floor drain into the drainage system. Instead, the floor drains should be tied into a drywell (Fig. 4-2) from which there will be no gases. Many building departments and plumbing codes prohibit the connection of floor drains to the sewage drainage system.

The water seal may also be broken if there is a great deal of air pressure turbulence in the pipes. To reduce the turbulence and to tend to equalize the pressure

FIGURE 3-3 / Integral trap

FIGURE 3-4 / Trap cleanout   FIGURE 3-5 / Trap connection

throughout the system, it is opened to the outside at the top and sufficient air is supplied throughout the system through *vent pipes*.

VENTS

Vent pipes allow gases in the sewage drainage system to discharge to the outside and sufficient air to enter the system to reduce the air turbulence in the system. Also, without a vent, once the water discharges from a fixture, the moving waste tends to siphon the water from other fixture traps as it goes through the pipes. This means that the vent piping must serve the various fixtures, or groups of fixtures, as well as the rest of the sewage drainage system. The vent from a fixture or group of fixtures ties in with the main vent stack (Fig. 3-7) or the stack vent (Fig. 3-8) which goes to the exterior. Vent piping may be copper, plastic, cast iron, or steel.

A *stack vent* is that portion of the vertical sewage drainage pipe (which may be a soil or waste stack) which extends above the highest horizontal drain that is connected to it (Fig. 3-9). It extends through the roof to the exterior of the building.

A *vent stack* is used in multistory buildings where a pipe is required to provide the flow of air throughout the drainage system. The vent stack begins at the soil or

FIGURE 3-6 / Floor drain   FIGURE 3-7 / Vent to vent stack

FIGURE 3-8 / Vent to stack vent

waste pipe, just below the lowest horizontal connection, and may go through the roof (Fig. 3-10) or connect back into the soil or waste pipe not less than 6 in. above the top of the highest fixture.

FIXTURE BRANCHES

The fixtures at a floor level are connected horizontally to the stack by a drain called a *fixture branch* (Fig. 3-1). Beginning with the fixture farthest from the stack, the branch must slope ⅛ to ½ in. per ft for proper flow of wastes through the branch. Branch piping which serves urinals, water closets, showers, or tubs is usually run in the floor (Fig. 3-11). When these fixtures are not on the branch, the piping may be run in the

FIGURE 3–9 / Vent stack to stack vent

MULTISTORY

FIGURE 3-10 / Vent stack to soil stack

SINGLE FLOOR

FIGURE 3-11 / Typical drainage piping

floor or in the wall behind the fixtures (Fig. 3-12). Branch piping may be copper, plastic, galvanized steel, or cast iron.

SOIL AND WASTE STACKS

The fixture branches feed into a vertical pipe referred to as a *stack*. When the waste that the stack will carry includes human waste from water closets (or from fixtures which have similar functions), the stack is referred to as a *soil stack*. When the stack will carry all wastes *except* human waste, it is referred to as a *waste stack*. Soil and waste stacks may be copper, plastic, galvanized steel, or cast iron. These stacks service the

FIGURE 3-12 / Individual fixture drainage

MULTISTORY

fixture branches beginning at the top branch and go vertically to the building drain (Fig. 3-13).

In larger buildings, the point where the stack ties into the building drain rests on a masonry pier or steel post so that the downward pressure of the wastes will not cause the piping system to sag. In addition, the stack must be supported at 10-ft intervals to limit movement of the pipe. When a stack length is greater than 80 ft, horizontal offsets are used to reduce free fall velocity and air turbulence. Connections to fixture branches and the building drain should be angled 45° or more to allow the smooth flow of wastes.

Most designers try to lay out plumbing fixtures to line up vertically floor after floor so that a minimum number of stacks will be required. Many times a central core of a multistory building will be used as a plumbing core, and a *pipe chase,* a space which is left to put the pipes in, runs from the first floor to the roof of the building (Fig. 3-14).

BUILDING DRAINS (ALSO CALLED HOUSE DRAINS)

The soil or waste stacks feed into a horizontal pipe referred to as the *building drain.* The building drain slopes ⅛ to ¼ in. per ft as it feeds the waste into the building sewer outside the building. By definition, the building drain extends to a point 3 ft *outside* the wall of the building (Fig. 3-13).

Provision is made to allow cleaning of the building drain by putting a *cleanout* at the end of the drain (Fig. 3-13). Another cleanout is sometimes placed just inside the building wall in case it is necessary to clean the building drain or sewer line. Cleanouts should also be placed no more than 50 ft apart in long building drains.

Location of the building drain in the building depends primarily on the location (elevation) below grade of the community sewer. Ideally, all of the plumbing wastes of the building will flow into the sewer (whether it is a community or a private sewer system) by gravity. Typically, the drain is placed below the first floor (Fig. 3-13) or below the basement floor (Fig. 3-15). If the height of the sewer requires the drain to be placed above the lowest fixtures (Fig. 3-16), it will be necessary for the low fixtures to drain into a sump pit. When the level in the sump pit rises to a certain point, an

FIGURE 3-13 / Stack locations

FIGURE 3-14 / Pipe chase

automatic float or control will activate a pump which raises the waste out of the pit and into the building drain.

Building drains are usually made of plastic, copper (for above the floor), or extra-heavy cast iron (for below the floor) pipe.

BUILDING TRAPS (ALSO CALLED HOUSE TRAPS) AND FRESH AIR INLETS

Some codes may require a *building trap* on the building drain near the building wall (Fig. 3-17). This trap acts as a seal to keep gases and vermin (rats and mice) from entering the sewage system from the sewer line. The *National Standard Plumbing Code* and most regional and state codes do not feel a building trap is necessary; instead it is felt that this trap will impede the flow of wastes in the system. However, when required by local, state, or regional codes, it must be put in the system. When a building trap is used, a *fresh air inlet* (Fig. 3-17) is required to allow fresh air into the system to be certain that the trap seal is not siphoned through. The fresh air inlet must be a minimum of 4 in. or one-half the diameter of the building drain, whichever is larger.

FIGURE 3-15 / Underfloor building drain

3 / PLUMBING DRAINAGE

Laundry tub

Sump pump

FIGURE 3-16 / Sump pump

FIGURE 3-17 / Building trap

3-4 PIPES AND FITTINGS

Drainage lines and vents make use of most of the same types of piping used in the water supply system, except that vitrified clay tile may be used in the building sewer line. Copper tubing, type DWV, is very commonly used in drainage piping but is *not* used in water supply. The *DWV* on the tubing means it can be used for drainage, waste and venting on the job. Type M copper may be used above grade and type L copper below grade. Plastic piping is used extensively in drainage systems because of its low cost and speedy installation. Other piping sometimes used in the building sewer line includes concrete, asbestos-cement and bituminous pipes. Fittings used in drainage systems are shown in Fig. 3-18.

3-5 PLUMBING DRAINAGE DESIGN

First, a complete review of the project being designed must be made. In this case, the four-story apartment building used for the water supply problem in Sec. 2–10 is used. A review of the drawings for the apartments shows that each floor contains two bathroom groups and two kitchen sinks. Assume the project will be connected to a community sewer.

In this project, it has been decided that there will be two plumbing stacks, one for each tier of apartments (Fig. 3-19).

STEP-BY-STEP APPROACH

1.   The first step will be to sketch an isometric of the drainage piping. It will be easiest to follow if you first locate the stack on the plan (Fig. 3-19). Then sketch the vertical stack (Fig. 3-20), and beginning at the top floor, sketch the fixture branch and then the connection at each fixture.

Next, sketch in the other three floors as shown in Fig. 3-21.

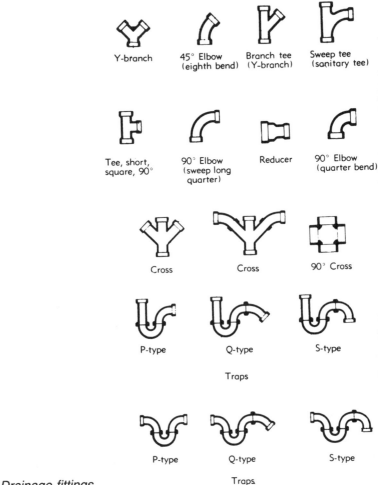

The figure labels read:

Y-branch   45° Elbow (eighth bend)   Branch tee (Y-branch)   Sweep tee (sanitary tee)

Tee, short, square, 90°   90° Elbow (sweep long quarter)   Reducer   90° Elbow (quarter bend)

Cross   Cross   90° Cross

P-type   Q-type   S-type

Traps

P-type   Q-type   S-type

Traps

FIGURE 3-18 / Drainage fittings

Now, add the vent stack from a point just below the bottom fixture branch to a point above the top fixture and the building drain (Fig. 3-22).

2. Next, the minimum trap size for each fixture is selected from Fig. 3-46 and the trap size noted on the schematic pipe layout, as shown in Fig. 3-23. Assume the kitchen sink has a small P.O. (plumbing outlet) plug.

3. The fixture branch is the first drainage pipe to be sized. The first portion of the branch to be sized is from the fixture farthest from the stack to the next fixture, as shown in Fig. 3-24. Begin by determining the fixture units that this short piece of pipe will serve from Fig. 3-24.

In this problem, the branch serves a bathtub with a fixture-unit value of 2, based on Fig. 3-42.

84   *3 / PLUMBING DRAINAGE*

FIGURE 3-19 / Stack location

Note:

⌣ Trap
required

⌐ No trap
required

FIGURE 3-20 / Sketch soil stack

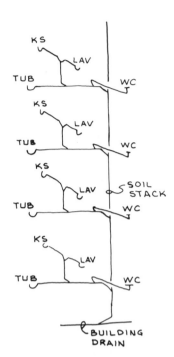

FIGURE 3-21 / Add fixture
branches

4.   Next, select the branch size to serve the bathtub from the table of sizes in Fig.
     3-43. Be sure to check the figures for horizontal fixture branches and stacks each
     time you use Fig. 3-43. The left row of numbers gives the various diameters of
     pipe which may be used. The rest of the columns list the maximum number of
     fixture units which can be connected to a given pipe size. Each of the fixture-unit
     columns defines the type of piping being selected.

> In this case, the horizontal fixture branch size is being selected so go
> to that column. As shown in Fig. 3-25, go down the column until the
> fixture-unit number is the same as or more than the amount being
> served—in this case, 3 f.u., which is greater than the 2 f.u. value of
> the bathtub. Now, move horizontally to the left and select the min-
> imum pipe size required—in this case, 1½ in. Now, note the infor-
> mation accumulated in tabular form as shown:

	f.u.	PIPE SIZE
#1-tub	2	1½ in.

5.   For all fixtures, there is a maximum horizontal distance between the fixture trap
     and a vent. The distance depends on the pipe size being used and is listed in Fig.
     3-47. For a 1½-in. pipe, the maximum distance from trap to vent is 5 ft. Add this
     information to the tabular form:

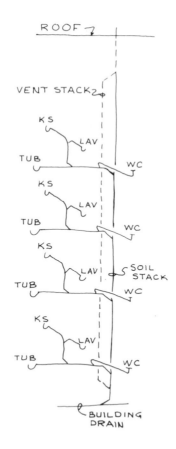

FIGURE 3-22 / Add vent stack

	f.u.	PIPE SIZE	DISTANCE
#1-tub to lav.	2	1½ in.	5 ft.

There are many different ways to vent a fixture or group of fixtures. A few of these methods are shown in this example, and many more are shown and discussed in Sec. 3-6. For now, the information needed has been accumulated.

6. Now, size that portion of the pipe which serves the lavatory and kitchen sink down to the branch. In Fig. 3-24, this length is labeled as #2. From Fig. 3-42, the number of fixture units for the kitchen sink being served is 2 f.u. and for the lavatory 1 f.u. for a total of 3 f.u. Referring to Fig. 3-43, the minimum pipe size would be 1½ in., and from Fig. 3-47, the maximum horizontal distance from fixture trap to vent is limited to 5 ft. Now, list the accumulated information.

FIGURE 3-23 / Add trap sizes

FIGURE 3-24 / Typical fixture branch

	f.u.	PIPE SIZE	DISTANCE
#2-k.s. & lav. to branch	3	1½ in.	5 ft

7. The section of branch marked #3 serves the tub, kitchen sink, and lavatory. From Fig. 3-42:

Bathtub	2 f.u.
Kitchen sink	2 f.u.
Lavatory	1 f.u.
Total	5 f.u.

From Fig. 3-43 the pipe size is 2 in.

Add this information to the tabular form.

HORIZONTAL FIXTURE BRANCHES AND STACKS

Maximum Number of Fixture Units that may be Connected to:

Diameter of Pipe	Any Horizontal Fixture Branch[1]	One Stack of Three Branch Intervals or Less	Stacks with More Than Three Branch Intervals	
			Total for Stack	Total at One Branch Interval
Inches	dfu	dfu	dfu	dfu
1½	3	4	8	2
2	6	10	24	6
2½	12	20	42	9
3	20[2]	48[2]	72[2]	20[2]
4	160	240	500	90
5	360	540	1,100	200
6	620	960	1,900	350
8	1,400	2,200	3,600	600
10	2,500	3,800	5,600	1,000
12	3,900	6,000	8,400	1,500
15	7,000			

[1]Does not include branches of the building drain.

[2]Not more than 2 water closets or bathroom groups within each branch interval nor more than 6 water closets or bathroom groups on the stack.

[3]Stacks shall be sized according to the total accumulated connected load at each story or branch interval and may be reduced in size as this load decreases to a minimum diameter of ½ of the largest size required.

Extracted from the *1987 National Standard Plumbing Code* with permission of PHCC.

FIGURE 3-25 / Sizing the horizontal fixture branch

	f.u.	PIPE SIZE
#3-k.s., lav., & tub	5	2 in.

8. Now, the last section (#4) is calculated and tabulated. At this point, the branch services all of the fixtures which are a fixture group and a kitchen sink. From Fig. 3-42 the fixture units are:

1 bathroom group	6 f.u.
1 kitchen sink	2 f.u.
Total	8 f.u.

From Fig. 3-43, the pipe size is 2½ in., but since the pipe cannot be smaller than the largest fixture trap, a 3-in. pipe is required (water closet, 3-in. trap).

	f.u.	PIPE SIZE
#4-bathroom group & k.s.	8	3 in.

9. Now, all of the branch sizes are tabulated (Fig. 3-26). Note the sizes on the isometric sketch, as shown in Fig. 3-27. Since each floor is exactly the same, all of the branches are the same size, and all floors are noted on the isometric. If any of the branches were different, the procedure just explained would be followed to get the branch pipe sizes.

10. The stack size is selected next. Because the stack handles human waste, it is a *soil* stack. The stack must be selected and sized for the total fixture units that it must handle. As noted on sketch in Fig. 3-28, each floor has a total of 8 f.u. for an overall total of 32 f.u. The soil stack is selected from Fig. 3-43 under the column ''More than 3 branch intervals'' since we are dealing with the entire stack height.

> Based on 32 f.u. for the entire stack, the minimum stack size from the chart would be 2½ in., except that the stack must be at least as large as the fixture branch—in this design, 3 in. Note the stack size on the sketch as shown and tabulated in Fig. 3-29.

11. The vent stack is sized next, using the table in Fig. 3-44. To use the table, it is necessary to know the maximum size of the soil stack (left column) and the fixture units connected to the vent stack; the maximum length of vent stack is noted in ft. The soil stack has already been sized, and the fixture units have been totaled as 32 for this stack. The developed length of the vent stack is the lineal ft of pipe required from the lowest point where it connects with the soil stack to the point where it terminates outside the building, as illustrated in Fig. 3-30.

The next step is to determine the size and location of the main (vent) stack. The code requires that every building ''shall have at least one main stack.'' This main stack must be sized to handle the total fixture units on the system.

> In this problem, the developed length is about 52 ft. Use of the table to size the stack is shown in Fig. 3-31; find the soil stack size (4 in.) and then move horizontally to the right to check the fixture-unit column. At this point, you should note that there are three listings for a 3-in. soil stack, all with different fixture-unit values. In this case, there are 64 f.u., which means that the listing of 100 must be used. Now move to the right; the next number represents the developed length of vent in the design—in this case, 52 lineal ft. In the table, it is more than 35, so the 100 column is used. From the 100, move vertically up to read a vent size of 2½ in.
>
> The plumbing code states that the main vent and vent stack shall be sized in accordance with the table ''and be not less than 3 in.

	Fu	Pipe	Dist. to Vent
#1 Tub to Lav	2	1½"	3'–6"
#2 KS, Lav to Tub	3	1½"	5'–0"
#3 KS, Lav, Tub to WC	5	2"	8'–0"
#4 KS, Lav, Tub, WC to Stack	8	3"	10'–0"

FIGURE 3-26 / Horizontal branch tabulation

in diameter.'' In addition, it states that the size of the vent stack must not be reduced all the way through the roof. So in this design, the minimum vent stack size of 3 in. is used.

Code requirements also stipulate that the vent stack will terminate no less than 6 in. above the roof (Fig. 3-32), and if the roof is to be used for other than weather protection (for example, as a terrace or balcony), the vent stack must run at least 5 ft above the roof. Most codes require at least a 3-in. vent through the roof (Fig. 3-32).

12. The next step in the design is to size the building drain. At this point, review the basic system being designed.

The building drain must be sized for the total amount of fixture units connected to the point at which the main vent (step 11) is connected.

In this problem, there are two stacks serving the building, which means that the two stacks must be connected to the building drain. A sketch similar to Fig. 3-33 helps to prevent any confusion or the possibility that a stack may be forgotten. On the sketch, and in tabular form, list the accumulated fixture units.

Next, the slope of the drain must be determined and noted on the sketch; in this case, a ⅛-in. slope per ft is used. Building drain sizes are found in Fig. 3-45. The pipe size is listed on the left, the slope of the pipe (referred to as *fall per ft*) is listed along the top right and the fixture units are listed below the fall per ft. Use of the table for this design is shown in Fig. 3-34. In this design, the main vent is considered to be the end vent, as noted in Fig. 3-35, so the entire building drain must be sized for 64 f.u.

FIGURE 3-27 / Horizontal branch sketch

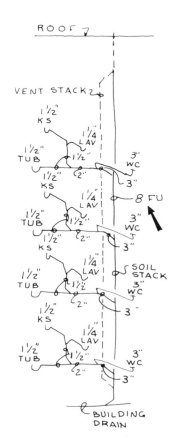

FIGURE 3-28 / Stack fixture units

13. The plumbing drainage system has now been designed, with the exception of checking the location of the vent in relation to the fixtures. As the fixture branch sizes were being selected, the maximum distance from the trap to a vent was also tabulated (Fig. 3-26). While an experienced designer would make a tentative decision as to vent locations early in the design, it has been left to the end here so that a more thorough explanation of the various methods of venting and possible venting solutions may be given.

In reviewing the fixture branch and trap sizes in Fig. 3-26, each of the tub, lavatory, and sink traps can be no more than 5 ft from a vent, and the water closet no more than 10 ft. A check of the floor plan shows that the total width of the bathroom is 7 ft-6 in. This means that the vent could be located in the wall near the lavatory and be within the limits of all listed horizontal distances.

If fixtures are so spread out that one or more fixtures are beyond the maximum horizontal distance, there are two options:

a. Increase the size of the horizontal fixture branch which automatically increases the horizontal distance. For example, change length #1 from 1½

STACK SIZE			
Floor	fu	Accum. fu	Pipe size
4	8	8	3''
3	8	16	3''
2	8	24	3''
1	8	32	3''

FIGURE 3-29 / Stack sizes

in. to 2 in., and it changes the horizontal distance from 5 ft to 8 ft. Many times this is the most economical solution.

b.   Add more vents. Instead of trying to service a group of fixtures with one vent, perhaps a vent should be added to service any fixtures which are beyond the allowable distance. A variety of venting solutions for various groups of fixtures is shown in Figs. 3-36 through 3-39.

ROOF

VENT STACK

SOIL
STACK

BUILDING
DRAIN

Length of pipe
required equals
developed
length

FIGURE 3-30 / Vent stack, developed length

In this design, a single vent off the top of the lavatory–kitchen sink fixtures (referred to as a *wet vent* and discussed in Sec. 3-6) will be used.

The size of the wet vent is selected from Fig. 3-44. But a little explanation is needed. First, a review of the sketch in Fig. 3-36 shows that the portion of the vent referred to as a *wet vent* is actually a part of the drainage system for the lavatory and the kitchen sink. Because it acts as both a *vent* and a *drainage* pipe, it is referred to as a *wet vent*. For single bathroom groups, selection of the wet vent is based on the number of fixture units that the wet vent serves. A careful check of the code requirements for wet venting a multistory bathroom group (Fig. 3-38) indicates that a wet vent and its extension must be 2 in. in diameter and can serve the kitchen sink, lavatory and bathtub. In Fig. 3-39 it states that "each water closet below the top floor is individually back vented" unless wet vented as illustrated in Fig. 3-39. When the minimum size of the vent is larger

Size of soil or waste stack	Fixture Units Connected	Diameter of Vent Required (Inches)								
		1-¼	1-½	2	2-½	3	4	5	6	8
		Maximum Length of Vent (Feet)								
Inches										
1½	8	50	150							
2	12	30	75	200						
2	20	26	50	150						
2½	42		30	100	300					
3	10		30	100	100	600				
3	30			60	200	500				
3	60			50	80	400				
4	100			35	100	260	1000			
4	200			30	90	250	900			
4	500			20	70	180	700			
5	200				35	80	350	1000		
5	500				30	70	300	900		
5	1100				20	50	200	700		
6	350				25	50	200	400	1300	
6	620				15	30	125	300	1100	
6	960					24	100	250	1000	
6	1900					20	70	200	700	
8	600						50	150	500	1300
8	1400						40	100	400	1200
8	2200						30	80	350	1100
8	3600						25	60	250	800
10	1000							75	125	1000
10	2500							50	100	500
10	3800							30	80	350
10	5600							25	60	250

Extracted from the *1987 National Standard Plumbing Code* with permission of PHCC.

FIGURE 3-31 / *Size and length of vents*

than the waste sizes previously selected, the larger size must be used.

Note the size of the venting required on the schematic sketch, and the plumbing drainage design is completed for this project.

3-6 VENTING

The basics of venting have been outlined in Sec. 3-3 and in the design worked out in Sec. 3-5. A further explanation and several illustrations to show methods of venting are included in this section.

Most codes require at least
a 3" vent through the roof
beginning at least one foot
below the roof.

FIGURE 3-32 / Vent termination

3-7   PLUMBING ECONOMY

Economies in plumbing are possible through the careful planning and location of fixtures in clusters, back-to-back or otherwise grouped to form as few wet-walls (walls in which the plumbing pipes are located) as possible.

In multistory construction, locating fixtures above each other saves considerable money since a minimum amount of piping and the smallest sizes possible may be used for both supply and disposal.

In residences designed with low cost as a primary objective, it is even possible to use the same wet-wall for a back-to-back bathroom and kitchen (Fig. 3-40). For middle-priced and custom-designed residences, the primary concern is the location of fixtures where they will best suit the plan. Most designers find no problem in planning and designing a building so that a certain amount of economy is achieved at no sacrifice to the overall plan. Some typical bathroom layouts are shown in Fig. 3-40.

While the plumbing designer is not an architect (and, typically, he will be working on a layout designed by the architect), he should not hesitate to make suggestions that might save money for the client or provide for more effective use of the space.

3 / PLUMBING DRAINAGE

STACK	FU	ACCUM. FU
#1	32	32
#2	32	64

STACK #2
32 FU

STACK #1
32 FU

BUILDING DRAIN
SLOPE 1/8" PER FOOT

FIGURE 3-33 / Building drain sketch

The designer should also check the plans to be certain that the fixtures will fit properly in the space and that there are at least the minimum clearances required.

3-8   TESTING THE SYSTEM

Plumbing permits and inspection are also discussed in Chapter 2. Once again, any inspections should be made after the system is roughed in and before it is covered.

The inspectors always pay close attention to the waste system to be certain that the layout conforms with the code. The system must also be checked to be certain it is watertight. The watertight test involves introducing an air pressure of 5 psi into the system. If it holds the pressure for 15 minutes, it is considered watertight. The system can also be checked with a water test. For the water test, all openings are plugged, the system filled with water and then inspected for leaks.

FIGURE 3-34 / Building drains and sewers[1]

Diameter of Pipe	Maximum Number of Fixture Units That May Be Connected to Any Portion of the Building Drain or the Building Sewer.			
	Slope Per Foot			
	1/16-Inch	1/8-Inch	1/4-Inch	1/2-Inch
Inches				
2			21	26
2½			24	31
3			42[2]	50[2]
4		180	216	250
5		390	480	575
6		700·	840	1,000
8	1,400	1,600	1,920	2,300
10	2,500	2,900	3,500	4,200
12	2,900	4,600	5,600	6,700
15	7,000	8,300	10,000	12,000

[1]On site sewers that serve more than one building may be sized according to the current standards and specifications of the Adminstrative Authority for public sewers.
[2]Not over two water closets or two bathroom groups, except that in single family dwellings, not over three water closets or three bathroom groups may be installed.

Extracted from the *1987 National Standard Plumbing Code* with permission of PHCC.

QUESTIONS

3-1. What is a *trap*, where is it located, and how does it work?

3-2. Why are vents required on the waste system? Where are they located in reference to the fixture?

3-3. What is a *wet vent*, and how does it differ from other types of vents?

3-4. What is the difference between a *stack vent* and a *vent stack*? Using a sketch, show the location of a stack vent and a vent stack in a multistory design.

FIGURE 3-35 / Building drain size tabulation

To roof vent
⎱ Soil stack vent

USE OF SOIL STACK

To roof vent
⎱ Waste stack vent

⎱ Waste stack

USE OF WASTE STACK

Fixtures above

⎲ Revent

Waste stack
Vent stack

USE OF REVENT
(Continuous vent)

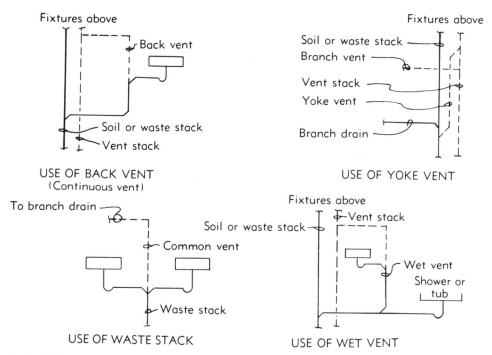

Fixtures above

Back vent

Soil or waste stack
Vent stack

USE OF BACK VENT
(Continuous vent)

Fixtures above

Soil or waste stack
Branch vent

Vent stack
Yoke vent

Branch drain

USE OF YOKE VENT

To branch drain

Common vent

Waste stack

USE OF WASTE STACK

Fixtures above

Vent stack

Soil or waste stack

Wet vent
Shower or tub

USE OF WET VENT

FIGURE 3-36 / Vents

FIGURE 3-37 / *Vent for a one-family dwelling*

3-5. What is the difference between a *soil stack* and a *waste stack?*

3-6. Sketch and locate the house (building) drain and the sewer.

3-7. What provisions must be made to provide drainage for fixtures located below the level of the building drain and the sewer?

3-8. Why are sketches of the drainage piping made by the designer?

3-9. Sketch a typical drainage piping design for a residence with a single bathroom with a kitchen sink on the other side of the wall (Fig. E3-9).

3-10. What is the difference between a *flush tank* and *flush valve* water closet?

FIGURE E3–9

3 / PLUMBING DRAINAGE

Wet vented single bathroom and single bathroom and kitchen fixture group on a stack or at the top floor of a stack serving multistory bathroom groups.

FIGURE 3-38 / Wet venting—top floor

Design Exercises:

3-11. Design the plumbing drainage for the apartment building in Appendix B. Use copper pipe and tubing for this design problem.

3-12. Design the plumbing drainage for the residence in Appendix C. Use copper pipe for this design problem.

3-13. Design the plumbing drainage for the residence in Appendix D. Use copper pipe for this design problem.

3-14. Design the plumbing drainage for the school bathrooms shown in Fig. E3-14.

FIGURE E3-14

WET VENTING

Single Bathroom Groups—A single bathroom group of fixtures may be installed with the drain from an individually vented lavatory serving as a wet vent for a bathtub or shower stall and for the water closet, provided that: (1) not more than one fixture unit is drained into a 1½-inch diameter wet vent or not more than four fixture units drain into a 2-inch diameter wet vent, and (2) the horizontal branch shall be a minimum of 2 inches and connect to the stack at the same level as the water closet drain or below the water-closet drain when installed on the top floor. It may also connect to the water-closet bend.

Multistory Bathroom Group—On the lower floors of a multistory building, the waste pipe from one or two lavatories may be used as a wet vent for one or two bathtubs or showers provided that: the wet vent and its extension to the vent stack is 2 inches in diameter; each water closet below the top floor is individually back vented.

SIZE OF VENT STACKS

Number of wet-vented fixtures	Diameter of vent stacks in inches
1 or 2 bathtubs or showers	2
3 to 5 bathtubs or showers	2½
6 to 9 bathtubs or showers	3
10 to 16 bathtubs or showers	4

In multistory bathroom groups, wet vented in accordance with the paragraph above, water closets below the top floor group need not be individually vented if the 2-inch wet vent connects directly into the water-closet bend at a 45-degree angle to the horizontal portion of the bend and in the direction of flow.

FIGURE 3-39 / Wet venting—below top floor

Assume that the building is 2 floors high and that the average floor-to-floor height is 12 ft.

3-15. Now resize the building drain in Exercise 3-14 to serve the stack design in Exercise 3-14 plus five other stacks exactly like it plus one stack which serves two service sinks and one drinking fountain on each floor. The building drain slope is ⅛ in. per ft.

FIGURE 3-39 (Continued) / Wet venting—below top floor

3-16. Design the plumbing drainage for the restrooms shown in Fig. E3-16. Assume that the building is three stories high and that 9 ft-6 in. is the average floor-to-floor height.

3-17. Size the building drain to serve the stack in Exercise 3-16 plus two other stacks exactly like it. The building drain slope is ½ in. per ft.

FIGURE E3–16

FIGURE 3-40 / Plumbing back to back

Piping symbols:

Vent — — — — — — — — — — — —

Cold water ——— · — · — · — · —

Hot water ——— ·· — ·· — ·· — ··

Hot water return — — —— — — —

Gas ——— G ——— G ———

Soil, waste or leader ———————
   (above grade)

Soil, waste or leader — — — — —— —
   (below grade)

Fixture symbols:

Symbol	
Baths	
Water closet (with tank)	
Water closet (flush valve)	
Shower	
Lavatory	
DW Dishwasher	
SS Service sink	
HWH Hot water heater	

HWT   Hot water tank

HWT

DF   Drinking fountain

M   Meter

HB   Hose bib

C O   CO   Cleanouts

FD   Floor drain

RD   Roof drain

90 Elbow

Gate valve

Reducer

Check valve

Tee (up)

Tee (down)

90° Elbow (up)

90 Elbow (down)

A.F.D.   area floor drain
B.W.V.   backwater valve
CODP.   deck plate cleanout
C.W.   cold water

FIGURE 3-41 / Plumbing symbols

C.W.R.	cold water return	H.W.S.	hot water supply
DEG.	degree	H.W.P.	hot water pump
D.F.	drinking fountain	I.D.	inside diameter
D.H.W.	domestic hot water	LAV.	lavatory
DR.	drain	LDR.	leader
D.W.	dishwasher	O.D.	outside diameter
F.	fahrenheit	(R)	roughing only
FDR.	feeder	R.D.	roof drain
FIXT.	fixture	S.C.	sill cock
F.D.	floor drain	S.S.	service sink
F.H.	fire hose	TOIL.	toilet
F.E.	fire extinguisher unit	UR.	urinal
H.W.	hot water	V.	vent
H.W.C.	hot water circulating line	W.C.	water closet
H.W.R.	hot water return	W.H.	wall hydrant

FIGURE 3-41 (Continued) / *Plumbing symbols*

DRAINAGE FIXTURE UNIT VALUES FOR VARIOUS PLUMBING FIXTURES

Type of Fixture or Group of Fixtures	Drainage Fixture Unit Value (d.f.u.)
Automatic clothes washer 2" standpipe and trap required—direct connection	3
Bathroom group consisting of a water closet, lavatory and bathtub or shower stall:	6
Bathtub[1] (with or without overhead shower)	2
Bidet	1
Clinic Sink	6
Combination sink-and-tray with food waste grinder	4
Combination sink-and-tray with one 1-1/2$_0$ trap	2
Combination sink-and-tray with separate 1-1/2$_0$ traps	3
Dental unit or cuspidor	1
Dental lavatory	1
Drinking fountain	1/2
Dishwasher, domestic	2
Floor drains with 2$_0$ waste	3
Kitchen sink, domestic, with one 1-1/2$_0$ trap	2
Kitchen sink, domestic, with food waste grinder	2
Kitchen sink, domestic, with food waste grinder and dishwaster 1-1/2$_0$ trap	3
Kitchen sink, domestic, with dishwasher 1-1/2$_0$ trap	3
Kitchen sink, domestic, with dishwasher 1-1/2$_0$ trap	3
Lavatory with 1-1/4$_0$ waste	1
Laundry trap (1 or 2 compartments)	2
Shower stall, domestic	2
Showers (group) per head[2]	2
Sinks:	
Surgeon's	3
Flushing rim (with valve)	6
Service (trap standard)	3
Service (P trap)	2
Pot, scullery, etc.[2]	4
Urinal, syphon jet blowout	6
Urinal, wall lip	4
Urinal, stall, washout	4
Urinal trough (each 6-ft. section)	2
Wash sink (circular or multiple) each set of faucets	2
Water closet, private	4
Water closet, public	6
Fixtures not listed above:	
Trap Size 1-1/4" or less	1
Trap Size 1-1/2"	2
Trap Size 2"	3
Trap Size 2-1/2"	4
Trap Size 3"	5
Trap Size 4"	6

[1]A shower head over a bathtub does not increase the fixture unit value.

[2]See Section 11.4.2 for method of computing equivalent fixture unit values for devices or equipment which discharge continuous or semi-continuous flows into sanitary drainage systems.

Extracted from the *1987 National Standard Plumbing Code* with permission of PHCC.

FIGURE 3-42 / Drainage fixture unit values for various plumbing fixtures

HORIZONTAL FIXTURE BRANCHES AND STACKS

Maximum Number of Fixture [...] may be Connected to:

	Any Horizontal Fixture Branch	One Stack of Three Branch Intervals or Less	Stacks with More Than Three Branch Intervals	
			Total for Stack	Total at One Branch Interval
			dfu	dfu
			8	2
			24	6
			42	9
			72^2	20^2
			500	90
			1,100	200
			1,900	350
			3,600	600
			5,600	1,000
			8,400	1,500

[...] building drain.

[...] not more than [...] water closets or bathroom groups within each branch interval nor more than [...] water closets or bathroom groups on the stack.

[...] Stacks shall be sized according to the total accumulated connected load at each story or branch interval and may be reduced in size as this load decreases to a minimum diameter of ½ of the largest size required.

Extracted from the *1987 National Standard Plumbing Code* with permission of PHCC.

FIGURE 3-43 / Horizontal fixture branches and stacks

SIZE AND LENGTH OF VENTS

Size of soil or waste stack	Fixture Units Connected	Diameter of Vent Required (Inches)								
		1-¼	1-½	2	2-½	3	4	5	6	8
		Maximum Length of Vent (Feet)								
Inches										
1½	8	50	150							
2	12	30	75	200						
2	20	26	50	150						
2½	42		30	100	300					
3	10		30	100	100	600				
3	30			60	200	500				
3	60			50	80	400				
4	100			35	100	260	1000			
4	200			30	90	250	900			
4	500			20	70	180	700			
5	200				35	80	350	1000		
5	500				30	70	300	900		
5	1100				20	50	200	700		
6	350				25	50	200	400	1300	
6	620				15	30	125	300	1100	
6	960					24	100	250	1000	
6	1900					20	70	200	700	
8	600						50	150	500	1300
8	1400						40	100	400	1200
8	2200						30	80	350	1100
8	3600						25	60	250	800
10	1000							75	125	1000
10	2500							50	100	500
10	3800							30	80	350
10	5600							25	60	250

Extracted from the *1987 National Standard Plumbing Code* with permission of PHCC.

FIGURE 3-44 / Vent size and length

BUILDING DRAINS AND SEWERS[1]

Diameter of Pipe	Maximum Number of Fixture Units That May Be Connected to Any Portion of the Building Drain or the Building Sewer.			
	Slope Per Foot			
	1/16-Inch	1/8-Inch	1/4-Inch	1/2-Inch
Inches				
2			21	26
2½			24	31
3			42[2]	50[2]
4		180	216	250
5		390	480	575
6		700·	840	1,000
8	1,400	1,600	1,920	2,300
10	2,500	2,900	3,500	4,200
12	2,900	4,600	5,600	6,700
15	7,000	8,300	10,000	12,000

[1]On site sewers that serve more than one building may be sized according to the current standards and specifications of the Adminstrative Authority for public sewers.
[2]Not over two water closets or two bathroom groups, except that in single family dwellings, not over three water closets or three bathroom groups may be installed.

Extracted from the *1987 National Standard Plumbing Code* with permission of PHCC.

FIGURE 3-45 / *Building drains and sewers*[1]

MINIMUM SIZE OF NON-INTEGRAL TRAPS

Plumbing Fixture	Trap Size in Inches
Bathtub (with or without overhead shower)	1-1/2
Bidet	1-1/4
Combination sink and wash (laundry) tray	1-1/2
Combination sink and wash (laundry) tray with food waste grinder unit	1-1/2*
Combination kitchen sink, domestic, dishwasher, and food waste grinder	1-1/2
Dental unit or cuspidor	1-1/4
Dental lavatory	1-1/4
Drinking fountain	1-1/4
Dishwasher, commercial	2
Dishwasher, domestic (non-integral trap)	1-1/2
Floor drain	2
Food waste grinder—Commercial Use	2
Food waste grinder—Domestic-Use	1-1/2
Kitchen sink, domestic, with food waste grinder unit	1-1/2
Kitchen sink, domestic	1-1/2
Kitchen sink, domestic, with dishwasher	1-1/2
Lavatory, common	1-1/4
Lavatory (barber shop, beauty parlor or surgeon's)	1-1/2
Lavatory, multiple type (wash fountain or wash sink)	1-1/2
Laundry tray (1 or 2 compartments)	1-1/2
Shower stall or drain	2
Sink (surgeon's)	1-1/2
Sink flushing rim type, flush valve supplied)	3
Sink (service type with floor outlet trap standard)	3
Sink (service trap with P trap)	2
Sink, commercial (pot, scullery, or similar type)	2
Sink, commercial (with food grinder unit)	2

*Separate trap required for wash tray and separate trap required for sink compartment with food waste grinder unit.

Extracted from the *1987 National Standard Plumbing Code* with permission of PHCC.

FIGURE 3-46 / Minimum size of non-integral traps

MAXIMUM LENGTH OF TRAP ARM

Diameter of Trap Arm Inches	Distance—Trap to Vent
1¼	3′ 6″
1½	5′
2	8′
3	10′
4	12′

NOTE: THIS TABLE HAS BEEN EXPANDED IN THE "LENGTH" REQUIREMENTS TO REFLECT EXPAN-ED APPLICATION OF THE WET VENTING PRINCIPLES. SLOPE SHALL NOT EXCEED ¼″ PER FOOT.

Extracted from the *1987 National Standard Plumbing Code* with permission of PHCC.

FIGURE 3-47 / Maximum length of trap arm

CHAPTER 4
STORM DRAINAGE

4-1 TYPES OF SYSTEMS

Whenever it rains, the drainage and runoff from roofs, courtyards, and paved areas (such as parking lots) must be carried away from the building and properly disposed of. This water may be directed to drains in the building roofs, parking areas, courtyards, and the like, and then be directed into:

1. A community storm sewer line.
2. A private storm sewer and drywell, or be run off onto a low portion of the client's land or into a creek, stream, lake, or pond.
3. A community sewer line.

4-2   COMMUNITY STORM SEWER

If the water is directed to a community storm sewer system, the only concern will be that the elevation of the sewer line is low enough that the private storm line can run into it (Fig. 4-1). Many communities have such systems which are also used to drain rainwater from the streets and safely away.

4-3   PRIVATE STORM SEWER-DRYWELL

If the water is collected into a private storm sewer line, the line can:

1.   Be directed into drywells (Fig. 4-2) which allow the water to be absorbed into the ground.

2.   Be run so that it will empty into an area of low elevation on the plot.

3.   Be run into a nearby creek or stream.

4.   Be run into a public or private lake or pond.

If the line serves a large area, the force of the water, after a rain, may cause considerable damage where it runs out the end of the line. This should be carefully considered by an engineer with experience in drainage.

Running the private line into a creek, stream, or lake may require a permit and may not be allowed in some areas. Usually, before approval, the design of the system will be checked to be certain there is no possibility of sewage wastes (chemical, human, or industrial wastes) getting into the storm sewer line and contaminating a lake, stream, or creek.

FIGURE 4-1 / Community storm sewer

Community
storm sewer

6" coarse gravel

2" layer of straw

Effective diameter

Effective depth

Concrete block laid with cells horizontal

6" coarse gravel

PLAN

SECTION

FIGURE 4-2 / Drywell

Many times on large projects, the storm water is run into a pond so that the water will be available for nonpotable uses such as watering lawns and gardens and circulating in fountains.

4-4   COMMUNITY SEWER LINE

In many cities, especially in the more urban sections, the storm sewers from the city streets and the private buildings, driveways, and parking areas all run into the city sewer line which is used for sewage waste; this is called a *combined sewer*. This should be done only if no other solution is available and if the city allows storm lines to be tied into its sewage lines. This storm water creates a tremendous excess work load for the city (county or municipality) sewage treatment plant. This unnecessary burden often requires that the sewage treatment plants built be much larger than they would be if only sewage were to be treated. In cities with such systems, the cost to separate the storm and sewage lines now would be prohibitive. However, in many cities there are separate storm and sewage lines, and it is illegal to tie storm drainage lines into sewage lines. Cities with only sewage lines may or may not allow storm water to be introduced into the sewage lines, and this should be carefully checked with the local authorities.

When designing drainage for driveways, parking lots, and surrounding ground, the site plan of the project must be checked to determine what effect the existing and revised contours will have on the flow of the surface water after a rain. It is most important that the flow of water be away from the building and not toward it (Fig. 4-3). On large projects (usually not individual residences), the ground should be contoured so water will flow toward the storm sewer system (usually a catch basin for collecting the water, Fig. 4-4). On projects without a storm sewer system, the water should be directed away from buildings, driveways, and parking lots.

4 / STORM DRAINAGE

FIGURE 4-3 / Slope of land

The detail for the construction of driveways and parking lots should also be checked. When the water is simply being allowed to run off onto the surrounding ground, the driveway and any curbs should be constructed higher than the surrounding ground (Fig. 4-5) so that the water will run off and onto the ground. When a storm sewer system will be used to collect and carry away the water, the driveway and curbs

Flow of
storm water

FIGURE 4-4 / Catch basins

FIGURE 4-5 / High driveways   FIGURE 4-6 / Low driveways

may be set lower than the surrounding ground (Fig. 4-6) and should be generally pitched toward the catch basins which collect the water. When this detail is used and there is no storm sewer system, the driveways and parking lots become shallow "swimming pools."

4-5 ROOF DRAINAGE DESIGN

The water from the roof may be taken into consideration by any of three methods:

1. Install roof drains.
2. Install gutters.
3. Allow the water to run off without drains or gutters.

Roof drains (Fig. 4-7) are commonly placed in "flat" or built-up roofs to be certain that the water will not stay on the roof after a rain. Because it is generally considered detrimental to the roofing materials to have water left on the roof, the roof should not be flat but have at least a small pitch (slope) to it. When placed in a flat roof, it is very important that the roof surface be pitched toward the drain to be certain that *all* the water is drained off the roof. This slope may be accomplished on a "flat" roof deck by the use of a layer of lightweight concrete or asphalt. When the deck is made of poured gypsum or concrete, the slope is put in as the deck is poured.

Properly installed roof drains are quite effective in draining a roof. The drains connect to pipes (called *leaders*) which carry the water away from the drain and into a horizontal storm drain (Fig. 4-8) or to the exterior of the building (Fig. 4-9). The leaders may be concealed in the walls or columns (Fig. 4-10) if the sight of an exposed pipe is objectionable. However, once enclosed, it is more expensive to make repairs if necessary. Leaders are usually made of cast iron, galvanized steel, galvanized wrought iron, copper, brass, lead, or plastic pipe.

FIGURE 4-7 / Roof drain

FIGURE 4-8 / Storm leader to drain   FIGURE 4-9 / Leader through wall

    The method used to size roof drain leaders and horizontal storm drains is described later in this section.

    If the leader runs to the outside of the building and empties, some precautions must be taken so that the water will be directed away from the building. Immediately adjacent to the building, a concrete pad or splashblock (Fig. 4-11) or other similar device is required so that the water coming from the end of the pipe will not hit the soil with such force that it will wash it away, causing soil erosion

FIGURE 4-10 / Concealed leaders   FIGURE 4-11 / Splashblocks and permitting the possibility of wet foundation walls. Undermining of the construction is even possible in extreme cases. Minor problems such as staining the building may also occur. Once the water is directed away from the building in some manner, be certain that the surrounding contours keep the water moving *away* from the building.

In locales where the leaders can be tied into the sewage system, the system is referred to as a *combined* sewer. Figure 4-12 illustrates how the leader might be tied into the building drain (discussed in Sec. 4-4). In this situation, most codes require a trap on the leader (storm sewer systems seldom require traps, mainly with combined sewers), and they may specify that the trap shall be a minimum of 10 ft from any stack.

Sizing of the leader for a combined sewer and its effect on the building drain are discussed in Sec. 4-6.

The water may also be directed off the roof into gutters. The roof surface should be pitched to direct the flow of water toward the gutter. The gutters are tied to leaders (often called *downspouts*) which may be tied to a storm sewer line (either community or private) or which may empty outside the building onto a pad, splashback or other means to disperse the water (Fig. 4-13).

Another possible solution is to run the leader into a small catch basin or disposal area filled with gravel (Fig. 4-14). This may be effectively used on smaller buildings, such as residences, but it is important that the catch basin be located at least 10 ft from the foundation walls to reduce any chance for wet walls from the water.

Gutters and leaders commonly used may be made of copper, steel, aluminum, or vinyl. Vinyl gutters can be made in one piece (without seams), but if the gutters are properly installed, seams are no problem (too often they are not properly installed). It is most important that the gutters be installed with a definite slope toward the leaders.

FIGURE 4-12 / Leaders and soil stacks to building drain

FIGURE 4-13 / Leader and splashblock

4 / STORM DRAINAGE

FIGURE 4-14 / *Leaders to drywell and disposal field*

SIZING ROOF DRAINS AND LEADERS—STEP-BY-STEP APPROACH

1. The first step in the design is to review the building.

    The roof of the apartment building shown in Appendix A is generally flat. The area of roof is calculated as 40 ft × 80 ft = 3,200 sq ft.

2. Next, the number of roof drains to be used must be determined. If two drains are used, each will have to handle 3,200 sq ft ÷ 2 = 1,600 sq ft of roof; if three are used, 1,067 sq ft each; if four are used, 800 sq ft each; and so on.

    At this time, a preliminary decision is made to use three roof drains (Fig. 4-15), each serving 1,067 sq ft.

3. The leader size required for this situation is selected from Fig. 4-24 and is based on the square footage of roof area the leader must handle.

    In this design, a 3-in. leader is required for each roof drain. In reviewing the decision for three drains, if two had been used, a 3-in.

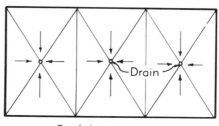

FIGURE 4-15 / *Roof drain plan*

Roof drainage

Roof Drainage Design / 4-5

leader would have been required, and if four had been used, a 2½-in. leader would have been required. In this design, we will continue with the three roof drains (any of the others could also have been used). The horizontal storm drain, if used, is sized later in this section.

SIZING ROOF GUTTERS AND LEADERS—STEP-BY-STEP APPROACH

1. Gutters are also sized according to the square footage of roof they serve.

   Using the four-story apartment building as a design problem (Appendix A), assume that the roof is pitched to the back (Fig. 4-16) and that a gutter is installed to collect the water. This means that the gutter will serve the entire 3,200 sq ft of roof area.

FIGURE 4-16 / Sloped roof and gutters and leaders

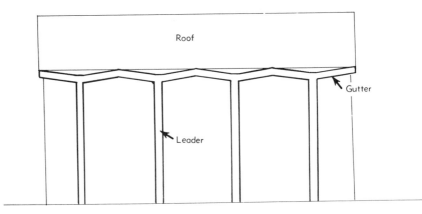

2. Next, the leaders are selected (in the same manner as discussed above). The leaders' size is based on the number of leaders used and the square footage each leader will serve.

> In this design, assume four leaders will be used, each serving 3,200 sq ft ÷ 4 = 800 sq ft. From Fig. 4-24, each leader would be 2½ in. in diameter. If the leaders are connected to a horizontal storm drain, the drain is then sized as discussed later in this section.

3. The gutter size depends on the area of the roof which each portion of the gutter serves and the slope of the gutter when it is installed.

> In this design, each of the four leaders serves 800 sq ft. The layout would be such that the gutter would feed into the leader from two sides, so that each portion of the gutter would serve 400 sq ft of roof area. Assuming a ¹⁄₁₆-in. slope per foot, from Fig. 4-25 a 6-in. diameter is selected for the gutters.

SIZING THE HORIZONTAL STORM DRAIN—STEP-BY-STEP APPROACH

Once the roof drains or gutters and leaders have been selected and sized, the next step is to size the horizontal storm drain (if one is to be used).

1. The horizontal storm drain is sized from Fig. 4-25; its size depends on the square footage being served and the slope at which the pipe is installed. The pipe may be increased in size as it collects the leaders so the first step will be to make a sketch of the system (Fig. 4-17).

> Next, add the square footage that each leader serves and the slope selected for the horizontal drain to the sketch.

> In this design, three leaders are used (Sec. 4-6), serving 1,067 sq ft each, and the slope is ¼ in. per ft.

FIGURE 4-17 / Horizontal storm drain location

HORIZONTAL STORM DRAIN			
	s.f.	Accum. s.f.	Pipe size
#1	1067	1067	
#2	1067	2134	
#3	1066	3200	

FIGURE 4-18 / Horizontal storm drain size

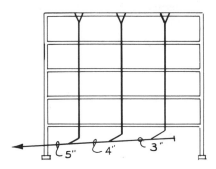

HORIZONTAL STORM DRAIN			
	s.f.	Accum. s.f.	Pipe size
# 1	1067	1067	3"
# 2	1067	2134	4"
# 3	1066	3200	5"

Slope ¼" per foot

2. With this information, the first length of drain (labeled #1 on sketch) is sized from Fig. 4-25 as a 3-in. pipe. Be certain that you use the column for a ¼-in. slope, in this case. The next length of drain (#2) services 2,134 sq ft and is a 4-in. pipe, while the last length (#3) serves 3,200 sq ft and is a 5-in. pipe. Note the pipe sizes on the sketch as shown in Fig. 4-18.

4-6   SIZING A COMBINED SEWER

If the roof leaders (from Sec. 4-5) are to be connected to the building drain (Fig. 4-19), it will be necessary to convert the roof area into an equivalent number of fixture units so that the building drain can be sized to reflect the increased load. (Building drains were sized for sewage waste from the stacks in Sec. 3–5.)

STEP-BY-STEP APPROACH

1. First, a schematic sketch of the stacks, leaders and building drain should be made so that the relationship of the stacks and the leaders to the building drain can be seen.

    In this design, we will continue with the four-story apartment building. The stacks have also been previously sized (Sec. 3–5), and a schematic of the design would look similar to Fig. 4-20.

    The f.u. of each of the stacks is taken from Sec. 3–6 and added to the sketch, as is the slope of the building drain selected (⅛-in. slope).

2. Next, the fixture units served by each stack must be converted into equivalent square feet. The code sets up a ratio of f.u. and equivalent square feet (Fig.

FIGURE 4-19 / Combined sewer

FIGURE 4–20 / Combined sewer schematic

4-27). The equivalent square feet, based on the code, for the first 256 f.u. is 1,000 sq ft.

$$256 \text{ f.u.} = 1,000 \text{ sq ft.}$$

Any additional f.u. are converted into equivalent square feet as the basis that 1 f.u. equals 3.9 sq ft.

In this design, the 64 f.u. would be the equivalent of 1,000 sq ft.

3. Add the equivalent square feet to the roof area being collected for the total area being served by the building drain.

    The total area is 3,200 sq ft + 1,000 equivalent sq ft = 4,200 sq ft. This is noted on the schematic in Fig. 4-21.

    From Fig. 4-28, the building drain size is determined. Based on a ⅛ in. slope, the building drain must be 5 in. to the main stack. The complete tabulation is shown in Fig. 4-22.

    A review of the sketch in Fig. 4-20 indicates that there is less than 200 ft developed length.

4. The equivalent square feet are based on a rainfall of 4 in. per hr. A check of the local weather service will indicate whether the rainfall in the proposed building location is more or less. If so, then the equivalent square feet must be adjusted proportionally.

    Assume the rainfall rate in the proposed location for the apartment is 5 in. per hr. How many equivalent square feet would the 64 f.u. equal? At 4 in. per hour:

$$64 \text{ f.u.} = 1,000 \text{ equivalent sq ft}$$

5 in. per hour:

$$64 \text{ f.u.} = 1,000 \times \frac{5}{4} = 1,250 \text{ equivalent sq ft}$$

FIGURE 4-21 / Leader and riser fixture units

Building drain slope 1/8″ per foot

FIGURE 4–23 / Foundation drains

BUILDING DRAIN			
	s.f.	Accum. s.f.	Pipe size
No. 1	1067	1067	3″
No. 2	1000	2067	4″
No. 3	1067	3134	4″
No. 4	1000	4134	5″
No. 5	1067	5200	5″

Slope 1/8″ per foot

FIGURE 4-22 / Building drain tabulation

4-7 FOUNDATION DRAINS

Many times drains are placed around the foundation of a building (Fig. 4-23) to direct water away from the building (usually after a rain). These footing drains may be of hard fibrous materials with holes, of plastic pipe with holes, or of clay tile spaced about ¼ in. apart with the upper half of the joint covered. The pipes are laid on a layer of gravel, with the holes toward the bottom, and then gravel is placed over the pipe or tile. The drain must be installed at a slope so the water will run to a low point and then run into a drywell or storm sewer. Whenever possible, this drain should not be connected to the sewer system.

QUESTIONS

4-1. What methods may be used to dispose of the water from roofs, courtyards, and parking lots?

4-2. What is a *combined sewer,* and under what conditions should this system of storm drainage be used?

4-3. What methods are commonly used for roof drainage?

4-4. Why should flat roofs be avoided?

4-5. When the roof drainage water is run into roof drains or gutters, what solutions may be used to disperse the water at the end of the leader?

Design Exercises

4-6. Design the storm drainage system for the apartment building in Appendix B. In this design, use four roof drains on the roof and size the leaders and horizontal storm drainage piping (¼-in. slope) to a community storm drainage system and a 4-in. per hr rainfall.

4-7. Design the storm drainage system for the apartment building in Appendix B. In this design, assume a sloped roof (Fig. 4-16) with gutters (¼-in. slope) and leaders to the ground and a 3-in. per hr rainfall.

4-8. Design the storm drainage system for the building in Appendix B. Use three roof drains and size the leaders and horizontal storm drainage piping (½-in. slope) to a community storm drainage system and a 5-in. per hr rainfall.

4-9. Design the storm drainage system for the residence in Appendix C. Use gutters (⅛-in. slope) and leaders to the ground, and assume a 4-in. per hr rainfall.

4-10. Design the storm drainage system for the residence in Appendix D. Use gutters (¼-in. slope) and leaders to the ground, and assume a 3-in. per hr rainfall.

FIGURE 4-24 / Size of vertical conductors and leaders[1]

Diameter of leader or conductor[2]	Maximum projected roof area	
Inches	Square feet	gpm
2	544	23
2½	987	41
3	1,610	67
4	3,460	144
5	6,280	261
6	10,200	424
8	22,000	913

[1]Table is based upon a maximum rate of rainfall of 4 inches per hour and on the hydraulic capacities of vertical circular pipes flowing between one-third and one-half full at terminal velocity, computed by the method of NBS Mono. 31. Where maximum rates are more or less than 4 inches per hour, the figures for drainage area shall be adjusted by multiplying by 4 and dividing by the local rate in inches per hour.

[2]The area of rectangular leaders shall be equivalent to that of the circular leader or conductor required. The ratio of width to depth of rectangular leaders shall not exceed 3 to 1

Extracted from the *1987 National Standard Plumbing Code* with permission of PHCC.

FIGURE 4-25 / Size of horizontal storm drains[1]

Diameter of Drain Inches	Maximum Projected Area for Drains of Various Slopes					
	1/8 in. Slope		1/4 in. Slope		1/2 in. Slope	
	Square Feet	gpm	Square Feet	gpm	Square Feet	gpm
3	822	34	1,160	48	1,644	68
4	1,880	78	2,650	110	3,760	156
5	3,340	139	4,720	196	6,680	278
6	5,350	222	7,550	314	10,700	445
8	11,500	478	16,300	677	23,000	956
10	20,700	860	29,200	1,214	41,400	1,721
12	33,300	1,384	47,000	1,953	66,600	2,768
15	59,500	2,473	84,000	3,491	119,000	4,946

[1]Table is based upon a maximum rate of rainfall of 4 inches per hour. Where maximum rates are more or less than 4 inches per hour, the figures for drainage area shall be adjusted by multiplying by 4 and dividing by the local rate in inches per hour.

Extracted from the *1987 National Standard Plumbing Code* with permission of PHCC.

FIGURE 4-26 / Size of roof gutters[1]

Diameter of Gutter[2] Inches	Maximum Projected Roof Area for Gutters	
	1/16 in. Slope[3]	
	Sq. Ft.	gpm
3	170	7
4	360	15
5	625	26
6	960	40
7	1,380	57
8	1,990	83
10	3,600	150

[1]Table is based upon a maximum rate of rainfall of 4 inches per hour. Where maximum rates are more or less than 4 inches per hour, the figures for drainage area shall be adjusted by multiplying by 4 and dividing by the local rate in inches per hour.

[2]Gutters other than semicircular may be used provided they have an equivalent cross-sectional area.

[3]Capacities given for slope of 1/16 inch per foot shall be used when designing for greater slopes.

Extracted from the *1987 National Standard Plumbing Code* with permission of PHCC.

When the total fixture unit load on the combined drain is less than 256 fixture units, the equivalent drainage area in horizontal projection shall be taken as 1000 square feet.

When the total fixture unit load exceeds 256 fixture units, each fixture unit shall be considered the equivalent of 3.9 square feet of drainage area.

If the rainfall to be provided for is more or less than 4 inches per hour, the 1000 square foot equivalent and the 3.9 shall be adjusted by dividing by 4 and multiplying by the rainfall per hour to be provided for.

FIGURE 4–27 / Roof area to fixture units

Extracted from *1987 National Standard Plumbing Code* with permission of PHCC.

FIGURE 4-28 / Roof area[1] for horizontal drains[2] pressure system-head[3]

Size	Slope[4] and Developed Length[5]					
	1/16		1/8		1/4	
	200	400	200	400	200	400
2			600	550	750	720
3			1,700	1,520	2,100	1,920
4			3,600	3,400	4,600	4,200
5			6,200	5,800	7,900	7,200
6	9,100	7,200	10,300	9,100	12,500	12,000
8	19,200	14,600	21,600	19,200	26,400	24,000
10	36,000	26,400	38,400	36,000	48,000	45,600
12	55,200	40,800	60,000	55,200	74,400	72,000

[1]Area in sq. ft. rounded off

[2]Based on 4″/hr precipitation rate

[3]Discharge terminal open to atmosphere

[4]Slope—in/ft

[5]Developed length—ft

Extracted from the *1987 National Standard Plumbing Code* with permission of PHCC.

4 / STORM DRAINAGE

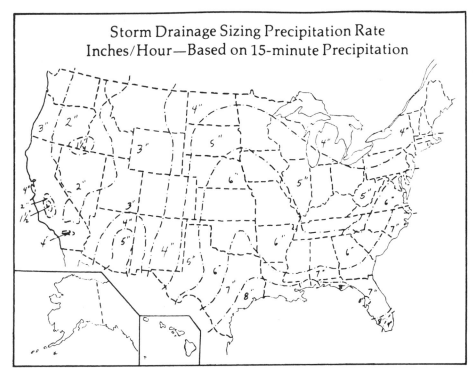

Extracted from the *1987 National Standard Plumbing Code* with permission of PHCC.

FIGURE 4-29 / Storm drainage sizing precipitation rate (inches/hour—based on 15-minute precipitation)

CHAPTER 5
PRIVATE SEWAGE DISPOSAL

5-1 TYPES OF SYSTEMS

Whenever possible, the sanitary drainage system should connect to a community (public) sewer, but when no community sewer is available, a private sewage disposal system must be installed. This is particularly true in surburban and rural areas and is one of the initial items that the designer should check. The information contained in this chapter is based on the *National Standard Plumbing Code,* but the codes in force in the geographic area of construction should always be checked *before* the system is designed. In some areas, the municipality will not only specify exactly where on the site the system will be placed but will also simply state the size of all equipment required and the installation method. In addition, many areas limit the minimum lot size on which a private sewage disposal system might be placed (often one-half acre) and the minimum size if both a sewage disposal system and a well are required (often about one acre). Most of these requirements are established because of the type of soil in the area and because there is always a concern that the potable water supply might be contaminated by a sewage disposal system (either the system serving this project or a neighbor's sewage system).

5-2   PRIVATE SYSTEMS

Private sewage disposal systems (Fig. 5-1) usually consist of the building sewer which leads from the project into a septic tank and then the line into a distribution box which feeds the fluid (effluent) into the disposal or leach fields. There are variations on this design: as shown in Fig. 5-2, the septic tank may feed into a seepage pit(s), and the packaged unit in Fig. 5-3 is designed to serve larger complexes.

The watertight septic tank is placed underground where it receives the sewage from the building and holds it for about a day while the suspended solids settle to the bottom and putrefy. The liquids pass out of the tank at the other end into the distribution box. Septic tanks may be concrete and of rectangular shape (Fig. 5-4) or asphalt-protected steel, usually round (Fig. 5-5).

The size of the septic tank will be one of the first considerations in private sewage disposal design. For individual residences, the tank design is based on the number of bedrooms and the maximum number of persons served and on whether a garbage disposal is used (Fig. 5-16); for institutional and commercial projects, it is based on the estimated sewage flow in gallons per day (Fig. 5-17).

A three-bedroom home which will have five people living in it will require a septic tank size of 1,000 gal minimum (Fig. 5-16). In many locales the tank sizes available may be limited, and it may be necessary to use a larger tank than the minimum. Using a larger tank will not interfere with the operation of the system. If a larger capacity is required than is available in one tank (for example, if 1,000 gal is required and only 600-gal tanks are available), two 600-gal tanks may be connected (Fig. 5-6). The tanks should be set close enough together that a single length of pipe (with no joints) can be used to join the outlet of the first tank to the inlet of the second.

FIGURE 5-1 / Private sewage system

FIGURE 5-2 / Septic tank to seepage pit

FIGURE 5-3 / Package sewage unit

Courtesy of Demco

Many municipalities require tanks larger than those recommended by the *National Standard Plumbing Code*. It is the designer's responsibility to know or find out local requirements *before* designing the system. When the designer is working in an area where he is not familiar with local codes and requirements, he must visit the local authorities and discuss the design, obtain local requirements in writing, or perhaps call to determine what codes are in effect in the locale.

The code also sets minimum distances for the location of the various parts of the private sewage disposal system (Fig. 5-18); the septic tank must be a minimum of 50 ft from any well or suction line (Fig. 5-7), and when possible, the tank is put even farther away. Many local codes require longer distances and therefore must be checked; in general, about 100 ft is the preferred distance, but this is not always feasible. These distances greatly reduce the danger of contaminating drinking water if leaks should occur in the tank or pipes (lines).

The depth of the tank will be determined by the depth of the sewer line from the building to the tank. It is important that the sewer line be sloped gradually toward the tank (about ⅛ to ¼ in. per ft). Too much slope and the sewage will flow into the tank too rapidly and disturb the natural action in the tank. Too little slope and the sewer line may become clogged. The top of the tank is usually located 12 to 36 in. below the ground surface so it can be serviced as required.

Institutions and commercial projects base their sewage treatment system sizes on the expected flow of sewage from the project in a day. The table in Fig. 5-17 lists various types of building uses and the gallons per person per day the system must be designed for.

EXAMPLE

In designing a private sewage system for the four-story apartment building (Appendix A), the first step is to determine the number of apartments. Reviewing the plans, there are two 2-bedroom apartments per floor or a total of 8 apartments with 16 bedrooms.

5 / *PRIVATE SEWAGE DISPOSAL*

PLAN

Cover

Location marker

Baffle (in lieu
of sanitary tee)

Optional sloping
bottom

SECTION

FIGURE 5-4 / Rectangular septic
tank

The required tank capacity may be obtained from Figs. 5-8 and 5-16.

8 bedrooms (one-bedroom units)   = 3,000 gallons
8 extra bedrooms at 150 gallons each = 1,200 gallons
Minimum septic tank capacity   = 4,200 gallons

The *distribution box* receives the effluent from the septic tank and distributes it equally to each individual line of the disposal field (as illustrated in Fig. 5-9). The box is connected to the septic tank with a tight sewer line.

 Disposal or tile fields are the preferred method for distributing the effluent. They consist of rows (called *lines*) of pipe through which the effluent passes. The lines may be made of clay tile (usually 12 in. long), bituminized pipe or plastic pipe. The clay tiles are laid with about ¼ in. of space between them (Fig. 5-10) to allow the effluent

Baffle

PLAN

Crushed stone
or gravel

SECTION

FIGURE 5-5 / Steel septic tank

to be absorbed into the gravel fill the tile is placed on. The top portion of the ¼-in.
space (Fig. 5-10) is covered with a piece of felt so that soil will not fall into the pipe
and clog or stop the flow of effluent. Most fields installed today use the bituminized or
plastic pipes which have holes in them. These pipes are installed much faster and do
not have any open joints to be covered with felt as the tile does. These pipes are
installed with the holes down, and as the effluent flows through the pipes, it is absorbed
into the gravel.

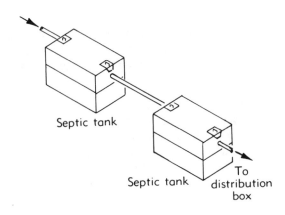

Septic tank

Septic tank

To
distribution
box

FIGURE 5-6 / Septic tanks in
series

5 / PRIVATE SEWAGE DISPOSAL

FIGURE 5-7 / Private disposal
system distances

The tile or pipe is set into a trench which varies from 18 to 30 in. in depth and 24 to 36 in. in width (Fig. 5-10). Trenches must be sloped in the direction of flow; the code limits the maximum slope to 6 in. in 100 ft so that the effluent will not simply flow to the end of the line and then back up. The bottom of the trench is filled with a layer of filter material not less than 6 in. deep below the pipe line, extending the full width of the trench and a minimum of 2 in. above the pipe, and covered with a layer of straw. The code also limits any individual line to a length of 100 ft and sets the minimum

FIGURE 5-8 / Capacity of septic tanks*

Extracted from the *1987 National Standard plumbing Code* with permission of PHCC.

CAPACITY OF SEPTIC TANKS*

Single family dwellings-number of bedrooms	Multiple dwellings units or apartments-one bedroom each	Other uses; maximum fixture units served	Minimum septic tank capacity in gallons
1-3		20	1000
4	2 units	25	1200
5 or 6	3	33	1500
7 or 8	4	45	2000
	5	55	2250
	6	60	2500
	7	70	2750
	8	80	3000
	9	90	3250
	10	100	3500

Extra bedroom, 150 gallons each.
Extra dwelling units over 10, 250 gallons each.
Extra fixture units over 100, 25 gallons per fixture unit.

FIGURE 5-9 / *Distribution box*

separation between lines at 6 ft. The disposal field may take any of a number of shapes (Fig. 5-11), depending on the contours (slope) of the ground, the size of the lot and the location of any well or stream on the property. The minimum distance between the field and the building is 10 ft, between field and property line 10 ft, between field and stream 25 ft and between field and well 100 ft. If the well has an outside watertight casing which extends down to a depth of 50 ft or more, the minimum separation between field and well may be reduced to 50 ft.

The length of line required in the disposal field depends on the ability of the soil to absorb sewage. The subsurface conditions are checked first by digging a hole about 5 ft below final grade to observe the type of soil encountered and whether any groundwater is evident. Next, a soil percolation test is made to measure the ability of the soil to absorb sewage. The procedure for making the soil percolation test is:

1. Dig a hole about 12 in. in diameter and 30 in. deep, keeping the sides of the hole vertical (Fig. 5-12).

2. Presoak the hole by filling it with water and allowing it to completely seep away.

FIGURE 5-10 / *Disposal field*

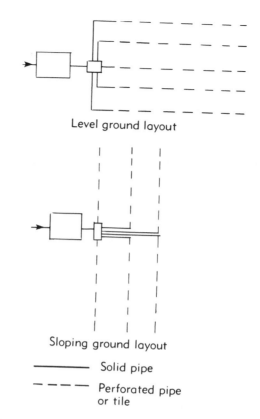

Level ground layout

Sloping ground layout

—————— Solid pipe

- - - - Perforated pipe
or tile

*FIGURE 5-11 / Disposal field
patterns*

The hole should be presoaked several hours before the test and again at the time
of the test.

3. After presoaking, remove any loose soil that might have fallen in from the sides
of the hole.

4. Carefully fill the hole to a depth of 6 in. with clean water with as little splashing
as possible.

Ruler or measuring stick
indicating 5" and 6" intervals

Water level at
start of test

Water level at
end of test

FIGURE 5-12 / Percolation pit

5. Record the time (in minutes) that it takes for the water level to drop 1 in. (from 6 in. to 5 in.)

6. Now, repeat the test a minimum of three times until the time it takes the water to drop 1 in. for two successive tests is approximately the same. Then take the last test as the stabilized rate of percolation; it is the time recorded for this test which will be used to size the disposal field.

The tile field length is sized from Fig. 5-17, which lists the gallons per day per person, and Fig. 5-19 which lists the time required for the water to drop 1 in. and the square feet of trench required per 100 gallons of sewage per day.

EXAMPLE

Assuming a soil percolation time of 5 minutes, from Fig. 5-17, the gallons per day per person required is 75. For a three-bedroom residence with four people, 300 gpd of sewage flow is generated. Using Fig.5-19, 42 s.f. of tile length is required per 100 gpd. For 300 gpd, 126 s.f. is required.

Institutional and commercial projects are sized from Figs. 5-17 and 15-19, which lists the time required for percolation in minutes and the absorption of the soil for tile fields and seepage pits in *gallons per square foot per day*.

EXAMPLE

Continuing with the four-story apartment building (Appendix A) with 8 apartments, averaging 2.5 persons per apartment. From Fig. 5-17, a rate of 75 gpd per person must be used (the same as individual residences), for 1,500 gpd. Adding 50% for food waste disposals increases it to 2,250 gpd. Assuming a soil percolation time of 3 minutes, from Fig. 5-19, the amount that the soil can absorb is 100 gpd per 35 sq ft. To determine the amount of square footage required, divide the sewage flow by 100 times the sq ft required. In this design, divide 2,250 gpd by 100 times 35 gal per sq ft and 788 sq ft of absorption area are required. Using a trench width of 3 ft, 263 lineal ft of line are required.

Seepage pits (also referred to as *leaching pits* and illustrated in Fig. 5-13) may be used instead of tile fields. They are preferable where the soil becomes more porous below a depth of 2 or 3 ft and where the property does not have sufficient space for all buildings, driveways, parking areas and the drain field. They cannot be used in areas with high water tables since the bottom of the pit must be at least 2 ft above the water table.

The seepage pit is usually made of concrete block or is a precast concrete unit (Fig. 5-14). Typically, 8-in. thick blocks are used, and they are laid with the cells

6" coarse gravel

Concrete block laid with cells horizontal

PLAN

2" layer of straw

Effective diameter

Effective depth

6" coarse gravel

SECTION

ABSORPTION AREAS					
Diam.	Depth				
	4'	5'	6'	8'	10'
4'	50.2	62.8	75.3	100.4	125.6
5'	62.8	78.5	94.2	125.6	157.0
6'	75.4	94.2	113.0	150.7	188.4
8'	100.4	125.6	150.7	200.9	251.2

FIGURE 5-13 / Typical seepage pit

(holes) placed horizontally (Fig. 5-13) to allow the effluent to seep into the ground. The tapered cells of the block are set with the widest area to the outside to reduce the amount of loose material behind the lining that might fall into the pit. The typical precast concrete seepage pit shown in Fig. 5-14 is the same unit used for drywells (Sec. 4-3). The bottom of the pit is lined with coarse gravel a minimum of 1 ft deep before the block or concrete is placed. Between the block or concrete and the soil is a minimum of 6 in. of clean crushed stone or gravel. Straw is placed on top of the gravel to keep sand from filtering down and reducing the effectiveness of the gravel. The top of the pit should have an opening with a watertight cover to provide access to the pit if necessary. The construction of the pit above the inlet pipe should be watertight.

When more than one seepage pit is used, the pipe from the settling tank must be laid out so that the effluent will be spread uniformly to the pits. To provide equal distribution, a distribution box with separate laterals (Fig. 5-15)—each lateral feeding no more than two pits—provides the best results. The distance between the outside walls of the pits should be a minimum of 3 pit diameters and not less than 10 ft.

The size of the seepage pit is based on the outside area of the walls. The areas

FIGURE 5-14 / Precast seepage pit

for pits of various diameters are given in Fig. 5-13. Many designers exclude the bottom area of the pit from the absorption area required to allow for a safety factor, while others calculate the total area available and then size the system to allow some safety factor. The latter approach is used in this text.

Seepage pits are sized from Fig. 5-21, which lists the time required for percolation and the absorption area required per 100 sq. ft. The four-story apartment building has a sewage flow of 2,250 gpd (sized earlier in this section). Assuming a soil percolation of 3 minutes, from Fig. 5-21, the soil can absorb 100 gal per 45 sq ft per day. To determine the amount of absorption area required, divide the sewage flow by 100, times the absorption rate. In this design:

$$\frac{2250}{100} \times 45 = 1013 \text{ sq. ft.}$$

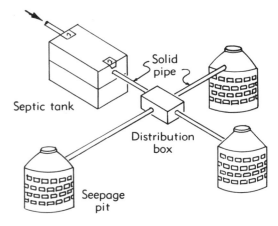

FIGURE 5-15 / Distribution box to seepage pits

The size of the pits to be used is selected from Fig. 5-13, and seepage pits 6 ft in diameter and 8 ft deep are selected. Other combinations may be used depending on the area required to place the pits, the sizes available locally, whether precast concrete is used, and the designer's own preference.

5-3   SEWAGE PROBLEMS

The uncertainty of exactly how much the soil will actually absorb is reflected in the values given in the various tables and charts. Even so, many designers prefer to oversize the system slightly to allow for poor absorption and also to allow for future increased amounts of effluent either because more people are using the facility than anticipated or because of an addition to the individual residence or an addition of various water-using fixtures which may not have been included in the original design.

One of the most wasteful uses of the private system is the connection of a washing machine to it. Many times the tying-in of a washing machine to an older system has resulted in more water flow than the ground could handle through the system installed. It is suggested that when a washing machine is installed (especially where there are several children in the family), a drywell should be installed. Problems may also occur if all of the family washing is done on one day. This puts a tremendous additional flow into the system for a brief period, and as a result, the system may back up into the house. One of the simplest solutions to this is to spread the washing out over several days, giving the ground a chance to absorb the water. Other solutions are to connect the washer to a drywell, to increase the size of the disposal field or to add a seepage pit.

The connection of gutters, storm drainage and roof drains may also cause periodic overloads on the private sewage system. When these are connected, the designer must increase the size of the system to accommodate the periodic additional flow. Most designers prefer to run such connections into drywells if no storm drain system is available.

QUESTIONS

5-1. When are private sewage systems generally used?

5-2. Draw a sketch of the major parts of a private sewage system in relation to a residence.

5-3. Why do most codes set minimum distances between the parts of the sewage system and wells and streams?

5-4. What is the function of a distribution box?

5-5. How is the ability of the soil to absorb sewage determined?

5-6. What are *seepage pits,* and when are they used?

5-7. Why should the designer consider not connecting pipes carrying certain waste water (such as water from washing machines) to the private sewage system?

5-8. How would the reuse water system discussed in Sec. 1-10 and illustrated in Fig. 1–25 affect sewage treatment system designs, both private and community?

Design Exercises:

5-9. Design a private sewage system (septic tank and disposal field) for the apartment building in Appendix B. In this design, use the sewage flows in Fig. 5-17 and an absorption rate of 6 to 7 minutes.

5-10. Design a private sewage system (seepage pits) for the apartment building in Appendix B. In this design, use the sewage flows in Fig. 5-17 and an absorption rate of 8 to 10 minutes. Due to the water table, limit the seepage pits to a 6 ft maximum depth.

5-11. Design a private sewage system (septic tank and disposal field) for the building in Appendix C. In this design, use the sewage flows in Fig. 5-16 and 5-17 and an absorption rate of 5 minutes.

5-12. Redesign Exercise 5-11 with a seepage pit system.

5-13. Design a private sewage system (septic tank and disposal field) for the building in Appendix D. In this design use an absorption rate of 4 minutes.

FIGURE 5-16 / Capacity of septic tanks[*]

Extracted from the 1988 Supplement to the *1987 National Standard Plumbing Code* with permission of PHCC.

* Septic tank sizes all for connection of food waste disposable units

CAPACITY OF SEPTIC TANKS*

Single family dwellings-number of bedrooms	Multiple dwellings units or apartments-one bedroom each	Other uses; maximum fixture units served	Minimum septic tank capacity in gallons
1-3		20	1000
4	2 units	25	1200
5 or 6	3	33	1500
7 or 8	4	45	2000
	5	55	2250
	6	60	2500
	7	70	2750
	8	80	3000
	9	90	3250
	10	100	3500

Extra bedroom, 150 gallons each.
Extra dwelling units over 10, 250 gallons each.
Extra fixture units over 100, 25 gallons per fixture unit.

5 / *PRIVATE SEWAGE DISPOSAL*

Type of Establishment	Gal. per day per person
Schools (toilet and lavatories only)	15 Gal. per day per person
Schools (with above plus cafeteria)	25 Gal. per day per person
Schools (with above plus cafeteria and showers)	35 Gal. per day per person
Day workers at schools and offices	15 Gal. per day per person
Day Camps	25 Gal. per day per person
Trailer parks or tourist camps (with built-in bath)	50 Gal. per day per person
Trailer parks or tourist camps (with central bathhouse)	35 Gal. per day per person
Work or construction camps	50 Gal. per day per person
Public picnic parks (toilet wastes only)	5 Gal. per day per person
Public picnic parks (bathhouse, showers and flush toilets)	10 Gal. per day per person
Swimming pools and beaches	10 Gal. per day per person
Country Clubs	25 Gal. per locker
Luxury residences and estates	150 Gal. per day per person
Rooming houses	40 Gal. per day per person
Boarding houses	50 Gal. per day per person
Hotels (with connecting baths)	50 Gal. per day per person
Hotels (with private baths—2 persons per room)	100 Gal. per day per person
Boarding Schools	100 Gal. per day per person
Factories (gallons per person per shift—exclusive of industrial wastes)	25 Gal. per day per person
Nursing Homes	75 Gal. per day per person
General Hospitals	150 Gal. per day per person
Public Institutions (other than hospitals)	100 Gal. per day per person
Restaurants (toilet and kitchen wastes per unit of serving capacity)	25 Gal. per day per person
Kitchen wastes from hotels, camps, boarding houses, etc. Serving three meals per day	10 Gal. per day per person
Motels	50 Gal. per bed space
Motels with bath, toilet, and kitchen wastes	60 Gal. per bed space
Drive-in theaters	5 Gal. per car space
Stores	400 Gal. per toilet room
Service stations	10 Gal. per vehicle served
Airports	3-5 Gal. per passenger
Assembly Halls	2 Gal. per seat
Bowling Alleys	75 Gal. per lane
Churches (small)	3-5 Gal. per sanctuary seat
Churches (large with kitchens)	5.7 Gal. per sanctuary seat
Dance Halls	2 Gal. per day per person
Laundries (coin operated)	400 Gal. per machine
Service Stations	1000 Gal. (First Bay)
	500 Gal. (Each add. Bay)
Subdivisions or individual homes	75 Gal. per day per person
Marinas—Flush toilets	36 Gal. per fixture per hr
Urinals	10 Gal. per fixture per hr
Wash basins	15 Gal. per fixture per hr
Showers	150 Gal. per fixture per hr

* Add 50% for food disposal units

Extracted from the 1988 Supplement to the *1987 National Standard Plumbing Code* with permission of PHCC.

FIGURE 5-17 / *Sewage flows according to type of establishment**

MINIMUM *DISTANCE BETWEEN* COMPONENTS OF AN INDIVIDUAL SEWAGE DISPOSAL SYSTEM (In Feet)[1]

	Shallow Well	Deep Well	Single Suction Line	Septic Tank	Distribution Box	Disposal Field	Seepage Pit	Dry Well	Property Line	Bldg.
Bldg. Sewer other than cast iron	(50)	(50)	(50)	–	–	–				
Bldg. Sewer cast iron	(10)	(10)	(10)							
Septic Tank	(100)	(50)	(50)	–	5	10	10	10	(10)[1]	(10)
Distribution Box	(100)	(50)	(50)	5	–	5	5	5	(10)	(20)
Disposal Field	(100)	(50)	(50)	10	5	–	–	–	(10)	(20)
Seepage Pit	(100)	(50)	(50)	10	5	–	–	–	(10)	(20)
Dry Well	(100)	(50)	(50)	10	5	–	–	–	(10)	(20)
Shallow Well	–	–	–	(100)	(100)	(100)	(100)	(100)		
Deep Well	–	–	–	(50)	(50)	(50)	(50)	(50)		
Suction Line	–	–	–	(50)	(50)	(50)	(50)	(50)		

[1]May be closer to building when permission is given by the Administrative Authority.

Extracted from the 1988 Supplement to the *1987 National Standard Plumbing Code* with permission of PHCC.

FIGURE 5-18 / Minimum distances for location of components of a private sewage disposal system

Time in Minutes for 1-inch Drop	Tile Length for Trench Widths of		
	1-foot	2-feet	3-feet
1	25	13	9
2	30	15	10
3	35	18	12
5	42	21	14
10	59	30	20
15	74	37	25
20	91	46	31
25	105	53	35
30	125	63	42

Extracted from the 1988 Supplement to the *1987 National Standard Plumbing Code* with permission of PHCC.

FIGURE 5-19 / *Tile length for each 100 gallons of sewage per day*

FIGURE 5-20 / *Size and spacing for disposal fields*

Width of Trench at Bottom	Recommended Depth of Trench	Spacing Tile Lines[1]	Effective Absorption Area per Lineal Foot of Trench
Inches	Inches	Feet	Square Feet
18	18 to 30	6.0	1.5
24	18 to 30	6.0	2.0
30	18 to 36	7.6	2.5
36	24 to 36	9.0	3.0

[1]A greater spacing is desirable where available area permits.

Time in Minutes for 1-inch Drop	Effective Absorption Area Square Feet
1	32
2	40
3	45
5	56
10	75
15	96
20	108
25	139
30	167

Note: Minimum 125 s.f. required. Bottom of pit shall not be considered part of the absorption area.

Extracted from the 1988 Supplement to the *1987 National Standard Plumbing Code* with permission of PHCC.

FIGURE 5-21 / Effective absorption area in seepage pits for each 100 gallons of sewage per day

CHAPTER 6
COMFORT

6-1 COMFORT

Comfort means different conditions to different people. Inside any room it means being able to carry on any desired activity without being either chilly or too hot. Most people don't care what combination of factors cause them to be comfortable as long as they feel comfortable.

6-2 TRANSFER OF BODY HEAT

Since we are concerned here with people, a short study of the body, its heat and how it is transferred is required. Body heat is transferred to the surrounding air and surfaces by three natural processes which usually occur at the same time. These natural processes are:

1. Convection.

2. Radiation.

3. Evaporation.

Convection

The process of heat transfer by convection is based on two fundamental principles:

1. Heat flows from a hot to a cold surface.

2. Heat rises.

   Applying these principles to the body (Fig. 6-1):

1. As the body gives off heat, it will flow to the surrounding cooler air.

2. As the surrounding air warms, it moves in an upward direction.

3. As the warm air moves upward, cooler air is pulled in behind it; then the cooler air heats and flows upward and more cool air moves in as the cycle of convection continues.

Radiation

The process of heat transfer by radiation is based on one fundamental principle (Fig. 6-2):

   Heat flows from a hot to a cold surface.

But radiation is different from convection in one respect: no air movement is required to transfer the heat. In the process of radiation *heat rays* transfer the heat from the heat source, just as the sun's rays heat any surface they touch. The only difference is that, in this case, people are the heat source.

FIGURE 6-1 / Convection

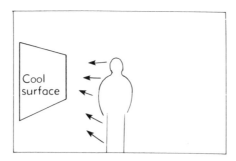

FIGURE 6-2 / Radiation

Evaporation

The process of heat transfer by evaporation is based on one fundamental principle (Fig. 6-3):

Moisture evaporates from a warm surface.

The evaporation of moisture from a warm surface removes heat from the surface and cools it. As moisture is given off through the pores of the skin, it evaporates, removing heat from the body.

AIR TEMPERATURE AND BODY HEAT

The amount of body heat given off is affected by the air temperature surrounding it in the following ways:

1. *Convection.* Cool air increases the rate of heat loss by convection while warm air slows the rate.

2. *Radiation.* Cool air will lower the surface temperature of the surroundings, increasing the rate of heat loss by radiation; warm air raises the temperature of the surfaces, lowering the rate of heat loss due to radiation.

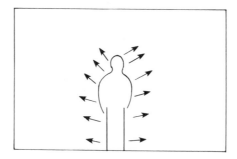

FIGURE 6-3 / Evaporation

3. *Evaporation*. Generally, cool air increases the rate of evaporation while warm air reduces the rate; however, the rate of evaporation also depends on the relative humidity (the amount of moisture in the air) and the amount of air movement.

6-3 SPACE CONDITIONS AFFECTING COMFORT

The conditions within a space (room) which affect the comfort of the occupant, because they affect the rate of heat loss from the body, are:

1. Room air temperature (also called dry-bulb temperature).

2. Humidity or moisture content of the room.

3. Surface temperature of surrounding surfaces in the room (also called mean radiant temperature or MRT).

4. Rate of air motion.

The occupant will feel comfortable when each of these is within a certain range.

The room air temperature affects the rate of convective and evaporative body heat losses. Since the room temperature will be below the body temperature of 98.6°F, there will be convective heat loss from the body. Generally, the body feels most comfortable in a temperature range of 72° to 78°F in the winter and 72° to 76°F in the summer. Of course, the range of comfortable temperatures varies with each individual and also is affected by what the person is wearing and how active he is.

The humidity (moisture content) of the air affects the rate of evaporative heat loss from the body. A high humidity (often occurring in the summer) will cause the surrounding air to absorb less heat from the body, making the occupant feel warmer. A low humidity (often occurring in the winter) allows the air to absorb greater quantities of body heat, making the occupant feel cooler. As discussed later in the text, part of the design problem may be to lower the summer humidity and increase the winter humidity.

The surface temperatures of surrounding surfaces affect the radiant heat loss from the body. The surface temperatures in the room may vary widely. Windows and exterior walls will probably be cooler in the winter than interior walls and the furniture. The temperatures of the floors and ceilings will depend on the air temperature on the other side of the construction. Comfort can be increased (in the winter) by directing the flow of warm air over the colder surfaces. This is why most heating elements (registers, baseboard heaters) are located under a window.

The rate of air motion affects the transfer of body heat by convection and evaporation. In the summer increased air motion increases the evaporation rate of heat from the body to help keep it cool. This is why buildings without air conditioners use fans to increase the movement of the air on hot days. In the winter a slower rate of air motion is desired, or the occupants will feel cool due to evaporative heat loss. But even in the winter it is desirable to have a flow of air to keep the air from becoming stagnant.

The building occupant will feel comfortable within certain ranges of air temperature, humidity, surface temperatures of surrounding surfaces and air motion.

Experiments were made by ASHRAE (The American Society of Heating, Refrigerating and Air Conditioning Engineers) to determine the ranges of these variable conditions which feel comfortable to the occupants. The results were then tabulated and made into the "comfort chart" shown in Fig. 6-4. Generally, the results show that there is a definite link between humidity and air temperature when both air movement and surface temperatures remain constant. This air temperature to humidity relationship shows that to produce comfort, as the temperature increases, the humidity should decrease. This means that in the winter, it would be most economical to provide comfort with lower air temperature and higher humidity.

FIGURE 6-4 / Comfort ranges

Reprinted with permission from ASHRAE, *Fundamentals Handbook,* 1989.

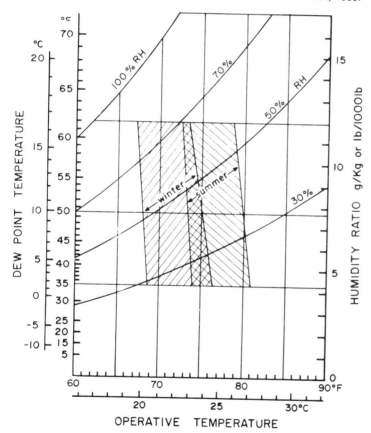

While the experiments and chart were done for central heating systems and have other design limitations noted by ASHRAE, they do show the important humidity/air temperature relationships. But first an explanation of how to read the chart will be helpful. The chart has five basic parts listed here and identified in Fig. 6-4:

1. Dry-bulb temperature (along the bottom).

2. Dew point temperature (along the left side).

3. Relative humidity in percent (across the chart from the lower left to the upper right, with percentages in the upper right).

4. The shaded areas show the range of conditions in which most people will feel comfortable.

6-5   WINTER COMFORT

Use of the comfort chart to determine winter comfort is shown in Fig. 6-4.

1. Determine the most likely dry-bulb temperature for the space along the bottom of the chart.

2. From the dry-bulb temperature move up into the comfort areas on the chart.

3. Determine the range of relative humidity which will provide comfort to the most occupants.

This will be used to determine the various combinations of dry-bulb temperature and relative humidity which will provide comfort and still provide an effective temperature of about 70° to 77°F.

Using a dry-bulb (room air) temperature of 70°F, what relative humidity would be required? Use of the chart to determine various dry-bulb to humidity relationships is shown in Fig. 6-4.

1. Find 76°F dry-bulb temperature along the bottom of the chart (point 1).

2. Move vertically up to the point where the 76°F dry-bulb line intersects the shaded area.

3. Read the relative humidity off as about 25% to 65% lines, where individuals will be most comfortable.

Homes with no humidity control will tend to have low relative humidity in the winter. So, with a winter heating condition and a 70°F dry-bulb reading, it is necessary to have about 30% relative humidity for the highest percentage of occupants to feel comfortable.

The approximate humidity inside a building can be found by putting a hygrometer (Fig. 6-5) in the space; it will show the percentage of humidity just as a thermometer shows temperature. Also, the chart in Fig. 6-6 shows the relationship of outside air temperature and relative humidity to heated interior air. For example, with an outside temperature of 45°F and a relative humidity of 80%, the indoor relative humidity will be only 30%.

It becomes obvious that it is often necessary to add moisture to the air in the winter. Humidity can be introduced into the space by installing humidifiers in the ducts of forced air systems and by placing large portable humidifiers in spaces with water, steam, or electric baseboard or panel heat.

6-6   SUMMER COMFORT

Summer comfort ranges can also be found on the comfort chart (Fig. 6-4).

1.   Determine the most likely dry-bulb temperature for the space along the bottom of the chart.

2.   Follow the dry-bulb line from that point on the chart where it enters the comfort areas.

This is the effective temperature at which the largest percentage of occupants feel comfortable, and it is used to determine the various comfortable combinations of dry-bulb temperature and relative humidity.

FIGURE 6-5 / Hygrometer (humidity meter)

INDOOR RELATIVE HUMIDITY CONVERSION CHART

OUTDOOR RELATIVE HUMIDITY	−20°	−10°	−5°	0°	+5°	+10°	+15°	+20°	+25°	+30°	+35°	+40°	+45°	+50°
100%	2%	3%	4%	6%	7%	9%	11%	14%	17%	21%	26%	31%	38%	46%
95%	2%	3%	4%	5%	7%	8%	10%	13%	16%	20%	24%	30%	36%	44%
90%	2%	2%	4%	5%	6%	8%	10%	12%	15%	19%	23%	28%	34%	41%
85%	2%	2%	4%	5%	6%	8%	9%	12%	15%	18%	22%	27%	32%	39%
80%	2%	2%	4%	5%	6%	7%	9%	11%	14%	17%	20%	25%	30%	36%
75%	2%	2%	3%	4%	5%	7%	8%	10%	13%	16%	19%	23%	28%	32%
70%	1%	2%	3%	4%	5%	6%	8%	10%	12%	15%	18%	22%	26%	32%
65%	1%	2%	3%	4%	5%	6%	7%	8%	11%	14%	17%	20%	25%	30%
60%	1%	2%	3%	3%	4%	5%	7%	8%	10%	13%	15%	19%	23%	28%
55%	1%	1%	2%	3%	4%	5%	6%	8%	9%	12%	14%	17%	21%	25%
50%	1%	1%	2%	3%	4%	4%	6%	7%	9%	10%	13%	16%	19%	23%
45%	1%	1%	2%	3%	3%	4%	5%	6%	8%	9%	12%	14%	17%	21%
40%	1%	1%	2%	2%	3%	4%	4%	6%	7%	8%	10%	12%	15%	18%
35%	1%	1%	2%	2%	3%	3%	4%	5%	6%	7%	9%	11%	13%	16%
30%	1%	1%	1%	2%	2%	3%	3%	4%	5%	6%	8%	9%	11%	14%
25%	1%	1%	1%	1%	2%	2%	3%	3%	4%	5%	6%	8%	10%	12%
20%	+%	1%	1%	1%	1%	2%	2%	3%	3%	4%	5%	6%	8%	10%
15%	+%	+%	1%	1%	1%	1%	2%	2%	3%	3%	4%	5%	6%	7%
10%	+%	+%	+%	1%	1%	1%	1%	1%	2%	2%	3%	3%	4%	5%
5%	+%	+%	+%	+%	+%	+%	1%	1%	1%	1%	1%	1%	2%	2%
0%	0%	0%	0%	0%	0%	0%	0%	0%	0%	0%	0%	0%	0%	0%

OUTDOOR TEMPERATURE

To find indoor relative humidity when outside air is heated to 70 degrees, find outdoor RH at left and outdoor temperature along the bottom. Indoor RH that results in where lines cross.

FIGURE 6-6 / Humidity conversion

A range of about 25% to 55% relative humidity (Fig. 6-6) and a dry-bulb range of 74° to 80°F is required for the highest percentage of occupants to feel comfortable.

During the summer, homes with no humidity control will tend to have high relative humidity. Yet during the summer, a low humidity will make higher temperatures feel comfortable and save cooling costs (where used). However, humidity control is often more expensive than cooling the air.

6-7 OVERALL COMFORT

The overall comfort will still vary from person to person, as well as with air velocity, types of heating and cooling systems, and types and materials of construction.

Women will generally prefer higher effective temperatures than men. Similarly, older people prefer higher effective temperatures, as do people who live in southern climates. Of course, whether a person will be comfortable or not also depends on the type of clothing the individual wears and how active he is. A person with a sweater on who is cleaning the house will need a lower effective temperature than someone with a short-sleeved shirt or blouse on who is watching television.

The suggested inside winter dry-bulb temperatures for a wide variety of spaces are shown in Fig. 6-7. Those spaces in which people will be relatively inactive, such as classrooms and hospital rooms, will require higher temperatures than spaces in which people will be active.

In the summer, comfort is also greatly affected by the relationship of indoor-outdoor temperatures. This is especially true in spaces which people occupy for short periods of time. A person who is in his residence or office for a long period of time becomes used to a 75°F temperature and is comfortable in it. But when a person occupies a space for short durations, generally up to 1 hr., he will be most comfortable

Type of Building	F
SCHOOLS—	
Classrooms..	72–74
Assembly rooms	68–72
Gymnasiums	55–65
Toilets and baths..	70
Wardrobe and locker rooms	65–68
Kitchens	66
Dining and lunch rooms...	65–70
Playrooms..	60–65
Natatoriums...	75
HOSPITALS—	
Private rooms...	72–74
Private rooms (surgical)..	70–80
Operating rooms	70–95
Wards..	72–74
Kitchens and laundries..	66
Toilets..	68
Bathrooms	70–80
THEATERS—	
Seating space...	68–72
Lounge rooms	68–72
Toilets..	68
HOTELS—	
Bedrooms and baths..	75
Dining rooms..	72
Kitchens and laundries..	66
Ballrooms	65–68
Toilets and service rooms..	68
HOMES...	73–75
STORES..	65–68

FIGURE 6-7 / Inside winter dry-bulb temperatures

if there is just a 10° to 15°F difference between the outside and the inside temperatures. So, if it is 95°F outside, it should be about 80°F inside stores and shops for a person to feel comfortable. The common practice in stores, shops, grocery markets, etc., of setting their cooling at a 68° to 70°F inside temperature does not make for comfortable conditions. This is obvious when you see the number of people who must take sweaters into grocery stores, fast food restaurants, and other stores and shops during the summer. Also, notice that the customers who didn't bring sweaters are almost always shivering. Yet, it is comfortable to some of those working there since it is likely that there is a low temperature/high humidity relationship.

Also, no matter how much heat is introduced into a space, it is very difficult for the occupant to feel comfortable if he is sitting next to a very cold surface, such as a window. The combination of the body heat loss on the side of the body nearest the window and the cold air coming through any cracks around the window makes a difficult situation. In one case, the temperature in a person's office was turned up to 76°F and he still felt uncomfortable. By rearranging the office so that there was an interior wall at his back instead of a window, he felt comfortable at 72°F.

6-8   AIR CONDITIONING

Whenever the term *air conditioning* is used, almost everyone automatically thinks of a cool building on a hot day. However, in a technical sense, air conditioning means exactly what it implies—conditioning the air inside a space; this means heating, cooling, humidity control, ventilation, filtering, and any other conditioning that may be required. While realizing that manufacturers will continue to sell air coolers as air conditioners and that when a client says he wants (or doesn't want) air conditioning, he means cooling, the technician and the engineer must be aware of the real meaning of the term.

Modern building design has increased the need for air conditioning since there is an increased tendency to build glass buildings which don't have a window that opens (no operable sash). Even in northern states, which have only short periods of warm weather, total air conditioning is often required since there are no windows to open for fresh air and ventilation.

6-9   VENTILATION

Many times it is necessary to ventilate (introduce outside air into a space) in order for the occupants to be comfortable. This is particularly true in any spaces where smoking is permitted and where dust or fumes are present.

Ventilation requirements, as set by ASHRAE, are shown in Fig. 6-8, and many times the codes in force also have ventilation requirements. Rooms with exterior exposures, windows, and exterior doors and with low occupancy may get all the

Functional Area	Air Changes per Hour	Cfm/ Person	Functional Area	Air Changes per Hour	Cfm/ Person
Anesthesia, hospital	8-12	—	Kitchens	10-30	—
Animal room	12-16	—	Laundries	10-60	—
Auditorium	10-20	10	Libraries	15-25	10
Autopsy, hospital	8-12	10	Locker room	2-15	—
Bakery	20-60	—	Machine shop	8-12	—
Bowling alley	15-30	30	Mechanical equipment	8-12	—
Churches	15-25	5	Media room, hospital	6-10	—
Cystoscopy, hospital	8-10	20	Nursery	10-15	—
Classroom	10-30	40	Offices	6-20	10
Conference	25-35	—	Operating room, hospital	10-15	—
Corridors	3-10	—	Ozalid room	8-12	—
Delivery room, hospital	8-12	—	Paint finishing	18-22	—
Dairies	5-15	—	Radiology	6-10	—
Dishwashing	30-60	—	Restaurant (dining room)	6-20	10
Drycleaning	20-40	—	Retail stores	18-22	10
Foundries	5-20	—	Residences	5-20	—
Gymnasiums	—	1½ sq ft	Telephone equipment	6-10	—
Garages	6-30	—	Traffic and flight cont.	18-22	10
Hydrotherapy, hospital	6-10	—	Toilets	8-20	—
Isolation ward	6-10	—	Transmitter, receiver		
Janitor and cleaning	8-12	—	and electronic	10° rise	—
			Welding	18-22	—

NOTE—Individual design conditions may cause variation in these values of considerable magnitude.

FIGURE 6-8 / Ventilation design criteria

ventilation they need through air leakage around the windows and doors. Rooms without exterior exposures commonly need ventilation so they will not become stale with cigarette smoke and other odors.

Many buildings with forced air systems leave the fan on even when the heating and cooling system is not operating. This provides ventilation throughout the building and reduces the possibility of stagnant air layers in a room.

QUESTIONS

6-1. Sketch and label the three natural processes by which body heat is transferred.

6-2. Briefly describe the three natural processes by which body heat is transferred and how they affect comfort.

6-3. In what ways does the surrounding air temperature affect the amount of body heat given off?

6-4. What are the three space conditions which affect the comfort of the occupant of the space?

6-5. What effect does humidity have on the comfort of a body?

6-6. What is meant by *effective temperature* in relation to comfort?

CHAPTER 7

HEATING AND AIR-CONDITIONING SYSTEMS

7-1 TYPES OF SYSTEMS

The selection of a heating system and the possible inclusion of a cooling system will depend on local climate conditions, degree of comfort desired, client's budget and fuel costs. An increasing number of clients want a system which incorporates total year-round air conditioning.

There are three basic methods of delivering heat to a space: forced air, hot water, and radiant electric. Of these three, only one, forced air, is used for central air conditioning in residences.

In *forced air systems,* the air is heated or cooled in a central unit and then delivered to the room through supply ducts. Air is returned to the central unit for treatment (to heat, cool, add humidity, or purify) and then recirculated through the rooms. (Chapter 9 contains a complete discussion and description of forced air systems for heating and cooling.)

Hot water heating systems heat the water in a central unit and pass it through pipes to a heating device in the room. As the water goes through the pipes and devices, it cools, and then it goes back through the central unit to be reheated. Cooling with water follows the same principle. Hot water heating is discussed in Chapter 10.

Radiant electric heat delivers the heat by electricity running through a cable, and the resistance produced gives off the heat. The radiant heating devices are actually in the room and may be ceiling, floor, or baseboard units. There is a complete discussion on radiant electric systems in Chapter 11.

In addition, *infrared heaters* use a lamp (bulb) which transfers heat by radiation to any people or objects which its heat rays come in contact with. It is effectively used when it is necessary to warm people, yet the surrounding air need not be heated or, perhaps, cannot be effectively heated. They are commonly used in bathrooms where for a short period of time (such as when a person steps out of a hot shower in the winter) extra heat is needed for the person to feel comfortable. Other locations include covered walkways and entries to commercial and industrial buildings.

Water may be delivered either hot or chilled, and chilled water systems are used for air conditioning in many larger projects. *Chilled water systems* cool the water at a central point, in a condenser, and then distribute chilled water throughout the building—either to convectors in the space or through pipes embedded in the floor or ceiling.

7-2 HEATING SYSTEM COMBINATIONS

It is not unusual for industrial and commercial buildings to use different types of systems to heat and cool different areas of a building. The systems may vary in use of hot water heat, with finned tube units being used in offices and convector units being used in storage or warehouse areas. Similarly, completely different systems may be used, with radiant hot water heat in the floor of an office area and electric unit heaters in the warehouse or storage areas. Any combination may be used, and the selection may vary, depending on the type of heat required, the type of fuels available, and to a great extent, how much heat is required, how often it is required, and what method of supplying the heat will provide the best results in the designer's opinion.

Residential designs may use combinations of systems such as hot water for heat and forced air for cooling, hot water or forced air heat with electric supplements (particularly in bathrooms or kitchens), and finned tube units with supplemental hot water unit heaters in areas such as a kitchen or basement.

As mentioned previously, chilled water may be used to provide cooling in a building by running it through the same pipes used for hot water heating. This means that once the system is changed over from one function to the other—say, from heating to cooling as summer approaches—it is not easily reversed if cold weather comes for several days. This type of system has little flexibility in that it provides either heating or cooling and cannot provide both at one time.

However, different uses, activities, type of exterior wall construction, and location in the building (especially larger buildings) may make it desirable to have heating

7 / HEATING AND AIR-CONDITIONING SYSTEMS

in some spaces while cooling is required in others. This may be accomplished by putting in separate pipes for hot and chilled water. In this manner, areas which require cooling can get chilled water while those requiring heat can get hot water. Of course, there is the extra cost of piping and controls to regulate the flow of the water to the desired location.

The actual design of any particular system will involve the size of the building, amount of insulation, doors, windows, climate in the area, and fuel to be used.

7-3   FUELS

The most commonly used sources of building heat are the sun, electricity, gas, oil, and coal. Use of the sun as an energy source is discussed in Chapter 14. The decision on which of the other four fuels to use is based on availability and cost of operation. In this section, we will review the advantages and disadvantages of each fuel and the method used to determine the cost of operation.

ELECTRICITY

Electricity is used as a fuel for a variety of heating systems, including baseboard radiant heat and electric coils in the ceiling and/or walls (refer to Chapter 11). In addition, there are electric furnaces for forced hot air systems, and it is used with heat pumps both to operate the system and to provide supplemental electric resistance heat for the system. Electricity has as its advantage its simplicity. It requires no chimney to remove toxic gases, and when baseboard strips and ceiling and wall coils are used, the system has individual room controls, providing a high degree of flexibility and comfort. Electric systems cost significantly less to install than other systems (including electric furnaces for forced hot air), and all electric systems (except heat pumps) require much less upkeep and maintenance than those using the other fuels.

The primary disadvantage of electric heat is its yearly cost of operation when compared with those of other fuels. Electricity rates vary tremendously throughout the country, and the rates are continuing to climb. It is necessary to determine the rates in the geographical area of construction to do a cost analysis. Electric heat is quite popular, and generally most economical, in the southern regions since winter is shorter and heat bills are generally lower. It is also used extensively in apartments, offices, and similar buildings where the developer is primarily interested in building the units as inexpensively as possible and where the cost of heating is usually paid by the person renting the space. Its minimal need for maintenance and repairs is also a factor in such construction. Builders of some homes, especially those which they may want to be able to sell at the lowest price, may use electric baseboard heat.

GAS

Gas, also a popular fuel for heating, is used to heat the water in hot water systems and the air in forced air systems. Gas fuels available include natural gas, which is piped to the residence or building, and propane gas, which is delivered in pressurized cylinders in trucks and tanks and stored in tanks at or near the building. Since natural gas is simply available as needed, with no storage or individual delivery required, it is considered simpler to use. However, it is not available in many areas, and the more suburban the area, the less likely it is that natural gas will be available. So the designer must first determine if natural gas is available. Secondly, at the present time, there is a shortage of natural gas. While this shortage may be alleviated in the future, many areas do not permit any new natural gas customers. In periods of shortages, the residential customer can be reasonably assured that he will have sufficient natural gas for his use, but industrial and commercial customers cannot be so assured. Since 1975, hundreds of businesses have been faced with the option of converting to another fuel or closing, and many did close for the winter months. While the reasons for such shortages may be debated as to whether they are real or contrived—caused by government, industry, or both—the designer is concerned with one thing: Is it available, and will it continue to be available, or not?

The primary advantages of natural gas have been its relatively low cost and its simple and clean burning which reduces the maintenance required on the heating unit. As with all of the fuels, as costs go up in the future, it is difficult to say which will be the most economical.

Propane gas is equally as clean as natural gas, and its availability is not limited to areas where supply pipes have been installed. To date the cost of propane gas has generally been higher than that of natural gas.

OIL

Oil is one of the most popular fuels, and it is used extensively in the Northeast. The primary reason for its use has been its availability and historic low cost. It does require delivery by trucks to storage tanks located in or near the building, and the heating unit will generally require more maintenance than a gas heating unit. The selection of oil as a heating fuel has diminished somewhat since the oil embargo in the early 1970s. In addition, the cost of this fuel has risen dramatically since that time. Costs of other fuels have also risen, but it is the fear of not having oil if another embargo is imposed that is one of the most important concerns.

Oil is available in various weights (Fig. 7-1) with various heating values and at different costs. Generally, the lower the number, the more refined it is and the higher the cost. Number 2 oil is commonly used in residences while numbers 4, 5, and 6 are commonly used in commercial and industrial projects.

COAL

Coal is rarely used for residential heating in new construction, and its use in industrial and commercial construction fluctuates. Its primary advantage is that it is available and

7 / HEATING AND AIR-CONDITIONING SYSTEMS

Commercial standard number	Weight (lb./gal.)	Btu per gallon	Btu average
1	6.675-7.076	132,900-138,800	136,000
2	6.870-7.481	135,800-144,300	140,000
4	7.529-8.212	145,000-153,000	149,000
5	7.627-8.328	146,200-154,600	150,000
6	7.909-8.448	149,700-156,000	154,000

FIGURE 7-1 / Fuel characteristics

there are ample supplies so that a shortage seems unlikely at this time. Generally, its cost is competitive with those of other fuels. Its disadvantages lie in the amount of space required for storage and the fact that it does not burn as completely as oil or gas, thus producing more pollution. Government regulations for clean air have also limited the use of some more polluting coals for industrial purposes.

Coal's decreased use for heating residences is due to the handling required in delivery and the inconvenience of having a coal bin as part of a basement. Also, originally the coal had to be shoveled into the furnace by the occupant of the house, which is sufficient reason to change to oil, gas, or electricity. Now, coal heating units are fed by automatic stokers which require no hand shoveling.

Since coal is used so little as a residential and small commercial heating fuel, it will not be considered further.

7-4   COOLING PRINCIPLES

While the principle of providing heat to a source (water or air) which is then used to heat the space is easily understood, the principles of providing cooling should be discussed. The fundamental principles on which the cooling process is based are derived from physics:

1.   As a gas is compressed, it will liquefy at a given point, and as it liquefies, it will *release* a large amount of latent *heat* from within the gas/liquid.

2.   As the pressure on the liquid is lowered, it vaporizes back to a gas, and as it boils through the vaporizing process, it *absorbs* a large amount of latent heat into the liquid/gas.

The refrigerant medium in the cooling system is cycled through three components (Fig. 7-2):

1.   A *compressor* which will compress the refrigerant, causing it to liquefy.

2.   A heat transfer surface which will distribute the *heat released* to a surrounding medium such as water or air. This heat transfer surface is called a *condenser*.

3.   A second heat transfer surface which will *extract heat* from the surrounding medium, such as water or air, as it is *absorbed* into the refrigerant. This heat transfer surface is called an *evaporator*.

The refrigerant is run continuously through the cycle while the system is in operation:

1.   The refrigerant is compressed to a liquid in the compressor, generally located in or near the condenser.

2.   The liquid passes through the condenser which allows the latent heat to be released. The condenser is often located on the exterior of the building. For most residences and small commercial projects, it is located on the ground; however, it may be located on the roof, often the case on larger projects. The heat is released through the condenser to a surrounding medium. This surrounding medium is the outside air for most installations, but water, such as a pond, can be used. In the typical installation, the condenser unit has a fan which pushes the air past the refrigerant to take as much heat away from it as possible.

3.   The refrigerant then passes out of the condenser to the second heat transfer surface (the evaporator) which will extract heat from the surrounding medium. So, as the liquid vaporizes to a gas, it draws heat out of the surrounding medium as it passes through the evaporator. The surrounding medium may be air or water. In a forced air system, air would be the medium, and this drawing of heat from the air and into the refrigerant causes the air to cool. As the air is forced

FIGURE 7-2 / Refrigerant cycle

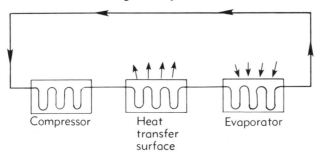

Compressor   Heat   Evaporator
                    transfer
                    surface

back through the system, it is cool air. When water is used as the medium, the heat is drawn from the water, making it cool or chilled; the water is then circulated through the system to cool the space.

These basic principles apply for all types of cooling systems. Some equipment, such as a room air conditioner, may be designed to combine all the components in one unit (Fig. 7-3), or they may be separate pieces of equipment. These principles are also the basic principles of heat pump operation (Sec. 14-8).

FIGURE 7-3 / Single unit cooling

QUESTIONS

7-1. What three basic methods are used to deliver heat to a space?

7-2. Why might combinations of systems be used in a building?

7-3. What type of system is most commonly used for residential cooling?

7-4. When might a chilled water system be used?

7-5. Describe the advantages and disadvantages of electricity as a fuel.

7-6. Why is electric heat often used in projects such as apartments?

7-7. List the fuels most commonly used for heating in a residence.

7-8. What are the two fundamental principles on which the cooling process is based?

7-9. Describe the three components used in the refrigeration process.

7-10. What types of surrounding mediums are generally used to take the heat from the refrigerant?

CHAPTER 8
HEAT LOSS

8-1   HEAT LOSS

The amount of heat lost from the building to the surrounding air will determine the size of the heating plant, the size of the heat convectors (radiators, ducts, etc.), and the heating cost per year. The amount of heat loss is measured in BTU (British Thermal Units); a BTU is defined as *the amount of heat required to raise 1 pound of water 1 degree Fahrenheit*. Heat loss will depend on the type of construction assembly, the types of doors and windows used, and the climate in the geographical area where the building is being constructed.

8-2   FACTORS IN CALCULATING HEAT LOSS

Heat is lost from a space by transmission, infiltration, and ventilation.

1. Before the heat loss for a building can be calculated, the places at which the losses occur must be identified. Since the heat inside will flow to colder areas, the heat will pass through walls, floors, ceilings, doors, and windows.

166

2. The heat loss is calculated separately for each room. Therefore, it is necessary to determine each type of assembly of materials used.

3. For each room, the area of each type of material assembly which has one side exposed to the inside of the room and the other side exposed to a lower temperature space—such as the exterior, attic, basement, or crawl space or a colder room such as a garage or enclosed porch which is not heated—must be calculated. This heat loss is referred to as *heat transmission*. Calculations for heat transmission loss are shown in this chapter.

4. In every building, no matter how well constructed, there is a certain amount of cold air which leaks into the building, referred to as *infiltration heat loss*, and an equal amount of hot air which leaks out. Most commonly infiltration will occur around doors and windows. The tight construction of the building will save the building owner a considerable amount of money over the life of the building. Some suggestions to reduce infiltration heat loss are discussed in Sec. 8-8; calculations for infiltration heat loss are also shown in Sec. 8-8.

5. *Ventilation* is the introduction of fresh air into the building, or parts of the building, at a controlled rate. Many times the air used to ventilate the building is heated before it is introduced into the building, and this must be considered in the design of the system.

8-3   RESISTANCE RATINGS

Since heat passes through different materials at different rates, each material is considered to have a certain resistance to the flow of heat through it. In general, the heavier and denser the material, the less resistance it has to the flow of heat through it and the lower its resistance (R) value is; for lighter, less dense materials, the higher the R value, the better its insulating value. For example, a 6-in.-thick poured concrete wall has an R value of about 0.48 while a 1-in. thickness of cork has an R value of about 3.70. Increasing the thickness of the material also affects the insulating value of the material in proportion to its original value. For example, doubling the 6-in. concrete wall to 12 in. will double the R value from 0.48 to 0.96. Doubling the cork thickness from 1 in. to 2 in. will double its R value from 3.70 to 7.40. To determine the heat flow of an assembly of materials (U value), it is first necessary to find the R value for each material and total them.

The resistance listings for most materials can be found in Fig. 8-46. When materials not listed here are encountered, the heat flow characteristics will have to be determined from the manufacturer.

There are four values used to measure the heat resistance of a material; they are the *U, R, C,* and *k* values. Each of the values is related, and the designer must understand the relationships:

1. The *k* value of the material used in the construction measures heat flow conductance in terms of how effective it is *per inch of thickness (t)*.

2. The C (conductance) value of the material measures the material's ability to conduct heat in terms of how effective it is for the *thickness being used*. The more effective the material, the lower the C value ($C = k \div t$).

3. The R (resistance) value of the material measures heat flow resistance in terms of how effective it is for the *thickness being used*. (This term is inversely related to the C value.) The more effective the material, the higher the R value ($R = 1 \div C$).

4. The U value of the entire assembly of materials measures heat flow resistance in terms of how effective it is for the type and thickness of the materials used in the total assembly ($U = 1 \div R$).

EXAMPLE

To show the relationship of the values we will use a 2-in.-thick piece of polystyrene foam insulation (Fig. 8-1). Polystyrene foam has a k value of 0.26 per inch of thickness. Since it is 2 in. thick, its insulating value is given as a C value as 0.13 (or one-half the k value). These values are directly proportional to each other, based on the thickness of material used. The *lower* these values, the better the material is as a heat insulator. The R value is equal to 1 divided by the C value. So for the 2-in.-thick polystyrene foam, $R = 1/C = 1 \div 0.13 = 7.7$. This indicates the resistance value of that particular material.

It is quite unlikely that a wall would be built only of 2-in. polystyrene foam; this insulating material is often used with other materials, such as metal facings, masonry, and concrete. For this example, assume that the wall is made of 6-in. poured concrete, gravel aggregate, 2-in. polystyrene foam and ⅜-in. gypsum board (Fig. 8-2). From Fig. 8-46, the resistance values listed are:

⅜-in. gypsum board	0.32
6-in. concrete, gravel (0.08 per in.)	0.48
2-in. polystyrene foam (3.45 per in.)	7.70
Outside air film (see Sec. 8-4)	0.17
Inside air film (see Sec. 8-4)	0.68
Total resistance R	9.35

FIGURE 8-1 / Heat flow terms

$$k = 0.26$$
$$C = \frac{k}{t} = \frac{0.26}{2} = 0.13$$
$$R = \frac{1}{c} = \frac{1}{0.13} = 7.7$$
$$R = \frac{t}{k} = \frac{2}{0.26} = 7.7$$

6" CONCRETE
GRAVEL
AGGREGATE

2" POLYSTYRENE
FOAM

3/8" GYPSUM
BOARD

FIGURE 8-2 / Wall section

SECTION

Heat flow from the interior of the building to the cooler exterior is determined by multiplying the heat flow characteristics of a given assembly of materials (referred to as the *U value*) times the area (*A*) of the material involved times the difference between the inside temperature desired and the average low temperature on the other side of the construction (referred to as ΔT and given in °F). In equation form:

$$U \times A \times \Delta T = BTU/hr(Btuh)$$

In the above equation, the U value is the most important item since it can vary so much, depending on the material assembly used. With any given A and ΔT, the number of Btuh required will vary in direct relationship with the U value for the assembly of materials used. The U value is determined by adding the R values of each material plus the resistance to heat flow caused by the flow of air inside and outside the building and then dividing 1 by the total $R (U = 1 \div R = 1/R)$.

$$U = 1/R = 1 \div 9.35 = 0.107 \text{ (use 0.11)}$$

The U value must be determined for walls, floors, and ceilings and for each material or assembly of materials used in the construction.

The area used in the formula is the *net exposed area* of the material assembly being considered. If a room has two different material assemblies (Fig. 8-3), each must

Resistance Ratings / 8-3

Calculate each
area separately

FIGURE 8-3 / Different wall
assemblies

be considered separately since each has a different U value. Likewise, the area of windows and doors must be deducted from the total area to obtain the net exposed wall area of the particular material assembly being considered. Assuming that the room being designed has two exposed walls 8 ft high (Fig. 8-4) with a total of 36 lineal ft, this would give a gross square footage of 288. Deduct the two 3 ft x 4 ft windows for a net exposed wall area of 288 sq ft − 24 sq ft = 264 sq ft.

The ΔT is the difference between the inside temperature desired and the temperature on the cold side of the construction in °F. If the cold side of the construction is the outside air, then the average low temperature expected during the year is used. This varies considerably, depending on the geographical area of construction. Some typical outside design temperatures for various areas are listed in Fig. 8-54. Assuming an indoor design temperature of 70°F, if the building is being built in Rutland, Vermont, with an outside design temperature of −8°F, the ΔT will be 78°F (Fig. 8-5). If the same building is constructed in Raleigh, North Carolina, the outside design temperature is 20°F and the ΔT will be 50°F. Assuming that similar buildings are being

FIGURE 8-4 / Room plan   FIGURE 8-5 / Calculating ΔT

built in Raleigh and Rutland, the heat loss for the walls in that one room would be:

Raleigh $U \times A \times \Delta T = 0.11 \times 264 \times 50 = 1{,}452$ Btuh

Rutland $U \times A \times \Delta T = 0.11 \times 264 \times 78 = 2{,}265$ Btuh

It is important that the designer become proficient in calculating U values for various assemblies of materials. The flow of heat through any barrier—in this case, the construction of the walls—is resisted by the materials used for the construction, the inside and outside air films, and any air spaces left. It is, therefore, important that the designer carefully review the drawings, especially wall sections and details, to determine what materials will be used on the project. In addition, the designer should check to be certain exactly what the materials being specified actually *are*. For example, the wall section (Fig. 8-6) may show 2 in. of rigid insulation. The designer must also know exactly what type of rigid insulation is going to be used and must be certain that the material the calculations were based on is actually specified on the project and, even further, that no material substitution is allowed. This is because if the rigid insulation

FIGURE 8-6 / Wall section

in Fig. 8-6 is urethane, it is about twice as effective as polystyrene foam insulation.

EXAMPLE

Problem: Determine the resistance values for each of the materials in the wall section shown in Fig. 8-7.

First, list all of the materials of construction; then list their resistance values next to them. When necessary, convert the C and k values to R values.

$$R = 1/C \text{ and } R = t/k$$

(t = thickness of the material, in inches)

The materials and R values for the wall section shown in Fig. 8-7 are indicated in Fig. 8-8.

8-4   AIR FILMS

Both inside a room and outside the building, there is a movement of air over the surfaces, creating a film of air which causes the air and wall to exchange convective heat. This air film helps resist the flow of heat through the construction. The air film's resistance value depends first on whether it is an *inside* air film (inside the room) or an *outside* air film (on the outside of the wall).

FIGURE 8-7 / Wall section

4″ Brick	0.44		4″ Brick	0.44
8″ Block, Gravel	1.11		8″ Block, Gravel	1.11
2″ Urethane	14.30		2″ Urethane	14.30
			→ Inside Air Film	0.68

FIGURE 8-8 / Material R values

FIGURE 8-9 / Inside air film resistance

The resistance values of inside air films are shown in Fig. 8-47. These values are based on still air (no wind), and proper selection from the table is based on:

1. Surface position or orientation. (Is it a vertical wall, horizontal ceiling or floor?)

2. Direction of heat flow—for a wall, horizontal; for a ceiling, upward; for a floor over a basement, downward. (In what direction is the heat flowing in the room in which the heat loss is being calculated?)

3. Surface emissivity. (Is the surface reflective or not? Most surfaces used in buildings, such as gypsum board painted with flat paint and concrete block, are not reflective. Use the nonreflective or reflective value, depending on the wall finish to be used in the building.) (Fig. 8-50)

EXAMPLE

Given: For the wall section in Fig. 8-7, the interior wall is gypsum board which will be nonreflective (from Fig. 8-50, an emissivity value of 0.90).

Problem: Using Fig. 8-47, find the resistance value of the air film.

The resistance value of this inside air film—which is for a vertical, nonreflective wall, with horizontal heat flow—is taken from Fig. 8-47 as $R = 0.68$. This value is included with the tabulation of material resistance values from Fig. 8-8 and combined here (Fig. 8-9):

The resistance values of exterior air films are shown in Fig. 8-48. Proper selection of the R value is based on:

1. Winter: 15 mph air velocity; use $R = 0.17$.

2. Summer: 7½ mph air velocity; use $R = 0.25$.

This value is now included with the tabulation of resistance values for materials and inside air film (Fig. 8-9) and combined here (Fig. 8-10):

4″ Brick	0.44
8″ Block, Gravel	1.11
2″ Urethane	14.30
Inside Air Film	0.68
→ Outside Air Film	0.17

FIGURE 8-10 / Outside air film resistance

8-5 AIR SPACES

Many times an assembly of materials will have an air space left between the materials. For example, there is usually an air space between the brick veneer on a building and the material behind it. A review of the wall section in Fig. 8-7 shows that it calls for a ¾-in. air space. These air spaces also resist the flow of heat and have an *R* or a *C* value.

The resistance values of air spaces are shown in Fig. 8-49. Proper selection of an *R* value from the table is based on:

1. Position of air space (horizontal, 45° slope, vertical—for this wall, it is vertical).

2. Direction of heat flow (up, horizontal, down—for this wall, the heat flow is horizontal).

3. Air space thickness (thicknesses other than those listed may be interpolated from the values given: for thickness greater than 3.5 in., use the 3.5-in. value).

4. Value of *E* (emissivity) (Are the surfaces on each side of the wall space reflective or not? For nonreflective materials, use $E = 0.82$; for reflective materials, such as aluminum foil, use $E = 0.05$. In this case, there are only nonreflective surfaces.)

EXAMPLE

For the ¾-in. air space in the wall section (Fig. 8-7), with a vertical air space, horizontal flow of heat, nonreflective surfaces, *E* at 0.82, and 50°–30° temperature, the resistance value *R* is 0.94. This value is included in the tabulation of material resistance values from Fig. 8-10 and combined (Fig. 8-11).

8-6 TOTAL RESISTANCE VALUES

With all of the materials, air films, and air spaces listed with their appropriate *R* values, the next step is to total the *R* values of the wall and convert this total to the equivalent *U* value. The total resistance value of the wall is 17.64 with a *U* value of 0.057, as calculated and shown in Fig. 8-12.

4" Brick	0.44
8" Block, Gravel	1.11
2" Urethane	14.30
Inside Air Film	0.68
Outside Air Film	0.17
→ ¾" Air Space	0.94

FIGURE 8-11 / Air space resistance

4" Brick	0.44
8" Block, Gravel	1.11
2" Urethane	14.30
Inside Air Film	0.17
Outside Air Film	0.17
¾" Air Space	0.94
Total R	17.64

$$U = \frac{1}{R} = \frac{1}{17.64} = 0.057$$

FIGURE 8-12 / Calculate total R and U values

8-7   CALCULATING R AND U VALUES

The method described in Secs. 8-3 through 8-6 of combining the R values for each separate material, for the inside and outside air films, and for any air spaces gives the total R value of the assembly. It is this total R of the assembly which is used to calculate the U value for the particular assembly and is used in the basic heat loss formula:

$$U \times A \times \Delta T = \text{Btuh}$$

To become proficient in the use of the tables and to be certain that the basic relationships of the various R values are understood, examples for floors and ceilings are given next. Keep in mind that:

1. The higher the R value, the more effective the material at resisting the flow of heat.

2. The higher the R value, the lower the heat loss. The lower the heat loss, the less expensive the entire installation in terms of the yearly fuel bills.

EXAMPLE

Problem: Calculate the R and U values for the wall assembly shown in Fig. 8-13.

The tabulations are shown in Fig. 8-14.

EXAMPLE

Problem: Calculate the R and U values for the roof assembly shown in Fig. 8-15.

The tabulations are also shown in Fig. 8-16. Note that the R values for the inside and

FIGURE 8-13 / Wall assembly

3½" BATT INSULATION (R-11)
½" GYPSUM BOARD
4" BRICK
½" PLYWOOD
¾" AIR SPACE

FIGURE 8-14 / R and U calculations

½" Plywood	0.62
4" Brick	0.44
3½" Batt Insul.	11.00
½" Gypsum Board	0.45
Inside Air Film	0.68
Outside Air Film	0.17
¾" Air Space	0.94
Total R	14.30

$$U = \frac{1}{R} = \frac{1}{14.30} = 0.07$$

outside air films are different from those used for the wall assembly and that there is no air space.

EXAMPLE

Problem: Calculate the R and U values for the floor assembly shown in Fig. 8-17.

Note that the tabulation (Fig. 8-18) shows R values for outside and inside air films different from those used for the wall and roof assemblies.

FIGURE 8-15 / Ceiling assemblies

BUILT-UP ROOF
2" MINERAL FIBERBOARD
3" GYPSUM FIBER CONCRETE

3" Gyp. Conc.	1.80
2" Fiberboard Insul.	5.88
Built-up Roof	0.33
Outside Air Film	0.17
Inside Air Film	0.61
Total R	8.79

$$U = \frac{1}{R} = \frac{1}{8.79} = 0.114$$

FIGURE 8-16 / Ceiling R and U calculations

Carpet, Rubber Pad	1.23
⅝" Plywood	0.77
6" Batt Insul.	19.00
Inside Air Film	0.92
Outside Air Film	0.92
Total R	22.84

$$U = \frac{1}{R} = \frac{1}{22.84} = 0.044$$

FIGURE 8-18 / Floor R and U calculations

CARPET AND RUBBER PAD

⅝" PLYWOOD

6" BATT INSUL. (R-19)

FIGURE 8-17 / Floor assembly

In reviewing the various assemblies, it becomes obvious that as more and better insulation is used, the R values of the other materials in the assembly become relatively less important.

EXAMPLE

In Fig. 8-12, the total R value is 17.64 with a U value of 0.057. If the concrete block were changed to lightweight block, the R value of the block would change from 1.11 to 2.00. This would cause the total R to change from 17.64 to 18.53 and the U value to change from 0.057 to 0.054. In terms of real savings, this is extremely little and unnecessary.

The designer must be able to see that small changes in the R value will have little effect on overall R value, on U value, and on subsequent heat loss of the building. This is particularly important when reading technical "sales sheets" and talking to materials salesmen. As an example of what is meant, on one residential project, it was proposed to use ½-in.-thick asphalt-impregnated fiberboard instead of ½-in.-thick plywood over the 2 x 4 studs because the fiberboard has a higher insulation value. A review of Fig. 8-46 quickly shows that:

½-in. sheathing (vegetable fiberboard)	$R = 1.32$
½-in. plywood	$R = 0.62$

Now, while the point could be made that the impregnated sheathing is twice as resistant as the plywood, it must be judged in relation to the entire wall.

A review of the tabulations (Fig. 8-14) indicates that the wall with ½-in. plywood has an R of 14.30; if ½-in. impregnated sheathing were used, the R value would increase by 0.69 (1.32 − 0.63) to 15.00 (Fig. 8-19)—about a 5% increase in the total

Calculating R and U Values / 8-7

FIGURE 8-19 / Material comparisons

½" Sheathing	1.32
4" Brick	0.44
3½" Batt Insul.	11.00
½" Gypsum Bd.	0.45
Inside Air Film	0.68
Outside Air Film	0.17
¾" Air Space	0.94
Total R	15.00

R. There may be other reasons to use the impregnated sheathing (because it is less expensive, for example), but not because it is a better insulation. The designer (as well as the architect, engineer, and owner) is subjected to this type of logic much of the time, and newspapers, magazines, television, and direct mailings send this type of logic into every household and business.

There is one other type of *R* value information that the designer should be aware of. To illustrate the type of analysis required, the following example has been prepared (this is a fictitious example and not taken from any manufacturer's brochure or data sheet):

Heat flow: Horizontal

R value:

¾-in. 4-in. air space + ½-in. impregnated fiber sheathing board = 2.24

Now, this in itself is not misrepresentation since the *R* value would be 2.24. But the *R* value of the board is 1.32 and the air space is about 0.92, so any comparison of materials should be based on the *R* of the 1.32, not 2.24. Also, the designer who is familiar with construction would realize that in the brick veneer construction shown in Fig. 8-20, the air space would easily be available; but the wood frame construction,

FIGURE 8-20 / Air space

with plywood panel facing, shown in Fig. 8-21 would not have an air space at the sheathing unless special construction methods were used. This is because R-11 insulation is 3½ in. thick, filling the entire space of the 2 x 4 studs; the sheathing is attached to the studs and the exterior finish material attached to the sheathing and studs. The only way there would be a ¾- to 4-in. air space is to use 2¼-in.-thick batt insulation which has an R of about 7.

FIGURE 8-21 / No air space

8-8   INFILTRATION HEAT LOSS FACTORS

Air leaks into a building through cracks around windows and doors, between the foundation wall and the sill plate, and at many of the connections between walls made of different types of materials. This air leakage is caused by a combination of the wind pressure on the building and the difference in temperature between the inside and the outside. As the wind velocity increases, the amount of air leakage also increases.

The infiltration heat loss (Btuh) will be calculated by multiplying LF (the lineal feet of window and door infiltration cracks or crackage, as outlined in this section) times Q (the air volume in cubic feet per hour, or cfh) times 0.018 (Btuh per cubic foot to raise 1°F) times ΔT (the design temperature difference).

$$\text{Btuh} = LF \times Q \times 0.018 \times \Delta T$$

Window air infiltration is determined primarily by the type of window. The lineal feet of infiltration through which air leaks occur is measured by finding the total length of crackage in the window parts for the type of window used. For example, a double-hung window (Fig. 8-22) is made so that both the top and bottom sash open, and this means that air can infiltrate around the entire perimeter of the window as well as the space where the stiles meet. For a 3-ft-wide x 5-ft-high double-hung wood window, the lineal feet of infiltration will be three times the width (w) plus two times the length (l) or

$$3w + 2l = 3(3 \text{ ft}) + 2(5 \text{ ft}) = 9 \text{ ft} + 10 \text{ ft} = 19 \text{ lineal ft of infiltration cracks}$$

There are two general guidelines to be followed regarding what is measured:

1. For a room with *one wall* of exterior exposure, list the totals for each type of window and door *separately*. Since different types of windows and doors have different infiltration factors (IF), it is important to list each type separately.

2. For a room with *two or more* exterior walls, only the wall with the most infiltration is used. Since the infiltration factor (amount of infiltration) will vary considerably for different types of doors and windows, it will be necessary to total the infiltration for each wall separately. The amount of infiltration loss will be taken as the total loss of the wall having the most loss *or* one-half of the total infiltration, whichever is more.

This approach to two or more exposed walls is taken because as air infiltrates into a building it must also be leaving at the same rate (otherwise, the building would blow

FIGURE 8-22 / Infiltration dimensions

up like a balloon). So, while a portion of the crackage allows air to infiltrate, the air is escaping through other cracks. Typically, the cold air infiltrates on whatever side the wind is blowing.

The air volume (Q) is a measure of the amount of outdoor air entering the building per lineal foot of crack. This value will vary considerably, depending on the type and material of the windows and doors, whether they fit well or poorly, and whether they are weatherstripped or not. Typical air volume values are listed in Fig. 8-52, and the appropriate values will be used in the infiltration loss formula (Btuh = $LF \times Q \times 0.018 \times \Delta T$).

For the 3-ft-wide x 5-ft-high double-hung wood window with 19 lineal feet of crackage (calculated earlier in this section), assuming a 15-mph wind velocity from Fig. 8-52, the air volume (Q) is taken as 14 cfh. The total infiltration Btuh for the window (assuming $\Delta T = 60$) is:

$$19 \times 14 \times 0.018 \times 60 = 288 \text{ Btuh}$$

In new construction, it is natural to assume that the windows will be tight fitting. This may or may not be the case since it depends a great deal on the window being used. Usually the more expensive the window, the better it fits, but for a window that has the sash slide (such as a double-hung window), a good fit would be considered average since if it is too tight, it will not open. Many of the better-quality windows also have built-in weatherstripping, and it is important to check the specifications to determine whether it is actually called for or not.

Door fit may also be considered average or poor. This depends to a great extent on the builder (or worker) who installs the door. All exterior doors should be weatherstripped since it is difficult to get a good fit on doors. The weatherstripping can then fill the cracks and reduce the air infiltration tremendously. The designer must check the building specifications to be certain that all exterior doors will get weatherstripping.

When designing a heating system for an existing building, the designer can see what is actually used on the building and the fit is more easily checked. In addition, the visual inspection shows if any of the cracks are larger than usual; if this is the case, it will be necessary to allow for the increased infiltration, and this must be considered in the calculations. For such a situation, values two, three or four times the values in Fig. 8-52 are used. Many times the designer will recommend storm windows, sealing of cracks with a sealant, weatherstripping, and perhaps even new windows. But it is important that a heating system design based on these recommended changes not be implemented until the changes are made. This is because the owner might install the new heating system, not make the recommended changes, and then have a cold building.

Construction cracks many times occur at the connection of different materials in the construction, such as the point where the sill plate of the floor construction attaches to the foundation wall (Fig. 8-23). To seal this crack, a roll of compressible plastic filler may be placed on the top of the foundation wall and then the sill plate put on top of it. In this way, the compressible filler seals the space. This type of situation can occur even more frequently in commercial construction at material junctions, such as the precast concrete plank on the top of the masonry wall (Fig. 8-24). Similar situations can occur throughout the construction of a building. It is the responsibility of the designer to analyze the drawings and specifications and to be familiar enough with the builder to know if his work is of good quality or not and, if an architect or engineer is involved, to know him well enough to determine whether he will insist that the building be built in accordance with the drawings and specifications. If there is any doubt in the designer's mind, he will have to take this information into account as the heating system for the building is designed.

Residential construction cracks most commonly occur between the window and door frames and the wood which forms the openings. To more effectively seal these cracks, a sealant should be applied so that as the window or door frame is installed, it will compress the sealant against the wood construction (Fig. 8-25) and seal the crack. In addition, all exterior wood trim should have two beads (rows) of sealant along the full length of the back of the trim or along the construction material it will be attached to. This further reduces any infiltration of air around the frame. Too often the exterior trim simply covers the cracks between the frame and the construction, and air can still infiltrate.

Note: As you review various manuals and books, you may find that they contain information on estimating air infiltration based on the air change method. This shortcut method is becoming increasingly popular in the heat loss calculation manuals and in ASHRAE.

8-9   TEMPERATURES IN UNHEATED SPACES

To determine the heat loss from a heated room to an unheated room or space, it is first necessary to determine the temperature in the unheated space, after which the ΔT can be calculated. The temperature in the unheated space will fall somewhere between the

FIGURE 8-23 / Construction cracks   *FIGURE 8-24 / Construction cracks*

FIGURE 8-25 / Caulk frames and trim

outside and inside temperatures and will vary depending on the amount of surface area adjacent to heated rooms compared to the amount of surface area adjacent to the exterior.

TEMPERATURES IN SPACES OTHER THAN ATTICS

All unheated spaces, except attics, use the equation:

$$t_u = \frac{t_i(A_1U_1 + A_2U_2 + \ldots) + t_o(A_aU_a + A_bU_b + \ldots)}{(A_1U_1 + A_2U_2 + \ldots) + (A_aU_a + A_bU_b + \ldots)}$$

where

t_u = temperature in unheated space (°F)
t_i = indoor design temperature of heated room (°F)
t_o = outdoor design temperature (°F)
$A_1, A_2, A_3, \ldots$ = areas of the surfaces which are exposed to the heated space (sq ft)
$A_a, A_b, A_c, \ldots$ = areas of the surfaces which are exposed to the exterior (sq ft)
$U_1, U_2, U_3, \ldots$ = coefficients of heat transmission for the material assemblies in $A_1, A_2, A_3, \ldots$
$U_a, U_b, U_c, \ldots$ = coefficients of heat transmission for the material assemblies in $A_a, A_b, A_c \ldots$

Each of the areas involved, and their U values, must be considered in the formula.

EXAMPLE

Given: The residence shown in Appendix C.

Problem: Calculate the temperature in the unheated garage adjoining the kitchen.

1.   Determine the area of the cold wall.

From the floor plan, the cold wall has a total length of 22 ft 0 in. (the same as the depth of the garage) and is 8 ft high—for a gross wall area of:

22 ft × 8 ft = 176 sq ft

Now the net wall area is determined by deducting any door or window openings. In this design, there is one 2 ft 8 in. x 6 ft 8 in. door with an area of 18 sq ft.

Gross wall area	176 sq ft
Opening area	− 18 sq ft
Net wall area	158 sq ft

2.   Determine the U value of the cold wall.

From Fig. 8-35, the U value of the cold wall is 0.076.

3.   The door area has been calculated as 18 sq ft in Step 1 of this example, and the door U value is taken as 0.61, the same as that used in determining the glass heat loss (Fig. 8-35).

4.   At this point, all of the areas and U values of the cold wall have been calculated and accumulated. Put this cold wall information in the equation.

$$t_u = \frac{70[(158 \times 0.076) + (18 \times 0.61) + t_o(A_aU_a + A_bU_b + \ldots)]}{(158 \times 0.076) + (18 \times 0.61) + (A_aU_a + A_bU_b + \ldots)}$$

5.   Next, the areas and U values of the surfaces which are exposed to the outside are determined. Begin by listing each of the material assemblies which must be considered.

Ceiling
Wall
Floor (slab on grade, neglected)
Doors

6.   Determine the area of the exterior wall.

In this design, the exterior walls referred to are the exterior walls of the garage. From the floor plan in Appendix C, the garage has a total exterior wall length of 14 ft 6 in. + 22 ft 0 in. + 14 ft 6 in., or 51 lineal feet. Using an 8-ft-high ceiling:

Gross exterior wall area = 51 ft × 8 ft = 408 sq ft

Now the net exterior wall area is determined by deducting the areas of any door or window openings.

In this design, there are two doors, one 3 ft 0 in. x 6 ft 8 in. and one 8 ft 0 in. x 7 ft 0 in. Thus, the door opening area is:

(3.0 ft × 6.7 ft) + (8.0 ft × 7.0 ft) = 20 sq ft + 56 sq ft = 76 sq ft

Gross wall area	408 sq ft
Opening area	−76 sq ft
Net wall area	332 sq ft

7. Determine the U value of the exterior wall. Many times this information is not as readily available to the designer as is the information for the material assembly for the heated portion of the building. Check the drawings and specifications carefully to determine if insulation is required in these walls and, if so, how thick it must be. Quite often insulation is not required in these exterior walls.

In this example, the exterior garage walls have the same material assembly as the rest of the exterior walls, and the U value of 0.07 is taken from Fig. 8-35.

8. Determine the area of the ceiling.

In this design, the ceiling referred to is the ceiling in the garage. This ceiling has an area of:

14 ft 6 in. × 22 ft 0 in. = 14.5 ft × 22 ft = 319 sq ft

9. Determine the U value of the ceiling.

In this design, the ceiling is insulated and has the same U value as the ceiling assembly used when determining the residence heat loss, 0.047 from Fig. 8-35.

10. The door area has been calculated as 76 sq ft in Step 6 of this example, and the door U value is taken as 0.61, the same as that used in determining the residence heat loss (Fig. 8-35).

11. Determine the temperature of the unheated space. Gather all of the accumulated information and put it into the equation:

$$t_u = \frac{70[(158 \times 0.076) + (18 \times 0.61) + 10[(332 \times 0.07) + (319 \times 0.047) + (76 \times 0.61)]}{(158 \times 0.076) + (18 \times 0.61) + (332 \times 0.07) + (319 \times 0.047) + (76 \times 0.61)}$$

$$= \frac{70 (12 + 11) + 10 (23 + 15 + 46)}{12 + 11 + 23 + 15 + 46} = \frac{1{,}610 + 840}{107}$$

$$= 22.8°F \text{ or } 23°F$$

TEMPERATURES IN ATTICS

To calculate the heat loss of the ceiling area of a building which has an uninsulated attic, it is necessary to estimate the temperature in the attic.

The attic temperature will fall somewhere between the outside and inside temperatures and will vary depending on the amount of surface area adjacent to heated rooms compared to the amount of surface area adjacent to the exterior.

To estimate the attic temperature, use the equation:

$$t_a = \frac{A_c U_c t_i + t_o(A_r U_r + A_w U_w + A_g U_g)}{A_c U_c + A_r U_r + A_w U_w + A_g U_g}$$

where

t_a = attic temperature (°F)
t_i = indoor temperature near top floor ceiling (°F)
t_o = outdoor design temperature (°F)
A_c = area of ceiling (sq ft)
A_r = area of roof (sq ft)
A_w = net area of vertical attic wall surface (sq ft)
A_g = area of attic glass (sq ft)
U_c = coefficient of heat transmission of ceiling
U_r = coefficient of heat transmission of roof
U_w = coefficient of heat transmission of vertical wall surface
U_g = coefficient of heat transmission of glass

EXAMPLE

Given: The residence shown in Appendix C.

Problem: Calculate the temperature in the attic.

1. Determine the area of the ceiling.

    From the floor plan, the total area of the ceiling in heated spaces is:

    36 ft 0 in. × 61 ft 6 in. = 2,214 sq ft

2. Determine the U value for the ceiling.

    From Fig. 8-35, the U value of the ceiling is 0.047.

3. Determine the area of the roof.

    To determine the area of the roof, it will be necessary to check the drawings in Appendix C. The quickest approach is to simply measure the length of the rafter from the outside edge of the wall to the ridge (highest point). This will give one-half the width of the roof. In this design, the roof measures about 20.2 ft, so the total roof width would be about 40.4 ft. The length of the roof is taken as the length of the building or 61.5 ft.

$$\text{Roof area} = 40.4 \text{ ft} \times 61.5 \text{ ft} = 2{,}485 \text{ sq ft}$$

4. Determine the U value for the roof construction.

In this example, the construction of the roof is shown in Appendix C. The U value is taken from Fig. 8-35 as 0.48.

5. Determine the area of the vertical wall surface (at the gable ends).

The area of the vertical wall surface may also be measured from the drawings. In this design, the triangular wall surface has a base dimension of 36 ft 0 in. and a height of about 9 ft 0 in.; there are two such surfaces (one at each end of the house). The area of vertical wall surface is:

$$\frac{bh}{2} \times 2 = \frac{36 \text{ ft} \times 9 \text{ ft}}{2} \times 2 = 324 \text{ sq ft}$$

6. Determine the U value of the vertical walls.

Many times this information is not as readily available to the designer as is the information for the material assembly for the heated portion of the building. Check the drawings and specifications carefully to determine if insulation is required in these walls and, if so, how thick it must be. Quite often insulation is not required in these exterior walls.

In this example, the vertical walls are constructed of the same basic materials as the rest of the walls, but without the insulation in the walls. To calculate the U value of the construction, it is necessary to take the R value of the wall with insulation, 14.26 from Fig. 8-35; deduct the R value of the insulation; and add the R value of the air space left where the insulation was.

Making use of the R values of the materials to calculate the R value of the wall in Fig. 8-35:

½-in. plywood	0.63
4-in. brick	0.44
Outside air	0.68
Inside air	0.17
	$R = \overline{1.92}$

$$U = 1 \div R = 0.52$$

7. Determine the temperature of the unheated attic. Gather all of the accumulated information and put it into the equation:

$$T_a = \frac{(2,214 \times 0.047 \times 70) + 10[(2,485 \times 0.48) + (324 \times 0.52)]}{(2,214 \times 0.047) + (2,485 \times 0.48) + (324 \times 0.52)}$$

$$= \frac{7,284 + 10\,(1,193 + 169)}{104 + 1,193 + 169} = \frac{7,284 + 13,620}{1,466}$$

$$= 14.26°F$$

What we find in determining unheated attic temperatures is that when the ceiling of the building is very well insulated and when there is no insulation in the roof and vertical walls, the temperature will be quite close to the outside design temperature.

The added flow of air through attic vents or louvers will further bring the temperature down.

The only times that the unheated attic temperature is significantly above the outside design temperature are:

1. When the ceiling of the building is not well insulated.

2. When the ceiling is well insulated and the roof is insulated also.

TEMPERATURES BELOW FLOORS

To calculate the heat loss through the floor area of a building, it is necessary to estimate the temperature in the basement or crawl space below the floor. Since the temperature cannot be readily calculated, the designer should use the following guidelines:

1. Basements and crawl spaces located almost entirely below ground will normally have a temperature midway between the inside and outside design temperatures being used.

2. If the basement has windows, the temperature will be lower than if it does not have windows.

3. If the heating unit (boiler or furnace) is located in the basement, the temperature will be higher than if the heater were located elsewhere.

4. The crawl space temperature will be affected by the size and number of vents; the presence of heating unit, hot water heater, piping and ductwork; and the amount of insulation used.

In short, the designer must use his judgment in determining the basement or crawl space temperature to use in the heat loss calculation.

8-10 DESIGNER RESPONSIBILITIES

The designer of the heating system for a building will have to review carefully all drawings and specifications for the construction. It is important that the designer not simply accept the word of the builder, general contractor, architect, or owner that certain materials, assemblies of materials, details, windows, and glass will be used. Whenever possible, all these things should be properly shown and specified for the designer's review.

In addition, the designer should clearly note on his design proposal the assemblies of materials, insulation, window types, and any other items on which the design is based. This is done because many times changes which may greatly affect the design are made and the designer is never told. Common changes include the type of windows, number of windows, type or thickness of insulation, ceiling height, materials in walls, ceilings, and floors, and type of window glass. Sometimes even room sizes are changed without letting the designer know. For these reasons, it is important that the designer make every attempt to keep in close contact with the others involved in the construction.

The designer has a further responsibility to the others in the sense that he should make recommendations on methods of construction and changes in materials which can reduce heat loss and save money.

8-11 OBTAINING BUILDING DIMENSIONS

When calculating the heat loss of a proposed building, the dimensions used are taken from the written dimensions on the drawings of the building. If written dimensions are incomplete, check the scale at which the drawings are made, and then check at least one dimension in each direction to be certain that it is drawn fairly close to scale. Be very careful since in many architectural and engineering offices, once the building has been drawn, if there are any small changes in room or building sizes, they simply change the written dimensions and do not revise the scale drawing. The written dimension takes precedence over any scaled dimension and should be used. Of course, if large discrepancies are found, check with whoever drew the plans to find out what is correct.

ROOM MEASUREMENTS

For heat loss calculations, the inside dimensions of a room are used when available. When working from the floor plan, the dimensions given are used. They should be accurate to the nearest foot for walls; for example, a wall 12 ft 8 in. long is considered 13 ft. Ceiling heights should be accurate to the nearest one-half foot; a 7 ft 10 in. ceiling height is considered 8 ft.

When calculating the areas, the following guidelines are used:

1. Any closet is figured as a part of the room that it opens into. Any exposed closet wall, ceiling, or floor is included as part of the heat loss of the room. Dressing rooms and walk-in closets are generally considered separate rooms with their own heat loss and will require heat to be supplied to them.

2. Any cabinets, bookshelves, or other types of pantry or closet areas are ignored when calculating the heat loss of a room. The calculations will be made as if they are not on the walls.

3. When two or more types of wall assemblies are used in one room (Figs. 8-3 and 8-26), the wall areas must be calculated separately since each assembly will have a different heat transmission value.

Many times special care must be taken in calculating the area of a wall, floor, or ceiling because part of the area may be a cold partition, floor, or ceiling. Typical *cold*

Calculate each area separately

FIGURE 8-26 / Wall assemblies

partitions are found between a heated room and an adjoining unheated space, such as any unheated garage, enclosed porch, attic or cellar stairway, crawl space, basement, or storage area. The area of cold partitions must be carefully separated from the areas of partitions which are exposed to the exterior since they will have different ΔT's.

Cold ceilings are found between a heated room and an unheated attic, storage area, or other unheated space. In a one-story house, all of the rooms have cold ceilings. In some two-story designs (such as Fig. 8-27), the second-story rooms have cold ceilings while some of the first-floor rooms may have full or partial cold ceilings. That area of the ceiling located below an unheated space must be calculated by multiplying the length times the width and then recorded. The ceiling portions of any first-floor rooms that are under heated second-floor rooms have no heat loss since the temperature would be balanced on each side of the ceiling (Fig. 8-28).

Cold floors are found between a first-floor room and an unheated basement or crawl space, and the area of these floors must be calculated. Floors over heated basements are not considered cold floors. If the basement is heated, check to be certain that it is completely heated since quite often only a portion is heated and part is left unheated. Any floor over the unheated portion is considered a cold floor. Cold floors also occur when a second-floor heated room is fully or partially over an unheated, enclosed first-floor space such as an enclosed porch or a garage. The area of the floor exposed to the cold must be calculated also.

When the floor construction is a concrete slab at or near the grade, calculate and record the lineal feet of exposed edge of slab around the building. In addition, the square footage of floor area is calculated and recorded. The heat loss factor for slab construction is given in Fig. 8-53.

WINDOW AND DOOR MEASUREMENTS

Windows and doors are measured inside the casings (Fig. 8-29), and while they are measured to the nearest inch, they are usually recorded to the nearest 0.1 ft, since it will be necessary to determine their area in square feet. A window 3 ft 4 in. x 5 ft 8 in. would be recorded as 3.3 ft x 5.7 ft. Greater accuracy in recording is not required since the area need be calculated only to the nearest 0.1 sq ft. The area of a 3.3-ft x

FIGURE 8-27 / Cold floor and ceilings

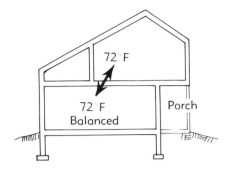

FIGURE 8-28 / Temperature balance

5.7-ft window is 18.8 sq ft. The values used in Fig. 8-30 may be used in place of inches as the dimensions are recorded. When totalling up the door and window areas of the room, these measurements should be rounded off to the nearest square foot. If the window area calculated is 38.6 sq ft use 39 sq ft while if it is 44.2 sq ft use 44 sq ft. The door and window areas should be kept separate. Many windows and doors come in stock (standardized) sizes; the commonly used sizes, with the area of window listed, are given in Fig. 8-31.

When recording the area of windows, note whether a storm window (SW) or insulating glass (IG) is specified (Fig. 8-32) since this will greatly affect the heat transmission value of the window. Similarly, note also the type of exterior door used and whether or not there is a storm door.

8-12   HEAT LOSS CALCULATIONS

The actual procedure in estimating heat loss is best illustrated by doing the calculations for a typical building. For this example, the single-story house shown in Appendix C is used. Throughout these calculations, keep in mind that accuracy should be limited

FIGURE 8-29 / Infiltration dimensions

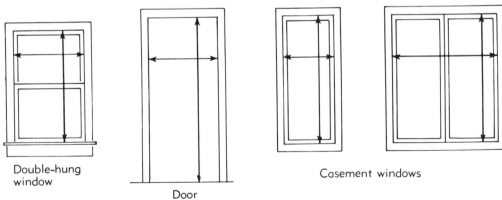

Double-hung window

Door

Casement windows

Actual dimension (in.)	Recorded dimension (ft.)
1	0.1
2	0.2
3	0.3
4	0.3
5	0.4
6	0.5
7	0.6
8	0.7
9	0.8
10	0.8
11	0.9

FIGURE 8-30 / Dimension conversion

Window Type	Size	Infiltration length (ft.)
Double-hung	2'-0" x 3'-10"	13.7
	2'-0" x 4'-2"	14.3
	2'-4" x 3'-10"	14.7
	2'-4" x 4'-2"	15.3
	2'-4" x 4'-6"	16.0
	2'-8" x 3'-10"	15.7
	2'-8" x 4'-2"	16.3
	2'-8" x 4'-6"	17.0
	3'-0" x 4'-2"	17.3
	3'-0" x 4'-6"	18.0
	3'-0" x 5'-2"	19.3
	3'-4" x 5'-2"	20.3
	3'-4" x 5'-6"	21.0
Casement	2'-0" x 3'-0"	10.0
	2'-0" x 3'-6"	11.0
	2'-0" x 4'-0"	12.0
	2'-0" x 5'-0"	14.0
	2'-0" x 6'-0"	16.0
	2'-4" x 3'-6"	11.7
	2'-4" x 4'-0"	12.7
Awning	3'-0" x 2'-0"	10.0
	3'-0" x 3'-6"	13.0
	4'-0" x 2'-0"	12.0

FIGURE 8-31 / Infiltration lengths

2-3'-0" × 4'0" Double Hung Wood
Windows, Insulating Glass
or
2-3/0 × 4/0 D.H., Wood, I.G.

FIGURE 8-32 / Window notation

to the first three figures since this is an *estimate* of the heat loss, *not* an exact measurement. Similarly, those using calculators should not use such accuracy that the Btuh might be listed as 587.236; instead, 587 or 588, even 590, would be a logical answer.

STEP-BY-STEP APPROACH

To record the heat loss, some type of form is required; the one shown in Fig. 8-33 is typical. Whatever form is used should be set up to list the rooms separately. Begin the heat loss estimate by putting the name of the project, the date and the designer's initials on the form and on the sheet of paper which will be used for calculations. Now, the actual heat loss estimate may begin:

1. Select the outdoor design temperature for the geographical area of construction (Fig. 8-54).

    In this case, the geographical area is 35° latitude, and the outdoor design temperature is 10°F.

2. Select the indoor design temperature for the design.

    Typically this is about 70°F for all residences or living quarters; occasionally it may vary slightly in an office design.

3. Calculate the design temperature difference. This is the difference between the outdoor and indoor design temperatures.

    In this design, the difference is 70°F minus 10°F, or 60°F.

    Note: Take care; if the outdoor design temperature were − 10°F, then the difference would be 80°F (Fig. 8-34).

FIGURE 8-33 / Typical heat loss form

Room	Portion considered	Dimensions	Height	Gross area or l.f.	Openings	Opening area	Net area or l.f.	U IF value	ΔT	Heat loss (Btuh)	Room heat loss (Btuh)

FIGURE 8-34 / Calculating ΔT

4. Locate and identify the construction of all walls, ceilings, floors and windows from the drawings.

    From Appendix C: *Exterior walls* are wood frame, with brick, plywood sheathing, 2 x 4 studs, 3½-in. blanket or batt insulation with a vapor barrier and ½-in. gypsum board finish. The *cold partition* is a frame partition, with ½-in. gypsum board on each side and 3½-in. batt-type insulation. *Ceilings* are ½-in. gypsum board, 6-in. batt-type insulation and ½-in. plywood. The *attic* is vented and unheated. *Floors* are ⅜-in. plywood on ½-in. plywood on wood joists, with 3½-in. batt-type insulation with a vapor barrier and no ceiling below. The *crawl space* is vented and unheated. *Windows* are wood, double-hung, with insulating glass (³⁄₁₆-in. air space) and weather-stripped. *Exterior doors* are weatherstripped and have storm doors.

5. The *U* values of the construction must be found next—either directly from the *U* value tables at the end of the chapter or by totalling up the resistances of the assembly of materials. Calculations should be made on the plain sheet and then the *U* value recorded in the table under the appropriate column.

    From Fig. 8-35, the *U* values are:

    Walls: 0.07
    Cold Partition: 0.076
    Ceiling: 0.047
    Floor: 0.066
    Windows: 0.61

    Doors: Glass and wood door: group with window area; allow the same *U* value

Design Temperatures	Inside	Outside	ΔT
Exterior Walls	70° F	10° F	60° F
Cold Walls	70° F	23° F	47° F
Ceiling	70° F	14° F	56° F
Crawl Space	70° F	35° F	35° F

U Values:

Exterior Wall

½″ Plywood	0.63
4″ Brick	0.44
3½″ Batt Insul.	11.00
½″ Gypsum Bd.	0.45
Inside Air Film	0.68
Outside Air Film	0.17
¾″ Air Space	0.94
Total R =	14.30

$$U = \frac{1}{R} = \frac{1}{14.30} = 0.07$$

Floor

Carpet	2.08
½″ Plywood	0.63
3½ Batt Insul.	11.00
Inside Air	0.61
Outside Air	0.92
Total R =	15.23

$$U = \frac{1}{R} = \frac{1}{15.23} = 0.066$$

Roof

Shingles	0.44
Bldg. Paper	0.06
⅝″ Plywood	0.77
Inside Air	0.17
Outside Air	0.61
Total R =	2.05

$$U = \frac{1}{R} = \frac{1}{2.05} = 0.48$$

Ceiling

½″ Gypsum Bd.	0.45
6″ Batt Insul.	19.00
Inside Air	0.61
Outside Air	0.61
Total R =	21.67

$$U = \frac{1}{R} = \frac{1}{21.67} = 0.047$$

Cold Wall

½″ Gypsum Bd.	0.45
3½″ Batt Insul.	11.00
½″ Gypsum Bd.	0.45
Inside Air	0.68
Outside Air	0.68
	13.26

$$U = \frac{1}{R} = \frac{1}{13.26} = 0.076$$

Glass, I.G., 0.1875″ Air Space
$$U = 0.62$$
Door, Same as Window

Infiltration

Doors and Windows,
IF = 14 CFH
Kitchen Door
IF = 7 CFH

FIGURE 8-35 / R *and* U *values calculated*

6. Next, the infiltration factors for the windows and doors should be determined and then recorded on the table.

From Fig. 8-52, the Q values are:

Windows: 14

Doors: 14 (door from kitchen to garage: use 7)

7. Next, the gross wall area of each room is calculated and recorded in the table.

    The dimensions are taken from the floor plan(s) of the building (Appendix C) as discussed in Sec. 8-11. Record the gross wall area of each room in the table.

8. Calculate the window and door areas for each room separately and record them in the table.

    Sizes are taken from the floor plan(s) and from the window and door schedules of the building. Record the gross area of windows and doors for each room in the table.

9. Calculate the net exposed wall area by subtracting the windows and doors from the gross wall area for each room. Record the net exposed wall area for each room in the table.

10. Calculate the area of any cold partitions, ceiling and floors (discussed in Sec. 8-11) and record the net area for any such rooms.

11. Calculate the total lineal feet of window and door crackage for each room as outlined in Sec. 8-11. Record the lineal feet of crackage of the windows and doors separately in the table.

12. Calculate the design heat loss for each of the areas of heat loss in the room. For the transmission heat loss, multiply the U value times the area times the design temperature difference:

$$U \times A \times \Delta T = \text{Btuh}$$

    For infiltration heat loss, multiply the infiltration air volume times the lineal feet of crackage times the design temperature difference:

$$0.018 \times Q \times LF \times \Delta T = \text{Btuh}$$

    The design heat losses calculated are recorded in the table.

13. Calculate the total heat loss for each room by adding the design heat losses obtained for each room in Step 12. Each room is totalled separately and recorded in the table.

14. Calculate the total heat loss for the entire building by adding the heat losses of each room together, and record this total in the table. This total heat loss will be used later when the heating unit (furnace) size is being selected; however, this value is *not* the heating unit's size (sizing of heating units is discussed in Sec. 9–6).

    The total heat loss for the building in Appendix C is shown in Figs. 8-35 and 8-36.

ROSE RESIDENCE 1/8/—

Room	Portion considered	Dimensions	Height	Gross area or lf	Openings	Opening area	Net area or lf	U / IF value	ΔT	Heat loss (Btuh)	Room heat loss (Btuh)
LIVING-FAMILY	EXT.WALL	32.25+7.0	8	314	2.6/0x6/8	80	234	0.07	60	983	
	COLD WALL	12.7	8	104			104	0.076	47	372	
	FLOOR	32.25x18.8		603			603	0.066	35	1393	
	CEILING	32.25x18.8		603			603	0.047	56	1587	
	GLASS	2-6/0x6/8		80			80	0.061	60	2928	
	INF-DOORS	18 / 31.4x2		63			63	(14x) 0.018	60	953	8216
KITCHEN	EXT.WALL	15.8+7.0	8	183	w2-4.0x3.0	12	171	0.07	60	718	
2x4=8	COLD WALL	10.3	8	82	3.0x6.8	21	61	0.076	47	218	
4x3=12 =20 l.f.	FLOOR	15.8x17.3		274			274	0.066	35	633	
	CEILING			274			274	0.047	56	721	
3'	GLASS	4.0x3.0	12				12	0.61	60	439	
4'	INF-GLASS		20				20	14x	60	302	
								0.018			
	DOOR		21				21	0.61	47	602	
Door to garage →	INF-DOOR		20				20	7x	47	119	3752
DINING ROOM	EXT.WALL	14.5	8	116	6.0x5.0	30	86	0.07	60	360	
6x5=30	FLOOR	14.5x13.3		193			193	0.066	35	446	
6x2=12 =42	CEILING	14.5x13.3		193			193	0.047	56	508	
	GLASS	6.0x5.0	30				30	0.61	60	1098	
	INF-GLASS		42				42	14x	60	635	3047
ENTRY & HALL	EXT.WALL	7.5+2.5	8	80	6.0x6.8	40	40	0.07	60	168	
	FLOOR	7.5+2.5x		289			289	0.066	35	668	
NO INF-GLASS, FIXED GLASS	CEILING	13.3+3.0x39		289			289	0.047	56	761	
	GLASS	2.8x6.7		21			19	0.61	60	696	
	DOOR			21			21	0.61	60	769	
	INF-DOOR						21	14x	60	302	
								0.018			3364
BEDROOM 3	EXT.WALL	14.5+6.8+68	8	225	4.0x4.0	16	209	0.07	60	878	
	FLOOR	14.5x13.3+		239			239	0.066	35	552	
		6.8x6.8									
	CEILING			239			239	0.047	56	629	
6x4=24 l.f.	GLASS	4.0x4.0		16			16	0.61	60	586	
	INF-GL			24			24	14x	60	363	
								0.018			3008

FIGURE 8-36 / Total heat loss

Room	Portion considered	Dimensions	Height	Gross area or l.f.	Openings	Opening area	Net area or l.f.	U IF value	ΔT	Heat loss (Btuh)	Room heat loss (Btuh)
BEDROOM 1 (INC. 2 CLOSETS)	EXT.WALL	12.7+18.7+ 2.5	8	272	4.0×4.0+ 3.0×4.0	28	244	0.07	60	1025	
	FLOOR	12.7+18.7+ 2.5×4.0+ 4.0×6.0		271	—	—	271	0.066	35	626	
				—			—	—	—	—	
	CEILING	—		271			271	0.047	56	713	
	GLASS	—		28			28	0.62	60	1025	
	INF.- GL.	—		46			46	14×	60	696	
								0.018	—	—	4085
BEDROOM 2 (INC. 2 CLOSETS)	EXT.WALL	11.5+ 2.5	8	112	3.0×4.0	12	100	0.07	60	420	
	FLOOR	11.5×18.8+ 2.5×4.0		226	—	—	226	0.066	35	522	
				—			—	—	—	—	
	CEILING	—		226			226	0.047	56	595	
	GLASS	—		12			12	0.62	60	440	
	INF.- GL.	—		22			22	14×	60	333	
								0.018	—	—	2310
BATH	EXT.WALL	10.5		84	2.0×2.0	4	80	0.07	60	336	
	FLOOR	10.5×6.8		72			72	0.066	35	166	
	CEILING	—		72			72	0.047	56	190	
	GLASS	—		4			4	0.62	60	147	
	INF.- GL.	—		8			8	14×	60	121	
				—			—	0.081	—	—	960
INTERIOR BATH (MAY ADD TO BEDROOM)	FLOOR	8.0×5.0		40			40	0.066	35	93	
	CEILING	—		40			40	0.047	56	105	198

TOTAL HEAT LOSS 28,940 BTUH

FIGURE 8-36 (Continued) / Total heat loss

Actual sizing of the system is discussed separately for the various types of heating systems commonly used. Water heating is discussed in Chapter 9; water cooling in Chapter 7; forced air heating in Chapter 10; forced air cooling in Chapter 13; electric baseboard, ceiling, and wall heating in Chapter 11; and solar heating in Chapter 14.

The total heat loss calculated for the residence in Appendix C may seem quite low in comparison to calculations in various other reference books and manuals. This large difference is attributed to the thicknesses of insulation used in this text and to the limited amount of window area used. In addition, many of the other references use an air-change method of calculating infiltration which is not readily adaptable to the smaller windows used in this design.

8-13   SEALING THE CRACKS

It is most important that the space (cracks) between different materials be properly sealed so that air will not infiltrate through them. This is a common problem in commercial buildings after about five years. One of the most common points of this air infiltration tends to be around the outside frame of a window or door where it rests against the surrounding wall (Fig. 8-37). Whether the window is operable (opens) or fixed has no effect on this infiltration since it occurs around the edges of the frame. This tendency can be reduced by any one or a combination of several methods:

1.   Detail the window and door to rest against a protruding portion of the structure or wall, as illustrated in Fig. 8-38. This reduces the chance of frame and wall separation which commonly occurs when a detail such as Fig. 8-37 is used and when the building undergoes expansion and contraction.

2.   When using detail such as Fig. 8-39, place a compressible filler between the wall and the window frame. This filler will reduce the chance of air flow as materials contract.

3.   All exterior cracks should be filled with a sealant designed to remain flexible so that it will hold to both the frame and the wall during periods of material contraction. Sealants should be called for in details, as shown in Fig. 8-39, and,

FIGURE 8-37 / Frame details

FIGURE 8-38 / Frame details   WINDOW   DOOR

when possible, they are used in combination with compressible fillers. It is important that caulking not be used since it will eventually dry and crack, allowing the air to infiltrate the building. Not only should sealants be specified inside and out, but also the designer must be certain that they are used on the job and that caulking is not substituted.

These suggestions should be followed whenever different materials meet and at junctions in the walls, walls and floor, and walls and roof.

The importance of such air flow can be verified in any older building. On a cold day, especially if the wind is blowing, the air infiltrating between the frame and wall can be felt by placing your hand at the juncture of materials. This cool flow of air is usually not considered in the design calculations, yet there it is. In some buildings, with large amounts of glass and glass frame, the air infiltration becomes so great on a cold, windy day that it is impossible to heat the space to the design temperature. This can be solved in new construction by the use of the installation methods outlined. In existing buildings, it can be corrected by removing the dried caulking, resealing around the frames with compressible filler, and using a sealant inside and out.

It is important to realize that the designer of the heating system *must* review the drawings, details, and specifications to determine what is being called for on the project. But just as important, the designer has a responsibility to make suggestions for the architect to consider which will improve the heat flow characteristics.

Once the designer has reviewed the drawings and specifications and carefully taken into consideration his experience with the builder, architect, or owner, he must make a decision on how to calculate possible air infiltration through the construction. When the designer feels that typical good construction methods and practices will be

FIGURE 8-39 / Frame details

Sealing the Cracks / 8-13

used, he has the option of ignoring the infiltration through the construction and calculating only the infiltration around operable windows and doors as outlined in Sec. 8-8. If construction cracks must be considered, the lineal feet of cracks must be determined in the same manner as for windows and doors (Sec. 8-8). The infiltration factor used will be determined largely by the designer and in relation to the IF values given for windows and doors in Fig. 8-52.

8-14 FIREPLACES

Since heat rises, a fireplace in a room has a tendency to allow the warm inside air to flow up the chimney. Once that begins, a natural flow of air will occur, continuously drawing warm air up the chimney and pulling in cooler air from the exterior through infiltration (Fig. 8-40). This natural flow of air can be greatly reduced if the fireplace is equipped with a tight-fitting damper that is kept *closed* when the fireplace is not in use. This flow of air increases greatly when there is a fire in the fireplace, and the constant draft of air up the chimney may result in warm air in adjoining rooms being pulled toward the fireplace; these rooms then become cool as air is pulled into them through infiltration cracks. At the same time, the room with the fireplace will become quite warm, even overheated.

FIGURE 8-40 / Flow of warm air toward fireplace

When the fuels used to provide heat were relatively inexpensive, little attention was paid to the heat loss through the fireplace. But the tremendous increases in fuel costs to date, along with even higher costs projected for the future, make it necessary to reduce heat loss as much as possible. This does not mean that fireplaces should no longer be built or used. It does mean that a few precautions must be taken to prevent some of the heat from escaping up the chimney.

1. Be certain that the fireplace has a tight-fitting damper and that the damper is closed when the fireplace is not being used.

2. Consider the use of a glass enclosure in front of the fireplace. This reduces the flow of air up the chimney, thus reducing the heat loss.

3. Consider a "snuff box" to put out the fire instead of leaving the fire to go out by itself. Even if the fire is almost out when you go to bed at night, the fire in the fireplace will probably still have hot ashes or coals in the morning. This means that all night long the air from inside the house flows up the chimney. The fire can be extinguished with a metal box that is placed over the fire to smother it. Then the damper can be closed and the flow of air reduced.

There are no calculations that a designer can make for fireplace heat loss. The designer must simply take this into consideration while designing the system by providing slightly more heat in surrounding rooms and by keeping the thermostat away from the fireplace, preferably in another room, to reduce the effect of fireplace heat on it.

8-15 MISCELLANEOUS HEAT LOSS

There are several other places where heat loss may occur that the designer should be aware of, even though he will not calculate the loss in designing the system.

1. Electrical boxes in exterior (or cold) walls and ceilings should be insulated around and in back (Fig. 8-41) to reduce the flow of cold air.

2. Medicine cabinets recessed into exterior (or cold) walls leave little or no space for insulation between the cabinet and the exterior wall sheathing (Fig. 8-42). A recessed medicine cabinet should be located in an interior wall when possible. If located in an exterior wall, consider placing a thin sheet of rigid insulation, such as polystyrene, between the cabinet and the sheathing (Fig. 8-43).

3. The exhaust fan for a cooking area that is vented to the exterior will draw heat out of the space. Consider using a charcoal filter exhaust which cleans the air but blows it back into the room. This way heat from the space is not exhausted to the

FIGURE 8-41 / Insulated electrical
box

FIGURE 8-42 / Recessed medicine
cabinet

exterior, and the fact that the heat from the stove and range is put into the room
instead of exhausted to the exterior is an extra bonus.

4. Exhaust fans in bathrooms do an excellent job of reducing humidity in the space
and are also effective in eliminating odors. Since the air being exhausted is
heated, it will increase the heat loss in the building. However, this can be greatly
reduced if the fan is on a switch separate from the light switch (Fig. 8-44) so that
it can be shut off when no longer needed.

5. All doorways to attics and cellars or other cold areas should have weatherstripping to reduce infiltration.

6. If the attic is reached through an access door or "hatch" in the ceiling of a heated
space, be certain that the access door is insulated and weatherstripped to reduce
heat loss.

7. Folding stairways into attics from heated spaces should also be insulated and
weatherstripped to reduce heat loss.

These are just several of the many places that miscellaneous heat loss can occur.
Any place that a pipe, duct, or any material passes from a cold to a warm space is a
possible location for heat loss, and it should be tightly installed and sealed and compressible filler used.

8-16   HEAT LOSS CONSIDERATIONS

There is an increased tendency to design buildings with as low a heat loss as possible
to conserve fuel and reduce fuel costs. Increasingly, the R values are approaching 20
and sometimes higher, resulting in a 0.05 U factor for the assembly. Similar savings

FIGURE 8-43 / Insulated recessed
medicine cabinet

FIGURE 8-44 / Separate switches

are being realized by increased use of insulating glass and weather-stripping, and use of smaller amounts of glass. While taking all of these factors into account in the sizing of the system, the designer must be particularly careful since the U values for material assemblies used will result in a total system which is much smaller than for designs based on U values of 0.10 to 0.15. Care must be taken so that the system will have sufficient capacity to provide any extra heat (above that calculated) that may be required due to:

1. The possibility that the materials will not be carefully installed. For example, insulation may not be packed in the smaller areas around windows and doors. Similar problems may occur when windows and doors are not installed snugly into the construction, allowing more infiltration than had been calculated.

2. The possibility that the builder (contractor) may use different materials from those on which the designer based his calculations (this may even be done with the architect's approval).

3. The probability that over the years the construction may deteriorate, allowing increased infiltration loss. This is a particular problem in buildings with window frames caulked into the wall similar to the detail shown in Fig. 8-37. If the sealant separates from the frame or the wall as the building settles, or if the sealant dries, cracks, and separates for any reason, the increased infiltration will require substantial extra heat. Obviously, the owner should have the windows resealed, but the initial separation occurs slowly, and the heat loss will slowly increase.

8-17 DEGREE DAYS

Degree days are a measure of approximately how much the ΔT is per year, and they are determined by finding the *daily* difference between the 65°F inside temperature and the average outside temperature during a 24-hour period (not the low temperature but the *average* over the 24 hours). For example, if the average outside temperature is 40°F, then the ΔT for that day is 65°F − 40°F = 25°F. The ΔT for each day is added for a yearly total which is given as degree days.

Figure 8-54 lists degree days for various cities; if one near your locale is not listed, contact the closest weather bureau for information. From Fig. 8-54, note the variations in degree days based on climate. For example, Albany, N.Y., has 6,900 degree days, while Raleigh, N.C., has 3,440 degree days at the airport. These degree days show the relative amount of heat and fuel which will be required. Since airports are located in the suburbs, and generally in open areas where they are more exposed to the climate, they have more degree days than the city where the buildings help protect one another and where the buildings and streets store heat during the day which they radiate at night.

8-18 FUEL COST COMPARISONS

The amount of fuel required for one year to heat a residence is determined by the following formula:

$$\frac{\text{Heat loss} \times \text{Degree days} \times 24 \text{ hours (a constant)}}{\text{Overall efficiency of fuel} \times \Delta T \times \text{Heating value of fuel}} = \begin{array}{c} \text{Amount of fuel required} \\ \text{in a year} \end{array}$$

For this example, assume 62,500 Btuh for baseboard, ceiling, or partition electric resistance heat and 75,000 Btuh for all other types of systems. The higher amount allows for an additional heat loss in the heating unit and in the pipes or ducts used to distribute the heat to the rooms.

Using the heating values and efficiency from Fig. 8-45, the amount of fuel required each year for a given residence would be:

Fuel	Btu	Unit	Efficiency (%)
Oil	140,000	Gal.	65-85
Natural gas	100,000	ccf	70-90
Propane	2,300	cf	70-90
Electricity	3,413	kw	100

FIGURE 8-45 / Heating values and efficiencies

cf = cubic feet
ccf = 100 cubic feet

Oil

$$\frac{(75{,}000)\ (3{,}440)\ (24)}{(0.80)\ (60)\ (140{,}000)} = 922\ \text{gal}$$

Natural gas

$$\frac{(75{,}000)\ (3{,}440)\ (24)}{(0.85)\ (60)\ (100{,}000)} = 1{,}215\ \text{ccf (hundred cubic feet)}$$

Propane

$$\frac{(75{,}000)\ (3{,}440)\ (24)}{(0.85)\ (60)\ (2{,}300)} = 52{,}788\ \text{c.f. or } 528\ \text{ccf}$$

Electric forced air

$$\frac{(75{,}000)\ (3{,}440)\ (24)}{(1.00)\ (60)\ (3{,}413)} = 30{,}237\ \text{kWh}$$

Electric baseboard, ceiling, partition

$$\frac{(62{,}500)\ (3{,}440)\ (24)}{(1.00)\ (60)\ (3{,}413)} = 25{,}198\ \text{kWh}$$

Now the fuel costs per year can be estimated by multiplying the amount of fuel used times its cost. This is when the designer *must check the fuel costs in the locale where the building will be built since it is these costs which determine which is the most economical system.* Fuel costs vary considerably and are constantly changing, so call and get local prices for comparison purposes.

Oil	$1.10 per gallon
Natural Gas	$0.60 per ccf
Propane Gas	$2.40 per ccf
Electricity	$0.068 per kWh

The fuel costs per year are:
Oil

922 gal × $1.10 per gal = $1,014.20 per year

Natural gas

1,215 ccf × $0.60 per ccf = $ 729 per year

Propane gas

528 ccf × $2.40 per ccf = $1,267.20 per year

Electric forced air

$$30{,}237 \text{ kWh} \times \$0.068 \text{ per kwh} = \$2{,}056.12 \text{ per year}$$

Electric baseboard, ceiling, partition

$$25{,}198 \text{ kWh} \times \$0.068 \text{ per kwh} = \$1{,}713.47 \text{ per year}$$

A comparison of the figures makes it obvious that oil and natural gas are the preferred methods of heating a building. Electricity does not become cost competitive until systems such as a heat pump are used (Sec. 14-8). In the future, costs will continue to vary, but the chances are that they will remain, proportionally, about the same. When one fuel price goes up, all others do also. After the oil embargo, the retail price of oil went up about 100% due to increased prices paid for the oil; it is significant that the prices of coal, gas and electricity all went up about the same percentage. This is because manufacturers and suppliers price their product based on what the alternatives are. The coal used is mined here near its point of use; the only reason the price of coal doubled is that the price of oil doubled. It is likely that this trend will continue in the future. (This is true in all business, not simply fuels, and it is mentioned here to explain how businesses operate, disregarding who may be involved.) This increasing cost of fuel is the primary reason that such an emphasis is being placed on heating with solar energy. It has greatly stimulated research and development in the solar energy field and has made solar energy systems a practical investment now.

8-19 CONTROLLING HEAT LOSS

Basically, all residences should be insulated in all portions of the building which are exposed to colder temperatures. By observing several considerations, the total heat loss of the building is reduced by one-half (and more) in the typical home built before 1976. Basically, the heat loss is reduced by:

1. 6 in. of insulation in the crawl space or basement ($R = 19$).

2. 6 in. of insulation in the exterior walls ($R = 19$). (Use 2-in. x 6-in. studs for framing the walls instead of 2 x 4s.)

3. 12 in. of insulation in the ceiling ($R = 38$).

4. Insulated glass windows.

5. A window area limited to 8% of the floor area. (This does away with the large glass windows and sliding glass doors which have such high heat losses. In the past it is estimated that the average home had windows which totalled 12% of the floor area.)

6. An insulated metal entry door with 1¾-in. polyurethane insulation.

7. Humidity controlled by a humidifier and a dehumidifier.

8. Locating forced air heating ducts in the heated area. (Drop the ceilings in corridors and install ducts along the upper perimeters of interior walls to reduce the heat loss from the ducts.)

Comparative studies of actual homes built in Arkansas show that heat loss can be reduced by much more than one-half. The real significance of this study is that for very little additional money actually spent on a house, significant savings can be realized. The type of construction, together with a solar heating system or with solar-assisted heat pumps, provides a major basis for future energy savings. A full report on "The Arkansas Story," *Report No. 1 Energy Conservation Ideas to Build On* is available through Owens-Corning Fiberglass Corp., Insulation Operating Division, Fiberglass Tower, Toledo, Ohio 43659. This report belongs in your library.

Another interesting investigation of energy conservation ideas, including the use of solar energy, was conducted by NASA (National Aeronautics and Space Administration) with similar results. However, the use of solar energy *and* water conservation techniques makes it doubly interesting. Copies of this study, "Technical support package for Tech. Brief LAR—12134," NASA Technology Utilization House, are available from Technology Utilization Office, NASA Langley Research Center, Hampton, Virginia 23665.

QUESTIONS

8-1. Describe the factors used in calculating heat loss.

8-2. What are the relationships of R, C, k, and U values?

8-3. How is the outside design temperature determined?

8-4. What is meant by *infiltration heat loss,* where does it occur and how is it calculated?

8-5. Why must the designer check the architect's specifications and drawings?

8-6. What is meant by the term *degree days,* and how will it affect the amount of fuel used per year?

8-7. List some of the ways in which the heat loss of a building can be controlled.

8-8. Why is limiting of window areas important in keeping the heat loss low?

Design Exercises:

8-9. The *U* value of an uninsulated wall is 0.29 and of the same wall insulated, 0.08. What is the resistance value of the insulation?

8-10. Using resistance values, what is the *U* value of the wall construction shown in Fig. E8-10?

8-11. What would be the *U* value for the wall used in Exercise 8-10 if 3-in. batt insulation is installed in the studs?

8-12. Using resistance values, what is the *U* value of the wall construction shown in Fig. E8-12?

8-13. What would be the *U* value for the wall used in Exercise 8-12 if 1-in. urethane and ⅜-in. gypsum board were glued to the inside of the wall?

8-14. Using resistance values, what is the *U* value of the wall construction shown in Fig. E8-14?

8-15. Calculate the heat loss for the residence in Appendix D. Assume the residence will be built in Richmond, Virginia.

8-16. Compare fuel costs, based on the cost of fuels in *your* locale, for the heat loss calculated in Exercise 8-15.

1"FIBERBOARD SHEATHING

½" GYPSUM BOARD

WOOD SIDING

FIGURE E8-10

FIGURE E8-12

8-17. Calculate the heat loss for a top floor apartment and an apartment which is below the top floor using the apartment building in Appendix A. Assume the apartment building will be built in Seattle, Washington.

FIGURE E8-14

Description	Density, lb/ft³	Conductivity[b] (k), Btu·in. / h·ft²·°F	Conductance (C), Btu / h·ft²·°F	Resistance [c](R) Per inch thickness (1/k), °F·ft²·h / Btu·in.	Resistance [c](R) For thickness listed (1/C), °F·ft²·h / Btu	Specific Heat, Btu / lb·°F
BUILDING BOARD						
Asbestos-cement board	120	4.0	—	0.25	—	0.24
Asbestos-cement board .... 0.125 in.	120	—	33.00	—	0.03	
Asbestos-cement board .... 0.25 in.	120	—	16.50	—	0.06	
Asbestos-cement board .... 0.375 in.	120	—	3.10	—	0.32	0.26
Gypsum or plaster board .... 0.5 in.	50	—	2.22	—	0.45	
Gypsum or plaster board .... 0.625 in.	50	—	1.78	—	0.56	
Plywood (Douglas Fir)[d]	50	0.80	—	1.25	—	0.29
Plywood (Douglas Fir) .... 0.25 in.	34	—	3.20	—	0.31	
Plywood (Douglas Fir) .... 0.375 in.	34	—	2.13	—	0.47	
Plywood (Douglas Fir) .... 0.5 in.	34	—	1.60	—	0.62	
Plywood (Douglas Fir) .... 0.625 in.	34	—	1.29	—	0.77	
Plywood or wood panels .... 0.75 in.	34	—	1.07	—	0.93	0.29
Vegetable Fiber Board	34	—	—	—	—	0.31
Sheathing, regular density[e] .... 0.5 in.	18	—	0.76	—	1.32	0.31
.... 0.78125 in.	18	—	0.49	—	2.06	
Sheathing intermediate density[e] .... 0.5 in.	22	—	0.92	—	1.09	0.31
Nail-base sheathing[e] .... 0.5 in.	25	—	0.94	—	1.06	0.31
Shingle backer .... 0.375 in.	18	—	1.06	—	0.94	0.31
Shingle backer .... 0.3125 in.	18	—	1.28	—	0.78	
Sound deadening board .... 0.5 in.	15	—	0.74	—	1.35	0.30
Tile and lay-in panels, plain or acoustic	18	0.40	—	2.50	—	0.14
.... 0.5 in.	18	—	0.80	—	1.25	
.... 0.75 in.	18	—	0.53	—	1.89	
Laminated paperboard	30	0.50	—	2.00	—	0.33
Homogeneous board from repulped paper	30	0.50	—	2.00	—	0.28
Hardboard[e]						
Medium density	50	0.73	—	1.37	—	0.31
High density, service temp. service underlay	55	0.82	—	1.22	—	0.32
High density, std. tempered	63	1.00	—	1.00	—	0.32
Particleboard[e]						
Low density	37	0.71	—	1.41	—	0.31
Medium density	50	0.94	—	1.06	—	0.31
High density	62.5	1.18	—	0.85	—	0.31
Underlayment .... 0.625 in.	40	—	1.22	—	0.82	0.29
Waferboard	37	0.63	—	1.59	—	0.33
Wood subfloor .... 0.75 in.	—	—	1.06	—	0.94	0.33
BUILDING MEMBRANE						
Vapor—permeable felt	—	—	16.70	—	0.06	
Vapor—seal, 2 layers of mopped 15-lb felt	—	—	8.35	—	0.12	
Vapor—seal, plastic film	—	—	—	—	Negl.	
FINISH FLOORING MATERIALS						
Carpet and fibrous pad	—	—	0.48	—	2.08	0.34
Carpet and rubber pad	—	—	0.81	—	1.23	0.33
Cork tile .... 0.125 in.	—	—	3.60	—	0.28	0.48
Terrazzo .... 1 in.	—	—	12.50	—	0.08	0.19
Tile—asphalt, linoleum, vinyl, rubber	—	—	20.00	—	0.05	0.30
vinyl asbestos						0.24
ceramic						0.19
Wood, hardwood finish .... 0.75 in.	—	—	1.47	—	0.68	
INSULATING MATERIALS						
Blanket and Batt[f,g]						
Mineral Fiber, fibrous form processed from rock, slag, or glass						
approx. 3-4 in.	0.3–2.0	—	0.091	—	11	
approx. 3.5 in.	0.3–2.0	—	0.077	—	13	
approx. 5.5-6.5 in.	0.3–2.0	—	0.053	—	19	
approx. 6-7.5 in.	0.3–2.0	—	0.045	—	22	
approx. 9-10 in.	0.3–2.0	—	0.033	—	30	
approx. 12-13 in.	0.3–2.0	—	0.026	—	38	
Board and Slabs						
Cellular glass	8.5	0.35	—	2.86	—	0.18
Glass fiber, organic bonded	4.0–9.0	0.25	—	4.00	—	0.23
Expanded perlite, organic bonded	1.0	0.36	—	2.78	—	0.30
Expanded rubber (rigid)	4.5	0.22	—	4.55	—	0.40

Reprinted with permission from ASHRAE, *Fundamentals Handbook,* 1989.

FIGURE 8-46 / *Thermal properties of typical building and insulating materials—design values*[a]

Description	Density, lb/ft³	Conductivity[b] (k), Btu·in / h·ft²·°F	Conductance (C), Btu / h·ft²·°F	Resistance [c](R) Per inch thickness (1/k), °F·ft²·h / Btu·in	Resistance [c](R) For thickness listed (1/C), °F·ft²·h / Btu	Specific Heat, Btu / lb·°F
Expanded polystyrene, extruded						
(smooth skin surface) (CFC-12 exp.)	1.8–3.5	0.20	—	5.00	—	0.29
Expanded polystyrene, molded beads..............	1.0	0.26	—	3.85	—	—
	1.25	0.25	—	4.00	—	—
	1.5	0.24	—	4.17	—	—
	1.75	0.24	—	4.17	—	—
	2.0	0.23	—	4.35	—	—
Cellular polyurethane/polyisocyanurate[h]						
(CFC-11 exp.)(unfaced)........................	1.5	0.16–0.18	—	6.25–5.56	—	0.38
Cellular polyisocyanurate[h]						
(CFC-11 exp.)(gas-permeable facers)	1.5–2.5	0.16–0.18	—	6.25–5.56	—	0.22
Cellular polyisocyanurate[i]						
(CFC-11 exp.)(gas-impermeable facers)	2.0	0.14	—	7.20	—	0.22
Cellular phenolic						
(closed cell)(CFC-11, CFC-113 exp.)	3.0	0.12	—	8.20	—	—
Cellular phenolic						
(open cell)	1.8–2.2	0.23	—	4.40	—	—
Mineral fiber with resin binder	15.0	0.29	—	3.45	—	0.17
Mineral fiberboard, wet felted						
Core or roof insulation	16–17	0.34	—	2.94	—	
Acoustical tile	18.0	0.35	—	2.86	—	0.19
Acoustical tile	21.0	0.37	—	2.70	—	
Mineral fiberboard, wet molded						
Acoustical tile[j]	23.0	0.42	—	2.38	—	0.14
Wood or cane fiberboard						
Acoustical tile[j]...........................0.5 in.	—	—	0.80	—	1.25	0.31
Acoustical tile[j].........................0.75 in.	—	—	0.53	—	1.89	
Interior finish (plank, tile)	15.0	0.35	—	2.86	—	0.32
Cement fiber slabs (shredded wood						
with Portland cement binder	25–27.0	0.50–0.53	—	2.0–1.89	—	—
Cement fiber slabs (shredded wood						
with magnesia oxysulfide binder)	22.0	0.57	—	1.75	—	0.31
Loose Fill						
Cellulosic insulation (milled paper or						
wood pulp)	2.3–3.2	0.27–0.32	—	3.70–3.13	—	0.33
Perlite, expanded	2.0–4.1	0.27–0.31	—	3.7–3.3	—	0.26
	4.1–7.4	0.31–0.36	—	3.3–2.8	—	
	7.4–11.0	0.36–0.42	—	2.8–2.4	—	
Mineral fiber (rock, slag, or glass)[g]						
approx. 3.75–5 in.	0.6–2.0	—	—	—	11.0	0.17
approx. 6.5–8.75 in.........................	0.6–2.0	—	—	—	19.0	
approx. 7.5–10 in.	0.6–2.0	—	—	—	22.0	
approx. 10.25–13.75 in.......................	0.6–2.0	—	—	—	30.0	
Mineral fiber (rock, slag, or glass)[g]						
approx. 3.5 in. (closed sidewall application)	2.0–3.5	—	—	—	12.0–14.0	
Vermiculite, exfoliated..........................	7.0–8.2	0.47	—	2.13	—	0.32
	4.0–6.0	0.44	—	2.27	—	
Masonry Units						
Brick, common	80	2.2–3.2	—	0.45-0.31	—	—
	90	2.7–3.7	—	0.37-0.27	—	—
	100	3.3–4.3	—	0.30-0.23	—	—
	110	3.5–5.5	—	0.29-0.18	—	—
	120	4.4–6.4	—	0.23-0.16	—	0.19
	130	5.4–9.0	—	0.19-0.11	—	—
Clay tile, hollow						
1 cell deep ....3 in.	—	—	1.25	—	0.80	0.21
1 cell deep ....4 in.	—	—	0.90	—	1.11	
2 cells deep ....6 in.	—	—	0.66	—	1.52	—
2 cells deep ....8 in.	—	—	0.54	—	1.85	—
2 cells deep ....10 in.	—	—	0.45	—	2.22	—
3 cells deep ....12 in.	—	—	0.40	—	2.50	—
Concrete blocks[k]						
Limestone aggregate						
8 in., 36 lb, 138 lb/ft³ concrete, 2 cores	—	—	—	—	—	—
Same with perlite filled cores	—	—	0.48	—	2.1	—
12 in., 55 lb, 138 lb/ft³ concrete, 2 cores	—	—	—	—	—	—
Same with perlite filled cores	—	—	0.27	—	3.7	—

Reprinted with permission from ASHRAE, *Fundamentals Handbook,* 1989.

FIGURE 8-46 / *Thermal properties of typical building and insulating materials—design values[a] (continued)*

Description	Density, lb/ft³	Conductivity[b] (k), Btu·in / h·ft²·°F	Conductance (C), Btu / h·ft²·°F	Resistance [c](R) Per inch thickness (1/k), °F·ft²·h / Btu·in	Resistance [c](R) For thickness listed (1/C), °F·ft²·h / Btu	Specific Heat, Btu / lb·°F
Normal weight aggregate (sand and gravel)						
8 in., 33-36 lb, 126-136 lb/ft³ concrete, 2 or 3 cores	—	—	0.90-1.03	—	1.11-0.97	0.22
Same with perlite filled cores	—	—	0.50	—	2.0	—
Same with verm. filled cores	—	—	0.52-0.73	—	1.92-1.37	—
12 in., 50 lb, 125 lb/ft³ concrete, 2 cores	—	—	0.81	—	1.23	0.22
Medium weight aggregate (combinations of normal weight and lightweight aggregate)						
8 in., 26-29 lb, 97-112 lb/ft³ concrete, 2 or 3 cores	—	—	0.58-0.78	—	1.71-1.28	—
Same with perlite filled cores	—	—	0.27-0.44	—	3.7-2.3	—
Same with verm. filled cores	—	—	0.30	—	3.3	—
Same with molded EPS (beads) filled cores	—	—	0.32	—	3.2	—
Same with molded EPS inserts in cores	—	—	0.37	—	2.7	—
Lightweight aggregate (expanded shale, clay, slate or slag, pumice)						
6 in., 16-17 lb 85-87 lb/ft³ concrete, 2 or 3 cores	—	—	0.52-0.61	—	1.93-1.65	—
Same with perlite filled cores	—	—	0.24	—	4.2	—
Same with verm. filled cores	—	—	0.33	—	3.0	—
8 in., 19-22 lb, 72-86 lb/ft³ concrete, ...	—	—	0.32-0.54	—	3.2-1.90	0.21
Same with perlite filled cores	—	—	0.15-0.23	—	6.8-4.4	—
Same with verm. filled cores	—	—	0.19-0.26	—	5.3-3.9	—
Same with molded EPS (beads) filled cores	—	—	0.21	—	4.8	—
Same with UF foam filled cores	—	—	0.22	—	4.5	—
Same with molded EPS inserts in cores	—	—	0.29	—	3.5	—
12 in., 32-36 lb, 80-90 lb/ft³ concrete, 2 or 3 cores	—	—	0.38-0.44	—	2.6-2.3	—
Same with perlite filled cores	—	—	0.11-0.16	—	9.2-6.3	—
Same with verm. filled cores	—	—	0.17	—	5.8	—
Stone, lime, or sand.........................	—	12.50	—	0.08	—	0.19
Gypsum partition tile						
3 by 12 by 30 in., solid	—	—	0.79	—	1.26	0.19
3 by 12 by 30 in., 4 cells	—	—	0.74	—	1.35	—
4 by 12 by 30 in., 3 cells	—	—	0.60	—	1.67	—

METALS
(See Chapter 39, Table 3)

ROOFING

Description	Density, lb/ft³	Conductivity (k)	Conductance (C)	Per inch thickness (1/k)	For thickness listed (1/C)	Specific Heat
Asbestos-cement shingles..........................	120	—	4.76	—	0.21	0.24
Asphalt roll roofing	70	—	6.50	—	0.15	0.36
Asphalt shingles	70	—	2.27	—	0.44	0.30
Built-up roofing ....0.375 in.	70	—	3.00	—	0.33	0.35
Slate...............................0.5 in.	—	—	20.00	—	0.05	0.30
Wood shingles, plain and plastic film faced	—	—	1.06	—	0.94	0.31

Spray Applied

Description	Density	Conductivity	Conductance	Per inch thickness	For thickness listed	Specific Heat
Polyurethane foam..............................	1.5-2.5	0.16-0.18	—	6.25-5.56	—	
Ureaformaldehyde foam	0.7-1.6	0.22-0.28	—	4.55-3.57	—	
Cellulosic fiber	3.5-6.0	0.29-0.34	—	3.45-2.94	—	
Glass fiber	3.5-4.5	0.26-0.27	—	3.85-3.70	—	

PLASTERING MATERIALS

Description	Density	Conductivity	Conductance	Per inch thickness	For thickness listed	Specific Heat
Cement plaster, sand aggregate	116	5.0	—	0.20	—	0.20
Sand aggregate ....0.375 in.	—	—	13.3	—	0.08	0.20
Sand aggregate ....0.75 in.	—	—	6.66	—	0.15	0.20
Gypsum plaster:						
Lightweight aggregate ....0.5 in.	45	—	3.12	—	0.32	
Lightweight aggregate ....0.625 in.	45	—	2.67	—	0.39	
Lightweight agg. on metal lath ....0.75 in.	—	—	2.13	—	0.47	
Perlite aggregate	45	1.5	—	0.67	—	0.32
Sand aggregate ....0.5 in.	105	5.6	—	0.18	—	0.20
Sand aggregate ....0.5 in.	105	—	11.10	—	0.09	
Sand aggregate ....0.625 in.	105	—	9.10	—	0.11	
Sand aggregate on metal lath ....0.75 in.	—	—	7.70	—	0.13	
Vermiculite aggregate..........................	45	1.7	—	0.59	—	

MASONRY MATERIALS

Concretes

Description	Density	Conductivity	Conductance	Per inch thickness	For thickness listed	Specific Heat
Cement mortar	105-135	5.0-10.5	—	0.20-0.10	—	—
Gypsum-fiber concrete 87.5% gypsum, 12.5% wood chips	51	1.66	—	0.60	—	0.21
Lightweight aggregates including expanded shale, clay or slate; expanded slags; cinders; pumice; vermiculite; also cellular concretes	120	5.5-11.0	—	0.18-0.09	—	—
	100	3.7-5.9	—	0.27-0.17	—	0.20
	80	2.5-3.5	—	0.40-0.29	—	0.20
	60	1.6-1.8	—	0.63-0.56	—	—
	40	0.93-1.11	—	1.08-0.90	—	—

Reprinted with permission from ASHRAE, *Fundamentals Handbook*, 1989.

FIGURE 8-46 / Thermal properties of typical building and insulating materials—design values[a] (continued)

Description	Density, lb/ft³	Conductivity[b] (k), Btu·in / h·ft²·°F	Conductance (C), Btu / h·ft²·°F	Resistance[c] (R) Per inch thickness (1/k), °F·ft²·h / Btu·in	Resistance[c] (R) For thickness listed (1/C), °F·ft²·h / Btu	Specific Heat, Btu / lb·°F
	30	0.75-0.91	—	1.33-1.10	—	0.20
	20	0.63-0.83	—	1.59-1.20	—	—
Perlite, expanded	50	1.4-1.8	—	0.71-0.56	—	—
	40	0.93	—	1.08	—	0.10
	30	0.71	—	1.41	—	—
	20	0.50	—	2.00	—	0.32
Sand and gravel or stone aggregate (oven dried)	140	8.0-16.0	—	0.13-0.06	—	0.18-0.22
Sand and gravel or stone aggregate (not dried)	140	10.0-20.0	—	0.10-0.05	—	0.19-0.24
Stucco	116	5.0	—	0.20	—	—
SIDING MATERIALS (on flat surface)						
Shingles						
Asbestos-cement	120	—	4.75	—	0.21	0.31
Wood, 16 in., 7.5 exposure	—	—	1.15	—	0.87	0.31
Wood, double, 16-in., 12-in. exposure	—	—	0.84	—	1.19	0.28
Wood, plus insul. backer board, 0.3125 in.	—	—	0.71	—	1.40	0.31
Siding						
Asbestos-cement, 0.25 in., lapped	—	—	4.76	—	0.21	0.24
Asphalt roll siding	—	—	6.50	—	0.15	0.35
Asphalt insulating siding (0.5 in. bed.)	—	—	0.69	—	1.46	0.35
Hardboard siding, 0.4375 in.	—	—	1.49	—	0.67	0.28
Wood, drop, 1 by 8 in.	—	—	1.27	—	0.79	0.28
Wood, bevel, 0.5 by 8 in., lapped	—	—	1.23	—	0.81	0.28
Wood, bevel, 0.75 by 10 in., lapped	—	—	0.95	—	1.05	0.28
Wood, plywood, 0.375 in., lapped	—	—	1.59	—	0.59	0.29
Aluminum or Steel[l], over sheathing						
Hollow-backed	—	—	1.61	—	0.61	0.29
Insulating-board backed nominal 0.375 in.	—	—	0.55	—	1.82	0.32
Insulating-board backed nominal 0.375 in., foil backed			0.34		2.96	
Architectural glass	—	—	10.00	—	0.10	0.20
WOODS (12% Moisture Content)[e,m]						
Hardwoods						0.39[n]
Oak	41.2-46.8	1.12-1.25	—	0.89-0.80	—.	
Birch	42.6-45.4	1.16-1.22	—	0.87-0.82	—	
Maple	39.8-44.0	1.09-1.19	—	0.92-0.84	—	
Ash	38.4-41.9	1.06-1.14	—	0.94-0.88	—	
Softwoods						0.39[n]
Southern Pine	35.6-41.2	1.00-1.12	—	1.00-0.89	—	
Douglas Fir-Larch	33.5-36.3	0.95-1.01	—	1.06-0.99	—	
Southern Cypress	31.4-32.1	0.90-0.92	—	1.11-1.09	—	
Hem-Fir, Spruce-Pine-Fir	24.5-31.4	0.74-0.90	—	1.35-1.11	—	
West Coast Woods, Cedars	21.7-31.4	0.68-0.90	—	1.48-1.11	—	
California Redwood	24.5-28.0	0.74-0.82	—	1.35-1.22	—	

aValues are for a mean temperature of 75°F. Representative values for dry materials are intended as design (not specification) values for materials in normal use. Thermal values of insulating materials may differ from design values depending on their in-situ properties (e.g., density and moisture content, orientation, etc.) and variability experienced during manufacture. For properties of a particular product, use the value supplied by the manufacturer or by unbiased tests.

bTo obtain thermal conductivities in Btu/h·ft·°F, divide the k-factor by 12 in./ft.

cResistance values are the reciprocals of C before rounding off C to two decimal places.

dLewis (1967).

eU.S. Department of Agriculture (1974).

fDoes not include paper backing and facing, if any. Where insulation forms a boundary (reflective or otherwise) of an airspace, see Tables 2 and 3 for the insulating value of an airspace with the appropriate effective emittance and temperature conditions of the space.

gConductivity varies with fiber diameter. (See Chapter 20, "Factors that Affect Thermal Performance.") Batt, blanket, and loose-fill mineral fiber insulations are manufactured to achieve specified R-values, the most common of which are listed in the table. Due to differences in manufacturing processes and materials, the product thicknesses, densities, and thermal conductivities vary over considerable ranges for a specified R-value.

hFor additional information, see Society of Plastics Engineers (SPI) Bulletin U108. Values are for aged, unfaced board stock. For change in conductivity with age of expanded polyurethane/polyisocyanurate, see Chapter 20, "Factors that Affect Thermal Performance."

iValues are for aged products with gas-impermeable facers on the two major surfaces. An aluminum foil facer of 0.001 in. thickness or greater is generally considered impermeable to gases. For change in conductivity with age of expanded polyisocyanurate, see Chapter 20, "Factors that Affect Thermal Performance," and SPI Bulletin U108.

jInsulating values of acoustical tile vary, depending on density of the board and on type, size, and depth of perforations.

kValues for fully grouted block may be approximated using values for concrete with a similar unit weight.

lValues for metal siding applied over flat surfaces vary widely, depending on amount of ventilation of airspace beneath the siding; whether airspace is reflective of nonreflective; and on thickness, type, and application of insulating backing-board used. Values given are averages for use as design guides, and were obtained from several guarded hot box tests (ASTM C236) or calibrated hot box (ASTM C976) on hollow-backed types and types made using backing-boards of wood fiber, foamed plastic, and glass fiber. Departures of ± 50% or more from the values given may occur.

mSee Adams (1971), MacLean (1941), and Wilkes (1979). The conductivity values listed are for heat transfer across the grain. The termal conductivity of wood varies linearly with the density and the density ranges listed are those normally found for the wood species given. If the density of the wood species is not known, use the mean conductivity value. For extrapolation to other moisture contents, the following empirical equation developed by Wilkes (1979) may be used:

FIGURE 8-46 / Thermal properties of typical building and insulating materials—design values[a] (continued)

Position of Surface	Direction of Heat Flow	Surface *Emittance*					
		Non-reflective $\varepsilon = 0.90$		Reflective $\varepsilon = 0.20$		Reflective $\varepsilon = 0.05$	
		h_i	R	h_i	R	h_i	R
STILL AIR							
Horizontal ..... Upward	1.63	0.61	0.91	1.10	0.76	1.32
Sloping—45 deg	Upward	1.60	0.62	0.88	1.14	0.73	1.37
Vertical	Horizontal	1.46	0.68	0.74	1.35	0.59	1.70
Sloping—45 deg	Downward	1.32	0.76	0.60	1.67	0.45	2.22
Horizontal	Downward	1.08	0.92	0.37	2.70	0.22	4.55

FIGURE 8-47 / Inside air film

Reprinted with permission from ASHRAE, *Fundamentals Handbook*, 1989.

Position of Surface	Direction of Heat Flow	Surface *Emittance*					
		Non-reflective $\varepsilon = 0.90$		Reflective $\varepsilon = 0.20$		Reflective $\varepsilon = 0.05$	
		h_0	R	h_0	R	h_0	R
MOVING AIR (Any Position)							
15-mph Wind (for winter)	Any	6.00	0.17				
7.5-mph Wind (for summer)	Any	4.00	0.25				

FIGURE 8-48 / Outside air film

Reprinted with permission from ASHRAE, *Fundamentals Handbook*, 1989.

Position of Airspace	Direction of Heat Flow	Airspace Mean Temp.[d] °F	Airspace Temp. Diff.[d] °F	0.5-in. Airspace[c] Effective Emittance, $E^{d,e}$ 0.03	0.05	0.2	0.5	0.82	0.75-in. Airspace[c] Effective Emittance, $E^{d,e}$ 0.03	0.05	0.2	0.5	0.82
Horiz.	Up ←	90	10	2.13	2.03	1.51	0.99	0.73	2.34	2.22	1.61	1.04	0.75
		50	30	1.62	1.57	1.29	0.96	0.75	1.71	1.66	1.35	0.99	0.77
		50	10	2.13	2.05	1.60	1.11	0.84	2.30	2.21	1.70	1.16	0.87
		0	20	1.73	1.70	1.45	1.12	0.91	1.83	1.79	1.52	1.16	0.93
		0	10	2.10	2.04	1.70	1.27	1.00	2.23	2.16	1.78	1.31	1.02
		−50	20	1.69	1.66	1.49	1.23	1.04	1.77	1.74	1.55	1.27	1.07
		−50	10	2.04	2.00	1.75	1.40	1.16	2.16	2.11	1.84	1.46	1.20
45° Slope	Up ↗	90	10	2.44	2.31	1.65	1.06	0.76	2.96	2.78	1.88	1.15	0.81
		50	30	2.06	1.98	1.56	1.10	0.83	1.99	1.92	1.52	1.08	0.82
		50	10	2.55	2.44	1.83	1.22	0.90	2.90	2.75	2.00	1.29	0.94
		0	20	2.20	2.14	1.76	1.30	1.02	2.13	2.07	1.72	1.28	1.00
		0	10	2.63	2.54	2.03	1.44	1.10	2.72	2.62	2.08	1.47	1.12
		−50	20	2.08	2.04	1.78	1.42	1.17	2.05	2.01	1.76	1.41	1.16
		−50	10	2.62	2.56	2.17	1.66	1.33	2.53	2.47	2.10	1.62	1.30
Vertical	Horiz. →	90	10	2.47	2.34	1.67	1.06	0.77	3.50	3.24	2.08	1.22	0.84
		50	30	2.57	2.46	1.84	1.23	0.90	2.91	2.77	2.01	1.30	0.94
		50	10	2.66	2.54	1.88	1.24	0.91	3.70	3.46	2.35	1.43	1.01
		0	20	2.82	2.72	2.14	1.50	1.13	3.14	3.02	2.32	1.58	1.18
		0	10	2.93	2.82	2.20	1.53	1.15	3.77	3.59	2.64	1.73	1.26
		−50	20	2.90	2.82	2.35	1.76	1.39	2.90	2.83	2.36	1.77	1.39
		−50	10	3.20	3.10	2.54	1.87	1.46	3.72	3.60	2.87	2.04	1.56
45° Slope	Down ↗	90	10	2.48	2.34	1.67	1.06	0.77	3.53	3.27	2.10	1.22	0.84
		50	30	2.64	2.52	1.87	1.24	0.91	3.43	3.23	2.24	1.39	0.99
		50	10	2.67	2.55	1.89	1.25	0.92	3.81	3.57	2.40	1.45	1.02
		0	20	2.91	2.80	2.19	1.52	1.15	3.75	3.57	2.63	1.72	1.26
		0	10	2.94	2.83	2.21	1.53	1.15	4.12	3.91	2.81	1.80	1.30
		−50	20	3.16	3.07	2.52	1.86	1.45	3.78	3.65	2.90	2.05	1.57
		−50	10	3.26	3.16	2.58	1.89	1.47	4.35	4.18	3.22	2.21	1.66
Horiz.	Down →	90	10	2.48	2.34	1.67	1.06	0.77	3.55	3.29	2.10	1.22	0.85
		50	30	2.66	2.54	1.88	1.24	0.91	3.77	3.52	2.38	1.44	1.02
		50	10	2.67	2.55	1.89	1.25	0.92	3.84	3.59	2.41	1.45	1.02
		0	20	2.94	2.83	2.20	1.53	1.15	4.18	3.96	2.83	1.81	1.30
		0	10	2.96	2.85	2.22	1.53	1.16	4.25	4.02	2.87	1.82	1.31
		−50	20	3.25	3.15	2.58	1.89	1.47	4.60	4.41	3.36	2.28	1.69
		−50	10	3.28	3.18	2.60	1.90	1.47	4.71	4.51	3.42	2.30	1.71

Reprinted with permission from ASHRAE, *Fundamentals Handbook*, 1989.

FIGURE 8-49 / Thermal resistances of plane[a] air space[b,c] (h • ft² • F/Btu)

Thermal Resistances of Plane Airspaces[a,b,c], °F · ft² · h/Btu (*Concluded*)

Position of Airspace	Direction of Heat Flow	Airspace Mean Temp.[d], °F	Airspace Temp. Diff.[d], °F	1.5-in. Airspace[c] Effective Emittance, E[d,e]					3.5-in. Airspace[c] Effective Emittance, E[d,e]				
				0.03	0.05	0.2	0.5	0.82	0.03	0.05	0.2	0.5	0.82
Horiz.	Up	90	10	2.55	2.41	1.71	1.08	0.77	2.84	2.66	1.83	1.13	0.80
		50	30	1.87	1.81	1.45	1.04	0.80	2.09	2.01	1.58	1.10	0.84
		50	10	2.50	2.40	1.81	1.21	0.89	2.80	2.66	1.95	1.28	0.93
		0	20	2.01	1.95	1.63	1.23	0.97	2.25	2.18	1.79	1.32	1.03
		0	10	2.43	2.35	1.90	1.38	1.06	2.71	2.62	2.07	1.47	1.12
		−50	20	1.94	1.91	1.68	1.36	1.13	2.19	2.14	1.86	1.47	1.20
		−50	10	2.37	2.31	1.99	1.55	1.26	2.65	2.58	2.18	1.67	1.33
45° Slope	Up	90	10	2.92	2.73	1.86	1.14	0.80	3.18	2.96	1.97	1.18	0.82
		50	30	2.14	2.06	1.61	1.12	0.84	2.26	2.17	1.67	1.15	0.86
		50	10	2.88	2.74	1.99	1.29	0.94	3.12	2.95	2.10	1.34	0.96
		0	20	2.30	2.23	1.82	1.34	1.04	2.42	2.35	1.90	1.38	1.06
		0	10	2.79	2.69	2.12	1.49	1.13	2.98	2.87	2.23	1.54	1.16
		−50	20	2.22	2.17	1.88	1.49	1.21	2.34	2.29	1.97	1.54	1.25
		−50	10	2.71	2.64	2.23	1.69	1.35	2.87	2.79	2.33	1.75	1.39
Vertical	Horiz. →	90	10	3.99	3.66	2.25	1.27	0.87	3.69	3.40	2.15	1.24	0.85
		50	30	2.58	2.46	1.84	1.23	0.90	2.67	2.55	1.89	1.25	0.91
		50	10	3.79	3.55	2.39	1.45	1.02	3.63	3.40	2.32	1.42	1.01
		0	20	2.76	2.66	2.10	1.48	1.12	2.88	2.78	2.17	1.51	1.14
		0	10	3.51	3.35	2.51	1.67	1.23	3.49	3.33	2.50	1.67	1.23
		−50	20	2.64	2.58	2.18	1.66	1.33	2.82	2.75	2.30	1.73	1.37
		−50	10	3.31	3.21	2.62	1.91	1.48	3.40	3.30	2.67	1.94	1.50
45° Slope	Down	90	10	5.07	4.55	2.56	1.36	0.91	4.81	4.33	2.49	1.34	0.90
		50	30	3.58	3.36	2.31	1.42	1.00	3.51	3.30	2.28	1.40	1.00
		50	10	5.10	4.66	2.85	1.60	1.09	4.74	4.36	2.73	1.57	1.08
		0	20	3.85	3.66	2.68	1.74	1.27	3.81	3.63	2.66	1.74	1.27
		0	10	4.92	4.62	3.16	1.94	1.37	4.59	4.32	3.02	1.88	1.34
		−50	20	3.62	3.50	2.80	2.01	1.54	3.77	3.64	2.90	2.05	1.57
		−50	10	4.67	4.47	3.40	2.29	1.70	4.50	4.32	3.31	2.25	1.68
Horiz.	Down	90	10	6.09	5.35	2.79	1.43	0.94	10.07	8.19	3.41	1.57	1.00
		50	30	6.27	5.63	3.18	1.70	1.14	9.60	8.17	3.86	1.88	1.22
		50	10	6.61	5.90	3.27	1.73	1.15	11.15	9.27	4.09	1.93	1.24
		0	20	7.03	6.43	3.91	2.19	1.49	10.90	9.52	4.87	2.47	1.62
		0	10	7.31	6.66	4.00	2.22	1.51	11.97	10.32	5.08	2.52	1.64
		−50	20	7.73	7.20	4.77	2.85	1.99	11.64	10.49	6.02	3.25	2.18
		−50	10	8.09	7.52	4.91	2.89	2.01	12.98	11.56	6.36	3.34	2.22

[a]See Chapter 20, section on "Factors Affecting Heat Transfer Across Airspaces." Thermal resistance values were determined from the relation, $R = 1/C$, where $C = h_c + Eh_r$; h_c is the conduction-convection coefficient, Eh_r is the radiation coefficient $\cong 0.00686E[(t_m + 460)/100]^3$, and t_m is the mean temperature of the airspace. Values for h_c were determined from data developed by Robinson et al. (1954). Equations 5 through 7 in Yarbrough (1983) show the data in Table 2 in analytic form. For extrapolation from Table 2 to airspaces less than 0.5 in. (as in insulating window glass), assume

$$h_c = 0.159(1 + 0.0016\, t_m)/l$$

where l is the airspace thickness in in., and h_c is heat transfer through the airspace only.

[b]Values are based on data presented by Robinson et al. (1954). (Also see Chapter 3, Tables 3 and 4, and Chapter 39.) Values apply for ideal conditions, i.e., airspaces of uniform thickness bounded by plane, smooth, parallel surfaces with no air leakage to or from the space. When accurate values are required, use overall U-factors determined through calibrated hot box (ASTM C 976) or guarded hot box (ASTM C 236) testing. Thermal resistance values for multiple airspaces must be based on careful estimates of mean temperature differences for each airspace.

[c]A single resistance value cannot account for multiple airspaces; each airspace requires a separate resistance calculation that applies only for the established boundary conditions. Resistances of horizontal spaces with heat flow downward are substantially independent of temperature difference.

[d]Interpolation is permissible for other values of mean temperature, temperature difference, and effective emittance E. Interpolation and moderate extrapolation for airspaces greater than 3.5 in. are also permissible.

[e]Effective emittance E of the airspace is given by $1/E = \epsilon_1 + 1/\epsilon_2 - 1$ where ϵ_1 and ϵ_2 are the emittances of the surfaces of the airspace (see Table 3).

Reprinted with permission from ASHRAE, *Fundamentals Handbook*, 1989.

FIGURE 8-49 / Thermal resistances of plane[a] air space[b,c] (h · ft² · F/Btu) (continued)

Emittance Values of Various Surfaces and Effective Emittances of Airspaces[a]

Surface	Average Emittance ϵ	Effective Emittance, E of Airspace	
		One surface emittance ϵ; the other 0.9	Both surfaces emittance ϵ
Aluminum foil, bright	0.05	0.05	0.03
Aluminum foil, with condensate just visible (> 0.7gr/ft²)	0.30[b]	0.29	—
Aluminum foil, with condensate clearly visible (> 2.9 gr/ft²)	0.70[b]	0.65	—
Aluminum sheet	0.12	0.12	0.06
Aluminum coated paper, polished	0.20	0.20	0.11
Steel, galvanized, bright	0.25	0.24	0.15
Aluminum paint	0.50	0.47	0.35
Building materials: wood, paper, masonry, nonmetallic paints	0.90	0.82	0.82
Regular glass	0.84	0.77	0.72

[a]These values apply in the 4 to 40 μm range of the electromagnetic spectrum.
[b]Values are based on data presented by Bassett and Trethowen (1984).

FIGURE 8-50 / Surface values of reflectivity and emissivity

FIGURE 8-51 / Vertical glass U values

VERTICAL GLASS V values

DESCRIPTION	WINTER	SUMMER
Flat glass,		
single	1.10	1.04
insulating glass		
double, 0.1875-in. air space	0.62	0.65
double, 0.25-in. air space	0.58	0.61
triple, 0.25-in. air space	0.39	0.44
Storm windows, 1-in. to 4-in. air space	0.50	0.50

Infiltration Through Double-Hung Wood Windows
Expressed in cubic feet per (hour) (foot of Crack)[d]

Type of Window	Pressure Difference (Inches of Water)				
	0.10	0.20	0.30	0.40	0.50
A. Wood Double-Hung Window (Locked)	25	50	25	100	125
(Leakage expressed as cubic feet per hour per foot of sash crack; only leakage around sash and through frame given)					
1. Nonweatheredstripped, loose fit[a]	77[d]	122[d]	150[d]	194[d]	225[d]
2. Nonweatheredstripped, average fit[b]	27[d]	43[d]	57[d]	69[d]	80[d]
3. Weatherstripped, loose fit	28[d]	44[d]	58[d]	70[d]	81[d]
4. Weatherstripped, average fit	14[d]	23[d]	30[d]	36[d]	42[d]
B. Frame-Wall Leakage[c]					
(Leakage is that passing between the frame of a wood double-hung window and the wall)					
1. Around frame in masonry wall, not caulked	17[d]	26[d]	34[d]	41[d]	48[d]
2. Around frame in masonry wall, caulked	3[d]	5[d]	6[d]	7[d]	8[d]
3. Around frame in wood frame wall	13[d]	21[d]	29[d]	35[d]	42[d]

[a] A 0.094-in. crack and clearance represent a poorly fitted window, much poorer than average.

[b] The fit of the average double-hung wood window was determined as 0.0625-in. crack and 0.047-in. clearance by measurements on approximately 600 windows under heating season conditions.

[c] The values given for frame leakage are per foot of sash perimeter, as determined for double-hung wood windows. Some of the frame leakage in masonry walls originates in the brick wall itself, and cannot be prevented by caulking. For the additional reason that caulking is not done perfectly and deteriorates with time, it is considered advisable to choose the masonry frame leakage values for caulked frames as the average determined by the caulked and non-caulked tests.

[d] Multiply by 0.0258 for l/s per metre of crack.

Wind vs Velocity Pressure and Velocity in FPM

Reprinted with permission from ASHRAE, *Fundamentals Handbook,* 1989.

FIGURE 8-52 / *Infiltration*

Heat Loss of Concrete Floors at or Near Grade Level per Foot of Exposed Edge

Outdoor Design Temperature, F	Heat Loss per Foot of Exposed Edge, Btuh	
	Recommended 2-in. Edge Insulation	1-in. Edge Insulation
−20 to −30	50	55
−10 to −20	45	50
0 to −10	40	45
Outdoor Design Temperature, F	1-in. Edge Insulation	No Edge Insulation[a]
−20 to −30	60	75
−10 to −20	55	65
0 to −10	50	60

[a] This construction not recommended; shown for comparison only.

Floor Heat Loss to be Used When Warm Air Perimeter Heating Ducts Are Embedded in Slabs[a]
Btuh per (linear foot of heated edge)

Outdoor Design Temperature, F	Edge Insulation		
	1-in. Vertical Extending Down 18 in. Below Floor Surface	1-in. L-Type Extending at Least 12 in. Deep and 12 in. Under	2-in. L-Type Extending at Least 12 in. Down and 12 in. Inder
−20	105	100	85
−20	95	90	75
0	85	80	65
10	75	70	55
20	62	57	45

[a] Factors include loss downward through inner area of slab.
Reprinted with permission from ASHRAE, Fundamentals Hand book, 1977

FIGURE 8-53 / Slab edge losses

FIGURE 8-54 / Outdoor design conditions for United States and Canada
(Design grains based on an inside design temperature of 75°F)

Location	WINTER			SUMMER				
	Latitude Degrees	97½% Design db	Heating D.D. Below 65°F	2½% Design db	Coincident Design wb	Grains Difference 55% RH	Grains Difference 50% RH	Daily Range
ALABAMA								
Alexander City	33	22	. . . .	93	76	37	44	21 M
Anniston AP	33	22	2810	94	76	35	42	21 M
Auburn	32	22	. . . .	93	76	37	44	21 M
Birmingham AP	33	21	2710	94	75	30	37	21 M
Decatur	34	16	3050	93	74	25	32	22 M
Dothan AP	31	27	1400	92	76	39	46	20 M
Florence AP	34	21	3199	94	74	23	30	22 M
Gadsden	34	20	3000	94	75	30	37	22 M
Huntsville AP	34	16	3190	93	74	25	33	23 M
Mobile AP	30	29	1620	93	77	44	51	18 M
Mobile CO	30	29	1620	93	77	44	51	16 M
Montgomery AP	32	25	2250	95	76	33	40	21 M
Selma-Craig AFB	32	26	2160	95	77	38	47	21 M
Talladega	33	22	. . . .	94	76	33	42	21 M
Tuscaloosa AP	33	23	2590	96	76	32	39	22 M
ALASKA								
Anchorage AP	61	−18	10860	68	58	0	0	15 L
Barrow (S)	71	−41	20265	53	50	0	0	12 L
Fairbanks AP (S)	64	−47	14290	78	60	0	0	24 M
Juneau AP	58	1	9080	70	58	0	0	15 L
Kodiak	57	13	8860	65	56	0	0	10 L
Nome AP	64	−27	14170	62	55	0	0	10 L
ARIZONA								
Douglas AP	31	31	2630	95	63	0	0	31 H
Flagstaff AP	35	4	7290	82	55	0	0	31 H
Fort Huachuca AP (S)	31	28	2551	92	62	0	0	27 H
Kingman AP	35	25	. . . .	100	64	0	0	30 H
Nogales	31	32	2150	96	64	0	0	31 H
Phoenix AP (S)	33	34	1680	107	71	0	0	27 H
Prescott AP	34	9	. . . .	94	60	0	0	30 H
Tuscon AP (S)	32	32	1700	102	66	0	0	26 H
Winslow AP	35	10	4780	95	60	0	0	32 H
Yuma AP	32	39	970	109	72	0	0	27 H
ARKANSAS								
Blytheville AFB	36	15	3760	94	77	42	49	21 M
Camden	33	23	. . . .	96	76	32	39	21 M

AP = Airport
CO = City Office
S = Solar Data Available

Reprinted with permission of ACCA, *Manual J* 1986.

8 / HEAT LOSS

FIGURE 8-54 / Outdoor design conditions for United States and Canada (continued)
(Design grains based on an inside design temperature of 75°F)

Location	Latitude Degrees	WINTER 97½% Design db	WINTER Heating D.D. Below 65°F	SUMMER 2½% Design db	SUMMER Coincident Design wb	SUMMER Grains Difference 55% RH	SUMMER Grains Difference 50% RH	Daily Range
El Dorado AP	33	23	2300	96	76	32	39	21 M
Fayetteville AP	36	12	3840	94	73	18	25	23 M
Fort Smith AP	35	17	3290	98	76	29	36	24 M
Hot Springs	34	23	2729	97	77	37	44	22 M
Jonesboro	35	15	....	94	77	42	49	21 M
Little Rock AP (S)	34	20	3170	96	77	39	46	22 M
Pine Bluff AP	34	22	2588	97	77	37	44	22 M
Texarkana AP	33	23	2530	96	77	39	46	21 M
CALIFORNIA								
Bakersfield AP	35	32	2150	101	69	0	0	32 H
Barstow	34	29	2203	104	68	0	0	37 H
Blythe AP	33	33	....	110	71	0	0	28 H
Burbank AP	34	39	1700	91	68	0	2	25 M
Chico	39	30	2835	101	68	0	0	36 H
Concord	38	27	3035	97	68	0	0	32 H
Covina	34	35	....	95	68	0	0	31 H
Crescent City AP	41	33	....	65	59	0	0	18 M
Downey	34	40	....	89	70	9	16	22 M
El Cajon	32	44	....	80	69	17	24	30 H
El Centro AP (S)	32	38	925	110	74	0	4	34 H
Escondido	33	41	....	85	68	4	11	30 H
Eureaka/Arcata AP	41	33	4640	65	59	0	0	11 L
Fairfield-Travis AFB	38	32	2725	95	67	0	0	34 H
Fresno AP (S)	36	30	2610	100	69	0	0	34 H
Hamilton AFB	38	32	3311	84	66	0	3	28 H
Laguna Beach	33	43	....	80	68	13	20	18 M
Livermore	37	27	3035	97	68	0	0	24 M
Lompoc, Vandenburg AFB	34	38	3451	70	61	0	0	20 M
Long Beach AP	33	43	1803	80	68	13	20	22 M
Los Angeles AP (S)	34	43	1960	80	68	13	20	15 L
Los Angeles CO (S)	34	40	1960	89	70	9	16	20 M
Merced-Castle AFB	37	31	2470	99	69	0	0	36 H
Modesto	37	30	....	98	68	0	0	36 H
Monterey	36	38	2750	71	61	0	0	20 M
Napa	38	32	....	96	68	0	0	30 H
Needles AP	34	33	....	110	71	0	0	27 H
Oakland AP	37	36	2940	80	63	0	0	19 M
Oceanside	33	43	....	80	68	13	20	13 L
Ontario	34	33	2009	99	69	0	5	36 H

AP = Airport
CO = City Office
S = Solar Data Available

Reprinted with permission of ACCA, *Manual J* 1986.

FIGURE 8-54 / Outdoor design conditions for United States and Canada (continued)
(Design grains based on an inside design temperature of 75°F)

Location	Latitude Degrees	WINTER 97½% Design db	Heating D.D. Below 65°F	SUMMER 2½% Design db	Coincident Design wb	Grains Difference 55% RH	Grains Difference 50% RH	Daily Range
Oxnard	34	36	....	80	64	0	0	19 M
Palmdale AP	34	22	2929	101	65	0	0	35 H
Palm Springs	33	35	....	110	70	0	0	35 H
Pasadena	34	35	1694	95	68	0	0	29 H
Petaluma	38	29	....	90	66	0	0	31 H
Pomona CO	34	30	2166	99	69	0	0	36 H
Redding AP	40	31	....	102	67	0	0	32 H
Redlands	34	33	....	99	69	0	0	33 H
Richmond	38	36	....	80	63	0	0	17 M
Riverside-March AFB (S)	33	32	2162	98	68	0	0	37 H
Sacramento AP	38	32	2700	98	70	0	2	36 H
Salinas AP	36	32	....	70	60	0	0	24 M
San Bernadino, Norton AFB	34	33	1978	99	69	0		38 H
San Diego AP	32	44	1500	80	69	17	24	12 L
San Fernando	34	39		91	68	0	2	38 H
San Francisco AP	37	38	3040	77	63	0	0	20 M
San Francisco CO	37	40	3040	71	62	0	3	14 L
San Jose AP	37	36	2416	81	65	0	3	26 H
San Luis Obispo	35	35	2472	88	70	10	17	26 H
Santa Ana AP	33	39	1675	85	68	4	11	28 H
Santa Barbara MAP	34	36	2470	77	66	7	14	24 M
Santa Cruz	37	38	....	71	61	0	0	28 H
Santa Maria AP (S)	34	33	2930	76	63	0	2	23 M
Santa Monica CO	34	43	....	80	68	13	20	16 M
Santa Paula	34	35	....	86	67	0	4	36 H
Santa Rosa	38	29	3065	95	67	0	0	34 H
Stockton AP	37	30	2806	97	68	0	0	37 H
Ukiah	39	29	....	95	68	0	0	40 H
Visalia	36	30	....	100	69	0	0	38 H
Vreka	41	17	....	92	64	0	0	38 H
Yuba City	39	31	....	101	67	0	0	36 H
COLORADO								
Alamosa AP	37	− 6	8529	82	57	0	0	35 H
Boulder	40	0	....	91	59	0	0	27 H
Colorado Springs AP	38	2	6410	88	57	0	0	30 H
Denver AP	39	1	6150	91	59	0	0	28 H
Durango	37	− 1	....	87	59	0	0	30 H
Fort Collins	40	1	....	91	59	0	0	28 H

AP = Airport
CO = City Office
S = Solar Data Available

Reprinted with permission of ACCA, *Manual J* 1986.

FIGURE 8-54 / Outdoor design conditions for United States and Canada (continued)
(Design grains based on an inside design temperature of 75°F)

Location	Latitude Degrees	WINTER 97½% Design db	Heating D.D. Below 65°F	SUMMER 2½% Design db	Coincident Design wb	Grains Difference 55% RH	Grains Difference 50% RH	Daily Range
Grand Junction AP (S)	39	7	5660	94	59	0	0	29 H
Greeley	40	4	....	94	60	0	0	29 H
LaJunta AP	38	3	5132	98	68	0	0	31 H
Leadville	39	− 14	....	81	51	0	0	30 H
Pueblo AP	38	0	5480	95	61	0	0	31 H
Sterling	40	− 2	....	93	62	0	0	30 H
Trinidad AP	37	3	5330	91	61	0	0	32 H
CONNECTICUT								
Bridgeport AP	41	9	5617	84	71	22	29	18 M
Hartford, Brainard Field	41	7	6170	88	73	28	35	22 M
New Haven AP	41	7	5890	84	73	33	40	17 M
New London	41	9	....	85	72	26	33	16 M
Norwalk	41	9	....	84	71	22	29	19 M
Norwich	41	7	....	86	73	31	38	18 M
Waterbury	41	2	6672	85	71	20	27	21 M
Windsor Locks, Bradley Field (S)	42	4	6350	88	72	22	29	22 M
DELAWARE								
Dover AFB	39	15	4700	90	75	36	43	18 M
Wilmington AP	39	14	4930	89	74	41	38	20 M
DISTRICT OF COLUMBIA								
Andrews AFB	38	14	....	90	74	30	37	18 M
Washington National AP	38	17	4240	91	74	29	36	18 M
FLORIDA								
Belle Glade	26	44	....	91	76	41	48	16 M
Cape Kennedy AP	28	38	711	88	78	59	66	15 L
Daytona Beach AP	29	35	879	90	77	49	56	15 L
Fort Lauderdale	26	46	244	91	78	53	60	15 L
Fort Myers AP	26	44	442	92	78	51	58	18 M
Fort Pierce	27	42	....	90	78	55	62	15 L
Gainesville AP (S)	29	31	1081	93	77	45	51	18 M
Jacksonville AP	30	32	1230	94	77	42	49	19 M
Key West AP	24	57	110	90	78	55	62	9 L
Lakeland CO (S)	28	41	661	91	76	51	48	17 M

AP = Airport
CO = City Office
S = Solar Data Available

Reprinted with permission of ACCA, *Manual J* 1986.

Heat Loss / 8

FIGURE 8-54 / Outdoor design conditions for United States and Canada (continued)
(Design grains based on an inside design temperature of 75°F)

Location	Latitude Degrees	WINTER		SUMMER				Daily Range
		97½% Design db	Heating D.D. Below 65°F	2½% Design db	Coincident Design wb	Grains Difference 55% RH	Grains Difference 50% RH	
Miami AP (S)	25	47	200	90	77	49	56	15 L
Miami Beach CO	25	48	200	89	77	51	58	10 L
Ocala	29	34	....	93	77	44	51	18 M
Orlando AP	28	38	720	93	76	37	44	17 M
Panama City, Tyndall AFB	30	33	1390	90	77	49	56	14 L
Pensacola CO	30	29	1480	93	77	44	51	14 L
St. Augustine	29	35	1051	89	78	57	64	16 M
St. Petersburg	28	40	670	91	77	47	54	16 M
Sanford	28	38	....	93	76	37	44	17 M
Sarasota	27	42	....	92	77	45	52	17 M
Tallahassee AP (S)	30	30	1520	92	76	39	46	19 M
Tampa AP (S)	28	40	700	91	77	47	54	17 M
West Palm Beach AP	26	45	270	91	78	53	60	16 M
GEORGIA								
Albany, Turner AFB	31	29	1760	95	76	33	40	20 M
Americus	32	25	....	94	76	35	42	20 M
Athens	34	22	2929	92	74	27	34	21 M
Atlanta AP (S)	33	22	2990	92	74	27	34	19 M
Augusta AP	33	23	2410	95	76	33	40	19 M
Brunswick	31	32	1531	89	78	57	64	18 M
Columbus, Lawson AFB	32	24	2380	93	76	37	44	21 M
Dalton	34	22	....	93	76	37	44	22 M
Dublin	32	25	....	93	76	37	44	20 M
Gainesville	34	21	....	91	74	29	36	21 M
Griffin (S)	33	22	....	90	75	36	43	21 M
La Grange	33	23	....	91	75	35	42	21 M
Macon AP	32	25	2160	93	76	37	44	22 M
Marietta, Dobbins AFB	34	21	3080	92	74	27	34	21 M
Moultrie	31	30	....	95	77	40	47	20 M
Rome AP	34	22	3326	93	76	37	44	23 M
Savannah-Travis AP	32	27	1850	93	77	44	51	20 M
Valdosta-Moody AFB	31	31	1520	93	77	43	49	20 M
Waycross	31	29	....	94	77	43	49	20 M
HAWAII								
Hilo AP (S)	19	62	0	83	72	30	37	15 L
Honolulu AP	21	63	0	86	73	31	38	12 L
Kaneohe Bay MCAS	21	66	0	84	74	40	47	12 L
Wahaiwa	21	59	10	85	72	26	33	14 L

AP = Airport
CO = City Office
S = Solar Data Available

Reprinted with permission of ACCA, *Manual J* 1986.

FIGURE 8-54 / Outdoor design conditions for United States and Canada (continued)
(Design grains based on an inside design temperature of 75°F)

Location	Latitude Degrees	WINTER 97½% Design db	Heating D.D. Below 65°F	SUMMER 2½% Design db	Coincident Design wb	Grains Difference 55% RH	Grains Difference 50% RH	Daily Range
IDAHO								
Boise AP (S)	43	10	5830	94	64	0	0	31 H
Burley	42	2	....	95	61	0	0	35 H
Coeur D'Alene AP	47	− 1	6660	86	61	0	0	31 H
Idaho Falls AP	43	− 6	7890	87	61	0	0	38 H
Lewiston AP	46	6	5500	93	64	0	0	32 H
Moscow	46	0	....	87	62	0	0	32 H
Mountain Home AFB	43	12	6120	97	63	0	0	36 H
Pocatello AP	43	− 1	7030	91	60	0	0	35 H
Twin Falls AP (S)	42	2	6730	95	61	0	0	34 H
ILLINOIS								
Aurora	41	− 1	6660	91	76	41	48	20 M
Belleville, Scott AFB	38	6	4480	92	76	39	49	21 M
Bloomington	40	− 2	....	90	74	30	37	21 M
Carbondale	37	7	....	93	77	44	51	21 M
Champaign/Urbana	40	2	5800	92	74	27	34	21 M
Chicago, Midway AP	41	0	6160	91	73	23	29	20 M
Chicago, O'Hare AP	42	− 4	6640	89	74	31	38	20 M
Chicago CO	41	2	6640	91	74	29	36	15 L
Danville	40	1	5538	90	74	30	37	21 M
Decatur	39	2	5480	91	74	29	36	21 M
Dixon	41	− 2	....	90	74	30	37	23 M
Elgin	42	− 2	....	88	74	33	40	21 M
Freeport	42	− 4	....	89	73	26	33	24 M
Galesburg	41	− 2	6005	91	75	35	42	22 M
Greenville	39	4	....	92	75	33	40	21 M
Joliet	41	0	6180	90	74	30	37	20 M
Kankakee	41	1	6040	90	74	30	37	21 M
LaSalle/Peru	41	− 2	....	91	75	35	42	22 M
Macomb	40	0	....	92	76	39	46	22 M
Moline AP	41	− 4	6410	91	75	35	42	23 M
Mt. Vernon	38	5	....	92	75	33	40	21 M
Peoria AP	40	− 4	6070	89	74	31	38	22 M
Quincy AP	40	3	5267	93	76	37	44	22 M
Rantoul, Chanute AFB	40	1	5966	91	74	29	36	21 M
Rockford	42	− 4	6840	89	73	26	33	24 M
Springfield AP	39	2	5530	92	74	27	34	21 M
Waukegan	42	− 3	....	89	74	31	37	21 M

AP = Airport
CO = City Office
S = Solar Data Available

Reprinted with permission of ACCA, *Manual J* 1986.

(Design grains based on an inside design temperature of 75°F)

Location	Latitude Degrees	WINTER 97½% Design db	WINTER Heating D.D. Below 65°F	SUMMER 2½% Design db	SUMMER Coincident Design wb	SUMMER Grains Difference 55% RH	SUMMER Grains Difference 50% RH	Daily Range
INDIANA								
Anderson	40	6	5580	92	75	33	40	22 M
Bedford	38	5	....	92	75	33	40	22 M
Bloomington	39	5	4860	92	75	33	40	22 M
Columbus, Bakalar AFB	39	7	5132	92	75	33	40	22 M
Crawfordsville	40	3	....	91	74	29	36	22 M
Evansville AP	38	9	4500	93	75	31	38	22 M
Fort Wayne AP	41	1	6220	89	72	20	27	24 M
Goshen AP	41	1	....	89	73	26	33	23 M
Hobart	41	2	....	88	73	26	33	21 M
Huntington	40	1	....	89	72	20	27	23 M
Indianapolis AP (S)	39	2	5630	90	74	30	37	22 M
Jeffersonville	38	10	....	93	74	25	33	23 M
Kokoma	40	0	5590	90	73	24	31	22 M
Lafayette	40	3	5820	91	73	23	30	22 M
LaPorte	41	3	....	90	74	30	37	22 M
Marion	40	0	....	90	73	24	31	23 M
Muncie	40	2	5950	90	73	24	31	22 M
Peru, Bunker Hill AFB	40	−1	....	88	73	28	35	22 M
Richmond AP	39	2	....	90	74	30	37	22 M
Shelbyville	39	3	....	91	74	29	36	22 M
South Bend AP	41	1	6460	89	73	26	33	22 M
Terre Haute AP	39	4	5360	92	74	27	34	22 M
Valparaise	41	3	....	90	74	30	37	22 M
Vincennes	38	6	....	92	74	27	34	22 M
IOWA								
Ames (S)	42	−6	....	90	74	30	37	23 M
Burlington AP	40	−3	6120	91	75	35	43	22 M
Cedar Rapids AP	41	−5	6600	88	75	38	45	23 M
Clinton	41	−3	....	90	75	36	33	23 M
Council Bluffs	41	−3	6610	91	75	35	42	22 M
Des Moines AP	41	−5	6610	91	74	29	36	23 M
Debuque	42	−7	7380	88	73	28	35	22 M
Fort Dodge	42	−7	7070	88	74	33	40	23 M
Iowa City	41	−6	6404	89	76	44	51	22 M
Keokuk	40	0	6404	92	75	33	40	22 M
Marshalltown	42	−7	6850	90	75	36	43	23 M
Mason City AP	43	−11	7790	88	74	33	40	24 M
Newton	41	−5	....	91	74	29	36	23 M

AP = Airport
CO = City Office
S = Solar Data Available

Reprinted with permission of ACCA, *Manual J* 1986.

8 / HEAT LOSS

FIGURE 8-54 / Outdoor design conditions for United States and Canada (continued)
(Design grains based on an inside design temperature of 75°F)

Location	Latitude Degrees	WINTER 97½% Design db	WINTER Heating D.D. Below 65°F	SUMMER 2½% Design db	SUMMER Coincident Design wb	SUMMER Grains Difference 55% RH	SUMMER Grains Difference 50% RH	Daily Range
Ottumwa AP	41	−4	....	91	74	29	36	22 M
Sioux City AP	42	−7	6960	92	74	27	34	24 M
Waterloo	42	−10	7370	89	75	38	45	23 M
KANSAS								
Atchison	39	2	....	93	76	37	44	23 M
Chanute AP	34	7	4566	97	74	19	26	23 M
Dodge City AP (S)	37	5	....	97	69	0	0	25 M
El Dorado	37	7	4990	98	73	11	18	24 M
Emporia	38	5	....	97	74	19	26	25 M
Garden City AP	38	4	....	96	69	0	0	28 H
Goodland AP	39	0	6140	96	65	0	0	31 H
Great Bend	38	4	....	98	73	11	18	28 H
Hutchinson AP	38	8	4680	99	72	3	10	28 H
Liberal	37	7	....	96	68	0	0	28 H
Manhattan, Fort Riley (S)	39	3	5306	95	75	28	35	24 M
Parsons	37	9	4158	97	74	19	26	23 M
Russel AP	38	4	....	98	73	11	18	29 H
Salina	38	5	4970	100	74	13	20	26 H
Topeka AP	39	4	5210	96	75	26	33	24 M
Wichita AP	37	7	4640	98	73	11	18	23 M
KENTUCKY								
Ashland	38	10	4555	91	74	29	36	22 M
Bowling Green AP	37	10	4280	92	75	33	40	21 M
Corbin AP	37	9	....	92	73	21	28	23 M
Covington AP	39	6	5260	90	72	19	26	22 M
Hopkinsville, Campbell AFB	36	10	4290	92	75	33	40	21 M
Lexington AP (S)	38	8	4760	91	73	23	30	22 M
Louisville AP	38	10	4610	93	74	25	33	23 M
Madisonville	37	10	....	93	75	31	38	22 M
Owensboro	37	10	4200	94	75	30	37	23 M
Pudacah AP	37	12	3650	95	75	28	35	20 M
LOUISIANA								
Alexandria AP	31	27	2000	94	77	43	49	20 M
Baton Rouge AP	30	29	1610	93	77	44	51	19 M
Bogalusa	30	28	....	93	77	44	51	19 M

AP = Airport
CO = City Office
S = Solar Data Available

Reprinted with permission of ACCA, *Manual J* 1986.

Heat Loss / 8

FIGURE 8-54 / Outdoor design conditions for United States and Canada (continued)
(Design grains based on an inside design temperature of 75°F)

Location	Latitude Degrees	WINTER 97½% Design db	Heating D.D. Below 65°F	SUMMER 2½% Design db	Coincident Design wb	Grains Difference 55% RH	Grains Difference 50% RH	Daily Range
Houma	29	35	....	93	78	50	57	15 L
Lafayette AP	30	30	1550	94	78	49	56	18 M
Lake Charles AP (S)	30	31	1490	93	77	44	51	17 M
Minden	32	25	....	96	76	32	38	20 M
Monroe AP	32	25	2310	96	76	32	38	20 M
Natchitoches	31	26	....	95	77	40	47	20 M
New Orleans AP	30	33	1400	92	78	51	58	16 M
Shreveport AP (S)	32	25	2160	96	76	32	39	20 M
MAINE								
Augusta AP	44	−3	7826	85	70	15	23	22 M
Bangor, Dow AFB	44	−6	8220	83	68	8	15	22 M
Caribou AP (S)	46	−13	9770	81	67	7	14	21 M
Lewiston	44	−2	7690	85	70	15	22	22 M
Millinocket AP	45	−9	8533	83	68	8	15	22 M
Portland (S)	43	−1	7570	84	71	23	29	22 M
Waterville	44	−4	....	84	69	11	18	22 M
MARYLAND								
Baltimore AP	39	13	4680	91	75	35	42	21 M
Baltimore CO	39	17	....	89	76	43	51	17 M
Cumberland	39	10	5070	89	74	31	38	22 M
Frederick AP	39	12	5030	91	75	35	42	22 M
Hagerstown	39	12	5130	91	74	29	36	22 M
Salisbury (S)	38	16	4220	91	75	35	42	18 M
MASSACHUSETTS								
Boston AP (S)	42	9	5630	88	71	16	23	16 M
Clinton	42	2	....	87	71	18	25	17 M
Fall River	41	9	5774	84	71	22	29	18 M
Framingham	42	6	....	86	71	19	26	17 M
Gloucester	42	5	....	86	71	19	26	15 L
Greenfield	42	−2	....	85	71	20	27	23 M
Lawrence	42	0	6195	87	72	23	30	22 M
Lowell	42	1	6060	88	72	22	29	21 M
New Bedford	41	9	5400	82	71	26	33	19 M
Pittsfield AP	42	−3	7580	84	70	16	23	23 M
Springfield, Westover AFB	42	0	5840	87	71	18	25	19 M
Tauton	41	9	....	86	72	25	32	18 M
Worcester AP	42	4	6970	84	70	16	23	18 M

AP = Airport
CO = City Office
S = Solar Data Available

Reprinted with permission of ACCA, *Manual J* 1986.

Location	Latitude Degrees	WINTER 97½% Design db	Heating D.D. Below 65°F	SUMMER 2½% Design db	Coincident Design wb	Grains Difference 55% RH	Grains Difference 50% RH	Daily Range
MICHIGAN								
Adrian	41	3	....	88	72	22	29	23 M
Alpena AP	45	−6	8510	85	70	15	22	27 H
Battle Creek AP	42	5	6580	88	72	22	29	23 M
Benton Harbor AP	42	5	....	88	72	22	29	20 M
Detroit	42	6	6290	88	72	22	29	20 M
Escanaba	45	−7	8481	83	69	13	20	17 M
Flint AP	42	1	7200	87	72	23	30	25 M
Grand Rapids AP	42	5	6890	88	72	22	29	24 M
Holland	42	6	....	86	71	19	26	22 M
Jackson AP	42	5	....	88	72	22	29	23 M
Kalamazoo	42	5	....	88	72	22	29	23 M
Lansing AP	42	1	6940	87	72	23	30	24 M
Marquette CO	46	−8	8390	81	69	16	23	18 M
Mt. Pleasant	43	4	....	87	72	23	30	24 M
Muskegon AP	43	6	6700	84	70	16	23	21 H
Pontiac	42	4	....	87	72	23	30	21 M
Port Huron	43	4	6564	87	72	23	30	21 H
Saginaw AP	43	4	7120	87	72	23	30	23 M
Sault Ste. Marie AP (S)	46	−8	9050	81	69	16	23	23 M
Traverse City AP	44	1	7700	86	71	19	26	22 M
Yipsilanti	42	5	6424	89	71	15	22	22 M
MINNESOTA								
Albert Lea	43	−12	....	87	72	23	30	24 M
Alexandria AP	45	−16	....	88	72	22	29	24 M
Bemidji AP	47	−26	10203	85	69	9	16	24 M
Brainerd	46	−16	....	87	71	18	25	24 M
Duluth AP	46	−16	9890	82	68	10	17	22 M
Fairbault	44	−12	....	88	72	22	27	24 M
Fergus Falls	46	−17	....	88	72	22	27	24 M
International Falls AP	48	−25	10600	83	68	8	15	26 M
Mankato	44	−12	8310	88	72	22	29	24 M
Minneapolis / St. Paul AP	44	−12	8250	89	73	26	33	22 M
Rochester AP	44	−12	8295	87	72	23	30	24 M
St. Cloud AP (S)	45	−11	8890	88	72	22	29	24 M
Virginia	47	−21	....	83	68	8	15	23 M

AP = Airport
CO = City Office
S = Solar Data Available

Reprinted with permission of ACCA, *Manual J* 1986.

Heat Loss / 8

FIGURE 8-54 / Outdoor design conditions for United States and Canada (continued)
(Design grains based on an inside design temperature of 75°F)

		WINTER		SUMMER				
Location	Latitude Degrees	97½% Design db	Heating D.D. Below 65°F	2½% Design db	Coincident Design wb	Grains Difference 55% RH	Grains Difference 50% RH	Daily Range
Wilmar	45	−11	....	88	72	22	29	24 M
Winona	44	−10	....	88	73	28	35	24 M
MISSISSIPPI								
Biloxi, Keesler AFB	30	31	1500	92	79	58	65	16 M
Clarksdale	34	19	....	94	77	42	49	21 M
Columbus AFB	33	20	2890	93	77	44	51	22 M
Greenville AFB	33	20	2580	93	77	44	51	21 M
Greenwood	33	20	....	93	77	44	51	21 M
Hattiesburg	31	27	1840	94	77	42	49	21 M
Jackson AP	32	25	2260	95	76	33	40	21 M
Laurel	31	27	....	94	77	42	49	21 M
McComb AP	31	26	....	94	76	35	42	18 M
Meridian AP	32	23	2340	95	76	33	40	22 M
Natchez	31	27	1800	94	78	49	56	21 M
Tupelo	34	19	....	94	77	42	49	22 M
Vicksburg CO	32	26	2040	95	78	47	54	21 M
MISSOURI								
Cape Girardeau	37	13	....	95	75	28	35	21 M
Columbia AP (S)	39	4	5070	94	74	23	30	22 M
Farmington AP	37	8	....	93	75	31	38	22 M
Hannibal	39	3	5512	93	76	37	44	22 M
Jefferson City	38	7	4620	95	74	21	28	23 M
Joplin AP	37	10	4090	97	73	13	20	24 M
Kansas City AP	39	6	4750	96	74	20	27	20 M
Kirksville AP	40	0	....	93	74	25	32	24 M
Mexico	39	4	....	94	74	23	30	22 M
Moberly	39	3	....	94	74	23	30	23 M
Poplar Bluff	36	16	3910	95	76	32	40	22 M
Rolla	38	9	....	91	75	35	42	22 M
St. Joseph AP	39	2	5440	93	76	37	44	23 M
St. Louis AP	38	6	4900	94	75	30	37	21 M
St. Louis CO	38	8	....	94	75	30	37	18 M
Sedalia, Whiteman AFB	38	4	5012	92	76	39	46	22 M
Sikeston	36	15	....	95	76	33	40	21 M
Springfield AP	37	9	4900	93	74	25	32	23 M

AP = Airport
CO = City Office
S = Solar Data Available

Reprinted with permission of ACCA, *Manual J* 1986.

(Design grains based on an inside design temperature of 75°F)

Location	Latitude Degrees	WINTER 97½% Design db	WINTER Heating D.D. Below 65°F	SUMMER 2½% Design db	SUMMER Coincident Design wb	SUMMER Grains Difference 55% RH	SUMMER Grains Difference 50% RH	Daily Range
MONTANA								
Billings AP	45	−10	7150	91	64	0	0	31 H
Bozeman	45	−14	....	87	60	0	0	32 H
Butte AP	46	−17	9730	83	56	0	0	35 H
Cut Bank AP	48	−20	9033	85	61	0	0	35 H
Glasgow AP (S)	48	−18	9000	89	63	0	0	29 H
Glendive	47	−13	....	92	64	0	0	29 H
Great Falls AP (S)	47	−15	7670	88	60	0	0	28 H
Havre	48	−11	8880	90	64	0	0	33 H
Helena AP	46	−16	8190	88	60	0	0	32 H
Kalispell AP	48	−7	8150	87	61	0	0	34 H
Lewiston AP	47	−16	8586	87	61	0	0	30 H
Livingston AP	45	−14	....	87	60	0	0	32 H
Miles City AP	46	15	7810	95	66	0	0	30 H
Missoula AP	46	−6	8000	88	61	0	0	36 H
NEBRASKA								
Beatrice	40	−2	....	95	74	21	28	24 M
Chadron AP	42	−3	7100	94	65	0	0	30 H
Columbus	41	−2	....	95	73	16	23	M
Fremont	41	−2	....	95	74	21	28	22 M
Grand Island AP	41	−3	6440	94	71	6	13	28 H
Hastings	40	−3	6070	94	71	6	13	27 H
Kearney	40	−4	....	93	70	2	9	28 H
Lincoln CO (S)	40	−2	6050	95	74	21	28	24 M
McCook	40	−2	....	95	69	0	0	28 H
Norfolk	42	−4	7010	93	74	25	32	30 H
North Platte AP (S)	41	−4	6680	94	69	0	2	28 H
Omaha AP	41	−3	6290	91	75	35	42	22 M
Scottsbluff AP	41	−3	6670	92	65	0	0	31 H
Sidney AP	41	−3	7030	92	65	0	0	31 H
NEVADA								
Carson City	39	9	5753	91	59	0	0	42 H
Elko AP	40	−2	7430	92	59	0	0	42 H
Ely AP (S)	39	−4	7710	87	56	0	0	39 H
Las Vegas AP (S)	36	28	2610	106	65	0	0	30 H
Lovelock AP	40	12	....	96	63	0	0	42 H
Reno AP (S)	39	10	6150	92	60	0	0	45 H
Reno CO	39	11	....	93	60	0	0	45 H

AP = Airport
CO = City Office
S = Solar Data Available

Reprinted with permission of ACCA, *Manual J* 1986.

Heat Loss / 8

FIGURE 8-54 / Outdoor design conditions for United States and Canada (continued)
(Design grains based on an inside design temperature of 75°F)

Location	Latitude Degrees	WINTER 97½% Design db	Heating D.D. Below 65°F	SUMMER 2½% Design db	Coincident Design wb	Grains Difference 55% RH	Grains Difference 50% RH	Daily Range
Tonapah AP	38	10	5900	92	59	0	0	40 H
Winnemucca AP	40	3	6760	94	60	0	0	42 H
NEW HAMPSHIRE								
Berlin	44	−9	8270	84	69	11	18	22 M
Claremont	43	−4	7850	86	70	14	21	24 M
Concord AP	43	−3	7360	87	70	12	19	26 H
Keene	43	−7	7460	87	70	12	19	24 M
Laconia	43	−5	7560	86	70	14	21	25 M
Manchester, Grenier AFB	43	−3	7100	88	71	16	23	24 M
Portsmouth, Pease AFB	43	2	6710	85	71	20	27	22 M
NEW JERSEY								
Atlantic City CO	39	13	4810	89	74	31	38	18 M
Long Branch	40	13	. . . .	90	73	24	31	18 M
Newark AP	40	14	4900	91	73	23	30	20 M
New Brunswick	40	10	5400	89	73	26	33	19 M
Paterson	40	10	5360	91	73	23	30	21 M
Phillipsburg	40	6	. . . .	89	72	20	27	21 M
Trenton CO	40	14	4980	88	74	33	40	19 M
Vineland	39	11	. . . .	89	74	31	38	19 M
NEW MEXICO								
Alamagordo Holloman AFB	32	19	3240	96	64	0	0	30 H
Albuquerque AP (S)	35	16	4250	94	61	0	0	27 H
Artesia	32	19	. . . .	100	67	0	0	30 H
Carlsbad AP	32	19	2835	100	67	0	0	28 H
Clovis AP	34	13	4200	93	65	0	0	28 H
Farmington AP	36	6	5713	93	62	0	0	30 H
Gallup	35	5	. . . .	89	58	0	0	32 H
Grants	35	4	. . . .	88	58	0	0	32 H
Hobbs AP	32	18	. . . .	99	66	0	0	29 H
Las Cruces	32	20	3194	96	64	0	0	30 H
Los Alamos	35	9	. . . .	87	60	0	0	32 H
Raton AP	36	1	6228	89	60	0	0	34 H
Roswell, Walker AFB	33	18	3680	98	66	0	0	33 H

AP = Airport
CO = City Office
S = Solar Data Available

Reprinted with permission of ACCA, *Manual J* 1986.

FIGURE 8-54 / Outdoor design conditions for United States and Canada (continued)
(Design grains based on an inside design temperature of 75°F)

Location	Latitude Degrees	WINTER 97½% Design db	WINTER Heating D.D. Below 65°F	SUMMER 2½% Design db	SUMMER Coincident Design wb	SUMMER Grains Difference 55% RH	SUMMER Grains Difference 50% RH	Daily Range
Santa Fe CO	35	10	6120	88	61	0	0	28 H
Silver City AP	32	10	3705	94	60	0	0	30 H
Socorro AP	34	17	....	95	62	0	0	30 H
Tucumcari AP	35	13	4047	97	66	0	0	28 H
NEW YORK								
Albany AP (S)	42	−1	6900	88	72	22	29	23 M
Albany CO	42	1	....	88	72	22	29	20 M
Auburn	43	2	....	87	71	18	25	22 M
Batavia	43	5	....	87	71	18	25	22 M
Binghamton AP	42	1	7340	83	69	13	20	20 M
Buffalo AP	43	6	6960	85	70	15	22	21 M
Cortland	42	0	....	85	71	20	27	23 M
Dunkirk	42	9	6851	85	72	26	33	18 M
Elmira AP	42	1	....	86	71	19	26	24 M
Geneva (S)	42	2	....	87	71	18	20	22 M
Glen Falls	42	−5	7270	85	71	20	27	23 M
Gloversville	43	−2	....	86	71	19	26	23 M
Hornell	42	0	....	85	70	15	22	24 M
Ithaca (S)	42	0	7052	85	71	20	27	24 M
Jamestown	42	3	6849	86	70	14	21	20 M
Kingston	42	2	....	88	72	22	29	22 M
Lockport	43	7	6724	86	72	25	32	21 M
Massena AP	45	−8	....	83	69	13	20	20 M
Newburg-Stewart AFB	41	4	6336	88	72	22	29	21 M
NYC-Central Park (S)	40	15	4880	89	73	26	33	17 M
NYC-Kennedy AP	40	15	5219	87	72	23	30	16 M
NYC-La Guardia AP	40	15	4811	89	73	26	33	16 M
Niagara Falls AP	43	7	6688	86	72	25	32	20 M
Olean	42	2	....	84	71	22	29	23 M
Oneonta	42	−4	....	83	69	13	20	24 M
Oswego CO	43	7	6792	83	71	24	31	20 M
Plattsburg AFB	44	−8	8044	83	69	13	20	22 M
Poughkeepsie	41	6	5820	89	74	31	38	21 M
Rochester AP	43	5	6760	88	71	16	23	22 M
Rome-Griffiss AFB	43	−5	7331	85	70	15	22	22 M
Schenectady (S)	42	1	6650	87	72	23	30	22 M
Suffolk County AFB	40	10	5951	83	71	24	31	16 M
Syracuse AP	43	2	6720	87	71	18	25	20 M

AP = Airport
CO = City Office
S = Solar Data Available

Reprinted with permission of ACCA, *Manual J* 1986.

Heat Loss / 8

(Design grains based on an inside design temperature of 75°F)

Location	WINTER			SUMMER				
	Latitude Degrees	97½% Design db	Heating D.D. Below 65°F	2½% Design db	Coincident Design wb	Grains Difference 55% RH	Grains Difference 50% RH	Daily Range
Utica	43	−6	7200	85	71	20	27	22 M
Watertown	44	−6	7300	83	71	24	31	20 M
NORTH CAROLINA								
Ashville AP	35	14	4130	87	72	23	30	21 M
Charlotte AP	35	22	3200	93	74	25	32	20 M
Durham	36	20	....	92	75	33	40	20 M
Elizabeth City AP	36	19	3207	91	77	47	54	18 M
Fayetteville, Pope AFB	35	20	3080	92	76	39	46	20 M
Goldsboro, Seymour-Johnson AFB	35	21	3124	91	76	41	48	18 M
Greensboro AP (S)	36	18	3810	91	73	23	30	21 M
Greenville	35	21	....	91	76	41	48	19 M
Henderson	36	15	....	92	76	39	46	20 M
Hickory	35	18	....	90	72	19	26	21 M
Jacksonville	34	24	....	90	78	55	62	18 M
Lumberton	34	21	....	92	76	39	46	20 M
New Bern AP	35	24	....	90	78	55	62	18 M
Raleigh/Durham AP (S)	35	20	3440	92	75	33	40	20 M
Rocky Mount	36	21	....	91	76	41	48	19 M
Wilmington AP	34	26	2380	91	78	53	60	18 M
Winston-Salem AP	36	20	3650	91	73	23	30	20 M
NORTH DAKOTA								
Bismark AP (S)	46	−19	8960	91	68	0	2	27 H
Devil's Lake	48	−21	9901	88	68	0	7	25 M
Dickinson AP	46	−17	8942	90	66	0	0	25 M
Fargo AP	46	−18	9250	89	71	15	22	25 M
Grands Forks AP	48	−22	9930	87	70	12	19	25 M
Jamestown AP	47	−18	....	90	69	2	9	26 H
Minot AP	48	−20	9610	89	67	0	0	25 M
Williston	48	−21	9180	88	67	0	1	25 M
OHIO								
Akron-Canton AP	41	6	6140	86	71	19	26	21 M
Ashtabula	41	9	....	85	72	26	33	18 M
Athens	39	6	....	92	74	27	34	22 M
Bowling Green	41	2	....	89	73	26	33	23 M

AP = Airport
CO = City Office
S = Solar Data Available

Reprinted with permission of ACCA, *Manual J* 1986.

(Design grains based on an inside design temperature of 75°F)

Location	Latitude Degrees	WINTER 97½% Design db	Heating D.D. Below 65°F	SUMMER 2½% Design db	Coincident Design wb	Grains Difference 55% RH	Grains Difference 50% RH	Daily Range
Cambridge	40	7	....	90	74	30	37	23 M
Chilicothe	39	6	....	92	74	27	34	22 M
Cincinnati CO	39	6	4830	90	72	19	26	21 M
Cleveland AP (S)	41	5	6200	88	72	22	29	22 M
Columbus AP (S)	40	5	5670	90	73	24	31	24 M
Dayton AP	39	4	5620	89	72	20	27	20 M
Defiance	41	4	....	91	73	23	30	24 M
Findlay AP	41	3	....	90	73	24	31	24 M
Fremont	41	1	....	88	73	28	35	24 M
Hamilton	39	5	....	90	72	19	26	22 M
Lancaster	39	5	....	91	73	23	30	23 M
Lima	40	4	5870	91	73	23	30	24 M
Mansfield AP	40	5	6403	87	72	23	30	22 M
Marion	40	5	....	91	73	23	30	23 M
Middletown	39	5	....	90	72	19	26	22 M
Newark	40	5	5655	92	73	21	28	23 M
Norwalk	41	1	....	88	73	28	35	22 M
Portsmouth	38	10	4410	92	74	27	34	22 M
Sandusky CO	41	6	5796	91	72	17	24	21 M
Springfield	40	3	4284	89	73	26	33	21 M
Stubenville	40	5	....	86	71	19	26	22 M
Toledo AP	41	1	6430	88	73	28	35	25 M
Warren	41	5	....	87	71	18	25	23 M
Wooster	40	6	....	86	71	19	26	22 M
Youngstown AP	41	4	6370	86	71	19	26	23 M
Zanesville AP	40	7	....	90	74	30	37	23 M
OKLAHOMA								
Ada	34	14	....	97	74	19	26	23 M
Altus AFB	34	16	3190	100	73	7	14	25 M
Ardmore	34	17	3060	98	74	17	24	23 M
Bartlesville	36	10	....	98	74	17	24	23 M
Chickasha	35	14	....	98	74	17	24	24 M
Enid-Vance AFB	36	13	3971	100	74	13	20	24 M
Lawton AP	34	16	3250	99	74	15	22	24 M
McAlester	34	19	3255	96	74	20	27	23 M
Muskogee AP	35	15	....	98	75	23	30	23 M
Norman	35	13	3247	96	74	20	27	24 M

AP = Airport
CO = City Office
S = Solar Data Available

Reprinted with permission of ACCA, *Manual J* 1986.

Location	Latitude Degrees	WINTER 97½% Design db	Heating D.D. Below 65°F	SUMMER 2½% Design db	Coincident Design wb	Grains Difference 55% RH	Grains Difference 50% RH	Daily Range
Oklahoma City AP	35	13	3700	97	74	19	26	23 M
Ponca City	36	9	3850	97	74	19	26	24 M
Seminole	35	15	....	96	74	20	27	23 M
Stillwater (S)	36	13	....	96	74	20	27	24 M
Tulsa AP	36	13	3730	98	75	23	30	22 M
Woodward	36	10	....	97	73	13	20	26 H
OREGON								
Albany	44	22	....	89	66	0	0	31 H
Astoria AP (S)	46	29	5190	71	62	0	4	16 M
Baker AP	44	6	....	89	61	0	0	30 H
Bend	44	4	....	87	60	0	0	33 H
Corvallis (S)	44	22	4854	89	66	0	0	31 H
Eugene AP	44	22	4740	89	66	0	0	31 H
Grants Pass	42	24	4375	96	68	0	0	33 H
Klamath Falls AP	42	9	6810	87	60	0	0	36 H
Medford AP (S)	42	23	4880	94	67	0	0	35 H
Pendleton AP	45	5	4700	93	64	0	0	29 H
Portland AP	45	23	4635	85	67	0	7	23 M
Portland CO	45	24	....	86	67	0	4	21 M
Roseburg AP	43	23	4491	90	66	0	0	30 H
Salem AP	45	23	4760	88	66	0	0	31 H
The Dalles	45	19	....	89	68	3	10	28 H
PENNSYLVANIA								
Allentown AP	40	9	5810	88	72	22	29	22 M
Altoona CO	40	5	6192	87	71	18	25	23 M
Butler	40	6	....	87	72	23	30	22 M
Chambersburg	40	8	5170	90	74	30	37	23 M
Erie AP	42	9	6540	85	72	26	33	18 M
Harrisburg AP	40	11	5280	91	74	29	36	21 M
Johnstown	40	2	7804	83	70	19	26	23 M
Lancaster	40	8	5560	90	74	30	37	22 M
Meadville	41	4	....	85	70	15	32	21 M
New Castle	41	7	5800	88	72	22	30	23 M
Philadelphia AP	39	14	5180	90	74	30	37	21 M
Pittsburgh AP	40	5	5950	86	71	19	26	22 M
Pittsburgh CO	40	7	....	88	71	16	22	19 M
Reading CO	40	13	4960	89	72	20	22	19 M
Scranton/Wilkes-Barre	41	5	6160	87	71	18	25	19 M

AP = Airport
CO = City Office
S = Solar Data Available

Reprinted with permission of ACCA, *Manual J* 1986.

FIGURE 8-54 / *Outdoor design conditions for United States and Canada (continued)*
(Design grains based on an inside design temperature of 75°F)

Location	Latitude Degrees	WINTER 97½% Design db	WINTER Heating D.D. Below 65°F	SUMMER 2½% Design db	SUMMER Coincident Design wb	SUMMER Grains Difference 55% RH	SUMMER Grains Difference 50% RH	Daily Range
State College (S)	40	7	6160	87	71	18	25	23 M
Sunbury	40	7	. . . .	89	72	20	27	22 M
Uniontown	39	9	. . . .	88	73	28	35	22 M
Warren	41	4	. . . .	86	71	19	26	24 M
West Chester	40	13	. . . .	89	74	31	38	20 M
Williamsport AP	41	7	5950	89	72	20	27	23 M
York	40	12	. . . .	91	74	29	36	22 M
RHODE ISLAND								
Newport (S)	41	9	5800	85	72	26	33	16 M
Providence AP	41	9	5950	86	72	25	32	19 M
SOUTH CAROLINA								
Anderson	34	23	. . . .	92	74	27	34	21 M
Charleston AFB (S)	32	27	2070	91	78	53	60	18 M
Charleston CO	32	28	2146	92	78	51	58	13 L
Columbia AP	34	24	2520	95	75	28	35	22 M
Florence AP	34	25	2480	92	77	45	52	21 M
Georgetown	33	26	2228	90	78	55	62	18 M
Greenville AP	34	22	3070	91	74	29	36	21 M
Greenwood	34	22	2890	93	74	25	32	21 M
Orangeburg	33	24	. . . .	95	75	28	35	20 M
Rock Hill	35	23	. . . .	94	74	23	30	20 M
Spartanburg AP	35	22	. . . .	91	74	29	36	20 M
Sumter-Shaw AFB	34	25	2453	92	76	39	46	21 M
SOUTH DAKOTA								
Aberdeen AP	45	-15	8620	91	72	17	24	27 H
Brookings	44	-13	. . . .	92	72	15	22	25 M
Huron AP	44	-14	8220	93	72	13	20	28 H
Mitchel	43	-10	. . . .	93	71	7	14	28 H
Pierre AP	44	-10	7550	95	71	4	11	29 H
Rapid City AP (S)	44	- 7	7370	92	65	0	0	28 H
Sioux Falls AP	43	-11	7840	91	72	17	24	24 M
Watertown AP	45	-15	8390	91	72	17	24	26 H
Yankton	43	- 7	. . . .	91	72	17	24	25 M
TENNESSEE								
Athens	33	18	. . . .	92	73	21	28	22 M
Bristol-Tri City AP	36	14	4143	89	72	20	27	22 M

AP = Airport
CO = City Office
S = Solar Data Available

Reprinted with permission of ACCA, *Manual J* 1986.

Heat Loss / *8*

(Design grains based on an inside design temperature of 75°F)

Location	WINTER			SUMMER				
	Latitude Degrees	97½% Design db	Heating D.D. Below 65°F	2½% Design db	Coincident Design wb	Grains Difference 55% RH	Grains Difference 50% RH	Daily Range
Chattanooga AP	35	18	3380	93	74	25	32	22 M
Clarksville	36	12	....	93	74	25	32	21 M
Columbia	35	15	....	94	74	23	30	21 M
Dyersburg	36	15	....	94	77	42	49	21 M
Greenville	35	16	....	90	72	19	26	22 M
Jackson AP	35	16	3350	95	75	28	35	21 M
Knoxville AP	35	19	3510	92	73	21	28	21 M
Memphis AP	35	18	3210	95	76	33	48	21 M
Murfreesboro	35	14	....	94	74	23	30	22 M
Nashville AP (S)	36	14	3610	94	74	23	30	21 M
Tullahoma	35	13	3577	93	73	19	26	22 M
TEXAS								
Abilene AP	32	20	2620	99	71	0	5	22 M
Alice AP	27	34	....	98	77	35	42	20 M
Amarillo AP	35	11	4140	95	67	33	40	26 H
Austin AP	30	28	1720	98	74	23	30	22 M
Bay City	29	33	....	94	77	42	49	16 M
Beaumont	30	31	1370	93	78	50	57	19 M
Beeville	28	33	1189	97	77	37	44	18 M
Big Springs AP (S)	32	20	....	97	69	0	0	26 H
Brownsville AP (S)	25	39	600	93	77	44	51	18 M
Brownwood	31	22	2437	99	73	9	16	22 M
Bryan AP	30	29	1640	96	76	32	39	20 M
Corpus Christi AP	27	35	930	94	78	49	56	19 M
Corsicana	32	25	....	98	75	23	30	21 M
Dallas AP	32	22	2320	100	75	20	27	20 M
Del Rio, Laughlin AFB	29	31	1520	98	73	11	18	24 M
Denton	33	22	....	99	74	15	22	22 M
Eagle Pass	28	32	1423	99	73	9	16	24 M
El Paso AP (S)	31	24	2680	98	64	0	0	27 H
Fort Worth AP (S)	32	22	2390	99	74	15	22	22 M
Galveston AP	29	36	1270	89	79	63	70	10 L
Greenville	33	22	....	99	74	15	22	21 M
Harlingen	26	39	693	94	77	42	49	19 M
Houston AP	29	32	1410	94	77	42	49	18 M
Houston CO	29	33	....	95	77	40	47	18 M
Huntsville	30	27	....	98	75	23	30	20 M
Killeen-Gray AFB	31	25	....	97	73	13	20	22 M
Lamesa	32	17	....	96	69	0	0	26 H

AP = Airport
CO = City Office
S = Solar Data Available

Reprinted with permission of ACCA, *Manual J* 1986.

FIGURE 8-54 / *Outdoor design conditions for United States and Canada (continued)*
(Design grains based on an inside design temperature of 75°F)

		WINTER			SUMMER			
Location	Latitude Degrees	97½% Design db	Heating D.D. Below 65°F	2½% Design db	Coincident Design wb	Grains Difference 55% RH	Grains Difference 50% RH	Daily Range
Laredo AFB	27	36	800	101	73	6	13	23 M
Longview	32	24	....	97	76	30	37	20 M
Lubbock AP	33	15	3570	96	69	0	0	26 H
Lufkin AP	31	29	1940	97	76	30	37	20 M
McAllen	26	39	....	95	77	40	47	21 M
Midland AP (S)	32	21	2600	98	69	0	0	26 H
Mineral Wells AP	32	22	....	99	74	15	22	22 M
Palestine CO	31	27	....	98	76	29	36	20 M
Pampa	35	12	....	96	67	0	0	26 H
Pecos	31	21	....	98	69	0	0	27 H
Plainview	34	13	....	96	68	0	0	26 H
Port Arthur AP	30	31	1447	93	78	50	57	19 M
San Angelo, Goodfellow AFB	31	22	2220	99	71	0	5	24 M
San Antonio AP (S)	29	30	1560	97	73	13	20	19 M
Sherman-Perrin AFB	33	20	2837	98	75	23	30	22 M
Snyder	32	18	....	98	70	0	1	26 M
Temple	31	27	....	99	74	15	22	22 M
Tyler AP	32	24	....	97	76	30	37	21 M
Vernon	34	17	....	100	73	7	14	24 M
Victoria AP	28	32	1160	96	77	39	46	18 M
Waco AP	31	26	2040	99	75	21	28	22 M
Wichita Falls AP	34	18	2900	101	73	6	13	24 M
UTAH								
Cedar City AP	37	5	5680	91	60	0	0	32 H
Logan	41	2	6750	91	61	0	0	33 H
Moab	38	11	....	98	60	0	0	30 H
Ogden AP	41	5	6012	91	61	0	0	33 H
Price	39	5	....	91	60	0	0	33 H
Provo	40	6	5720	96	62	0	0	32 H
Richfield	38	5	....	91	60	0	0	34 H
St. George CO	37	21	....	101	65	0	0	33 H
Salt Lake City AP (S)	40	8	5990	95	62	0	0	32 H
Vernal AP	40	0	....	89	60	0	0	32 H
VERMONT								
Barre	44	-11	....	81	69	16	23	23 M
Burlington AP (S)	44	-7	8030	85	70	15	22	23 M
Rutland	43	-8	7440	84	70	16	23	23 M

AP = Airport
CO = City Office
S = Solar Data Available

Reprinted with permission of ACCA, *Manual J* 1986.

| | | WINTER | | SUMMER | | | | |
| | | | | | | | | |
Location	Latitude Degrees	97½% Design db	Heating D.D. Below 65°F	2½% Design db	Coincident Design wb	Grains Difference 55% RH	Grains Difference 50% RH	Daily Range
VIRGINIA								
Charlottsville	38	18	4220	91	74	29	36	23 M
Danville AP	36	16	3510	92	73	21	28	21 M
Fredericksburg	38	14	. . . .	93	75	31	38	21 M
Harrisonburg	38	16	. . . .	91	72	17	24	23 M
Lynchburg AP	37	16	4166	90	74	30	37	21 M
Norfolk AP	36	22	3440	91	76	41	48	18 M
Petersburg	37	17	. . . .	92	76	39	46	20 M
Richmond AP	37	17	3910	92	76	39	46	21 M
Roanoke AP	37	16	4150	91	72	17	24	23 M
Staunton	38	16	4307	91	72	17	24	23 M
Winchester	39	10	4780	90	74	30	37	21 M
WASHINGTON								
Aberdeen	47	28	5316	77	62	0	0	16 M
Bellingham AP	48	15	5420	77	65	2	9	19 M
Bremerton	47	25	5432	78	64	0	3	20 M
Ellensburg AP	47	6	. . . .	91	64	0	0	34 H
Everett-Paine AFB	47	25	5940	76	64	0	7	20 M
Kennewick	46	11	. . . .	96	67	0	0	30 H
Longview	46	24	5064	85	67	0	7	30 H
Moses Lake, Larson AFB	47	7	. . . .	94	65	0	0	32 H
Olympia AP	47	22	5236	83	65	0	0	32 H
Port Angeles	48	27	. . . .	69	61	0	3	18 M
Seattle-Boeing Fld	47	26	. . . .	81	66	1	8	24 M
Seattle CO (S)	47	27	4424	82	66	0	7	19 M
Seattle-Tacoma AP (S)	47	26	5190	80	64	0	0	22 M
Spokane AP (S)	47	2	6770	90	63	0	0	28 M
Tacoma-McChord AFB	47	24	5287	82	65	0	2	22 M
Walla Walla AP	46	7	4800	94	66	0	0	27 H
Wenatchee	47	11	. . . .	96	66	0	0	32 H
Yakima AP	46	5	5950	93	65	0	0	36 H
WEST VIRGINIA								
Beckley	37	4	5615	81	69	16	23	22 M
Bluefield AP	37	4	5000	81	69	16	23	22 M
Charleston AP	38	11	4510	90	73	24	31	20 M

AP = Airport
CO = City Office
S = Solar Data Available

Reprinted with permission of ACCA, *Manual J* 1986.

| Location | WINTER | | | SUMMER | | | | |
	Latitude Degrees	97½% Design db	Heating D.D. Below 65°F	2½% Design db	Coincident Design wb	Grains Difference 55% RH	Grains Difference 50% RH	Daily Range
Clarksburg	39	10	4590	90	73	24	31	21 M
Elkins AP	38	6	5680	84	70	16	23	22 M
Huntington CO	38	10	4340	91	74	29	36	22 M
Martinsburg AP	39	10	5231	90	74	30	37	21 M
Morgantown AP	39	8	5100	87	73	29	36	22 H
Parkersburg CO	39	11	4780	90	74	30	37	21 M
Wheeling	40	5	5220	86	71	19	26	21 M
WISCONSIN								
Appleton	44	-9	. . . .	86	72	25	32	23 M
Ashland	46	-16	. . . .	82	68	10	17	23 M
Beloit	42	-3	. . . .	90	75	36	43	24 M
Eau Claire AP	44	-11	7970	89	73	26	33	23 M
Fond du Lac	43	-8	. . . .	86	72	25	32	23 M
Green Bay AP	44	-9	8100	85	72	26	33	23 M
LaCrosse AP	43	-9	7530	88	73	28	35	22 M
Madison AP (S)	43	-7	7720	88	73	28	35	22 M
Manitowoc	44	-7	. . . .	86	72	25	32	21 M
Marinette	45	-11	. . . .	84	71	32	29	20 M
Milwaukee AP	43	-4	7470	87	73	29	36	21 M
Racine	42	-2	. . . .	88	73	28	35	21 M
Sheboygan	43	-6	. . . .	86	73	31	38	20 M
Stevens Point	43	-11	. . . .	89	73	26	33	23 M
Waukesha	43	-5	. . . .	87	73	29	36	22 M
Wausau AP	44	-12	8490	88	72	22	29	23 M
WYOMING								
Casper AP	42	-5	7510	90	57	0	0	31 H
Cheyene AP	41	-1	7370	86	58	0	0	30 H
Cody AP	44	-13	. . . .	86	60	0	0	32 H
Evanston	41	-3	. . . .	84	55	0	0	32 H
Lander AP (S)	42	-11	7870	88	61	0	0	32 H
Laramie AP (S)	41	- 6	7560	81	56	0	0	28 H
Newcastle	43	-12	. . . .	87	63	0	0	30 H
Rawlins	41	- 4	. . . .	83	57	0	0	40 H
Rock Springs AP	41	- 3	8430	84	55	0	0	32 H
Sheridan AP	44	- 8	7740	91	62	0	0	32 H
Torrington	42	- 8	. . . .	91	62	0	0	30 H

AP = Airport
CO = City Office
S = Solar Data Available

Reprinted with permission of ACCA, *Manual J* 1986.

CHAPTER 9
HOT WATER HEATING SYSTEMS AND DESIGN

9-1 TYPES OF SYSTEMS

For heat, the water is heated in a boiler to the preset temperature (180° to 210°F). Then a circulating pump is automatically cut on, and the hot water is circulated through the system of pipes, passing through any of a variety of convector types (Sec. 9-4). As it circulates, it gives off the heat, primarily through the convectors; then the pipes return the water to the boiler to be reheated and circulated again. Most of the convectors used can be regulated slightly by opening or closing adjustable dampers. A compression tank is included in the system to adjust for the varying pressure in the system since water expands as it is heated.

Circulating hot water systems are also referred to as *hydronic* heating systems, and the four different hot water piping systems commonly used are series loop, one-pipe, and two-pipe systems and radiant panels.

SERIES LOOP SYSTEMS

Most commonly used for residences and small buildings, the convectors in the series loop system are fed by a single pipe which goes through the convector and makes a

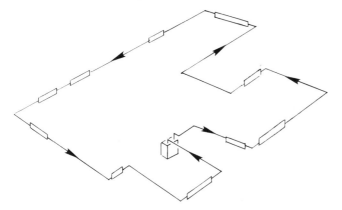

FIGURE 9-1 / Series loop isometric

loop around the building, or one portion of the building (Fig. 9-1 and 9-2). The pipe acts as supply and return with the water getting cooler as it progresses through the system. To the designer this means that larger convectors are required to obtain the same amount of heat at the end of the loop as compared to convectors at the beginning because the water is cooler. Also, the longer the run of piping and the more convectors

FIGURE 9-2 / Series loop plan

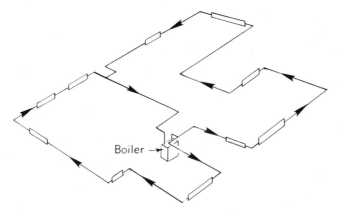

FIGURE 9-3 / Series loop (zoned) isometric

it serves, the cooler the water will become. For more even heat, the building may be broken into zones (Fig. 9-3), each with its own series loop system activated by its individual thermostat. It is economical to install, but any control of individual convectors is minimal. Only heating is supplied with this system.

ONE-PIPE SYSTEMS

As shown in Figs. 9-4 and 9-5, the one-pipe system has a single pipe going around the building, or a zone of the building. A portion of the hot water is diverted through a special tee at each convector so that a portion of the hot water is diverted through the convector where it gives off heat to the room, thereby cooling the water. Then the water is returned to the supply pipe. Upon entering the supply pipe, it will slightly reduce the temperature of the water in that pipe. The primary advantage of this system

FIGURE 9-4 / One-pipe (zoned) isometric

FIGURE 9-5 / One-pipe plan

over the series loop is that each individual convector may be controlled by a valve to turn it on, off or in between. The convectors may be placed above the pipe (upfeed) or below it (downfeed). The upfeed is more effective since the water tends to be diverted more easily in that direction. This system is more expensive than the series loop since it requires additional piping, fittings and valves. It may also be zoned for larger buildings where the temperature drop over a long pipe run would be excessive.

TWO-PIPE SYSTEMS

For large installations the supply of hot water needs to be kept separate from that water which has been cooled by passing through a convector. To accomplish this, one pipe is used to supply the hot water, which then empties into another pipe used for return. This type of system provides the water at as high a temperature as possible. The return may be classified as *reverse return* (Fig. 9-6) or *direct return* (Fig. 9-7). The reverse return results in a more even flow of water because the supply and return are of equal length, resulting in equal friction losses. The direct return requires slightly less piping. Individual convector control is available by the installation of valves. This is the best system available and also the most expensive. It would be unnecessary to put this system in a residence.

Reprinted with permission from ASHRAE, Fundamentals Handbook, 1985

FIGURE 9-6 / Two-pipe (zoned) reverse return

RADIANT PANELS

The hot water may be circulated through pipes located, usually, in the floor or ceiling of a building. The pipes are laid in a coil or grid arrangement (Fig. 9-8); for a floor system they are embedded in concrete, whereas for a ceiling they are attached to the framing and plastered or drywalled over. They may also be used on walls, but this is not common. The basic disadvantage with this type of system is that while it provides uniform heat over an entire room, heat is not uniformly lost; most of it is lost at exterior walls, usually at the window. This situation tends to cause drafts and a feeling of being

FIGURE 9-7 / Two-pipe (zoned) direct return

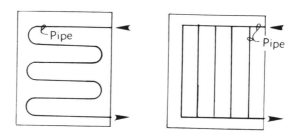

FIGURE 9-8 / Radiant panels

cold near the windows. The floor panels have a tendency to make the occupant's feet hot and uncomfortable, while the heat coming down from the ceiling tends to stay high (since heat rises), and a person's legs under a table will probably feel cool. (This is also true of electric ceiling and wall radiant panels.)

9-2   PIPING AND FITTINGS

The piping used for hot water heating is usually copper, but steel pipe is sometimes used. Copper is preferred because it is lightweight and easy to work with— characteristics described in Sec. 2-4. The types of copper piping used for hot water heating systems are Type L pipe and tubing and Type M pipe.

The most commonly used fittings for the system are the same as those used in plumbing systems (Sec. 2-5, Figs. 2-3 through 2-5).

9-3   BOILER AND SYSTEM CONTROLS

BOILER

The boiler (furnace, Fig. 9-9) heats the water for circulation through the system. It may be rectangular or square (occasionally even round) and made of steel or cast iron. A boiler is rated by the amount of heat it can produce in an hour. The maximum amount of heat the system can put out is limited first by the size of the boiler selected. Boiler efficiency increases when the boiler runs for long periods of time, so the unit selected should not be oversized or it will run intermittently and thus be less efficient. Hot water boilers may use oil, gas, propane gas, coal, or electricity as fuel. In residences oil and gas boilers are most commonly used.

For a hot water heating system, the temperature that the water is heated to in the boiler is of prime importance since it has a direct relationship to the amount of heat which the radiation or convector units will give off. Typically, the thermostat should be set at about 180°F but temperatures as high as 220°F are possible. The thermostat which controls the water temperature (Fig. 9-10) is located somewhere on the boiler

FIGURE 9-9 / Typical boiler installation

FIGURE 9-10 / Boiler thermostat control

9 / HOT WATER HEATING SYSTEMS AND DESIGN

(usually in plain sight, sometimes behind a small sheet-metal cover plate) and should be checked, after installation, by the designer.

THERMOSTAT

The thermostat, which controls the air temperature in the space (Fig. 9-11), is placed in the building. With hot water heat, there will be one thermostat for each zone. The temperature desired is set on the thermostat, and when the temperature in the room falls below the desired temperature, the thermostat turns on the boiler and the circulating pump. When the desired temperature is reached, the thermostat will turn the boiler and the pump off. The thermostat has a temperature differential within which it will call for heat and then cut it off. Typically, this temperature differential is about 1°F, which means that the thermostat will call for heat at 69°F and shut it off at 70°F. This differential may be adjusted on a small calibration setting inside the thermostat housing (Fig. 9-12). The less the differential, the more comfortable the space will feel. But it also means that the boiler will be turned on and off more frequently (to maintain a close tolerance of temperature) which will lower the efficiency of the boiler operation.

Thermostats used for hot water systems are usually either the single-setting thermostat (Fig. 9-11) or the day-night thermostat (Fig. 9-13).

The single-setting thermostat is the one most commonly used. The desired temperature is set and the thermostat will operate the cycles of the heating system. The temperature may be changed at any time by simply adjusting the temperature setting on the thermostat.

A day-night thermostat permits the setting of one temperature for the daytime and another (usually lower) for nighttime. With this thermostat a clock is set for a given

FIGURE 9-11 / Thermostat

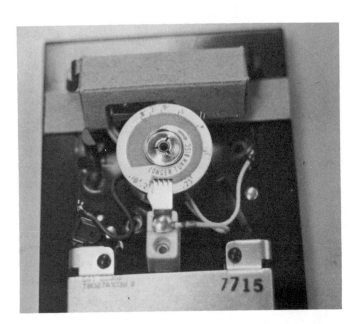

FIGURE 9-12 / Thermostat calibration

FIGURE 9-13 / Day-night thermostat

9 / *HOT WATER HEATING SYSTEMS AND DESIGN*

time (say, 8 A.M.) and at that time the temperature will go to the daytime setting (perhaps 72°F); then at the other time set (say, 5 P.M.) the temperature will go to the nighttime setting (perhaps 60°F). The times and temperatures are set on the thermostat and may be changed as desired.

The day-night thermostat is used in residences, stores, offices, apartments, institutions and commercial and industrial projects. In a residence, the temperature differential may be 3°F or 4°F, set to begin to cool just before bedtime and to heat up as the occupants arise. In apartments where the heat is furnished and paid for by the apartment owner and not the renter, this type of thermostat is commonly used to control heat costs for the owner. In this case, the thermostat used would have two parts, one located in the apartments to sense the temperature and the second located in a place the renters cannot enter which controls the temperature desired and the times of operation. Since many stores and offices are open only limited hours, perhaps 8 A.M. to 5 P.M., it would be foolish to maintain the temperature needed during hours of operation through the hours in which the space is not in use. Rather than depend on someone to turn down the temperature before he leaves (which he may forget to do) and to turn up the temperature in the morning (no one will begin work until it warms up), the day-night thermostat takes care of these functions automatically. In locations where the possibility of people tampering with the thermostats is a problem, the unit may have a cover which locks it or may be designed so that the temperature settings can be changed only with a special keying device.

Thermostats are usually placed about 5 ft up on a wall. The location should be carefully checked to be certain that the thermostat will provide a true representation of the temperature in the spaces it serves. Guidelines used in thermostat location include the following:

1. Always mount it on an inside wall (on an outside wall, the cold air outside will affect the readings).

2. Keep it away from the cold air drafts (such as near a door or window), away from any possible warm air drafts (near a radiation unit, fireplace or stove) and away from any direct sunlight.

EXPANSION TANK

The expansion tank (also called a *compression tank*) allows for the expansion of the water in the system as it is heated. It is located above the boiler.

AUTOMATIC FILLER VALVE

When the pressure in the system drops below 12 psi, this valve opens, allowing more water into the system; then the check valve automatically closes as the pressure increases. This maintains a minimum water level in the system.

CIRCULATING PUMP

The hot water is circulated from the boiler through the pipes and back to the boiler by a pump. The pump provides fast distribution of hot water through the system, thus delivering heat as quickly as possible. The circulating pump size is based on the delivery of water required, in gpm, and the amount of friction head allowed. Circulating pumps are not used on gravity systems.

FLOW CONTROL VALVE

The flow control valve closes to stop the flow of hot water when the pump stops, so that the hot water will not flow through the system by gravity. Any gravity flow of the water would cause the temperature in the room to continue to rise.

BOILER RELIEF VALVE

When the pressure in the system exceeds 30 psi, a spring-loaded valve opens, allowing some of the water to bleed out of the system and allowing the pressure to drop. The valve should be located where the discharge will not cause any damage.

BOILER RATING

Boiler manufacturers list both gross and net Btuh ratings of the boiler. The gross Btuh is the heat input to the boiler by the fuel, and the net Btuh is the usable heat output which is available for use in the hot water system.

9-4 HOT WATER HEATING DEVICES

Some type of heating device must be used to distribute the heat efficiently from the hot water to the room being heated. These devices are classified as *radiant* and *convector*, according to the way in which they transfer the heat.

Radiant heating units have the heat transfer surface exposed so that the heat is transferred to radiation to the surrounding objects and by natural convection to the surrounding air. A typical radiant unit is shown in Fig. 9-14.

FIGURE 9-14 / Radiant heating device

CAST IRON BASEBOARD

FIN TYPE BASEBOARD

FIN TYPE RADIATOR

FIGURE 9-15 / Convector heating devices

Convector heating units have the heat transfer surface enclosed in a cabinet or other enclosure (Fig. 9-15). The transfer of heat occurs primarily through convection as air flows through the enclosure, and past the heat transfer surface, by gravity. For institutional and commercial projects, the convectors used may have several rows of large finned-tube radiators in the cabinet (Fig. 9-16).

Unit heaters use a fan to distribute the air through the space. The unit usually consists of a heating coil and a fan enclosed in a cabinet (Fig. 9-17). The heat may be supplied by hot water or even steam when available. Often this type of unit is suspended from the ceiling in areas such as a warehouse, a storage area or any large room situation, especially one with high ceilings. Such a unit is sized according to heat output, and the layout of these units to provide adequate coverage of the space with warm air must be carefully checked. This type of unit is also effective when the room is deep with a relatively small outside wall area for a convector or radiation unit. A typical situation would be that of a motel room (Fig. 9-18) where the unit heater is placed under the glass area in the exterior wall and the air is fan-blown through the room. Unit heaters may be recessed, surface mounted, or suspended from the ceiling or wall, or recessed or surface mounted on the floor (Fig. 9-19).

FIGURE 9-16 / High output convector

Hot Water Heating Devices / 9-4

255

Ceiling unit

Floor unit

Concealed
in ceiling

Concealed
in wall

FIGURE 9-17 / Unit heaters

9-5 HEATING DEVICE RATINGS

All radiant, convector and unit heaters are rated in terms of the amount of heat they will give off in an hour; the capacity ratings are given in Btuh for small devices and in MBH (thousands of Btuh) for larger devices. The heating capacities vary, depending on the type of pipe, the size of the finned tube, the number of fins per foot of radiation and

Heat

Unit heater

FIGURE 9-18 / Unit heater

Recessed unit   Floor mounted

FIGURE 9-19 / Floor unit heaters

the temperature of the water. Each manufacturer's specifications (or technical data report) should be checked for heating capacity of a particular unit.

Baseboard radiation units may be cast-iron radiation units or finned-tubed convectors. A typical manufacturer's specification rating is shown in Fig. 9-20. The various types of elements available from this manufacturer are shown in the left column and the heat ratings, for the various water temperatures, on the right. Notice that the heating capacity of the unit increases as the water temperature increases. Comparing the copper-aluminum elements, the capacity for the 2¾-in. x 5-in. x 0.020 x 40/ft 1¼-in. tube element (the second entry on left) at 180°F is 850 Btuh, while at 200°F the capacity is 1,030 Btuh. The capacity is increased by 180 Btuh simply by increasing the temperature of water that will flow through the element. This 180-Btuh increase represents a 21% gain in the heating capacity at no increase in the cost of boiler or heating device, only an increase in the temperature of the water. The effects of the fins and tube on the heating capacity of an element can be seen by comparing the first and third listings under the copper-aluminum elements. The smaller top element (2¾-in. x 3¾-in. x 0.011 x 50/ft 1-in. tube) has a capacity of 840 Btuh at 180°F, while the third listing (2¾-in. x 5-in. x 0.020 x 50/ft 1¼-in. tube) has a capacity of 910 Btuh. This is an increase of 70 Btuh or about 8.33%. The copper-aluminum elements may be compared with the steel elements by checking the second copper-aluminum listing against the second steel element listing. The second copper-aluminum listing (2¾-in. x 5-in. x 0.020 x 40/ft 1¼-in. tube) has a capacity of 850 Btuh at 180°F, and the second steel element listing has a capacity of 710 Btuh at 180°F. The copper-aluminum element capacity is 140 Btuh or 19.7% higher than that of the steel element.

As initial selections of heating devices are made, the various ratings must be checked. It may be necessary to use different sizes of heating devices in different rooms (usually depending on the amount of wall space available for mounting the devices), but once a basic decision is made as to type of material (steel or copper-aluminum), this will usually be used throughout.

To make an economical selection, the designer should also consider the relative costs of the devices per foot and then compare these costs to the heating capacities of the units. Prices vary considerably, but unless the steel elements, installed, cost about 20% less than the copper-aluminum elements, they will not be as economical to install. It is part of the designer's responsibility to provide the best system at the lowest cost.

Heating Device Ratings / 9-5

	Hot Water Output* 1 gal. flow rate (for 5 gal. flow rate use factor 1.067)				
Copper-Aluminum Elements	220°	210°	200°	190°	180°
2¾" x 3¾" x .011 x 50/ft. 1" tube	1240	1120	1020	930	840
2¾" x 5" x .020 x 40/ft. 1¼" tube	1250	1120	1030	940	850
2¾" x 5" x .020 x 50/ft. 1¼" tube	1340	1200	1100	1000	910
Steel Elements					
2¾" x 5 x 24 ga. x 40/ft. 1" tube (IPS)	1020	920	840	770	690
2¾" x 5 x 24 ga. x 40/ft. 1¼" tube (IPS)	1040	940	860	780	710

*Based on 65° entering air.

FIGURE 9-20 / Finned tube ratings

9-6   HOT WATER HEATING SYSTEM DESIGN

The first thing which must be done is to decide whether the hot water heating system will be a series loop, one-pipe, two-pipe or radiant panel system. The following step-by-step approach will work for any of the systems (except radiant panels) which are discussed in Sec. 9-1. Completed heat loss tabulations calculated for the residences in Chapter 8 are in Fig. 8-36.

STEP-BY-STEP APPROACH

1.   Determine the heat loss of each room and list them (Fig. 9-21).

   Heat losses for this residence are determined in Chapter 8.

2.   Next, determine whether a series loop, a one-pipe or a two-pipe system will be used.

9   /   HOT WATER HEATING SYSTEMS AND DESIGN

Trunk	28,940	BTUH	Zone 2	
Zone 1			Bedroom 3	3,008
Entry		3,364	Bath	960
Dining		3,047	Bedroom 1	4,085
Kitchen		3,752	Bedroom 2	2,310
Living		8,216	Int. Bath	198
		18,379		10,561

FIGURE 9-21 / Zone heat loss totals

For this design a series loop system has been selected.

3. Using a floor plan, locate the approximate position of the heating devices in each room.

The heating devices have been located on the plan in Fig. 9-22.

4. Locate the boiler on the plan (Fig. 9-23).
5. Determine how many zones will be used in the design.

FIGURE 9-22 / Series loop system

FIGURE 9–23 / Locate boiler on plan

In this design, two zones will be used, as shown in Fig. 9-24.

6.   Determine the actual length of the longest zone (circuit).

       From Fig. 9-25, the actual length of the longest zone is taken as 145 lineal ft.

7.   Assume an average pipe size for the system. *This pipe size is a preliminary selection which will be rechecked later.*

       Assume ¾-in. copper tubing for this design.

8.   Determine the velocity of the water in the system from Fig. 9-43 for steel pipe and from Fig. 9-44 for copper tubing, based on the heat to be conveyed per hour in the zone or on gpm of hot water. Also, note the friction.

       Note: The Btuh requirement may be converted to gpm by dividing Btuh by 10,000 (based on a 20°F temperature drop). Zone 1 requires 18,379 Btuh or 1.8 gpm.

       Use of the copper tubing chart is shown in Fig. 9-26. Based on this design, with the largest zone serving 18,379 Btuh, a ¾-in., Type L

FIGURE 9-24 / Determine zones

pipe would have a velocity of 1.7 ft per second (fps). Also from the chart it is determined that:

$$\text{Friction} = 1.4 \text{ ft per 100 ft}$$
$$= 168 \text{ millinches, per ft}$$

FIGURE 9-25 / Determine actual length of zone

9. List the fittings which the hot water will pass through in the complete circuit [beginning with the heating unit and going through the longest circuit (zone) and back to the heating unit] (Fig. 9-27).

10. Determine the equivalent elbows for each fitting from Fig. 9-45. Each fitting is converted into the equivalent length of pipe by first converting the fitting into an equivalent number of 90° elbows and then converting the elbows into equivalent length.

> In this design (Fig. 9-28), from Fig. 9-45, one boiler is equal to four 90° copper elbows or three 90° iron elbows. The equivalent length will be found in step 11.

11. Determine the total equivalent length of the fittings from Fig. 9-46. This table is based on the pipe size and the velocity in feet per second. The pipe was tentatively selected in step 7 and the velocity noted in step 8.

> In this design, a ¾-in. pipe and 1.7 fps have been selected. From Fig. 9-46, there is an equivalent length of 1.9 ft of pipe for every elbow. The equivalent length of the fittings is 154 ft (81 elbows × 1.9). Use of the table is shown in Fig 9-29.

12. Add the length of the longest circuit (zone), step 6, to the total equivalent length of fittings for the circuit, step 11.

> In this design, the longest circuit is 145 lineal ft (step 6), and the equivalent length of fittings is 154 lineal ft (step 11), for a total equivalent length of 299 lineal ft.

13. Determine the pressure head, using the friction head selected, step 8, and the total equivalent length of pipe, step 12, and Fig. 9-46.

9 / HOT WATER HEATING SYSTEMS AND DESIGN

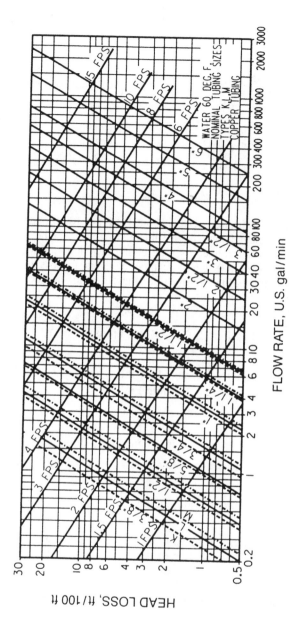

FLOW RATE, U.S. gal/min

Friction Loss for Water in Copper Tubing (Types K, L, M)

Reprinted with permission from ASHRAE, *Fundamentals Handbook*, 1989.

FIGURE 9-26 / Copper tubing friction loss

Longest Zone	Fittings No.
Boiler	1
Convectors	5
90° Elbows	17
Check Valves	2

FIGURE 9-27 / Fittings

In this design, the friction head is about 1.4 ft per 100 ft (step 8) and the total equivalent length is 299 lineal ft (step 12). The pressure head required is determined by multiplying the friction loss per 100 ft times the equivalent length of the pipe. Note that the loss is *per 100 ft*, and the equivalent length must be adjusted to the number of 100 ft required (299 lf = 2.99).

1.4 ft per 100 ft × 2.99 = 4.2 ft pressure head

14. Select the rest of the pipe sizes required for the system, using the friction head selected and the heat it must supply, from Fig. 9-44.

    Using 1.4 ft per 100 ft:
    Zone 2: 10,561 Btuh (1.1 gpm) = ¾-in. pipe required
    Main: 28,940 Btuh (2.9 gpm) = 1-in. main (Fig. 9-30)

    Return: After the two zones join, same as main = 1-in. pipe

15. Select the pump size required, using the gpm necessary with the required pressure head, from Fig. 9-47.

    In this design, the gpm is noted in step 8 as 1.8 gpm and the pressure head in step 13 as 4.2 ft. Use of the pump chart is shown in Fig. 9-31. Find the gpm along the bottom and move vertically; now find the pressure head along the left and move horizontally until they meet. On this chart an A pump would provide a pressure head of about 6.0 ft. (Do not use this chart for actual design; secure the manufacturer's performance ratings.)

16. Find the temperature drop for the total circuit based on the total friction head in millinches (friction times total equivalent length) times the design temperature drop for the system divided by the pressure head (pressure head in millinches equals pressure head in feet times 12,000).

Longest Zone Fittings

	No.	Equiv Elbows
Boiler	1	4
Convectors	5	20
90° Elbows	17	17
Check Valves	2	40
		81

FIGURE 9-28 / Equivalent elbows

$$\frac{\text{Friction head (millinches)} \times \text{Total equivalent length (ft)} \times \text{Design temperature}}{\text{Pressure head (ft)} \times 12,000}$$

In this design, the friction head is 168 millinches, the total equivalent length is 299 ft, the design temperature drop is 20°F and the pressure head is 4.2 ft.

$$\frac{168 \times 299 \text{ ft} \times 20°F}{4.2 \text{ ft} \times 12,000} = 19.9°F \text{ temperature drop in circuit}$$

17.   The next phase of the design is to determine how many lineal feet of exterior wall are available for radiation units of some type (Fig. 9-32). In a room with little or no exterior wall available, it may be necessary to use interior wall space.

FIGURE 9-29 / Equivalent lengths

Reprinted with permission from ASHRAE, *Fundamentals Handbook,* 1989.

Equivalent Length of Pipe for 90-Deg Elbows

Vel. Fps	Pipe Size														
	½	¾	1	1¼	1½	2	2½	3	3½	4	5	6	8	10	12
1	1.2	1.7	2.2	3.0	3.5	4.5	5.4	6.7	7.7	8.6	10.5	12.2	15.4	18.7	22.2
2	1.4	1.9	2.5	3.3	3.9	5.1	6.0	7.5	8.6	9.5	11.7	13.7	17.3	20.8	24.8
3	1.5	2.0	2.7	3.6	4.2	5.4	6.4	8.0	9.2	10.2	12.5	14.6	18.4	22.3	26.5
4	1.5	2.1	2.8	3.7	4.4	5.6	6.7	8.3	9.6	10.6	13.1	15.2	19.2	23.2	27.6
5	1.6	2.2	2.9	3.9	4.5	5.9	7.0	8.7	10.0	11.1	13.6	15.8	19.8	24.2	28.8
6	1.7	2.3	3.0	4.0	4.7	6.0	7.2	8.9	10.3	11.4	14.0	16.3	20.5	24.9	29.6
7	1.7	2.3	3.0	4.1	4.8	6.2	7.4	9.1	10.5	11.7	14.3	16.7	21.0	25.5	30.3
8	1.7	2.4	3.1	4.2	4.9	6.3	7.5	9.3	10.8	11.9	14.6	17.1	21.5	26.1	31.0
9	1.8	2.4	3.2	4.3	5.0	6.4	7.7	9.5	11.0	12.2	14.9	17.4	21.9	26.6	31.6
10	1.8	2.5	3.2	4.3	5.1	6.5	7.8	9.7	11.2	12.4	15.2	17.7	22.2	27.0	32.0

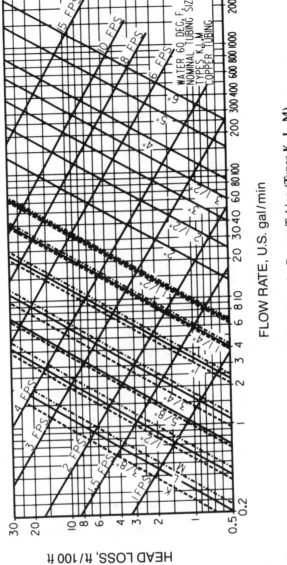

Friction Loss for Water in Copper Tubing (Types K, L, M)

Reprinted with permission from ASHRAE, *Fundamentals Handbook*, 1989.

FIGURE 9-30 / Main sizing

9 / *HOT WATER HEATING SYSTEMS AND DESIGN*

CAPACITY IN GALLONS PER MINUTE

Courtesy of The Hydronics Institute.

FIGURE 9-31 / Pump performance

18. Calculate the temperature drop for each radiation unit served through the circuit, and record it in the tabulated form (Fig. 9-33) under "System Temperature Drop." The formula used to calculate the temperature drop for each radiation unit(s) is:

$$\frac{\text{Radiation unit(s) heating capacity}}{\text{Circuit (zone) capacity}} \times \text{Temperature drop in total system}$$

19. Calculate the temperature in the circuit main, in a series loop or after the water returns from the radiation unit(s) served. Tabulate this temperature in the main

	BTUH Req.	L.F. of Ext. Wall
Entry	3,364	—
Dining	3,047	12
Kitchen	3,752	—
Living Room	8,216	10

FIGURE 9-32 / Exterior wall available

$$\text{ENTRY} \quad \frac{3{,}364}{18{,}379} \times 16.4 = 3.0°F$$

$$\text{DINING} \quad \frac{3{,}447}{18{,}379} \times .16.4 = 2.7°F$$

$$\text{KITCHEN} \quad \frac{3{,}752}{18{,}379} \times 16.4 = 3.4°F$$

$$\text{LIVING ROOM} \quad \frac{8{,}216}{18{,}379} \times 16.4 = 7.3°F$$

FIGURE 9-33 / Calculate temperature drop

in the form under "Main Temperature." *This is the entering temperature for each of the radiation units* (Fig. 9-34).

Note: If designing a series loop system, go directly to step 21a.

20. *Note: This step is used only in the one-pipe system. For all other systems go to step 21.*

Calculate the temperature drop of the water which is diverted through the radiation unit(s) and through the fitting used. The amount of water diverted depends on the size of the fitting used and location of the main above or below the radiation unit; Fig. 9-42 is used for this percentage of diversion.

$$\text{Radiation unit(s) temp. drop} = \frac{\text{Temp. drop in circuit (zone)}}{\text{Percent diversion}} \times 100$$

Note: The 100 is a constant and changes the percentage to a decimal equivalent.

Tabulate the temperature drop for the radiation unit(s) in the form (Fig. 9-35) under "Radiation Unit Temperature Drop."

FIGURE 9-34 / Calculate temperature in main

	ENTER TEMP ° F	TEMP LOSS IN CONVECTOR °F
ENTRY	200.0	3.0
DINING	197.0	2.7
KITCHEN	194.3	3.4
LIVING ROOM	190.7	7.3

ROOM OR UNIT	ENTER TEMP	RADIATION UNIT TEMP DROP

FIGURE 9-35 / Calculate temperature drop in devices

21. Calculate the average temperature.

   a. *Series loop only.* Calculate the average temperature in the radiation unit(s) by subtracting one-half of the temperature drop from the entering temperature of the circuit main. Tabulate the average temperature in the form under ''Average Radiation Temperature.''

   b. *All except series loop.* Calculate the average temperature in the radiation unit(s) by subtracting one-half of the temperature drop which occurs in the radiation units (from step 16) from the entering temperature of the circuit main. Tabulate the average temperature in the form under ''Average Radiation Temperature.''

22. Next, the heat emission rate of radiation required is determined by dividing the heat loss for each room by the available length of exterior wall.

23. Select the type of radiation unit(s) to be used based on the maximum emission rate required.

24. Determine the length or amount of radiation unit(s) required to evenly heat each room by dividing the heat loss of the room by the heat emission rate of the radiation unit(s) selected. Tabulate the lengths on the form.

25. Size the compression tank by determining the entire volume of water in the system and then finding the amount of expansion based on a temperature rise of 150°F (from 50°F entering to 200°F heated) times $(0.0041t - 0.0466)$ the net coefficient of expansion of the water. The compression tank must be sized to accommodate this water expansion. The volume of water in the system is determined from the table in Fig. 9-40.

FIGURE 9–36 / Calculate average temperature drop

	ENTER	LEAVE	AVE.
ENTRY	200.0	197.0	198.5
DINING	197.0	194.3	196.6
KITCHEN	194.3	190.9	192.6
LIVING ROOM	190.9	187.2	189.0
LIVING ROOM	187.2	183.6	185.4

	BTUH REQ.	L.F. OF EXT. WALL	HEAT EMISSION RATE
ENTRY	3,364	—	—
DINING	3,047	12	254
KITCHEN	3,752	—	—
LIVING ROOM	8,216	10	822

FIGURE 9–37 / *Required heat emission rate*

9-7   BOILERS

In residences the boiler (furnace) which provides the heat (either hot water or forced air) is commonly located in the basement or crawl space or in a first-floor utility room, but it may also be in the attic. Boilers are most commonly fired by natural gas or oil, and occasionally by electricity, coal or bottled gas.

The boiler selected must be large enough to supply all of the heat loss in the spaces as calculated. The boiler must also have enough extra capacity to compensate for heat loss which will occur in the pipes which circulate the hot water through the system (called pipe loss or pipe tax). In addition, an extra reserve capacity is required so that the boiler can provide heat quickly to warm up a ''cooled off'' space. This ''pickup'' allowance also provides some extra heating capacity when it is necessary to increase the temperature of a space several degrees, not merely to maintain a temperature. For example, a store which closes at 5 P.M. may turn its thermostat back to 60°F before closing. Then in the morning as the thermostat is raised to 68° or 70°F, it is necessary to have some extra capacity in the boiler to provide this extra heat as quickly as possible. Many buildings have automatic, timed thermostats which are used to regulate the temperatures throughout the day.

Typically, the designer allows about 33⅓% for the heat loss in the pipes and an additional 15% to 20% as a pick-up allowance, in addition to the calculated heat loss of the building. For example, in the residence being designed:

Calculated heat loss	29,000 Btuh
Piping loss (33⅓%)	+ 9,700
	38,700
Pick-up allowance (20%)	+ 7,700
Total	46,400 Btuh

Spaces which are heated intermittently, such as a church or an auditorium, will have to have a much larger pick-up allowance, perhaps as much as 50%. This is because the temperature will often be allowed to drop quite low (perhaps 50°F) when the space is not in use, and then when the heat is raised to 70°F, it must heat up quickly.

While most designers simply allow a certain percentage for piping loss, it can be calculated—but only once the piping layout is finalized and the installation decided

Hot Water Output*
1 gal. flow rate
(for 5 gal. flow rate use factor 1.067)

Copper-Aluminum Elements	220°	210°	200°	190°	180°
2¾" × 3¾" × .011 × 50/ft. 1" tube	1240	1120	1020 ←	930	840
2¾" × 5" × .020 × 40/ft. 1¼" tube	1250	1120	1030	940	850
2¾" × 5" × .020 × 50/ft. 1¼" tube	1340	1200	1100	1000	910

FIGURE 9-38 / Select radiation unit(s)

	BTUH REQ.	L.F.OF EXT.WALL	AVE. TEMP	AVE.HEAT EMISSION	LENGTH REQ.
ENTRY	3,364	—	198.5	1006	3.35'
DINING	3,047	12	196.6	989	3.08'
KITCHEN	3,752	—	192.6	953	3.93'
LIVING ROOM	4,108	10	189.0	921	4.46'
LIVING ROOM	4,108	—	185.4	888	4.68'

FIGURE 9-39 / Determine lengths of radiation unit(s)

upon and specified. From the piping layout it would be necessary to determine the length of pipe and the various temperatures of the air through which the pipe travels. Where the pipe travels through an unheated basement or attic, the heat loss would be much greater than the heat loss of the same pipe traveling through a heated space.

Once the piping loss and the pick-up allowance have been taken into account, the boiler size may be selected. The boiler selected should be as close to the total Btuh as

FIGURE 9-40 / Size expansion tank

Volume of Water
in Standard Pipe and Tube

Nominal Pipe Size In.	Standard Steel Pipe			Type L Copper Tube	
	Schedule No.	Inside Dia In.	Gallons per Lin Ft	Inside Dia In.	Gallons per Lin Ft
3/8	—	—	—	0.430	0.0075
1/2	40	0.622	0.0157	0.545	0.0121
5/8	—	—	—	0.666	0.0181
3/4	40	0.824	0.0277	0.785	0.0251
1	40	1.049	0.0449	1.025	0.0429
1 1/4	40	1.380	0.0779	1.265	0.0653
1 1/2	40	1.610	0.106	1.505	0.0924
2	40	2.067	0.174	1.985	0.161
2 1/2	40	2.469	0.249	2.465	0.248
3	40	3.068	0.384	2.945	0.354
3 1/2	40	3.548	0.514	3.425	0.479
4	40	4.026	0.661	3.905	0.622
5	40	5.047	1.04	4.875	0.970
6	40	6.065	1.50	5.845	1.39
8	30	8.071	2.66	7.725	2.43
10	30	10.136	4.19	9.625	3.78
12	30	12.090	5.96	11.565	5.46

Reprinted with permission from ASHRAE, *HVAC Handbook*, 1987.

9 / HOT WATER HEATING SYSTEMS AND DESIGN

possible to provide the most efficient operation. Keep in mind that the outside design temperature used will not actually occur very often, that the boiler will be operating at less than full capacity during most of the time and that the pickup allowance also gives a little extra capacity. Also, oversizing the boiler will probably be of little value during any unusually long cold spells with temperatures well below the outside design temperature unless the radiation or convector units selected are able to put out additional heat.

In large projects (institutional and commercial) quite often two boilers are used. Since boilers are more efficient the longer they operate, the first boiler would be designed to satisfy about 60% of the heat required, and the second would supply the balance. In this way, the first unit would come on and supply the heat required for about 75% of the days that heat is needed. Only during colder weather would the second unit turn on. The more efficient operation of the smaller first unit (when compared with the operation of a single boiler) pays for the added cost of a second unit. Also, this provides a backup unit in case one of the boilers requires repairs.

9-8 INSTALLED AND EXISTING SYSTEMS

No matter how carefully a system is designed and laid out, there is the possibility that at least a portion of the building is not being heated satisfactorily. This, of course, is also true of many existing systems. Quite often the problems in these systems can be corrected easily and relatively inexpensively after a careful analysis of the system.

First, carefully take notes as to exactly what the problem is, what time of day it is most noticeable, what the outside temperature is during the time that sufficient heat is not being properly distributed and whether the boiler is running continuously or intermittently.

For example, in Fig. 9-41, note first that the general complaint is that the temperature of the entire house dropped to about 60° to 62°F during the night. During the day, it warmed up to the 70°F reading desired. The outside temperature that night reached a low of about −10°F, well below the design temperature of 0°F used for Albany, N.Y. (the location of the residence).

FIGURE 9-41 / Complaints

Complaint: Temperature in house 60° to 62°F during night, it raised to desired temperature during the day.

Heating equipment: hot water, working alright
Outside temperature —20°F
Wind: light
Boiler water temperature: 180°F

The first observation is that the outside temperature during the night was about 10°F below the outside design temperature and the inside temperature registers about 8°F below the thermostat setting. So, the problem is how to get more heat out of the baseboard convector radiators installed in the house. The first possibility is to check the temperature to which the boiler is heating the hot water. Each boiler has a thermostat which sets the highest temperature to which it can heat the water, and then the boiler will shut off while the circulating pumps continue to push hot water through the system.

It is most important to know whether or not the boiler was operating continuously or intermittently. Quite often the occupant confuses the fact that the pipes were hot and the hot water was being circulated with the actual boiler operation. It may be necessary to have the occupant obtain more information about the boiler operation before the system is corrected. If the boiler is operating continuously, it indicates that no matter how hard the boiler works, it cannot heat the water to the thermostat setting. When the boiler operates intermittently, it means that the boiler has heated the water to the thermostat setting and is waiting for cooler water to circulate to it before starting again. Intermittent operation is most commonly found and will be discussed first.

Typically, the boiler thermostat is set at 170° or 180°F during installation. Keeping in mind that the amount of heat delivered by the convectors will increase with hotter water (Sec. 9-5, Fig. 9-20), the solution may be to increase the thermostat setting of the boiler. The hot water, in a closed heating system such as this, can be heated as high as 220°F. Generally, for every increase of 10°F in water temperature, the heat output of the radiation or convector units is increased about 10%. Intermittent operation is the most common problem and, fortunately, this is the most common solution.

If the temperature *is* set high and the boiler is operating intermittently, the next solution is to provide additional heat in each room by some means. In most rooms the length of fin-tubed radiators may be increased, thus increasing the amount of heat which is put into the room. Many rooms have convector covers all along a wall, but check inside the cover; a great deal of that length may be plain tube and not finned tube. In such a case a plumber can add some fin-tubed element. It may be necessary to add extra lengths of finned tube on an interior wall or to put a convector or unit heater up in a wall where baseboard space is not available. Any revision or addition of this type must be carefully planned and may be costly. Unfortunately, I don't know of anyone who has marketed a snap-on finned tube which the occupants or owners could install themselves in such situations.

QUESTIONS

9-1. What are the differences between series loop and one-pipe hot water systems, and what are the advantages of each?

9-2. Discuss the two-pipe system, how it works and its advantages and disadvantages.

9-3. Why are multiple heating circuits (zones) often used?

9-4. How does a radiant hot water heating panel work?

9-5. What types of heating devices are available to distribute heat to a space?

9-6. What is the one variable which affects the amount of heat given out by a finned-tube convector?

9-7. What type of system is most commonly used in a residence?

Design Exercises

9-8. Design a series loop system, two zones, for the residence in Appendix C, page 531, based on the heat loss calculations from Exercise 8-15.

9-9. Design a one-pipe system, two zones, for the residence in Appendix B, page 530, based on the heat loss calculations from Exercise 8-15.

9-10. Design a series loop system, one zone, for the apartments in Appendix A, page 529, based on the heat loss calculations from Exercise 8-17.

Notes: 1. The chart is based on straight tees, that is, branches A, B, and C are the same size.

2. Head loss in desired circuit is obtained by selecting proper curve according to illustrations, determining the flow at the circled branch, and multiplying the head loss for the same size elbow at the flow rate in the circled branch by the equivalent elbows indicated.

3. When the size of an outlet is reduced the equivalent elbows shown in the chart do not apply. The maximum loss for any circuit for any flow will not exceed 2 elbow equivalents at the maximum flow (gpm) occurring in any branch of the tee.

4. The top curve of the chart is the average of 4 curves, one for each of the tee circuits illustrated.

Elbow Equivalents of Tees at
Various Flow Conditions[1,4]

Reprinted with permission from ASHRAE, *Fundamentals Handbook,* 1989.

FIGURE 9–42 / Elbow equivalents of tees

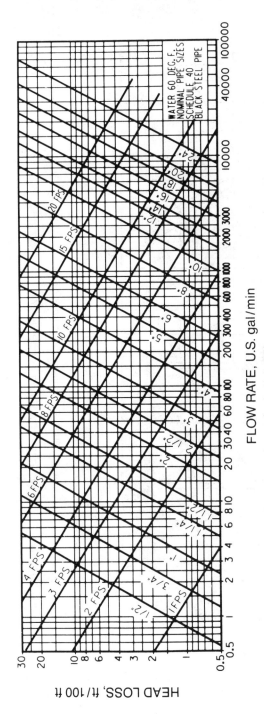

FLOW RATE, U.S. gal/min

Reprinted with permission from ASHRAE, *Fundamentals Handbook*, 1989.

FIGURE 9-43 / Friction loss for water in commercial steel pipe

277

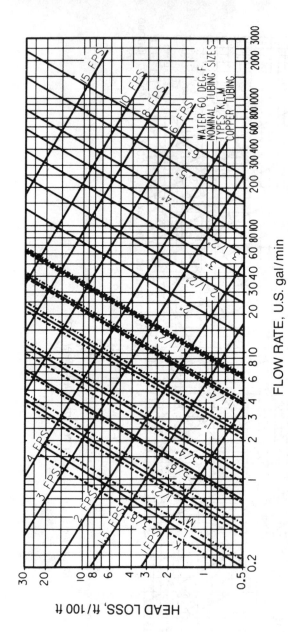

FLOW RATE, U.S. gal/min

HEAD LOSS, ft/100 ft

Reprinted with permission from ASHRAE, *Fundamentals Handbook*, 1989.

FIGURE 9-44 / Friction loss for water in copper tubing

Iron and Copper Elbow Equivalents

Fitting	Iron Pipe	Copper Tubing
Elbow, 90-deg	1.0	1.0
Elbow, 45-deg	0.7	0.7
Elbow, 90-deg long turn...	0.5	0.5
Elbow, welded, 90-deg....	0.5	0.5
Reduced coupling	0.4	0.4
Open return bend........	1.0	1.0
Angle radiator valve......	2.0	3.0
Radiator or convector	3.0	4.0
Boiler or heater	3.0	4.0
Open gate valve	0.5	0.7
Open globe valve	12.0	17.0

Reprinted with permission from ASHRAE, *Fundamentals Handbook,* 1989.

FIGURE 9-45 / Elbow equivalents

FIGURE 9-46 / Equivalent length of pipe
Reprinted with permission from ASHRAE, *Fundamentals Handbook,* 1989.

Equivalent Length of Pipe for 90-Deg Elbows

Vel. Fps.	½	¾	1	1¼	1½	2	2½	3	3½	4	5	6	8	10	12
1	1.2	1.7	2.2	3.0	3.5	4.5	5.4	6.7	7.7	8.6	10.5	12.2	15.4	18.7	22.2
2	1.4	1.9	2.5	3.3	3.9	5.1	6.0	7.5	8.6	9.5	11.7	13.7	17.3	20.8	24.8
3	1.5	2.0	2.7	3.6	4.2	5.4	6.4	8.0	9.2	10.2	12.5	14.6	18.4	22.3	26.5
4	1.5	2.1	2.8	3.7	4.4	5.6	6.7	8.3	9.6	10.6	13.1	15.2	19.2	23.2	27.6
5	1.6	2.2	2.9	3.9	4.5	5.9	7.0	8.7	10.0	11.1	13.6	15.8	19.8	24.2	28.8
6	1.7	2.3	3.0	4.0	4.7	6.0	7.2	8.9	10.3	11.4	14.0	16.3	20.5	24.9	29.6
7	1.7	2.3	3.0	4.1	4.8	6.2	7.4	9.1	10.5	11.7	14.3	16.7	21.0	25.5	30.3
8	1.7	2.4	3.1	4.2	4.9	6.3	7.5	9.3	10.8	11.9	14.6	17.1	21.5	26.1	31.0
9	1.8	2.4	3.2	4.3	5.0	6.4	7.7	9.5	11.0	12.2	14.9	17.4	21.9	26.6	31.6
10	1.8	2.5	3.2	4.3	5.1	6.5	7.8	9.7	11.2	12.4	15.2	17.7	22.2	27.0	32.0

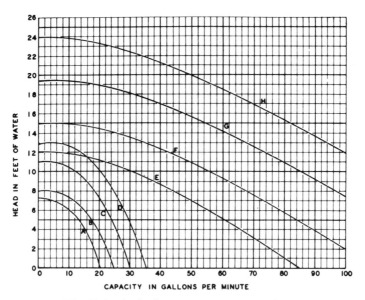

Courtesy of The Hydronics Institute.

FIGURE 9-47 / Pump performance

CHAPTER 10
FORCED AIR SYSTEM DESIGN (HEAT)

10-1   FORCED AIR SYSTEMS (HEATING)

A motor-driven fan is used to circulate filtered, heated air from a central heating unit through supply ducts to each of the rooms. As the hot air is delivered through the ducts and into the room through the supply outlet, cooler air from the space (room) is being returned through return grilles, into ducts, and back through the central heating unit to be heated and sent back to the space. The ducts may be circular or rectangular, and their size depends on the amount of heated air which must flow through them to maintain the desired temperature of the room. A variety of duct systems, or basic designs, may be used; several of the most common are shown in Fig. 10-1.

Forced air heating systems are economical and generally easy to install. Filters are put in the system to reduce the amount of dust in the air. The furnace (heating unit) may be located wherever convenient in the building including the basement, crawl space, attic, utility room, or garage, and in larger buildings it is sometimes located on the roof or in the structural systems.

Extended plenum supply

Individual supply system

Perimeter-loop system

FIGURE 10-1 / *Typical heating duct systems*

Humidifiers (discussed in Sec. 6-5) are recommended for use in most heating systems. They provide extra comfort at a minimal cost, making them a good investment. The humidifier will fit right into the duct system as it is being installed.

10-2 DUCTS AND FITTINGS

The ductwork is used to take the forced warm air from the furnace to the supply outlet and the cooler air from the return register back to the furnace.

The most commonly used materials for ducts are galvanized iron and aluminum. Both materials are relatively lightweight and easily shaped to whatever size duct is required, either round or rectangular. Minimum metal thicknesses required of these materials vary according to the size of the duct required and are shown in Fig. 10-2. These ducts may have to be insulated as discussed in Sec. 10-3.

Another very popular ductwork material is glass fiber, molded duct board. These ducts are available in a large variety of sizes, both round and rectangular. Its principal advantage is that for installations which need insulating (Sec. 10-3), it is less expensive and installed in one operation, as opposed to metal ducts which are installed in one operation and insulated in a second operation. The round fiber ducts are compatible with standard round metal ducts and may be used as part of a system which also uses metal ducts. The round fiber duct makes use of metal fittings to connect, reduce and make elbows as shown in Fig. 10-3. Another advantage of this type of duct is its excellent acoustic properties to ensure a quiet system. Fiber duct is also sometimes

10 / *FORCED AIR SYSTEM DESIGN (HEAT)*

Round Ducts Diameter, In.	Minimum Thickness		Minimum Weight of Tinplate
	Galv. Iron, U.S. Gage	Aluminum, B&S Gage	
Less than 14	30	26	
14 or more	28	24	IX (135 lb)
Rectangular Ducts Width, In.	Minimum Thickness		Minimum Weight of Tinplate
	Galv. Iron, U.S. Gage	Aluminum, B&S Gage	
Ducts Enclosed in Partions			
14 or less	30	26	
Over 14	28	24	IX (135 lb)
Ducts Not Enclosed in Partions			
Less than 14	28	24	—
14 or more	26	23	—

Note: The table is in accordance with Standard 90B of the National Board of Fire Underwriters.® Industry practice is to use heavier gage metals where maximum duct widths exceed 24 in (see also NBFU No 90A). Reprinted with permission from ASHRAE, Systems Handbook, 1976

FIGURE 10-2 / Metal duct thicknesses

used for the section of ductwork connecting the main trunk supply and the return lines to the furnace (Fig. 10-4).

Where the ducts will be in and under a concrete slab, an asbestos-cement round duct is most commonly used. Ducts placed below a slab must be made from a material which is not subject to moisture transmission or corrosion by concrete, will not float as the concrete is poured and is noncombustible. The asbestos-cement duct is available with inside diameters from 4 to 36 in. The ducts are joined with an impermeable rubber sleeve and two stainless steel straps (Fig. 10-5). The tees, wyes, elbows, reducers, and end caps are also made of asbestos-cement. This type of duct material is much more expensive than the fiber glass or metal and is rarely used except, for example, for installations in or under a concrete slab.

Oftentimes the ducts are made an integral part of the construction of the building, especially the returns which handle cooler air. In large buildings (hospitals, nursing

FIGURE 10-3 / Fiber duct connections

FIGURE 10-4 / Fiber duct as connection

FIGURE 10-5 / Asbestos-cement
duct connection

homes, office buildings) the ceiling area over a corridor is sometimes used as an air return (also called an *air plenum*.). A typical section through a corridor with an air plenum above it is shown in Fig. 10-6. The ceiling used should be tight fitting so that the air will not "leak" out of the space. Quite often gypsum board is used. The spaces between joists may also be used for air returns, with the bottom usually formed from sheet metal nailed to the bottom of the joists (Fig. 10-7). If the joist runs through cold spaces, it may be desirable to insulate the underside of the return. Also, the designer must check to be certain that the joists run in the direction which the return air must run.

A wide variety of fittings may be used to make all of the reductions, branch take-offs, turns, and bends required in many duct systems. Ideally, the best system layout has the fewest and simplest duct fittings since fittings restrict the flow of the forced air and increase the friction in the system. The friction of the various fittings used must be included in the duct size calculations. In order to calculate the amount of pressure lost in a fitting, it is estimated as the number of feet of straight run that would equal the friction loss in that fitting. It is called *equivalent length*.

EXAMPLE

The friction loss of boot fitting A (which is the piece used to connect the branch duct to the supply register) is listed in Fig. 10-33 as A-30. This means that the friction loss in the best fitting is the equivalent length of 30 ft of straight duct.

During the duct design, it will be necessary to make preliminary selections of fittings so that the duct design will be as accurate as possible. Fittings and their equivalent lengths are given in Fig. 10-33.

FIGURE 10-6 / Return air plenum

FIGURE 10-7 / Joists as ducts

Supply ducts should be equipped with an adjustable locking-type damper (Fig. 10-8) so that the air volume can be controlled. The damper should be located in an accessible spot in the branch duct as far from the supply outlet as possible. This allows a measure of control over the flow of the air and also allows a branch to be shut off when desired.

Splitter dampers (Fig. 10-9) are used to direct part of the air into the branch where it is taken off the trunk. They do not give precise volume control.

Squeeze dampers (Fig. 10-10) are placed in a duct to provide a means to control the air volume in the duct.

Turning vanes may be used to direct the flow of air smoothly around a corner or a bend, as shown in Fig. 10-11.

The entire system should be checked to be certain that proper attention has been given to the elimination of as much noise as possible from the system. The following suggestions will help keep noise to a minimum (see also Chapter 20).

1. The furnace and metal ducts should be connected with a flexible fire-resistant fabric. In this manner, any noises or vibrations will not be transmitted directly through the system (Fig. 10-12).

FIGURE 10-8 / Adjustable dampers

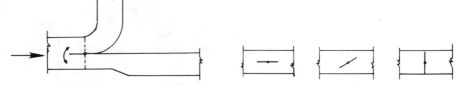

FIGURE 10-9 / Splitter damper   FIGURE 10-10 / Squeeze dampers

2.   All electrical conduits and pipes should have flexible connections to the furnace.

3.   Do not locate the return air immediately adjacent to the furnace.

4.   Do not install a fan directly below the return air grille.

10-3   DUCT INSULATION

Ducts which are located in heated spaces do not need to be insulated. But ducts which run through enclosed, unheated spaces or in spaces which are exposed to outdoor temperatures should be insulated. While glass fiber ducts are made of an insulating material (the glass fiber), sheet metal ducts must be wrapped in an insulation. Thicknesses of insulation recommended are:

Supply ducts:

1.   When located in enclosed, unheated spaces—1 in. of insulation.

2.   When located in a space in which it is exposed to outdoor temperatures—2 in. of insulation.

Return ducts: When not located in a heated space, use 1 in. of insulation.

The most commonly used insulation on residential and small commercial buildings is fiberglass with a facing of reinforced aluminum foil vapor-barrier which goes to the outside. In large buildings, the ducts may be sprayed with an insulating/fire-resistant coating.

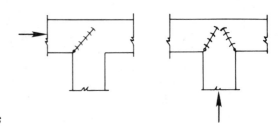

FIGURE 10-11 / Turning vanes

FIGURE 10-12 / Boiler-duct connection

| Return duct | | Furnace | | Supply duct |

10-4   SUPPLY AND RETURN LOCATIONS

This information given on the location of supply and return ducts is for installations where only heating will be supplied or in areas where heat is required much of the time while any cooling requirements are small. (For example, in an upstate New York residence, heat will probably be required regularly for about six to seven months, October 15–May 15, and air conditioning intermittently for two months.)

The supply registers should be located in the floor, 4 in. out from the baseboard, or be very low in an exterior wall (Fig. 10-13) and near or under windows, in exterior walls and near exterior doors. In effect, put the heat supplying registers as close as possible to the spots where the most heat is lost. These registers should have both vertical and horizontal dampers (Fig. 10-14) so that the air will be directed downward at the floor by the horizontal dampers and diffused to the sides by the vertical dampers.

Returns are often located on interior walls, in hallways, and in exposed corners.

A low baseboard location is required for a return on the floor, and a centrally located return, perhaps one for a small residence and two for a large one, provides satisfactory results. If there is only one central return, it is important to put it in a location where it will be able to draw return air from as much of the building as possible. This is why they are frequently located in hallways. More expensive, individual room exhausts may be used if the designer feels that the layout of rooms may cause an uneven return of air or that the air flow from the rooms to the return (under doorways or through adjoining rooms) may cause a problem. For example, if there is a central return in the hallway and the door to a bedroom is closed all night, it will be very difficult for air to flow from the room to the return, unless the bottom of the door

FIGURE 10-13 / Register location

Floor register   Low wall register

Horizontal dampers

Vertical dampers

FIGURE 10-14 / Register dampers

is trimmed (undercut) up about an inch or so. Unless air is drawn from the room as the supply keeps bringing air into the room, a slight pressure is built up in the room, reducing the amount of warm air coming through the supply outlets, and the room will tend to be cool. The same situation will occur in any other room closed off from the return. If the designer is aware that such a problem may exist, the solution would be to put a separate return in the room.

The returns are covered with grilles which are put over the opening primarily to "cover it up" so there won't be a big hole in the wall. There are no movable dampers. The type of grille used will determine the required grille size (in conjunction with the cfm required for the system). This is because air can only flow through the openings in the grille (called the *face openings*) and not through the material. Therefore, the percentage of face opening for the grille used must be determined from the manufacturer's specifications. The register must be proportionally larger than the return duct, based on the percentage of face opening of the grille required. For example, if a grille with 50% face opening is used on a 20-in. x 14-in. duct carrying 1,400 cfm, it will be necessary to have a grille twice as large as the duct branch (or trunk).

10-5 FURNACE LOCATION

Furnaces for forced air systems are available in various designs so that they may be located in the basement, crawl space, attic, or first floor of the building. In addition, each is usually classified in terms of the direction in which the air is delivered. The three basic types are *upflow, counter flow,* and *horizontal,* and there are several variations depending on the actual installation (Fig. 10-15). A lowboy-style (upflow) furnace (Fig. 10-15) is installed in the basement of a building, and the air is delivered to the building through ducts from the top of the boiler.

The highboy (upflow) furnace (Fig. 10-15) is used primarily in single-level homes when the ducts are placed in the attic. This may be because of the slab on grade construction or because there is limited crawl space. The furnace may be located in a closet or recessed area in the wall. The air enters the furnace through a low side entry or through the bottom, and it leaves through the top.

The counterflow (downflow) furnace (Fig. 10-15) is used primarily where it is preferable to have the furnace in the building, on the first floor, and not in a crawl space. The air enters the furnace at the top, and it leaves through the bottom. It is usually used with crawl spaces and slabs on grade. While it may be used in a building

Lowboy (upflow)

Highboy (upflow)

Counterflow

Horizontal

Horizontal

FIGURE 10-15 / Boiler locations

with a basement, such buildings usually have the furnace located in the basement.

The horizontal furnace (Fig. 10-15) is used primarily in homes with crawl spaces or concrete slab floors (i.e., no basement). The furnace may be set off the ground in the crawl space, placed in the attic or suspended from posts in an attic or utility room. The air enters the furnace at one end, and it leaves through the opposite end.

Combinations of systems are often used in larger homes and in many industrial, commercial or institutional buildings. In a two-story home it may be desirable to heat the first floor with an upflow furnace in the basement and the second floor with a horizontal furnace in the attic.

Furnace Location / 10-5

STEP-BY-STEP APPROACH

1.   Determine the heat loss of each individual room and list them.

From Chapter 8 the heat loss for each room is taken as:

2.   Next, determine the location and number of supply outlets (in this case, located on outside walls under windows; read Sec. 10-4 for a complete discussion) and return air intakes. Sketch the proposed locations on the floor plan as shown in Fig. 10-17. As a general rule, in residential design, no one supply outlet should supply more than 8,000 Btuh.

   Figure 10-17 has a proposed layout for the ductwork. The ducts are shown as single lines and the outlets as rectangles, and the Btuh for each outlet is listed.

   Figure 10-18 has a tabulation of each supply outlet and the Btuh.

3.   Note on the sketch the types of fittings which will be used and the actual length of each duct. The fittings may be selected from Fig. 10-33, which also gives the equivalent length for each type of fitting. The plan in Fig. 10-18 shows the fittings and their equivalent lengths.

   Now, on the sketch, note the actual length of each run. Then add the equivalent and actual lengths for each run to obtain the total equiv-

FIGURE 10-16 / Room heat loss

	BTUH
Entry	3,364
Dining	3,047
Kitchen	3,752
Living	8,216
Bedroom 3	3,008
Bath	960
Bedroom 1	4,085
Bedroom 2	2,310
Int. Bath	198
	28,940

FIGURE 10-17 / Duct schematic

alent length for each run from the bonnet to the supply outlet (Fig. 10-19).

The tabulated total equivalent length of each run is:

4. Furnace size and cfm.

a. A tentative furnace size should be selected and the manufacturer's specifications give the cfm. The total cfm should not be less than 400 cfm per 12,000 Btuh.

$$\frac{28,940}{12,000} \times 400 = 965 \text{ cfm minimum (use 1,000)}$$

5. Calculate the cfm required from each of the supply outlets by dividing the Btuh of each supply outlet by the total Btuh and multiplying by the total air flow (cfm).

In this design, for bedroom 1:

$$\frac{4,283}{28,940} \times 1,000 = 148 \text{ cfm}$$

Supply Outlet	Heat Loss (BTUH)
Bedroom #1	4,283
Bedroom #2	2,310
Living	4,108
Living	4,108
Kitchen	3,752
Dining	3,047
Entry	1,682
Hall	1,682
Bedroom #3	3,008
Bath	960
Total	28,940

FIGURE 10-18 / Heat loss for each outlet

Following this example, calculate the required cfm for each room and tabulate as shown (Fig. 10-20).

6. Bonnet pressure.

   a. The bonnet pressure is selected next. The approximate bonnet pressure required for a trunk (main duct) to carry the maximum volume of air (cfm) is found in Fig. 10-36.

   In this design, the total cfm required is 1,000 (the total of all the supply outlets). From Fig. 10-36, for quiet operation in a residence (Type A), the suggested bonnet pressure is a minimum of 0.10 in. of water.

   b. If a furnace has been selected, the rated capacity of the unit must be checked, and its pressure used. In this design assume a furnace with 0.12 in. of water was selected.

7. The available bonnet pressure is divided proportionally by length between the supply and return runs. In perimeter heating (Fig. 10-1), the supply runs are longer than the returns, and a 0.12 in-pressure might be divided with 75% on the supply and 25% on the return. For other systems the sketch plan layout shows the approximate proportion of supply to return runs.

Outlet	Equivalent length	Actual length	Total equivalent length
Bedroom (1)	F 35 B 15 G 30 80	36	116
Bedroom (2)	F 35 + 25 B 15 G 30 105	26	131
Living 1	F 35 B 15 + 25 G 30 105	33	138
2	F 35 B 15 G 30 80	55	135
Kitchen	F 35 B 15 G 30 80	46	126
Dining	F 35 + 25 B 15 G 30 105	27	132
Entry 1	F 35 + 25 B 15 E 10 G 30 115	16	131
2	F 35 B 15 G 30 80	10	90
Bedroom (3)	F 35 + 25 B 15 G 30 105	30	135
Bath	F 35 B 15 E 10 G 30 90	25	115

FIGURE 10-19(a) / Equivalent lengths

Supply Outlet	Heat Loss (BTUH)	Actual Length (ft)	Equivalent Length (ft)	Total Equiv. Length (ft)
Bedroom #1	4,283	36	80	116
Bedroom #2	2,310	26	105	131
Living	4,108	33	105	138
Living	4,108	55	80	135
Kitchen	3,752	46	80	126
Dining	3,047	27	105	132
Entry	1,682	16	115	131
Hall	1,682	10	80	90
Bedroom #3	3,008	30	105	135
Bath	960	25	90	115
Totals	28,940			

FIGURE 10-19(b) / Total equivalent lengths (continued)

The sketch plan layout in Fig. 10-17 shows that there are longer supply than return runs, so a division of 0.09 in. for supply and 0.03 in. for return is selected and tabulated (Fig. 10-21).

Note: If later during the design the proportion selected does not provide satisfactory results, it can be reapportioned between supply and return.

8. Next, the supply outlet size and its pressure loss are selected from the manufacturer's engineering data. A typical example of the manufacturer's data is shown

Supply Outlet	Heat Loss (BTUH)	Actual Length (ft)	Equivalent Length (ft)	Total Equiv. Length (ft)	Heating CFM
Bedroom #1	4,283	36	80	116	148
Bedroom #2	2,310	26	105	131	80
Living	4,108	33	105	138	142
Living	4,108	55	80	135	142
Kitchen	3,752	46	80	126	130
Dining	3,047	27	105	132	105
Entry	1,682	16	115	131	58
Hall	1,682	10	80	90	58
Bedroom #3	3,008	30	105	135	104
Bath	960	25	90	115	33
Totals	28,940				1,000

FIGURE 10-20 / Heating cfm required

in Fig. 13–14. Typically, the pressure loss will range from 0.01 to 0.02 in., and many designers simply allow 0.02 in.

In this design the pressure loss has been tabulated in Fig. 10-22.

9. Next, the actual pressure which is available for duct loss is obtained by subtracting the supply outlet loss (step 8) from the total pressure available for supply runs (Fig. 10-22).

In this design, the pressure for supply runs is 0.09 in. Beginning with the bedroom 1 supply run, from step 8 the supply outlet loss is 0.02 in., so for this run, the pressure available for actual duct loss is 0.09 in. − 0.02 in. = 0.07 in. Calculate the actual pressure available for duct loss for each of the supply runs, and tabulate the information as shown (Fig. 10-23):

10. In order to make a workable table of duct sizes, the pressure drop for duct loss must be calculated as the pressure drop per *100 ft* of the duct. Since the various supply runs are all different lengths, it is necessary to find the allowable *pressure drop per 100 ft* based on the *allowable duct loss* and the *total equivalent length*

Supply Outlet	Heat Loss (BTUH)	Actual Length (Ft)	Equivalent Length (Ft)	Total Equiv. Length (Ft)	Heating CFM	Supply Air Pressure
Bedroom #1	4,283	36	80	116	148	0.09
Bedroom #2	2,310	26	105	131	80	0.09
Living	4,108	33	105	138	142	0.09
Living	4,108	55	80	135	142	0.09
Kitchen	3,752	46	80	126	130	0.09
Dining	3,047	27	105	132	105	0.09
Entry	1,682	16	115	131	58	0.09
Hall	1,682	10	80	90	58	0.09
Bedroom #3	3,008	30	105	135	104	0.09
Bath	960	25	90	115	33	0.09
Totals	28,940				1,000	

FIGURE 10-21 / Supply air pressure

of the supply run. This allowable pressure drop is calculated by using the equation:

$$\text{Allowable pressure drop per 100 ft} = \frac{\text{Allowable duct loss} \times 100}{\text{Total equivalent length}}$$

In this design, the bedroom 1 supply run has an allowable duct loss of .07 in. (step 11) and an equivalent length of 116 ft (step 3). Using the formula to determine the allowable pressure drop per 100 ft,

$$\text{Allowable pressure drop per 100 ft} = \frac{0.07 \text{ in.} \times 100 \text{ ft.}}{116 \text{ ft}} = 0.60 \text{ in.}$$

Calculate the allowable pressure drop per 100 ft for each supply run, and tabulate the information as shown (Fig. 10-24):

11. The branch duct sizes may be determined by using the table in Fig. 10-34 or by using an air duct calculator (Fig. 10-25) if one is available. The table in Fig.

10 / FORCED AIR SYSTEM DESIGN (HEAT)

Supply Outlet	Heat Loss (BTUH)	Actual Length (Ft)	Equivalent Length (Ft)	Total Equiv. Length (Ft)	Heating CFM	Supply Air Pressure	Supply Outlet Pressure Loss
Bedroom #1	4,283	36	80	116	148	0.09	0.02
Bedroom #2	2,310	26	105	131	80	0.09	0.02
Living	4,108	33	105	138	142	0.09	0.02
Living	4,108	55	80	135	142	0.09	0.02
Kitchen	3,752	46	80	126	130	0.09	0.02
Dining	3,047	27	105	132	105	0.09	0.02
Entry	1,682	16	115	131	58	0.09	0.02
Hall	1,682	10	80	90	58	0.09	0.02
Bedroom #3	3,008	30	105	135	104	0.09	0.02
Bath	960	25	90	115	33	0.09	0.02
Totals	28,940				1,000		

FIGURE 10-22 / Supply outlet pressure

10-34 gives the size of the round duct based on the cfm required and the allowable pressure drop per 100 ft (step 12). The size of the round duct may be converted to an equivalent rectangular duct size which will handle the required cfm within the allowable pressure drop.

In this design, the bedroom 1 supply run has an allowable duct loss of 0.06 in. per 100 ft (step 12) and a required cfm of 148 (step 7). Using the table in Fig. 10-34 (partially reproduced for this design in Fig. 10-26), a 8.0 in. round duct would be selected. Figure 10-26 shows the use of the table. Begin by finding the pressure drop per 100 ft across the bottom; then move up the right side to the required cfm; then move horizontally to the left and vertically from the bottom (friction loss) to read the round duct size required.

From Fig. 10-34, determine the round duct sizes for each of the supply runs, and tabulate the information as shown in Fig. 10-27.

The air duct calculator is used to obtain required round duct sizes by aligning the required air volume and the allowable pressure drop (friction) per 100 ft of duct and reading the round duct diameter directly from the calculator.

12. The round duct sizes selected in step 11 may be changed to equivalent rectangular duct sizes, carrying the same cfm required while maintaining the allowable

Supply Outlet	Heat Loss (BTUH)	Actual Length (Ft)	Equivalent Length (Ft)	Total Equiv. Length (Ft)	Heating CFM	Supply Air Pressure	Supply Outlet Pressure Loss	Pressure Avail. for Duct Loss
Bedroom #1	4,283	36	80	116	148	0.09	0.02	0.07
Bedroom #2	2,310	26	105	131	80	0.09	0.02	0.07
Living	4,108	33	105	138	142	0.09	0.02	0.07
Living	4,108	55	80	135	142	0.09	0.02	0.07
Kitchen	3,752	46	80	126	130	0.09	0.02	0.07
Dining	3,047	27	105	132	132	0.09	0.02	0.07
Entry	1,682	16	115	131	58	0.09	0.02	0.07
Hall	1,682	10	80	90	58	0.09	0.02	0.07
Bedroom #3	3,008	30	105	135	104	0.09	0.02	0.07
Bath	960	25	90	115	33	0.09	0.02	0.07
Totals	28,940				1,000			

FIGURE 10-23 / Available duct pressure

pressure drops. Using the table in Fig. 10-35, the 8.0-in. round duct for bedroom 1 can be changed to a rectangular duct of 10 in. x 5.5 in., 11 in. x 5 in. or 13 in. x 4.5 in. and others.

The rectangular duct sizes are found with one dimension along the top of the table and another along the side. Their circular equivalent is found where the two sizes intersect. For example, a 10″ x 5″ rectangular duct has a circular (round) duct equivalent of 7.6″.

To convert round ducts to rectangular find the circular equivalent in the center of the table and find the rectangular equivalents by reading up and to the side. Several different rectangular sizes can be used.

The actual size selected depends to a large extent on the space available for installation of the duct.

From Fig. 10-34 determine a rectangular duct size for each supply run which could be used instead of the round duct previously selected. Tabulate the rectangular duct sizes as shown (Fig. 10-29):

13. Add the air volumes of all of the branch supply runs from each trunk duct. When there is more than one trunk duct (such as in this design), keep the totals for each trunk duct separate.

Supply Outlet	Heat Loss (BTUH)	Actual Length (Ft)	Equivalent Length (Ft)	Total Equiv. Length (Ft)	Heating CFM	Supply Air Pressure	Supply Outlet Pressure Loss	Pressure Avail. for Duct Loss	Pressure Avail. Per 100 Ft
Bedroom #1	4,283	36	80	116	148	0.09	0.02	0.07	0.060
Bedroom #2	2,310	26	105	131	80	0.09	0.02	0.07	0.054
Living	4,108	33	105	138	142	0.09	0.02	0.07	0.051
Living	4,108	55	80	135	142	0.09	0.02	0.07	0.052
Kitchen	3,752	46	80	126	130	0.09	0.02	0.07	0.056
Dining	3,047	27	105	132	105	0.09	0.02	0.07	0.053
Entry	1,682	16	115	131	58	0.09	0.02	0.07	0.054
Hall	1,682	10	80	90	58	0.09	0.02	0.07	0.078
Bedroom #3	3,008	30	105	135	104	0.09	0.02	0.07	0.052
Bath	960	25	90	115	33	0.09	0.02	0.07	0.061
Totals	28,940				1,000				

FIGURE 10-24 / Pressure available (per 100 ft)

In this design, there are two trunk ducts (one toward the living room and kitchen, the other toward the bedrooms). Tabulate and total the air volume for each trunk duct as shown (Fig. 10-30).

14. For best air flow distribution through the ducts, it is important that the friction losses per 100 ft be approximately equal in both trunk ducts.

Using the table in Fig. 10-34, select the trunk sizes required. When there is more than one trunk duct, size each separately using the required air volume (cfm) and the allowable duct friction (step 10).

The bedroom trunk must handle 365 cfm with an allowable pressure drop of 0.54 in. per 100 ft. Using Fig. 10-34, the bedroom trunk duct will be an 8 inch round duct.

The living space trunk duct has 142 cfm and an allowable 0.051 in. per 100 ft pressure drop. Using Fig. 10-34, the living space trunk duct will be an 8-in. round duct.

Since the trunk ducts have been sized separately, based on cfm and allowable pressure drop, they are balanced.

The round duct sizes may be converted to rectangular duct sizes using Fig. 10-35. Once again, the space available for installa-

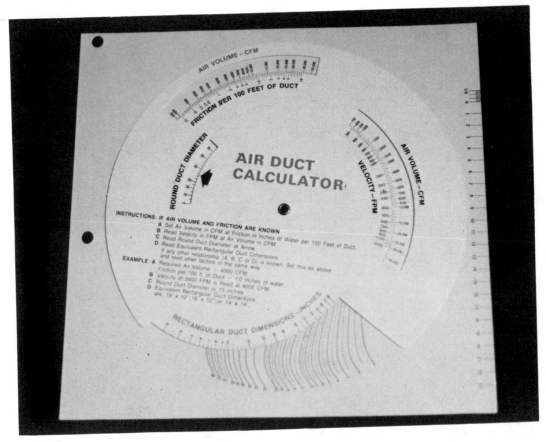

FIGURE 10-25 / Air duct calculator

tion will have a large influence on the shape of the rectangular duct
selected. Tabulate the trunk duct sizes as shown in Fig. 10-31:

15. Review the supply trunk duct to determine if it is desirable to reduce the size of
the duct as each duct leaves the trunk. Generally, such a reduction is suggested
so that the velocity of air through the duct will not drop too low. Using the
remaining air volume in the trunk duct, after each branch, and the allowable
pressure drop per 100 ft of duct (step 10), select the reduced trunk sizes from Fig.
10-34.

    Using tables in Fig. 10-34 and 10-35, determine the reduced trunk
    duct sizes for both the bedroom and the living space ducts, and
    tabulate the sizes as shown:

16. Next, the design turns to the return ducts. The first step is to select an allowable
return air pressure drop. This was previously decided (step 10), but it is reviewed

10 / FORCED AIR SYSTEM DESIGN (HEAT)

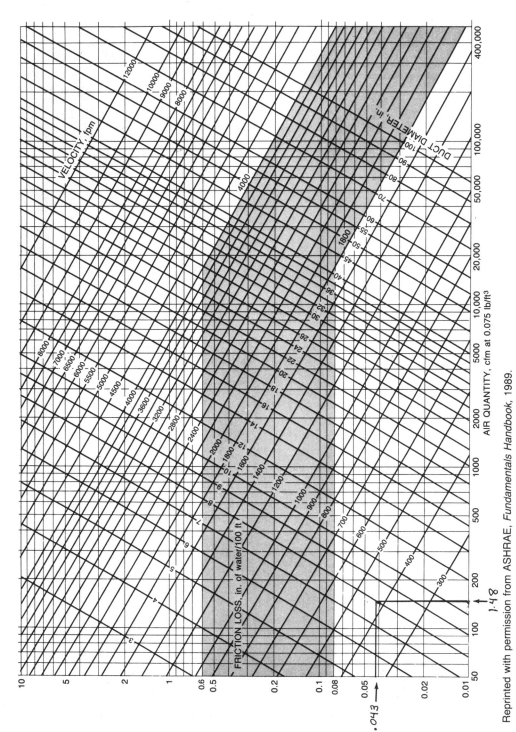

Reprinted with permission from ASHRAE, *Fundamentals Handbook*, 1989.

FIGURE 10-26 / Round duct selection

Supply Outlet	Heat Loss (BTUH)	Actual Length (Ft)	Equivalent Length (Ft)	Total Equiv. Length (Ft)	Heating CFM	Supply Air Pressure	Supply Outlet Pressure Loss	Pressure Avail. for Duct Loss	Pressure Avail. Per 100 Ft	Round Duct Size (In.)
Bedroom #1	4,283	36	80	116	148	0.09	0.02	0.07	0.060	8.0
Bedroom #2	2,310	26	105	131	80	0.09	0.02	0.07	0.054	7.0
Living	4,108	33	105	138	142	0.09	0.02	0.07	0.051	8.0
Living	4,108	55	80	135	142	0.09	0.02	0.07	0.052	8.0
Kitchen	3,752	46	80	126	130	0.09	0.02	0.07	0.056	8.0
Dining	3,047	27	105	132	105	0.09	0.02	0.07	0.053	7.0
Entry	1,682	16	115	131	58	0.09	0.02	0.07	0.054	6.0
Hall	1,682	10	80	90	58	0.09	0.02	0.07	0.078	4.0
Bedroom #3	3,008	30	105	135	104	0.09	0.02	0.07	0.052	7.0
Bath	960	25	90	115	33	0.09	0.02	0.07	0.061	5.0
Totals	28,940				1,000					

FIGURE 10-27 / Tabulated round duct sizes

at this point as the designer reviews the supply trunk and branch duct sizes to see if he might want to increase the duct sizes (reducing the allowable air pressure drop) or perhaps to reduce the duct sizes (increasing the allowable air pressure drop for the supply runs). Remember that a change in allowable air pressure drop for the supply will affect the allowable air pressure drop for the return runs.

A review of the supply duct sizes is made, and it is decided that they will not be revised. Therefore, the original decision, in step 7, to use 0.03 in. as the allowable pressure drop for the return is unchanged, and the return design will be based on it.

17. The return trunk duct size is determined by the air volume it must handle and the allowable pressure drop. This allowable pressure drop must be converted to allowable pressure drop *per 100 ft* just as was done for the supply runs. Using the air volume and the allowable pressure drop per 100 ft, the round return duct size may be selected from Fig. 10-34.

The rectangular duct of equivalent size may be found in Fig. 10-35. The return trunk duct will have to handle an air volume equal to what the supply trunk duct handled; from step 5 this was 1,000 cfm. The allowable pressure drop selected for the return was 0.03 in. (step 7). First, the allowable pressure drop must be converted into the allow-

Circular Equivalents of Rectangular Duct for Equal Friction and Capacity[a]

Lgth Adj[b]	4.0	4.5	5.0	5.5	6.0	6.5	7.0	7.5	8.0	9.0	10.0	11.0	12.0	13.0	14.0	15.0	16.0
											Length of One Side of Rectangular Duct (a), in.						
3.0	3.8	4.0	4.2	4.4	4.6	4.7	4.9	5.1	5.2	5.5	5.7	6.0	6.2	6.4	6.6	6.8	7.0
3.5	4.1	4.2	4.6	4.8	5.0	5.2	5.3	5.5	5.7	6.0	6.3	6.5	6.8	7.0	7.2	7.5	7.7
4.0	4.4	4.6	4.9	5.1	5.3	5.5	5.7	5.9	6.1	6.4	6.7	7.0	7.3	7.6	7.8	8.0	8.3
4.5	4.6	4.9	5.2	5.4	5.7	5.9	6.1	6.3	6.5	6.9	7.2	7.5	7.8	8.1	8.4	8.6	8.8
5.0	4.9	5.2	5.5	5.7	6.0	6.2	6.4	6.7	6.9	7.3	7.6	8.0	8.3	8.6	8.9	9.1	9.4
5.5	5.1	5.4	5.7	6.0	6.3	6.5	6.8	7.0	7.2	7.6	8.0	8.4	8.7	9.0	9.3	9.6	9.9

Length of One Side of Rectangular Duct (a), in.

Lgth Adj[b]	6	7	8	9	10	11	12	13	14	15	16	17	18	19	20	22	24	26	28	30	Lgth Adj[b]
6	6.6																				6
7	7.1	7.7																			7
8	7.6	8.2	8.7																		8
9	8.0	8.7	9.3	9.8																	9
10	8.4	9.1	9.8	10.4	10.9																10
11	8.8	9.5	10.2	10.9	11.5	12.0															11
12	9.1	9.9	10.7	11.3	12.0	12.6	13.1														12
13	9.5	10.3	11.1	11.8	12.4	13.1	13.7	14.2													13
14	9.8	10.8	11.4	12.2	12.9	13.5	14.2	14.7	15.3												14
15	10.1	11.0	11.8	12.6	13.3	14.0	14.6	15.3	15.8	16.4											15
16	10.4	11.3	12.2	13.0	13.7	14.4	15.1	15.7	16.4	16.9	17.5										16
17	10.7	11.6	12.5	13.4	14.1	14.9	15.6	16.2	16.8	17.4	18.0	18.6									17
18	11.0	11.9	12.9	13.7	14.5	15.3	16.0	16.7	17.3	17.9	18.5	19.1	19.7								18
19	11.2	12.2	13.2	14.1	14.9	15.7	16.4	17.1	17.8	18.4	19.0	19.6	20.2	20.8							19
20	11.5	12.6	13.5	14.4	15.2	16.0	16.8	17.5	18.2	18.9	19.5	20.1	20.7	21.3	21.9						20
22	12.0	13.0	14.1	15.0	15.9	16.8	17.6	18.3	19.1	19.8	20.4	21.1	21.7	22.3	22.9	24.0					22
24	12.4	13.5	14.6	15.6	16.5	17.4	18.3	19.1	19.9	20.6	21.3	22.0	22.7	23.3	23.9	25.1	26.2				24
26	12.8	14.0	15.1	16.2	17.1	18.1	19.0	19.8	20.6	21.4	22.1	22.9	23.5	24.2	24.9	26.1	27.3	28.4			26
28	13.2	14.5	15.6	16.7	17.7	18.7	19.6	20.5	21.3	22.1	22.9	23.7	24.4	25.1	25.8	27.1	28.3	29.5	30.6		28
30	13.6	14.9	16.1	17.2	18.3	19.3	20.2	21.1	22.0	22.9	23.7	24.4	25.2	25.9	26.6	28.0	29.3	30.5	31.7	32.8	30
32	14.0	15.3	16.5	17.7	18.8	19.8	20.8	21.8	22.7	23.5	24.4	25.2	26.0	26.7	27.5	28.9	30.2	31.5	32.7	33.9	32
34	14.4	15.7	17.0	18.2	19.3	20.4	21.4	22.4	23.3	24.2	25.1	25.9	26.7	27.5	28.3	29.7	31.0	32.4	33.7	34.9	34
36	14.7	16.1	17.4	18.6	19.8	20.9	21.9	22.9	23.9	24.8	25.7	26.6	27.4	28.2	29.0	30.5	32.0	33.3	34.6	35.9	36
38	15.0	16.5	17.8	19.0	20.2	21.4	22.4	23.5	24.5	25.4	26.4	27.2	28.1	28.9	29.8	31.3	32.8	34.2	35.6	36.8	38
40	15.3	16.8	18.2	19.5	20.7	21.8	22.9	24.0	25.0	26.0	27.0	27.9	28.8	29.6	30.5	32.1	33.6	35.1	36.4	37.8	40
42	15.6	17.1	18.5	19.9	21.1	22.3	23.4	24.5	25.6	26.6	27.6	28.5	29.4	30.3	31.2	32.8	34.4	35.9	37.3	38.7	42
44	15.9	17.5	18.9	20.3	21.5	22.7	23.9	25.0	26.1	27.1	28.1	29.1	30.0	30.9	31.8	33.5	35.1	36.7	38.1	39.5	44
46	16.2	17.8	19.3	20.6	21.9	23.2	24.4	25.5	26.6	27.7	28.7	29.7	30.6	31.6	32.5	34.2	35.9	37.4	38.9	40.4	46
48	16.5	18.1	19.6	21.0	22.3	23.6	24.8	26.0	27.1	28.2	29.2	30.2	31.2	32.2	33.1	34.9	36.6	38.2	39.7	41.2	48
50	16.8	18.4	19.9	21.4	22.7	24.0	25.2	26.4	27.6	28.7	29.8	30.8	31.8	32.8	33.7	35.5	37.2	38.9	40.5	42.0	50
52	17.1	18.7	20.2	21.7	23.1	24.4	25.7	26.9	28.0	29.2	30.3	31.3	32.3	33.3	34.3	36.2	37.9	39.6	41.2	42.8	52
54	17.3	19.0	20.6	22.0	23.5	24.8	26.1	27.3	28.5	29.7	30.8	31.8	32.9	33.9	34.9	36.8	38.6	40.3	41.9	43.5	54
56	17.6	19.3	20.9	22.4	23.8	25.2	26.5	27.7	28.9	30.1	31.2	32.3	33.4	34.4	35.4	37.4	39.2	41.0	42.7	44.3	56
58	17.8	19.5	21.2	22.7	24.2	25.5	26.9	28.2	29.4	30.6	31.7	32.8	33.9	35.0	36.0	38.0	39.8	41.6	43.3	45.0	58
60	18.1	19.8	21.5	23.0	24.5	25.9	27.3	28.6	29.8	31.0	32.2	33.3	34.4	35.5	36.5	38.5	40.4	42.3	44.0	45.7	60
62		20.1	21.7	23.3	24.8	26.3	27.6	28.9	30.2	31.5	32.6	33.8	34.9	36.0	37.1	39.1	41.0	42.9	44.7	46.4	62
64		20.3	22.0	23.6	25.1	26.6	28.0	29.3	30.6	31.9	33.1	34.3	35.4	36.5	37.6	39.6	41.6	43.5	45.3	47.1	64
66		20.6	22.3	23.9	25.5	26.9	28.4	29.7	31.0	32.3	33.5	34.7	35.9	37.0	38.1	40.2	42.2	44.1	46.0	47.7	66
68		20.8	22.6	24.2	25.8	27.3	28.7	30.1	31.4	32.7	33.9	35.2	36.3	37.5	38.6	40.7	42.8	44.7	46.6	48.4	68
70		21.1	22.8	24.5	26.1	27.6	29.1	30.4	31.8	33.1	34.4	35.6	36.8	37.9	39.1	41.2	43.3	45.3	47.2	49.0	70
72			23.1	24.8	26.4	27.9	29.4	30.8	32.2	33.5	34.8	36.0	37.2	38.4	39.5	41.7	43.8	45.8	47.8	49.6	72
74			23.3	25.1	26.7	28.2	29.7	31.2	32.5	33.9	35.2	36.4	37.7	38.8	40.0	42.2	44.4	46.4	48.4	50.3	74
76			23.6	25.3	27.0	28.5	30.0	31.5	32.9	34.3	35.6	36.8	38.1	39.3	40.5	42.7	44.9	47.0	48.9	50.9	76
78			23.8	25.6	27.3	28.8	30.4	31.8	33.3	34.6	36.0	37.2	38.5	39.7	40.9	43.2	45.4	47.5	49.5	51.4	78
80			24.1	25.8	27.5	29.1	30.7	32.2	33.6	35.0	36.3	37.6	38.9	40.2	41.4	43.7	45.9	48.0	50.1	52.0	80
82				26.1	27.8	29.4	31.0	32.5	34.0	35.4	36.7	38.0	39.3	40.6	41.8	44.1	46.4	48.5	50.6	52.6	82
84				26.4	28.1	29.7	31.3	32.8	34.3	35.7	37.1	38.4	39.7	41.0	42.2	44.6	46.9	49.0	51.1	53.2	84
86				26.6	28.3	30.0	31.6	33.1	34.6	36.1	37.4	38.8	40.1	41.4	42.6	45.0	47.3	49.6	51.7	53.7	86
88				26.9	28.6	30.3	31.9	33.4	34.9	36.4	37.8	39.2	40.5	41.8	43.1	45.5	47.8	50.0	52.2	54.3	88
90				27.1	28.9	30.6	32.2	33.8	35.3	36.7	38.2	39.5	40.9	42.2	43.5	45.9	48.3	50.5	52.7	54.8	90
92					29.1	30.8	32.5	34.1	35.6	37.1	38.5	39.9	41.3	42.6	43.9	46.4	48.7	51.0	53.2	55.3	92
96					29.6	31.4	33.0	34.7	36.2	37.7	39.2	40.6	42.0	43.3	44.7	47.2	49.6	52.0	54.2	56.4	96

Reprinted with permission from ASHRAE, *Fundamentals Handbook,* 1989.

FIGURE 10–28 / Rectangular ducts

Supply Outlet	Heat Loss (BTUH)	Actual Length (Ft)	Equivalent Length (Ft)	Total Equiv. Length(Ft)	Heating CFM	Supply Air Pressure	Supply Outlet Pressure Loss	Pressure Avail. for Duct Loss	Pressure Avail. Per 100 Ft	Round Duct Size (In.)	Rectangular Duct Size (In.)
Bedroom #1	4,283	36	80	116	148	0.09	0.02	0.07	0.060	8.0	6 x 9
Bedroom #2	2,310	26	105	131	80	0.09	0.02	0.07	0.054	7.0	6 x 7
Living	4,108	33	105	138	142	0.09	0.02	0.07	0.051	8.0	6 x 9
Living	4,108	55	80	135	142	0.09	0.02	0.07	0.052	8.0	6 x 9
Kitchen	3,752	46	80	126	130	0.09	0.02	0.07	0.056	8.0	6 x 9
Dining	3,047	27	105	132	105	0.09	0.02	0.07	0.053	7.0	6 x 7
Entry	1,682	16	115	131	58	0.09	0.02	0.07	0.054	6.0	6 x 5
Hall	1,682	10	80	90	58	0.09	0.02	0.07	0.078	4.0	3 x 4.5
Bedroom #3	3,008	30	105	135	104	0.09	0.02	0.07	0.052	7.0	6 x 7
Bath	960	25	90	115	33	0.09	0.02	0.07	0.061	5.0	6 x 3.5
Totals	28,940				1,000						

FIGURE 10-29 / Tabulated rectangular duct sizes

able pressure drop *per* 100 ft: (0.03 in. × 100 ft) ÷ 82 ft = 0.036 in. per 100 ft allowable pressure drop.

Using this information (1,000 cfm, 0.036 in. per 100 ft) select the round return duct size from the table in Fig. 10-34 and its equivalent rectangular size from Fig. 10-35. Tabulate the information as shown (Fig. 10-32):

If the return trunk sizes are too large, they may be reduced in size by:

a. Reapportioning the pressure drop available so there is less drop allowed for the supply runs and more pressure allowed for the return runs. This may require a revision of supply branch and trunk duct sizes.

b. Checking to see if the return air grille can be located closer to the furnace, which would reduce the actual length of duct. This increases the allowable pressure drop per 100 ft, resulting in a smaller duct size.

18. The size of the blower on the furnace is determined from the total air volume (the total cfm to be delivered) and the total static pressure requirements.

The total static pressure of a furnace-blower combination unit is the total

Duct		CFM
Main		
	A-B	1,000
Bedroom Branch		
	B-C	365
	C-D	285
	D-E	181
	E-F	33
Living Branch		
	B-G	635
	G-H	577
	H-I	519
	I-J	414
	J-K	272
	K-L	142

FIGURE 10-30 / Trunk duct volumes

of the actual pressure drops in the supply and return ducts. Most residential and small commercial buildings have furnace-blower combination units.

When the blowers are selected separately from the furnace, the total static pressure is the sum of the actual pressure losses in the supply and return ducts, the filter loss, the casing loss and losses through any devices which are put on the system, such as air washers and purifiers.

In this design, the 0.12-in. pressure drop, on which the designs of ducts were based, has been selected to provide a standard blower-furnace combination. While the actual pressure drop was slightly less than 0.12 in., the actual drop was not calculated since each duct selected is large enough to handle the air volume within the allowable pressure drop.

19. The capacity of the furnace to be selected is found next. The first step is to determine the Btuh requirements of all supply outlets.

The total Btuh for this building is 28,940 Btuh, calculated in Sec. 8-3.

20. Determine the required bonnet capacity of the furnace in Btuh or MBH.

When all the ductwork for a building will be located within heated spaces (spaces in which heat loss is calculated), the required bonnet capacity will be the same as the calculated heat loss plus any allowance for "pickup load" in step 21.

When the furnace and ductwork will not be located in spaces included in the heat loss, the required bonnet capacity can be determined by the use of the formula:

$$Btuh = cfm \times \text{Unit temperature rise} \times 1.08$$

Duct		CFM	Supply Static Pressure*	Total Equiv. Length (Ft)	Supply Pressure Avail. Per 100 Ft	Round Duct Size (In.)	Rectangular Duct Size (In.)
Main	A-B	1,000	0.07	138	0.051	16.0	12 x 18
Bedroom Branch	B-C	365	0.07	131	0.054	12.0	8 x 16
	C-D	285				10.0	8 x 11
	D-E	181				9.0	8 x 9
	E-F	33				5.0	8 x 3
Living Branch	B-G	635	0.07	138	0.051	14.0	8 x 22
	G-H	577				14.0	8 x 22
	H-I	519				14.0	8 x 22
	I-J	414				12.0	8 x 16
	J-K	272				10.0	8 x 11
	K-L	142				8.0	8 x 7

* Allows 0.02 for supply outlet

FIGURE 10-31 / Tabulated trunk sizes

For this design, the bonnet capacity will be based on a furnace and ducts in an unheated space. The cfm to be used in the formula is taken from step 9 as 513 cfm. The 1.08 in the formula is a constant factor (it will not change) based on:

$$60 \text{ min/hr} \times 0.75 \text{ lb/cu ft (avg. air density)} \times$$
$$0.241 \text{ Btu/lb (specific heat of air)} = 1.08$$

FIGURE 10-32 / Return duct sizes

Duct	Cfm	Actual Length	Equivalent Length	Total Equivalent Length	Loss Per 100 Ft	Round Duct Size (in.)	Rectangular Duct Size (in.)
Return	1,000	12	70	82	0.036	18.0	12 x 24

The unit temperature rise is based on the difference between the temperature of the air as it leaves the bonnet (in step 4b, a 130°F temperature was decided on) and the temperature of the air as it re-enters the furnace to be heated (for this design, assume 65°F, which is slightly below the inside design temperature of 70°F). So the unit temperature rise will be 100°F − 65°F = 35°F. Therefore, the minimum required furnace size will be:

$$\text{Btuh} = 1000 \text{ cfm} \times 35°\text{F} \times 1.08 = 37{,}800 \text{ Btuh}$$

21. Add any allowance which is required for pickup load.

For this design, it has been decided to allow 10% for pickup load. Therefore, the total furnace Btuh required will be 39,614 Btuh (36,013 + 10% = 36,013 + 3,601 = 39,614). This will probably result in the selection of a furnace with a capacity of about 40,000 Btuh.

QUESTIONS

10-1. What are the advantages of a forced air system as compared to hot water?

10-2. What types of materials are most commonly used for forced air ducts?

10-3. What can be done to be certain that the system will be as quiet as possible?

10-4. What is the purpose of putting dampers and vanes in the ductwork?

10-5. When is insulation around the ductwork recommended?

10-6. When heating is the predominant function of the forced air system, what are the recommended locations for supply and return?

10-7. What types of furnaces are available for use in forced air systems, and where might each type be located?

10-8. How may humidity be introduced into the forced air system?

Design Exercises

10-9. Design a forced hot air system for the residence in Appendix B based on the heat loss calculations from Exercise 8-15.

Equivalent of Supply and Return Air Plenum Fittings[a]

Equivalent Length of Reducing Trunk Duct Fittings[a]

Reprinted with permission of ACCA, *Manual D*, 1984.

FIGURE 10-33 / Equivalent fittings

*Add 25 equivalent feet to each of the 3 fittings nearest the unit in each trunk duct after a reduction.

Equivalent Length of Extended Plenum Fittings[a,8]

*Add 25 equivalent feet to each of the 3 fittings nearest the unit in each trunk duct.

Equivalent Length of Round Trunk Duct Fittings[a,8]

12.7

[a] These values may also be used for floor diffuser boxes.

Equivalent Length of Boot Fittings[a,8]

Reprinted with permission of ACCA, *Manual D,* 1984.

FIGURE 10-33 / Equivalent fittings (continued)

O - 25   Return Air Liner To Duct.

P - 15   Stud Space To Liner.

Q - 25   Stud Space To Liner.

80 sq. ft.
R.A. GRILL AND FITTING.

2.5 sq ft
10 sq ft
R.A. GRILL TO STUD SPACE. R.A. GRILL ONLY.

20
FLOOR GRILL TO LINER

*Inside radius for A and B = 3 in., and for F and G = 5 in.

Equivalent Length of Angles and Elbows for Individual and Branch Ducts[a,b]

| A - 5 | B - 10 | C - 25 | D - 5 | E - 10 |

F - 5

G - 10 in. wide	10	H - 10 in. wide	40	I - 3¼ in. × 10 in.	60	J - 3¼ in. × 10 in.	75
G - 12 in. wide	15	H - 12 in. wide	55	I - 3¼ in. × 12 in.	75	J - 3¼ in. × 12 in.	90
G - 14 in. wide	15	H - 14 in. wide	55	I - 3¼ in. × 14 in.	75	J - 3¼ in. × 14 in.	90

| K - 125 | L - 35 | M - 10 | N - 95 |

Reprinted with permission of ACCA, *Manual D*, 1984.

FIGURE 10-33 / Equivalent fittings (continued)

10 / FORCED AIR SYSTEM DESIGN (HEAT)

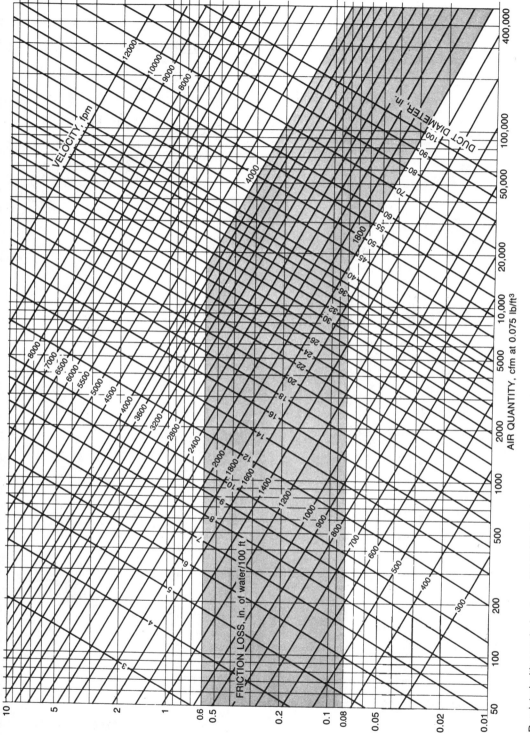

Reprinted with permission from ASHRAE, *Fundamentals Handbook*, 1989.

FIGURE 10-34 / Round duct sizes

Circular Equivalents of Rectangular Duct for Equal Friction and Capacity[a]

Lgth Adj[b]	Length of One Side of Rectangular Duct (a), in.																
	4.0	4.5	5.0	5.5	6.0	6.5	7.0	7.5	8.0	9.0	10.0	11.0	12.0	13.0	14.0	15.0	16.0
3.0	3.8	4.0	4.2	4.4	4.6	4.7	4.9	5.1	5.2	5.5	5.7	6.0	6.2	6.4	6.6	6.8	7.0
3.5	4.1	4.2	4.6	4.8	5.0	5.2	5.3	5.5	5.7	6.0	6.3	6.5	6.8	7.0	7.2	7.5	7.7
4.0	4.4	4.6	4.9	5.1	5.3	5.5	5.7	5.9	6.1	6.4	6.7	7.0	7.3	7.6	7.8	8.0	8.3
4.5	4.6	4.9	5.2	5.4	5.7	5.9	6.1	6.3	6.5	6.9	7.2	7.5	7.8	8.1	8.4	8.6	8.8
5.0	4.9	5.2	5.5	5.7	6.0	6.2	6.4	6.7	6.9	7.3	7.6	8.0	8.3	8.6	8.9	9.1	9.4
5.5	5.1	5.4	5.7	6.0	6.3	6.5	6.8	7.0	7.2	7.6	8.0	8.4	8.7	9.0	9.3	9.6	9.9

Lgth Adj[b]	Length of One Side of Rectangular Duct (a), in.																				Lgth 30 Adj[b]
	6	7	8	9	10	11	12	13	14	15	16	17	18	19	20	22	24	26	28	30	
6	6.6																				6
7	7.1	7.7																			7
8	7.6	8.2	8.7																		8
9	8.0	8.7	9.3	9.8																	9
10	8.4	9.1	9.8	10.4	10.9																10
11	8.8	9.5	10.2	10.9	11.5	12.0															11
12	9.1	9.9	10.7	11.3	12.0	12.6	13.1														12
13	9.5	10.3	11.1	11.8	12.4	13.1	13.7	14.2													13
14	9.8	10.8	11.4	12.2	12.9	13.5	14.2	14.7	15.3												14
15	10.1	11.0	11.8	12.6	13.3	14.0	14.6	15.3	15.8	16.4											15
16	10.4	11.3	12.2	13.0	13.7	14.4	15.1	15.7	16.4	16.9	17.5										16
17	10.7	11.6	12.5	13.4	14.1	14.9	15.6	16.2	16.8	17.4	18.0	18.6									17
18	11.0	11.9	12.9	13.7	14.5	15.3	16.0	16.7	17.3	17.9	18.5	19.1	19.7								18
19	11.2	12.2	13.2	14.1	14.9	15.7	16.4	17.1	17.8	18.4	19.0	19.6	20.2	20.8							19
20	11.5	12.6	13.5	14.4	15.2	16.0	16.8	17.5	18.2	18.9	19.5	20.1	20.7	21.3	21.9						20
22	12.0	13.0	14.1	15.0	15.9	16.8	17.6	18.3	19.1	19.8	20.4	21.1	21.7	22.3	22.9	24.0					22
24	12.4	13.5	14.6	15.6	16.5	17.4	18.3	19.1	19.9	20.6	21.3	22.0	22.7	23.3	23.9	25.1	26.2				24
26	12.8	14.0	15.1	16.2	17.1	18.1	19.0	19.8	20.6	21.4	22.1	22.9	23.5	24.2	24.9	26.1	27.3	28.4			26
28	13.2	14.5	15.6	16.7	17.7	18.7	19.6	20.5	21.3	22.1	22.9	23.7	24.4	25.1	25.8	27.1	28.3	29.5	30.6		28
30	13.6	14.9	16.1	17.2	18.3	19.3	20.2	21.1	22.0	22.9	23.7	24.4	25.2	25.9	26.6	28.0	29.3	30.5	31.7	32.8	30
32	14.0	15.3	16.5	17.7	18.8	19.8	20.8	21.8	22.7	23.5	24.4	25.2	26.0	26.7	27.5	28.9	30.2	31.5	32.7	33.9	32
34	14.4	15.7	17.0	18.2	19.3	20.4	21.4	22.4	23.3	24.2	25.1	25.9	26.7	27.5	28.3	29.7	31.0	32.4	33.7	34.9	34
36	14.7	16.1	17.4	18.6	19.8	20.9	21.9	22.9	23.9	24.8	25.7	26.6	27.4	28.2	29.0	30.5	32.0	33.3	34.6	35.9	36
38	15.0	16.5	17.8	19.0	20.2	21.4	22.4	23.5	24.5	25.4	26.4	27.2	28.1	28.9	29.8	31.3	32.8	34.2	35.6	36.8	38
40	15.3	16.8	18.2	19.5	20.7	21.8	22.9	24.0	25.0	26.0	27.0	27.9	28.8	29.6	30.5	32.1	33.6	35.1	36.4	37.8	40
42	15.6	17.1	18.5	19.9	21.1	22.3	23.4	24.5	25.6	26.6	27.6	28.5	29.4	30.3	31.2	32.8	34.4	35.9	37.3	38.7	42
44	15.9	17.5	18.9	20.3	31.5	22.7	23.9	25.0	26.1	27.1	28.1	29.1	30.0	30.9	31.8	33.5	35.1	36.7	38.1	39.5	44
46	16.2	17.8	19.3	20.6	21.9	23.2	24.4	25.5	26.6	27.7	28.7	29.7	30.6	31.6	32.5	34.2	35.9	37.4	38.9	40.4	46
48	16.5	18.1	19.6	21.0	22.3	23.6	24.8	26.0	27.1	28.2	29.2	30.2	31.2	32.2	33.1	34.9	36.6	38.2	39.7	41.2	48
50	16.8	18.4	19.9	21.4	22.7	24.0	25.2	26.4	27.6	28.7	29.8	30.8	31.8	32.8	33.7	35.5	37.2	38.9	40.5	42.0	50
52	17.1	18.7	20.2	21.7	23.1	24.4	25.7	26.9	28.0	29.2	30.3	31.3	32.3	33.3	34.3	36.2	37.9	39.6	41.2	42.8	52
54	17.3	19.0	20.6	22.0	23.5	24.8	26.1	27.3	28.5	29.7	30.8	31.8	32.9	33.9	34.9	36.8	38.6	40.3	41.9	43.5	54
56	17.6	19.3	20.9	22.4	23.8	25.2	26.5	27.7	28.9	30.1	31.2	32.3	33.4	34.4	35.4	37.4	39.2	41.0	42.7	44.3	56
58	17.8	19.5	21.2	22.7	24.2	25.5	26.9	28.2	29.4	30.6	31.7	32.8	33.9	35.0	36.0	38.0	39.8	41.6	43.3	45.0	58
60	18.1	19.8	21.5	23.0	24.5	25.9	27.3	28.6	29.8	31.0	32.2	33.3	34.4	35.5	36.5	38.5	40.4	42.3	44.0	45.7	60
62		20.1	21.7	23.3	24.8	26.3	27.6	28.9	30.2	31.5	32.6	33.8	34.9	36.0	37.1	39.1	41.0	42.9	44.7	46.4	62
64		20.3	22.0	23.6	25.1	26.6	28.0	29.3	30.6	31.9	33.1	34.3	35.4	36.5	37.6	39.6	41.6	43.5	45.3	47.1	64
66		20.6	22.3	23.9	25.5	26.9	28.4	29.7	31.0	32.3	33.5	34.7	35.9	37.0	38.1	40.2	42.2	44.1	46.0	47.7	66
68		20.8	22.6	24.2	25.8	27.3	28.7	30.1	31.4	32.7	33.9	35.2	36.3	37.5	38.6	40.7	42.8	44.7	46.6	48.4	68
70		21.1	22.8	24.5	26.1	27.6	29.1	30.4	31.8	33.1	34.4	35.6	36.8	37.9	39.1	41.2	43.3	45.3	47.2	49.0	70
72			23.1	24.8	26.4	27.9	29.4	30.8	32.2	33.5	34.8	36.0	37.2	38.4	39.5	41.7	43.8	45.8	47.8	49.6	72
74			23.3	25.1	26.7	28.2	29.7	31.2	32.5	33.9	35.2	36.4	37.7	38.8	40.0	42.2	44.4	46.4	48.4	50.3	74
76			23.6	25.3	27.0	28.5	30.0	31.5	32.9	34.3	35.6	36.8	38.1	39.3	40.5	42.7	44.9	47.0	48.9	50.9	76
78			23.8	25.6	27.3	28.8	30.4	31.8	33.3	34.6	36.0	37.2	38.5	39.7	40.9	43.2	45.4	47.5	49.5	51.4	78
80			24.1	25.8	27.5	29.1	30.7	32.2	33.6	35.0	36.3	37.6	38.9	40.2	41.4	43.7	45.9	48.0	50.1	52.0	80
82				26.1	27.8	29.4	31.0	32.5	34.0	35.4	36.7	38.0	39.3	40.6	41.8	44.1	46.4	48.5	50.6	52.6	82
84				26.4	28.1	29.7	31.3	32.8	34.3	35.7	37.1	38.4	39.7	41.0	42.2	44.6	46.9	49.0	51.1	53.2	84
86				26.6	28.3	30.0	31.6	33.1	34.6	36.1	37.4	38.8	40.1	41.4	42.6	45.0	47.3	49.6	51.7	53.7	86
88				26.9	28.6	30.3	31.9	33.4	34.9	36.4	37.8	39.2	40.5	41.8	43.1	45.5	47.8	50.0	52.2	54.3	88
90				27.1	28.9	30.6	32.2	33.8	35.3	36.7	38.2	39.5	40.9	42.2	43.5	45.9	48.3	50.5	52.7	54.8	90
92					29.1	30.8	32.5	34.1	35.6	37.1	38.5	39.9	41.3	42.6	43.9	46.4	48.7	51.0	53.2	55.3	92
96					29.6	31.4	33.0	34.7	36.2	37.7	39.2	40.6	42.0	43.3	44.7	47.2	49.6	52.0	54.2	56.4	96

Reprinted with permission from ASHRAE, *Fundamentals Handbook*, 1989.

FIGURE 10-35 / Rectangular duct sizes

Lgth Adj.[b]	Length of One Side of Rectangular Duct (a), in.																			Lgth 88 Adj.[b]
	32	34	36	38	40	42	44	46	48	50	52	56	60	64	68	72	76	80	84	
32	35.0																			32
34	36.1	37.2																		34
36	37.1	38.2	39.4																	36
38	38.1	39.3	40.4	41.5																38
40	39.0	40.3	41.5	42.6	43.7															40
42	40.0	41.3	42.5	43.7	44.8	45.9														42
44	40.9	42.2	43.5	44.7	45.8	47.0	48.1													44
46	41.8	43.1	44.4	45.7	46.9	48.0	49.2	50.3												46
48	42.6	44.0	45.3	46.6	47.9	49.1	50.2	51.4	52.5											48
50	43.6	44.9	46.2	47.5	48.8	50.0	51.2	52.4	53.6	54.7										50
52	44.3	45.7	47.1	48.4	49.7	51.0	52.2	53.4	54.6	55.7	56.8									52
54	45.1	46.5	48.0	49.3	50.7	52.0	53.2	54.4	55.6	56.8	57.9									54
56	45.8	47.3	48.8	50.2	51.6	52.9	54.2	55.4	56.6	57.8	59.0	61.2								56
58	46.6	48.1	49.6	51.0	52.4	53.8	55.1	56.4	57.6	58.8	60.0	62.3								58
60	47.3	48.9	50.4	51.9	53.3	54.7	56.0	57.3	58.6	59.8	61.0	63.4	65.6							60
62	48.0	49.6	51.2	52.7	54.1	55.5	56.9	58.2	59.5	60.8	62.0	64.4	66.7							62
64	48.7	50.4	51.9	53.5	54.9	56.4	57.8	59.1	60.4	61.7	63.0	65.4	67.7	70.0						64
66	49.4	51.1	52.7	54.2	55.7	57.2	58.6	60.0	61.3	62.6	63.9	66.4	68.8	71.0						66
68	50.1	51.8	53.4	55.0	56.5	58.0	59.4	60.8	62.2	63.6	64.9	67.4	69.8	72.1	74.3					68
70	50.8	52.5	54.1	55.7	57.3	58.8	60.3	61.7	63.1	64.4	65.8	68.3	70.8	73.2	75.4					70
72	51.4	53.2	54.8	56.5	58.0	59.6	61.1	62.5	63.9	65.3	66.7	69.3	71.8	74.2	76.5	78.7				72
74	52.1	53.8	55.5	57.2	58.8	60.3	61.9	63.3	64.8	66.2	67.5	70.2	72.7	75.2	77.5	79.8				74
76	52.7	54.5	56.2	57.9	59.5	61.1	62.6	64.1	65.6	67.0	68.4	71.1	73.7	76.2	78.6	80.9	83.1			76
78	53.3	55.1	56.9	58.6	60.2	61.8	63.4	64.9	66.4	67.9	69.3	72.0	74.6	77.1	79.6	81.9	84.2			78
80	53.9	55.8	57.5	59.3	60.9	62.6	64.1	65.7	67.2	68.7	70.1	72.9	75.4	78.1	80.6	82.9	85.2	87.5		80
82	54.6	56.4	58.2	59.9	61.6	63.3	64.9	66.5	68.0	69.5	70.9	73.7	76.4	79.0	81.5	84.0	86.3	88.5		82
84	55.1	57.0	58.8	60.6	62.3	64.0	65.6	67.2	68.7	70.3	71.7	74.6	77.3	80.0	82.5	85.0	87.3	89.6	91.8	84
86	55.7	57.6	59.4	61.2	63.0	64.7	66.3	67.9	69.5	71.0	72.5	75.4	78.2	80.9	83.5	85.9	88.3	90.7	92.9	86
88	56.3	58.2	60.1	61.9	63.6	65.4	67.0	68.7	70.2	71.8	73.3	76.3	79.1	81.8	84.4	86.9	89.3	91.7	94.0	96.2 ... 88
90	56.8	58.8	60.7	62.5	64.3	66.0	67.7	69.4	71.0	72.6	74.1	77.1	79.9	82.7	85.3	87.9	90.3	92.7	95.0	97.3 ... 90
92	57.4	59.3	61.3	63.1	64.9	66.7	68.4	70.1	71.7	73.3	74.9	77.9	80.8	83.5	86.2	88.8	91.3	93.7	96.1	98.4 ... 92
94	57.9	59.9	61.9	63.7	65.6	67.3	69.1	70.8	72.4	74.0	75.6	78.7	81.6	84.4	87.1	89.7	92.3	94.7	97.1	99.4 ... 94
96	58.4	60.5	62.4	64.3	66.2	68.0	69.7	71.5	73.1	74.8	76.3	79.4	82.4	85.3	88.0	90.7	93.2	95.7	98.1	100.5 ... 96

[a] Table based on $D_e = 1.30(ab)^{0.625}/(a+b)^{0.25}$
[b] Length of adjacent side of rectangular duct (b), in.

Reprinted with permission from ASHRAE, *Fundamentals Handbook,* 1989.

FIGURE 10-35 / *Rectangular duct sizes (continued)*

Duct	Cfm	Actual length	Equivalent length	Total equivalent length	Loss per 100'	Round duct size	Rectangular duct size
Return	513	12	70	82	.10	11.0"	12" x 5" 18" x 6" 15" x 7"13" x 8"

CFM	TYPE A	TYPE B	TYPE C
1000	0.10	0.15	0.20
1500	.12	.17	.22
2000	.13	.18	.24
2500	.14	.20	.27
3000	.16	.22	.29
3500	.17	.24	.31
4000	.18	.26	.33
4500	0.20	0.28	0.36
5000	.21	.29	.38
5500	.22	.31	.40
6000	.24	.33	.42
6500	.25	.34	.45
7000	.27	.36	.47
7500	.28	.38	.49
8000	0.29	0.39	0.51
8500	.30	.41	.53
9000	.32	.43	.56
9500	.34	.45	.58
10,000	.34	.47	.60
10,500	.37	.48	.60
11,000	.39	.50	.60
11,500	0.40	0.50	0.60
12,000	.40	.50	.60
12,500	.40	.50	.60
13,000	.40	.50	.60
14,000	.40	.50	.60

CFM = Maximum cfm in any one duct.
Type A = Systems for quiet operation in residences, churches, concert halls, broadcasting studios, funeral homes, etc.
Type B = Systems for schools, theaters, public buildings, etc.
Type C = Systems for industrial buildings.

FIGURE 10-36 / Suggested bonnet and return pressures

CHAPTER 11
ELECTRIC HEAT DESIGN

11-1 TYPES OF SYSTEMS

The advantages of an electric heating system include low installation cost, individual room control, quiet operation, and cleanliness, and when cable or panels are used, there are no exposed heating units. The primary disadvantage of electric heat is its high cost of operation in almost all areas. A specialist is required to give honest figures for comparing electric heat costs with those of other types of fuels. Electrically operated boilers (furnaces) are not discussed in this chapter since they are not different systems but rather a different forced air unit with electricity as a fuel.

Most electric ratings are given in watts and Btuh. There are 3,413 Btuh for every 1,000 watts (1 kilowatt = 1,000 watts), and often the ratings will be given or noted as MBH (thousand Btuh) and kW (kilowatts), such as 6.8 MBH and 2 kW.

OVERALL SYSTEMS

Baseboard
Electric baseboard units have a heating element enclosed in a metal case. This system offers individual room control, but furniture arrangement and draperies must not in-

terfere with the operation of the units by blocking the natural flow of air. This system is economical for a builder to install and is especially popular in low-cost housing and housing built for speculation (to try to sell), although the cost of operation is generally higher than most other fuels.

Resistance Cable

With this system, electric heating cable is stapled to the drywall in a grid pattern and covered with plaster or gypsum board. Individual thermostats control the heat in each room. However, since the cable is usually installed on the ceiling, the disadvantages of heat rising and cold feet must be considered.

Drawings are not usually done for this type of heating system; instead, the amount of heat required is noted for each space. The cable system allows complete freedom in furniture and drapery placement.

Panels

The prefabricated ceiling and wall panels used in this system have the heating wire sandwiched in rubber with an asbestos board backing. They are only ¼ in. thick and may be plastered, painted, or wallpapered over. The panels come in a standard size (usually 2 ft x 4 ft) and cannot be cut. They are often used in hung suspension ceilings. A panel system has the same basic advantages and disadvantages as a resistance cable system, including flexibility of furniture and drapery arrangement.

UNIT HEATERS

There are a variety of electric unit heaters available which may be used to supplement other heat sources in a space or to completely heat a room. In residences, such a unit heater is quite often installed in the bathroom, often to supplement other heat sources, since a temperature higher than 72°F is necessary to feel comfortable when washing and after bathing.

Unit heaters are also commonly installed in spaces where the heat is only used periodically, such as a basement, workshop or garage work area.

So that the warm air will be quickly spread throughout the area to be heated, unit heaters are equipped with a fan. It is preferable if the fan switch is the type which will not start until after the unit comes on and the air has warmed to a preset temperature; in this way, cold air is not pushed around the room.

Units are generally available for use in walls (recessed into the wall), and ceiling recessed units are also available.

SYSTEM COMBINATIONS

Quite often in order to provide the best results, the design may incorporate more than one type of system. For example, a building may be predominantly heated with baseboard units, but in spaces where there is little free wall space, such as a kitchen, it may be desirable to use a unit heater in the ceiling or the wall under the cabinets. Another possibility for the kitchen might be to use resistance cables or panels in the ceiling. Bathrooms may be heated with unit heaters to provide added comfort.

CODES AND INSTALLATION

While a hot water heating system is installed by the heating contractor, an electrical heating system is installed by an electrical contractor. ASHRAE publishes guides which discuss the use of the units for proper heating conditions and the installation, but the *National Electric Code* (NEC) also governs the installation of the resistance cable. The designer must have both the NEC code and ASHRAE available for reference.

11-2   BASEBOARD SYSTEM DESIGN

A baseboard electric system transfers heat to the space primarily by convection. It consists of baseboard units which may be mounted on the wall or recessed into the wall (Fig. 11-1). In selecting a baseboard unit, the designer must consider the direction in which the air will be discharged from the baseboard unit (Fig. 11-2).

Baseboard units are rated in watts and Btuh. These ratings, which may vary for different manufacturers, are given *for the length specified* and not per lineal foot. For example, in Fig. 11-3, the very first listing specifies a 36-in. (3-ft) length and a rating of 500 watts and 1,707 Btuh for the 3-ft length. The manufacturer often has several models, sizes and ratings available, and the ratings will probably vary with other manufacturers. In Figs 11-4 and 11-5, two separate series are listed; both have the same outside dimensions and the B series has a rating about 100% higher for each length than the A series. In addition, many manufacturers make larger units, with higher ratings, which are normally used in commercial, industrial and institutional buildings. A 3-ft length of this style may range from 750 to 2,250 watts.

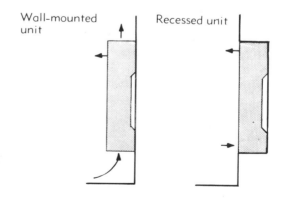

Wall-mounted unit   Recessed unit

FIGURE 11-1 / Baseboard mounting

FIGURE 11-2 / Baseboard air discharge

In designing an electric baseboard system, it may be necessary to use the larger units in some areas in order to provide the Btuh required.

STEP-BY-STEP APPROACH

1. Using the calculations from Fig. 8–36, do a heat loss calculation on each individual space, and tabulate them as shown (Fig. 11-6):

FIGURE 11-3 / Baseboard ratings

Length	Watts	Btuh
36" (3'-0")	500	1,707
52" (4'-4")	750	2,560
68" (5'-8")	1,000	3,413
100" (8'-4")	1,500	5,120

FIGURE 11-4 / High output baseboard ratings

Length	Watts	Btuh
36" (3'-0")	750	2,560
48" (4'-0")	1,000	3,413
60" (6'-0")	1,250	4,269
72" (6'-0")	1,500	5,120
96" (8'-0")	2,000	6,830

A Series

Length	Watts	Btuh
36" (3'-0")	1,500	5,120
48" (4'-0")	2,000	6,830
60" (5'-0")	2,500	8,538
72" (6'-0")	3,000	10,245
96" (8'-0")	4,000	13,660
	B Series	

FIGURE 11-5 / High output baseboard ratings

2. List the lineal feet of exterior wall that are available for baseboard convector units for each separate space, and tabulate them as shown (Fig. 11-7):

3. Using the manufacturer's ratings (Figs. 11-3 and 11-4 are typical), determine the length and corresponding rating that will be used to provide heat to each space.

> Some walls, such as those in the living room of this design, will require two or more lengths of baseboard. All that is important is that the Btuh of heat loss calculated for each room is put back into that room.

> In some rooms, such as a kitchen, where there is little exterior wall space, it may be necessary to put a unit on an interior wall, or a larger unit which has a higher capacity may be used.

4. Tabulate the baseboard convector units selected for each room; list their lengths, wattage ratings and Btuh ratings.

> Based on the heat loss calculations, the units have been selected and tabulated as shown (Fig. 11-8):

FIGURE 11-6 / Room heat loss

Room	Heat loss (Btuh)	Exterior wall (l.f.)	Watts	(Btuh ÷ 3.413)	Radiation unit selected
BEDROOM 1	4,085				
BEDROOM 2	2,310				
LIVING	8,216				
KITCHEN	3,752				
DINING	3,047				
ENTRY & HALL	3,364				
BEDROOM 3	3,008				
BATH	960				
INTERIOR BATH	198				

Room	Heat loss (Btuh)	Exterior wall (l.f.)	Watts (Btuh ÷ 3.413)	Radiation unit selected
BEDROOM 1	4,085	30.0		
BEDROOM 2	2,310	11.0		
LIVING	8,216	23.3		
KITCHEN	3,752	—		
DINING	3,047	14.0		
ENTRY & HALL	3,364	—		
BEDROOM 3	3,008	14.0		
BATH	960	—		
INTERIOR BATH	198	—		

FIGURE 11-7 / Exterior wall available

Note: Since exterior wall space for radiant baseboard units is likely to be limited in some areas, it may be desirable to use other units or devices to supplement or take the place of the radiant baseboards. The kitchen and bathrooms quite often have unit heaters recessed in the wall (Fig. 11-1). Kitchen heat may also be supplemented by a "kickspace" heater which is placed in the kickspace under the kitchen cabinets.

Room	Heat loss (Btuh)	Exterior wall (l.f.)	Watts (Btuh ÷ 3.413)	Radiation unit selected
BEDROOM 1	4,085	30.0	1197	1-500W, 3' 1-750W, 4'-4"
BEDROOM 2	2,310	11.0	677	1-750W, 4'-4"
LIVING	8,216	23.3	2407	2-1000W, 5'-8"; 1-500W, 3'
KITCHEN	3,752	—	1100	1-500W, 3' 1-750W, 4'-4"
DINING	3,047	14.0	893	2-500W, 3'
ENTRY & HALL	3,364	—	986	2-500W, 3'
BEDROOM 3	3,008	14.0	881	2-500W, 3'
BATH	960	—	281	1-500W, 3'
INTERIOR BATH	198	—	58	USE UNIT HEATER

FIGURE 11-8 / Select and tabulate baseboard units

11-3   RESISTANCE CABLE SYSTEM DESIGN

The amount of heat given off by the cables will vary with the amount of heating cable used in the installation.

The electric cable used for ceiling installations comes in rolls; it is stapled to the ceiling and then covered with gypsum or plasterboard in accordance with the manufacturer's specifications and the code requirements. Basically, the cable must not be installed within 6 in. of any wall, within 8 in. of the edge of any junction box or outlet, or within 2 in. of any recessed lighting fixtures.

Cable assemblies are usually rated at 2.75 watts per lineal foot, with generally available ratings from 400- to 5,000-watt lengths in 200-watt increments, but the manufacturer's specifications should be checked to determine what is available. A typical list of available lengths, watts and Btuh from one manufacturer is shown in Fig. 11-9. The cables have insulated coverings which are resistant to medium temperatures, water absorption and the effects of aging and chemical reactions (concrete, plaster, etc.); a polyvinyl chloride covering with a nylon jacket is most commonly used. Each separate cable has an individual thermostat, providing flexible control throughout the building.

A typical cable installation in a plastered ceiling is shown in Fig. 11-10. The space between the rows of heating cable is generally limited to a minimum of 1.5 in., and some manufacturers recommend a 2-in. minimum spacing when drywall construction is used. Another limitation on the spacing of the cable is a 2.5-in. clearance required between cables under each joist (Fig. 11-11), and a review of the layout in Fig. 11-10 shows that the cable is installed parallel (in the same direction) as the joists.

To be certain the required amount of Btuh is obtained, it is sometimes desirable

Btuh	Watts	Length Ft.
1365	400	145
2047	600	218
2730	800	292
3413	1000	362
4095	1200	436
5461	1600	582
6143	1800	654
6826	2000	728
7509	2200	800
8533	2500	910
10,239	3000	1090
11,287	3600	1310
15,700	4600	1672

FIGURE 11-9 / Typical cable ratings

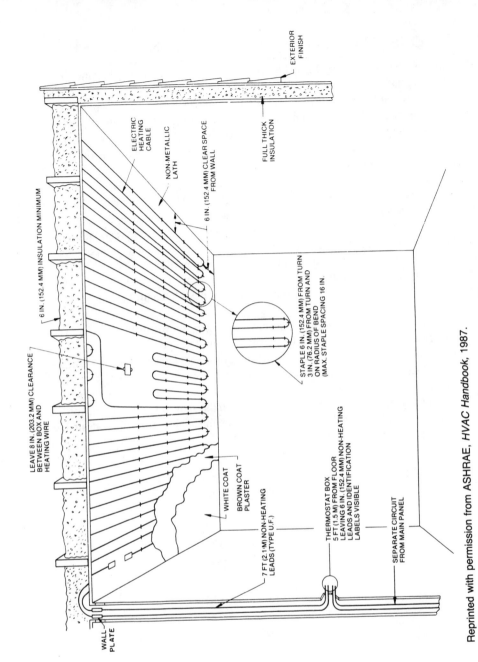

EXTERIOR FINISH

ELECTRIC HEATING CABLE

NON-METALLIC LATH

6 IN. (152.4 MM) CLEAR SPACE FROM WALL

FULL THICK INSULATION

6 IN. (152.4 MM) INSULATION MINIMUM

LEAVE 8 IN. (203.2 MM) CLEARANCE BETWEEN BOX AND HEATING WIRE

STAPLE 6 IN. (152.4 MM) FROM TURN 3 IN. (76.2 MM) FROM TURN AND ON RADIUS OF BEND (MAX. STAPLE SPACING 16 IN.

WHITE COAT

BROWN COAT PLASTER

THERMOSTAT BOX 5 FT (1.5 M) FROM FLOOR LEAVING 6 IN. (152.4 MM) NON-HEATING LEADS AND IDENTIFICATION LABELS VISIBLE

SEPARATE CIRCUIT FROM MAIN PANEL

7 FT (2.1M) NON-HEATING LEADS (TYPE U.F.)

WALL PLATE

Reprinted with permission from ASHRAE, HVAC Handbook, 1987.

FIGURE 11-10 / Electric heating panel for wet plaster ceiling

322

FIGURE 11-11 / Cable detail

to specify the maximum spacing of heat cable allowed in a room. This maximum spacing may be determined by using the formula:

$$s = 12 \, (An/C)$$

where

s = cable spacing (in.)
An = net available area for heat cables (sq ft)
C = length of a cable required to deliver required Btuh (ft)
12 = constant (used to change ft to in.)

The net available area for heating cables is equal to the total ceiling area minus any area in which cable cannot be placed (due to borders, ceiling obstructions, cabinets and any similar items). While a small lighting fixture may be neglected, if the ceiling has several, their area should be deducted.

EXAMPLE

Given: Assume that bedroom 1 illustrated in Fig. 11-12 is about 18 ft 3 in. by 12 ft 3 in. and requires 4,024 Btuh. From the available cable lengths given in Fig. 11-9, a 1,200-watt, 4,095-Btuh, 436-ft cable is selected. Assume one ceiling fixture which is neglected in the calculation and a 6-in. border required between the cable and the intersection of wall.

Problem: Determine the net area available for heating cables and the maximum cable spacing.

FIGURE 11-12 / Floor plan

FIGURE 11-13 / Cable area calculations

$$An = 18 \text{ ft-3 in.} \times 12 \text{ ft-3 in.} - (6 \text{ in. around the perimeter of room}) \text{ (Fig. 11-13)}$$

$$17.25 \text{ ft} \times 11.25 \text{ ft} = 194 \text{ sq ft}$$

$$s = 12 (194 \text{ sq ft}/436 \text{ ft}) = 5.34 \text{ in. maximum spacing}$$

Bedroom 1 (Fig. 11-12) requires a maximum cable spacing of 5.34 in.

This is the procedure used to determine cable ceiling heat requirements for a building.

STEP-BY-STEP APPROACH

1. Determine the heat loss of each individual room and tabulate them.

    The heat loss has already been calculated (Sec. 8–12) for the residence being designed and they are tabulated by room as shown in Fig. 11-14.

2. Select the cable required to provide the Btuh required for each room. Do not use a cable which will provide less Btuh than calculated.

    From Fig. 11-9, select the required cable for each room and tabulate each cable rating (Btuh, watts, length) as shown in Fig. 11-15.

11 / ELECTRIC HEAT DESIGN

Room	Heat loss (Btuh)	Cable selected (Btuh)	Cable length (ft.)	Ceiling space available (ft.)	Ceiling area (s.f.)	Maximum spacing (in.)
BEDROOM 1	4,085					
BEDROOM 2	2,310					
LIVING	8,216					
KITCHEN	3,752					
DINING	3,047					
ENTRY & HALL	3,364					
BEDROOM 3	3,008					
BATHROOM	960					
INTERIOR BATH	198					

FIGURE 11-14 / Room heat loss

3.   Calculate the net ceiling area for each room.

Calculate the net ceiling area for each room based on a 6-in. border. In the kitchen deduct for the wall cabinets and the fluorescent light. Tabulate the net ceiling area for each room as shown in Fig. 11-16.

4.   Calculate the maximum cable spacing which can be used in each space.

Using the formula $s = 12 (An/C)$, calculate the cable spacing for each room and tabulate the information as shown in Fig. 11-17.

This information is often given on the drawings in tabulated form, similar to that shown in Fig. 11-17. The location of each thermostat must be shown on the drawing and may be put on the general construction (architectural) drawings; but often the

FIGURE 11-15 / Select and tabulate cable lengths

Room	Heat loss (Btuh)	Cable selected (Btuh)	Cable length (ft.)	Ceiling space available (ft.)	Ceiling area (s.f.)	Maximum spacing (in.)
BEDROOM 1	4,085	4,095	436			
BEDROOM 2	2,310	2,730	292			
LIVING	8,216	8,533	910			
KITCHEN	3,752	4,095	436			
DINING	3,047	3,413	362			
ENTRY & HALL	3,364	3,413	362			
BEDROOM 3	3,008	3,413	362			
BATHROOM	960	1,365	145			
INTERIOR BATH	198	USE ELECTRIC UNIT HEATER				

Room	Heat loss (Btuh)	Cable selected (Btuh)	Cable length (ft.)	Ceiling space available (ft.)	Ceiling area (s.f.)	Maximum spacing (in.)
BEDROOM 1	4,085	4,095	436	17.25×11.25	194	
BEDROOM 2	2,310	2,730	292	14.3 × 11	157	
LIVING	8,216	8,533	910	17×27.6	470	
KITCHEN	3,752	4,095	436	15×12	160	
DINING	3,047	3,413	362	13 × 11.5	150	
ENTRY & HALL	3,364	3,413	362	7×11.5 + 3×30	170	
BEDROOM 3	3,008	3,413	362	13×11.5	150	
BATHROOM	960	1,365	145	5×9	45	
INTERIOR BATH	198	USE ELECTRIC	UNIT HEATER			

FIGURE 11-16 / Calculate net ceiling areas

information is put on the electrical drawings since the electrician will locate and install the thermostat and tie the cable circuit into the power panel which serves it.

11-4   RADIANT PANEL SYSTEM DESIGN

The heating rates for radiant ceiling panels are generally given in watts per panel, Btuh per panel or both. As shown in Fig. 11-18, the ratings for a 2-ft x 4-ft panel may vary from about 500 to 750 watts per panel, depending on the panel selected and the manufacturer. Since 1 kW = 3,413 Btuh, 500 watts = 1,707 Btuh and 750 watts = 2,560 Btuh. It is important that the designer get accurate ratings by checking the engineering specifications for the type of panel which will actually be used on the project.

FIGURE 11-17 / Calculate maximum cable spacing

Room	Heat loss (Btuh)	Cable selected (Btuh)	Cable length (ft.)	Ceiling space available (ft.)	Ceiling area (s.f.)	Maximum spacing (in.)
BEDROOM 1	4,085	4,095	436	17.25×11.25	194	5.4
BEDROOM 2	2,310	2,730	292	14.3 × 11	157	6.4
LIVING	8,216	8,533	910	17×27.6	470	6.2
KITCHEN	3,752	4,095	436	15×12	160	4.4
DINING	3,047	3,413	362	13 × 11.5	150	4.9
ENTRY & HALL	3,364	3,413	362	7×11.5 + 3×30	170	5.6
BEDROOM 3	3,008	3,413	362	13×11.5	150	4.9
BATHROOM	960	1,365	145	5×9	45	3.7
INTERIOR BATH	198	USE ELECTRIC	UNIT HEATER			

Watts	Btuh	Size
500	1707	2'-0"x4'-0"
750	2560	2'-0"x4'-0"
560	1911	2'-0"x4'-0"
700	3019	2'-0"x5'-0"
500	1707	2'-0"x3'-0"
750	2560	2'-0"x3'-0"
1000	3413	2'-0"x3'-0"

FIGURE 11-18 / Radiant ceiling panel ratings

STEP-BY-STEP APPROACH

To design ceiling panels for the residence for which the heat loss was calculated in Sec. 8-12:

1. The first step in the design is to tabulate the Btuh for each space, as shown in Fig. 11-19.

2. List the square feet of ceiling area available for use in each space (Fig. 11-19).

    Any space which does not have sufficient ceiling area for the panels must have supplemental heat provided by adding wall panels or electric baseboard or wall unit heaters. Another solution would be to use another type of system, such as baseboard or unit heaters, and not put any ceiling panels in the space.

    It may be decided to put unit heaters in certain spaces where it is desirable to have a fan circulate the air through the space. Bathrooms are a typical example of where a unit heater might be used for this reason.

Room	Heat loss (Btuh)	Net ceiling area (s.f.)	Watts (Btuh ÷ 3413)	No. of panels
BEDROOM 1	4,085	194		
BEDROOM 2	2,310	157		
LIVING	8,216	470		
KITCHEN	3,752	160		
DINING	3,047	150		
ENTRY & HALL	3,364	170		
BEDROOM 3	3,008	150		
BATH	960	45		
INTERIOR BATH	198	14		

FIGURE 11-19 / Tabulate Btuh

Room	Heat loss (Btuh)	Net ceiling area (s.f.)	Watts (Btuh ÷ 3413)	No. of panels
BEDROOM 1	4,085	194	1197	
BEDROOM 2	2,310	157	677	
LIVING	8,216	470	2407	
KITCHEN	3,752	160	1100	
DINING	3,047	150	893	
ENTRY & HALL	3,364	170	986	
BEDROOM 3	3,008	150	881	
BATH	960	45	281	
INTERIOR BATH	198	14	58	

FIGURE 11-20 / Tabulate watts

3. Select the heating capacity for the space (Fig. 11-20).

4. Determine the number of ceiling panels required for each space (Fig. 11-21).

5. Determine the location of the thermostat, keeping in mind the location guides given in Sec. 9-3.

The biggest disadvantage of ceiling panels is that there is a tendency for the heat to stay high in the space (keep in mind that heat rises), requiring higher temperature settings to achieve comfort since feet will feel cold. Also, this type of heating will not heat "hidden" air spaces, such as under a table or desk; these will feel quite cool.

But from the builder's standpoint, it is an acceptable system because of its low initial cost, individual room control and "invisibility" (there are no portions of the system exposed except the thermostat).

Ceiling panels may be installed so that the heat is effectively put into the space at the place where most of it is lost—at the windows. In general, best results are

Room	Heat loss (Btuh)	Net ceiling area (s.f.)	Watts (Btuh ÷ 3413)	No. of panels
BEDROOM 1	4,085	194	1197	1-500W, 1-750W
BEDROOM 2	2,310	157	677	1-750W
LIVING	8,216	470	2407	1-500W, 1-1000W
KITCHEN	3,752	160	1100	1-500W, 1-750W
DINING	3,047	150	893	2-500W
ENTRY & HALL	3,364	170	986	2-500W
BEDROOM 3	3,008	150	881	2-500W
BATH	960	45	281	UNIT HEATER
INTERIOR BATH	198	14	58	UNIT HEATER

FIGURE 11-21 / Tabulate number of panels

11 / ELECTRIC HEAT DESIGN

obtained with this type of unit when the rooms are generally small (such as in rental apartments) and when the glass area is limited.

QUESTIONS

11-1. Discuss the advantages and disadvantages of using electric heating systems.

11-2. What is the primary reason that electric heating systems are used?

11-3. What are the most common types of electric heat installations used?

11-4. Why is it important to have well-insulated construction when electric heat will be used?

Design Exercises

11-5. Design an electric baseboard heating system for the residence in Appendix D, based on the heat loss calculations in Exercise 8-15.

11-6. Design a resistance cable heating system for the residence in Appendix D, based on the heat loss calculations in Exercise 8-15.

11-7. Design an electric baseboard heating system for a typical apartment (not the top floor) in Appendix A, based on the heat loss calculations in Exercise 8-17.

11-8. Design a resistance cable heating system for the residence in Appendix D, based on the heat loss calculations in Exercise 8-17.

CHAPTER 12
HEAT GAIN

12-1   GENERAL

Heat gain deals with the amount of heat which a space will accumulate during warm weather. To adequately cool the air inside the space, it is necessary to estimate the amount of heat which will build up in the space. Many of the heat gain factors are basically the same as those considered in heat loss (Chapter 8):

1.   Transmission (through walls, ceilings, and floors).
2.   Infiltration (through windows and doors).

While the terms *transmission* and *infiltration* are the same terms as are used for heat loss, and the general principles the same, there are some important differences in the time of day considered and the method of calculation. And for *total* heat gain, several other factors must also be considered:

1. Solar radiation.

2. Heat produced in the space.

3. Latent heat.

12-2   SENSIBLE AND LATENT HEAT

The heat gain of the building is a combination of *sensible* and *latent* heat, which together give the total heat gain, or total cooling load, of the building.

Sensible heat is heat which a substance absorbs, and while its temperature goes up, the substance *does not change its state*. For example, if some water (at, say, 50°F) is placed in the sunshine, the water will absorb the heat from the sun and warm up, but it will still be water.

Latent heat is heat which is absorbed or given off by a substance *when changing its state*. As a substance changes from a solid to a liquid or from a liquid to a gas, it *absorbs* heat, and as a substance changes from a gas to a liquid or from a liquid to a solid, it *gives off* heat.

12-3   TRANSMISSION

While the greatest heat loss will probably occur at night, the greatest heat gain will occur during a sunny day. Heat gain calculations make use of a heat transfer multiplier (HTM) (Fig. 12-6) which takes into account:

1. The temperature differential (between the inside of a building and the outside).

2. The type of construction (considering insulation value, mass of the type of construction, and thermal time lag) and the ability of the construction to hold heat.

Some typical heat transfer multipliers are listed in Fig. 12-6. To determine the heat gain by transmission, simply multiply the area of construction by the HTM for the type of construction.

When the HTM for a particular material is not listed in the table, it can be found by multiplying the *U* value by the equivalent temperature differential (ETD) (Fig. 12-11). Summer design conditions are listed in Fig. 8–54.

12-4   INFILTRATION

Heat gain *infiltration* is calculated in the same manner as heat loss infiltration—by multiplying the lineal feet of crackage by the infiltration factor. However, air leakage into structures is much smaller in the summer than in the winter. This is because winter air leakage is caused by a combination of wind direction and velocity which, when combined with the inside–outside temperature difference, creates a "chimney" effect of heat loss. This type of loss does not occur in the summer, and most localities have lower wind velocities in the summer.

Since there is much less air leakage in the summer, when calculating heat gain, ASHRAE suggests use of the air change or ventilation approach. The air change method is based on the assumption that the average air leakage will occur at a rate of one-half air change per hour. In this case, the heat gain is calculated in terms of Btuh per square foot of gross exposed wall area, using the Btuh per square foot values given in Fig. 12-7.

Using bedroom 1 for the residence in Appendix C (Fig. 12-1), it would have an outside exposed area of 34 ft x 8 ft or 272 sq ft. Based on the Btuh per square foot values given in Fig. 12-7, the value for a 95°F outside design temperature is 1.5 Btuh per sq ft. Based on this, the heat gain for the room is 272 sq ft x 1.5 Btuh per sq ft = 408 Btuh due to infiltration.

When mechanical ventilation is used, the amount of heat gain is based on the volume of air change in cfm. Assuming one air change per hour (the rate most commonly used), a room 12 ft-3 in. x 18 ft-3 in. x 8 ft high with 1,789 cu ft would ventilate 1,789 cu ft ÷ 60 min = 29.3 cfm. The heat gain is based on the Btuh of sensible heat per cfm of ventilating air shown in Fig. 12-7 and is selected from the table according to the outside design temperature used. With a 95°F outside design temperature, the heat gain would be 22 Btuh per cfm. So the heat gain of this room would be 29.8 cfm × 22 Btuh per cfm = 656 Btuh.

12-5 OCCUPANCY LOADS

The amount of heat given off by people (Fig. 12-8) and appliances must also be considered in any cooling load considerations. Since the number of occupants and appliances and the amount of appliance use which will occur will vary and cannot be predicted, the cooling load they will create must be estimated.

FIGURE 12-1 / Room plan

For residences, the occupant heat release is 225 Btuh per occupant. To estimate the number of occupants as accurately as possible, it is necessary to consider how much the owner entertains large groups of people and whether such entertaining occurs during the heat of the day or in the cooler evening. Many times this information is not available, and the designer will simply have to assume that there will be two occupants for each bedroom in the house.

The heat gain from occupants is then distributed equally among the living spaces of the house since during the time when the maximum heat gain will occur, the occupants will be using the living spaces and not the sleeping areas.

Appliance values are generally limited to the kitchen areas of the residence. ASHRAE suggests a heat gain load of 1,200 Btuh for the appliances. The intermittent use of appliances, along with the use of kitchen ventilating fans, makes it difficult to calculate exactly what the heat gain value should be. Appliances which are major sources of latent and sensible heat gain loads must be vented to the exterior. It would be very difficult to provide sufficient cooling to overcome the heat gain which an unvented clothes dryer would produce.

12-6   SOLAR RADIATION

Solar radiation consists primarily of heat gain through the windows. The window heat gain for both *absorbed solar energy* and *transmitted heat gain* are calculated together by use of a heat gain multiplier. This multiplier (Fig. 12-9) takes into consideration glass orientation (the direction the window faces), type of glass, type of shading, and outside design temperature, and the result is expressed in Btuh per square foot.

Glass which is protected by permanent shading, such as a wide roof overhang, is generally calculated as glass facing north. The overhang probably only protects part of the glass area, and in making the heat gain calculations, it is necessary to separate the square foot of glass which will be shaded from that portion which won't be shaded. The amount of shaded area varies with the direction the window faces, the length of the overhang and the geographic latitude (in degrees, Fig. 8–46) of the building. The table in Fig. 12-10 lists *shade line factors* which give the distance below the bottom of the fascia which the shadow will cover for every foot of overhang. The shade line factors shown are the average for the 5 hr of maximum solar intensity which would occur. Windows which face northeast and northwest cannot be effectively protected with roof overhangs, and they are considered to be in full sunshine with no shade.

EXAMPLE

Given: Using the wall section in Fig. 12-2 (from Appendix C), *note* that the top of the window is located at the same elevation (level) as the bottom of the fascia. Assume this is a 4-ft-wide, 4-ft-high, regular double-glass window, facing SE, with draperies, and that the building is located at about latitude 35°.

FIGURE 12-2 / Wall section

Problem: Determine the area in shade and the area in sunlight, and then the amount of heat gain through the window. Assume a 95°F design temperature with medium temperature range.

Shade line factor (from Fig. 12-10)   = 1.4
Roof overhang (from the wall section in Fig. 12-2) = 2 ft
Shade distance below overhang = 2 ft x 1.4   = 2.8 ft

Since the top of the window lines up with the bottom of the fascia, the top 2.8 ft of the window are considered in shade and calculated as facing N.
    Area of window in shade:

2.8 ft x 4.0 ft = 11.2 sq ft

Area of window in sun:

$$(4.0 \text{ ft} - 2.8 \text{ ft}) \times 4.0 \text{ ft} = 1.2 \text{ ft} \times 4.0 \text{ ft} = 4.8 \text{ sq ft}$$

Calculate the heat gain based on Fig. 12-9. Using an outdoor design temperature of 95°F, the heat gain through shaded glass is:

$$11.2 \text{ sq ft (in shade)} \times 17 \text{ Btuh/sq ft (N, draperies)} = 191 \text{ Btuh}$$

The heat gain through unshaded glass is:

$$4.8 \text{ sq ft (in sun)} \times 40 \text{ Btuh/sq ft (SE, draperies)} = 192 \text{ Btuh}$$

Therefore, the total heat gain through the window is:

$$191 \text{ Btuh} + 192 \text{ Btuh} = 383 \text{ Btuh}$$

EXAMPLE

Given: Using the wall section in Fig. 12-3, *note* that the top of the window is 8 in. below the bottom of the fascia (overhang). Assume that this is a 3 ft-6 in.-wide, 4 ft-6 in.-high single-glass window, facing E, with draperies, and that the building is located at about latitude 35° where the outside design temperature is 95°F.

Problem: Determine the total heat gain through the window.

```
Shade line factor (from Fig. 12-10)              = 0.8
Roof overhang (from the wall section in Fig. 12-4) = 3 ft
Shade distance below overhang = 3 ft x 0.8       = 2.4 ft
```

Since the window beings 8 in. (0.67 ft) below the overhang, this distance must be subtracted from the shade distance to determine how much of the window is covered by the shade (Fig. 12-4).

Area of window in shade:

$$(2.4 \text{ ft} - 0.67 \text{ ft}) \times 3.5 \text{ ft} = 1.73 \text{ ft} \times 3.5 \text{ ft} = 6.1 \text{ sq ft}$$

Area of window in sun:

$$(4.5 \text{ ft} - 1.73 \text{ ft}) \times 3.5 \text{ ft} = 2.77 \text{ ft} \times 3.5 \text{ ft} = 9.7 \text{ sq ft}$$

FIGURE 12-3 / Wall section   FIGURE 12-4 / Shade line

Calculate the heat gain based on Fig. 12-9. Using an outside design temperature of
95°F, the heat gain through shaded glass is:

6.1 sq ft (in shade) × 23 Btuh/sq ft (N, draperies) = 140.3 (140) Btuh

The heat gain through shaded glass is:

9.7 sq ft (in sun) × 56 Btuh/sq ft (E, draperies) = 545.2 (545) Btuh

Therefore, the total heat gain through the window is:

140 Btuh + 545 Btuh = 685 Btuh

12-7 LATENT HEAT GAIN

Heat gain in buildings also occurs due to latent heat. In residential cooling the latent heat is generally estimated to be about 30 percent of the total sensible heat calculated. While this percentage is an approximation, there are numerous moisture sources in a residence. Since it would be very difficult to precisely evaluate the latent heat which will occur, ASHRAE has determined that the 30 percent results in a design system which will be comfortable.

12-8 TOTAL COOLING LOAD

The total heat gain of the building is the sum of the sensible and latent heat gains. This total cooling load in a residence is calculated as 1.3 times the total sensible heat load.
    The sensible heat gain is the total of:

1.   The heat transmitted through the floors, ceilings and walls.

2.   The occupants' body heat.

3.   The appliance heat, including lights.

4.   The heat gain through glass, by both absorption and solar radiation.

5.   Infiltration.

12-9 HEAT GAIN CALCULATIONS

Heat gain calculations are similar to heat loss calculations (Chapter 8). The heat gain for the residence in Appendix C (the same one for which the heat loss was calculated) is calculated in Fig. 12-5. One major difference that must be considered is that during the summer roof temperatures outside could be as high as 140–150°F when the building has a dark roof, making its ΔT value very high compared to that of the walls. This must be taken into account when selecting the HTM value.

QUESTIONS

12-1. What factors must be considered when determining heat gain in buildings?

12-2. Define *sensible* and *latent heat*.

12-3. How does the orientation of the windows in the building affect the heat gain?

12-4. Why must the number of occupants and the type of activity be considered in a heat gain calculation?

12-5. What factors does a heat transfer multiplier take into account?

12-6. How is infiltration calculated for heat gain, and how does this compare with infiltration calculations in heat loss?

Design Exercises

12-7. Calculate the heat gain for the residence in Appendix D. Assume the residence will be built in Richmond, Virginia.

12-8. Calculate the heat gain for a top floor apartment and one on a lower floor (use the apartment with most of the windows facing south and west in Appendix A). Assume the apartments will be built in Seattle, Washington.

HTM (From Fig. 12–6)
Medium 95°F
Walls 1.9
Cold walls (medium 90°F) 1.4
Ceilings 1.8 (dark)
Floors, no heat gain
Infiltration 1.5 Btuh/sq. ft gross
   exposed wall

Windows
Determine shade line
From Appendix C—location, 35° lat.
From Appendix C—orientation
   Front of house faces northeast,
     all in sun
   Rear of house faces southwest
Roof overhang 2'0"
Shade line factor (Fig. 12-10)
   Southwest 1.4
Draperies—all except kitchen
Window HTM (Fig. 12-9)
   Northeast 32 (with draperies)
             51 (without draperies)
   Southwest 17 (shade & draperies)
             40 (sun & draperies)
   Southeast 40 (sun & draperies,
              no overhang)

Occupants
2 @ 225 Btuh in kitchen
4 @ 225 Btuh in living-family

FIGURE 12—5 / Heat Gain

Room	Portion considered	Dimensions	Height	Gross area or l.f.	Openings	Opening area	Net area or l.f.	HTM U value	ETD	Heat gain (Btuh)	Room heat gain (Btuh)
BEDROOM 1 INC. 2 CLOSETS AND BATH	EXTERIOR WALL	12.7+18.7+2.5	8	272	4.0×4.0 / 3.0×4.0	28	244	1.9		464	
	CEILING	12.7×18.7+	8	323			323	1.8		582	
	SM. CLOSET	2.5×4.0+									
	CLOS. BATH	5.0×14.7									
	GLASS, S.W.SUN	4.0×1.2		4.8			4.8	40		192	
	SHADE	4.0×2.8		11.2			11.2	17		191	
	S.E. SUN	3.0×4.0		12			12	32		384	2221
	INFILTRATION			272			272	1.5		408	
BEDROOM 2 INC. 1 CLOSET	EXT. WALL	11.5+2.5	8	112	3.0×4.0	12	100	1.9		190	
	CEILING	11.5×18.8+ / 2.5×4.0		226			226	1.8		407	
	INFIL.	11.5+2.5	8	112			112	1.5		168	1148
	GLASS, S.W.SUN	3.0×1.2		3.6			3.6	40		115	
	SHADE	3.0×2.8		8.4			8.4	17		143	
LIVING (4 PEOPLE)	EXT. WALL	32.25+7.0	8	314	2-6.0×6.7	80	234	1.9		445	
	COLD WALL	18.8-7.0	8	95			95	1.4		133	
	CEILING	18.75×32.25		605			605	1.8		1089	
	INFIL.			314			314	1.5		471	5481
	GLASS, S.W.SUN	12×3.9		46.8			46.8	40		1872	
	SHADE	12×2.8		33.6			33.6	17		571	
	2 PEOPLE									900	
KITCHEN (2 PEOPLE)	EXT. WALL	15.8+7.0	8	183	4.0×3.0	12	171	1.9		291	
	COLD WALL	10.3	8	82	3.0×6.8	21	61	1.4		86	
	CEILING	15.8×17.3		274			274	1.8		493	
	INFIL			183			183	1.5		275	3604
	GLASS, N.E.SUN			12			12	51		612	
	DOOR										
	APPLIANCES									1200	
	1 PERSON			21			21	9.4		197	
DINING	EXT. WALL	14.5	8	116	6.0×5.0	30	86	1.9		164	
	CEILING	14.5×13.3		193			193	1.8		375	3604
	INFIL			116			116	1.5		174	
	GLASS, N.E.SUN			30			30	32		960	1673

FIGURE 12-5 / Heat gain for building

Room	Portion considered	Dimensions	Height	Gross area or l.f.	Openings	Opening area	Net area or l.f.	HTM U value	ETD	Heat gain (Btuh)	Room heat gain (Btuh)
ENTRY (AND HALL)	EXT. WALL	7.5+2.5	8	80	DISIDELTS.	40	40	1.9		76	
					6.0×6.8			1.8		520	
	CEILING	4.0×37.0+ / 13.2×(7.5+2.5)		289			289	1.5		120	
	INFIL			80			80	1.5		120	
	GLASS, N.E.			20			20	32		640	
	DOOR			20			20	12		240	1596
BEDROOM 3	EXT. WALL	14.5+6.8+ / 6.8	8	225	4.0×4.0	16	209	1.9		397	
	CEILING	14.5×13.3 / 6.8×6.8		239			239	1.8		430	
	INFIL			225			225	1.5		338	
	GLASS, N.E.			16			16	32		512	1677
BATH	EXT. WALL	10.5	8	84	2.0×2.0	4	80	1.9		152	
	CEILING	10.5×6.8		72			72	1.8		130	
	INFIL			84			84	1.5		126	
	GLASS, S.W.			4			4	32		128	536

CALCULATED SENSIBLE HEAT GAIN   17,936 BTUH
TOTAL HEAT GAIN = SENSIBLE HEAT GAIN × 1.3 (LATENT HEAT)
17,936 × 1.3 = 23,317 BTUH

BEDROOM 1   = 2221 × 1.3 = 2887
BEDROOM 2   = 1148 × 1.3 = 1492
LIVING   = 5481 × 1.3 = 7125
KITCHEN   = 3604 × 1.3 = 4685
DINING   = 1673 × 1.3 = 2175
ENTRY (AND HALL) = 1596 × 1.3 = 2075
BEDROOM 3   = 1677 × 1.3 = 2188
BATH   = 536 × 1.3 = 697

FIGURE 12-5 / Heat gain for building (continued)

TABLE 6

HEAT GAIN FACTORS FOR ROOFS, CEILINGS, FLOORS AND INFILTRATION

Btuh per Square Foot

Outdoor Design Dry-Bulb Temperature	90		95			100		105		110
Daily Temperature Range	Low	Med.	Low	Med.	High	Med.	High	Med.	High	High
WALLS AND DOORS										
1. Frame and Veneer-on-Frame										
(a) Wood sheathing or 1/2" insulating sheathing	6.0	4.8	7.2	6.0	4.8	7.5	6.0	8.7	7.5	8.7
(b) 25/32" insulating sheathing or one reflective air space	4.3	3.5	5.1	4.5	3.5	5.4	4.5	6.3	5.4	6.3
(c) Same as (a) or (b) plus either 1" or 2" insulation or 2 reflective air spaces	2.9	2.4	3.6	3.1	2.4	3.7	3.1	4.4	3.7	4.4
(d) Same as (a) or (b) plus either more than 2" insulation, or 3 reflective air spaces	1.8	1.5	2.2	1.9	1.5	2.3	1.9	2.7	2.3	2.7
2. Masonry Walls, 8" Block or Brick										
(a) Plastered or plain	7.2	5.4	9.7	7.9	5.4	10.4	7.9	12.5	10.4	12.5
(b) Furred, no insulation	4.6	3.4	6.0	4.9	3.4	6.3	4.9	7.9	6.3	7.9
(c) Furred, with less than 1" insulation, or one reflective air space	3.1	2.3	4.3	3.3	2.3	4.3	3.3	5.4	4.3	5.4
(d) Furred, with 1" to 2" insulation, or two reflective air spaces	2.1	1.6	2.8	2.3	1.6	3.0	2.3	3.7	3.0	3.7
(e) Furred, with more than 2" insulation, or three reflective air spaces	1.4	1.0	1.8	1.5	1.0	1.9	1.5	2.4	1.9	2.4
3. Partitions										
(a) Frame, finished one side only, no insulation	8.5	6.0	11.4	9.1	6.0	12.0	9.1	15.0	12.0	15.0
(b) Frame, finished both sides, no insulation	4.8	3.4	6.6	5.1	3.4	6.9	5.1	8.5	6.9	8.5
(c) Frame, finished both sides, more than 1" insulation or two reflective air spaces	2.0	1.4	2.7	2.1	1.4	2.8	2.1	3.5	2.8	3.5
(d) Masonry, plastered one side, no insulation	2.6	1.2	4.4	3.0	1.2	4.7	3.0	6.6	4.7	6.6
4. Wood Doors (Consider glass areas of doors as windows)	11.4	9.4	14.0	12.0	9.4	14.0	12.0	17.0	14.0	17.0
CEILING OR ROOFS										
5. Ceilings under naturally vented attic, or vented flat roof										
(a) Uninsulated ... Dark	10.0	9.1	11.0	10.0	9.1	11.4	10.0	12.5	11.4	12.5
Light	8.2	7.2	9.1	8.2	7.2	9.4	8.2	10.4	9.4	10.4
(b) Less than 2" insulation or reflective air space ... Dark	4.3	3.9	4.8	4.4	3.9	4.9	4.4	5.4	4.9	5.4
Light	3.5	3.1	4.1	3.6	3.1	4.1	3.6	4.6	4.1	4.6
(c) 2" to 4" insulation, or two reflective air spaces ... Dark	2.6	2.3	2.9	2.6	2.3	2.9	2.6	3.2	2.9	3.2
Light	2.1	1.9	2.4	2.2	1.9	2.5	2.2	2.8	2.5	2.8
(d) More than 4" insulation or three or more reflective air spaces ... Dark	1.8	1.6	1.9	1.8	1.6	2.0	1.8	2.2	2.0	2.2
Light	1.4	1.2	1.6	1.4	1.2	1.6	1.4	1.8	1.6	1.8
6. Built-up Roof, No Ceiling										
(a) Uninsulated ... Dark	17.0	16.0	19.0	18.0	16.0	20.0	18.0	22.0	20.0	22.0
Light	14.0	12.5	16.0	14.0	12.5	16.0	14.0	18.0	16.0	18.0
(b) 2" Roof insulation ... Dark	8.5	7.9	9.7	8.7	7.9	9.7	8.7	11.0	9.7	11.0
Light	6.9	6.3	7.9	7.2	6.3	8.2	7.2	9.1	8.2	9.1
(c) 3" Roof insulation ... Dark	6.0	5.4	6.6	6.3	5.4	6.9	6.3	7.5	6.9	7.5
Light	4.9	4.3	5.6	5.1	4.3	5.6	5.1	6.3	5.6	6.3
7. Ceilings under rooms which are not cooled	2.7	1.9	3.6	2.9	1.9	3.8	2.9	4.8	3.8	4.8
FLOORS										
8. Over rooms which are not cooled	3.4	2.4	4.6	3.6	2.4	4.8	3.6	6.0	4.8	6.0
9. Over basement, enclosed crawl space, or concrete slab on ground	0	0	0	0	0	0	0	0	0	0
10. Over open crawl space	4.8	3.4	6.6	5.1	3.4	6.9	5.1	8.5	6.9	8.5
INFILTRATION										
11. Btuh per sq. ft. of gross exposed wall area	1.1	1.1	1.5	1.5	1.5	1.9	1.9	2.2	2.2	2.6
MECHANICAL VENTILATION										
12. Btuh per cfm	16.0	16.0	22.0	22.0	22.0	27.0	27.0	32.0	32.0	38.0

Courtesy of the Hydronics Institute.

FIGURE 12-6 / Heat transfer multipliers

Heat Gain Calculations / 12-9

No. 10 - Wood Doors	Summer Temperature Difference and Daily Temperature Range												
	10		15			20			25		30	35	U
	L	M	L	M	H	L	M	H	M	H	H	H	
	HTM (Btuh per sq. ft.)												
A. Hollow Core	9.9	7.6	12.7	10.4	7.6	15.5	13.2	10.4	16.0	13.2	16.0	18.8	.560
B. Hollow Core & Wood Storm	5.8	4.5	7.5	6.1	4.5	9.1	7.8	6.1	9.4	7.8	9.4	11.1	.330
C. Hollow Core & Metal Storm	6.3	4.9	8.1	6.7	4.9	9.9	8.5	6.7	10.3	8.5	10.3	12.1	.360
D. Solid Core	8.1	6.3	10.4	8.6	6.3	12.7	10.9	8.6	13.2	10.9	13.2	15.5	.460
E. Solid Core & Wood Storm	5.1	3.9	6.6	5.4	3.9	8.0	6.8	5.4	8.3	6.8	8.3	9.7	.290
F. Solid Core & Metal Storm	5.6	4.4	7.2	6.0	4.4	8.8	7.6	6.0	9.2	7.6	9.2	10.8	.320
G. Panel	11.8	9.1	15.1	12.5	9.1	18.5	15.8	12.5	19.2	15.8	19.2	22.5	.670
H. Panel & Wood Storm	6.3	4.9	8.1	6.7	4.9	9.9	8.5	6.7	10.3	8.5	10.3	12.1	.360
I. Panel & Metal Storm	7.2	5.6	9.3	7.6	5.6	11.3	9.7	7.6	11.7	9.7	11.7	13.8	.410

No. 11 - Metal Doors	10		15			20			25		30	35	U
	L	M	L	M	H	L	M	H	M	H	H	H	
	HTM (Btuh per sq. ft.)												
A. Fiberglass Core	10.4	8.0	13.3	11.0	8.0	16.3	13.9	11.0	16.9	13.9	16.9	19.8	.590
B. Fiberglass Core & Storm	6.5	5.0	8.3	6.8	5.0	10.1	8.7	6.8	10.5	8.7	10.5	12.3	.367
C. Polystyrene Core	8.3	6.4	10.6	8.7	6.4	13.0	11.1	8.7	13.4	11.1	13.4	15.8	.470
D. Polystyrene Core & Storm	5.6	4.3	7.2	5.9	4.3	8.7	7.5	5.9	9.1	7.5	9.1	10.7	.317
E. Urethane Core	3.3	2.6	4.3	3.5	2.6	5.2	4.5	3.5	5.4	4.5	5.4	6.4	.190
F. Urethane Core & Storm	3.0	2.3	3.8	3.2	2.3	4.7	4.0	3.2	4.9	4.0	4.9	5.7	.170

No. 12 Wood Frame Exterior Walls With Sheathing and Siding or Brick Veneer or Other Exterior Finish.	10		15			20			25		30	35	U
	L	M	L	M	H	L	M	H	M	H	H	H	
	HTM (Btuh per sq. ft.)												
A. None ½" Gypsum Board (R-0.5)	4.8	3.7	6.1	5.0	3.7	7.5	6.4	5.0	7.8	6.4	7.8	9.1	.271
B. None ½" Asphalt Board (R-1.3)	3.8	3.0	4.9	4.0	3.0	6.0	5.1	4.0	6.2	5.1	6.2	7.3	.217
C. R-11 ½" Gypsum Board (R-0.5)	1.6	1.2	2.0	1.7	1.2	2.5	2.1	1.7	2.6	2.1	2.6	3.0	.090
D. R-11 ½" Asphalt Board (R-1.3) R-11 ½" Bead Brd. (R-1.8) R-13 ½" Gypsum Brd. (R-0.5)	1.4	1.1	1.8	1.5	1.1	2.2	1.9	1.5	2.3	1.9	2.3	2.7	.080
E. R-11 ½" Extr Poly Brd. (R-2.5) R-11 ¾" Bead Brd. (R-2.7) R-13 ½" Asphalt Brd. (R-1.3) R-13 ½" Bead Brd. (R-1.8)	1.3	1.0	1.7	1.4	1.0	2.1	1.8	1.4	2.1	1.8	2.1	2.5	.075
F. R-11 1" Bead Brd. (R-3.6) R-11 ¾" Extr Poly Brd. (R-3.8) R-13 ½" Extr Poly Brd (R-2.5) R-13 ¾" Bead Brd. (R-2.7)	1.2	1.0	1.6	1.3	1.0	1.9	1.7	1.3	2.0	1.7	2.0	2.4	.070
G. R-13 ¾" Extr Poly Brd (R-3.8) R-13 1" Bead Brd (R-3.6)	1.1	.9	1.5	1.2	.9	1.8	1.5	1.2	1.9	1.5	1.9	2.2	.065
H. R-11 1" Extr Brd. (R-5.0) R-13 1" Extr Poly Brd. (R-5.0) R-19 ½" Gypsum Brd. (R-0.5)	1.1	.8	1.4	1.1	.8	1.7	1.4	1.1	1.7	1.4	1.7	2.0	.060
I. R-19 ½" Asphalt Brd. (R-1.3) R-19 ½" Bead Brd. (R-1.8)	1.0	.7	1.2	1.0	.7	1.5	1.3	1.0	1.6	1.3	1.6	1.8	.055
J. R-11 R-8 Sheathing R-13 R-8 Sheathing R-19 ½" or ¾" Extr Poly R-19 ¾" or 1" Bead Brd.	.9	.7	1.1	.9	.7	1.4	1.2	.9	1.4	1.2	1.4	1.7	.050
K. R-19 1" Extr Poly Brd (R-5.0)	.8	.6	1.0	.8	.6	1.2	1.1	.8	1.3	1.1	1.3	1.5	.045
L. R-19 R-8 Sheathing	.7	.5	.9	.7	.5	1.1	.9	.7	1.1	.9	1.1	1.3	.040
M. R-27 Wall	.7	.5	.8	.7	.5	1.0	.9	.7	1.1	.9	1.1	1.2	.037
N. R-30 Wall	.6	.4	.7	.6	.4	.9	.8	.6	.9	.8	.9	1.1	.033
O. R-33 Wall	.5	.4	.7	.6	.4	.8	.7	.6	.9	.7	.9	1.0	.030

Reprinted with permission of ACCA, *Manual J*, 1986.

FIGURE 12-6 / Heat transfer multipliers (continued)

No. 13 - Partitions Between Conditioned and Unconditioned Space - Wood Frame Partitions

Summer Temperature Difference and Daily Temperature Range

	10		15			20			25		30	35	U
	L	M	L	M	H	L	M	H	M	H	H	H	
						HTM (Btuh per sq. ft.)							
A. None ½" Gypsum Board (R-0.5)	2.4	1.4	3.8	2.7	1.4	5.1	4.1	2.7	5.4	4.1	5.4	6.8	.271
B. None ½" Asphalt Board (R-1.3)	2.0	1.1	3.0	2.2	1.1	4.1	3.3	2.2	4.3	3.3	4.3	5.4	.217
C. R-11 ½" Gypsum Board (R-0.5)	.8	.4	1.3	.9	.4	1.7	1.3	.9	1.8	1.3	1.8	2.2	.090
D. R-11 ½" Asphalt Board (R-1.3); R-11 ½" Bead Brd. (R-1.8); R-13 ½" Gypsum Brd. (R-0.5)	.7	.4	1.1	.8	.4	1.5	1.2	.8	1.6	1.2	1.6	2.0	.080
E. R-11 ½" Extr Poly Brd. (R-2.5); R-11 ¾" Bead Brd. (R-2.7); R-13 ½" Asphalt Brd. (R-1.3); R-13 ½" Bead Brd. (R-1.8)	.7	.4	1.0	.8	.4	1.4	1.1	.8	1.5	1.1	1.5	1.9	.075
F. R-11 1" Bead Brd. (R-3.6); R-11 ¾" Extr Poly Brd. (R-3.8); R-13 ½" Extr Poly Brd. (R-2.5); R-13 ¾" Bead Brd. (R-2.7)	.6	.4	1.0	.7	.4	1.3	1.0	.7	1.4	1.0	1.4	1.8	.070
G. R-13 ¾" Extr Poly Brd. (R-3.8); R-13 1" Bead Brd. (R-3.6)	.6	.3	.9	.6	.3	1.2	1.0	.6	1.3	1.0	1.3	1.6	.065
H. R-11 1" Extr Brd. (R-5.0); R-13 1" Extr Poly Brd. (R-5.0); R-19 ½" Gypsum Brd. (R-0.5)	.5	.3	.8	.6	.3	1.1	.9	.6	1.2	.9	1.2	1.5	.060
I. R-19 ½" Asphalt Brd. (R-1.3); R-19 ½" Bead Brd. (R-1.8)	.5	.3	.8	.5	.3	1.0	.8	.5	1.1	.8	1.1	1.4	.055
J. R-11 R-8 Sheathing; R-13 R-8 Sheathing; R-19 ½" or ¾" Extr Poly; R-19 ¾" or 1" Bead Brd.	.4	.2	.7	.5	.2	.9	.7	.5	1.0	.7	1.0	1.2	.050
K. R-19 1" Extr Poly Brd. (R-5.0)	.4	.2	.6	.4	.2	.9	.7	.4	.9	.7	.9	1.1	.045
L. R-19 R-8 Sheathing	.4	.2	.6	.4	.2	.8	.6	.4	.8	.6	.8	1.0	.040

No. 13 - Partitions Between Conditioned & Unconditioned Space. Brick or Brick Partitions

	10		15			20			25		30	35	U
	L	M	L	M	H	L	M	H	M	H	H	H	
						HTM (Btuh per sq. ft.)							
M. 8" Brick, No Insul., Unfinished	1.3	0	3.8	1.8	0	6.4	4.3	1.8	6.9	4.3	6.9	9.4	.510
N. 8" Brick R-5	.4	0	1.1	.5	0	1.8	1.2	.5	1.9	1.2	1.9	2.7	.144
O. 8" Brick R-11	.2	0	.6	.3	0	1.0	.7	.3	1.0	.7	1.0	1.4	.077
P. 8" Brick R-19	.1	0	.4	.2	0	.6	.4	.2	.6	.4	.6	.9	.048
Q. 4" Brick 8" Block, No Insul.	1.0	0	3.0	1.4	0	5.0	3.4	1.4	5.4	3.4	5.4	7.4	.400
R. 4" Brick 8" Block R-5	.3	0	1.0	.5	0	1.7	1.1	.5	1.8	1.1	1.8	2.5	.133
S. 4" Brick 8" Block R-11	.2	0	.6	.3	0	.9	.6	.3	1.0	.6	1.0	1.4	.074
T. 4" Brick 8" Block R-19	.1	0	.4	.2	0	.6	.4	.2	.6	.4	.6	.9	.047

No. 14 - Masonry Walls, Block or Brick Finished or Unfinished - Above Grade

	10		15			20			25		30	35	U
	L	M	L	M	H	L	M	H	M	H	H	H	
						HTM (Btuh per sq. ft.)							
A. 8" or 12" Block, No Insul., Unfinished	5.3	3.2	7.8	5.8	3.2	10.4	8.3	5.8	10.9	8.3	10.9	13.4	.510
B. 8" or 12" Block + R-5	1.5	.9	2.2	1.6	.9	2.9	2.3	1.6	3.1	2.3	3.1	3.8	.144
C. 8" or 12" Block + R-11	.8	.5	1.2	.9	.5	1.6	1.3	.9	1.6	1.3	1.6	2.0	.077
D. 8" or 12" Block + R-19	.5	.3	.7	.5	.3	1.0	.8	.5	1.0	.8	1.0	1.3	.048
E. 4" Brick + 8" Block, No Insul.	4.1	2.5	6.1	4.5	2.5	8.1	6.5	4.5	8.5	6.5	8.5	10.5	.400
F. 4" Brick + 8" Block + R-5	1.4	.8	2.0	1.5	.8	2.7	2.2	1.5	2.8	2.2	2.8	3.5	.133
G. 4" Brick + 8" Block + R-11	.8	.5	1.1	.8	.5	1.5	1.2	.8	1.6	1.2	1.6	1.9	.074
H. 4" Brick + 8" Block + R-19	.5	.3	.7	.5	.3	1.0	.8	.5	1.0	.8	1.0	1.2	.047

Reprinted with permission of ACCA, *Manual J*, 1986.

FIGURE 12-6 / Heat transfer multipliers (continued)

No. 15 - Masonry Walls, Block or Brick Below Grade -

Summer Temperature Difference and Daily Temperature Range												
10		15			20			25		30	35	U
L	M	L	M	H	L	M	H	M	H	H	H	
HTM (Btuh per sq. ft.)												

All

L	M	L	M	H	L	M	H	M	H	H	H	U
0.0	0.0	0.0	0.0	0.0	0.0	0.0	0.0	0.0	0.0	0.0	0.0	

No. 16 - Ceilings Under a Ventilated Attic Space.
Light Colored Roof

	10		15			20			25		30	35	U
	L	M	L	M	H	L	M	H	M	H	H	H	
	HTM (Btuh per sq. ft.)												
A. No Insulation	13.1	11.4	15.3	13.5	11.4	17.5	15.7	13.5	17.9	15.7	17.9	20.1	.437
B. R-7 Insulation	3.4	2.9	3.9	3.5	2.9	4.5	4.0	3.5	4.6	4.0	4.6	5.2	.112
C. R-11 Insulation	2.5	2.2	2.9	2.6	2.2	3.3	3.0	2.6	3.4	3.0	3.4	3.8	.083
D. R-19 Insulation	1.6	1.4	1.9	1.6	1.4	2.1	1.9	1.6	2.2	1.9	2.2	2.4	.053
E. R-22 Insulation	1.4	1.2	1.7	1.5	1.2	1.9	1.7	1.5	2.0	1.7	2.0	2.2	.048
F. R-26 Insulation	1.1	1.0	1.3	1.2	1.0	1.5	1.4	1.2	1.6	1.4	1.6	1.7	.038
G. R-30 Insulation	1.0	.9	1.2	1.0	.9	1.3	1.2	1.0	1.4	1.2	1.4	1.5	.033
H. R-38 Insulation	.8	.7	.9	.8	.7	1.0	.9	.8	1.1	.9	1.1	1.2	.026
I. R-44 Insulation	.7	.6	.8	.7	.6	.9	.8	.7	.9	.8	.9	1.1	.023
J. R-57 Insulation	.5	.4	.6	.5	.4	.7	.6	.5	.7	.6	.7	.8	.017
K. Wood Decking, No Insulation	8.6	7.5	10.0	8.9	7.4	11.4	10.3	8.9	11.8	10.3	11.8	13.2	.287

No. 16 - Ceilings Under a Ventilated Attic (Btuh per sq. ft.)
Dark Colored Roof

	10		15			20			25		30	35	U
	L	M	L	M	H	L	M	H	M	H	H	H	
	HTM (Btuh per sq. ft.)												
A. No Insulation	16.6	14.9	18.8	17.0	14.9	21.0	19.2	17.0	21.4	19.2	21.4	23.6	.437
B. R-7 Insulation	4.3	3.8	4.8	4.4	3.8	5.4	4.9	4.4	5.5	4.9	5.5	6.0	.112
C. R-11 Insulation	3.2	2.8	3.6	3.2	2.8	4.0	3.7	3.2	4.1	3.7	4.1	4.5	.083
D. R-19 Insulation	2.0	1.8	2.3	2.1	1.8	2.5	2.3	2.1	2.6	2.3	2.6	2.9	.053
E. R-22 Insulation	1.8	1.6	2.1	1.9	1.6	2.3	2.1	1.9	2.4	2.1	2.4	2.6	.048
F. R-26 Insulation	1.4	1.3	1.6	1.5	1.3	1.8	1.7	1.5	1.9	1.7	1.9	2.1	.038
G. R-30 Insulation	1.3	1.1	1.4	1.3	1.1	1.6	1.5	1.3	1.6	1.5	1.6	1.8	.033
H. R-38 Insulation	1.0	.9	1.1	1.0	.9	1.2	1.1	1.0	1.3	1.1	1.3	1.4	.026
I. R-44 Insulation	.9	.8	1.0	.9	.8	1.1	1.0	.9	1.1	1.0	1.1	1.2	.023
J. R-57 Insulation	.6	.6	.7	.7	.6	.8	.7	.7	.8	.7	.8	.9	017
K. Wood Decking, No Insulation	10.9	9.8	12.3	11.2	9.8	13.8	12.6	11.2	14.0	12.6	14.0	15.5	.287

No. 17 - Roof on Exposed Beams or Rafters
Light Colored Roof

	10		15			20			25		30	35	U
	L	M	L	M	H	L	M	H	M	H	H	H	
	HTM (Btuh pr sq. ft.)												
A. 1½" Wood Decking, No Insul	8.8	7.6	10.3	9.1	7.6	11.8	10.6	9.1	12.1	10.6	12.1	13.5	.294
B. 1½" Wood Decking R-4	4.2	3.6	4.9	4.3	3.6	5.6	5.0	4.3	5.7	5.0	5.7	6.4	.140
C. 1½" Wood Decking R-5	3.6	3.1	4.2	3.7	3.1	4.8	4.3	3.7	4.9	4.3	4.9	5.5	.119
D. 1½" Wood Decking R-6	3.2	2.8	3.7	3.3	2.8	4.2	3.8	3.3	4.3	3.8	4.3	4.9	.106
E. 1½" Wood Decking R-8	2.6	2.3	3.1	2.7	2.3	3.5	3.2	2.7	3.6	3.2	3.6	4.0	.088
F. 2" Shredded Wood Planks	6.2	5.4	7.2	6.4	5.4	8.3	7.5	6.4	8.5	7.5	8.5	9.5	.207
G. 3" Shredded Wood Planks	4.6	4.0	5.4	4.3	4.0	6.2	5.5	4.8	6.3	5.5	6.3	7.1	.154
H. 1½" Fiber Board Insulation	5.1	4.4	5.9	5.2	4.4	6.8	6.1	5.2	6.9	6.1	6.9	7.8	.169
I. 2" Fiber Board Insulation	4.0	3.5	4.7	4.2	3.5	5.4	4.9	4.2	5.5	4.9	5.5	6.2	.135
J. 3" Fiber Board Insulation	2.9	2.5	3.4	3.0	2.5	3.9	3.5	3.0	4.0	3.5	4.0	4.5	.097
K. 1½" Wood Decking R-13	1.8	1.6	2.1	1.9	1.6	2.4	2.2	1.9	2.5	2.2	2.5	2.8	.060
L. 1½" Wood Decking R-19	1.2	1.1	1.4	1.3	1.1	1.6	1.5	1.3	1.7	1.5	1.7	1.9	.041

Reprinted with permission of ACCA, *Manual J*, 1986.

FIGURE 12-6 / Heat transfer multipliers (continued)

No. 17 - Roof on Exposed Beams or Rafters — Dark Colored Roof

	10		15			20			25		30	35	U
Summer Temperature Difference and Daily Temperature Range	L	M	L	M	H	L	M	H	M	H	H	H	
HTM (Btuh per sq. ft.)													
A. 1½" Wood Decking, No Insul.	11.2	10.0	12.6	11.5	10.0	14.1	12.9	11.5	14.4	12.9	14.4	15.9	.294
B. 1½" Wood Decking R-4	5.3	4.8	6.0	5.5	4.8	6.7	6.2	5.5	6.9	6.2	6.9	7.6	.140
C. 1½" Wood Decking R-5	4.5	4.0	5.1	4.6	4.0	5.7	5.2	4.6	5.8	5.2	5.8	6.4	.119
D. 1½" Wood Decking R-6	4.0	3.6	4.6	4.1	3.6	5.1	4.7	4.1	5.2	4.7	5.2	5.7	.106
E. 1½" Wood Decking R-8	3.3	3.0	3.8	3.4	3.0	4.2	3.9	3.4	4.3	3.9	4.3	4.8	.088
F. 2" Shredded Wood Planks	7.9	7.0	8.9	8.1	7.0	9.9	9.1	8.1	10.1	9.1	10.1	11.2	.207
G. 3" Shredded Wood Planks	5.9	5.2	6.6	6.0	5.2	7.4	6.8	6.0	7.5	6.8	7.5	8.3	.154
H. 1½" Fiber Board Insulation	6.4	5.7	7.3	6.6	5.7	8.1	7.4	6.6	8.3	7.4	8.3	9.1	.169
I. 2" Fiber Board Insulation	5.1	4.6	5.8	5.3	4.6	6.5	5.9	5.3	6.6	5.9	6.6	7.3	.136
J. 3" Fiber Board Insulation	3.7	3.3	4.2	3.8	3.3	4.7	4.3	3.8	4.8	4.3	4.8	5.2	.097
K. 1½" Wood Decking R-13	2.3	2.0	2.6	2.3	2.0	2.9	2.6	2.3	2.9	2.6	2.9	3.2	.060
L. 1½" Wood Decking R-19	1.6	1.4	1.8	1.6	1.4	2.0	1.8	1.6	2.0	1.8	2.0	2.2	.041

No. 18 - Roof-Ceiling Combination - Light Colored Roof

	10		15			20			25		30	35	U
	L	M	L	M	H	L	M	H	M	H	H	H	
HTM (Btuh per sq. ft.)													
A. No Insulation	8.6	7.5	10.0	8.9	7.5	11.5	10.3	8.9	11.8	10.3	11.8	13.2	.287
B. R-11 Batts	2.2	1.9	2.5	2.2	1.9	2.9	2.6	2.2	3.0	2.6	3.0	3.3	.072
C. R-19 Batts	1.5	1.3	1.7	1.5	1.3	2.0	1.8	1.5	2.0	1.8	2.0	2.3	.049
D. R-22 Batts (2" x 8" Rafters)	1.3	1.2	1.6	1.4	1.2	1.8	1.6	1.4	1.8	1.6	1.8	2.1	.045
E. R-26 Batts (2" x 8" Rafters)	1.2	1.0	1.4	1.2	1.0	1.6	1.4	1.2	1.6	1.4	1.6	1.8	.040
F. R-30 Batts (2" x 10" Rafters)	1.0	.9	1.2	1.1	.9	1.4	1.3	1.1	1.4	1.3	1.4	1.6	.035

No. 18 - Roof-Ceiling Combination - Dark Colored Roof

	10		15			20			25		30	35	U
	L	M	L	M	H	L	M	H	M	H	H	H	
HTM (Btuh per sq. ft.)													
A. No Insulation	10.9	9.8	12.3	11.2	9.8	13.8	12.6	11.2	14.1	12.6	14.1	15.5	.287
B. R-11 Batts	2.7	2.4	3.1	2.8	2.4	3.5	3.2	2.8	3.5	3.2	3.5	3.9	.072
C. R-19 Batts	1.9	1.7	2.1	1.9	1.7	2.4	2.2	1.9	2.4	2.2	2.4	2.6	.049
D. R-22 Batts (2" x 8" Rafters)	1.7	1.5	1.9	1.8	1.5	2.2	2.0	1.8	2.2	2.0	2.2	2.4	.045
E. R-26 Batts (2" x 8" Rafters)	1.5	1.4	1.7	1.6	1.4	1.9	1.8	1.6	2.0	1.8	2.0	2.2	.040
F. R-30 Batts (2" x 10" Rafters)	1.3	1.2	1.5	1.4	1.2	1.7	1.5	1.4	1.7	1.5	1.7	1.9	.035

No. 19 - Floors Over a Basement or Enclosed Crawl Space

	10		15			20			25		30	35	U
	L	M	L	M	H	L	M	H	M	H	H	H	
HTM (Btuh per sq. ft.)													
All	0.0	0.0	0.0	0.0	0.0	0.0	0.0	0.0	0.0	0.0	0.0	0.0	

No. 20 - Floors Over an Open Crawl Space or Garage

	10		15			20			25		30	35	U
	L	M	L	M	H	L	M	H	M	H	H	H	
HTM (Btuh per sq. ft.)													
A. Hardwood Floor, No Insulation	3.5	1.9	5.4	3.9	1.9	7.3	5.8	3.9	7.7	5.8	7.7	9.6	.386
B. Hardwood Floor R-11	.8	.4	1.2	.8	.4	1.6	1.3	.8	1.7	1.3	1.7	2.1	.084
C. Hardwood Floor R-13	.7	.4	1.1	.8	.4	1.4	1.1	.8	1.5	1.1	1.5	1.9	.076
D. Hardwood Floor R-19	.5	.3	.8	.5	.3	1.0	.8	.5	1.1	.8	1.1	1.3	.054
E. Hardwood Floor R-30	.3	.2	.5	.4	.2	.7	.6	.4	.7	.6	.7	.9	.037
F. Carpet Floor No Insulation	2.3	1.3	3.5	2.5	1.3	4.8	3.8	2.5	5.1	3.8	5.1	6.3	.253
G. Carpet Floor R-11	.7	.4	1.0	.8	.4	1.4	1.1	.8	1.5	1.1	1.5	1.9	.075
H. Carpet Floor R-13	.6	.3	1.0	.7	.3	1.3	1.0	.7	1.4	1.0	1.4	1.7	.068
I. Carpet Floor R-19	.4	.2	.7	.5	.2	.9	.7	.5	1.0	.7	1.0	1.2	.050
J. Carpet Floor R-30	.3	.2	.5	.4	.2	.7	.5	.4	.7	.5	.7	.9	.035

No. 21 - 23 Basement Floors, Concrete Slab on Grade

	10		15			20			25		30	35	U
	L	M	L	M	H	L	M	H	M	H	H	H	
HTM													
All	0.0	0.0	0.0	0.0	0.0	0.0	0.0	0.0	0.0	0.0	0.0	0.0	

Notes to Table — Heat Transfer Multipliers
1. The HTM shown in this table do not include credit for infiltration.
2. Wall U values include wood framing equal to 20% of the opaque wall area.
3. Ceiling U values include wood framing equal to 10% of the opaque ceiling area.
4. Floor U values include wood framing equal to 15% of the opaque floor area.
5. Summer HTM values include the effects of solar radiation and thermal mass!

Reprinted with permission of ACCA, *Manual J*, 1986.

FIGURE 12-6 / Heat transfer multipliers (continued)

Design Temperature, F	85	90	95	100	105	110
Infiltration, Btuh per sq ft of gross exposed wall area	0.7	1.1	1.5	1.9	2.2	2.6
Mechanical Ventilation, Btuh per cfm	11.0	16.0	22.0	27.0	32.0	38.0

Courtesy of the Hydronics Institute.

FIGURE 12-7 / Infiltration values

Rates of Heat Gain from Occupants of Conditioned Spaces[a,b,c]

Degree of Activity	Typical Application	Total Heat Adults, Male, Btu/h	Total Heat Adjusted,[d] Btu/h	Sensible Heat, Btu/h	Latent Heat, Btu/h
Seated at theater	Theater—Matinee	390	330	225	105
Seated at theater	Theater—Evening	390	350	245	105
Seated, very light work	Offices, hotels, apartments	450	400	245	155
Moderately active office work	Offices, hotels, apartments	475	450	250	200
Standing, light work; walking	Department store, retail store	550	450	250	200
Walking; standing	Drug store, bank	550	500	250	250
Sedentary work	Restaurant[e]	490	550	275	275
Light bench work	Factory	800	750	275	475
Moderate dancing	Dance hall	900	850	305	545
Walking 3 mph; light machine work	Factory	1000	1000	375	625
Bowling[e]	Bowling alley	1500	1450	580	870
Heavy work	Factory	1500	1450	580	870
Heavy machine work; lifting	Factory	1600	1600	635	965
Athletics	Gymnasium	2000	1800	710	1090

[a]Tabulated values are based on 75°F room dry-bulb temperature. For 80°F room dry-bulb, the total heat remains the same, but the sensible heat values should be decreased by approximately 20%, and the latent heat values increased accordingly.

[b]Also refer to Table 1, Chapter 8.

[c]All values are rounded to nearest 5 Btu/h.

[d]Adjusted heat gain is based on normal percentage of men, women, and children for the application listed, with the postulate that the gain from an adult female is 85% of that for an adult male, and that the gain from a child is 75% of that for an adult male.

[e]Adjusted total heat gain for Sedentary work, Restaurant, includes 60 Btu/h for food per individual (30 Btu/h sensible and 30 Btu/h latent).

[f]For Bowling, figure one person per alley actually bowling, and all others as sitting (400 Btu/h) or standing and walking slowly (550 Btu/h).

Reprinted with permission from ASHRAE, Fundamentals Handbook, 1989.

FIGURE 12-8 / Rates of heat gain from occupants of conditioned spaces[a]

Design Cooling Load Factors through Glass (Btu/h·ft²)

Outdoor Design Temp.	Regular Single Glass						Regular Double Glass						Heat Absorbing Double Glass						Clear Triple Glass					
Design Temp.	85	90	95	100	105	110	85	90	95	100	105	110	85	90	95	100	105	110	85	90	95	100	105	110
No Awnings or Inside Shading																								
North	23	27	31	35	39	44	21	24	26	28	30	33	12	14	17	19	21	23	17	19	20	21	22	23
NE and NW	56	60	64	68	72	77	48	51	53	55	57	61	27	29	32	34	36	38	42	43	44	46	47	49
East and West	81	85	89	93	97	102	70	73	75	77	79	82	42	44	47	49	51	53	62	63	64	66	68	70
SE and SW	70	74	78	82	86	91	61	64	66	68	70	73	35	37	40	42	44	46	53	55	56	57	59	61
South	40	44	48	52	56	61	35	38	40	42	44	46	19	21	24	26	28	31	30	31	32	33	35	37
Horiz. Skylight	160	164	168	172	176	181	141	144	146	148	150	153	89	91	94	96	98	100	126	127	129	—	—	—
Draperies or Venetian Blinds																								
North	15	19	23	27	31	36	14	17	19	21	23	26	9	11	14	16	18	20						
NE and NW	32	36	40	44	48	53	29	32	34	36	38	41	20	22	25	27	29	31						
East and West	48	52	56	60	64	69	44	47	49	51	53	56	30	32	35	37	39	41						
SE and SW	40	44	48	52	56	61	37	40	42	44	46	48	24	26	29	31	33	35						
South	23	27	31	35	39	44	22	25	27	29	31	34	15	17	20	22	24	26						
Roller Shades Half-Drawn																								
North	18	22	26	30	34	39	17	20	22	24	26	29	10	12	15	17	19	21						
NE and NW	40	44	48	52	56	61	40	43	45	47	49	52	24	26	29	31	33	35						
East and West	61	65	69	73	77	82	56	59	61	63	65	68	35	37	40	42	44	46						
SE and SW	52	56	60	64	68	73	48	51	53	55	57	59	30	32	35	37	39	41						
South	29	33	37	41	45	50	29	32	34	36	38	40	18	20	23	25	27	29						
Awnings																								
North	20	24	28	32	36	41	18	19	20	21	22	24	10	11	12	13	14	15						
NE and NW	21	25	29	33	37	42	19	21	21	23	23	25	11	12	13	14	15	16						
East and West	22	26	30	34	38	43	19	21	21	23	23	25	11	12	13	14	15	16						
SE and SW	21	25	29	33	37	42	18	20	21	22	23	24	10	11	12	13	14	15						
South	21	24	28	32	36	41	18	20	21	22	23	24	10	11	12	13	14	15						

Courtesy of the Hydronics Institute.

FIGURE 12-9 / Solar heat gain

Shade Line Factors

Direction Window Faces	Latitude, Degrees						
	25	30	35	40	45	50	55
E	0.8	0.8	0.8	0.8	0.8	0.8	0.8
SE	1.9	1.6	1.4	1.3	1.1	1.0	0.9
S	10.1	5.4	3.6	2.6	2.0	1.7	1.4
SW	1.9	1.6	1.4	1.3	1.1	1.0	0.9
W	0.8	0.8	0.8	0.8	0.8	0.8	0.8

Note: Distance shadow line falls below the edge of the overhang equals shade line factor multiplied by width of overhang. Values are averages for five hours of greatest solar intensity on August 1.

Reprinted with permission of ACCA, *Manual D,* 1984.

FIGURE 12-10 / Shade line factors

Design Equivalent Temperature Differences

Design Temperature, F	85		90			95			100		105	110
Daily Temperature Range[a]	L	M	L	M	H	L	M	H	M	H	H	H
WALLS AND DOORS												
1. Frame and veneer-on-frame	17.6	13.6	22.6	18.6	13.6	27.6	23.6	18.6	28.6	23.6	28.6	33.6
2. Masonry walls, 8-in. block or brick	10.3	6.3	15.3	11.3	6.3	20.3	16.3	11.3	21.3	16.3	21.3	26.3
3. Partitions, frame	9.0	5.0	14.0	10.0	5.0	19.0	15.0	10.0	20.0	15.0	20.0	25.0
masonry	2.5	0	7.5	3.5	0	12.5	8.5	3.5	13.5	8.5	13.5	18.5
4. Wood doors	17.6	13.6	22.6	18.6	13.6	27.6	23.6	18.6	28.6	23.6	28.6	33.6
CEILINGS AND ROOFS[b]												
1. Ceilings under naturally vented attic or vented flat roof—dark	38.0	34.0	43.0	39.0	34.0	48.0	44.0	39.0	49.0	44.0	49.0	54.0
—light	30.0	26.0	35.0	31.0	26.0	40.0	36.0	31.0	41.0	36.0	41.0	46.0
2. Built-up roof, no ceiling—dark	38.0	34.0	43.0	39.0	34.0	48.0	44.0	39.0	49.0	44.0	49.0	54.0
—light	30.0	26.0	35.0	31.0	26.0	40.0	36.0	31.0	41.0	36.0	41.0	46.0
3. Ceilings under unconditioned rooms	9.0	5.0	14.0	10.0	5.0	19.0	15.0	10.0	20.0	15.0	20.0	25.0
FLOORS												
1. Over unconditioned rooms	9.0	5.0	14.0	10.0	5.0	19.0	15.0	10.0	20.0	15.0	20.0	25.0
2. Over basement, enclosed crawl space or concrete slab on ground	0	0	0	0	0	0	0	0	0	0	0	0
3. Over open crawl space	9.0	5.0	14.0	10.0	5.0	19.0	15.0	10.0	20.0	15.0	20.0	25.0

[a] Daily Temperature Range

    L (Low) Calculation Value: 12   M (Medium) Calculation Value: 20   H (High) Calculation Value: 30

    Applicable Range: Less than 15 deg.   Applicable Range: 15 to 25 deg.   Applicable Range: More than 25 deg.

[b] Ceilings and Roofs: For roofs in shade, eight-hour average = 11 deg temperature differential. At 90 F design and medium daily range, equivalent temperature differential for light-colored roof equals $11 + (0.71)(39 − 11) = 31$ deg.

Reprinted with permission of ACCA, *Manual J*, 1986.

FIGURE 12-11 / Equivalent temperature differences

Table 8 Recommended Rate of Heat Gain from Selected Restaurant Equipment[a]

Appliance	Size	Input Rating, Btu/h		Recommended Rate of Heat Gain, Btu/h			
				Without Hood			With Hood
		Max.	Standby[b]	Sens.	Latent	Total	Sensible
Electric, No Hood Required							
Blender, per quart of capacity	1 to 4 qt	1550		1000	520	1520	480
Cabinet (large hot holding)	16.2 to 17.3 ft³	7100		610	340	960	290
Cabinet (small hot holding	3.2 to 6.4 ft³	3070		270	140	410	130
Coffee brewer	12 cups/2 brnrs	5660		3750	1910	5660	1810
Coffee brewing urn (large), per quart of capacity	23 to 40 qt	2130		1420	710	2230	680
Coffee heater, per warming burner	1 to 2 brnrs	340		230	110	340	110
Dishwasher (hood type chemical sanitizing), per 100 dishes/h	950 to 2000 dishes/h	1300		170	370	540	170
Dishwasher (conveyor type water sanitizing), per 100 dishes/h	5000 to 9000 dishes/h	1160		150	370	520	170
Display case (refrigerated), per ft³ of interior	6 to 67 ft³	154		62	0	62	0
Food warmer (infrared bulb), per lamp	1 to 6 bulbs	850		850	0	850	850
Food warmer (well type), per ft³ of well	0.7 to 2.5 ft³	3620		1200	610	1810	580
Freezer (large)	73 ft³	4570		1840	0	1840	0
Griddle/grill (large), per ft² of cooking surface	4.6 to 11.8 ft²	9200		620	340	960	340
Hot plate (high speed double burner)		16720		7810	5430	13240	6240
Ice maker (large)	220 lb/day	3720		9320	0	9320	0
Microwave oven (heavy duty commercial)	0.7 ft³	8970		8970		8970	0
Mixer (large), per quart of capacity	80 qt	94		94	0	94	0
Refrigerator (large), per 100 ft³ of space	25 to 74 ft³	750		300	0	300	0
Rotisserie	300	10920		7200	3720	10920	3480
Serving cart (hot), per ft³ of well	1.8 to 3.2 ft³	2050		680	340	1020	330
Steam kettle (large), per quart of capacity	80 to 320 qt	300		23	16	40	13
Toaster (large pop-up)	10 slice	18080		9590	8500	18080	5800
Electric, Exhaust Hood Required							
Charbroiler, per ft² of cooking surface	1.5 to 4.6 ft²	7320					3310
Fryer (deep fat), per lb of fat capacity	15 to 15 to 70 lb	1270					14
Fryer (pressurized), per lb of fat capacity	13 to 33	1570					59
Oven (large convection), per ft³ of oven space	7 to 19 ft³	4450					180
Oven (small convection), per ft³ of oven space	1.4 to 5.3 ft³	10340					150
Range (burners), per 2 burner section	2 to 10 burners	7170					2660
Gas, No Hood Required							
Broiler, per ft² of broiling area	2.7 ft²	14770	61	5310	2860	8170	1220
Dishwasher (hood type chemical sanitizing), per 100 dishes/h	950 to 2000 dishes/h	1740	660[b]	510	200	710	230
Dishwasher (conveyor type water sanitizing), per 100 dishes/h	5000 to 9000 dishes/h	1370	660[b]	370	80	450	140
Griddle/grill (large), per ft² of cooking surface	4.6 to 11.8 ft²	17000	330	1140	610	1750	460
Oven (pizza), per ft² of hearth	6.4 to 12.9 ft²	4740	61[b]	620	220	840	84
Gas, Exhaust Hood Required							
Braising pan, per quart of capacity	105 to 140 qt	9840	620				2430
Charbroiler (large), per ft² of cooking area	4.6 to 11.8 ft²	16440	510				790
Fryer (deep fat), per lb of fat capacity	11 to 70 lb	2270	300[b]				160
Oven (convection), per ft³ of oven space	7.4 to 19.4 ft³	8670	19[b]				250
Oven (pizza), per ft² of oven hearth	9.3 to 25.8 ft²	7240	61[b]				130
Range (burners), per 2 burner section	2 to 10 burners	33600	1325				6590
Range (hot top/fry top), per ft² of cooking surface	3 to 8 ft²	11800	330				3390
Steam							
Compartment steamer, per lb of food/h	46 to 450 lb	280		22	14	36	11
Dishwasher (hood type chemical sanitizing), per 100 dishes/h	950 to 2000 dishes/h	3150		880	380	1260	410
Dishwasher (conveyor water sanitizing), per 100 dishes/h	5000 to 9000 dishes/h	1180		150	370	520	170
Steam kettle, per quart capacity	13 to 32 qt .	500		39	25	64	19

[a] In cases where heat gain is given per unit of capacity the heat gain is calculated by multiplying the capacity by the recommended heat gain per unit of capacity.
[b] Standby input rating is for the entire appliance regardless of size.

Reprinted with permission form ASHRAE, *FUNDAMENTALS HANDBOOK*, 1989.

FIGURE 12-12 / Appliance heat gain

CHAPTER 13

FORCED AIR SYSTEM DESIGN (AIR CONDITIONING)

13-1 FORCED AIR SYSTEMS (AIR CONDITIONING)

A motor-driven fan is used to circulate filtered, heated or cooled air from a central unit through supply ducts to each of the rooms. When hot air is supplied, cold air is returned through return registers and ducts to be warmed. When cold air is supplied, warm air is returned to be cooled. The ductwork supplies air into main trunks and then smaller ducts branch off these to feed the rooms, or individual ducts to each room may be used. The ducts may be circular or rectangular, and their size depends on the amount of heated or cooled air required to maintain the desired temperature of the room.

A variety of duct layout designs for the various duct systems is available, several of which are indicated in Fig. 13-1. These types of systems quickly deliver heating or cooling when required, and are economical and easy to install. Filters are put in these systems to reduce the amount of dust in the air. Heating and cooling units may be located anywhere in the building including basement, crawl space, utility room, attic,

Extended plenum supply

Individual supply system

Perimeter-loop system

FIGURE 13-1 / Duct layouts

small closets, garage, and even on the roof (commonly done in commercial, institutional, and industrial buildings where flat roofs are used).

The location of the supply registers (also called *diffusers*) and return registers varies, depending on whether warm or cool air is the most important portion of the system. Ideally, the air registers should be located below a window so that the heat will counteract the cold outside air which infiltrates and transmits the most at windows. In this case, the registers would be located on the floor or slightly up the wall. Be certain the registers will not be covered by furniture or drapes, or their usefulness will be seriously reduced. Where cold air is of prime importance, the suggested locations are in the ceiling and high in the wall.

Warm air furnaces may use oil, natural or bottled gas, or electricity as a fuel. The air-conditioning equipment may be a part of a heating and cooling package called a unitary system or a package which has part of the unit on the furnace and the condenser package outside (split system).

Forced air systems may have humidifiers which are controlled by a *humidistat* inside the building, and moisture is added to the air when required. Another option being used increasingly is an electronic air purifier which removes impurities such as dust from the air.

Ducts and fittings for forced air systems are discussed thoroughly in Sec. 10-2 and 10-3, and apply to ducts used for cooling and heating with one additional item: all insulation used should have a vapor-barrier covering to protect against any possibility of moisture condensation developing.

The forced air heating and cooling system may obtain its heat from a furnace, just as is used in forced air systems which supply only heat, with an added-on package of cooling coils placed next to the furnace bonnet and a condenser located outside the building (Fig. 13-2). The other unit which is becoming increasingly popular is the heat pump (Sec. 14-8) which produces both warm and cool air. Use of a heat pump means a furnace is not necessary.

In this section, the furnace with a separate cooling unit (commonly called an air conditioner) will be discussed. The size of the cooling unit is rated according to its cooling capacity in Btuh, often referred to as "tons." One ton is equal to 12,000 Btuh (so a 3-ton unit would have a capacity of 36,000 Btuh). The rating of the unit selected should be adequate to provide cooling Btuh equal to, or slightly more than, what the heat gain calculations call for. The wide range of sizes commonly available allows for the selection of a unit with the rated cooling capacity close to the required cooling calculated. Selection of a much larger unit will result in less efficient operation, and thus higher costs (due to the inefficiency of the on-off cycles, the time it takes to begin to cool and the warming of the system as it is off, only to be cooled again as it is turned back on). But if a unit is too small, it may not be able to provide sufficient cool air. This becomes especially critical if any of the design assumptions (such as the amount of moisture, insulation or the size or type glass used) varies, and the designer is not aware of the change. Also, the "tightness" of the construction, how well it is built, is assumed by the designer to be average. If it is not, there may be more heat gain than was calculated.

The unit selected for use should also be checked for its energy efficiency. Most manufacturers have more than one type of unit available. It is important to get the most efficient model available. The tables in Fig. 13-3 give the manufacturer's specifications for "standard" and "high efficiency" models.

The efficiency of the models is checked by comparing the EER (energy efficiency ratio) listed for each model. This EER rating is obtained by dividing the total Btuh of the unit by its watts; the higher the number, the more efficient the unit. Note that the standard 24,000-Btuh model in Fig. 13-3 has an EER of 6.3, while the highest-efficiency 24,000-Btuh model has an EER of 8.9. This indicates that the highest-efficiency model is slightly more than 40% more efficient than the standard model. This means that the fuel bill for cooling will be about 40% less when using the highest-

FIGURE 13-2 / Split system

Cooling capacity (Btuh)	Watts	EER (Btuh per watt)	Cooling capacity (Btuh)	Watts	EER (Btuh per watt)
24,000	2750	8.9	24,000	3800	6.3
29,000	3100	9.4	30,000	4600	6.3
36,000	4050	9.0	36,000	5800	6.2
42,000	5000	8.4	42,000	7100	5.9

Highest efficiency   Standard

FIGURE 13-3 / Energy efficiency ratios

efficiency model, compared to the standard. High-efficiency units typically cost 50% more than the standard, but in terms of dollars, it may only be $200 to $300. The EER ratings shown are typical, but each manufacturer must be checked since they will vary.

13-3   DUCT DESIGN

STEP-BY-STEP APPROACH

1. Determine the heat loss and heat gain of each individual room, and tabulate them.

    The heat loss (Sec. 8-12) and heat gain (Sec. 12-9) have already been calculated for the residence being designed, and they are tabulated as shown in Fig. 13-4.

2. The cooling unit size is selected based on the heat gain calculated. The unit selected should be as close as possible to the heat gain which was calculated.
    When the heat gain calculations are more than the capacity of an available unit, yet going to the next available unit would provide far too much capacity, the designer may want to review the calculations and suggest changes (perhaps in insulation, type of glass or sunshields) that will reduce the load.
    For example, assume the heat gain calculations require a cooling unit of about 2 tons. Units available are generally limited to 2, 2½, 3, 5, 7, 8 and 10 tons.

    From step 1, the heat gain calculations are 23,447 Btuh (2.1 tons). A 2½-ton unit is selected to provide enough capacity to allow for a pick-up allowance and for cooling lost in the duct-work.

Room	Heat gain (Btuh)	Heat loss (Btuh)
BEDROOM 1	2,887	4,283
BEDROOM 2	1,492	2,310
LIVING	3,571	4,108
LIVING	3,571	4,108
KITCHEN	4,685	3,752
DINING	2,175	3,047
ENTRY	1,038	1,682
HALL	1,037	1,682
BEDROOM 3	2,188	3,008
BATH	697	960
TOTALS	23,447	28,940

FIGURE 13-4 / Tabulate heat loss and gain

3. Next, determine the location and number of supply outlets and return air intakes. The layout should allow:

> Heat loss: no more than 8,000 Btuh per outlet.
> Heat gain: no more than 4,000 Btuh per outlet.

Extra outlets may be desirable in some rooms to provide the best air distribution. This is particularly true in large rooms.

4. Note on the sketch the types of fittings which will be used and the actual length of each run from the furnace to the outlet. The fittings are the same as those used for heating (Chapter 10) and are also included at the end of this chapter. Fittings may be selected from Fig. 13-21, and the equivalent lengths are given for each type of fitting shown in the illustrations. Note the equivalent length of each fitting on the sketch.

> The sketch in Fig. 13-5 shows the actual length of duct, the type of fitting and each fitting's equivalent length.

5. Determine the total equivalent length of each run from bonnet to outlet by adding the actual length and the equivalent length of each fitting in the run, and tabulate the totals.

> The tabulated total equivalent length of each run is calculated in Fig. 13-6 and Fig. 13-7.

13 / FORCED AIR SYSTEM DESIGN (AIR CONDITIONING)

FIGURE 13-5 / Duct layout

6. Determine the air volume (cfm) required per MBH (1,000 Btuh) for the system from the table in Fig. 13-8. The largest cfm (heating or cooling) is used.

   In this design the cfm for heating is

   $$408 \times \frac{23,447}{12,000} = 906 \text{ cfm}$$

   The cfm for cooling is

   $$\frac{400 \times 28,940}{12,000} = 965 \text{ cfm (use 1,000 cfm)}$$

7. The heating Btuh for each supply outlet is found by dividing the number of outlets in each room into the heat loss of each room.

   In this problem only the living room has two outlets; it is noted twice in Fig. 13-4.

8. Calculate the air volume which will be delivered through each supply outlet. The air volume is calculated by dividing the Btuh for the outlet by the total Btuh of heat loss (or heat gain) and then multiplying it times the total cfm.

   In Bedroom 1, the heat gain is 2,887. With a total heat gain of 23,447, the system is 1,000 cfm.

   $$\frac{2,887}{23,447} \times 1,000 = 123 \text{ cfm}$$

Outlet	Equivalent length	Actual length	Total equivalent length
BEDROOM (1)	F 35 B 15 G 30 80	36	116
BEDROOM (2)	F 35 + 25 B 15 G 30 105	26	131
LIVING 1	F 35 B 15 + 25 G 30 105	33	138
2	F 35 B 15 G 30 80	55	135
KITCHEN	F 35 B 15 G 30 80	46	126
DINING	F 35 + 25 B 15 G 30 105	27	132
ENTRY 1	F 35 + 25 B 15 E 10 G 30 115	16	131
2	F 35 B 15 G 30 80	10	90
BEDROOM (3)	F 35 + 25 B 15 G 30 105	30	135
BATH	F 35 B 15 E 10 G 30 90	25	115

FIGURE 13-6 / Equivalent length tabulation

13 / FORCED AIR SYSTEM DESIGN (AIR CONDITIONING)

Supply Outlet	Heat Gain (BTUH)	Heat Loss (BTUH)	Actual Length (ft)	Equivalent Length (ft)	Total Equiv. Length (ft)
Bedroom #1	2,887	4,283	36	80	116
Bedroom #2	1,492	2,310	26	105	131
Living	3,571	4,108	33	105	138
Living	3,571	4,108	55	80	135
Kitchen	4,685	3,752	46	80	126
Dining	2,175	3,047	27	105	132
Entry	1,038	1,682	16	115	131
Hall	1,037	1,682	10	80	90
Bedroom #3	2,188	3,008	30	105	135
Bath	697	960	25	90	115
Totals	23,447	28,940			

FIGURE 13-7 / Duct lengths

This is repeated for each outlet, for both heat gain and heat loss, and tabulated as shown in Fig. 13-9.

9. The bonnet pressure is selected next. The approximate bonnet pressure required for a trunk (main duct) to carry the maximum volume of air (either heating or cooling cfm, whichever is larger) is found in Fig. 13-22.

In this design, the total cfm required is 1,000 cfm. From Fig. 13-22 for quiet operation in a residence (Type A), the suggested bonnet pressure is about 0.10 in. of water; assume a system with .10 is selected.

FIGURE 13-8 / Air flow volume

Air Flow	cfm/ton
Typical*	400
Some Heat Pumps	450
Humid Areas	360
Dry Areas	429

* For normal residential cooling (70% sensible and 30% latent heat)
Reprinted with permission from ASHRAE, *HVAC Handbook*, 1987.

Supply Outlet	Heat Gain (BTUH)	Heat Loss (BTUH)	Actual Length (ft)	Equivalent Length (ft)	Total Equiv. Length (ft)	Cooling cfm	Heating cfm
Bedroom #1	2,887	4,283	36	80	116	123	148
Bedroom #2	1,492	2,310	26	105	131	64	80
Living	3,571	4,108	33	105	138	153	142
Living	3,571	4,108	55	80	135	153	142
Kitchen	4,685	3,752	46	80	126	200	130
Dining	2,175	3,047	27	105	132	95	105
Entry	1,038	1,682	16	115	131	44	58
Hall	1,037	1,682	10	80	90	44	58
Bedroom #3	2,188	3,008	30	105	135	94	104
Bath	697	960	25	90	115	30	33
Totals	23,447	28,940				995	1,000

FIGURE 13-9 / Branch cfm

10. Next, the supply outlet size and its pressure loss are selected from the manufacturer's engineering data. A typical example of a manufacturer's data is shown in Fig. 13-10. The exact pressure loss will depend on variables such as the duct velocity and the angles at which the register blades are set. Typically, the pressure loss will range from 0.01 to 0.02 in.; many designers assume a 0.02-in. loss and make a final selection later.

The selected supply outlet pressure losses are tabulated in Fig. 13-11.

11. The available bonnet pressure is divided between the supply and the return runs. It should be divided in proportion to the amount of supply and return runs on the project. A review of the sketch plan layout shows the approximate proportions of supply to return runs.

A review of the sketch plan layout (Fig. 13-6) shows that there are considerably more supply than return runs, so a division of 0.07 in. for supply and 0.03 in. for return is selected.

Note: If later during the design the proportion selected does not provide satisfactory results, the available bonnet pressure can be reapportioned between supply and return.

LISTED WIDTH

	6	8	10	12	14	16	18	20	22	24	26	28	30	32	34	36
6		4														
6		8	6	5		4										
		8	6	5		6		5	4							
		10	8		6		8									
		12	10								5					4

V = Duct Vel.	300			400			500			600				
Blade Set°	0	22½	45	0	22½	45	0	22½	45	0	22½	45		
P_t	.01	.012	.027	.014	.021	.050	.023	.034	.082	.034	.051	.120		
CFM	75			100			125			150			T	PWL-NC
													8	L
CFM	130			180			220			260			T	PWL-NC
													9	L
CFM	210			280			350			400			T	PWL-NC
													13	L
CFM	300			400			500			600			T	PWL-NC
	10			13			16			20			15	
	13			17			21			24				
	17			20			25			29				
								26			28			
											32		4	

SYMBOLS:

V = Duct velocity in fpm.
CFM = Quantity of air in cubic ft./min.
NC = Noise criteria (8 db room attenuation).
D = Drop in feet.
P_t = Total pressure inches H₂O
T = Throw in Feet
PWL-NC INDEX = A single number which expresses the PWL (sound power level) in relation to NC (noise criteria) curves.

FIGURE 13-10 / Supply outlet data

361

Supply Outlet	Heat Gain (BTUH)	Heat Loss (BTUH)	Actual Length (ft)	Equivalent Length (ft)	Total Equiv. Length (ft)	Cooling cfm	Heating cfm	Supply Air Presssure	Supply Outlet Pressure Loss	Pressure Avail. for Duct Loss
Bedroom #1	2,887	4,283	36	80	116	123	148	0.07	0.02	0.05
Bedroom #2	1,492	2,310	26	105	131	64	80	0.07	0.02	0.05
Living	3,571	4,108	33	105	138	153	142	0.07	0.02	0.05
Living	3,571	4,108	55	80	135	153	142	0.07	0.02	0.05
Kitchen	4,685	3,752	46	80	126	200	130	0.07	0.02	0.05
Dining	2,175	3,047	27	105	132	95	105	0.07	0.02	0.05
Entry	1,038	1,682	16	115	131	44	58	0.07	0.02	0.05
Hall	1,037	1,682	10	80	90	44	58	0.07	0.02	0.05
Bedroom #3	2,188	3,008	30	105	135	94	104	0.07	0.02	0.05
Bath	697	960	25	90	115	30	33	0.07	0.02	0.05
Totals	23,447	28,940				995	1,000			

FIGURE 13-11 / Typical tabulated duct sizes

12. Determine the pressure available for duct loss by subtracting the supply outlet loss (step 10) from the total pressure available for supply runs (step 11).

> In this design, the pressure allowed for supply runs is 0.07 in. (step 11). Beginning with the supply run in bedroom 1, the supply outlet loss is 0.02 in. (step 11) and the pressure available for duct drop is 0.05 in. Calculate the pressure available for duct loss for each of the supply runs, and tabulate the information as shown in Fig. 13-11.

13. In order to make a workable table of duct sizes, the pressure drop for duct loss must be calculated as the pressure drop *per 100 ft* of duct.

> Since the various supply runs are all of different lengths, it is necessary to find the *allowable pressure drop per 100 ft* based on the *allowable duct loss* and the *total equivalent length* of the supply run. This allowable pressure drop may be calculated by using the equation:

$$\text{Allowable pressure drop per 100 ft} = \frac{\text{Allowable duct loss} \times 100}{\text{Total equivalent length}}$$

> In this design, in bedroom 1 the supply run has an allowable duct loss of 0.05 in. (Step 12) and an equivalent length of 116 ft.

Using the formula, the allowable pressure drop per 100 ft is:

$$\text{Allowable pressure drop per 100 ft} = \frac{0.05 \text{ in. } (100)}{116 \text{ ft}} = 0.0431 \text{ in.}$$

Calculate the allowable pressure drop per 100 ft for each supply run, and tabulate the information as shown in Fig. 13-12.

14. The branch duct sizes may be determined by using the table in Fig. 13-23 or by using an air duct calculator if one is available. The table in Fig. 13-23 gives the size of round ducts based on the larger cfm required (either heating or cooling) and the allowable pressure drop per 100 ft (step 13). The size of the round duct may be converted to an equivalent rectangular duct size which will handle the required cfm within the allowable pressure drop.

In this design, bedroom 1 has an allowable duct loss of 0.043 in. per 100 ft (step 13). Using the table in Fig. 13-23 (partially reproduced

FIGURE 13-12 / Typical tabulated pressure available

Supply Outlet	Heat Gain (BTUH)	Heat Loss (BTUH)	Actual Length (ft)	Equivalent Length (ft)	Total Equiv. Length (ft)	Cooling cfm	Heating cfm	Supply Air Pressure	Supply Outlet Pressure Loss	Pressure Avail. for Duct Loss	Pressure Avail. Per 100 ft
Bedroom #1	2,887	4,283	36	80	116	123	148	0.07	0.02	0.05	0.043
Bedroom #2	1,492	2,310	26	105	131	64	80	0.07	0.02	0.05	0.038
Living	3,571	4,108	33	105	138	153	142	0.07	0.02	0.05	0.036
Living	3,571	4,108	55	80	135	153	142	0.07	0.02	0.05	0.037
Kitchen	4,685	3,752	46	80	126	200	130	0.07	0.02	0.05	0.040
Dining	2,175	3,047	27	105	132	95	105	0.07	0.02	0.05	0.038
Entry	1,038	1,682	16	115	131	44	58	0.07	0.02	0.05	0.038
Hall	1,037	1,682	10	80	90	44	58	0.07	0.02	0.05	0.055
Bedroom #3	2,188	3,008	30	105	135	94	104	0.07	0.02	0.05	0.037
Bath	697	960	25	90	115	30	33	0.07	0.02	0.05	0.043
Totals	23,447	28,940				995	1,000				

cfm = 400 cfm/ton

$$400 \times \frac{28,940}{12,000} = 965 \text{ cfm (use 1,000)}$$

to show the use of the table in this example in Fig. 13-13) a 9.0-in. round duct is selected.

a. Find the allowable pressure drop of 0.043 in. across the bottom. (Friction loss, in $H_2O/100$ ft).

b. Air quantity, ft^3/min (cfm), is found along the right side. Find 148 cfm.

c. Move vertically from the friction loss and horizontally from the air quantity until the two lines meet.

d. This intersection will occur on or near the diagonal lines which will give the duct diameters required (sizes along the left). If it falls right on the line, using that size duct will use the amount of friction loss available. If it falls between two lines, using the larger duct will use slightly less friction loss (the smaller duct would use more).

From the table in Fig. 13-23, determine the round duct sizes for each of the supply runs and tabulate the information as shown in Fig. 13-14.

The air duct calculator is used to obtain required round duct sizes by aligning the required air volume (cfm) and the allowable pressure drop (friction) per 100 ft of duct (0.043 in.) and reading the round duct diameter directly from the calculator (about 8.3 in., rounded off to 9.0 in.).

15. Round duct sizes selected in step 14 may be changed to equivalent rectangular duct sizes, carrying the same cfm required while maintaining the allowable pressure drops, by using the table in Fig. 13-24 or by using an air-duct calculator:

In this design, the 9.0-in. round duct for bedroom 1 can be changed to a comparable rectangular duct by using Fig. 13-24. To use the table, the sizes of the rectangular duct are found with one dimension along the top and the other along the side. Their circular equivalent is the number in the middle of the page where the two sizes intersect. For example, a 10 in. × 5 in. rectangular duct has a circular equivalent of 7.6 in.

To convert circular ducts to rectangular, find the circular equivalent in the center of the table and get the rectangular equivalents by reading up and to the side. There are many different sizes which can be used. Figure 13-15 shows the use of the table for bedroom 1; the 9.0-in. round duct for bedroom 1 can be changed to a rectangular duct of 13 in. × 5½ in., 6 in. × 12 in., 7 in. × 10 in., or 8 in. × 9 in. The actual size selected depends to a large extent on the space available for installation of the duct.

From Fig. 13-24, determine a rectangular size for each supply run which could be used instead of the round duct previously selected. Tabulate the rectangular duct size as shown in Fig. 13-16.

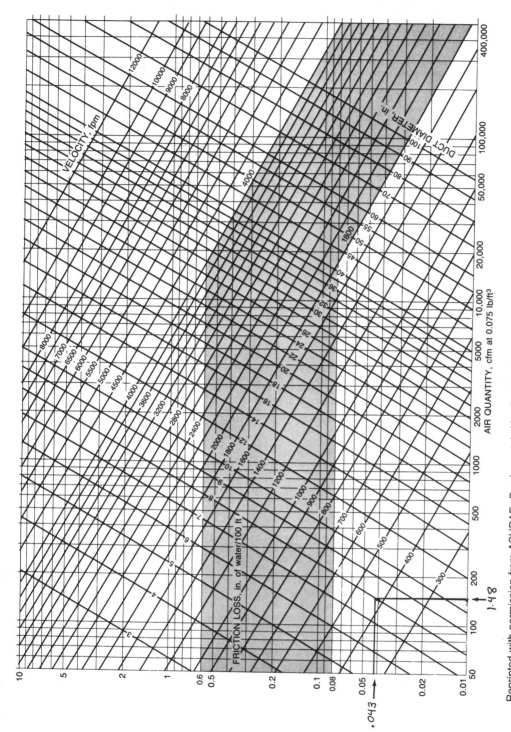

Reprinted with permission from ASHRAE, *Fundamentals Handbook*, 1989.

FIGURE 13-13 / Friction chart

Supply Outlet	Heat Gain (BTUH)	Heat Loss (BTUH)	Actual Length (ft)	Equivalent Length (ft)	Total Equiv. Length (ft)	Cooling cfm	Heating cfm	Supply Air Pressure	Supply Outlet Pressure Loss	Pressure Avail. for Duct Loss	Pressure Avail. Per 100 ft	Round Duct Size (in.)
Bedroom #1	2,887	4,283	36	80	116	123	148	0.07	0.02	0.05	0.043	9.0
Bedroom #2	1,492	2,310	26	105	131	64	80	0.07	0.02	0.05	0.038	8.0
Living	3,571	4,108	33	105	138	153	142	0.07	0.02	0.05	0.036	9.0
Living	3,571	4,108	55	80	135	153	142	0.07	0.02	0.05	0.037	9.0
Kitchen	4,685	3,752	46	80	126	200	130	0.07	0.02	0.05	0.040	9.0
Dining	2,175	3,047	27	105	132	95	105	0.07	0.02	0.05	0.038	9.0
Entry	1,038	1,682	16	115	131	44	58	0.07	0.02	0.05	0.038	7.0
Hall	1,037	1,682	10	80	90	44	58	0.07	0.02	0.05	0.055	6.0
Bedroom #3	2,188	3,008	30	105	135	94	104	0.07	0.02	0.05	0.037	7.0
Bath	697	960	25	90	115	30	33	0.07	0.02	0.05	0.043	6.0
Totals	23,447	28,940				995	1,000					

FIGURE 13-14 / Typical tabulated duct sizes

The air duct calculator is used to find rectangular duct sizes by aligning the required cfm (148) and the allowable drop per 100 ft (0.043 in.), and reading off the rectangular duct dimensions from the calculator. The aligned sizes provide the various sizes. When using sizes that do not quite align, go to the next larger size.

16. Add the air volume of all of the branch supply runs from each trunk duct. When there is more than one trunk duct (such as in Fig. 13-5), keep the totals for each trunk duct separate.

In this design, there are two trunk ducts (one toward the living room and kitchen, the other toward the bedrooms). Tabulate and total the air volume for each trunk duct.

17. For best air flow distribution through the ducts, it is important that the friction losses per 100 ft be approximately equal in both trunk ducts.

Using the table in Fig. 13-23, select the trunk sizes required. When there is more than one trunk duct, size each separately using the required air volume (cfm) and the allowable duct friction (step 12).

The bedroom trunk must handle 365 cfm with an allowable pressure drop of 0.038 in. per 100 ft. Using Fig. 13-23, the bedroom trunk duct will be a 12-in. round duct.

Circular Equivalents of Rectangular Duct for Equal Friction and Capacity[a]

Lgth Adj[b]	4.0	4.5	5.0	5.5	6.0	6.5	7.0	7.5	8.0	9.0	10.0	11.0	12.0	13.0	14.0	15.0	16.0
										Length of One Side of Rectangular Duct (a), in.							
3.0	3.8	4.0	4.2	4.4	4.6	4.7	4.9	5.1	5.2	5.5	5.7	6.0	6.2	6.4	6.6	6.8	7.0
3.5	4.1	4.2	4.6	4.8	5.0	5.2	5.3	5.5	5.7	6.0	6.3	6.5	6.8	7.0	7.2	7.5	7.7
4.0	4.4	4.6	4.9	5.1	5.3	5.5	5.7	5.9	6.1	6.4	6.7	7.0	7.3	7.6	7.8	8.0	8.3
4.5	4.6	4.9	5.2	5.4	5.7	5.9	6.1	6.3	6.5	6.9	7.2	7.5	7.8	8.1	8.4	8.6	8.8
5.0	4.9	5.2	5.5	5.7	6.0	6.2	6.4	6.7	6.9	7.3	7.6	8.0	8.3	8.6	8.9	9.1	9.4
5.5	5.1	5.4	5.7	6.0	6.3	6.5	6.8	7.0	7.2	7.6	8.0	8.4	8.7	9.0	9.3	9.6	9.9

Lgth Adj[b]	6	7	8	9	10	11	12	13	14	15	16	17	18	19	20	22	24	26	28	30	Lgth Adj[b]
						Length of One Side of Rectangular Duct (a), in.															
6	6.6																				6
7	7.1	7.7																			7
8	7.6	8.2	8.7																		8
9	8.0	8.7	9.3	9.8																	9
10	8.4	9.1	9.8	10.4	10.9																10
11	8.8	9.5	10.2	10.9	11.5	12.0															11
12	9.1	9.9	10.7	11.3	12.0	12.6	13.1														12
13	9.5	10.3	11.1	11.8	12.4	13.1	13.7	14.2													13
14	9.8	10.8	11.4	12.2	12.9	13.5	14.2	14.7	15.3												14
15	10.1	11.0	11.8	12.6	13.3	14.0	14.6	15.3	15.8	16.4											15
16	10.4	11.3	12.2	13.0	13.7	14.4	15.1	15.7	16.4	16.9	17.5										16
17	10.7	11.6	12.5	13.4	14.1	14.9	15.6	16.2	16.8	17.4	18.0	18.6									17
18	11.0	11.9	12.9	13.7	14.5	15.3	16.0	16.7	17.3	17.9	18.5	19.1	19.7								18
19	11.2	12.2	13.2	14.1	14.9	15.7	16.4	17.1	17.8	18.4	19.0	19.6	20.2	20.8							19
20	11.5	12.6	13.5	14.4	15.2	16.0	16.8	17.5	18.2	18.9	19.5	20.1	20.7	21.3	21.9						20
22	12.0	13.0	14.1	15.0	15.9	16.8	17.6	18.3	19.1	19.8	20.4	21.1	21.7	22.3	22.9	24.0					22
24	12.4	13.5	14.6	15.6	16.5	17.4	18.3	19.1	19.9	20.6	21.3	22.0	22.7	23.3	23.9	25.1	26.2				24
26	12.8	14.0	15.1	16.2	17.1	18.1	19.0	19.8	20.6	21.4	22.1	22.9	23.5	24.2	24.9	26.1	27.3	28.4			26
28	13.2	14.5	15.6	16.7	17.7	18.7	19.6	20.5	21.3	22.1	22.9	23.7	24.4	25.1	25.8	27.1	28.3	29.5	30.6		28
30	13.6	14.9	16.1	17.2	18.3	19.3	20.2	21.1	22.0	22.9	23.7	24.4	25.2	25.9	26.6	28.0	29.3	30.5	31.7	32.8	30
32	14.0	15.3	16.5	17.7	18.8	19.8	20.8	21.8	22.7	23.5	24.4	25.2	26.0	26.7	27.5	28.9	30.2	31.5	32.7	33.9	32
34	14.4	15.7	17.0	18.2	19.3	20.4	21.4	22.4	23.3	24.2	25.1	25.9	26.7	27.5	28.3	29.7	31.0	32.4	33.7	34.9	34
36	14.7	16.1	17.4	18.6	19.8	20.9	21.9	22.9	23.9	24.8	25.7	26.6	27.4	28.2	29.0	30.5	32.0	33.3	34.6	35.9	36
38	15.0	16.5	17.8	19.0	20.2	21.4	22.4	23.5	24.5	25.4	26.4	27.2	28.1	28.9	29.8	31.3	32.8	34.2	35.6	36.8	38
40	15.3	16.8	18.2	19.5	20.7	21.8	22.9	24.0	25.0	26.0	27.0	27.9	28.8	29.6	30.5	32.1	33.6	35.1	36.4	37.8	40
42	15.6	17.1	18.5	19.9	21.1	22.3	23.4	24.5	25.6	26.6	27.6	28.5	29.4	30.3	31.2	32.8	34.4	35.9	37.3	38.7	42
44	15.9	17.5	18.9	20.3	21.5	22.7	23.9	25.0	26.1	27.1	28.1	29.1	30.0	30.9	31.8	33.5	35.1	36.7	38.1	39.5	44
46	16.2	17.8	19.3	20.6	21.9	23.2	24.4	25.5	26.6	27.7	28.7	29.7	30.6	31.6	32.5	34.2	35.9	37.4	38.9	40.4	46
48	16.5	18.1	19.6	21.0	22.3	23.6	24.8	26.0	27.1	28.2	29.2	30.2	31.2	32.2	33.1	34.9	36.6	38.2	39.7	41.2	48
50	16.8	18.4	19.9	21.4	22.7	24.0	25.2	26.4	27.6	28.7	29.8	30.8	31.8	32.8	33.7	35.5	37.2	38.9	40.5	42.0	50
52	17.1	18.7	20.2	21.7	23.1	24.4	25.7	26.9	28.0	29.2	30.3	31.3	32.3	33.3	34.3	36.2	37.9	39.6	41.2	42.8	52
54	17.3	19.0	20.6	22.0	23.5	24.8	26.1	27.3	28.5	29.7	30.8	31.8	32.9	33.9	34.9	36.8	38.6	40.3	41.9	43.5	54
56	17.6	19.3	20.9	22.4	23.8	25.2	26.5	27.7	28.9	30.1	31.2	32.3	33.4	34.4	35.4	37.4	39.2	41.0	42.7	44.3	56
58	17.8	19.5	21.2	22.7	24.2	25.5	26.9	28.2	29.4	30.6	31.7	32.8	33.9	35.0	36.0	38.0	39.8	41.6	43.3	45.0	58
60	18.1	19.8	21.5	23.0	24.5	25.9	27.3	28.6	29.8	31.0	32.2	33.3	34.4	35.5	36.5	38.5	40.4	42.3	44.0	45.7	60
62		20.1	21.7	23.3	24.8	26.3	27.6	28.9	30.2	31.5	32.6	33.8	34.9	36.0	37.1	39.1	41.0	42.9	44.7	46.4	62
64		20.3	22.0	23.6	25.1	26.6	28.0	29.3	30.6	31.9	33.1	34.3	35.4	36.5	37.6	39.6	41.6	43.5	45.3	47.1	64
66		20.6	22.3	23.9	25.5	26.9	28.4	29.7	31.0	32.3	33.5	34.7	35.9	37.0	38.1	40.2	42.2	44.1	46.0	47.7	66
68		20.8	22.6	24.2	25.8	27.3	28.7	30.1	31.4	32.7	33.9	35.2	36.3	37.5	38.6	40.7	42.8	44.7	46.6	48.4	68
70		21.1	22.8	24.5	26.1	27.6	29.1	30.4	31.8	33.1	34.4	35.6	36.8	37.9	39.1	41.2	43.3	45.3	47.2	49.0	70
72			23.1	24.8	26.4	27.9	29.4	30.8	32.2	33.5	34.8	36.0	37.2	38.4	39.5	41.7	43.8	45.8	47.8	49.6	72
74			23.3	25.1	26.7	28.2	29.7	31.2	32.5	33.9	35.2	36.4	37.7	38.8	40.0	42.2	44.4	46.4	48.4	50.3	74
76			23.6	25.3	27.0	28.5	30.0	31.5	32.9	34.3	35.6	36.8	38.1	39.3	40.5	42.7	44.9	47.0	48.9	50.9	76
78			23.8	25.6	27.3	28.8	30.4	31.8	33.3	34.6	36.0	37.2	38.5	39.7	40.9	43.2	45.4	47.5	49.5	51.4	78
80			24.1	25.8	27.5	29.1	30.7	32.2	33.6	35.0	36.3	37.6	38.9	40.2	41.4	43.7	45.9	48.0	50.1	52.0	80
82				26.1	27.8	29.4	31.0	32.5	34.0	35.4	36.7	38.0	39.3	40.6	41.8	44.1	46.4	48.5	50.6	52.6	82
84				26.4	28.1	29.7	31.3	32.8	34.3	35.7	37.1	38.4	39.7	41.0	42.2	44.6	46.9	49.0	51.1	53.2	84
86				26.6	28.3	30.0	31.6	33.1	34.6	36.1	37.4	38.8	40.1	41.4	42.6	45.0	47.3	49.6	51.7	53.7	86
88				26.9	28.6	30.3	31.9	33.4	34.9	36.4	37.8	39.2	40.5	41.8	43.1	45.5	47.8	50.0	52.2	54.3	88
90				27.1	28.9	30.6	32.2	33.8	35.3	36.7	38.2	39.5	40.9	42.2	43.5	45.9	48.3	50.5	52.7	54.8	90
92					29.1	30.8	32.5	34.1	35.6	37.1	38.5	39.9	41.3	42.6	43.9	46.4	48.7	51.0	53.2	55.3	92
96					29.6	31.4	33.0	34.7	36.2	37.7	39.2	40.6	42.0	43.3	44.7	47.2	49.6	52.0	54.2	56.4	96

Reprinted with permission from ASHRAE, *Fundamentals Handbook*, 1989.

FIGURE 13-15 / Circular equivalents of rectangular ducts for equal friction and capacity[a]

Supply Outlet	Heat Gain (BTUH)	Heat Loss (BTUH)	Actual Length (ft)	Equivalent Length (ft)	Total Equiv. Length (ft)	Cooling cfm	Heating cfm	Supply Air Pressure	Supply Outlet Pressure Loss	Pressure Avail. for Duct Loss	Pressure Avail. Per 100 ft	Round Duct Size (in.)	Rectangular Duct Size (in.)
Bedroom #1	2,887	4,283	36	80	116	123	148	0.07	0.02	0.05	0.043	9.0	7 x 10
Bedroom #2	1,492	2,310	26	105	131	64	80	0.07	0.02	0.05	0.038	8.0	6 x 9
Living	3,571	4,108	33	105	138	153	142	0.07	0.02	0.05	0.036	9.0	7 x 10
Living	3,571	4,108	55	80	135	153	142	0.07	0.02	0.05	0.037	9.0	7 x 10
Kitchen	4,685	3,752	46	80	126	200	130	0.07	0.02	0.05	0.040	9.0	7 x 10
Dining	2,175	3,047	27	105	132	95	105	0.07	0.02	0.05	0.038	9.0	7 x 10
Entry	1,038	1,682	16	115	131	44	58	0.07	0.02	0.05	0.038	7.0	6 x 7
Hall	1,037	1,682	10	80	90	44	58	0.07	0.02	0.05	0.055	6.0	4.5 x 7
Bedroom #3	2,188	3,008	30	105	135	94	104	0.07	0.02	0.05	0.037	7.0	6 x 7
Bath	697	960	25	90	115	30	33	0.07	0.02	0.05	0.043	6.0	4.5 x 7
Totals	23,447	28,940				995	1,000						

FIGURE 13-16 / Typical rectangular tabulated duct sizes

The living space trunk duct has 635 cfm, and an allowable 0.038-in. pressure drop per 100 ft. Using Fig. 13-23, the living space trunk duct will be a 14.0-in. round duct.

Since the trunk ducts have been sized separately, based on the cfm and the allowable pressure drop, they are balanced.

The round duct sizes may be converted to rectangular duct sizes by use of Fig. 13-24. Once again, the space available for installation will have a large influence on the shape of the rectangular duct selected. For this design, a bedroom trunk duct of 16 in. × 8 in. and a living space trunk duct of 22 in. × 8 in. have been selected.

18. Review the supply trunk duct to determine if it is desirable to reduce its size as each branch duct leaves the trunk. Generally, such a reduction is suggested so that the velocity of air through the duct will not drop too low. Using the remaining air volume in the trunk duct, after each branch and the allowable pressure drop per 100 ft of duct (step 9), select the reduced trunk sizes from Figs. 13-23 and 13-24.

First, checking the bedroom trunk duct, the total cfm supplied is 365 (Fig. 13-17), with a 0.038-in. drop per 100 ft. Referring to the tabulated calculations (Fig. 13-16), the first branch to bedroom 2 has 80 cfm. This leaves 365 cfm − 80 cfm = 285 cfm in the trunk. Using 285 cfm and 0.022 pressure drop, select the reduced trunk duct from Fig. 13-23. The round duct size would be 6 in., and from Fig. 13-24, the rectangular size selected is 8 in. × 11 in. This process is repeated to the last branch.

Using the information in Fig. 13-18 and the tables in Figs. 13-23 and 13-24, determine the reduced trunk duct sizes for both the bedroom and the living space ducts, and tabulate the sizes as shown in Fig. 13-19.

19. Next, the design turns to the return ducts. The first step is to select an allowable return air pressure drop. This was previously decided (step 11), but it is reviewed at this point as the designer reviews the supply trunk and branch duct sizes to see if it is desirable to increase the duct sizes (reducing the allowable air pressure drop) or perhaps to reduce the duct sizes (increasing the allowable air pressure drop for the supply runs). Remember that a change in allowable air pressure drop for the supply will affect the allowable air pressure drop for the return runs (step 11).

A review of the supply duct sizes is made, and it is decided that they will not be revised since the duct sizes selected so far seem reasonable. Therefore, the original decision, in step 11, to use 0.03 in. as the allowable pressure drop for the return is unchanged, and the return design will be based on it.

20. The return trunk duct size is determined by the air volume it must handle and the allowable pressure drop. This allowable pressure drop must be converted to

FIGURE 13-17 / Tabulated main duct sizes

Duct	cfm	Supply Static Pressure*	Total Equiv. Length (ft)	Supply Pressure Avail. Per 100 ft	Round Duct Size (in.)	Rectangular Duct Size (in.)
Main Branch	1,000	0.05	138	0.036	18.0	12 x 24
Bedroom Branch	365	0.05	131	0.038	12.0	8 x 16
Living Branch	635	0.05	138	0.036	14.0	8 x 22

* Allows 0.02 for supply outlet

Duct		cfm	Supply Static Pressure	Total Equiv. Length (ft)	Supply Pressure Avail. Per 100 ft	Round Duct Size (in.)	Rectangular Duct Size (in.)
Main Branch	A-B	1,000	0.05	138	0.036	18.0	12 x 24
Bedroom Branch	B-C	365	0.05	131	0.038	12.0	8 x 16
	C-D	285					
	D-E	181					
	E-F	33					
Living Branch	B-G	635	0.05	138	0.036	14.0	8 x 22
	G-H	577					
	H-I	519					
	I-J	414					
	J-K	272					
	K-L	142					

FIGURE 13-18 / Reduced trunk sizes

allowable pressure drop *per 100 ft,* just as was done for the supply runs. Using the air volume and the allowable pressure drop per 100 ft, the round return duct size may be selected from Fig. 13-23. The rectangular duct of equivalent size may be found in Fig. 13-24.

The return trunk duct will have to handle an air volume equal to what the supply trunk duct handles; from Fig. 13-17, this is 1,000 cfm. The allowable pressure drop selected for the return is 0.03 in. (steps 11 and 12). First, the allowable pressure drop must be converted into the allowable pressure drop *per* 100 ft (step 13). The equivalent length is shown in Fig. 13-20.

$$(0.03 \text{ in.} \times 100) \div 82 \text{ ft} = 0.036 \text{ in.}$$
allowable pressure drop per 100 ft

Using this information (1,000 cfm, 0.036 in. per 100 ft) select the round return duct size from the table in Fig. 13-23 and its equivalent rectangular size from Fig. 13-24. Tabulate the information as shown in Fig. 13-20.

If the return trunk sizes are too large, they may be reduced in size by:

Duct		cfm	Supply Static Pressure	Total Equiv. Length (ft)	Supply Pressure Avail. Per 100 ft	Round Duct Size (in.)	Rectangular Duct Size (in.)
Main	A-B	1,000	0.05	138	0.036	18.0	12 x 24
Bedroom Branch	B-C	365	0.05	131	0.038	12.0	8 x 16
	C-D	285				10.0	8 x 11
	D-E	181				9.0	8 x 9
	E-F	33				6.0	8 x 4
Living Branch	B-G	635	0.05	138	0.036	14.0	8 x 22
	G-H	577				14.0	8 x 22
	H-I	519				12.0	8 x 16
	I-J	414				12.0	8 x 16
	J-K	272				10.0	8 x 11
	K-L	142				9.0	8 x 9

FIGURE 13-19 / Reduced trunk sizes

a. Reapportioning the pressure drop available so there is less drop allowed for the supply runs and more pressure allowed for the return runs. This may require a revision of supply branch and trunk duct sizes.

b. Checking to see if the return air grilles can be located closer to the furnace which would reduce the actual length of duct. This reduces the allowable pressure drop per 100 ft, resulting in a smaller duct size.

FIGURE 13-20 / Return duct sizes

Duct	Cfm	Actual length	Equivalent length	Total equivalent length	Loss per 100'	Round duct size (in.)	Rectangular duct size (in.)
Return	1000	12	70	82	0.036	20.0	12 X 30

21.   The size of the blower on the furnace is determined by the total air volume (the total cfm to be delivered) and the total static pressure requirements.

The total static pressure for furnace-blower combination units is the total of the actual pressure drops in the supply and return ducts. Most residential and small commercial buildings have furnace-blower combination units.

When the blowers are selected separately from the furnace, the total static pressure is the sum of the actual pressure losses in the supply and return ducts, filter loss, casing loss and losses through any devices which are put on the system, such as air washers and purifiers.

In this design, the 0.10-in. pressure drop, on which the designs of the ducts are based, is selected for a standard blower-furnace combination. While the actual pressure drop is slightly less than 0.10 in., the actual drop is not calculated since, as each duct is selected, it is large enough to handle the air volume within the allowable pressure drop.

22.   The capacity of the furnace to be selected is found next. The first step is to determine the Btuh requirements of all supply outlets.

The total Btuh for this building is 28,940 Btuh (calculated in Sec. 8-12).

23.   Determine the required bonnet capacity of the furnace in Btuh or MBH.

When all the ductwork for a building will be located within heated spaces (spaces on which heat losses are calculated), the required bonnet capacity will be the same as the calculated heat loss plus any allowance for "pick-up load."

When the furnace and ductwork will not be located in spaces included in the heat loss, the required bonnet capacity can be determined by the use of the formula:

$$\text{Btuh} = \text{cfm} \times \text{Unit temperature rise} \times 1.08$$

For this design, the bonnet capacity will be based on furnace and ducts in an unheated space. The cfm to be used in the formula is taken from step 7 as 1,000 cfm. The 1.08 in the formula is a constant factor (it will not change) based on 60 min/hr $\times$ 0.75 lb/cu ft (avg. air density) $\times$ 0.241 Btuh/lb (specific heat of air) = 1.08. The unit temperature rise is based on the difference between the temperature of the air as it leaves the bonnet (assume a 100°F temperature) and the temperature of the air as it re-enters the furnace to be heated (for this design, assume 65°F, which is slightly below the inside design temperature of 70°F). So the unit temperature rise will be 100°F − 65°F = 35°F. Therefore, the minimum required furnace size will be:

$$\text{Btuh} = 1,000 \text{ cfm} \times 35°\text{F} \times 1.08 = 37,800 \text{ Btuh}$$

24. Add any allowance which is required for pickup load (Sec. 8-12).

For this design, it has been decided to allow 10% for pickup load. Therefore, the total furnace Btuh required will be:

37,800 Btuh + 10% = 37,800 Btuh + 3,780 Btuh = 41,580 Btuh

QUESTIONS

13-1. What term is commonly used to refer to the cooling capacity of a cooling unit, and how does it relate to Btuh?

13-2. What does the term *EER* mean, and why is it important to check the EER of the cooling unit?

13-3. What type of equipment may be used when both heating and air conditioning are required?

13-4. What factors determine where the supplies and returns are located?

Design Exercises

13-5. Design a forced air heating and cooling system for the residence in Appendix D, based on the heat loss calculations in Exercise 8-15 and the heat gain calculations in Exercise 12-7.

13-6. Design a forced air heating and cooling system for one of the top floor apartments and one of the lower floor apartments in Appendix A. Base the design on the heat loss calculations in Exercise 8-17 and the heat gain calculations in Exercise 12–8.[23]

Equivalent of Supply and Return Air Plenum Fittings[8]

NOTE: D – 3" Throat Radius
F – No Radius
Q – Not Recommended

Equivalent Length of Reducing Trunk Duct Fittings[8]

Reprinted with permission of ACCA, *Manual D*, 1984.

FIGURE 13-21 / Equivalent fittings

13 / FORCED AIR SYSTEM DESIGN (AIR CONDITIONING)

^{a}Add 25 equivalent feet to each of the 3 fittings nearest the unit in each trunk duct after a reduction.

Equivalent Length of Extended Plenum Fittings^{a,B}

^{a}Add 25 equivalent feet to each of the 3 fittings nearest the unit in each trunk duct.

Equivalent Length of Round Trunk Duct Fittings^{a,B}

12.7

A – 30   B – 35   C – 60   D – 55   E – 70

F – 45   G – 30   H – 50   I – 5   J – 15

K – 30   L – 30   M – 5   N – 15   O – 15   P – 5

^{B}These values may also be used for floor diffuser boxes.

FIGURE 13-21 / Equivalent fittings (continued)

Duct Design / 13-3

O – 25

P – 15

Q – 25

Return Air Liner To Duct.

Stud Space To Liner.

Stud Space To Liner.

E

25 sq. ft.

F

10 sq. ft.

G

60 sq. ft.
R.A. GRILL AND FITTING. R.A. GRILL TO STUD SPACE. R.A. GRILL ONLY.

20
FLOOR GRILL TO LINER

^aInside radius for A and B = 3 in., and for F and G = 5 in.

Equivalent Length of Angles and Elbows for Individual and Branch Ducts[a,8]

Reprinted with permission from ASHRAE, Systems Handbook, 1976

Equivalent Length of Boot Fittings[a,8]

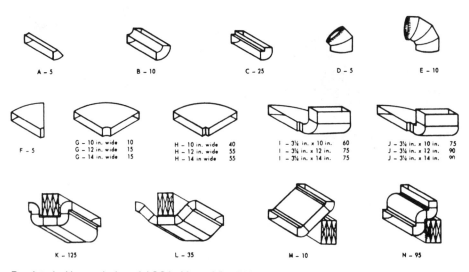

A – 5

B – 10

C – 25

D – 5

E – 10

F – 5

G – 10 in. wide	10
G – 12 in. wide	15
G – 14 in. wide	15

H – 10 in. wide	40
H – 12 in. wide	55
H – 14 in wide	55

I – 3¼ in. x 10 in.	60
I – 3¼ in. x 12 in.	75
I – 3¼ in. x 14 in.	75

J – 3¼ in. x 10 in.	75
J – 3¼ in. x 12 in.	90
J – 3¼ in. x 14 in.	90

K – 125

L – 35

M – 10

N – 95

Reprinted with permission of ACCA, *Manual D*, 1984.

FIGURE 13-21 / *Equivalent fittings (continued)*

CFM	Type A	Type B	Type C
1000	0.10	0.15	0.20
1500	.12	.17	.22
2000	.13	.18	.24
2500	.14	.20	.27
3000	.16	.22	.29
3500	.17	.24	.31
4000	.18	.26	.33
4500	0.20	0.28	0.36
5000	.21	.29	.38
5500	.22	.31	.40
6000	.24	.33	.42
6500	.25	.34	.45
7000	.27	.36	.47
7500	.28	.38	.49
8000	0.29	0.39	0.51
8500	.30	.41	.53
9000	.32	.43	.56
9500	.34	.45	.58
10,000	.34	.47	.60
10,500	.37	.48	.60
11,000	.39	.50	.60
11,500	0.40	0.50	0.60
12,000	.40	.50	.60
12,500	.40	.50	.60
13,000	.40	.50	.60
14,000	.40	.50	.60

CFM = Maximum cfm in any one duct.
Type A = Systems for quiet operation in residences, churches, concert halls, broadcasting studios, funeral homes, etc.
Type B = Systems for schools, theaters, public buildings, etc.
Type C = Systems for industrial buildings.

FIGURE 13-22 / Suggested bonnet and return pressures (inches of water)

Reprinted with permission from ASHRAE, *Fundamentals Handbook*, 1989.

FIGURE 13-23 / Friction chart

Length of One Side of Rectangular Duct (a), in.

Lgth Adj[b]	4.0	4.5	5.0	5.5	6.0	6.5	7.0	7.5	8.0	9.0	10.0	11.0	12.0	13.0	14.0	15.0	16.0
3.0	3.8	4.0	4.2	4.4	4.6	4.7	4.9	5.1	5.2	5.5	5.7	6.0	6.2	6.4	6.6	6.8	7.0
3.5	4.1	4.2	4.6	4.8	5.0	5.2	5.3	5.5	5.7	6.0	6.3	6.5	6.8	7.0	7.2	7.5	7.7
4.0	4.4	4.6	4.9	5.1	5.3	5.5	5.7	5.9	6.1	6.4	6.7	7.0	7.3	7.6	7.8	8.0	8.3
4.5	4.6	4.9	5.2	5.4	5.7	5.9	6.1	6.3	6.5	6.9	7.2	7.5	7.8	8.1	8.4	8.6	8.8
5.0	4.9	5.2	5.5	5.7	6.0	6.2	6.4	6.7	6.9	7.3	7.6	8.0	8.3	8.6	8.9	9.1	9.4
5.5	5.1	5.4	5.7	6.0	6.3	6.5	6.8	7.0	7.2	7.6	8.0	8.4	8.7	9.0	9.3	9.6	9.9

Length of One Side of Rectangular Duct (a), in.

Lgth Adj.[b]	6	7	8	9	10	11	12	13	14	15	16	17	18	19	20	22	24	26	28	30	Lgth Adj.[b]
6	6.6																				6
7	7.1	7.7																			7
8	7.6	8.2	8.7																		8
9	8.0	8.7	9.3	9.8																	9
10	8.4	9.1	9.8	10.4	10.9																10
11	8.8	9.5	10.2	10.9	11.5	12.0															11
12	9.1	9.9	10.7	11.3	12.0	12.6	13.1														12
13	9.5	10.3	11.1	11.8	12.4	13.1	13.7	14.2													13
14	9.8	10.8	11.4	12.2	12.9	13.5	14.2	14.7	15.3												14
15	10.1	11.0	11.8	12.6	13.3	14.0	14.6	15.3	15.8	16.4											15
16	10.4	11.3	12.2	13.0	13.7	14.4	15.1	15.7	16.4	16.9	17.5										16
17	10.7	11.6	12.5	13.4	14.1	14.9	15.6	16.2	16.8	17.4	18.0	18.6									17
18	11.0	11.9	12.9	13.7	14.5	15.3	16.0	16.7	17.3	17.9	18.5	19.1	19.7								18
19	11.2	12.2	13.2	14.1	14.9	15.7	16.4	17.1	17.8	18.4	19.0	19.6	20.2	20.8							19
20	11.5	12.6	13.5	14.4	15.2	16.0	16.8	17.5	18.2	18.9	19.5	20.1	20.7	21.3	21.9						20
22	12.0	13.0	14.1	15.0	15.9	16.8	17.6	18.3	19.1	19.8	20.4	21.1	21.7	22.3	22.9	24.0					22
24	12.4	13.5	14.6	15.6	16.5	17.4	18.3	19.1	19.9	20.6	21.3	22.0	22.7	23.3	23.9	25.1	26.2				24
26	12.8	14.0	15.1	16.2	17.1	18.1	19.0	19.8	20.6	21.4	22.1	22.9	23.5	24.2	24.9	26.1	27.3	28.4			26
28	13.2	14.5	15.6	16.7	17.7	18.7	19.6	20.5	21.3	22.1	22.9	23.7	24.4	25.1	25.8	27.1	28.3	29.5	30.6		28
30	13.6	14.9	16.1	17.2	18.3	19.3	20.2	21.1	22.0	22.9	23.7	24.4	25.2	25.9	26.6	28.0	29.3	30.5	31.7	32.8	30
32	14.0	15.3	16.5	17.7	18.8	19.8	20.8	21.8	22.7	23.5	24.4	25.2	26.0	26.7	27.5	28.9	30.2	31.5	32.7	33.9	32
34	14.4	15.7	17.0	18.2	19.3	20.4	21.4	22.4	23.3	24.2	25.1	25.9	26.7	27.5	28.3	29.7	31.0	32.4	33.7	34.9	34
36	14.7	16.1	17.4	18.6	19.8	20.9	21.9	22.9	23.9	24.8	25.7	26.6	27.4	28.2	29.0	30.5	32.0	33.3	34.6	35.9	36
38	15.0	16.5	17.8	19.0	20.2	21.4	22.4	23.5	24.5	25.4	26.4	27.2	28.1	28.9	29.8	31.3	32.8	34.2	35.6	36.8	38
40	15.3	16.8	18.2	19.5	20.7	21.8	22.9	24.0	25.0	26.0	27.0	27.9	28.8	29.6	30.5	32.1	33.6	35.1	36.4	37.8	40
42	15.6	17.1	18.5	19.9	21.1	22.3	23.4	24.5	25.6	26.6	27.6	28.5	29.4	30.3	31.2	32.8	34.4	35.9	37.3	38.7	42
44	15.9	17.5	18.9	20.3	31.5	22.7	23.9	25.0	26.1	27.1	28.1	29.1	30.0	30.9	31.8	33.5	35.1	36.7	38.1	39.5	44
46	16.2	17.8	19.3	20.6	21.9	23.2	24.4	25.5	26.6	27.7	28.7	29.7	30.6	31.6	32.5	34.2	35.9	37.4	38.9	40.4	46
48	16.5	18.1	19.6	21.0	22.3	23.6	24.8	26.0	27.1	28.2	29.2	30.2	31.2	32.2	33.1	34.9	36.6	38.2	39.7	41.2	48
50	16.8	18.4	19.9	21.4	22.7	24.0	25.2	26.4	27.6	28.7	29.8	30.8	31.8	32.8	33.7	35.5	37.2	38.9	40.5	42.0	50
52	17.1	18.7	20.2	21.7	23.1	24.4	25.7	26.9	28.0	29.2	30.3	31.3	32.3	33.3	34.3	36.2	37.9	39.6	41.2	42.8	52
54	17.4	19.0	20.6	22.0	23.5	24.8	26.1	27.3	28.5	29.7	30.8	31.8	32.9	33.9	34.9	36.8	38.6	40.3	41.9	43.5	54
56	17.6	19.3	20.9	22.4	23.8	25.2	26.5	27.7	28.9	30.1	31.2	32.3	33.4	34.4	35.4	37.4	39.2	41.0	42.7	44.3	56
58	17.8	19.5	21.2	22.7	24.2	25.5	26.9	28.2	29.4	30.6	31.7	32.8	33.9	35.0	36.0	38.0	39.8	41.6	43.3	45.0	58
60	18.1	19.8	21.5	23.0	24.5	25.9	27.3	28.6	29.8	31.0	32.2	33.3	34.4	35.5	36.5	38.5	40.4	42.3	44.0	45.7	60
62		20.1	21.7	23.3	24.8	26.3	27.6	28.9	30.2	31.5	32.6	33.8	34.9	36.0	37.1	39.1	41.0	42.9	44.7	46.4	62
64		20.3	22.0	23.6	25.1	26.6	28.0	29.3	30.6	31.9	33.1	34.3	35.4	36.5	37.6	39.6	41.6	43.5	45.3	47.1	64
66		20.6	22.3	23.9	25.5	26.9	28.4	29.7	31.0	32.3	33.5	34.7	35.9	37.0	38.1	40.2	42.2	44.1	46.0	47.7	66
68		20.8	22.6	24.2	25.8	27.3	28.7	30.1	31.4	32.7	33.9	35.2	36.3	37.5	38.6	40.7	42.8	44.7	46.6	48.4	68
70		21.1	22.8	24.5	26.1	27.6	29.1	30.4	31.8	33.1	34.4	35.6	36.8	37.9	39.1	41.2	43.3	45.3	47.2	49.0	70
72			23.1	24.8	26.4	27.9	29.4	30.8	32.2	33.5	34.8	36.0	37.2	38.4	39.5	41.7	43.8	45.8	47.8	49.6	72
74			23.3	25.1	26.7	28.2	29.7	31.2	32.5	33.9	35.2	36.4	37.7	38.8	40.0	42.2	44.4	46.4	48.4	50.3	74
76			23.6	25.3	27.0	28.5	30.0	31.5	32.9	34.3	35.6	36.8	38.1	39.3	40.5	42.7	44.9	47.0	48.9	50.9	76
78			23.8	25.6	27.3	28.8	30.4	31.8	33.3	34.6	36.0	37.2	38.5	39.7	40.9	43.2	45.4	47.5	49.5	51.4	78
80			24.1	25.8	27.5	29.1	30.7	32.2	33.6	35.0	36.3	37.6	38.9	40.2	41.4	43.7	45.9	48.0	50.1	52.0	80
82				26.1	27.8	29.4	31.0	32.5	34.0	35.4	36.7	38.0	39.3	40.6	41.8	44.1	46.4	48.5	50.6	52.6	82
84				26.4	28.1	29.7	31.3	32.8	34.3	35.7	37.1	38.4	39.7	41.0	42.2	44.6	46.9	49.0	51.1	53.2	84
86				26.6	28.3	30.0	31.6	33.1	34.6	36.1	37.4	38.8	40.1	41.4	42.6	45.0	47.3	49.6	51.7	53.7	86
88				26.9	28.6	30.3	31.9	33.4	34.9	36.4	37.8	39.2	40.5	41.8	43.1	45.5	47.8	50.0	52.2	54.3	88
90				27.1	28.9	30.6	32.2	33.8	35.3	36.7	38.2	39.5	40.9	42.2	43.5	45.9	48.3	50.5	52.7	54.8	90
92					29.1	30.8	32.5	34.1	35.6	37.1	38.5	39.9	41.3	42.6	43.9	46.4	48.7	51.0	53.2	55.3	92
96					29.6	31.4	33.0	34.7	36.2	37.7	39.2	40.6	42.0	43.3	44.7	47.2	49.6	52.0	54.2	56.4	96

Reprinted with permission from ASHRAE, *Fundamentals Handbook*, 1989.

FIGURE 13-24 / Circular equivalents of rectangular ducts for equal friction and capacity[a]

Circular Equivalents of Rectangular Duct for Equal Friction and Capacity[a] (Concluded)

Lgth Adj.[b]	32	34	36	38	40	42	44	46	48	50	52	56	60	64	68	72	76	80	84	88	Lgth Adj.[b]
32	35.0																				32
34	36.1	37.2																			34
36	37.1	38.2	39.4																		36
38	38.1	39.3	40.4	41.5																	38
40	39.0	40.3	41.5	42.6	43.7																40
42	40.0	41.3	42.5	43.7	44.8	45.9															42
44	40.9	42.2	43.5	44.7	45.8	47.0	48.1														44
46	41.8	43.1	44.4	45.7	46.9	48.0	49.2	50.3													46
48	42.6	44.0	45.3	46.6	47.9	49.1	50.2	51.4	52.5												48
50	43.6	44.9	46.2	47.5	48.8	50.0	51.2	52.4	53.6	54.7											50
52	44.3	45.7	47.1	48.4	49.7	51.0	52.2	53.4	54.6	55.7	56.8										52
54	45.1	46.5	48.0	49.3	50.7	52.0	53.2	54.4	55.6	56.8	57.9										54
56	45.8	47.3	48.8	50.2	51.6	52.9	54.2	55.4	56.6	57.8	59.0	61.2									56
58	46.6	48.1	49.6	51.0	52.4	53.8	55.1	56.4	57.6	58.8	60.0	62.3									58
60	47.3	48.9	50.4	51.9	53.3	54.7	56.0	57.3	58.6	59.8	61.0	63.4	65.6								60
62	48.0	49.6	51.2	52.7	54.1	55.5	56.9	58.2	59.5	60.8	62.0	64.4	66.7								62
64	48.7	50.4	51.9	53.5	54.9	56.4	57.8	59.1	60.4	61.7	63.0	65.4	67.7	70.0							64
66	49.4	51.1	52.7	54.2	55.7	57.2	58.6	60.0	61.3	62.6	63.9	66.4	68.8	71.0							66
68	50.1	51.8	53.4	55.0	56.5	58.0	59.4	60.8	62.2	63.6	64.9	67.4	69.8	72.1	74.3						68
70	50.8	52.5	54.1	55.7	57.3	58.8	60.3	61.7	63.1	64.4	65.8	68.3	70.8	73.2	75.4						70
72	51.4	53.2	54.8	56.5	58.0	59.6	61.1	62.5	63.9	65.3	66.7	69.3	71.8	74.2	76.5	78.7					72
74	52.1	53.8	55.5	57.2	58.8	60.3	61.9	63.3	64.8	66.2	67.5	70.2	72.7	75.2	77.5	79.8					74
76	52.7	54.5	56.2	57.9	59.5	61.1	62.6	64.1	65.6	66.9	68.4	71.1	73.7	76.2	78.6	80.9	83.1				76
78	53.3	55.1	56.9	58.6	60.2	61.8	63.4	64.9	66.4	67.9	69.3	72.0	74.6	77.1	79.6	81.9	84.2				78
80	53.9	55.8	57.5	59.3	60.9	62.6	64.1	65.7	67.2	68.7	70.1	72.9	75.4	78.1	80.6	82.9	85.2	87.5			80
82	54.6	56.4	58.2	59.9	61.6	63.3	64.9	66.5	68.0	69.5	70.9	73.7	76.4	79.0	81.5	84.0	86.3	88.5			82
84	55.1	57.0	58.8	60.6	62.3	64.0	65.6	67.2	68.7	70.3	71.7	74.6	77.3	80.0	82.5	85.0	87.3	89.6	91.8		84
86	55.7	57.6	59.4	61.2	63.0	64.7	66.3	67.9	69.5	71.0	72.5	75.4	78.2	80.9	83.5	85.9	88.3	90.7	92.9		86
88	56.3	58.2	60.1	61.9	63.6	65.4	67.0	68.7	70.2	71.8	73.3	76.3	79.1	81.8	84.4	86.9	89.3	91.7	94.0	96.2	88
90	56.8	58.8	60.7	62.5	64.3	66.0	67.7	69.4	71.0	72.6	74.1	77.1	79.9	82.7	85.3	87.9	90.3	92.7	95.0	97.3	90
92	57.4	59.3	61.3	63.1	64.9	66.7	68.4	70.1	71.7	73.3	74.9	77.9	80.8	83.5	86.2	88.8	91.3	93.7	96.1	98.4	92
94	57.9	59.9	61.9	63.7	65.6	67.3	69.1	70.8	72.4	74.0	75.6	78.7	81.6	84.4	87.1	89.7	92.3	94.7	97.1	99.4	94
96	58.4	60.5	62.4	64.3	66.2	68.0	69.7	71.5	73.1	74.8	76.3	79.4	82.4	85.3	88.0	90.7	93.2	95.7	98.1	100.5	96

Column heading: Length of One Side of Rectangular Duct (a), in.

[a] Table based on $D_e = 1.30(ab)^{0.625}/(a+b)^{0.25}$
[b] Length of adjacent side of rectangular duct (b), in.

Reprinted with permission from ASHRAE, *Fundamentals Handbook,* 1989.

FIGURE 13-24 / Circular equivalents of rectangular ducts for equal friction and capacity[a] (continued)

CHAPTER 14

SOLAR ENERGY AND HEAT PUMPS

14-1   OVERVIEW

The idea of harnessing the sun's energy for use in homes and factories is nothing new. Work began on solar furnaces more than two centuries ago—but with little success. In the United States solar hot water heaters were used in the early 1900s in Florida, Arizona, and California. The introduction of mass-produced hot water heaters which were low in cost and which used inexpensive oil, natural gas, and electricity all but stopped the further development of solar hot water heaters. The higher initial cost of the solar unit made it uneconomical except where the price of oil or electricity was high.

Since the 1930s limited experimentation continued in the application of solar energy, and interest increased markedly after World War II. But by 1960, the basic obstacle which had to be overcome was that the solar units were not "economically feasible" when compared with the low cost of other fuels. Not being "economically feasible" means that the amount of money saved on fuel costs is not sufficient to pay the increased cost of a solar system over a set period (say, 10 years).

Solar energy is being used to:

1. Heat hot water for use in buildings.
2. Provide heating for buildings.
3. Provide cooling for buildings.
4. Provide heating and cooling for buildings.
5. Provide heating and hot water for buildings.
6. Provide heating, cooling, and hot water for buildings (Fig. 14-1).

As outlined above, quite often the solar energy package will provide more than one service, usually at very little extra cost.

FIGURE 14-1 / Solar heating and cooling system

In this chapter, we will review some solar systems available, how they work and what they have to offer.

14-3   COLLECTORS AND STORAGE

All systems are made up of two basic components—collectors and storage areas.

COLLECTORS

First, all systems must have some type of collector. The flat-plate collector (shown in Fig. 14-2) is the collector most commonly used to gather in the heat from the sun. Basically, all collectors are similar in that they have a casing (or frame), insulation, plate, heat transfer medium (liquid or gas), and glazing. There is no one design that is used, however, and several different collector designs are shown in Fig. 14-3. But it is important to note there are two basic types of heat transfer mediums—*liquid and air*—and this makes for two basic types of collectors—liquid and air.

The collector is located outside and is angled to receive the maximum amount of sunshine possible (Fig. 14-4). To increase the amount of the sun's rays which hit the collector, some systems even use a reflective surface in front of the collector (Fig. 14-5), with the reflective panel placed either on an adjoining flat roof or in front of the collector. The collector is commonly located on the roof, and many units are also designed to be placed on the ground.

STORAGE MEDIUMS

Once the heat exchange medium (liquid or air) is warmed in the collector, the heat it absorbs is transferred to a storage medium for future use. The storage mediums most commonly used are coarse aggregates (clean, washed rock), water and a combination of the coarse aggregates and water (Fig. 14-6).

14-4   HEATING, COOLING, AND HOT WATER

The system shown in Fig. 14-1 utilizes a liquid heat transfer medium (water or water and anti-freeze), a collector on the roof, and water as the heat storage medium. Such a system is the most versatile, providing the most benefits to the owner. The system shown has auxiliary units for heating, cooling, and hot water for the time when the solar system cannot provide sufficient heat (or cooling).

HEATING

The heat transfer medium is heated in the collector and is then circulated through the storage tank, transferring its heat to the storage medium—in this case, water. This

Liquid collector

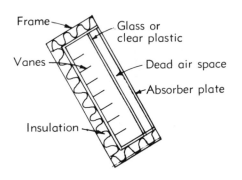

Air collector

FIGURE 14-2 / Flat plate collectors

14 / SOLAR ENERGY AND HEAT PUMPS

Reprinted with permission from ASHRAE, *HVAC Handbook*, 1987.

FIGURE 14-3 / *Variations of solar water and air heaters*

385

FIGURE 14-4 / *Collector angle*

heated water then circulates through the hot water heater tank to heat all or part of the hot water required for the building. The heated water then passes a fan which forces air past the hot water coils. The air passing the coils is warmed and circulates through the building.

There are many variations on the design; in Fig. 14-1, the water from the storage tank passes first through the fan and forced air and then through the hot water tank. A hot water heating system is shown in Fig. 14-7 and discussed in Sec. 14-5.

FIGURE 14-5 / *Reflection to collector*

14 / *SOLAR ENERGY AND HEAT PUMPS*

Collector

Collector

Water storage tank

Alternate water storage location

Storage of water and rock in basement

Collector

Rock storage

FIGURE 14-6 / Storage medium

COOLING

To provide cooling for the building, the system is, in effect, reversed. While the collectors used to gather the heat ideally face south, the radiators used to give off heat to the exterior face north. (Although some systems utilize the collectors already on the south, it is not as effective.)

In order to use the system for cooling, the storage medium must be made as low in temperature (cool) as possible; then it circulates past the refrigerant in the refrigeration unit which then circulates past the fan to blow cool air into the building. One method used is to have the heat pump transfer heat from the house to the heat storage medium and into the storage tank where the temperature of the entire storage medium slowly increases. Then at night, the radiation system turns on and the heat transfer medium cools the storage medium by absorbing the heat as it passes through the tank. Circulating it up through the night radiator collectors facing north, the collectors radiate the heat to the surrounding atmosphere and then the medium goes back to the storage tank to constantly repeat the process of lowering the water temperature in the storage tank so it can be used for cooling.

Heating, Cooling, and Hot Water / 14-4

Collector
(Roof or yard)

Heated

Cooled

Hot water
supply

Tank to
hold water

Heated medium
from collector
heats water in
tank

Tank—This tank could be used to just hold water heated by the collector medium or it could be a direct hot water heater used to supplement the collector during times when the collector cannot provide all of the hot water required.

FIGURE 14-7 / Hot water system

Another method used with a system of this type is to connect to a well; then if the water in the storage tank reaches a certain temperature (about 65°F), the system will automatically switch to the well as its source of cool water. Since many of the same controls (valves and pumps) are utilized in both the heating and the cooling operations, it is often this dual feature that makes the system economically feasible.

Another method used converts the sun's energy into the energy source used to power the cooling equipment. In this type of installation, storage batteries are charged during the daytime hours to operate a heat pump.

The use of solar energy for cooling is not nearly as advanced as its use for heating. A great deal more research is required before economical, dependable solar cooling units are available.

14-5   HOT WATER HEATING

Hot water solar systems are similar to the system described (in Sec. 14-4) except that the storage medium (water) is used to heat the hot water which is then circulated through the system (Fig. 14-7). An auxiliary heat source is still required to supplement the solar system. This system could also be used for cooling (similar to Fig. 14-1) if the devices in the building are selected to effectively handle chilled water. Realistically, this is rarely the case in residential work. Chilled water systems are discussed in Sec. 7-1. Solar hot water is also discussed in Sec. 2-17.

14-6   HOT AIR SYSTEM (HEATING)

A hot air heating system uses air as the heat transfer medium and rocks as the heat storage medium. As the diagram in Fig. 14-5 shows, the collector may be located on the ground. The air in the collector is heated as it is pulled across the vanes in the collector, and it is then pushed over the rocks in the storage medium, transferring much of the heat collected to the rocks. This continuous flow of air is constantly warmed in the collector and then cooled as it transfers its heat to the rocks (Fig. 14-8).

When the thermostat in the building calls for heat, the distribution fans come on and circulate the cooler air from the building over the rocks in the storage area, and this warmed air is then circulated back through the building (Fig. 14-9).

When both the collection and the distribution are on, the air flow from the building passes through the collector to provide heat directly from the collector. This commonly occurs when the building thermostat calls for heat during the daytime while the collector is also activated to gather the heat from the sun. With a system of this type, it is usually recommended that there be continuous air circulation in the building. A solar system of this type is designed to continuously circulate air in the building, that is relatively cooler than that from the forced air system using a furnace. In the solar system, the air will usually feel just slightly warm, or perhaps even a little cool to the touch since the air temperature will be lower than your body temperature. Studies of systems using continuous air circulation show that less heat is required when such a system is used.

Also important in this system is the fact that it is easily adaptable to existing forced air systems. In such an installation, the collector could be set on the ground.

14-7   SUPPLEMENTARY HEAT

Almost all solar systems are more expensive to install than conventional boiler or furnace systems. As discussed in Chapter 8, the conventional system is sized to deliver all of the heat required down to a particular design temperature ($-$ 10°F in Rutland,

FIGURE 14-8 / Hot air collection

NOTE Steps 1, 2 and 3 explain the collection air flow circuit

2. Hot air gives up its heat to the rock. ②

3. And is blown back across the collector to be heated again ③

1. Air is pulled across the collector, where it s heated, then blown into the rock.

Courtesy of Champion Home Builders Company

Steps 4, 5 and 6 explain the distribution air flow circuit.

6. And the distribution fan sends it back into the house.

5. Here the rocks heat the cool air.

4. When the house needs heat, cool air is drawn from the house cold air return ducts.

Courtesy of Champion Home Builders Company

FIGURE 14-9 / Hot air storage and transfer

Vt., and 20°F in Raleigh, N.C.). It is quite inexpensive to size the boiler or furnace to provide all of the heat required to meet those demands, even with an extra 10% pickup load added on. But keep in mind two things:

1. During most of the heating season, the temperatures are well above the design temperature used. (Many times it might reach the low during the night, but it warms up 15° to 25°F during the day.)

2. The solar system costs much more for the materials used.

This means that providing all of the heat required to keep a house warm in a northern city on *the coldest day ever recorded there* would require a solar unit about four times as large as one that would provide 90% of the heat required during the entire heating season.

For these reasons many of the solar systems have auxiliary or supplemental heating systems along with the solar system. In this situation the solar system would provide a certain percentage of the heat required (perhaps 40%, 50%, 60%, or more) and the supplemental heating boiler or furnace would provide the rest. In this manner the most economically feasible installation can be obtained, and the problem of allocating huge areas to contain the storage medium is overcome.

A solar system with supplemental heat can be designed to save a significant amount of the total heat bill, but it is important to realize that it is the *total annual fuel bill* being discussed, that the savings will be highest in the milder months and that the heat bills will increase in the colder months. So it is the "average" being discussed, as illustrated in Fig. 14-10.

While this type of system may not satisfy the "purist" in terms of total solar systems, it provides a very "cost effective" system which will save large amounts of fuel. In addition, it makes solar systems easily adaptable to existing installations where the existing system may be used as the supplemental system. It is most important not only that fuels be conserved in new construction but also that systems be developed that are adaptable to existing heating systems (hot water and air).

14-8   HEAT PUMPS

Use of refrigeration to provide cooling is discussed in Sec. 7-4, as are the basic principles which apply to such use. The use of refrigeration to provide both heating and cooling for a space is accomplished with a device called a *heat pump*. This increasingly popular form of heating and cooling a space requires explanation as to the principles involved and its advantages and disadvantages.

First, the discussion of the cooling principles of refrigerants in Sec. 7-4 must be carefully read and understood. In effect, it states that the refrigerant can take heat from one place (air or water) and move it to another by use of an evaporator, compressor and condenser.

Now, using those basic cooling principles and a valve control, it is possible to reverse the cycle, causing the refrigerant to absorb heat from an outside surrounding medium (usually air but water is sometimes used) and to release this heat inside the building (in the air or water being used to heat the building).

The reversing valve control allows the refrigerant to be used to provide cooling or heating, depending on the direction of flow after it leaves the compressor. If the

FIGURE 14-10 / Yearly heat supplied

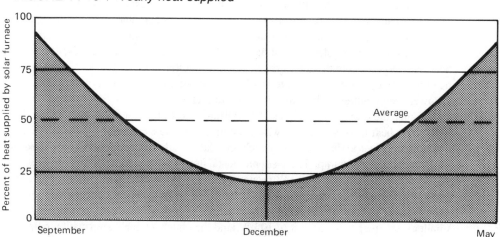

refrigerant flows to the condenser, it provides cooling; if it flows toward the evaporator section, it provides heating.

The most commonly used surrounding mediums are the outside air and the forced air in the ductwork.

Outside air is the surrounding medium most likely to be used to draw heat from in the winter for heating and to release heat to in the summer for cooling. The temperature of this outside air affects the efficiency of the unit in providing heating and cooling Btuh. Typically, in the winter as the outside air temperature goes down, the amount of heat which the heat pump will produce goes down also. In effect, the more heat needed in the space, the less Btuh the unit will provide.

At this point, it is important to realize that a heat pump is not electric heat. Actually, it is a type of solar heating which draws heat from the surrounding air. It requires electrical power to run the equipment, but it is more efficient than electric heat. The efficiency of the heat pump can be determined from the manufacturer's engineering data. While there are many sizes and capacities of units available, we will review the typical data for a 3-ton (36,000-Btuh) cooling capacity unit. Since each manufacturer's units vary, so will their data; and as more efficient units are developed, the result will be higher values from the heat pump.

Note in Fig. 14-11 that at a 60°F outside temperature, the unit will provide 41,000 Btuh for heating. As the temperature goes down to 40°F, the unit will supply 32,000 Btuh, and yet more heat is required inside the space at 40°F than at 60°F. When it gets cold—say, 20°F—outside, the unit will provide 21,000 Btuh. It is obvious that as the temperature goes down, so does the ability of the heat pump to produce heat.

It is when the heat pump alone is producing the heat that the unit is economical to operate. The coefficient of performance [(Btuh/watts) $\times$ 3.14] is not generally given by the manufacturer, but it has been calculated for the 3-ton unit in Fig. 14-11. This coefficient of performance offers a comparison of the heat pump and electric resistance heat. The table shows a COP of 2.46 at 60°F, dropping to 2.17 at 40°F and to 1.71 at 20°F. Due to this fluctuation, it is difficult to give an actual comparison with other fuels and systems. It depends very much on the geographic area it is being used in and how many hours it operates at the different temperatures.

For comparison, electric heat has a COP of 1.0. As shown in Sec. 8-18, electric heat tends to cost about twice as much as oil or natural gas. So, for the heat pump to be competitive, it needs to operate at a COP of about 2.0, and at 40°F it does this. But at lower temperatures, it becomes less and less efficient.

Since the heat pump puts out 21,000 Btuh at 20°F, the rest of the heat is supplied by electric heat resistance units, which mount inside the evaporator blower discharge area; or else electric duct heaters, which are placed right in the ductwork, are used to supplement the heat pump. These supplemental units run on electricity and provide the standard 3,413 Btuh per 1,000 W (watts) (1 k W). These electric resistance units are generally available in increments of 3, 5, 10, 15, and 20 kW, depending on the manufacturer. Many of the smaller heat pump units have space to install only the smaller sizes, perhaps to a limit of 10 kW, and the manufacturer's information must be

Typical 3-ton (36,000 Btuh) heat pump
Cooling capacity, 62° outside wet bulb,
85° air temperature entering evaporator.

Outside air temperature db°F	Cooling Btuh	Watts	EER
85	36,000	5,250	6.85
95	34,000	5,400	6.30
105	32,000	5,750	5.56

Heating capacity

Outside air temperature	Heating Btuh	Watts	COP
60	41,000	5,300	2.46
50	38,000	5,100	2.37
45	35,000	4,900	2.37
40	32,000	4,700	2.17
30	26,000	4,300	1.92
20	21,000	3,900	1.71
10	15,000	3,500	1.36
0	10,000	3,100	1.02

FIGURE 14-11 / Typical
3-ton heat pump

checked. The large units, such as the 3-ton unit being discussed here, will take the 15-kW unit.

The 15-kW unit would be made up of three 5-kW elements which would operate at three different stages set to provide the required heat to the space. The first stage is controlled by the room thermostat, and it operates on a 2°F differential from the setting on the room thermostat. This means that if the room thermostat is set, say, at 70°F, as the thermostat calls for heat, the heat pump goes on and begins to send heat to the space. If the temperature of the room falls below 68°F, then the first 5-kW unit would come on and begin to provide additional heat to supplement the heat pump. The second and third stages of electrical resistance heat are activated by outdoor thermostat settings which are adjustable (from 50° to 0°F).

This differential of 2°F between the thermostat setting and the room temperature, which activates the first stage, may mean that in cold weather the room temperature may stabilize at 68°F. This is because 68°F is the temperature at which the first stage shuts off; to get a 70°F reading on those days, it may be necessary to raise the thermostat reading to about 72°F.

The cooling efficiency of the heat pump should also be checked. Many times the less expensive units have much lower efficiency ratings than the individual cooling units discussed in Sec. 13-2. It is important that the most efficient model be selected. For example, the 3-ton unit being discussed in this section has its engineering data shown in Fig. 14-11. As the temperature goes up, the cooling Btuh provided goes down; at 85°F it produces 36,000 Btuh for cooling and 5,250 W, while at 95°F it produces 34,000 Btuh and 5,450 W. Its EER ranges from 6.85 to 5.56 as listed in the table. The EER most commonly used for comparison of cooling units is based on its performance at a 95°F temperature; based on that, this unit's EER would be 6.24.

In reviewing the operation and efficiency of the heat pump:

1. The heat pump is more efficient in warmer climates than in cooler areas. In Florida and southern California, for example, heat pumps are reasonably efficient. As you approach "mid-South" states, those states in a band from North Carolina and Virginia on the east to Northern California on the west, the efficiency begins to fall off. In northern states these units would depend on the electric resistance heat for so much of the time that efficiency is minimal.

2. Technology will continue to improve the efficiency of the heat pump. It is part of the designer's responsibility to keep abreast of developments in the field that will provide increased efficiency.

3. A comparison of the heat pump with the other fuels and systems must be made for each geographical area, and its complexity suggests that a computer be used. This type of analysis is available in many areas now. However, the designer should be aware that it is being made available by the same people who are selling heat pumps and perhaps by those who sell the electricity to run the unit. This is not to infer that it would not be "technically accurate"; only that the utmost caution should always be used when using calculations, analyses, claims, and the like from any interested party (such as the company selling the unit). The best idea is to check actual installations and compare the costs with those of comparable installations. But be certain that they are comparable installations, that the thermostats are set at about the same temperatures and that the actual electrical and fuel bills are available (don't rely on word of mouth).

4. While heat pumps are more efficient than electric resistance heat, in northern and mid-South states actual use has shown that it is not less expensive to heat with a heat pump than with oil and natural gas fuels.

5. While the currently available heat pump is a solar unit, it will probably soon be available with a solar collector panel which can be attached to it to provide greater efficiency. This may be one of the first practical, small and mid-sized solar system projects. Currently, at least one manufacturer is working on its development.

6. The shortage of fuel oil due to the embargo in the early 1970s, the shortage of natural gas available to the user and the general uncertainty over future supplies and prices of these fuels have caused many owners and designers to consider using the heat pump in many areas where it might not ordinarily be considered. In effect, most people feel that, one way or another, at least with the heat pump,

4-ton heat pump, heating capacity

Outside air temperature db°F	Heating Btuh	Watts
60	52,000	5,900
40	41,000	5,300
20	28,000	4,800
0	20,000	4.300

2-ton heat pump, heating capacity

Outside air temperature db°F	Heating Btuh	Watts
60	31,000	3,850
40	22,000	3,300
20	14,000	2,700
0	8,200	2,200

FIGURE 14-12 / 4-ton and 2-ton heat pumps

the fuel (the electricity) will be available to run the unit and provide the heating and cooling required.

7.   It is more efficient and generally less expensive, especially during the heating season, to use one large unit instead of two smaller units, unless one section of the house (or building) will be closed off. For example, based on the data in Fig. 14-12, if a building requires a 4-ton cooling unit at 20°F, the heat pump will provide 28,000 Btuh for heating while using 4,800 W. Using two 2-ton units, at 20°F each unit will provide 14,000 Btuh using 2,700 W, for a total of 28,000 Btuh using 5,400 W. Again, this is the type of analysis that the designer must consider. Now, if part of the building were to be closed off—say, a large bedroom wing—with the temperature set quite low (about 50°F), it might be more economical to have two units—in this case, one unit to serve the bedrooms and one for the rest of the building.

QUESTIONS

14-1. What factors have made solar energy more attractive in recent years?

14-2. What may solar energy be used for in a building?

14-3. Briefly describe what a *collector* is and how it works.

14-4. What are the two basic types of heat transfer mediums?

14-5. What are the basic components of a collector?

14-6. What are the commonly used storage mediums, and what is the function of a storage medium in the solar energy system?

14-7. Sketch a schematic of a solar energy system providing heating and hot water only; label all the parts.

14-8. Sketch a schematic of a solar energy system providing heating, cooling, and hot water; label all the parts.

14-9. Why is supplementary heat often *required* in solar heating systems?

14-10. Why might it be *desirable* to have supplemental heat with a solar heating system?

14-11. Describe briefly how a heat pump operates.

14-12. What happens to the heating and cooling outputs of a heat pump as the temperature varies?

CHAPTER 15
ELECTRICAL SYSTEMS

15-1   CODES

All buildings require electrical systems to provide power for the lights and to run various appliances and equipment. The safety of the system is of prime importance, and minimum requirements are included in building codes. Most applicable codes have separate electrical sections, or else completely separate electrical codes are prepared. In addition, many local codes make reference to the *National Electric Code* (NEC) or are based on the national code. The designer must first determine what code is applicable to the locale in which the building will be built, and then be certain that the electrical design is in accordance with the code. The NEC is used as a basis for this portion of the text. Generally, these codes place limitations on the type and size of the wiring to be used, the circuit size, the outlet spacings, the conduit requirements, and the like. The tables used in this text are from the 1990 NEC. Be certain that you always have a copy of the latest edition available for your use.

15-2   UNDERWRITERS LABORATORIES (UL)

UL is an independent organization which tests various electrical fixtures and devices to determine if they meet minimum specifications as set up by UL. The device to be tested is furnished by the manufacturer, and if the test shows that it meets the minimum specifications, it will be put on the UL official published list, referred to as "listed by Underwriters Laboratories, Inc." The approved device may then have a UL label on it. A typical UL seal is shown in Fig. 15-1, and many consumers will not buy any electrical device which does not have a UL label.

15-3   LICENSES

Most municipalities have laws which require that any person who wishes to engage in the business of installing electrical systems must be licensed (usually by the state or the province) to do so. This generally means that the person must have a minimum number of years of experience working with a licensed electrician and must pass a written test which deals primarily with the electrical code being used and with methods of installation.

By requiring a license, it is assured that the electrician knows, at a minimum, the code requirements and the installation procedures. There are areas where no laws require that only licensed electricians may install electrical systems, and, in effect, there is no protection for the consumer against an unskilled electrician. Always insist on licensed electricians for all installations.

15-4   PERMITS

Many municipalities require a permit before any electrical installations may be made on the project. Depending on the municipality, a complete electrical drawing may be required and may even be reviewed by the municipality before installation may begin, while others may require no drawings at all. In general, most municipalities that require electrical permits also require licensed electricians.

In addition, these municipalities will probably have electrical inspectors, trained personnel who check the project during regularly scheduled visits. Typically, they will want to inspect the installation after the rough wiring is in and before it is concealed in the construction, and again when all of the fixtures and devices are installed and wired back to the panel and the service and meter installed.

On large projects it may be necessary for many electrical inspections since the work may be done in stages. For example, conduit which will be encased in concrete may have to be checked before the concrete is poured, and conduit to be built into the masonry walls will have to be checked before the walls are begun. These types of covering up will occur throughout the project. Be certain that the installer and the

FIGURE 15-1 / Typical Underwriters Laboratories seal

designer are aware of when inspections are required and of what will be inspected. Also, it is important that close coordination and cooperation be maintained with the inspector since he could slow down the progress of the work if he does not make his inspections promptly. Whenever possible, he will need to know as early as possible when inspections will be necessary.

15-5   TERMINOLOGY

Circuit: Two or more wires which carry electricity from the source to an electrical device and back.

Circuit Breaker: A switch which automatically stops the flow of electricity in a particular circuit when the circuit is overloaded.

Conductor: The wire used to carry electricity.

Conduit: A channel or tube which is designed to carry the conductors in locations where the conductors need protection.

Convenience Outlet: An outlet which receives the plugs of electrical devices such as lamps, radios, clocks, etc. Also referred to as a *receptacle.*

Fixtures: The lighting fixtures used. They may be wall or ceiling mounted, recessed or surface mounted. Also included are table and floor lighting fixtures.

Ground: To minimize injuries from shock and possible damage from lightning, the electrical system should be equipped with a wire (called a ground) that connects to the earth.

Service Entrance: The wires, fittings and equipment which bring the electricity into the building.

Service Panel: The main panel which receives the electricity at the service entrance, breaks it down and distributes it through the various circuits.

Switch: The control used to turn the flow of electricity on or off to the electrical device to which it is connected.

15-6   SERVICE ENTRANCE

The service entrance furnishes electricity to a house; a three-wire service bringing in 120/240 volt, single-phase power is generally standard. These three wires attach to the house at a mast (Fig. 15-2), are installed underground (Fig. 15-3) and run through a metal conduit through the meter and into the service panel. The meter and service panel should be placed as close to the mast as possible. This will place the main breaker as close to the meter as possible.

FIGURE 15-2 / Overhead service

FIGURE 15-3 / Underground service

The location of the service entrance is generally controlled by economics. Often the service is located near the point of greatest power usage (in a house, this is usually the kitchen) since larger wires are needed where high usage is indicated, and the closer the entrance to the high-usage area, the less of the larger, more expensive wiring that is required (Fig. 15-4).

Electric meters are weatherproof and should be located on the outside of the house so readings can be taken by the power company without disturbing anyone or when no one is at home.

In many locales service is brought to the buildings in electrical wires below ground (Fig. 15-3). In this manner, unsightly wires, masts and fittings are concealed. When the entire community is served by underground service, the power poles and lines are never missed. However, this is more expensive than running services above ground.

The sizing of the service entrance, based on the amount of power it must supply, should be guided by the following information:

100 amperes: Adequate power to provide general-purpose circuits, water heater, electric laundry, and cooking.

150 amperes: Adequate power to provide general-purpose circuits, water heater, electric laundry, cooking, and for a small house, the air conditioning and heating.

200 amperes: Adequate power to provide general-purpose circuits, water heater, electric laundry and cooking, air conditioning and heating.

Once all of the circuits, fixtures, appliances and type of heating are determined, the size of the service entrance may be calculated by experienced personnel. It is best

Overhead service

Underground service

Alternate location

FIGURE 15-4 / Service location

to anticipate a little high when selecting the size of the service entrance. It is much more expensive to increase the size later than when the building is being built.

15-7   SERVICE PANEL

This distribution box is the main panel (Fig. 15-5) that receives the service electricity, breaks it down and distributes it through branch circuits to the places where the electricity is needed. Inside the panel is a main disconnect switch which cuts off power

Meter

Service panel

Overhead service

FIGURE 15-5 / Service panel

to the entire building and the circuit breakers (or fuses) which control the power to the individual circuits serving the house.

The circuit breakers (or fuses) are protective devices which will automatically cut off power to any circuit which is overloaded or short-circuited. The circuit breaker may be turned back on by flipping its surface-mounted switch; if the circuit is still overloaded, the switch will immediately flip off again. Fuses burn out when the circuit is overloaded and must be replaced to activate the circuit again. Circuit breakers and fuses are sized as to the amperage they will carry, and when replaced, the replacement should have the same rating.

The service panel is sized to match the service coming in, commonly 100, 150, or 200 amps. The number of circuits required in the building will determine the size of the panel. Panels are rated in amperage and poles, the poles being how many circuits it will handle. All 120-volt circuits, as required for most lighting, convenience outlets and appliances, require one pole each. All appliances such as ranges, clothes dryers, hot water heaters, large air conditioners and many motors require 240 volts, and two poles are required. The panel selected should have extra poles so that additional circuits may be run if and when they may be desired.

The panel may be surface mounted or recessed and should be conveniently located for easy servicing and resetting of circuit breakers and fuses as required. It should not be located anywhere there is a possibility of water being on the panel or on the floor around it. Typically, it is located in a garage, corridor, basement or utility room of the building.

15-8   FEEDER CIRCUITS

On large buildings where the wiring for circuits would have long runs, a feeder circuit may be run from the service panel to a subdistribution panel (Fig. 15-6 and Fig. 15-7). Locating the subdistribution panel conveniently to service the larger feeder conductors (wires) will allow a minimal voltage drop when compared with the excessive voltage drop that occurs when branch circuits are in excess of 75 to 100 ft long.

15-9   BRANCH CIRCUITS

The branch circuit connects the service panel to the electrical device it supplies (Fig. 15-8). It may supply power to a single device such as a water heater, range or air conditioner, or it may service a group or series of devices such as convenience outlets and lights. The branch circuit may have a variety of capacities, such as 15, 20, 30, 40, or 50 amps, depending on the requirements of the electrical devices serviced. The general-purpose circuits for lights and convenience outlets are usually sized at 15 or 20 amps. One general-purpose branch circuit will provide a maximum of 20 amps × 120 volts = 2,400 watts, of which the NEC allows 80%. There is a tendency for people to put higher wattage bulbs (luminaires) in lighting fixtures as they need replacing; a

FIGURE 15-6 / Feeder circuit

group of light fixtures totalling 1,200 to 1,600 watts may be placed on a circuit and still allow for additional future usage. The same is true with convenience outlets; generally no more than six should be on a circuit.

The wiring layout for most buildings shows the branch circuit arrangements. If not shown on the layout, it will be left to the electrical contractor to decide on groupings (Fig. 15-9).

15-10   RECEPTACLES

Receptacles, also referred to as convenience outlets (Fig. 15-10) are used to plug in lights and small appliances around the house. Each room should be laid out with no less than one outlet per wall and with outlets no more than 10 ft apart. The amount, location and type will vary with the room, depending on both the design of the room and the furniture layout. Duplex outlets (two receptacles) are most commonly used, but single and triple receptacles are also used. Also used are strips which allow movement of the

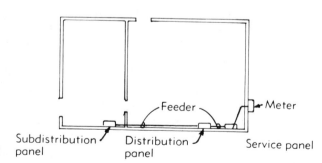

FIGURE 15-7 / Feeder circuit

FIGURE 15-8 / Typical branch circuit

receptacle to any desired location; these strips are available in 3-ft and 6-ft lengths and may even be used around the entire room. When specified, one of the receptacles may be controlled by a wall switch. This is particularly desirable in rooms where portable fixtures are used. Typical room layouts are shown in Fig. 15-11. Some room designs make it difficult to locate the outlets on the walls. Plans such as Fig. 15-12 require that furniture be located out from the wall and the space between the furniture and the wall used for pedestrian traffic out to the deck. If the outlets were placed on the exterior wall, the cords from lamps to the outlets would cross the traffic area, creating a safety hazard. Floor outlets may be used in this situation; these outlets may be located anywhere desired in the floor. A note of caution—they should be carefully planned so they will not interfere with furniture arrangement.

Ranges, dryers, large air conditioners, and other such electrical devices which require 240-volt service require special outlets. These special three-prong outlets (Fig. 15-10) are designed so that conventional 120-volt devices cannot be plugged into them. The symbol used will vary only slightly from that used for 120-volt convenience outlets in that there are three straight lines through the circle instead of two. Typically, each one of these special outlets is on a circuit by itself.

Two commonly used specialty outlets are the split-wired outlet and the weatherproof outlet. A split-wired outlet (Fig. 15-13) is any outlet which has the top outlet on a different circuit than the bottom or which has one outlet that may be switched off and on from a wall switch. The weatherproof outlet is used in all exterior locations because it resists damage from weather. It is noted on the plan by use of the standard outlet symbol and the letters WP next to it.

15-11 LUMINAIRES (LIGHTING FIXTURES)

The luminaires used in a residence must be carefully selected with the client. Lighting of some type will be required throughout the house, and quite often exterior lighting will also be required. The size, type, and location of fixtures throughout must be coordinated with the style of the house and the client's preferences. The lighting may come from built-in and surface-mounted ceiling and wall luminaires; floor and table lamps may be used as a supplement, or they may be preferred throughout.

The living areas of the house are where the client might prefer various types of accent and indirect lighting to achieve the various lighting effects desired.

Circuits not shown

FIGURE 15-9 / Circuit labeling (circuits not shown)

Fluorescent lighting (tubes) is more efficient than incandescent lighting (bulbs), and it is effective as indirect lighting in valances and coves around rooms and also where high lighting levels are desired such as in bathrooms, work areas in the kitchen, and workshop areas. Objections to fluorescent lighting include: its higher initial cost, slow starting, and a tendency to flicker.

Many clients prefer a permanent ceiling fixture that can be turned on from the wall switch, while others prefer that the wall switch activate a convenience outlet and they use a table or floor lamp in that outlet to light the room. Small rooms frequently

FIGURE 15-10 / Typical receptacles

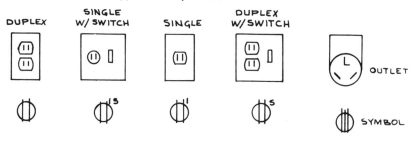

Luminaires (Lighting Fixtures) / 15-11

FIGURE 15-11 / Typical room layouts

have one central ceiling fixture activated by a wall switch. This provides the general illumination required and may be supplemented by wall, floor and table fixtures. Shallow closets generally don't require fixtures if there is average room illumination. However, many clients want fixtures in the closets, and, if so, a ceiling fixture may be used. The closet fixture may be operated by a pull chain, but, again, many clients prefer either a wall switch just outside the door or a door-operated switch which turns the light on when the door is opened and shuts it off when the door is closed. The lighting symbols used are shown in Fig. 15-14. For those fixtures activated by a switch, a line must be shown connecting the switch and the fixtures it controls.

FIGURE 15-12 / Floor receptacles

SPLIT WIRED TO SWITCH

SPLIT WIRED TO DIFFERENT CIRCUIT

FIGURE 15-13 / Split-wired outlets

15-12   SWITCHES

Wall switches are used to control lighting fixtures in the various rooms of the house, and they may also be used to control convenience outlets. The switch most commonly used is the *toggle switch* which has a small arm which is pushed up and down. Also used is the *mercury switch,* a completely noiseless switch which has mercury in a sealed tube; when the switch is turned on, the mercury completes the circuit.

Wall switches are located 4 ft above the floor and a few inches in from the door frame on the latch side (doorknob side) of the entry door into a room. Generally, they are located just inside the room.

Rooms with two entrances often have two switches controlling the fixture, referred to as three-way switches. When the fixture is to be controlled from three locations, it will require the use of two 3-way switches and one 4-way switch (Fig. 15-15).

A dimmer control is used when it is desirable to vary the intensity of the light being given off from very low to bright. A delayed action switch is used when it is desirable to have the lights go out about a minute after the switch is turned off.

FIGURE 15-14 / Fixture symbols

CEILING FIXTURE

A   B   DROP CORD   FLUORESCENT

WALL FIXTURE

A   C
LETTER OR NUMBER REPRESENTS TYPE OF FIXTURE

FIXTURE SCHEDULE		
NO.	TYPE	REMARKS

Fixture controlled by
two switches

Fixture controlled by
three switches

FIGURE 15-15 / Switches

LOW-VOLTAGE SWITCHING

The flexibility desired in home lighting systems has led to the development of low-voltage wiring which allows flexibility in the control of fixtures through the use of centrally located remote-control switches which control any or all of the lights in the house.

Low-voltage wiring (about the size of wiring used to wire a door chime) connects the wall switch to a relay center. When the switch is turned on, it sends a low voltage (usually 24 V) to the relay center; this triggers a relay switch which activates the line voltage (120 V) at the light. The savings in wiring costs, the convenience of a centrally located remote-control selector switch, and the elimination of any possible electric shocks at the switch make this increasingly popular in homes.

15-13   CONDUCTORS

The wires used to supply electricity throughout the system are called *conductors*. Copper has traditionally been used as the conductor material, and the wiring practices developed over the years have been based on its use. Aluminum conductors are also available and are allowed in many, but not all, codes. Further engineering study is now going on to be certain that all aluminum conductor installations will be as safe as possible. One of the biggest reasons for using aluminum conductors is that their costs range from one-third to one-half those of copper conductors. Aluminum conductors must be larger than copper conductors that carry the same amperage. This means that for installations requiring that the conductors be placed in conduit, the larger aluminum conductors may require larger conduits. (Conduits are discussed in Sec. 15-14.)

The various types of insulation which are placed on the conductor wires have been standardized and are listed in Fig. 15-16. The types of conductors are referred to by the type letter assigned to the insulation used. For example, RHW conductor has a moisture- and heat-resistant rubber insulation, with a maximum operating temperature of 75°C (167°F), and it may be used in both dry and wet locations. The maximum operating temperature has an effect on the allowable ampacities which the NEC will allow for the conductor (Fig. 15-24); the higher the maximum operating temperature, the higher the allowable ampacity. All individual conductors must be protected by raceways. Individual conductors in raceways are used extensively in commercial and industrial installations where changes in the electrical requirements are likely to occur.

When two or more conductors, each insulated separately, are grouped together in one common covering, they are referred to as *cables* (Fig. 15-17). These cables are used extensively in electrical wiring, particularly in residences. They are designated according to type of insulation used and where they are used; generally, they do not have to be protected by raceways.

All conductor sizes are given by an AWG or MCM number. Standard available conductor sizes are given in Fig. 15-24. Those conductor sizes based on the American Wire Gauge (from No. 16 to No. 4/0) are listed as AWG—for example, No. 12 AWG. The larger the AWG number, the smaller the conductor. The cross-sectional area of any conductor is listed in *circular* mils, with a circular mil defined as the area of a circle one mil in diameter; then the area is the square of the diameter (in mils). All conductors larger than 4/0 AWG are sized in direct relation to the circular mil and are labeled MCM or one thousand (M) circular mils. A wire with an area of 500,000 circular mils would be called 500 MCM.

15-14   RACEWAYS

A channel which is designed exclusively, and used solely, for holding wires, cables or bus bars is called a *raceway*. The raceway may be made of metal or insulating material. Metal raceways include rigid and flexible metal conduits, electric metallic tubing (EMT) and cellular metal raceways, and all may be concealed in the construction or exposed in the space. The most popular insulating raceways are made of cement, asbestos or impregnated fiber, all of which are commonly used in underground exposures since they are corrosion resistant.

TYPES

Rigid metal conduit is usually steel (ferrous) or aluminum (nonferrous). The steel conduit has its outside surface coated in zinc to galvanize it, making it resistant to

Perfluoro-alkoxy	PFA	90°C 194°F 200°C 392°F	Dry and damp locations. Dry locations — special applications.†	Perfluoro-alkoxy	14-10 .... 20 8-2 .... 30 1-4/0 45	None
Perfluoro-alkoxy	PFAH	250°C 482°F	Dry locations only. Only for leads within apparatus or within raceways connected to apparatus. (Nickel or nickel-coated copper only.)	Perfluoro-alkoxy	14-10 .... 20 8-2 .... 30 1-4/0 45	None
Heat-Resistant Rubber	RH	75°C 167°F	Dry and damp locations.	Heat-Resistant Rubber	**14-12 .... 30 10 .... 45 8-2 .... 60 1-4/0 .... 80 213-500 .... 95 501-1000 .... 110 1001-2000 .... 125 For 601-2000 volts, see Table 310-62.	*Moisture-resistant, flame-retardant, non-metallic covering
Heat-Resistant Rubber	RHH††	90°C 194°F	Dry and damp locations.			
Moisture- and Heat-Resistant Rubber	RHW††, †††	75°C 167°F	Dry and wet locations. For over 2000 volts insulation shall be ozone-resistant.	Moisture- and Heat-Resistant Rubber	14-10 .... 45 8-2 .... 60 1-4/0 .... 80 213-500 .... 95 501-1000 .... 110 1001-2000 .... 125 For 601-2000 volts, see Table 310-62.	*Moisture-resistant, flame-retardant, non-metallic covering

* Some rubber insulations do not require an outer covering.
** For 14-12 sizes RHH shall be 45 mils thickness insulation.
† Where environmental conditions require maximum conductor operating temperatures above 90°C.
†† Insulation and outer coverings that meet the requirements of flame-retardant, limited smoke and are so listed shall be permitted to be designated limited smoke with the suffix /LS after the Code type designation.
††† Listed wire types designated with the suffix –2 such as RHW-2 shall be permitted to be used at a continuous 90°C operating temperature wet or dry. Ampacities of these wire types are given in the 90°C column in the appropriate ampacity table.

Reprinted with permission from NFPA 70-1990, the *National Electrical Code,* Copyright © 1989, National Fire Protection Association, Quincy, MA 02269. This reprinted material is not the official position of the National Fire Protection Association, which is represented only by the standard in its entirety.

FIGURE 15-16 / Conductor application and insulations

Trade Name	Type Letter	Max. Operating Temp.	Application Provisions	Insulation	AWG or kcmil	Thickness of Insulation	Mils	Outer Covering****
Moisture- and Heat-Resistant Rubber	RHW-2	90°C 194°F	Dry and wet locations.	Moisture- and Heat-Resistant Rubber	14-10 8-2 1-4/0 213-500 501-1000 1001-2000 For 601-2000 volts, see Table 310-62.		45 60 80 95 110 125	*Moisture-resistant, flame-retardant, non-metallic covering
Silicone-Asbestos	SA	90°C 194°F / 125°C 257°F	Dry and damp locations. / For special application.†	Silicone Rubber	14-10 8-2 1-4/0 213-500 501-1000 1001-2000		45 60 80 95 110 125	Asbestos, glass or other suitable braid material
Synthetic Heat-Resistant	SIS††	90°C 194°F	Switchboard wiring only.	Heat-Resistant Rubber	14-10 8 6-2 1-4/0		30 45 60 80	None
Thermoplastic and Asbestos	TA	90°C 194°F	Switchboard wiring only.	Thermoplastic and Asbestos	14-8 6-2 1-4/0	Th'pl'. 20 30 40	Asb. 20 25 30	Flame-retardant, nonmetallic covering
Thermoplastic and Fibrous Outer Braid	TBS	90°C 194°F	Switchboard wiring only.	Thermoplastic	14-10 8 6-2 ! 4/0		30 45 60 80	Flame-retardant, nonmetallic covering

* Some rubber insulations do not require an outer covering.
**** Some insulations do not require an outer covering.
† Where environmental conditions require maximum conductor operating temperatures above 90°C.
†† Insulation and outer coverings that meet the requirements of flame-retardant, limited smoke and are so listed shall be permitted to be designated limited smoke with the suffix /LS after the Code type designation.

Reprinted with permission from NFPA 70-1990, the *National Electrical Code*, Copyright © 1989, National Fire protection Association, Quincy, MA 02269. This reprinted material is not the official position of the National Fire Protection Association, which is represented only by the standard in its entirety.

FIGURE 15-16 / Conductor application and insulations (continued)

Trade Name	Type Letter	Max. Operating Temp.	Application Provisions	Insulation	AWG or kcmil	Thickness of Insulation	Mils	Outer Covering****
Moisture- and Heat-Resistant Thermoplastic	THWN ††, †††	75°C 167°F	Dry and wet locations.	Flame-Retardant, Moisture- and Heat-Resistant Thermoplastic	14-12 10 8-6 4-2 1-4/0 250-500 501-1000		15 20 30 40 50 60 70	Nylon jacket or equivalent
Moisture-Resistant Thermoplastic	TW††	60°C 140°F	Dry and wet locations.	Flame-Retardant, Moisture-Resistant Thermoplastic	14-10 8 6-2 1-4/0 213-500 501-1000 1001-2000		30 45 60 80 95 110 125	None
Underground Feeder & Branch-Circuit Cable-Single Conductor. (For Type UF cable employing more than one conductor, see Article 339.)	UF	60°C 140°F **75°C 167°F	See Article 339.	Moisture-Resistant Moisture- and Heat-Resistant	14-10 8-2 1-4/0		*60 *80 *95	Integral with insulation

* Includes integral jacket.

** For ampacity limitation, see Section 339-5.

**** Some insulations do not require an outer covering.

† † Insulation and outer coverings that meet the requirements of flame-retardant, limited smoke and are so listed shall be permitted to be designated limited smoke with the suffix /LS after the Code type designation.

††† Listed wire types designated with the suffix –2 such as RHW-2 shall be permitted to be used at a continuous 90°C operating temperature wet or dry. Ampacities of these wire types are given in the 90°C column in the appropriate ampacity table.

Reprinted with permission from NFPA 70-1990, the *National Electrical Code*, Copyright © 1989, National Fire Protection Association, Quincy, MA 02269. This reprinted material is not the offical position of the National Fire Protection Association, which is represented only by the standard in its entirety.

FIGURE 15-16 / Conductor application and insulations (continued)

FIGURE 15-17 / Cable

rusting, and zinc is applied to the interior surface of the conduit to make it easier to pull the conductors through it. Steel conduit is also available dipped in a clear, elastic enamel. The enamel coating makes it easier to pull the conductors and provides some resistance to corrosion, but it should not be used outside or where severe corrosive conditions may be present. Rigid metal conduit is extensively used throughout the building and may be placed in the walls, ceiling and floors of the construction. In addition, corrosion-resistant metal conduit may also be used outside.

Flexible metal conduit is made of a continuous length of galvanized, spirally wound steel strip. It is used primarily when it is necessary to make connections from a junction box to machinery and to go around obstructions. Only the waterproof type may be used in wet locations.

Use of liquid-tight flexible metal conduit is restricted to connections of motors or portable equipment when the connections must be flexible. Further, its use is not allowed where it may be subjected to physical damage, where it may be in contact with rapidly moving parts, where temperatures exceed 60°C (140°F) and in hazardous locations.

Plastic-coated galvanized steel conduit is available for locations where the conduit will be subjected to the highly corrosive actions of fumes, gases, or chemicals. Polyvinyl chloride is extruded over the conduit, and all connections are taped with a vinyl, pressure-sensitive electrical insulating tape.

Also available for installations requiring high corrosion-resistance and high strength is an alloy of a mild carbon steel with 2% nickel and 1% copper. This provides a highly corrosion-resistant conduit which is available galvanized or enameled.

Electrical metallic tubing (EMT) is a thin-walled metallic conduit which weighs about one-third less than rigid metal conduits. It may be used anywhere except where it will be subject to severe physical damage during or after installation, in cinder concrete or fill underground, or in any hazardous locations. This type of conduit connects to its fittings with set screws, saving the time often required to put screw threads on rigid metal conduits.

Surface metal raceways (Fig. 15-18) must be installed in dry locations and must not be concealed in the construction. This type of raceway is used extensively with metal partitions (Fig. 15-19) where the raceway has a backplate which attaches to the metal stud and a snap-on cover. The NEC limits conductor sizes used in this type of

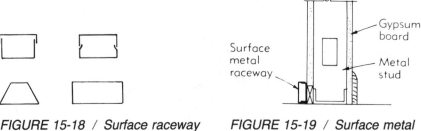

FIGURE 15-18 / Surface raceway
shapes

FIGURE 15-19 / Surface metal
raceway

raceway to No. 6 AWG and smaller. The number of conductors allowed must be taken
from the raceway manufacturer's data sheet and is based on the amount which Underwriters Laboratories will allow. This type of installation is used extensively when
remodeling, adding to existing systems, and building new additions where room arrangements will be subject to changes.

Underfloor raceways, made of metal or fiber, are commonly used in any building where periodic remodeling or a change in the occupancy may occur. This includes most office buildings and many institutional and industrial buildings. While
the size and number of conductors used will depend on the size of the raceway and
is controlled by UL, it may also be found in the manufacturer's data. Some typical
underfloor raceways are shown in Fig. 15-20. The NEC states that for raceways less
than 4 in. wide, a minimum of ¾ in. of wood or concrete must cover the raceway.
Raceways 4 to 8 in. wide and at least 1 in. apart (Fig. 15-21) must have at least a
1-in. concrete cover. When they are less than 1 in. apart, raceways must have a
1½-in. concrete cover. Also available are flush raceways with removable covers
(Fig. 15-22).

Cellular metal floor raceways are installed when the hollow spaces in cellular
metal floors are used for the distribution of conductors through the building (Fig.
15-23). The NEC limits conductor size to No. 1 AWG or less, and the number of
conductors which may be put in an individual cell (single, enclosed tubular space) is
limited to 40% of the cross-sectional cell area, except that the limit does not apply to
type AC metal-clad cable or to nonmetallic sheathed cable.

Wireways are sheet-metal troughs with hinged or removable covers. Wireways
are used primarily for exposed inside work; if they are used outside, they must be of
rain-tight construction. Conductor size is limited to 500 MCM, and the number of
conductors is limited to a maximum of 30. The total area of all conductors installed in
the wireway is limited to 20% of the interior cross-sectional area of the wireway.

Busways (also called bus ducts) are factory-assembled conductors mounted in a
steel housing. They have high current-carrying capacities and are often used as service-
entrance conductors, feeders and subfeeders and even as branch circuits where large
service loads are required. The NEC allows the use of busways only where they will
be exposed. They may not be concealed in the construction or installed where they may
be subjected to severe physical damage or corrosive vapors.

Standard header duct or trench duct may be used

Concrete slab

Metal deck

Trench duct

Header duct

(a)

Header duct fits
in depressed slab area

(b)

Trench duct

Metal deck

Electrical cell

Dual pre-set insert

(c)

FIGURE 15-20 / Raceways

FIGURE 15-21 / Raceway spacing

FIGURE 15-22 / Raceway

INSTALLATION

Rigid nonmetallic conduit used below ground must be moisture resistant and, when used above ground, also flame retardant and resistant to impact. When used for direct burial, not encased in concrete, the material must be strong enough to withstand any loads which may be placed on it after installation. Typical materials used below ground are fiber, asbestos cement, soapstone, rigid polyvinyl chloride, and high-density polyethylene. Rigid polyvinyl chloride is used above ground. This type of conduit should *not* be used:

1. Less than 8 ft above the ground, outdoors, unless protected from any possible physical damage.

2. In combustible construction where it is concealed (built into the walls, floors, ceilings).

3. In any location where it might be subject to physical damage.

4. In any location where the temperature may be higher than that which the conduit has been tested for.

5. Where the conductor's maximum insulation temperature is higher than that of the conduit being used.

6. If there is any possibility that the electrical service running through it may exceed 600 V, unless encased in a minimum of 2 in. of concrete.

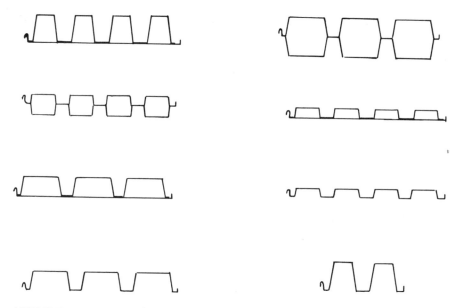

FIGURE 15-23 / Cellular metal raceways

7. In sunlight, unless the conduit being used has been tested and approved for such use.

8. In hazardous locations.

Rigid metal conduits are connected to their fittings by screwing the threaded fittings onto the threaded conduits. Whenever the conduit has been cut, it must be rethreaded to make the connection.

The number of conductors which may be put in a rigid metal conduit depends on the conductor and conduit sizes. The sizes are selected from Fig. 15-25, and typical examples are shown in Sec. 16-4.

The number of conductors which may be put in electrical metallic tubing again depends on the conductor and conduit sizes. The sizes are also selected from Fig. 15-25.

15-15   AMPS, OHMS, VOLTS

The design of electrical systems in a building requires that the designer have a "working familiarity" with amperes, ohms, and volts. These three electrical terms are often used by the designer to determine the total electrical load requirements of the building, and they are all related.

Ampere (Amp, Amperage—A):   A unit (or measure) of the flow of electrons passing through a circuit (current).

Volt (Voltage—V):   The unit of electrical pressure required to push the amperage through the circuit.

Ohm (Ω):   The unit of electrical resistance which resists the flow of electrons through the circuit. Ohm's law states that the current in an electrical circuit is equal to the pressure divided by the resistance.

$$Amps = \frac{Volts}{Ohms}$$

Watt (W):   The unit of electrical energy or electrical power. It indicates how much power has been used.

$$Watts = Amps \times Volts$$

Kilowatt (kW):   1,000 watts; for example, 9,500 W equals 9.5 kW.

QUESTIONS

15-1. Briefly describe what the Underwriters Laboratories does.

15-2. What does it mean when an electric fixture has a UL tag on it?

15-3. Define the following terms:
   a. Service entrance
   b. Service panel
   c. Feeder circuits
   d. Branch circuits
   e. Receptacles
   f. Luminaires

15-4. When is a *split-wired outlet* used?

15-5. What is the difference between conductors and cable?

15-6. When are raceways used, and what are three commonly used types?

15-7. Show, in a formula, the relationship between amps, volts, and ohms; then briefly describe each.

Ampacities of Single Insulated Conductors, Rated 0 through 2000 Volts, In Free Air Based on Ambient Air Temperature of 30°C (86°F)

Size	Temperature Rating of Conductor. See Table 310-13.								Size
	60°C (140°F)	75°C (167°F)	85°C (185°F)	90°C (194°F)	60°C (140°F)	75°C (167°F)	85°C (185°F)	90°C (194°F)	
AWG kcmil	TYPE †TW, †UF	TYPES †FEPW, †RH, †RHW, †THHW, †THW, †THWN, †XHHW, †ZW	TYPE V	TYPES TA, TBS, SA, SIS, †FEP, †FEPB, †RHH, †THHN, †THHW, †XHHW, MI	TYPE †TW, †UF	TYPES †RH, †RHW, †THHW, †THW, †THWN, †XHHW	TYPE V	TYPES TA, TBS, SA, SIS, †RHH, †THHN, †THHW, †XHHW, MI	AWG kcmil
	COPPER				ALUMINUM OR COPPER-CLAD ALUMINUM				
18	. . . .	. . . .	. . . .	18	. . . .	. . . .	. . . .	. . . .	18
16	. . . .	. . . .	23	24	. . . .	. . . .	. . . .	. . . .	16
14	25†	30†	30	35†	. . . .	. . . .	. . . .	. . . .	14
12	30†	35†	40	40†	25†	30†	30	35†	12
10	40†	50†	55	55†	35†	40†	40	40†	10
8	60	70	75	80	45	55	60	60	8
6	80	95	100	105	60	75	80	80	6
4	105	125	135	140	80	100	105	110	4
3	120	145	160	165	95	115	125	130	3
2	140	170	185	190	110	135	145	150	2
1	165	195	215	220	130	155	165	175	1
1/0	195	230	250	260	150	180	195	205	1/0
2/0	225	265	290	300	175	210	225	235	2/0
3/0	260	310	335	350	200	240	265	275	3/0
4/0	300	360	390	405	235	280	305	315	4/0
250	340	405	440	455	265	315	345	355	250
300	375	445	485	505	290	350	380	395	300
350	420	505	550	570	330	395	430	445	350
400	455	545	595	615	355	425	465	480	400
500	515	620	675	700	405	485	525	545	500
600	575	690	750	780	455	540	595	615	600
700	630	755	825	855	500	595	650	675	700
750	655	785	855	885	515	620	675	700	750
800	680	815	885	920	535	645	700	725	800
900	730	870	950	985	580	700	760	785	900
1000	780	935	1020	1055	625	750	815	845	1000
1250	890	1065	1160	1200	710	855	930	960	1250
1500	980	1175	1275	1325	795	950	1035	1075	1500
1750	1070	1280	1395	1445	875	1050	1145	1185	1750
2000	1155	1385	1505	1560	960	1150	1250	1335	2000

AMPACITY CORRECTION FACTORS

Ambient Temp. °C	For ambient temperatures other than 30°C (86°F), multiply the ampacities shown above by the appropriate factor shown below.								Ambient Temp. °F
21-25	1.08	1.05	1.04	1.04	1.08	1.05	1.04	1.04	70-77
26-30	1.00	1.00	1.00	1.00	1.00	1.00	1.00	1.00	79-86
31-35	.91	.94	.95	.96	.91	.94	.95	.96	88-95
36-40	.82	.88	.90	.91	.82	.88	.90	.91	97-104
41-45	.71	.82	.85	.87	.71	.82	.85	.87	106-113
46-50	.58	.75	.80	.82	.58	.75	.80	.82	115-122
51-55	.41	.67	.74	.76	.41	.67	.74	.76	124-131
56-60	. . . .	.58	.67	.71	. . . .	.58	.67	.71	133-140
61-70	. . . .	.33	.52	.58	. . . .	.33	.52	.58	142-158
71-80	. . . .	. . . .	.30	.41	. . . .	. . . .	.30	.41	160-176

† Unless otherwise specifically permitted elsewhere in this Code, the overcurrent protection for conductor types marked with an obelisk (†) shall not exceed 15 amperes for 14 AWG, 20 amperes for 12 AWG, and 30 amperes for 10 AWG copper; or 15 amperes for 12 AWG and 25 amperes for 10 AWG aluminum and copper-clad aluminum.

FIGURE 15-24 / Allowable ampacities

Maximum Number of Conductors in Trade Sizes of Conduit or Tubing

Type Letters	Conductor Size AWG, kcmil	½	¾	1	1¼	1½	2	2½	3	3½	4	5	6
RHW,	14	3	6	10	18	25	41	58	90	121	155		
	12	3	5	9	15	21	35	50	77	103	132		
	10	2	4	7	13	18	29	41	64	86	110	94	137
	8	1	2	4	7	9	16	22	35	47	60		
RHH	6	1	1	2	5	6	11	15	24	32	41	64	93
	4	1	1	1	3	5	8	12	18	24	31	50	72
(with	3	1	1	1	3	4	7	10	16	22	28	44	63
outer	2		1	1	3	4	6	9	14	19	24	38	56
covering)	1		1	1	1	3	5	7	11	14	18	29	42
	1/0		1	1	1	2	4	6	9	12	16	25	37
	2/0			1	1	1	3	5	8	11	14	22	32
	3/0			1	1	1	3	4	7	9	12	19	28
	4/0			1	1	1	2	4	6	8	10	16	24
	250				1	1	1	3	5	6	8	13	19
	300				1	1	1	3	4	5	7	11	17
	350				1	1	1	2	4	5	6	10	15
	400				1	1	1	1	3	4	6	9	14
	500				1	1	1	1	3	4	5	8	11
	600					1	1	1	2	3	4	6	9
	700					1	1	1	1	3	3	6	8
	750						1	1	1	3	3	5	8

FIGURE 15-25 / Conductors in conduit

CHAPTER 16
ELECTRICAL SYSTEM DESIGN

16-1 PRELIMINARY INFORMATION

Ideally, the electrical designer should be involved from the very beginning in the design of the project. It would be best, in some situations, if he could even be involved in the selection of the site for the project. On a large project it may be necessary to extend high-voltage lines to the project site. This will take time and the owner may have to pay part of the cost. The designer is the person who could best discuss the situation with the power company. All of the utilities (whether sewer, water storm sewer, natural gas lines, etc.) must be checked to determine if they are near the property and whether they can be brought to the property economically or not. Such information is needed early in the design stage.

Before actually beginning the design layout of the project, the designer will need to accumulate certain information:

1. Determine whether electrical service is available. If it is not, arrangements must be made with the power company to extend service to the building site. Large

projects may require more voltage or more wattage than existing service can supply. Each of these situations requires coordination with the power company as early in the design stage as possible. Costs which may have to be paid by the owner should be thoroughly discussed, written, and given to the owner.

2. Obtain a list from the owner of all the types of equipment, appliances, etc., to be used in the building which will require electricity. While the electrical designer will know the electrical requirements of much of the equipment, it may be necessary to find the manufacturer's specifications for certain items, such as motor sizes and power required.

3. Working with the architectural designer, locate all of the equipment and appliances on the floor plan. In commercial projects this sometimes takes many meetings with the architects, owners, and manufacturer's representatives. There are times when the type of equipment used and its location must be approved by governmental agencies.

4. Review with the architect where the basic mechanical equipment, such as the service entrance, the power and lighting panels, and the conduit or cable, will be located.

5. Discuss with the owners what future plans are as far as adding to the building, remodeling, constructing other buildings, increasing future equipment requirements, and anything else that could affect the size and location of the electrical service. Many times the service entrance must be sized to anticipate future expansion as well as present building plans. Once the basic information has been gathered, the designer can begin to design the system itself.

16-2 ELECTRICAL SYSTEM DESIGN

The system is designed by first drawing, or having a print made, of the floor plan of the building.

STEP-BY-STEP APPROACH

In this problem, the floor plan of the residence shown in Appendix C will be used to illustrate the design process:

1. The receptacles are located first, as discussed in Sec. 15–10. The various types of receptacles available are shown in Fig. 15–10, along with the symbols used to represent each. All switching, sizing of wire and circuit layout will be done later.

   Locate the receptacles and switches on the floor plan as shown in Fig. 16-1.

FIGURE 16-1 / Locate switches and receptacles

2.   Locate on the floor plan all connections to be made for appliances and equipment. This calls for close coordination with the architectural designer since each appliance and piece of equipment must be known in order to locate the receptacles properly. Many times the plans do not show everything which must be connected. For example, a garbage disposal must be connected to power and may even have a switch on the wall to turn it on and off; yet it is seldom shown on the floor plan. Specifically, the electrical designer should ask the architectural designer to list all appliances and equipment in a letter or on the drawing for complete coordination. A checklist of typical appliances that require electrical connections is listed in Fig. 16-2. In addition, the electrical designer will need to know the voltage and amperage required. Typical requirements for various appliances are shown in Fig. 16-3, but these may vary among different manufacturers and should be checked.

Also, check as to the number of appliances or equipment. For example, quite often two water heaters are used in residences and both will need connections. Also, in some residences and many commercial buildings, more than one heating and/or cooling unit may be used.

Using the appropriate symbols for the various receptacles required (Fig. 16—20), lay out the electrical requirements for appliances and equipment as shown in Fig. 16-4.

Device
Air conditioner, central
Air conditioner, room
Clothes dryer
Garbage disposal
Heat pump
Humidifier
Iron, hand
Lamp, incandescent
Lamp, fluorescent
Radio
Range
Range, oven
Range, top
Television
Water heaters

FIGURE 16-2 / Typical residential checklist

3. Locate the lighting fixtures.

As shown in Fig. 16-5, lay out on the floor plan all lighting fixtures, using the appropriate symbols from Fig. 15–14 for all wall and ceiling fixtures.

At the same time, the designer must make a list of what types of fixtures will be used throughout and how many watts each will use. This list will be used later when grouping circuits, and it must also be included in the specifications or on the drawings as a "Fixture Schedule" (Fig. 16-6). The list is also used by the electrical estimator when he is determining the cost to be charged for the work, then by the electrical purchasing agent when the material is ordered for the project and then by the electrician who actually installs the work. Many times the architectural designer decides what fixtures are to be used, often in coordination with the electrical designer.

When a minimum amount of illumination is required, the electrical de-

Device	Watts	
Air conditioner, central	3,000 to	5,000
Air conditioner, room	800 to	1,500
Clothes dryer	4,000 to	8,000
Garbage disposal	300 to	500
Heat pump	3,000 to	6,000
Humidifier	80 to	200
Iron, hand	600 to	1,200
Lamp, incandescent	10 to	250
Lamp, fluorescent	15 to	60
Radio	40 to	150
Range	8,000 to	14,000
Range, oven	4,000 to	6,000
Range, top	4,000 to	8,000
Television	200 to	400
Water heaters	2,000 to	5,000

FIGURE 16-3 / Residential appliance checklist

FIGURE 16-4 / Lay out power requirements

425

FIGURE 16-5 / Lay out fixtures (luminaires)

426

FIXTURE SCHEDULE		
NO.	TYPE	REMARKS

FIGURE 16-6 / Fixture schedule

Number or letter used on drawing

Fixture manufacturer and fixture number

signer may have to calculate the number and types of lighting fixtures which should be used. A complete discussion of this is given in Chapter 17.

4. The circuit layout may be an *individual branch circuit* which feeds only one receptacle, light, appliance or piece of equipment or a *branch circuit* which supplies power to two or more receptacles, lights, appliances, or equipment. An example of an individual branch circuit would be the circuit to a clothes dryer (240 V) and back to the electrical panel. The NEC states that an individual branch circuit should supply any load required to service that single item.

15- and 20-ampere branch circuits are used for receptacles, light fixtures, and small appliances. They are limited according to what will be connected to them.

a. When the circuit serves fixed appliances and light fixtures or portable appliances, the total of the fixed appliances shall be no more than 50% of the branch circuit rating. Assuming a 15-amp, 120-V branch circuit, it would have a maximum rating of 15 amps $\times$ 120 V = 1,800 W (refer to Sec. 15-15 for formula explanation). In this case, the fixed appliances would be limited to 900 W, leaving the other 900 W available to supply the light fixtures or portable appliances also served by the branch circuit. A 20-amp, 120-V branch circuit would have a maximum of 2,400 W.

b. When the load on the circuit will be a continuous operating load, such as for store lights, the total load should not exceed 80% of the circuit rating. The lighting load must include any ballasts, transformers or auto-transformers which are part of the lighting system. Since a 15-amp branch has a full rating of 1,800 W, the limit would be 80% or 12 amps and 1,440 W. A 20-amp, 2,400-W branch would be limited to 16 amps and 1,920 W of connected load.

c. When portable appliances will be used on a circuit, the limit for any one portable appliance is 80% of the branch circuit rating.

d. Receptacles are computed at a load of 1½ amps each and limited to 80% of the rating. This limits a branch circuit serving only receptacles to its rating divided by 1½ amps. For example, a 15-amp circuit is limited to a maximum of 8 outlets and a 20-amp circuit to 10 outlets.

e. A minimum of two 20-amp circuits is required for small appliances in the kitchen, laundry, dining room, family room and breakfast or dinette area. These are in addition to the other receptacles required, and no lights or fixed appliances should be connected to these circuits. A typical layout of the two circuits is shown in Fig. 16-7.

f. A minimum of one 20-amp circuit is required as an individual branch to the laundry room receptacle. Any other special requirements, such as an electric clothes dryer requiring 230-V service, must also be added.

The designer must be certain that he doesn't exceed the code requirements. In actual practice, the designer tends to be a little more conservative, generally limiting a 15-amp branch to 1,000 to 1,200 W and a 20-amp branch to 1,300 to 1,600 W. Receptacles are generally limited to about six on a circuit. This allows the circuit to take additional loads, such as when higher wattage bulbs are used to replace those originally installed and calculated. In addition, more and more small appliances and equipment are being purchased and connected to receptacles (for example, air purifiers, humidifiers, stereos, and the like). The designer must also try to anticipate any future requirements. Such a layout allows for the extension of a circuit if it is necessary to add a light or a receptacle instead of adding a whole new circuit from the panel. If it is possible that the occupant will want to install individual air conditioners, an individual branch circuit to each receptacle required may be desired.

Thirty-, 40-, 50- and 60-ampere branch circuits will be used for fixed appliances, equipment, and heavy-duty lampholders (in other than residential occupancies). Generally, the electrical requirements of the connected load must be determined, and the total load connected to the branch circuit should be limited to 80% of the branch circuit rating.

The code states that any branch circuit serving a single motor shall have an ampacity (amperage rating) of not less than 125% of the motor's full-load current rating (this is the same as saying that no motor can exceed 80% of the branch circuit rating).

For example, if the motor to operate the air conditioner requires 22 amps, it will require a minimum branch circuit of 22 amps $\times$ 1.25% = 27.5 amperes, and a 30-ampere branch circuit will be used. This means that the electrical

FIGURE 16-7 / Typical kitchen circuit layout

designer will need the manufacturers' data for all equipment and appliances selected to be certain the proper branch circuit sizes are used. Many times the fuse sizes required for individual branch circuits are listed in the manufacturers' data.

A typical circuit layout is shown in Fig. 16-8. Later each circuit group will have an arrow at the end of with a circuit number to be assigned later (Fig. 16-9).

5. Lay out the switches required to control the lights, appliances, equipment and any desired receptacles. The discussion of switches in Section 15-12 generally outlines where they are most commonly used and the symbols used.

    The plan in Fig. 16-9 shows the switches and circuits added to the floor plan.

6. Calculate the electrical load, the total of all general lighting, appliance and equipment loads in the building.

    a. *The general lighting load* is calculated for all types of occupancies (Fig. 16-21) based on the unit load given in the table (in watts) times the square footage of the building.

        The square footage shall be determined using the outside dimensions of the building involved and the number of stories. For dwellings do not include any open porches, garages or carports. Any unfinished or unused spaces do not have to be included in the square footage *unless* they are adaptable for future use.

        For the residence being designed, the lighting load is taken as 3 W per sq ft (Fig. 16-21). Since its outside dimensions (excluding garage) are 61 ft 6 in. × 36 ft, there are 2,214 sq ft.

Minimum general lighting load = 3 W/sq ft × 2,214 sq ft = 6,642 W

    b. *The appliance and laundry circuit load* is calculated next.

        Since the code requires two 20-amp branch circuits, the load would be based on 1,500 W (from the code) for each branch circuit. In addition, one 20-amp circuit is required for laundry room appliances. This results in a total of three 20-amp branch circuits for appliances.

Appliance and laundry load = 3 circuits × 1,500 W = 4,500 W

    c. *Subtotal* the general lighting, appliance, and laundry branch circuit loads.

FIGURE 16-8 / Typical branch circuit

430

Circuits shown and numbered

FIGURE 16-9 / Add light switches and circuits (circuits shown and numbered)

431

In this example:

General lighting	6,642 W
Appliance & laundry circuits	4,500 W
Subtotal	11,142 W

d. The *demand load* allowed by the code takes into account the fact that all of the electrical connections will not be in use at one time. While there are limits to this reduction for certain types of occupancies, in a dwelling the first 3,000 W are taken as 100%, and from 3,000 to 120,000 W, only 35% of the load is calculated (from Fig. 16-22).

For this example, the load subtotal is 11,142 W.

First 3,000 W at 100%	3,000 W
Remaining 8,142 W at 35%	2,850 W
Total demand load	5,850 W

The loads of all other appliances and equipment (motors) must be added to this demand load in order to determine the total service load on the system.

e. To determine the *appliance and equipment load,* all appliances and equipment which will not be on the lines discussed above must be listed along with their electrical requirements. While typical ratings are given in Fig. 16-4, it is most important that the manufacturer's data be used in the design.

For the residence being designed, the following is a list of fixed appliances and equipment and their ratings:

Water heater	3,800 W
Clothes dryer	4,400 W
Dishwasher	1,000 W
Range	11,700 W

The demand load for an *electric range,* consisting of an oven and a countertop cooking unit, is taken from Fig. 16-23.

For an electric range with a rating of 11.7 kW, the demand load would be 8 kW (or 8,000 W).

Electric range demand load = 8,000 W

The demand load for a *clothes dryer* is the total amount of power required according to the manufacturer's data.

In this case, the full 4,400 W must be used in the calculation.

Clothes dryer demand load = 4,400 W

The demand for *fixed appliances* (other than the range, clothes dryer and air conditioning and space heating equipment) is taken as 100% of the total amount they require; *except* that when there are four or more of these fixed appliances (other than those omitted), the demand load can be taken as 75% of the fixed appliance load.

In this design, there are only two of these fixed appliances, the water heater at 3,800 W and the dishwasher at 1,000 W. The total of the ratings is 4,800 W, also the demand load.

Fixed appliances demand load = 4,800 W

Motors, such as those used in *central air conditioners,* have their demand loads calculated as 125% of the motor rating.

In this case, the air conditioner is rated at 9,000 watts. The total demand load will be 9,000 W × 1.25% = 11,250 W.

Air conditioner demand load = 11,250 W

The demand load for all of the lighting and appliances has now been calculated, and it should be tabulated as shown (Fig. 16-10):

FIGURE 16-10 / Total demand load

GENERAL LIGHTING APPLIANCES & LAUNDRY	5,850
ELECTRIC RANGE	8,000
CLOTHES DRYER	4,400
FIXED APPLIANCES	4,800
AIR CONDITIONER	11,250
	34,300 WATTS

7. Size the minimum service entrance based on the demand load from step 6. Service entrances and the typical sizes used for residential work are discussed in Sec. 15-6. The service entrance size is found by dividing the demand load for the building by the voltage serving the building. Most commonly 240-V service is used.

In this design, the total demand load of 34,300 W is divided by the 240-V service for a minimum service entrance of 143 amps.

Minimum service entrance = 34,300 W ÷ 240 V = 142.9 or 143 amps

8. Sizing the feeder (the circuit conductors between the service equipment and the branch overcurrent device—circuit breaker or fuse) is the next step. The feeder size is based on the total demand load calculated. The size is then selected from the tables in Fig. 16-24. The tables list the size of the conductor in the left column and the different insulation temperature ratings across the top. Generally, conductors with insulation ratings of 60°, 75°, and 95°C (140°, 167°, and 185°F) are most commonly used.

    For example a No. 6 copper conductor, 60°C insulation, will carry 55 amps without subjecting the insulation to damaging heat. The same No. 6 conductor with 75°C insulation can safely carry 65 amps. These values must be adjusted using a correction factor from the lower portion of the table if the room temperatures are within certain ranges. For example, if the No. 6 conductor with 60°C insulation will carry 55 amps and if the room temperature is 45°C (113°F), the load-carrying capacity would be corrected by a factor of 0.58; 55 amps × 0.58 = 31 amps, the maximum safe allowable amperage.

    To size the feeder, assuming RHW conductor, copper (75°C, 167°F) and a 150-amp demand load, as calculated. From Fig. 16-24, a 1/0 AWG is selected as the feeder size for 150-amp, 240-V service.

    150-amp feeder demand load, 1/0 AWG, RHW, copper

    Most designers would review their design before using a feeder conductor size so close to its capacity. In this case, the calculated demand load is 143 amps, while the conductor's capacity is listed as 150 amps. It is probably a better design solution to use 2/0 AWG copper conductors with a rated capacity of 175 amps. This allows for future addition of appliances and other equipment by the occupant.

    The size of the *neutral feeder conductor* may be determined as 70% of the demand load calculated for the range (step 6) plus all other demand loads on the system.

    In this design, the neutral feeder demand load would be:

Range load (8,000 W × 70%)	5,600 W
All other demand loads	26,300 W
Neutral demand load	31,900 W

    Neutral net computed load = 31,900 W/240 V = 133 amps

    Select the size of the neutral feeder from Fig. 16-24:

    133-amp neutral feeder demand load, 1/0 AWG, RHW, copper

There are times when this calculation will result in smaller neutral feeder sizes, while at other times, it will not change.

Now size the feeder conduit. The minimum conduit size is determined for new work by using the table in Fig. 16-25. The conductor sizes are listed in the left column, and conduit (or tubing) sizes across the top. The numbers within the body of the table indicate the maximum number of conductors of any given size which can be put in the conduit in accordance with the NEC. First, find the conductor size being used in the left column. Then move to the right until the number shown is the same as, or larger than, the number of conductors to be placed in the conduit. Then move vertically upward and read the conduit size.

In this design, the three feeders are No. 2/0 AWG copper conductors. Using Fig. 15-28, find the 2/0 in the left column, and move horizontally to the right to the number 3 and then vertically up to the 2 in. The code requires a 2-in. conduit to carry three No. 2/0 AWG copper conductors.

9. Determine the minimum number of lighting circuits by dividing the general lighting load by the voltage, finding the amperage required and dividing the amperage into circuits.

In this design, the general lighting load is calculated in step 6 as 6,642 W, and the voltage used for the lighting is 120 V.

$$6,642 \text{ W} \div 120 \text{ V} = 56 \text{ amps}$$

Since the Code limits the branch circuit size to 80% of the rating, this may be broken up into four 20-amp branches for a total of 64 amps, or into five 15-amp branches for a total of 60 amps. Remember, this is the minimum number of branch circuits. In laying out the circuits, almost all designs will have more circuits than the minimum. This is because, as discussed in Sec. 15-9 and 16-2, step 4, most designers will limit each circuit to five or six receptacles, lights or a combination of receptacles and lights.

10. Lay out all branch circuits on the drawing. The branch circuits for receptacles and switching are discussed in Sec. 15-9 and 16-2. The symbols used for the circuits are shown in Fig. 15–13. Remember that all of these general-use receptacles and all lighting will use 120-V service.

A typical circuit layout is shown in Fig. 16-9. Note that each circuit is numbered, beginning with 1. It will be necessary to know the total number of 120- and 240-V circuits required.

In this design, there is a total of 14 circuits of which 11 are 120-V and 3 are 240-V.

11. Select the lighting panel based on the number of circuits and the required amperage. Be certain that all the pole space is not taken up so there is room for expansion. Remember that each 120-V circuit takes up one pole, while each 240-V circuit takes up two poles.

In this design, there are:

11 120-V circuits	11 poles
3 240-V circuits (3 × 2)	6 poles
Total poles required	17 poles

For this design, a 150-amp, 24-pole lighting panel would be selected.

12. Lay out the panel circuits, either on the drawing or in tabulated form as shown in Fig. 16-11. In large designs, with more than one panel, this provides the electrician with a schedule of what circuits will be served from what box. It is also used to note the size of the conductors used for circuits (step 8).

While a lighting panel layout is not often done for a residence, it is helpful to both the electrician and the designer if one is included. For commercial projects, a panel layout is almost always included. A typical commercial application is shown in Fig. 16-12. The panel drawing for the residence is shown in Fig. 16-14 with each of the branch circuits, and the circuit numbers, noted.

13. Size the conductors for all of the branch circuits, and note them on the panel drawing or in the tabulation. The conductors are sized just as the feeder conductor was sized in step 8.

Branch circuit conductors to general-purpose receptacles and light fixtures must be a minimum of No. 14 AWG when used with a 15-amp overcurrent

FIGURE 16-11 / Circuits and panels

LP-3

42 POLE

225 AMP MAIN LUG PANEL 120/208V 3∅, 4 WIRE		
13 - 20A 1∅ 120V	2#12 IN ¾"C	FAN COIL UNITS C-301, C-303 THRU C-313, C-315
2 - 20A 1∅ 120V	2#12 IN ¾"C	CABINET UNIT HEATERS C-302, C-314
30A 1∅ 208V	2#10 IN ¾"C	SPECIAL RECEPTACLE C-316
5 - 20A 1∅ 120V	2#12 IN ¾"C	ROOF EXHAUSTS C-317 THRU C-321
30A 1∅ 208V	2#10 IN ¾"C	RANGE C-322
4 - 20A 1∅ 120V	2#12 IN ¾"C	OUTSIDE LIGHTS C-323 THRU C-326
20A 1∅ 120V	2#12 IN ¾"C	TELEPHONE BOOTH C-327
20A 1∅ 120V	2#12 IN ¾"C	TELEPHONE COMPANY SIGN C-238
20A 1∅ 120V	2#12 IN ¾"C	DHW BURNER C-329
20A 1∅ 120V	2#12 IN ¾"C	DHW CIRC. PUMP C-330
20A 3∅ 208V	3#12 IN ¾"C	P-2 C-331
20A 3∅ 208V	3#12 IN ¾"C	AH-2 C-332
20A 1∅ 208V	2#12 IN ¾"C	TRICKLE CHARGE CKT. C-333
2 - 20A 1∅ 120V		SPARES

FIGURE 16-12 / Commercial panels and circuits

device (circuit breaker or fuse). Because No. 14 AWG conductors are limited to a maximum load of 1,725 W and a maximum circuit length of 30 ft, most designers use 20-amp breakers and No. 12 AWG conductors.

In this design, the conductors for the 20-amp branch circuits serving the receptacles and light fixtures are sized first. The conductor size selected from the table in Fig. 16-24 is No. 12 AWG, RHW, copper (see note at bottom of table). This is noted on the panel drawing as shown in Fig. 16-13.

Next, the conductor for each branch circuit is sized, based on the amperage required and the type of conductor being used. The NEC requires limiting of

```
                    ┌─────────────────────────────────────┐
              150 AMP, 24 POLE
                 SERVICE PANEL
     2-#12  │ RECEP. & LIGHTS │ RECEP. & LIGHTS │  2-#12
C1 ◄────────                                      ────────► C2
     2-#12  │ RECEP. & LIGHTS │ RECEP.          │  2-#12
C3 ◄────────                                      ────────► C4
     2-#12  │ RECEP.          │ RECEP.          │  2-#12
C5 ◄────────                                      ────────► C6
     2-#12  │ RECEP. & LIGHTS │ RECEP. & LIGHTS │  2-#12
C7 ◄────────                                      ────────► C8
     2-#12  │ RECEP.          │ RECEP. & LIGHTS │  2-#12
C9 ◄────────                                      ────────► C10
                    └─────────────────────────────────────┘
```

FIGURE 16-13 / Conductor notation

such loads to 80% of the ratings. To allow for this, the calculated amperage is multiplied by 1.25.

Air conditioner—11,250 W:

$$11,250 \text{ W} \div 240 \text{ V} = 46.9 \text{ amps}$$
$$46.9 \times 1.25 = 58.7 \text{ amps}$$

From Fig. 16-24, use No. 6 AWG, RHW, copper.
Water heater—3,800 W:

$$3,800 \text{ W} \div 240 \text{ V} = 15.8 \text{ amps}$$
$$15.8 \times 1.25 = 19.75 \text{ amps}$$

From Fig. 16-24, use No. 12 AWG, RHW, copper.
Clothes dryer—4,400 W:

$$4,400 \text{ W} \div 240 \text{ V} = 18.3 \text{ amps}$$
$$18.3 \times 1.25 = 22.9 \text{ amps}$$

From Fig. 16-24, use No. 10 AWG, RHW, copper.
Dishwasher—1,000 W:

$$1,000 \text{ W} \div 120 \text{ V} = 8.3 \text{ amps}$$
(a 20-amp breaker is used)

From Fig. 16-24, use No. 12 AWG, RHW, copper.
Range—11,700 W (nameplate rating):

$$11,700 \text{ W} \div 240 \text{ V} = 48.8 \text{ amps}$$
$$48.8 \times 1.25 = 61 \text{ amps}$$

From Fig. 16-24, use No. 6 AWG, RHW, copper.

Note the conductor sizes for each branch circuit on the panel drawing as shown in Fig. 16-14.

Whenever there will be more than three conductors in a raceway, the allowable ampacity of each conductor must be reduced. The amount of reduction required is shown in Fig. 16-24, note 8.

For example, if six No. 10 AWG copper conductors are placed in a 1-in. conduit, according to the reduction values in Fig. 16-24, the allowable ampacity will be reduced to 80% of the allowable values given in Fig. 16-24. The allowable ampacity for No. 10 AWG copper conductors is 30. Since this must be reduced by 80%:

$$30 \times 0.80 = 24 \text{ amps (allowed ampacity)}$$

The design of the electrical system for the residence in Appendix C is complete. The electrical system selected is 150-amp service with a 24-pole lighting panel. The feeders selected are three No. 2/0 AWG, RHW, copper conductors. The panel layout is shown in Fig. 16-14, with all branch circuits and their conductor sizes noted.

14. On commercial, industrial, and institutional projects, the electrical supply feeds into several panels, oftentimes broken up into *lighting panels* to serve light fixtures and general-purpose receptacles and *power panels* to supply the electricity to all appliances and equipment in the project. Quite often there are several of each type of panel.

FIGURE 16-14 / Conductor notation

In such a design, the circuits are labeled with a circuit number and a panel number. For example, C–3, LP–1 would be circuit 3 from lighting panel 1. Typical examples of this type of notation are shown in Fig. 16-15.

Also, in such a design, it is necessary to have a feeder from the service entrance to the main distribution panel which is in turn connected to the lighting and power panels by feeders (Fig. 16-16). Each of the feeders must be sized in accordance with the code.

16-3 OPTIONAL CALCULATION FOR A ONE-FAMILY RESIDENCE

There is an optional method of calculating the demand load for a residence, based on percentages of the loads listed in Fig. 16-17.

Fig. 16-18 is a list of loads calculated for the residence in Appendix C.

Under the optional method of calculating the demand load for a one-family residence, a much smaller service is required (117.6 amps compared with 143 amps), and a 150-amp service would still be used.

Based on amps, the feeder required (from Fig. 16-24) is a No. 1 AWG, RHW, copper conductor.

Neutral feeder calculations are the same as for the feeder *except* for the reduced range load.

16-4 CONDUIT SIZING

Conduits and raceways are discussed in Sec. 15-14, and in this section, the sizing of rigid metal conduit and electrical metallic tubing is covered. The size of the conduit is directly related to the number and size of the conductors which will be placed in it.

All of the tables to be used are based on the NEC's maximum percentages of the conduit that can be filled with conductors. Based on these percentages, the table in Fig. 16-25 gives the maximum number of conductors which can be placed in the trade (standard) sizes of conduit or tubing listed.

For example:

1. What size conduit is required to run three No. 3 AWG conductors in?

    From Fig. 16-25, 1¼-in. conduit or tubing is required for three No. 3 AWG conductors.

FIGURE 16-15 / Typical commer- cial notation

FIGURE 16-16 / Typical commercial panel layout

2.   How many No. 1 AWG conductors may be placed in 2-in. conduit or tubing?

A maximum of five No. 1 AWG conductors may be placed in 2-in.
conduit or tubing.

Remember that when more than three conductors are placed in any raceway
(including conduit or tubing), the allowable ampacity of each conductor is derated
(reduced) in accordance with note 8 for Fig. 16-24.

FIGURE 16-17 / Optional residential demand load (load in kVA)

Optional Calculation for Dwelling Unit
Load in kVA

Largest of the following four selections.

(1) 100 percent of the nameplate rating(s) of the air conditioning and cooling,
including heat pump compressors.

(2) 100 percent of the nameplate ratings of electric thermal storage and other
heating systems where the usual load is expected to be continuous at the full
nameplate value. Systems qualifying under this selection shall not be figured under
any other selection in this table.

(3) 65 percent of the nameplate rating(s) of the central electric space heating
including integral supplemental heating in heat pumps.

(4) 65 percent of the nameplate rating(s) of electric space heating if less than four
separately controlled units.

(5) 40 percent of the nameplate rating(s) of electric space heating of four or more
separately controlled units.

Plus: 100 percent of the first 10 kVA of all other load. 40 percent of the remainder of
all other load.

Conduit Sizing   /   16-4

	Watts
Air conditioner	9,000
General lighting 2213 x 3	6,642
2-20 amp appliance circuits	
2 @ 1500 each	3,000
1-20 amp laundry circuit	1,500
Water heater	3,800
Clothes dryer	4,400
Dishwasher	1,000
Range	11,700
Total	$\overline{41,042}$ = 41.04 kw

Optional demand load	
Air conditioner @ 100%	= 9,000
First 10kw @ 100%	10,000
Balance @ 40% (23.04 x 0.4)	9,216
	$\overline{28,216}$ watts

Service load
28,216 watts ÷ 240 volts = 117.6 amps

FIGURE 16-18 / Optional demand load calculations

16-5   VOLTAGE DROP

The NEC limits the amount of voltage drop (the loss of voltage due to resistance in the conductors) for power, heating and lighting, or any combination of these loads, to 3%. In addition, the maximum total voltage drop for feeders and branch circuits should be no more than 5%, leaving 2% for branch circuit loss.

In most residences, and small buildings, the voltage drop in the feeder is small because the length of the conductor is short.

The voltage drop can be calculated by using the formula:

$$\text{Voltage drop} = \frac{I \times L \times R}{1,000}$$

where

I = current carried in the conductor (amps)
L = length of current-carrying conductor (ft)
R = resistance of conductor (ohms per 1,000 ft)
1,000 = constant (converting R per 1,000 ft to R per ft)

EXAMPLE

Given: The commercial building shown in Fig. 16-19.

Problem: Determine the total voltage drop from the feeder to panel B.

FIGURE 16-19 / Voltage drop

The feeder to panel B has an I of 93 amps, and the conductor is No. 3 AWG copper. The length of the conductor from the main distribution panel to panel B is about 85 ft. Resistances for the various sizes of copper and aluminum conductors are given in Fig. 16-26. This table lists the DC resistances in ohms per M (1,000) ft at 25°C (77°F), which are then converted to AC resistances by multiplying by the factors also given in Fig. 16-27. For a No. 3 conductor, there is no revision; but note that as the conductors get larger, so do the factors. From Fig. 16-26, the resistance for a No. 3 conductor is 0.254 ohms per 1,000 ft.

The total voltage drop for the feeder to panel B is:

$$\frac{93 \text{ amps} \times 85 \text{ ft} \times 0.254 \text{ ohms}}{1,000} = 2.01 \text{ V}$$

The percentage of voltage drop, in this case, would be 2.01 V (voltage drop) divided by 240 (voltage), or less than 1%.

EXAMPLE

Given: The residence in Appendix C.

Problem: Check the voltage drop in the branch circuit to bedroom 1 since it is the one farthest from the panel.

The circuit has four receptacles on it, and its load is about 1,440 (4 duplex outlets at 180 W each = 4 × 2 × 180 = 1,440 W). This 1,440 W gives an amperage of 1,440 W ÷ 120 V = 12 amps. The approximate length of the branch circuit is 90 ft, and the resistance of a No. 12 AWG conductor (unstranded) is 2.01 ohms per 1,000 ft.

$$\frac{12 \text{ amps} \times 90 \text{ ft} \times 2.01 \text{ ohms}}{1,000} = 2.17 \text{ V}$$

The percentage of voltage drop, in this case, would be 2.17 V (voltage drop) divided by 120 (voltage) or about 1.8%, within the 2% drop that is considered good design practice.

QUESTIONS

16-1. What type of information will the designer need to accumulate before actually beginning to design the electrical system?

16-2. What is an *individual branch circuit,* and when is it used?

16-3. How many circuits are required to accommodate kitchen appliances?

16-4. What is meant by the *demand load* in reference to the electrical load of the building?

16-5. When selecting the panel size, what considerations for the future should be taken into account?

16-6. How is the general lighting load for a building determined?

16-7. How is the minimum service entrance determined?

16-8. In selecting the service entrance size, what should be considered?

Design Exercises

16-9. Design the electrical system for the residence in Appendix D.

16-10. Design the electrical system for one of the apartments in Appendix A. Calculate the total load and service for the apartment building.

Bell	
Buzzer	
Convenience outlet duplex	
Convenience outlet waterproof	WP
Lighting panel	LP
Power panel	PP
Outlet, floor	
Fixture, light (letter designates fixture type)	A or A or A
Motor	M
Outlet, range	R
Push button	
Outlet, special purpose (see specs.)	
Switch, single pole	
Switch, double pole	
Switch, three-way	
Switch and convenience outlet	S
Telephone	
Transformer	T

FIGURE 16-20 / Symbols

General Lighting Loads by Occupancies

Type of Occupancy	Unit Load per Sq. Ft. (Volt-Amperes)
Armories and Auditoriums	1
Banks	3½**
Barber Shops and Beauty Parlors	3
Churches	1
Clubs	2
Court Rooms	2
*Dwelling Units	3
Garages — Commercial (storage)	½
Hospitals	2
*Hotels and Motels, including apartment houses without provisions for cooking by tenants	2
Industrial Commercial (Loft) Buildings	2
Lodge Rooms	1½
Office Buildings	3½**
Restaurants	2
Schools	3
Stores	3
Warehouses (storage)	¼
In any of the above occupancies except one-family dwellings and individual dwelling units of two-family and multifamily dwellings: Assembly Halls and Auditoriums Halls, Corridors, Closets, Stairways Storage Spaces	1 ½ ¼

FIGURE 16-21 / General lighting loads by occupancies

Lighting Load Feeder Demand Factors

Type of Occupancy	Portion of Lighting Load to Which Demand Factor Applies (wattage)	Demand Factor Percent
Dwelling Units	First 3,000 or less at..................	100
	Next 3,001 to 120,000 at...........	35
	Remainder over 120,000 at.......	25
*Hosptials	First 50,000 or less at................	40
	Remainder over 50,000 at.........	20
*Hotels and Motels—Including Apartment Houses without Provision for Cooking by Tenants	First 20,000 or less at...............	50
	Next 20,001 to 100,000 at.........	40
	Remainder over 100,000 at.......	30
Warehouses (Storage)	First 12,500 or less at...............	100
	Remainder over 12,500 at.........	50
All Others	Total Wattage.............................	100

* The demand factors of this table shall not apply to the computed load of feeders to areas in hospitals, hotels, and motels where the entire lighting is likely to be used at one time: as in operating rooms, ballrooms, or dining rooms.

Reprinted with permission from NFPA 70-1990, the *National Electrical Code,* Copyright © 1989, National Fire Protection Association, Quincy, MA 02269. This reprinted material is not the official position of the National Fire Protection Association, which is represented only by the standard in its entirety.

FIGURE 16-22 / Demand factors

Demand Loads for Household Electric Ranges, Wall-Mounted Ovens, Counter-Mounted Cooking Units, and Other Household Cooking Appliances over 1¾ kW Rating, Column A to be used in all cases except as otherwise permitted in Note 3 below.

NUMBER OF APPLIANCES	Maximum Demand (See Notes)	Demand Factors Percent (See Note 3)	
	COLUMN A (Not over 12 kW Rating)	COLUMN B (Less than 3½ kW Rating)	COLUMN C (3½ kW to 8½ kW Rating)
1	8kW	80%	80%
2	11kW	75%	65%
3	14kW	70%	55%
4	17kW	66%	50%
5	20kW	62%	45%
6	21kW	59%	43%
7	22kW	56%	40%
8	23kW	53%	36%
9	24kW	51%	35%
10	25kW	49%	34%
11	26kW	47%	32%
12	27kW	45%	32%
13	28kW	43%	32%
14	29kW	41%	32%
15	30kW	40%	32%
16	31kW	39%	28%
17	32kW	38%	28%
18	33kW	37%	28%
19	34kW	36%	28%
20	35kW	35%	28%
21	36kW	34%	26%
22	37kW	33%	26%
23	38kW	32%	26%
24	39kW	31%	26%
25	40kW	30%	26%
26–30	15 kW plus 1kW	30%	24%
31–40	for each range	30%	22%
41–50	25 kW plus ½	30%	20%
51–60	kW for each	30%	18%
61 & over	range	30%	16%

Note 1. Over 12 kW through 27 kW ranges all of same rating. For ranges individually rated more than 12 kW but not more than 27 kW, the maximum demand in Column A shall be increased 5 percent for each additional kW of rating or major fraction thereof by which the rating of individual ranges exceeds 12 kW.

Note 2. Over 12 kW through 27 kW ranges of *unequal ratings.* For ranges individually rated more than 12 kW and of different ratings but none exceeding 27 kW an average value of rating shall be computed by adding together the ratings of all ranges to obtain the total connected load (using 12 kW for any range rated less than 12 kW) and dividing by the total number of ranges: and then the maximum demand in Column A shall be increased 5 percent for each kW or major fraction thereof by which this average value exceeds 12 kW.

Note 3. Over 1¾ kW through 8¼ kW. In lieu of the method provided in Column A, it shall be permissible to add the nameplate ratings of all ranges rated more than 1¼ kW but not more than 8¼ kW and multiply the sum by the demand factors specified in Column B or C for the given number of appliances.

Note 4. Branch-Circuit Load. It shall be permissible to compute the branch-circuit load for one range in accordance with Table 220-19. The branch-circuit load for one wall-mounted oven or one counter-mounted cooking unit shall be the nameplate rating of the appliance. The branch-circuit load for a counter-mounted cooking unit and not more than two wall-mounted ovens, all supplied from a single branch circuit and located in the same room, shall be computed by adding the nameplate rating of the individual appliances and treating this total as equivalent to one range.

Note 5. This table also applies to household cooking appliances rated over 1¼ kW and used in instructional programs.

See Table 220-20 for commercial cooking equipment.

FIGURE 16-23 / Demand load for electric ranges

Ampacities of Single Insulated Conductors, Rated 0 through 2000 Volts, In Free Air Based on Ambient Air Temperature of 30°C (86°F)

Size	Temperature Rating of Conductor. See Table 310-13.								Size
	60°C (140°F)	75°C (167°F)	85°C (185°F)	90°C (194°F)	60°C (140°F)	75°C (167°F)	85°C (185°F)	90°C (194°F)	
AWG kcmil	TYPE †TW, †UF	TYPES †FEPW, †RH, †RHW, †THHW, †THW, †THWN, †XHHW, †ZW	TYPE V	TYPES TA, TBS, SA, SIS, †FEP, †FEPB, †RHH, †THHN, †THHW, †XHHW, MI	TYPE †TW, †UF	TYPES †RH, †RHW, †THHW, †THW, †THWN, †XHHW	TYPE V	TYPES TA, TBS, SA, SIS, †RHH, †THHN, †THHW, †XHHW, MI	AWG kcmil
		COPPER				ALUMINUM OR COPPER-CLAD ALUMINUM			
18	....	....	....	18	....	....	....	....	
16	....	....	23	24	....	....	....	....	
14	25†	30†	30	35†	....	....	....	....	
12	30†	35†	40	40†	25†	30†	30	35†	12
10	40†	50†	55	55†	35†	40†	40	40†	10
8	60	70	75	80	45	55	60	60	8
6	80	95	100	105	60	75	80	80	6
4	105	125	135	140	80	100	105	110	4
3	120	145	160	165	95	115	125	130	3
2	140	170	185	190	110	135	145	150	2
1	165	195	215	220	130	155	165	175	1
1/0	195	230	250	260	150	180	195	205	1/0
2/0	225	265	290	300	175	210	225	235	2/0
3/0	260	310	335	350	200	240	265	275	3/0
4/0	300	360	390	405	235	280	305	315	4/0
250	340	405	440	455	265	315	345	355	250
300	375	445	485	505	290	350	380	395	300
350	420	505	550	570	330	395	430	445	350
400	455	545	595	615	355	425	465	480	400
500	515	620	675	700	405	485	525	545	500
600	575	690	750	780	455	540	595	615	600
700	630	755	825	855	500	595	650	675	700
750	655	785	855	885	515	620	675	700	750
800	680	815	885	920	535	645	700	725	800
900	730	870	950	985	580	700	760	785	900
1000	780	935	1020	1055	625	750	815	845	1000
1250	890	1065	1160	1200	710	855	930	960	1250
1500	980	1175	1275	1325	795	950	1035	1075	1500
1750	1070	1280	1395	1445	875	1050	1145	1185	1750
2000	1155	1385	1505	1560	960	1150	1250	1335	2000

AMPACITY CORRECTION FACTORS

Ambient Temp. °C	For ambient temperatures other than 30°C (86°F), multiply the ampacities shown above by the appropriate factor shown below.								Ambient Temp. °F
21-25	1.08	1.05	1.04	1.04	1.08	1.05	1.04	1.04	70-77
26-30	1.00	1.00	1.00	1.00	1.00	1.00	1.00	1.00	79-86
31-35	.91	.94	.95	.96	.91	.94	.95	.96	88-95
36-40	.82	.88	.90	.91	.82	.88	.90	.91	97-104
41-45	.71	.82	.85	.87	.71	.82	.85	.87	106-113
46-50	.58	.75	.80	.82	.58	.75	.80	.82	115-122
51-55	.41	.67	.74	.76	.41	.67	.74	.76	124-131
56-60	....	.58	.67	.71	....	.58	.67	.71	133-140
61-70	....	.33	.52	.58	....	.33	.52	.58	142-158
71-80	....	....	.30	.41	....	....	.30	.41	160-176

† Unless otherwise specifically permitted elsewhere in this Code, the overcurrent protection for conductor types marked with an obelisk (†) shall not exceed 15 amperes for 14 AWG, 20 amperes for 12 AWG, and 30 amperes for 10 AWG copper; or 15 amperes for 12 AWG and 25 amperes for 10 AWG aluminum and copper-clad aluminum.

Reprinted with permission from NFPA 70-1990, the *National Electrical Code,* Copyright © 1989, National Fire Protection Association, Quincy, MA 02269. This reprinted material is not the official position of the National Fire Protection Association, which is represented only by the standard in its entirety.

FIGURE 16-24 / Allowable ampacities

Ampacities of Insulated Conductors
Rated 0-2000 Volts, 60° to 90°C (140° to 194°F)
Not More Than Three Conductors in Raceway or Cable or Earth
(Directly Buried), Based on Ambient Temperature of 30°C (86°F)

Size	Temperature Rating of Conductor. See Table 310-13.								Size
	60°C (140°F)	75°C (167°F)	85°C (185°F)	90°C (194°F)	60°C (140°F)	75°C (167°F)	85°C (185°F)	90°C (194°F)	
AWG kcmil	TYPES †TW, †UF	TYPES †FEPW, †RH, †RHW, †THHW, †THW, †THWN, †XHHW †USE, †ZW	TYPE V	TYPES TA, TBS, SA SIS, †FEP, †FEPB, †RHH, †THHN, †THHW, †XHHW	TYPES †TW, †UF	TYPES †RH, †RHW, †THHW, †THW, †THWN, †XHHW †USE	TYPE V	TYPES TA, TBS, SA, SIS, †RHH, †THHW, †THHN, †XHHW	AWG kcmil
	COPPER				ALUMINUM OR COPPER-CLAD ALUMINUM				
18	....	....	....	14	....	....	....	....	....
16	....	....	18	18	....	....	....	....	....
14	20†	20†	25	25†	....	....	....	....	....
12	25†	25†	30	30†	20†	20†	25	25†	12
10	30	35†	40	40†	25	30†	30	35†	10
8	40	50	55	55	30	40	40	45	8
6	55	65	70	75	40	50	55	60	6
4	70	85	95	95	55	65	75	75	4
3	85	100	110	110	65	75	85	85	3
2	95	115	125	130	75	90	100	100	2
1	110	130	145	150	85	100	110	115	1
1/0	125	150	165	170	100	120	130	135	1/0
2/0	145	175	190	195	115	135	145	150	2/0
3/0	165	200	215	225	130	155	170	175	3/0
4/0	195	230	250	260	150	180	195	205	4/0
250	215	255	275	290	170	205	220	230	250
300	240	285	310	320	190	230	250	255	300
350	260	310	340	350	210	250	270	280	350
400	280	335	365	380	225	270	295	305	400
500	320	380	415	430	260	310	335	350	500
600	355	420	460	475	285	340	370	385	600
700	385	460	500	520	310	375	405	420	700
750	400	475	515	535	320	385	420	435	750
800	410	490	535	555	330	395	430	450	800
900	435	520	565	585	355	425	465	480	900
1000	455	545	590	615	375	445	485	500	1000
1250	495	590	640	665	405	485	525	545	1250
1500	520	625	680	705	435	520	565	585	1500
1750	545	650	705	735	455	545	595	615	1750
2000	560	665	725	750	470	560	610	630	2000

AMPACITY CORRECTION FACTORS									
Ambient Temp. °C	For ambient temperatures other than 30°C (86°F), multiply the ampacities shown above by the appropriate factor shown below.								Ambient Temp. °F
21-25	1.08	1.05	1.04	1.04	1.08	1.05	1.04	1.04	70-77
26-30	1.00	1.00	1.00	1.00	1.00	1.00	1.00	1.00	79-86
31-35	.91	.94	.95	.96	.91	.94	.95	.96	88-95
36-40	.82	.88	.90	.91	.82	.88	.90	.91	97-104
41-45	.71	.82	.85	.87	.71	.82	.85	.87	106-113
46-50	.58	.75	.80	.82	.58	.75	.80	.82	115-122
51-55	.41	.67	.74	.76	.41	.67	.74	.76	124-131
56-60	....	.58	.67	.71	....	.58	.67	.71	133-140
61-70	....	.33	.52	.58	....	.33	.52	.58	142-158
71-80	....	....	.30	.41	....	....	.30	.41	160-176

† Unless otherwise specifically permitted elsewhere in this Code, the overcurrent protection for conductor types marked with an obelisk (†) shall not exceed 15 amperes for 14 AWG, 20 amperes for 12 AWG, and 30 amperes for 10 AWG copper; or 15 amperes for 12 AWG and 25 amperes for 10 AWG aluminum and copper-clad aluminum after any correction factors for ambient temperature and number of conductors have been applied.

FIGURE 16-24 / Allowable ampacities (continued)

Ampacities of Three Single Insulated Conductors, Rated 0 through 2000 Volts, 110° to 250°C, in Raceway in Free Air

Based on Ambient Air Temperature of 40°C (104°F).

Size	Temperature Rating of Conductor. See Table 310-13.									Size
	110°C (230°F)	125°C (257°F)	150°C (302°F)	200°C (392°F)	250°C (482°F)	110°C (230°F)	125°C (257°F)	150°C (302°F)	200°C (392°F)	
AWG MCM	TYPES AVA, AVL	TYPES AI, AIA	TYPE Z	TYPES A, AA, FEP, FEPB, PFA	TYPES PFAH, TFE	TYPES AVA, AVL	TYPES AI, AIA	TYPE Z	TYPES A, AA	AWG MCM
	COPPER				NICKEL OR NICKEL-COATED COPPER	ALUMINUM OR COPPER-CLAD ALUMINUM				
14	29	31	34	36	39	. . . .	. . . .	. . . .	. . . .	14
12	36	39	43	45	54	25	27	30	35	12
10	46	50	55	60	73	37	40	44	47	10
8	64	69	76	83	93	48	52	57	65	8
6	81	87	96	110	117	63	68	75	86	6
4	109	118	120	125	148	85	92	94	98	4
3	129	139	143	152	166	96	104	109	119	3
2	143	154	160	171	191	111	120	124	133	2
1	168	181	186	197	215	131	141	145	154	1
1/0	193	208	215	229	244	150	162	169	183	1/0
2/0	229	247	251	260	273	179	193	198	208	2/0
3/0	263	284	288	297	308	205	221	227	238	3/0
4/0	301	325	332	346	361	235	253	260	275	4/0
250	345	372	. . . .	. . . .	. . . .	270	291	. . . .	. . . .	250
300	391	422	. . . .	. . . .	. . . .	306	330	. . . .	. . . .	300
350	436	470	. . . .	. . . .	. . . .	342	369	. . . .	. . . .	350
400	468	505	. . . .	. . . .	. . . .	368	397	. . . .	. . . .	400
500	531	573	. . . .	. . . .	. . . .	421	454	. . . .	. . . .	500
600	588	634	. . . .	. . . .	. . . .	471	508	. . . .	. . . .	600
700	645	696	. . . .	. . . .	. . . .	520	561	. . . .	. . . .	700
750	673	726	. . . .	. . . .	. . . .	545	588	. . . .	. . . .	750
800	699	754	. . . .	. . . .	. . . .	566	610	. . . .	. . . .	800
1000	785	846	. . . .	. . . .	. . . .	651	701	. . . .	. . . .	1000
1500	961	. . . .	. . . .	. . . .	. . . .	795	. . . .	. . . .	. . . .	1500
2000	1109	. . . .	. . . .	. . . .	. . . .	919	. . . .	. . . .	. . . .	2000

AMPACITY CORRECTION FACTORS

Ambient Temp. °C	For ambient temperatures other than 40°C (104°F), multiply the ampacities shown above by the appropriate factor shown below.									Ambient Temp. °F
41–50	.93	.94	.95	.97	.98	.93	.94	.95	.97	106–122
51–60	.85	.87	.90	.94	.95	.85	.87	.90	.94	124–140
61–70	.76	.80	.85	.90	.93	.76	.80	.85	.90	142–158
71–80	.65	.73	.80	.87	.90	.65	.73	.80	.90	160–176
81–90	.53	.64	.74	.83	.87	.53	.64	.74	.83	177–194
91–100	.38	.54	.67	.79	.85	.38	.54	.67	.79	195–212
101–120	. . . .	.24	.52	.71	.79	. . . .	.24	.52	.71	213–248
121–140	. . . .	. . . .	.30	.61	.72	. . . .	. . . .	.30	.61	249–284
141–160	. . . .	. . . .	. . . .	.50	.65	. . . .	. . . .	. . . .	.50	285–320
161–180	. . . .	. . . .	. . . .	.35	.58	. . . .	. . . .	. . . .	.35	321–356
181–200	. . . .	. . . .	. . . .	. . . .	.49	. . . .	. . . .	. . . .	. . . .	357–392
201–225	. . . .	. . . .	. . . .	. . . .	.35	. . . .	. . . .	. . . .	. . . .	393–437

FIGURE 16-24 / Allowable ampacities (continued)

451

Ampacities for Single Insulated Conductors, Rated 0 through 2000 Volts, 110° to 250°C, in Free Air

Based on Ambient Air Temperature of 40°C (104°F).

Size AWG MCM	Temperature Rating of Conductor. See Table 310-13.									Size AWG MCM
	110°C (230°F) TYPES AVA, AVL	125°C (257°F) TYPES AI, AIA	150°C (302°F) TYPE Z	200°C (392°F) TYPES A, AA, FEP, FEPB, PFA	250°C (482°F) TYPES PFAH, TFE	110°C (230°F) TYPES AVA, AVL	125°C (257°F) TYPES AI, AIA	150°C (302°F) TYPE Z	200°C (392°F) TYPES A, AA	
	COPPER				NICKEL OR NICKEL-COATED COPPER	ALUMINUM OR COPPER-CLAD ALUMINUM				
14	39	42	46	54	59	. . . .	. . . .	. . . .	. . . .	14
12	51	55	60	68	78	40	43	47	54	12
10	67	72	80	90	107	53	57	63	71	10
8	90	97	106	124	142	70	75	83	96	8
6	121	131	155	165	205	95	102	112	128	6
4	160	172	190	220	278	125	135	148	171	4
3	180	194	214	252	327	144	155	170	196	3
2	215	232	255	293	381	167	180	198	227	2
1	247	266	293	344	440	193	208	228	267	1
1/0	286	309	339	399	532	222	239	263	310	1/0
2/0	329	355	390	467	591	257	277	305	363	2/0
3/0	380	410	451	546	708	296	319	351	443	3/0
4/0	446	481	529	629	830	347	374	411	490	4/0
250	493	532	. . . .	. . . .	. . . .	384	414	. . . .	. . . .	250
300	552	595	. . . .	. . . .	. . . .	431	464	. . . .	. . . .	300
350	611	659	. . . .	. . . .	. . . .	477	514	. . . .	. . . .	350
400	663	715	. . . .	. . . .	. . . .	518	559	. . . .	. . . .	400
500	767	827	. . . .	. . . .	. . . .	600	647	. . . .	. . . .	500
600	860	928	. . . .	. . . .	. . . .	674	727	. . . .	. . . .	600
700	953	1028	. . . .	. . . .	. . . .	749	808	. . . .	. . . .	700
750	1000	1079	. . . .	. . . .	. . . .	786	848	. . . .	. . . .	750
800	1039	1121	. . . .	. . . .	. . . .	818	882	. . . .	. . . .	800
1000	1197	1291	. . . .	. . . .	. . . .	947	1021	. . . .	. . . .	1000
1500	1465	1580	. . . .	. . . .	. . . .	1160	1251	. . . .	. . . .	1500
2000	1692	1825	. . . .	. . . .	. . . .	1340	1444	. . . .	. . . .	2000

AMPACITY CORRECTION FACTORS

Ambient Temp. °C	For ambient temperatures other than 40°C (104°F), multiply the ampacities shown above by the appropriate factor shown below.									Ambient Temp. °F
41–50	.93	.94	.95	.97	.98	.93	.94	.95	.97	106–122
51–60	.85	.87	.90	.94	.95	.85	.87	.90	.94	124–140
61–70	.76	.80	.85	.90	.93	.76	.80	.85	.90	142–158
71–80	.65	.73	.80	.87	.90	.65	.73	.80	.87	160–176
81–90	.53	.64	.74	.83	.87	.53	.64	.74	.83	177–194
91–100	.38	.54	.67	.79	.85	.38	.54	.67	.79	195–212
101–120	. . . .	.24	.52	.71	.79	. . . .	.24	.52	.71	213–248
121–140	. . . .	. . . .	.30	.61	.72	. . . .	. . . .	.30	.61	249–284
141–160	. . . .	. . . .	. . . .	.50	.65	. . . .	. . . .	. . . .	.50	285–320
161–180	. . . .	. . . .	. . . .	.35	.58	. . . .	. . . .	. . . .	.35	321–356
181–200	. . . .	. . . .	. . . .	. . . .	.49	. . . .	. . . .	. . . .	. . . .	357–392
201–225	. . . .	. . . .	. . . .	. . . .	.35	. . . .	. . . .	. . . .	. . . .	393–437

FIGURE 16-24 / Allowable ampacities (continued)

Notes to Tables

1. Explanation of Tables. For explanation of Type Letters, and for recognized size of conductors for the various conductor insulations, see Section 310-13. For installation requirements, see Sections 310-1 through 310-10, and the various articles of this Code. For flexible cords, see Tables 400-4 and 400-5.

3. Three-Wire, Single-Phase Dwelling Services. In dwelling units, conductors, as listed below, shall be permitted to be utilized as three-wire, single-phase, service-entrance conductors and the three-wire, single-phase feeder that carries the total current supplied by that service. Grounded service-entrance conductors shall be permitted to be two AWG sizes smaller than the ungrounded conductors provided the requirements of Section 230-42 are met.

Conductor Types and Sizes
RH-RHH-RHW-THW-THWN-THHN-XHHW

Copper	Aluminum and Copper-Clad AL	Service Rating in Amps
AWG	AWG	
4	2	100
3	1	110
2	1/0	125
1	2/0	150
1/0	3/0	175
2/0	4/0	200

5. Bare Conductors. Where bare conductors are used with insulated conductors, their allowable ampacities shall be limited to that permitted for the adjacent insulated conductors.

6. Mineral-Insulated, Metal-Sheathed Cable. The temperature limitation on which the ampacities of mineral-insulated, metal-sheathed cable are based is determined by the insulating materials used in the end seal. Termination fittings incorporating unimpregnated, organic, insulating materials are limited to 90°C operation.

7. Type MTW Machine Tool Wire.

(FPN): For the ampacities of Type MTW wire, see Table 13-1(c) in the Electrical Standard for Industrial Machinery (NFPA 79-1985).

8. Ampacity Adjustment Factors.

(a) More than Three Conductors in a Raceway or Cable. Where the number of conductors in a raceway or cable exceeds three, the ampacities given in Tables 310-16, 310-18, 310-22, 310-26, 310-27, 310-28, 310-29, 310-30, and 310-31 shall be reduced as shown in the following table:

FIGURE 16-24 / Allowable ampacities (continued)

Number of Conductors	Percent of Values in Tables 310-16, 310-18, 310-22, 310-26, 310-27, 310-28, 310-29, 310-30, and 310-31, as Adjusted for Ambient Temperature if Necessary
4 thru 6	80
7 thru 9	70
10 thru 24*	70
25 thru 42*	60
43 and above*	50

* These factors include the effects of a load diversity of 50 percent.

Where single conductors or multiconductor cables are stacked or bundled longer than 24 inches (610 mm) without maintaining spacing and are not installed in raceways, the ampacity of each conductor shall be reduced as shown in the above table.

Exception No. 1: When conductors of different systems, as provided in Section 300-3, are installed in a common raceway the derating factors shown above shall apply to the number of power and lighting (Articles 210, 215, 220, and 230) conductors only.

Exception No. 2: For conductors installed in cable trays, the provisions of Section 318-11 shall apply.

Exception No. 3: Derating factors do not apply to conductors in nipples having a length not exceeding 24 inches (610 mm).

Exception No. 4: Derating factors do not apply to underground conductors entering or leaving an outdoor trench if those conductors have physical protection in the form of rigid metal conduit, intermediate metal conduit or rigid nonmetallic conduit Schedule 80 having a length not exceeding 10 feet (3.05 m) and the number of conductors in a conduit does not exceed 4.

(b) More than One Conduit, Tube, or Raceway. Spacing between conduits, tubing, or raceways shall be maintained.

9. Overcurrent Protection. Where the standard ratings and settings of overcurrent devices do not correspond with the ratings and settings allowed for conductors, the next higher standard rating and setting shall be permitted.

Exception: As limited in Section 240-3.

10. Neutral Conductor.

(a) A neutral conductor which carries only the unbalanced current from other conductors, as in the case of normally balanced circuits of three or more conductors, shall not be counted when applying the provisions of Note 8.

(b) In a 3-wire circuit consisting of 2-phase wires and the neutral of a 4-wire, 3-phase wye-connected system, a common conductor carries approximately the same current as the other conductors and shall be counted when applying the provisions of Note 8.

(c) On a 4-wire, 3-phase wye circuit where the major portion of the load consists of electric-discharge lighting, data processing, or similar equipment, there are harmonic currents present in the neutral conductor and the neutral shall be considered to be a current-carrying conductor.

11. Grounding or Bonding Conductor. A grounding or bonding conductor shall not be counted when applying the provisions of Note 8.

FIGURE 16-24 / Allowable ampacities (continued)

Maximum Number of Conductors in Trade Sizes of Conduit or Tubing

Type Letters	Conductor Size AWG, kcmil	½	¾	1	1¼	1½	2	2½	3	3½	4	5	6
RHW,	14	3	6	10	18	25	41	58	90	121	155		
	12	3	5	9	15	21	35	50	77	103	132		
	10	2	4	7	13	18	29	41	64	86	110		
	8	1	2	4	7	9	16	22	35	47	60	94	137
RHH	6	1	1	2	5	6	11	15	24	32	41	64	93
	4	1	1	1	3	5	8	12	18	24	31	50	72
(with	3	1	1	1	3	4	7	10	16	22	28	44	63
outer	2		1	1	3	4	6	9	14	19	24	38	56
covering)	1		1	1	1	3	5	7	11	14	18	29	42
	1/0		1	1	1	2	4	6	9	12	16	25	37
	2/0			1	1	1	3	5	8	11	14	22	32
	3/0			1	1	1	3	4	7	9	12	19	28
	4/0			1	1	1	2	4	6	8	10	16	24
	250				1	1	1	3	5	6	8	13	19
	300				1	1	1	3	4	5	7	11	17
	350				1	1	1	2	4	5	6	10	15
	400				1	1	1	1	3	4	6	9	14
	500				1	1	1	1	3	4	5	8	11
	600					1	1	1	2	3	4	6	9
	700				1	1	1	1	1	3	3	6	8
	750						1	1	1	3	3	5	8

Reprinted with permission from NFPA 70-1990, the *National Electrical Code,* Copyright © 1989, National Fire Protection Association, Quincy, MA 02269. This reprinted material is not the official position of the National Fire Protection Association, which is represented only by the standard in its entirety.

FIGURE 16-25 / Conductors in conduit

Table 8.   Conductor Properties

Size AWG/ kcmil	Area Cir. Mils	Stranding Quan-tity	Stranding Diam. In.	Overall Diam. In.	Overall Area In.^{2}	Copper Uncoated ohm/MFT	Copper Coated ohm/MFT	Aluminum ohm/ MFT
18	1620	1	—	0.040	0.001	7.77	8.08	12.8
18	1620	7	0.015	0.046	0.002	7.95	8.45	13.1
16	2580	1	—	0.051	0.002	4.89	5.08	8.05
16	2580	7	0.019	0.058	0.003	4.99	5.29	8.21
14	4110	1	—	0.064	0.003	3.07	3.19	5.06
14	4110	7	0.024	0.073	0.004	3.14	3.26	5.17
12	6530	1	—	0.081	0.005	1.93	2.01	3.18
12	6530	7	0.030	0.092	0.006	1.98	2.05	3.25
10	10380	1	—	0.102	0.008	1.21	1.26	2.00
10	10380	7	0.038	0.116	0.011	1.24	1.29	2.04
8	16510	1	—	0.128	0.013	0.764	0.786	1.26
8	16510	7	0.049	0.146	0.017	0.778	0.809	1.28
6	26240	7	0.061	0.184	0.027	0.491	0.510	0.808
4	41740	7	0.077	0.232	0.042	0.308	0.321	0.508
3	52620	7	0.087	0.260	0.053	0.245	0.254	0.403
2	66360	7	0.097	0.292	0.067	0.194	0.201	0.319
1	83690	19	0.066	0.332	0.087	0.154	0.160	0.253
1/0	105600	19	0.074	0.373	0.109	0.122	0.127	0.201
2/0	133100	19	0.084	0.419	0.138	0.0967	0.101	0.159
3/0	167800	19	0.094	0.470	0.173	0.0766	0.0797	0.126
4/0	211600	19	0.106	0.528	0.219	0.0608	0.0626	0.100
250	—	37	0.082	0.575	0.260	0.0515	0.0535	0.0847
300	—	37	0.090	0.630	0.312	0.0429	0.0446	0.0707
350	—	37	0.097	0.681	0.364	0.0367	0.0382	0.0605
400	—	37	0.104	0.728	0.416	0.0321	0.0331	0.0529
500	—	37	0.116	0.813	0.519	0.0258	0.0265	0.0424
600	—	61	0.099	0.893	0.626	0.0214	0.0223	0.0353
700	—	61	0.107	0.964	0.730	0.0184	0.0189	0.0303
750	—	61	0.111	0.998	0.782	0.0171	0.0176	0.0282
800	—	61	0.114	1.03	0.834	0.0161	0.0166	0.0265
900	—	61	0.122	1.09	0.940	0.0143	0.0147	0.0235
1000	—	61	0.128	1.15	1.04	0.0129	0.0132	0.0212
1250	—	91	0.117	1.29	1.30	0.0103	0.0106	0.0169
1500	—	91	0.128	1.41	1.57	0.00858	0.00883	0.0141
1750	—	127	0.117	1.52	1.83	0.00735	0.00756	0.0121
2000	—	127	0.126	1.63	2.09	0.00643	0.00662	0.0106

These resistance values are valid ONLY for the parameters as given. Using conductors having coated strands, different stranding type, and especially, other temperatures, change the resistance.

Formula for temperature change: $R_2 = R_1 [1+\alpha(T_2-75)]$ where: $\alpha_{cu} = 0.00323$, $\alpha_{AL} = 0.00330$.

Conductors with compact and compressed stranding have about 9 percent and 3 percent, respectively, smaller bare conductor diameters than those shown. See Table 5A for actual compact cable dimensions.

The IACS conductivities used: bare copper = 100%, aluminum = 61%.

Class B stranding is listed as well as solid for some sizes. Its overall diameter and area is that of its circumscribing circle.

(FPN): The construction information is per NEMA WC8-1976 (Rev 5-1980). The resistance is calculated per National Bureau of Standards Handbook 100, dated 1966, and Handbook 109, dated 1972.

FIGURE 16-26 / Conductor properties

**Multiplying Factors for Converting DC
Resistance to 60-Hertz AC Resistance**

Size	Multiplying Factor			
	For Nonmetallic-Sheathed Cables in Air or Nonmetallic Conduit		For Metallic-Sheathed Cables or all Cables in Metallic Raceways	
	Copper	Aluminum	Copper	Aluminum
Up to 3 AWG	1.	1.	1.	1.
2	1.	1.	1.01	1.00
1	1.	1.	1.01	1.00
0	1.001	1.000	1.02	1.00
00	1.001	1.001	1.03	1.00
000	1.002	1.001	1.04	1.01
0000	1.004	1.002	1.05	1.01
250 MCM	1.005	1.002	1.06	1.02
300 MCM	1.006	1.003	1.07	1.02
350 MCM	1.009	1.004	1.08	1.03
400 MCM	1.011	1.005	1.10	1.04
500 MCM	1.018	1.007	1.13	1.06
600 MCM	1.025	1.010	1.16	1.08
700 MCM	1.034	1.013	1.19	1.11
750 MCM	1.039	1.015	1.21	1.12
800 MCM	1.044	1.017	1.22	1.14
1000 MCM	1.067	1.026	1.30	1.19
1250 MCM	1.102	1.040	1.41	1.27
1500 MCM	1.142	1.058	1.53	1.36
1750 MCM	1.185	1.079	1.67	1.46
2000 MCM	1.233	1.100	1.82	1.56

FIGURE 16-27 / Multiplying factors

CHAPTER 17
LIGHTING

17-1 GENERAL

The basic reasons for providing light in a space are to make the objects in the space visible and to allow the conduct of activities which must take place in the space. Part of the light required may be provided by windows and skylights which allow sunlight to come into the space. Many times this sunlight is sufficient to provide all the light required on sunny days. However, as the sun moves, it shines first on the east portion of the building, and it moves toward the west as the day progresses. This means that windows facing the east are subjected to the strong rays of the sun in the morning, but must count on reflected light later in the day. Windows facing north get no direct sun, while windows facing south get a considerable amount. And on cloudy days, no direct sunlight is available. In effect, while natural light from windows and skylights can be counted on to provide some general light, it does not provide a controlled light source by which to perform activities.

Therefore, in most projects, at least some electric lighting must be introduced to provide a constant, controlled amount of light so that the space can be used whenever necessary, whether sunny or cloudy, day or night. This chapter discusses the terminology and procedures used to arrive at a lighting design that will provide the required amount of light.

Since lighting should be an integral part of the building, the lighting designer must work closely with the architect to achieve a lighting solution which blends with and becomes a part of the architectural design.

17-2   TERMINOLOGY

Light: That radiant energy which has a wavelength that the human eye can see. Light from the sun may be *sunlight* or it may be *skylight*. Light which is produced electrically should be referred to as *electric light* and not artificial light (as it is commonly called). This is because, even though it is there because of our technology, it is not "artificial."

Luminous Flux: The term used to refer to that portion of the radiant energy which the human eye can see (it produces the sensation of light in the human eye).

Lumen (lm):   A quantity of light used to express the total output of a light source. It is the unit of measure for luminous flux and for light. One lumen is the amount of light which falls on 1 sq ft of surface area when all points on the surface are 1 ft from a standard candle (Fig. 17-1).

Footlambert (fl):   The unit of measure for brightness for any perfectly diffused (spread out) surface which emits or reflects light. Footlamberts are expressed in lumens per square foot; 1 footlambert equals 1 lumen per sq ft. When lumens are measured from a light source (such as a light fixture or a reflecting wall or ceiling), they are referred to as footlamberts. (See "Footcandle" below.)

Reflectance: The ability of a surface to reflect light. It is expressed as the ratio of the light reflected by a surface to the amount of light which strikes the surface.

1' to any point
on the surface

FIGURE 17-1 / Lumen

One lumen is the amount of light which falls on 1 sq. ft. of surface area which is located 1' from a standard candle.

Transmission Factor: The ability of a surface or object to allow the light to transmit (pass through it). It is expressed as the ratio of the light transmitted through a body to the amount of light which strikes the surface.

Illumination: The density of light (luminous flux) on a surface. The amount of illumination is found by dividing the amount of luminous flux (in lumens) by the area over which the flux is distributed. The unit of measure for illumination is the footcandle.

Footcandle (fc):   The unit of measure for illumination, expressed in lumens per square foot, indicating how much light is actually on a surface. When lumens are measured at the surface where they will be ''used,'' such as a desk top, they are referred to as footcandles. (See ''Footlambert'' above.) The number of footcandles for a given surface is found by dividing the number of lumens on a surface by the area of surface in square feet. One footcandle is the equivalent of 1 lumen distributed uniformly over 1 sq ft of surface located 1 ft from a standard candle (Fig. 17-2). The number of footcandles required varies considerably with the use of the space or area being lit; some typical footcandle requirements are given in Fig. 17-3.

Brightness: The property of a surface. For example, the surface of a wall either absorbs or reflects light, exhibiting a certain amount of brightness. Technically, it is ''the luminous intensity of any surface in a given direction per unit of projected area of the surface viewed from that direction'' [Bertram Y. Kinzey, Jr., and Howard M. Sharp, *Environmental Technologies in Architecture* (Englewood Cliffs, N.J.: Prentice-Hall, Inc., 1963), p. 501.]

FIGURE 17-2 / Footcandle

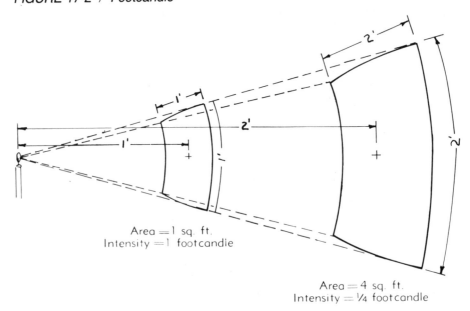

Area = 1 sq. ft.
Intensity = 1 footcandle

Area = 4 sq. ft.
Intensity = ¼ footcandle

Schools		Industrial	
corridors	20	general lighting	30-50
auditorium	20-30	laundries	30-50
study halls	70-80	locker rooms	30
classrooms	70	machines, rough	40-50
chalkboard area	150	machines, fine	80-100
drafting rooms	80-100	intricate work	150-400
laboratories	80	assembly areas	50-100
art	100	Theaters	
sewing	120-150	entrance, lobby	30-40
shop	100	foyer	30-40
gymnasium	50	auditorium	10
Stores		Post office	
circulation area	30	lobby	30
merchandise	100-150	mail sorting	100
showcases	150-200	corridors, storage	30

FIGURE 17-3 / Typical footcandle requirements

Candlepower (cp):   A measurement of the luminous intensity of the source of light, stated in terms of candles. The amount of candlepower from any light source varies with the direction from the source in which the measurement is taken. This is because different types of light sources give off their light in different directions, some aiming up to the ceiling and others toward the floor. Manufacturers have available a candle-power distribution curve which shows in what direction the light will go and how much. The typical candlepower distribution of various luminaires is shown in Fig. 17-19.

Lamp: A man-made source of light, commonly referred to as a bulb (for incandescent lamps) and a tube (fluorescent lamps).

Reflector: A device which redirects the light of a lamp by reflecting it to the desired location. As the light leaves the source, it hits the reflector (Fig. 17-4) and is directed in the direction that the reflector is aimed.

Globe: An enclosing device which covers all or part of the lamp. It may protect the lamp, diffuse the light, redirect the light or modify the color of the light.

Luminaire: A complete lighting unit consisting of a light source, globe, reflector, housing, wiring and any supporting brackets that are a part of the housing.

FIGURE 17-4 / Reflector

17-3 ELECTRIC LAMPS

The available electric light sources are grouped into two classes:

1. Incandescent light sources (which use a tungsten filament).

2. Gaseous discharge light sources (such as fluorescent, mercury vapor, sodium, and neon).

For general lighting purposes inside residences and commercial, industrial and institutional projects, the incandescent and fluorescent lamps are used. Mercury vapor, quartz and sodium lamps are predominantly used outside to light large areas such as parking lots and to serve as flood lights.

Incandescent lamps have three main parts: the filament, the base and the hollow-glass bulb which encloses the filament. The filament is made of tungsten and is connected by lead-in wires to the base. When the base is screwed into a socket and the power turned on, the circuit is complete. As the tungsten filament heats, the lamp gives off light.

The bulb bases most commonly used are the *medium* (usually up to 200 W) and the mogul (over 200 W). But other bases are also used, depending on the type and the size of the lamp.

The glass bulb is available with clear or frosted glass, coated inside or outside with a diffusing or reflecting material, or etched on the inside.

The typical luminous characteristics of an incandescent lamp with a frosted bulb are listed in Fig. 17-5. Among the advantages of incandescent lamps are:

1. They operate directly from the standard electrical distribution circuits.

2. A wide range of lighting distribution characteristics is available.

3. The standard sockets make them easily interchangeable.

4. Surrounding air temperature does not affect their performance.

5. Their radiation characteristics are good within the luminous range.

6. They can be easily equipped with a dimmer that can control the amount of light the lamp gives off from none to full outlet.

General Service Lamps for 115-, 120-, and 125-Volt Circuits (Will Operate in Any Position but Lumen Maintenance is Best for 40 to 1500 Watts When Burned Vertically Base-Up)

Watts	Bulb and Other Description	Base (see Fig. 8-9)	Filament (see Fig. 8-7)	Rated Average Life (hours)	Max Over-All Length (mm)	(inches)	Avg Light Center Length (mm)	(inches)	Approx Initial Filament Temp (K)	Max Bare Bulb Temp (°C)	(°F)	Base Temp (°C)	(°F)	Approx Initial Lumens	Rated Initial Lumens Per Watt	Lamp Lumen Depreciation (per cent)
10	S-14 inside frosted or clear	Med.	C-9	1500	89	3 1/2	64	2 1/2	2420	41	106	41	106	80	8.0	89
15	A-15 inside frosted	Med.	C-9	2500	89	3 1/2	60	2 3/8	—	—	—	—	—	126	8.4	83
25	A-19 inside frosted	Med.	C-9	2500	98	3 7/8	64	2 1/2	2550	43	110	42	108	230	9.2	79
34[a,b]	A-19 inside frosted	Med.	CC-6 or CC-8	1500	113	4 7/16	76	3	—	—	—	—	—	410	12.1	—
40	A-19 inside frosted and white¶	Med.	C-9	1500	108	4 1/4	75	2 15/16	2650	127	260	105	221	455	11.4	87.5
50[a]	A-19 inside frosted	Med.	CC-6	1000	113	4 7/16	79	3 3/8	—	—	—	—	—	680	13.6	—
52[a,c]	A-19 clear or inside frosted	Med.	CC-8	1000	113	4 7/16	79	3 3/8	—	—	—	—	—	800	15.4	—
55[a]	A-19 clear or white	Med.	CC-8	1000	113	4 7/16	79	3 3/8	—	—	—	—	—	870	15.8	93
60	A-19 inside frosted and white¶	Med.	CC-6	1000	113	4 7/16	79	3 3/8	2790	124	255	93	200	860	14.3	
67[a,d]	A-19 clear or inside frosted	Med.	CC-8	750	113	4 7/16	79	3 3/8	—	—	—	—	—	1130	16.9	—
70[a]	A-19 clear or white	Med.	CC-8	750	113	4 7/16	79	3 3/8	—	—	—	—	—	1190	17.0	92
75	A-19 inside frosted and white¶	Med.	CC-6	750	113	4 7/16	79	3 3/8	2840	135	275	96	205	1180	15.7	
90[a]	A-19 clear or inside frosted	Med.	CC-8	750	113	4 7/16	79	3 3/8	—	—	—	—	—	1620	18.0	—
95[a]	A-19 clear or white	Med.	CC-8	750	113	4 7/16	79	3 3/8	—	—	—	—	—	1710	18.0	90.5
100	A-19 inside frosted and white¶	Med.	CC-6	750	113	4 7/16	79	3 3/8	2905	149	300	98	208	1740	17.4	
100§	A-19 inside frosted and white	Med.	CC-8	1000	113	4 7/16	79	3 3/8	—	—	—	—	—	1680	16.8	—
100	A-21 inside frosted	Med.	CC-6	750	133	5 1/4	98	3 7/8	2880	127	260	90	194	1690	16.9	90
135[a]	A-21 clear or inside frosted	Med.	CC-8	750	139	5 1/2	101	4	—	—	—	—	—	2580	19.1	
150	A-21 inside frosted	Med.	CC-8	750	139	5 1/2	101	4	2960	—	—	—	—	2880	19.2	89
150	A-21 white	Med.	CC-8	750	139	5 1/2	101	4	2930	—	—	—	—	2790	18.6	89
150	A-23 inside frosted or clear or white	Med.	CC-6	750	157	6 3/16	117	4 5/8	2925	138	280	99	210	2780	18.5	89
150	PS-25 clear or inside frosted	Med.	C-9	750	176	6 15/16	133	5 1/4	2910	143	290	99	210	2660	17.7	87.5
200	A-23 inside frosted white or clear	Med.	CC-8	750	160	6 5/16	117	4 5/8	2980	174	345	107	225	4000	20.0	89.5
200	PS-25 clear or inside frosted	Med.	CC-6	750	176	6 15/16	133	5 1/4	—	—	—	—	—	3800	19.0	—

Reprinted with permission from IES, *IES Lighting Handbook, 1984 Reference Handbook.*

FIGURE 17-5 / Incandescent lamp characteristics

The incandescent lamp is used extensively in residences in ceiling, wall, floor and table luminaires. In commercial applications, it is primarily for specialty usage, such as spotlighting.

Fluorescent lamps are devices which convert invisible ultraviolet radiation into visible radiation. This conversion is made by the chemical phosphorus which is distributed over the inside of the tube.

The fluorescent lamp is used extensively in commercial, industrial and institutional projects. The typical fluorescent lamp has a cylindrical, sealed, glass tube which contains a mixture of low-pressure mercury vapor and an inert gas—usually argon (and phosphorus on the inside of the tube). Each end of the fluorescent tube has a cathode built in to supply the electrons which start, and maintain, the mercury arc. This mercury arc is absorbed by the phosphorus which re-radiates it as visible radiation.

The typical fluorescent lamp is available with straight tubes, for most commercial uses, and with circular, square, or U-shaped tubes, for specialty uses. Lamp lengths are given in inches. A range of lighting "colors" is available from the lamps; they may be referred to as "daylight" and "white," and some manufacturers use terms such as "cool white," "soft white," and "warm white." The "deluxe" lamp produces a warmer, more lifelike light for flesh tones by adding more red to the phosphor. This deluxe type of lamp is used extensively in retail stores.

The cathodes commonly used in fluorescent lamps are:

1. Instant start (Fig. 17-20).
2. Rapid start (Fig. 17-6).

The instant-start fluorescent lamp, of which the slimline lamp is the best known, makes use of a high-voltage transformer which strikes an arc without any of the cathode preheating that was necessary in early lamp designs. This type of lamp has only one pin at each end of the tube. While more expensive and slightly less efficient than the rapid-start lamp, it is manufactured in some lengths and currents which are not available with the rapid-start. Since it will operate at lower temperatures (below 50°F) than the rapid-start lamp, it is often used in outdoor situations or in any location where the temperature may be low (such as in many manufacturing facilities, outdoor loading docks and covered parking areas).

The rapid-start fluorescent lamp is the more popular of the two since it has a higher light output per foot and is slightly less expensive than the instant-start. This type of lamp has about a 1-sec starting time and operates on a cathode current which flows continuously from a separate ballast; no starter is needed.

Typical fluorescent lamp data are given in Fig. 17-6.

The advantages of fluorescent lamps are as follows:

1. They provide more light (lumens) for less operating cost than incandescent lamps.

Nominal length (millimeters)	1050	1600	1800	2400	1200	1500
(inches)	42	64	72	96	48	60
Bulb	T-6	T-6	T-8	T-8	T-12	T-17
Base	Single Pin	Single Pin	Single Pin	Single Pin	Med. Bipin	Mog. Bipin
Approx. lamp current (amperes)	0.200[f]	0.200[f]	0.200[f]	0.200[f]	0.425	0.425
Approx. lamp volts	150	233	220	295	104	107
Approx. lamp watts	25.5	38.5	38	51	40.5	42
Rated life (hours)[b]	7500	7500	7500	7500	7500–12000	7500–9000
Lamp lumen depreciation (LLD)[c]	76	77	83	89	83	89
Initial lumens[d]						
Cool White	1835	3000	3030	4265	3100	2900
Deluxe Cool White	1265	2100	2100	2910		2020
Warm White	1875	3050	3015	4215	3150	2940
Deluxe Warm White	1275	2100				1990
White	1900	2945	3050	4225	3150	2940
Daylight	1605	2600	2650	3525	2565	2410
Factors for Calculating Luminance[e]						
Candelas per Square Meter	6.1	3.93	2.55	1.87	2.65	1.5

[a] The life and light output ratings of fluorescent lamps are based on their use with ballasts that provide proper operating characteristics. Ballasts that do not provide proper electrical values may substantially reduce either lamp life or light output, or both.
[b] Rated life under specified test conditions at three hours per start. At longer burning intervals per start, longer life can be expected.
[c] Per cent of initial light output at 70 per cent rated life at three hours per start. Average for cool white lamps. Approximate values.
[d] At 100 hours. Where lamp is made by more than one manufacturer, light output is the average of manufacturers. For the lumen output of other colors of fluorescent lamps, multiply the cool white lumens by the relative light output value from the table below Fig. 8–116.

Reprinted with permission from IES, *IES Lighting Handbook, 1984 Reference Handbook.*

FIGURE 17-6 / Typical hot-cathode fluorescent lamps (rapid starting)[a]

2. Since they provide more light (lumens) per watt, less wattage is required, resulting in fewer branch circuits.

3. Less heat is given off by fluorescent lamps.

17-4   LIGHTING SYSTEMS

The luminaire may project *direct, indirect* or *semi-indirect* light on the surface or in the area to be lit. *Direct* lighting (Fig. 17-7) projects light directly onto the surface or object, and there is little reflection of the light rays. *Indirect* lighting projects all of its light onto a surface (usually a ceiling), and the light is reflected from that surface onto the object (Fig. 17-8). *Semi-indirect* lighting projects part of the light onto a surface to be reflected onto the object, and part of the light travels directly to the object (Fig. 17-9). Even when a direct lighting system is used, the light that falls onto an object or surface is usually a combination of light reflected from the walls, ceiling, and even floors as well as the direct light.

The use of diffusers below fluorescent lamps makes possible an even distribution of lighting without causing any glare. Thus, the tremendous selection and availability of such diffusers has made the direct lighting system the most popular in commercial, industrial, and institutional projects.

Lightly Loaded Lamps

	Circline				U-Shaped								
Nominal length (millimeters)	165 dia.	210 dia.	300 dia.	400 dia.	600	600	900	1200	1200	1200	900	1200	1500
(inches)	6½ dia.	8¼ dia.	12 dia.	16 dia.	24	24	36	48	48	48	36	48	60
Bulb	T-9	T-9	T-10	T-10	T-12	T-12	T-12	T-12	T-12	T-10	T-8	T-8	T-8
Base	4-Pin	4-Pin	4-Pin	4-Pin	Med. Bipin	Med. Bipin	Med. Bipin	Med. Bipin	Med. Bipin	Med. Bipin	Med. Bipin	Med. Bipin	Med. Bipin
Leg spacing					92 mm (3⅝ in)	152 mm (6 in)							
Approx. lamp current (amperes)	0.38	0.37	0.425	0.415	0.42	0.43	0.43	0.43	0.43	0.42	0.265	0.265	0.265
Approx. lamp volts	48	61	81	108	103	100	81	101	101	104	100	135	172
Approx. lamp watts[f]	20	22.5	33	41.5	41	40.5	32.4	41	41	41	25	32	40
Rated life (hours)[b]	12000	12000	12000	12000	12000	12000	18000	20000	15000	24000	20000	20000	20000
Lamp lumen depreciation (LLD)[c]		72	82	77	84	84	81	84					
Initial lumens[d]													
Cool White	800	1065	1870	2580	2900	2935	2210	3150	3250	3200	*	*	*
Deluxe Cool White		875	1425	2000	2020	2065	1555	2200		2270			
Warm White	825	1065	1835	2550	2850	2965	2235	3175	3250	3250			
Deluxe Warm White	630	800	1375	1950	1980	2040	1505	2165					
White		1100	1870	2650	2850	2965	2255	3185	3250	3250			
Daylight		906	1550	2165			1900	2615	2650	2700			
Factors for Calculating Luminance[e]													
Candelas per Square Meter	11.5	8.4	4.6	3.3	2.65	2.65	3.58	2.65	2.65	3.18	5.42	4.03	3.18
Candelas per Square Foot	1.07	0.78	0.43	0.31	0.25	0.25	0.33	0.25	0.25	0.30	0.50	0.37	0.30

Medium Loaded Lamps

Nominal length (millimeters)	600	750	900	1050	1200	1500	1600	1800	2100	2400
(inches)	24	30	36	42	48	60	64	72	84	96
Bulb	T-12	T-12	T-12	T-12	T-12	T-12	T-12	T-12	T-12	T-12
Base	Recess D.C.	Recess D.C.	Recess D.C.	Recess D.C.	Recess D.C.	Recess D.C.	Recess D.C.	Recess D.C.	Recess D.C.	Recess D.C.
Approx. lamp current (amperes)	0.8	0.8	0.8	0.8	0.8	0.8	0.8	0.78	0.8	0.79
Approx. lamp volts	41		59		78	98		117	135	153
Approx. lamp watts[f]	37		50		63	75.5		87	100	113
Rated life (hours)[b]	9000	9000	9000	9000	12000	12000	12000	12000	12000	12000
Lamp lumen depreciation (LLD)[c]	77		77	77	82	82	82	82	82	82
Initial lumens[d]										
Cool White	1700	2290	2885	3516	4300	5400	5800	6650	7800	9150
Deluxe Cool White					3050			4550		6533
Warm White	1700				4300	5500		6500		9200
Deluxe Warm White										6475
White								6475		9200
Daylight	1400		2476	3100	4300	4650	4900	5600	6867	7800
Factors for Calculating Luminance[e]										
Candelas per Square Meter	5.54	4.35	3.58	3.04	2.65	2.1	1.95	1.7	1.44	1.24
Candelas per Square Foot	0.51	0.40	0.33	0.28	0.25	0.20	0.18	0.16	0.13	0.12

Reprinted with permission from IES, IES Lighting Handbook, 1984 Reference Handbook.

FIGURE 17-6 / Typical hot-cathode fluorescent lamps (rapid starting) (continued)

466

Highly Loaded Lamps

	1200 48 T-10[g]	1800 72 T-10[g]	2400 96 T-10[g]	1200 48 T-12	1500 60 T-12	1800 72 T-12	2400 96 T-12	1200 48 PG-17	1800 72 PG-17	2400 96 PG-17
Base	Recess D.C.	Recess D.C.	Recess D.C.	Recess D.C.	Recess D.C.	Recess D.C.	Recess D.C.	Recess D.C.	Recess D.C.	Recess D.C.
Approx. lamp current (amperes)	1.5	1.5	1.5	1.5	1.5	1.52	1.5	1.5	1.5	1.5
Approx. lamp volts	80	120[h]	160[h]	84		125	163	84	125	163
Approx. lamp watts[f]	105[h]	150[h]	205[h]	116		168	215	116	168	215
Rated life (hours)[b]	9000	9000	9000	9000	9000	9000	9000	9000	9000	9000
Lamp lumen depreciation (LLD)[c]	66	66	66	69		72	72	69	69	69
Initial lumens[d]										
Cool White	6700[h]	10000[h]	14000[h]	6900	8950	10640	15250	7450	11500	16000
Deluxe Cool White	4690[h]	7000[h]	9800[h]	4900		7400	10750	5200		11200
Warm White				6700		10500	14650	7000		15000
White						10500	15000			
Daylight				5700		9300	12650	6000	9300	13300
Factors for Calculating Luminance[e]										
Candelas per Square Meter	3.18	2.04	1.49	2.65	2.1	1.7	1.24	1.91[j]	1.2[j]	0.89[j]
Candelas per Square Foot	0.30	0.19	0.14	0.25	0.20	0.16	0.12	0.18[j]	0.11[j]	0.08[j]

[a] The life and light output ratings of fluorescent lamps are based on their use with ballasts that provide proper operating characteristics. Ballasts that do not provide proper electrical values may substantially reduce either lamp life or light output, or both.

[b] Rated life under specified test conditions at three hours per start. At longer burning intervals per start, longer life can be expected.

[c] Per cent of initial light output at 70 per cent rated life at three hours per start. Average for cool white lamps. Approximate values.

[d] At 100 hours. Where lamp is made by more than one manufacturer, light output is the average of manufacturers. For the lumen output of other colors of fluorescent lamps, multiply the cool white lumens by the relative light output value from the table below.

[e] To calculate approximate lamp luminance, multiply the lamp lumens of the lamp color desired by the appropriate factor. Factors derived using method by E. A. Linsday, ''Brightness of Cylindrical Fluorescent Sources'', Illuminating Engineering, Vol. XXXIX, January, 1944, p. 23.

[f] Includes watts for cathode heat.

[g] A jacketed T-10 design is also available for use in applications where lamps are directly exposed to cold temperatures.

[h] Peak value. At 25 °C (77 °F) lumen and wattage values are lower.

[i] These lamps available in several variations (outdoor, low temperature, jacketed) with the same, or slightly different, ratings.

[j] Average luminance for center section of lamp. Parts of surface of lamp will have higher luminance.

Note: All electrical and lumen values apply only under standard photometric conditions.

[k] Initial Lumens for 3100 K and 4100 K color lamps (GTE Sylvania) are: 25-W, 2150; 32-W, 2900; and 40-W, 3650.

FIGURE 17-6 / Hot cathode lamp characteristics

FIGURE 17-7 / Direct lighting   FIGURE 17-8 / Indirect lighting

17-5 METHODS OF LIGHTING

The three methods of providing light to any space are localized, general and a combination of localized and general.

Localized lighting (Fig. 17-10) provides light only at the point where it is needed. This is accomplished primarily by providing individual luminaires in specific locations. For example, to provide the localized lighting necessary for reading a paper in a chair, a floor, ceiling or table luminaire would probably be used. Localized lighting generally produces pools or areas of light among larger areas of shadow. It is used primarily in residences and apartments, and to some extent in industrial plants.

General lighting (Fig. 17-11) provides a uniform level of lighting over an entire area. In this type of design, the luminaires are evenly distributed within the space. The luminaires may use various types of diffusing covers to spread the light. General lighting is often used in stores, classrooms, markets, factories, and other such general-use spaces.

Combination lighting (Fig. 17-12) provides enough general illumination for the entire space with additional localized lighting in areas where such things as desks, showcases, drafting tables, or machinery are located. With this type of lighting, the general lighting level would be lower than when only general lighting is used. Combination lighting is used in almost all types of buildings.

17-6 PRINCIPLES OF DESIGN

There are several basic principles of lighting design which should be discussed before the actual design is begun.

General lighting *requirements* must be determined for the surface; that is, the number of footcandles (lumens per square foot) must be determined for the use of the surface. Next, the designer will have to take into account the room area, the light loss

FIGURE 17-9 / Semi-indirect lighting

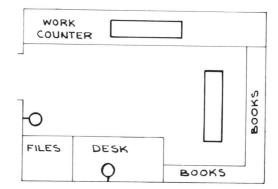

FIGURE 17-10 / Lighting combinations

due to room proportions, the color of the walls, the coefficient of utilization, and the maintenance factor.

The number of *footcandles* required for a variety of common uses is shown in Fig. 17-3. Selecting the required number of footcandles is among the first steps in the lighting design.

Next, the *room area* in square feet must be determined, taking the room dimensions from the drawings.

The *coefficient of utilization* is a measure of the amount of the total lumens put out by a luminaire that will actually reach the working plane, or the surface being lit. The higher the percentage of lumens that reach the surface, the higher the coefficient. The coefficient is a function of the room dimensions, the reflection factors of walls and ceilings and the characteristics of any particular luminaire. For any particular luminaire (such as those shown in Fig. 17-19), the two variables become the room ratio and the reflection factors of walls and ceilings.

Reflection factors of the floor, ceiling and walls must also be considered. The reflection factors of the surface finish materials, such as paints, ceiling tile, carpet, and wood, are easily found in the manufacturers' data sheets.

Ceiling reflection factors are usually taken as the reflection factor of the ceiling finish. When the ceiling has more than one finish, each finish must be considered in

FIGURE 17-11 / General and local
lighting

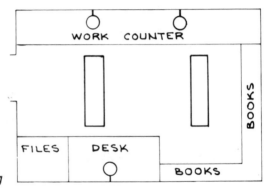

FIGURE 17-12 / Combined lighting

relation to the area it covers. Most ceiling factors are listed in manufacturers' brochures as 50%, 70%, and 80%.

Wall reflection factors must take into consideration not only the finish on the wall but also the other vertical reflection surfaces including doors, curtains (or other window coverings), windows (when they are not covered), cabinets, and any other items which may be on the walls such as a chalkboard or bulletin board. The wall factors listed in the manufacturers' material are 10%, 30%, and 50%. Average rooms have wall reflection factors of 30%, and it would be unlikely that any room would have a factor exceeding 50%.

Floor reflection factors also must be based on the reflection factor not only of the floor but also of all horizontal surfaces including furniture (desks, chairs, couches, files, and so on). A conservative factor of 10% is often used, but the increased use of lighter floor colors has caused many designers to use a floor value of 30%. Many manufacturers list both 10% and 30% floor reflection factors. As a compromise value, an effective floor cavity reflectance (p_{FC}) of 20% is used in the CU tables in Fig. 17-19. When the actual value of the floor cavity reflectance is more or less than the 20%, the CU values in Fig. 17-19 are adjusted by the appropriate factor from Fig. 17-18.

Since the lighting design is usually done before all the room finishes are selected, the designer must have a "feeling" for what will be done in the space. Many times paint colors, ceiling and floor tiles, and the other finishes will not be actually selected (as to color and style) until the project is well under construction. The designer will have to check carefully as to what each space will be used for and what colors and finishes the architect, owner, and decorator may use. From this information, the lighting designer must make an "educated guess," and when in doubt, he should use lower values to be on the safe side.

The *maintenance factor* takes into consideration all of the reasons that would cause a luminaire (with its lamp) to operate at less than 100% of its design and test capabilities after it is installed. Reasons for such decreased performance include:

1. The output of the luminaire decreases with age.

2. The voltage at the luminaire is generally less than the voltage at which it is rated.

3.   Longtime chemical changes and discolorations affect the reflecting surface and diffusing grilles.

4.   Dust and dirt affect the lamp, its reflecting surface and its diffusing grilles.

These loss of performance factors are grouped into:

LLD = Lamp Lumen Depreciation Factor
LDD = Luminaire Dirt Depreciation Factor

These two factors are combined (multiplied by each other) to obtain the maintenance factor.

This maintenance factor may be kept to a minimum by regularly cleaning the entire luminaire and periodically replacing the lamp, but it cannot be eliminated.

Values of lamp lumen depreciation (LLD) for various lamps are given in Figs. 17-5 and 17-20. The values are listed as the percentage of initial lumens produced at 70% of life for the various types of lamps in common use.

The luminaire dirt depreciation (LDD) categories range from I through VI and are listed in Fig. 17-17. Each category applies to certain types of luminaire and lamp situations. The appropriate LDD category classification to be used for each type is listed in the typical luminaire listings in Fig. 17-19.

The selection for cleanliness (very clean through very dirty) is a judgment factor based on the designer's anticipation of the quality of maintenance and housekeeping to which the luminaire will be subjected.

LDD values are listed as the percentage of initial lumens produced by the specific luminaire type.

> *Caution:*   Care must be used in selecting both the surface reflection factors and the maintenance factor. Many designers (and architects/engineers) have a tendency to use values which are too high so they will have to use fewer luminaires, saving money on the number of luminaires bought, the wiring, the circuits, and so on. This becomes false economy since the lighting system will not provide the light required in the space.

The breakdown of a space into the room cavities used to determine the coefficient of utilization is shown in Fig. 17-13.

The cavity ratios are used to determine how the proportions of a room will affect the characteristics of light flux. For example, a room that is narrow in relation to its height will allow less flux to reach the working plane (surface) than one that is wide.

Reprinted with permission from IES, *IES Lighting Handbook, 1984 Reference Handbook.*

FIGURE 17-13 / Cavities

The ceiling and floor cavity ratios (CCR and FCR respectively) are used in conjunction with the wall, ceiling, and floor reflectances. The ratios are used to combine separate wall and ceiling reflectances into a single effective ceiling cavity reflectance, p_{CC}, or to combine separate wall and floor reflectances into a single effective floor cavity reflectance, p_{FC}.

The RCR, CCR, and FCR may be calculated by use of the equation:

$$\text{Cavity ratio} = \frac{5h \,(\text{Room length} \,+\, \text{Room width})}{\text{Room length} \,\times\, \text{Room width}}$$

Where:

$$h = h_{RC} \text{ for the room cavity ratio (RCR)}$$
$$= h_{CC} \text{ for the ceiling cavity ratio (CCR)}$$
$$= h_{FC} \text{ for the floor cavity ratio (FCR)}$$

When the luminaire is surface mounted or recessed, the CCR = 0 and the ceiling reflectance is used as the p_{CC}.

Many cavity ratios are given in Fig. 17-14.

To determine the coefficient of utilization (CU) for a particular room size and luminaire, it is necessary to:

1. Determine the RCR, CCR, and FCR, either by calculating the ratio or by using Fig. 17-14.

2. Determine the effective ceiling cavity reflectance p_{CC} and the effective floor cavity reflectance p_{FC} (Fig. 17-15).

3. Determine the coefficient of utilization (CU) based on the RCR, p_{CC}, p_{FC} and wall reflectance (referred to as p_{WC}). The CUs for many typical luminaires are shown in Fig. 17-19. When the exact ratios and reflectances are not given in the tables, they may be interpolated (averaged from the values given).

4. When the effective floor cavity reflectance varies greatly from the 20% value used in Fig. 17-19, a multiplying factor is found in Fig. 17-18 by which the CU is adjusted.

EXAMPLE

Given:

> Room: 20 ft × 30 ft
> Fixture mounting height: 6 ft (above working plane)
> Working plane: 2 ft 6 in. above finished floor
> Footcandles desired: 100 fc (store, merchandise)
> Ceiling reflectance: 80%
> Wall reflectance: 50%
> Floor reflectance: 20%
> Maintenance factor: Fair
> Luminaires: Fluorescent, 40-W, instant-start, cool white (#40, Fig. 17-19) mounted 1 ft 0 in. from the ceiling

Problem: Find the total lumens and the number of luminaires required and the number of footcandles they provide.

1. Determine the heights (h) of the zonal cavities.

$$h_{CC} = 1.0$$
$$h_{RC} = 6.0$$
$$h_{FC} = 2.5$$

2. Determine the cavity ratios, using the formula or taking them directly from Fig. 17-4 if the room size is given.

$$CCR = 0.4$$
$$RCR = 2.5$$
$$FCR = 1.0$$

3. Determine the effective ceiling and floor cavity reflectances from Fig. 17-15 by use of the given reflectances and the calculated cavity ratios.

$$p_{CC} = 74\%$$
$$p_{WC} = 50\% \text{ (the given value)}$$
$$p_{FC} = 20\% \text{ (the given value)}$$

4. Determine the coefficient of utilization (CU) from the manufacturer's specifications or from Fig. 17-19. The RCR, p_{FC}, and p_{CC} must be interpolated (averaged) from the values given. From Fig. 17-19, the values are:

p_{CC}		80	70
RCR =	2.0	0.55	0.54
	3.0	0.48	0.47

You will need to do a two-way average of RCR 2.5 and p_{CC} 74%. First RCR: RCR 2.5 is midway between 2.0 and 3.0, so the interpolation to RCR 2.5 at p_{CC} 80 and 70 is:

At 80:

2.0	0.55
3.0	0.48

difference = 0.07
RCR 2.5   = 0.55 minus (0.5) times the difference
          = 0.515

At 70:

2.0	0.54
3.0	0.47

difference = 0.07
RCR 2.5   = 0.54 minus (0.5) times the difference
          = 0.505

$p_{CC} = 74\%$:
Using the values calculated at RCR, the p_{CC} can be interpolated to determine the coefficient of utilization.

RCR 2.5		
p_{CC}	80	70
CU	0.515	0.505

The coefficient of utilization is calculated by interpolating between the p_{CC} values.

$$CH = \text{(If subtracting from 80)}$$
$$0.515 - [\,(0.515 - 0.505) \times 0.6] = 0.51$$

5. Determine the lamp lumen depreciation (LLD) from the table in Fig. 17-16. Based on fluorescent lamps, 48″, 40 watt cool white:

$$LLD = 83\%$$

6. Determine the luminaire dirt depreciation (LDD) from Fig. 17-17. The luminaire selected (type 40, Fig. 17-19) lists an LDD maintenance category of V. Assuming a dirty maintenance (D), with a 24-month interval, the LDD from Fig. 17-17 is 0.7.

7. Determine the total lumens required for the space:

$$\text{Total lumens} = \frac{\text{Footcandles} \times \text{Room area}}{\text{CU} \times \text{LLD} \times \text{LDD}}$$

$$\text{Total lumens} = \frac{100\,(20 \times 30)}{0.51 \times 0.83 \times 0.70} = 202,491 \text{ lumens}$$

8. Determine the minimum number of lamps required by dividing the number of lumens per lamp into the total amount of lumens required. Since 40-W, instant start, cool white fluorescent lamps are used, from Fig. 17-20 the lumens per lamp are 3,100.

9. Determine the number of lamps required by dividing the total number of lumens required by the lumens per lamp:

$$\text{Lamps} = \frac{202{,}491}{3{,}100} = 65.3 = 66 \text{ lamps}$$

10. Determine the number of luminaires required by dividing the number of lamps required by the number of lamps in the luminaire selected.

$$\text{Luminaires} = \frac{66}{2} = 33 \text{ luminaires}$$

The designer has several choices in luminaire placement. Using a 4-ft luminaire, a maximum of 7 luminaires could be placed end to end in a row. To install the luminaires required in this manner would require 4.7 rows. The luminaires could also be placed in 5 alternate rows of 6 and 5 luminaires for a total of 33.

The spacing used should be checked against spacing-mounting-height ratios in Fig. 17-19. In this design, the mounting height above the working plane is 6 ft. Using Fig. 17-19, the maximum spacing (S) should be no more than the mounting height times 1.0:

$$\frac{\text{Max } S}{MH_{WP}} = 1.0$$

or

$$\text{Max } S = MH_{WP} \times 1.0$$

In this design, the maximum spacing should be 6.0 ft.

To calculate the number of footcandles, the original formula

$$\text{Lumens} = \frac{\text{Footcandles} \times \text{Room area}}{\text{Coefficient of utilization (cu)} \times \text{Maintenance factor (mf)}}$$

is rewritten:

$$\text{Footcandles} = \frac{\text{Lumens} \times \text{cu} \times \text{mf}}{\text{Room area}}$$

$$= \frac{3{,}100(66) \times 0.51 \times 0.83 \times 0.70}{600}$$

$$= 101 \text{ fc}$$

Since 100 fc are desired, the design is complete.

QUESTIONS

17-1. Why are fluorescent lamps used extensively in industrial and commercial projects?

17-2. What are the three types of light which may be projected by a luminaire onto a surface?

17-3. What is the difference between *localized* and *generalized lighting,* and where would you consider using each of them?

17-4. What is meant by the terms *room index* and *room ratio?*

17-5. How do the reflection factors of the space affect the number of luminaires required?

17-6. What must be considered when determining wall reflection factors?

17-7. What is meant by the *maintenance factor* when considering luminaires?

17-8. What does *coefficient of utilization* mean with regard to luminaires?

Design Exercises

17-9. Determine the total lumens and the number of luminaires required for the following problem:
Room: 24 ft × 48 ft
Fixture mounting height: 9 ft (above working plane), 1 ft 0 in. below ceiling
Working plane: 3 ft 0 in. above finished floor
Use: Laboratory, 120 fc
Ceiling reflectance: 70%
Wall reflectance: 50%
Floor reflectance: 30%
Maintenance factor: Clean, 12 months
Luminaires: Fluorescent, 40-W, instant-start, white, #29 (Fig. 17-19), 12 hours per start

17-10. Determine the total lumens and the number of luminaires required for the following problem:
Room: 18 ft × 24 ft
Fixture mounting height: 6 ft (above working plane), flush to ceiling
Working plane: 2 ft 6 in. above finished floor
Footcandles desired: 75 fc, study hall
Ceiling reflectance: 80%
Wall reflectance: 50%
Floor reflectance: 30%
Maintenance factor: Dirty, 24 months
Luminaires: Fluorescent, 40-W, instant-start, deluxe cool white, #34 (Fig. 17-19), 12 hours per start

Room Dimensions		Cavity Depth																		
Width	Length	1	1.5	2	2.5	3	3.5	4	5	6	7	8	9	10	11	12	14	16	20	25	30
8	8	1.2	1.9	2.5	3.1	3.7	4.4	5.0	6.2	7.5	8.8	10.0	11.2	12.5	—	—	—	—	—	—	—
	10	1.1	1.7	2.2	2.8	3.4	3.9	4.5	5.6	6.7	7.9	9.0	10.1	11.3	12.4	—	—	—	—	—	—
	14	1.0	1.5	2.0	2.5	3.0	3.4	3.9	4.9	5.9	6.9	7.8	8.8	9.7	10.7	11.7	—	—	—	—	—
	20	0.9	1.3	1.7	2.2	2.6	3.1	3.5	4.4	5.2	6.1	7.0	7.9	8.8	9.6	10.5	12.2	—	—	—	—
	30	0.8	1.2	1.6	2.0	2.4	2.8	3.2	4.0	4.7	5.5	6.3	7.1	7.9	8.7	9.5	11.0	—	—	—	—
	40	0.7	1.1	1.5	1.9	2.3	2.6	3.0	3.7	4.5	5.3	5.9	6.5	7.4	8.1	8.8	10.3	11.8	—	—	—
10	10	1.0	1.5	2.0	2.5	3.0	3.5	4.0	5.0	6.0	7.0	8.0	9.0	10.0	11.0	12.0	—	—	—	—	—
	14	0.9	1.3	1.7	2.1	2.6	3.0	3.4	4.3	5.1	6.0	6.9	7.8	8.6	9.5	10.4	12.0	—	—	—	—
	20	0.7	1.1	1.5	1.9	2.3	2.6	3.0	3.7	4.5	5.3	6.0	6.8	7.5	8.3	9.0	10.5	12.0	—	—	—
	30	0.7	1.0	1.3	1.7	2.0	2.3	2.7	3.3	4.0	4.7	5.3	6.0	6.6	7.3	8.0	9.4	10.6	—	—	—
	40	0.6	0.9	1.2	1.6	1.9	2.2	2.5	3.1	3.7	4.4	5.0	5.6	6.2	6.9	7.5	8.7	10.0	12.5	—	—
	60	0.6	0.9	1.2	1.5	1.7	2.0	2.3	2.9	3.5	4.1	4.7	5.3	5.9	6.5	7.1	8.2	9.4	11.7	—	—
12	12	0.8	1.2	1.7	2.1	2.5	2.9	3.3	4.2	5.0	5.8	6.7	7.5	8.4	9.2	10.0	11.7	—	—	—	—
	16	0.7	1.1	1.5	1.8	2.2	2.5	2.9	3.6	4.4	5.1	5.8	6.5	7.2	8.0	8.7	10.2	11.6	—	—	—
	24	0.6	0.9	1.2	1.6	1.9	2.2	2.5	3.1	3.7	4.4	5.0	5.6	6.2	6.9	7.5	8.7	10.0	12.5	—	—
	36	0.6	0.8	1.1	1.4	1.7	1.9	2.2	2.8	3.3	3.9	4.4	5.0	5.5	6.0	6.6	7.8	8.8	11.0	—	—
	50	0.5	0.8	1.0	1.3	1.5	1.8	2.1	2.6	3.1	3.6	4.1	4.6	5.1	5.6	6.2	7.2	8.2	10.2	—	—
	70	0.5	0.7	1.0	1.2	1.5	1.7	2.0	2.4	2.9	3.4	3.9	4.4	4.9	5.4	5.8	6.8	7.8	9.7	12.2	—
14	14	0.7	1.1	1.4	1.8	2.1	2.5	2.9	3.6	4.3	5.0	5.7	6.4	7.1	7.8	8.5	10.0	11.4	—	—	—
	20	0.6	0.9	1.2	1.5	1.8	2.1	2.4	3.0	3.6	4.2	4.9	5.5	6.1	6.7	7.3	8.6	9.8	12.3	—	—
	30	0.5	0.8	1.0	1.3	1.6	1.8	2.1	2.6	3.1	3.7	4.2	4.7	5.2	5.8	6.3	7.3	8.4	10.5	—	—
	42	0.5	0.7	1.0	1.2	1.4	1.7	1.9	2.4	2.9	3.3	3.8	4.3	4.7	5.2	5.7	6.7	7.6	9.5	11.9	—
	60	0.4	0.7	0.9	1.1	1.3	1.5	1.8	2.2	2.6	3.1	3.5	3.9	4.4	4.8	5.2	6.1	7.0	8.8	10.9	—
	90	0.4	0.6	0.8	1.0	1.2	1.4	1.6	2.0	2.5	2.9	3.3	3.7	4.1	4.5	5.0	5.8	6.6	8.3	10.3	12.4
17	17	0.6	0.9	1.2	1.5	1.8	2.1	2.3	2.9	3.5	4.1	4.7	5.3	5.9	6.5	7.0	8.2	9.4	11.7	—	—
	25	0.5	0.7	1.0	1.2	1.5	1.7	2.0	2.5	3.0	3.5	4.0	4.5	5.0	5.5	6.0	7.0	8.0	10.0	12.5	—
	35	0.4	0.7	0.9	1.1	1.3	1.5	1.7	2.2	2.6	3.1	3.5	3.9	4.4	4.8	5.2	6.1	7.0	8.7	10.9	—
	50	0.4	0.6	0.8	1.0	1.2	1.4	1.6	2.0	2.4	2.8	3.1	3.5	3.9	4.3	4.5	5.4	6.2	7.7	9.7	11.6
	80	0.4	0.5	0.7	0.9	1.1	1.2	1.4	1.8	2.1	2.5	2.9	3.3	3.6	4.0	4.3	5.1	5.8	7.2	9.0	10.9
	120	0.3	0.5	0.7	0.8	1.0	1.2	1.3	1.7	2.0	2.3	2.7	3.0	3.4	3.7	4.0	4.7	5.4	6.7	8.4	10.1
20	20	0.5	0.7	1.0	1.2	1.5	1.7	2.0	2.5	3.0	3.5	4.0	4.5	5.0	5.5	6.0	7.0	8.0	10.0	12.5	—
	30	0.4	0.6	0.8	1.0	1.2	1.5	1.7	2.1	2.5	2.9	3.3	3.7	4.1	4.5	4.9	5.8	6.6	8.2	10.3	12.4
	45	0.4	0.5	0.7	0.9	1.1	1.3	1.4	1.8	2.2	2.5	2.9	3.3	3.6	4.0	4.3	5.1	5.8	7.2	9.1	10.9
	60	0.3	0.5	0.7	0.8	1.0	1.2	1.3	1.7	2.0	2.3	2.7	3.0	3.4	3.7	4.0	4.7	5.4	6.7	8.4	10.1
	90	0.3	0.5	0.6	0.8	0.9	1.1	1.2	1.5	1.8	2.1	2.4	2.7	3.0	3.3	3.6	4.2	4.8	6.0	7.5	9.0
	150	0.3	0.4	0.6	0.7	0.8	1.0	1.1	1.4	1.7	2.0	2.3	2.6	2.9	3.2	3.4	4.0	4.6	5.7	7.2	8.6
24	24	0.4	0.6	0.8	1.0	1.2	1.5	1.7	2.1	2.5	2.9	3.3	3.7	4.1	4.5	5.0	5.8	6.7	8.2	10.3	12.4
	32	0.4	0.5	0.7	0.9	1.1	1.3	1.5	1.8	2.2	2.6	2.9	3.3	3.6	4.0	4.3	5.1	5.8	7.2	9.0	11.0
	50	0.3	0.5	0.6	0.8	0.9	1.1	1.2	1.5	1.8	2.2	2.5	2.8	3.1	3.4	3.7	4.4	5.0	6.2	7.8	9.4
	70	0.3	0.4	0.6	0.7	0.8	1.0	1.1	1.4	1.7	2.0	2.2	2.5	2.8	3.0	3.3	3.8	4.4	5.5	6.9	8.2
	100	0.3	0.4	0.5	0.6	0.8	0.9	1.0	1.3	1.6	1.8	2.1	2.4	2.6	2.9	3.1	3.7	4.2	5.2	6.5	7.9
	160	0.2	0.4	0.5	0.6	0.7	0.8	1.0	1.2	1.4	1.7	1.9	2.1	2.4	2.6	2.8	3.3	3.8	4.7	5.9	7.1
30	30	0.3	0.5	0.7	0.8	1.0	1.2	1.3	1.7	2.0	2.3	2.7	3.0	3.3	3.7	4.0	4.7	5.4	6.7	8.4	10.0
	45	0.3	0.4	0.6	0.7	0.8	1.0	1.1	1.4	1.7	1.9	2.2	2.5	2.7	3.0	3.3	3.8	4.4	5.5	6.9	8.2
	60	0.3	0.4	0.5	0.6	0.7	0.9	1.0	1.2	1.5	1.7	2.0	2.2	2.5	2.7	3.0	3.5	4.0	5.0	6.2	7.4
	90	0.2	0.3	0.4	0.6	0.7	0.8	0.9	1.1	1.3	1.6	1.8	2.0	2.2	2.5	2.7	3.1	3.6	4.5	5.6	6.7
	150	0.2	0.3	0.4	0.5	0.6	0.7	0.8	1.0	1.2	1.4	1.6	1.8	2.0	2.2	2.4	2.8	3.2	4.0	5.0	5.9
	200	0.2	0.3	0.4	0.5	0.6	0.7	0.8	1.0	1.1	1.3	1.5	1.7	1.9	2.0	2.2	2.6	3.0	3.7	4.7	5.6
36	36	0.3	0.4	0.6	0.7	0.8	1.0	1.1	1.4	1.7	1.9	2.2	2.5	2.8	3.0	3.3	3.9	4.4	5.5	6.9	8.3
	50	0.2	0.4	0.5	0.6	0.7	0.8	1.0	1.2	1.4	1.7	1.9	2.1	2.5	2.6	2.9	3.3	3.8	4.8	5.9	7.2
	75	0.2	0.3	0.4	0.5	0.6	0.7	0.8	1.0	1.2	1.4	1.6	1.8	2.0	2.3	2.5	2.9	3.3	4.1	5.1	6.1
	100	0.2	0.3	0.4	0.5	0.6	0.7	0.8	0.9	1.1	1.3	1.5	1.7	1.9	2.1	2.3	2.6	3.0	3.8	4.7	5.7
	150	0.2	0.3	0.3	0.4	0.5	0.6	0.7	0.9	1.0	1.2	1.4	1.6	1.7	1.9	2.1	2.4	2.8	3.5	4.3	5.2
	200	0.2	0.2	0.3	0.4	0.5	0.6	0.7	0.8	1.0	1.1	1.3	1.5	1.6	1.8	2.0	2.3	2.6	3.3	4.1	4.9
42	42	0.2	0.4	0.5	0.6	0.7	0.8	1.0	1.2	1.4	1.6	1.9	2.1	2.4	2.6	2.8	3.3	3.8	4.7	5.9	7.1
	60	0.2	0.3	0.4	0.5	0.6	0.7	0.8	1.0	1.2	1.4	1.6	1.8	2.0	2.2	2.4	2.8	3.2	4.0	5.0	6.0
	90	0.2	0.3	0.3	0.4	0.5	0.6	0.7	0.9	1.0	1.2	1.4	1.6	1.7	1.9	2.1	2.4	2.8	3.5	4.4	5.2
	140	0.2	0.3	0.3	0.4	0.5	0.5	0.6	0.8	0.9	1.1	1.2	1.4	1.5	1.7	1.9	2.2	2.5	3.1	3.9	4.6
	200	0.1	0.2	0.3	0.4	0.4	0.5	0.6	0.7	0.9	1.0	1.1	1.3	1.4	1.6	1.7	2.0	2.3	2.9	3.6	4.3
	300	0.1	0.2	0.3	0.3	0.4	0.5	0.5	0.7	0.8	0.9	1.1	1.3	1.4	1.5	1.7	1.9	2.2	2.8	3.5	4.2

Reprinted with permission from IES, *IES Lighting Handbook, 1984 Reference Handbook.*

FIGURE 17-14 / Cavity ratios

Room Dimensions		Cavity Depth																			
Width	Length	1	1.5	2	2.5	3	3.5	4	5	6	7	8	9	10	11	12	14	16	20	25	30
50	50	0.2	0.3	0.4	0.5	0.6	0.7	0.8	1.0	1.2	1.4	1.6	1.8	2.0	2.2	2.4	2.8	3.2	4.0	5.0	6.0
	70	0.2	0.3	0.3	0.4	0.5	0.6	0.7	0.9	1.0	1.2	1.4	1.5	1.7	1.9	2.0	2.4	2.7	3.4	4.3	5.1
	100	0.1	0.2	0.3	0.4	0.4	0.5	0.6	0.7	0.9	1.0	1.2	1.3	1.5	1.6	1.8	2.1	2.4	3.0	3.7	4.5
	150	0.1	0.2	0.3	0.3	0.4	0.5	0.5	0.7	0.8	0.9	1.1	1.2	1.3	1.5	1.6	1.9	2.1	2.7	3.3	4.0
	300	0.1	0.2	0.2	0.3	0.3	0.4	0.5	0.6	0.7	0.8	0.9	1.0	1.1	1.3	1.4	1.6	1.9	2.3	2.9	3.5
60	60	0.2	0.2	0.3	0.4	0.5	0.6	0.7	0.8	1.0	1.2	1.3	1.5	1.7	1.8	2.0	2.3	2.7	3.3	4.2	5.0
	100	0.1	0.2	0.3	0.3	0.4	0.5	0.5	0.7	0.8	0.9	1.1	1.2	1.3	1.5	1.6	1.9	2.1	2.7	3.3	4.0
	150	0.1	0.2	0.2	0.3	0.3	0.4	0.5	0.6	0.7	0.8	0.9	1.0	1.2	1.3	1.4	1.6	1.9	2.3	2.9	3.5
	300	0.1	0.1	0.2	0.2	0.3	0.3	0.4	0.5	0.6	0.7	0.8	0.9	1.0	1.1	1.2	1.4	1.6	2.0	2.5	3.0
75	75	0.1	0.2	0.3	0.3	0.4	0.5	0.5	0.7	0.8	0.9	1.1	1.2	1.3	1.5	1.6	1.9	2.1	2.7	3.3	4.0
	120	0.1	0.2	0.2	0.3	0.3	0.4	0.4	0.5	0.6	0.8	0.9	1.0	1.1	1.2	1.3	1.5	1.7	2.2	2.7	3.3
	200	0.1	0.1	0.2	0.2	0.3	0.3	0.4	0.5	0.5	0.6	0.7	0.8	0.9	1.0	1.1	1.3	1.5	1.8	2.3	2.7
	300	0.1	0.1	0.2	0.2	0.2	0.3	0.3	0.4	0.5	0.6	0.7	0.7	0.8	0.9	1.0	1.2	1.3	1.7	2.1	2.5
100	100	0.1	0.1	0.2	0.2	0.3	0.3	0.4	0.5	0.6	0.7	0.8	0.9	1.0	1.1	1.2	1.4	1.6	2.0	2.5	3.0
	200	0.1	0.1	0.1	0.2	0.2	0.3	0.3	0.4	0.4	0.5	0.6	0.7	0.7	0.8	0.9	1.0	1.2	1.5	1.9	2.2
	300	0.1	0.1	0.1	0.2	0.2	0.2	0.3	0.3	0.4	0.5	0.5	0.6	0.7	0.7	0.8	0.9	1.1	1.3	1.7	2.0
150	150	0.1	0.1	0.1	0.2	0.2	0.2	0.3	0.3	0.4	0.5	0.5	0.6	0.7	0.7	0.8	0.9	1.1	1.3	1.7	2.0
	300	—	0.1	0.1	0.1	0.1	0.2	0.2	0.2	0.3	0.3	0.4	0.5	0.5	0.6	0.6	0.7	0.8	1.0	1.2	1.5
200	200	—	0.1	0.1	0.1	0.1	0.2	0.2	0.2	0.3	0.3	0.4	0.5	0.5	0.6	0.6	0.7	0.8	1.0	1.2	1.5
	300	—	0.1	0.1	0.1	0.1	0.1	0.2	0.2	0.2	0.3	0.3	0.4	0.4	0.5	0.5	0.6	0.7	0.8	1.0	1.2
300	300	—	—	0.1	0.1	0.1	0.1	0.1	0.2	0.2	0.2	0.3	0.3	0.3	0.4	0.4	0.5	0.5	0.6	0.7	0.8
500	500	—	—	—	—	0.1	0.1	0.1	0.1	0.1	0.1	0.2	0.2	0.2	0.2	0.2	0.3	0.3	0.4	0.5	0.6

Reprinted with permission from IES, *IES Lighting Handbook, 1984 Reference Handbook.*

FIGURE 17-14 / Cavity ratios (continued)

Per Cent Effective Ceiling or Floor Cavity Reflectances for Various Reflectance Combinations
See Page 9–26 for Algorithms for Calculation of Effective Cavity Reflectance*

Per Cent Base† Reflectance	50										60										70										80										90									
Per Cent Wall Reflectance	90	80	70	60	50	40	30	20	10	0	90	80	70	60	50	40	30	20	10	0	90	80	70	60	50	40	30	20	10	0	90	80	70	60	50	40	30	20	10	0	90	80	70	60	50	40	30	20	10	0
Cavity Ratio																																																		
0.2	50	50	49	49	48	48	47	46	46	44	60	59	59	58	58	57	56	56	55	53	70	69	68	68	67	66	66	65	65	64	79	78	78	77	76	76	75	74	74	72	89	88	88	87	86	86	85	84	84	82
0.4	50	49	48	48	46	46	45	44	44	42	60	59	58	57	55	55	54	53	52	50	69	68	67	66	65	64	63	62	61	58	79	77	76	75	74	73	72	71	69	67	88	87	86	85	84	83	81	80	79	76
0.6	50	48	47	46	44	44	43	42	41	38	60	58	57	55	53	53	51	51	50	46	69	67	65	64	63	61	59	58	57	54	78	76	75	73	71	70	68	66	65	63	87	86	84	83	82	80	77	77	74	73
0.8	50	48	47	45	44	42	40	40	38	36	59	58	55	54	51	51	48	47	46	43	68	66	64	62	60	58	56	55	53	50	78	75	73	71	69	67	65	63	63	61	87	85	82	80	77	73	73	69	69	67
1.0	50	48	46	44	43	41	38	37	36	34	59	57	55	53	51	48	45	44	43	41	68	65	62	60	58	55	53	52	50	47	77	74	72	69	67	65	62	60	57	55	86	83	80	77	75	72	69	66	64	62
1.2	47	45	43	41	39	36	36	35	34	29	56	54	51	49	46	44	42	39	37	35	67	64	61	59	57	54	51	48	46	44	76	73	70	67	64	61	58	55	53	51	85	82	78	75	72	69	66	63	60	57
1.4	47	45	42	40	38	35	35	34	32	27	56	53	49	47	44	42	39	37	35	33	67	63	60	58	55	51	47	45	44	41	76	72	68	65	62	59	55	51	50	47	85	80	77	73	71	69	65	61	57	52
1.6	47	44	41	39	36	34	33	32	30	26	55	52	48	45	42	39	37	35	33	31	67	62	59	56	53	49	45	43	41	38	75	71	67	63	60	57	53	50	47	44	84	79	75	71	67	63	59	56	53	50
1.8	47	41	40	38	35	31	31	30	28	25	54	50	47	43	40	37	35	33	31	29	66	61	58	54	51	46	42	40	38	35	75	70	66	62	58	56	52	48	45	44	83	78	73	69	66	63	56	53	50	47
2.0	46	40	39	37	34	30	30	28	26	24	54	50	46	42	39	37	35	33	31	27	66	60	56	52	49	45	40	38	36	33	74	69	64	60	56	52	48	45	42	38	83	77	72	67	62	56	53	49	47	43
2.2	46	38	38	36	33	29	27	25	22	22	53	49	45	42	38	36	31	28	25	22	66	60	55	51	48	43	39	36	34	32	74	68	63	58	54	49	45	42	38	35	82	76	70	65	59	54	50	47	44	40
2.4	46	37	37	35	31	27	25	23	21	21	53	48	44	41	36	30	30	27	24	21	65	60	54	50	46	41	35	35	33	30	73	67	61	56	52	47	43	40	36	33	82	75	69	64	58	53	48	45	41	37
2.6	46	37	36	34	30	26	23	21	18	20	53	48	43	39	35	31	28	26	24	20	65	59	54	49	45	39	35	33	30	28	73	66	60	56	51	46	41	38	34	31	81	74	67	62	56	51	46	42	38	34
2.8	46	36	35	33	29	25	22	20	17	19	53	47	42	38	34	29	27	24	21	18	65	59	53	48	43	38	33	32	28	26	73	65	59	53	48	44	39	36	32	29	81	73	66	60	54	49	44	40	36	34
3.0	45	36	34	32	28	24	21	19	17	17	52	46	41	37	32	28	25	23	20	17	64	58	52	47	42	37	32	29	27	24	72	65	58	52	47	43	38	34	30	28	80	72	64	58	52	47	42	38	33	30
3.2	45	36	33	31	28	23	20	18	16	16	52	45	41	36	33	28	24	22	19	18	64	58	51	46	40	36	31	28	25	23	72	65	57	51	45	40	35	33	28	25	79	71	63	56	50	45	40	36	32	28
3.4	44	35	32	30	27	22	19	17	15	15	52	45	40	35	32	27	23	21	18	17	64	57	50	45	39	35	28	27	24	22	71	63	56	49	44	39	34	32	27	24	79	70	62	54	48	43	38	34	30	27
3.6	44	35	31	30	26	21	18	16	14	14	51	44	39	34	31	26	22	20	17	16	63	56	49	44	38	34	27	25	22	20	71	63	54	48	43	37	33	31	26	22	78	69	61	53	47	42	36	32	28	25
3.8	43	34	31	29	24	20	17	15	13	13	51	44	39	34	30	25	22	20	17	15	63	56	49	43	37	33	27	24	21	19	70	62	53	47	41	36	32	29	24	21	78	69	60	51	45	40	35	31	27	23
4.0	42	34	30	28	24	20	17	14	12	12	50	43	38	33	29	24	21	19	16	14	63	55	48	42	36	31	26	23	20	17	70	61	53	46	40	35	30	28	22	20	77	69	58	50	44	39	33	29	25	22
4.2	42	34	30	27	22	19	16	14	12	12	50	43	37	32	28	24	21	19	16	14	62	55	47	41	35	30	25	22	19	16	69	60	52	45	39	34	29	25	22	18	77	62	57	50	43	37	32	28	24	20
4.4	41	32	28	25	21	18	14	13	11	11	49	42	36	31	27	22	19	16	14	11	62	54	46	40	34	29	24	21	16	13	69	60	51	44	38	32	28	24	19	17	76	56	56	49	42	36	31	27	23	20
4.6	41	33	28	25	20	17	14	13	10	10	49	41	35	30	26	21	18	15	13	10	62	53	45	39	33	28	23	20	17	14	69	59	50	43	37	32	27	23	18	15	76	60	55	47	40	35	30	26	22	19
4.8	40	33	28	24	20	17	13	12	09	09	48	41	34	29	25	21	17	15	12	09	62	53	45	38	32	27	23	16	16	13	68	58	49	42	36	31	26	22	18	14	75	59	54	46	39	34	28	24	21	18
5.0	40	33	27	24	19	16	13	12	09	09	48	40	34	28	24	20	17	14	11	09	61	52	44	36	31	26	22	19	16	12	68	58	48	41	35	30	25	21	18	14	75	59	53	45	38	33	28	24	20	16
6.0	42	30	24	22	18	15	13	10	08	06	53	38	29	24	19	16	13	11	09	07	60	51	41	35	28	24	19	16	13	09	66	53	44	38	31	27	22	19	15	10	73	49	49	41	34	29	24	20	16	11
7.0	41	27	23	20	17	14	11	08	07	05	50	36	27	22	17	14	11	10	07	05	58	46	38	31	25	22	17	14	11	05	64	53	41	35	28	24	19	16	12	07	70	58	45	38	30	27	21	18	14	08
8.0	40	25	21	18	16	12	10	08	07	03	48	35	25	20	16	13	10	08	06	04	57	46	35	29	23	18	15	13	10	04	62	50	38	32	25	21	17	14	11	06	68	55	42	35	27	23	18	15	12	06
9.0	39	24	19	17	15	11	09	07	06	03	46	33	23	18	15	12	09	07	06	04	56	45	33	27	21	18	15	12	09	04	61	49	36	30	23	19	15	13	10	05	66	52	38	31	25	21	16	14	11	05
10.0	37	23	17	16	14	10	08	06	06	02	45	32	21	17	14	11	09	07	05	03	55	43	31	25	19	16	12	10	08	03	59	46	33	27	21	18	14	11	09	04	65	51	36	29	22	19	15	11	09	04

* Values in this table are based on a length to width ratio of 1.6.
† Ceiling, floor or floor of cavity.

Reprinted with permission from IES, IEs Lighting Handbook, 1984 Reference Handbook.

FIGURE 17-15 / Cavity reflectances (continued)

Per Cent Base† Reflectance / Per Cent Wall Reflectance / Cavity Ratio

Cavity Ratio	Base 40										Base 30										Base 20										Base 10										Base 0									
Wall Refl →	90	80	70	60	50	40	30	20	10	0	90	80	70	60	50	40	30	20	10	0	90	80	70	60	50	40	30	20	10	0	90	80	70	60	50	40	30	20	10	0	90	80	70	60	50	40	30	20	10	0
0.2	40	40	39	39	39	38	38	37	36	36	31	31	30	30	30	29	29	28	28	27	21	20	20	20	20	20	19	19	18	17	11	11	11	10	10	10	10	09	09	09	02	02	01	01	01	01	01	01	00	0
0.4	41	40	39	39	38	37	36	35	34	34	31	31	30	30	29	28	28	27	26	25	22	21	20	20	20	19	19	18	18	16	12	12	12	11	11	10	10	09	09	08	04	03	03	02	02	02	01	01	01	0
0.6	41	40	39	38	37	36	34	33	32	31	32	31	30	29	28	28	27	26	25	23	23	21	21	20	19	19	18	18	17	15	13	13	12	11	11	10	10	09	08	08	05	04	04	03	03	02	02	01	01	0
0.8	41	40	38	37	36	35	33	32	31	29	32	31	29	29	28	27	26	25	23	22	24	22	21	20	19	18	18	17	16	14	15	13	13	12	11	10	10	09	08	08	07	05	05	04	04	03	02	02	01	0
1.0	42	40	38	37	35	33	32	31	29	27	33	32	30	29	27	25	24	23	22	20	25	23	22	20	19	18	17	16	15	13	16	14	13	12	12	11	10	09	08	07	08	07	06	05	04	03	02	02	01	0
1.2	42	39	37	36	34	32	30	29	27	25	33	32	30	28	27	23	22	22	21	19	25	24	22	20	19	17	17	16	14	12	17	15	14	13	12	11	10	09	07	06	10	08	07	06	05	04	03	02	01	0
1.4	42	39	37	35	33	31	29	27	25	23	34	32	30	28	26	23	21	21	19	18	26	24	22	19	18	17	16	15	13	12	18	16	14	13	12	11	10	09	07	06	11	09	08	07	05	04	03	02	01	0
1.6	43	39	36	34	32	30	27	26	23	22	34	33	30	28	25	22	20	20	18	17	26	24	22	20	18	16	16	15	13	11	19	17	15	14	13	11	09	08	06	06	12	10	09	07	06	04	03	02	01	0
1.8	43	39	36	34	31	29	26	24	22	21	34	33	29	27	25	21	19	19	18	17	27	25	23	20	18	16	15	14	12	10	19	18	15	14	13	11	09	08	06	05	13	11	09	08	06	04	03	02	01	0
2.0	43	39	36	33	31	28	25	23	21	19	35	33	29	26	24	20	18	18	16	14	28	25	23	20	18	15	14	13	11	09	20	18	16	14	13	11	09	08	06	05	14	12	10	09	07	05	04	02	01	0
2.2	42	39	36	33	30	27	24	22	19	18	36	32	29	26	24	19	17	16	15	13	28	25	23	20	18	16	14	12	11	09	21	19	16	14	13	11	09	07	06	05	15	13	11	09	07	05	04	02	01	0
2.4	43	39	35	33	29	27	24	22	18	17	36	32	28	25	23	19	16	16	14	12	29	26	23	20	18	16	14	12	10	08	21	19	17	15	13	11	09	07	05	04	15	13	11	09	08	05	04	02	01	0
2.6	43	39	35	32	29	26	23	20	17	15	36	32	28	25	23	18	16	15	14	12	29	26	23	20	18	16	14	12	10	08	22	20	17	15	13	11	09	07	05	04	16	14	12	10	08	06	04	02	01	0
2.8	43	39	35	32	28	26	22	19	16	14	37	33	29	25	23	18	15	14	14	11	30	27	23	20	17	15	13	11	09	07	23	20	18	16	13	11	09	07	05	04	17	15	13	10	08	06	04	02	01	0
3.0	43	39	35	31	27	25	21	18	15	13	37	33	29	25	22	17	15	14	13	10	30	27	23	20	17	15	13	11	09	07	23	21	18	16	13	11	09	07	05	04	18	16	13	11	09	07	05	02	01	0
3.2	43	39	35	31	27	23	20	17	15	13	37	33	29	25	22	16	14	14	12	10	31	27	23	20	17	15	12	11	09	06	25	21	20	17	13	11	09	07	05	04	19	16	14	11	09	07	05	03	02	0
3.4	43	39	34	30	26	23	20	17	14	12	37	33	29	25	22	16	14	13	11	09	31	27	23	20	17	15	12	11	08	06	26	22	20	17	15	11	09	07	05	03	20	17	15	12	09	07	05	03	02	0
3.6	44	39	34	30	26	22	19	16	14	11	38	33	29	25	21	15	13	13	11	09	32	28	23	20	18	16	12	10	08	05	26	22	21	17	15	11	09	06	05	03	21	17	15	12	10	08	05	03	02	0
3.8	44	38	33	29	25	22	18	16	13	10	38	33	28	24	21	15	13	12	10	08	32	28	23	20	17	15	12	10	08	05	27	23	21	17	15	11	08	06	04	03	21	18	16	13	10	08	05	03	02	0
4.0	44	38	33	29	25	21	18	15	13	10	39	33	28	24	20	14	13	12	10	08	33	28	23	20	17	14	12	10	07	05	27	23	21	17	14	11	08	06	04	03	22	18	16	13	11	08	05	03	02	0
4.2	44	38	33	29	24	21	17	15	12	10	38	33	28	24	20	17	14	12	09	07	33	28	23	20	17	14	11	10	07	04	28	24	20	17	13	11	08	06	04	03	22	19	16	13	10	08	05	02	01	0
4.4	44	38	33	28	24	20	17	14	11	09	38	33	28	24	20	17	14	11	09	06	34	28	23	20	17	14	11	09	07	04	28	24	20	17	13	11	08	06	04	02	23	19	16	13	10	08	06	02	01	0
4.6	44	38	32	28	23	20	16	14	11	08	38	32	28	24	20	16	13	11	09	07	34	28	23	20	17	13	11	09	06	04	29	24	20	17	14	10	08	06	04	02	23	20	16	13	11	08	06	02	01	0
4.8	44	38	32	27	23	19	16	13	10	08	39	33	28	24	20	16	13	11	08	05	35	29	23	20	17	13	10	08	06	04	29	25	21	17	13	10	07	05	04	02	24	20	17	14	11	08	06	02	01	0
5.0	45	38	31	27	22	19	15	13	10	07	39	33	28	24	18	16	13	11	08	05	35	29	23	20	16	13	10	08	06	04	30	25	21	17	12	10	07	05	04	02	25	21	17	14	11	08	06	02	01	0
6.0	44	37	30	25	20	17	13	11	08	04	39	33	27	23	18	15	11	09	06	04	36	30	24	20	16	13	10	07	05	02	31	26	21	17	14	11	08	06	03	02	27	23	18	15	12	09	06	02	01	0
7.0	44	36	29	24	19	16	12	10	07	04	40	33	26	21	19	14	10	08	07	01	36	30	24	20	15	12	08	06	04	02	32	27	21	17	13	11	07	05	03	01	28	24	19	15	12	09	06	02	01	0
8.0	44	35	28	23	18	15	11	09	06	03	40	33	26	20	15	13	09	07	05	01	37	30	23	19	15	12	08	06	03	01	33	27	21	17	13	10	07	05	02	01	30	25	20	15	12	09	06	02	01	0
9.0	44	35	26	21	16	13	10	08	05	02	40	33	25	20	12	12	09	06	04	01	37	29	23	19	14	11	08	05	03	01	34	28	21	17	13	10	07	05	02	01	31	25	20	15	12	09	06	02	01	0
10.0	43	34	25	20	15	12	08	07	05	02	40	32	24	19	13	11	08	06	03	01	37	29	22	18	13	11	07	05	03	01	34	28	21	17	12	10	07	05	02	01	31	25	20	15	12	09	06	02	01	0

* Values in this table are based on a length to width ratio of 1.6.
† Ceiling, floor or floor of cavity.

Reprinted with permission from IES, IES Lighting Handbook, 1984 Reference Handbook.

FIGURE 17-15 / Cavity reflectances

Mainte-nance Category	Top Enclosure	Bottom Enclosure
I	1. None.	1. None
II	1. None 2. Transparent with 15 per cent or more uplight through apertures. 3. Translucent with 15 per cent or more uplight through apertures. 4. Opaque with 15 per cent or more uplight through apertures.	1. None 2. Louvers or baffles
III	1. Transparent with less than 15 per cent upward light through apertures. 2. Translucent with less than 15 per cent upward light through apertures. 3. Opaque with less than 15 per cent uplight through apertures.	1. None 2. Louvers or baffles
IV	1. Transparent unapertured. 2. Translucent unapertured. 3. Opaque unapertured.	1. None 2. Louvers
V	1. Transparent unapertured. 2. Translucent unapertured. 3. Opaque unapertured.	1. Transparent unapertured 2. Translucent unapertured
VI	1. None 2. Transparent unapertured. 3. Translucent unapertured. 4. Opaque unapertured.	1. Transparent unapertured 2. Translucent unapertured 3. Opaque unapertured

Reprinted with permission from IES, *IES Lighting Handbook, 1984 Reference Handbook.*

FIGURE 17-16 / Lamp lumen depreciation

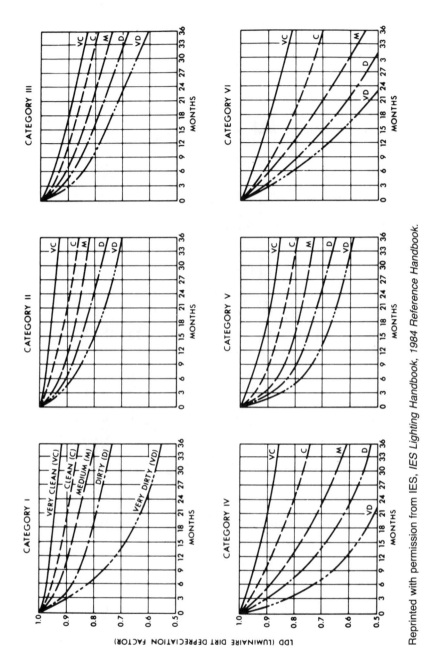

FIGURE 17-17 / Luminaire dirt depreciation factors

483

% Effective Ceiling Cavity Reflectance, ρ_{cc}	80				70				50			30			10		
% Wall Reflectance, ρ_w	70	50	30	10	70	50	30	10	50	30	10	50	30	10	50	30	10

For 30 Per Cent Effective Floor Cavity Reflectance (20 Per Cent = 1.00)

Room Cavity Ratio																	
1	1.092	1.082	1.075	1.068	1.077	1.070	1.064	1.059	1.049	1.044	1.040	1.028	1.026	1.023	1.012	1.010	1.008
2	1.079	1.066	1.055	1.047	1.068	1.057	1.048	1.039	1.041	1.033	1.027	1.026	1.021	1.017	1.013	1.010	1.006
3	1.070	1.054	1.042	1.033	1.061	1.048	1.037	1.028	1.034	1.027	1.020	1.024	1.017	1.012	1.014	1.009	1.005
4	1.062	1.045	1.033	1.024	1.055	1.040	1.029	1.021	1.030	1.022	1.015	1.022	1.015	1.010	1.014	1.009	1.004
5	1.056	1.038	1.026	1.018	1.050	1.034	1.024	1.015	1.027	1.018	1.012	1.020	1.013	1.008	1.014	1.009	1.004
6	1.052	1.033	1.021	1.014	1.047	1.030	1.020	1.012	1.024	1.015	1.009	1.019	1.012	1.006	1.014	1.008	1.003
7	1.047	1.029	1.018	1.011	1.043	1.026	1.017	1.009	1.022	1.013	1.007	1.018	1.010	1.005	1.014	1.008	1.003
8	1.044	1.026	1.015	1.009	1.040	1.024	1.015	1.007	1.020	1.012	1.006	1.017	1.009	1.004	1.013	1.007	1.003
9	1.040	1.024	1.014	1.007	1.037	1.022	1.014	1.006	1.019	1.011	1.005	1.016	1.009	1.004	1.013	1.007	1.002
10	1.037	1.022	1.012	1.006	1.034	1.020	1.012	1.005	1.017	1.010	1.004	1.015	1.009	1.003	1.013	1.007	1.002

For 10 Per Cent Effective Floor Cavity Reflectance (20 Per Cent = 1.00)

Room Cavity Ratio																	
1	.923	.929	.935	.940	.933	.939	.943	.948	.956	.960	.963	.973	.976	.979	.989	.991	.993
2	.931	.942	.950	.958	.940	.949	.957	.963	.962	.968	.974	.976	.980	.985	.988	.991	.995
3	.939	.951	.961	.969	.945	.957	.966	.973	.967	.975	.981	.978	.983	.988	.988	.992	.996
4	.944	.958	.969	.978	.950	.963	.973	.980	.972	.980	.986	.980	.986	.991	.987	.992	.996
5	.949	.964	.976	.983	.954	.968	.978	.985	.975	.983	.989	.981	.988	.993	.987	.992	.997
6	.953	.969	.980	.986	.958	.972	.982	.989	.977	.985	.992	.982	.989	.995	.987	.993	.997
7	.957	.973	.983	.991	.961	.975	.985	.991	.979	.987	.994	.983	.990	.996	.987	.993	.998
8	.960	.976	.986	.993	.963	.977	.987	.993	.981	.988	.995	.984	.991	.997	.987	.994	.998
9	.963	.978	.987	.994	.965	.979	.989	.994	.983	.990	.996	.985	.992	.998	.988	.994	.999
10	.965	.980	.989	.995	.967	.981	.990	.995	.984	.991	.997	.986	.993	.998	.988	.994	.999

For 0 Per Cent Effective Floor Cavity Reflectance (20 Per Cent = 1.00)

Room Cavity Ratio																	
1	.859	.870	.879	.886	.873	.884	.893	.901	.916	.923	.929	.948	.954	.960	.979	.983	.987
2	.871	.887	.903	.919	.886	.902	.916	.928	.926	.938	.949	.954	.963	.971	.978	.983	.991
3	.882	.904	.915	.942	.898	.918	.934	.947	.936	.950	.964	.958	.969	.979	.976	.984	.993
4	.893	.919	.941	.958	.908	.930	.948	.961	.945	.961	.974	.961	.974	.984	.975	.985	.994
5	.903	.931	.953	.969	.914	.939	.958	.970	.951	.967	.980	.964	.977	.988	.975	.985	.995
6	.911	.940	.961	.976	.920	.945	.965	.977	.955	.972	.985	.966	.979	.991	.975	.986	.996
7	.917	.947	.967	.981	.924	.950	.970	.982	.959	.975	.988	.968	.981	.993	.975	.987	.997
8	.922	.953	.971	.985	.929	.955	.975	.986	.963	.978	.991	.970	.983	.995	.976	.988	.998
9	.928	.958	.975	.988	.933	.959	.980	.989	.966	.980	.993	.971	.985	.996	.976	.988	.998
10	.933	.962	.979	.991	.937	.963	.983	.992	.969	.982	.995	.973	.987	.997	.977	.989	.999

Reprinted with permission from IES, *IES Lighting Handbook, 1984 Reference Handbook.*

FIGURE 17-18 / *Multiplying factors for other than 20 percent effective floor cavity reflectance*

Figure 17-19 — Coefficients of utilization

Typical Luminaire	Maint. Cat.	SC	RCR ↓	ρcc 80 / ρw 50	30	10	ρcc 70 / ρw 50	30	10	ρcc 50 / ρw 50	30	10	ρcc 30 / ρw 50	30	10	ρcc 10 / ρw 50	30	10	ρcc 0 / 0	WDRC	RCR ↓
1 — Pendant diffusing sphere with incandescent lamp (35½%↑, 45%↓)	V	1.5	0	.87	.87	.87	.81	.81	.81	.70	.70	.70	.59	.59	.59	.49	.49	.49	.45		0
			1	.71	.66	.62	.65	.61	.58	.55	.52	.49	.46	.44	.42	.38	.36	.34	.30	.368	1
			2	.60	.53	.48	.55	.50	.45	.47	.42	.38	.39	.35	.32	.31	.29	.26	.23	.279	2
			3	.52	.44	.38	.48	.41	.36	.40	.35	.31	.33	.29	.26	.27	.24	.21	.18	.227	3
			4	.45	.37	.32	.42	.35	.29	.35	.30	.25	.29	.25	.21	.23	.20	.17	.14	.192	4
			5	.40	.32	.27	.37	.30	.25	.31	.25	.21	.26	.21	.18	.21	.17	.14	.12	.166	5
			6	.35	.28	.23	.33	.26	.21	.28	.22	.18	.23	.19	.15	.19	.15	.12	.10	.146	6
			7	.32	.25	.19	.29	.23	.18	.25	.20	.16	.21	.16	.13	.17	.13	.11	.09	.130	7
			8	.29	.22	.17	.27	.20	.16	.23	.17	.14	.19	.15	.12	.15	.12	.09	.07	.117	8
			9	.26	.19	.15	.24	.18	.14	.21	.16	.12	.17	.13	.10	.14	.11	.08	.07	.107	9
			10	.24	.17	.13	.22	.16	.12	.19	.14	.11	.16	.12	.09	.13	.10	.08	.06	.098	10
2 — Concentric ring unit with incandescent silvered-bowl lamp (83%↑, 3½%↓)	II	N.A.	0	.83	.83	.83	.72	.72	.72	.50	.50	.50	.30	.30	.30	.12	.12	.12	.03		0
			1	.72	.69	.66	.62	.60	.57	.43	.42	.40	.26	.25	.25	.10	.10	.10	.03	.018	1
			2	.63	.58	.54	.54	.50	.47	.38	.35	.33	.23	.22	.20	.09	.09	.08	.02	.015	2
			3	.55	.49	.45	.47	.43	.39	.33	.30	.28	.20	.19	.17	.08	.07	.07	.02	.013	3
			4	.48	.42	.37	.42	.37	.33	.29	.26	.23	.18	.16	.15	.07	.06	.06	.02	.012	4
			5	.43	.36	.32	.37	.32	.28	.26	.23	.20	.16	.14	.12	.06	.06	.05	.01	.011	5
			6	.38	.32	.27	.33	.28	.24	.23	.20	.17	.14	.12	.11	.06	.05	.04	.01	.010	6
			7	.34	.28	.23	.30	.24	.21	.21	.17	.15	.13	.11	.09	.05	.04	.04	.01	.009	7
			8	.31	.25	.20	.27	.21	.18	.19	.15	.13	.12	.10	.08	.05	.04	.03	.01	.008	8
			9	.28	.22	.18	.24	.19	.16	.17	.14	.11	.10	.09	.07	.04	.03	.03	.01	.008	9
			10	.25	.20	.16	.22	.17	.14	.16	.12	.10	.10	.08	.06	.04	.03	.03	.01	.007	10
29 — Metal or dense diffusing sides with 45°CW × 45°LW shielding (39%↑, 32%↓)	II	1.1	0	.75	.75	.75	.69	.69	.69	.57	.57	.57	.46	.46	.46	.37	.37	.37	.32		0
			1	.66	.64	.62	.61	.59	.57	.51	.50	.48	.42	.41	.40	.33	.33	.32	.28	.094	1
			2	.59	.55	.52	.54	.51	.48	.46	.43	.41	.38	.36	.34	.30	.29	.28	.25	.091	2
			3	.52	.48	.44	.48	.44	.41	.41	.38	.35	.34	.32	.30	.27	.26	.25	.22	.085	3
			4	.47	.42	.38	.43	.39	.35	.37	.33	.31	.31	.28	.26	.25	.23	.22	.19	.079	4
			5	.42	.37	.33	.39	.34	.31	.33	.30	.27	.28	.25	.23	.23	.21	.20	.17	.073	5
			6	.38	.33	.29	.35	.31	.27	.30	.27	.24	.25	.23	.21	.21	.19	.18	.16	.068	6
			7	.35	.29	.26	.32	.28	.24	.28	.24	.21	.23	.21	.19	.19	.17	.16	.14	.063	7
			8	.32	.26	.23	.29	.25	.22	.25	.22	.19	.22	.19	.17	.18	.16	.15	.13	.059	8
			9	.29	.24	.21	.27	.23	.20	.23	.20	.17	.20	.17	.15	.17	.15	.13	.12	.056	9
			10	.27	.22	.19	.25	.21	.18	.22	.18	.16	.19	.16	.14	.16	.14	.12	.11	.052	10
34 — Prismatic bottom and sides, open top, 4-lamp suspended unit—see note 7 (33%↑ II, 50%↓ II)	VI	1.4/1.2	0	.91	.91	.91	.85	.85	.85	.74	.74	.74	.64	.64	.64	.54	.54	.54	.50		0
			1	.80	.77	.74	.75	.72	.70	.65	.63	.61	.57	.55	.54	.49	.47	.47	.43	.179	1
			2	.70	.65	.61	.66	.62	.58	.58	.54	.52	.50	.48	.46	.43	.42	.40	.37	.166	2
			3	.62	.56	.51	.58	.53	.49	.51	.47	.44	.45	.42	.39	.39	.37	.35	.32	.153	3
			4	.55	.49	.44	.52	.46	.42	.46	.41	.38	.40	.37	.34	.35	.32	.30	.27	.140	4
			5	.50	.43	.38	.47	.41	.36	.41	.37	.33	.36	.33	.30	.32	.29	.26	.24	.129	5
			6	.45	.38	.33	.42	.36	.32	.37	.33	.29	.33	.29	.26	.29	.26	.23	.21	.119	6
			7	.40	.34	.29	.38	.32	.28	.34	.29	.26	.30	.26	.23	.26	.23	.21	.19	.111	7
			8	.37	.30	.26	.35	.29	.25	.31	.26	.23	.28	.24	.21	.24	.21	.19	.17	.103	8
			9	.34	.27	.23	.32	.26	.22	.29	.24	.21	.25	.22	.19	.22	.19	.17	.15	.096	9
			10	.31	.25	.21	.29	.24	.20	.26	.22	.19	.23	.20	.17	.21	.18	.15	.14	.090	10
35 — 2-lamp prismatic wraparound—see note 7 (11½%↑, 58½%↓)	V	1.5/1.2	0	.81	.81	.81	.78	.78	.78	.72	.72	.72	.66	.66	.66	.61	.61	.61	.59		0
			1	.71	.68	.66	.68	.66	.63	.63	.61	.59	.58	.57	.56	.54	.53	.52	.50	.223	1
			2	.63	.58	.55	.60	.56	.53	.56	.53	.50	.52	.50	.47	.48	.46	.45	.43	.201	2
			3	.56	.50	.46	.54	.49	.45	.50	.46	.43	.47	.43	.41	.43	.41	.39	.37	.183	3
			4	.50	.44	.40	.48	.43	.39	.45	.40	.37	.42	.38	.35	.39	.36	.34	.32	.167	4
			5	.45	.39	.34	.43	.38	.34	.40	.36	.32	.38	.34	.31	.35	.32	.30	.28	.153	5
			6	.40	.34	.30	.39	.34	.30	.37	.32	.28	.34	.30	.27	.32	.29	.26	.25	.142	6
			7	.37	.31	.27	.35	.30	.26	.33	.29	.25	.31	.27	.24	.30	.26	.23	.22	.131	7
			8	.33	.28	.24	.32	.27	.23	.30	.26	.23	.29	.25	.22	.27	.24	.21	.20	.122	8
			9	.31	.25	.21	.30	.25	.21	.28	.24	.20	.26	.23	.20	.25	.22	.19	.18	.114	9
			10	.28	.23	.19	.27	.22	.19	.26	.21	.18	.24	.21	.18	.23	.20	.17	.16	.107	10
40 — Fluorescent unit dropped diffuser, 4-lamp 610 mm (2') wide—see note 7 (1%↑, 60½%↓)	V	1.2	0	.73	.73	.73	.71	.71	.71	.68	.68	.68	.65	.65	.65	.62	.62	.62	.60		0
			1	.63	.60	.58	.62	.59	.57	.59	.57	.55	.56	.55	.53	.54	.53	.51	.50	.259	1
			2	.55	.51	.47	.54	.50	.46	.51	.48	.45	.49	.46	.44	.47	.45	.43	.42	.236	2
			3	.48	.43	.39	.47	.42	.39	.45	.41	.38	.43	.40	.37	.42	.39	.36	.35	.212	3
			4	.43	.37	.33	.42	.37	.33	.40	.36	.32	.39	.35	.32	.37	.34	.31	.30	.191	4
			5	.38	.33	.29	.37	.32	.28	.36	.31	.28	.35	.31	.28	.33	.30	.27	.26	.173	5
			6	.34	.29	.25	.34	.29	.25	.33	.28	.24	.31	.27	.24	.30	.27	.24	.23	.158	6
			7	.31	.26	.22	.31	.26	.22	.30	.25	.22	.29	.25	.21	.28	.24	.21	.20	.144	7
			8	.28	.23	.20	.28	.23	.20	.27	.23	.19	.26	.22	.19	.25	.22	.19	.18	.133	8
			9	.26	.21	.18	.26	.21	.18	.25	.21	.17	.24	.20	.17	.24	.20	.17	.16	.123	9
			10	.24	.19	.16	.24	.19	.16	.23	.19	.16	.22	.19	.16	.22	.18	.16	.15	.115	10

Coefficients of Utilization for 20 Per Cent Effective Floor Cavity Reflectance (ρFC = 20)

FIGURE 17-19 / Coefficients of utilization

Luminaire 49

Typical Luminaire	Typical Intensity Distribution and Per Cent Lamp Lumens			ρcc → 80			70			50			30			10			0	WDRC	ρcc →
	Maint. Cat.	SC	ρw → / RCR ↓	50	30	10	50	30	10	50	30	10	50	30	10	50	30	10	0		RCR ↓
49	I	1.4/1.2	0	1.13	1.13	1.13	1.09	1.09	1.09	1.01	1.01	1.01	.94	.94	.94	.88	.88	.88	.85		
			1	.95	.90	.86	.92	.87	.83	.85	.82	.78	.79	.76	.74	.74	.72	.69	.66	.464	1
			2	.82	.74	.68	.79	.72	.66	.73	.68	.63	.68	.64	.60	.63	.60	.56	.53	.394	2
			3	.71	.62	.55	.69	.61	.54	.64	.57	.52	.59	.54	.49	.55	.51	.47	.44	.342	3
			4	.62	.53	.46	.60	.52	.45	.56	.49	.43	.52	.46	.41	.49	.44	.40	.37	.300	4
			5	.55	.46	.39	.54	.45	.39	.50	.43	.37	.47	.40	.36	.44	.38	.34	.32	.267	5
			6	.50	.41	.34	.48	.40	.33	.45	.38	.32	.42	.36	.31	.39	.34	.30	.27	.240	6
			7	.45	.36	.30	.43	.35	.29	.41	.34	.28	.38	.32	.27	.36	.30	.26	.24	.218	7
			8	.41	.32	.26	.40	.32	.26	.37	.30	.25	.35	.29	.24	.33	.27	.23	.21	.199	8
			9	.37	.29	.24	.36	.28	.23	.34	.27	.22	.32	.26	.22	.30	.25	.21	.19	.183	9
			10	.34	.26	.21	.33	.26	.21	.32	.25	.20	.30	.24	.20	.28	.23	.19	.17	.170	10

2-lamp fluorescent strip unit with 235° reflector fluorescent lamps
(12↓ 85↑)

Luminaires 50–53

Typical Luminaires	ρcc → 80			70			50			30			10			0
ρw → / RCR ↓	50	30	10	50	30	10	50	30	10	50	30	10	50	30	10	0
50 1	.42	.40	.39	.36	.35	.33	.25	.24	.23	Coves are not recommended for lighting areas having low reflectances.						
2	.37	.34	.32	.32	.29	.27	.22	.20	.19							
3	.32	.29	.26	.28	.25	.23	.19	.17	.16							
4	.29	.25	.22	.25	.22	.19	.17	.15	.13							
5	.25	.21	.18	.22	.19	.16	.15	.13	.11							
6	.23	.19	.16	.20	.16	.14	.14	.12	.10							
7	.20	.17	.14	.17	.14	.12	.12	.10	.09							
8	.18	.15	.12	.16	.13	.10	.11	.09	.08							
9	.17	.13	.10	.15	.11	.09	.10	.08	.07							
10	.15	.12	.09	.13	.10	.08	.09	.07	.06							
51 1				.60	.58	.56	.58	.56	.54							
2				.53	.49	.45	.51	.47	.43							
3				.47	.42	.37	.45	.41	.36							
4				.41	.36	.32	.39	.35	.31							
5				.37	.31	.27	.35	.30	.26							
6				.33	.27	.23	.31	.26	.23							
7				.29	.24	.20	.28	.23	.20							
8				.26	.21	.18	.25	.20	.17							
9				.23	.19	.15	.23	.18	.15							
10				.21	.17	.13	.21	.16	.13							
52 1				.71	.68	.66	.67	.66	.65	.65	.64	.62				
2				.63	.60	.57	.61	.58	.55	.59	.56	.54				
3				.57	.53	.49	.55	.52	.48	.54	.50	.47				
4				.52	.47	.43	.50	.45	.42	.48	.44	.42				
5				.46	.41	.37	.44	.40	.37	.43	.40	.36				
6				.42	.37	.33	.41	.36	.32	.40	.35	.32				
7				.38	.32	.29	.37	.31	.28	.36	.31	.28				
8				.34	.28	.25	.33	.28	.25	.32	.28	.25				
9				.30	.25	.22	.30	.25	.21	.29	.25	.21				
10				.27	.23	.19	.27	.22	.19	.26	.22	.19				
53 1							.51	.49	.48				.47	.46	.45	
2							.46	.44	.42				.43	.42	.40	
3							.42	.39	.37				.39	.38	.36	
4							.38	.35	.33				.36	.34	.32	
5							.35	.32	.29				.33	.31	.29	
6							.32	.29	.26				.30	.28	.26	
7							.29	.26	.23				.28	.25	.23	
8							.27	.23	.21				.26	.23	.21	
9							.24	.21	.19				.24	.21	.19	
10							.22	.19	.17				.22	.19	.17	

Coefficients of utilization for 20 Per Cent Effective Floor Cavity Reflectance, ρFC

50 Single row fluorescent lamp cove without reflector, mult. by 0.93 for 2 rows and by 0.85 for 3 rows.

51 ρcc from below ~65%
Diffusing plastic or glass.
1) Ceiling efficiency ~60%; diffuser transmittance ~50%; diffuser reflectance ~40%. Cavity with minimum obstructions and painted with 80% reflectance paint—use ρc = 70.
2) For lower reflectance paint or obstructions—use ρc = 50.

52 ρcc from below ~60%
Prismatic plastic or glass.
1) Ceiling efficiency ~67%; prismatic transmittance ~72%; prismatic reflectance ~18%. Cavity with minimum obstructions and painted with 80% reflectance paint—use ρc = 70.
2) For lower reflectance paint or obstructions—use ρc = 50.

53 ρcc from below ~45%
Louvered ceiling.
1) Ceiling efficiency ~50%; 45° shielding opaque louvers of 80% reflectance. Cavity with minimum obstructions and painted with 80% reflectance paint—use ρc = 50.
2) For other conditions refer to Fig. 6–18.

Reprinted with permission from IES, *IES Lighting Handbook, 1984 Reference Handbook.*

FIGURE 17-19 / Coefficients of utilization (continued)

Typical Hot-Cathode Fluorescent Lamps (Instant Starting)[a]

Nominal length (millimeters)	1050	1600	1800	2400	1200	1500	600	900	1050	1200	1500	1600	1800	2100	2400
(inches)	42	64	72	96	48	60	24	36	42	48	60	64	72	84	96
Bulb	T-6	T-6	T-8	T-8	T-12	T-17	T-12	T-12	T-12	T-12	T-12	T-12	T-12	T-12	T-12
Base	Single Pin	Single Pin	Single Pin	Single Pin	Med. Bipin	Mog. Bipin	Single Pin	Single Pin	Single Pin	Single Pin	Single Pin	Single Pin	Single Pin	Single Pin	Single Pin
Approx. lamp current (amperes)	0.200[f]	0.200[f]	0.200[f]	0.200[f]	0.425	0.425	0.425	0.425	0.425	0.425	0.425	0.425	0.425	0.425	0.425
Approx. lamp volts	150	233	220	295	104	107	53	77	88	100	123	131	149	172	197
Approx. lamp watts	25.5	38.5	38	51	40.5	42	21.5	30	34.5	39	48	50.5	57	66.5	75
Rated life (hours)[b]	7500	7500	7500	7500	7500–12000	7500–9000	7500–9000	7500–9000	7500–9000	7500–12000	7500–12000	7500–12000	7500–12000	7500–12000	12000
Lamp lumen depreciation (LLD)[c]	76	77	83	89	83	89	81	82	80	82	78	78	89	91	89
Initial lumens[d]															
Cool White	1835	3000	3030	4265	3100	2900	1065	2000	2350	3000	3585	3865	4650	5400	6300
Deluxe Cool White	1265	2100	2100	2910		2020				2065			3175		4465
Warm White	1875	3050	3015	4215	3150	2940	1150	2050	2500	3000		3950	4675		6500
Deluxe Warm White	1275	2100				1990				2050			3200		4365
White	1900	2945	3050	4225	3150	2940	1010	1715	2015	3000	3135	3250	4700		6400
Daylight	1605	2600	2650	3525	2565	2410				2500			3850	4450	5425
Factors for Calculating Luminance[e] Candelas per Square Meter	6.1	3.93	2.55	1.87	2.65	1.5	5.54	3.58	3.04	2.65	2.1	1.95	1.7	1.44	1.24

[a] The life and light output ratings of fluorescent lamps are based on their use with ballasts that provide proper operating characteristics. Ballasts that do not provide proper electrical values may substantially reduce either lamp life or light output, or both.
[b] Rated life under specified test conditions at three hours per start. At longer burning intervals per start, longer life can be expected.
[c] Per cent of initial light output at 70 per cent rated life at three hours per start. Average for cool white lamps. Approximate values.
[d] At 100 hours. Where lamp is made by more than one manufacturer, light output is the average of manufacturers. For the lumen output of other colors of fluorescent lamps, multiply the cool white lumens by the relative light output value from the table below Fig. 8–116.
[e] To calculate approximate lamp luminance, multiply the lamp lumens of the lamp color desired by the appropriate factor.
[f] These lamps can also be operated at 0.120 and 0.300 amperes.
Note: All electrical and lumen values apply only under standard photometric conditions.

Reprinted with permission from IES, IES Lighting Handbook, 1984 Reference Handbook.

FIGURE 17-20 / Instant starting fluorescent lamps

487

CHAPTER 18
SYSTEM INSTALLATION

18-1 GENERAL

Too often a building is designed with little or no concern for its plumbing, heating, and electrical systems. Many projects also have special requirements in terms of communications (telephones, nursing stations, etc.) or security that must be considered.

The materials and assemblies used in the construction of the building have an important impact on the ease of installation and cost of the mechanicals. The materials and assemblies most commonly used and the integration of the mechanicals into them are discussed in this chapter. The major areas of coordination between contractors are listed at the end of the chapter.

When considering the space required to run the mechanicals, the two primary considerations will be the size of the pipe connections, particularly of cast iron, and whether mechanicals cross each other, one in a horizontal direction and one in a vertical direction (the space required may be greater at that point than at any other).

18-2 POURED CONCRETE

If the concrete is poured on the job, it is often required that the mechanicals be embedded in the concrete. The conduit and boxes for electrical work, the pipes for heating and plumbing and the various inserts, sleeves, and straps are placed by the mechanicals in the area or form to be filled with concrete. Coordination is required with the general contractor since some of the mechanicals' materials should be installed before the reinforcing bars are positioned and some must be installed after.

Sleeves and inserts are often installed before the re-bars; therefore they must be securely fastened so they will not be disturbed by the bar-setter or by the concrete when it is placed. Sleeves are the holes left in the concrete so that pipes or other material may pass through. The sleeve is easily formed by nailing a metal cup to the form, placing a fiber cylinder over it and inserting a metal closure on the top of the cylinder. These fiber cylinders are available in a wide range of diameters. The fewer the number of nails required to attach materials to the form, the less chance of damaging the concrete surface. Wooden forms are used to block out chases and rectangular or square sleeves. An adhesive tape about ⅛ in. thick is available that will hold the inserts in place against the form. The insert and form must be clean and dry for the tape to stick properly, and when they are, it is very effective, it leaves no nail holes and the form is easily stripped.

Embedding conduit in concrete presents no problem except that care must be taken in placing the concrete so that the conduit is not damaged, allowing moisture to enter. The wiring is then easily pulled through the conduit when convenient.

All water, waste and vent pipes should be tested before they are covered—in this case, embedded—to determine if the entire system is watertight. Tests commonly run for water piping require that it be watertight under a hydrostatic water pressure of 125 psi for a minimum of 1 hr; any leaks that appear must be repaired with the joint compound used originally. Sanitary (waste) drainage and vent piping should be tested before any fixtures are installed and before connection is made to the sewer. The test consists of capping or plugging the opening, filling the entire system with water and allowing it to stand for 3 hr, during which time any leaks are repaired. The testing times must be coordinated with the general contractor, so they may be completed while the piping is completely exposed. Once the concrete is poured and the pipes embedded, it is very time-consuming and expensive to remove the concrete so that repairs to the pipe may be made.

Inserts and hangers are often embedded in concrete slabs to provide support for pipes running horizontally below them. Some typical inserts and hangers are shown in Fig. 18-1. These inserts eliminate or reduce the amount of piping embedded in the concrete; at the same time, the pipes installed below the concrete deck are either exposed to view, concealed by a suspended ceiling or enclosed in a soffit. Mechanicals exposed to view are acceptable in some areas, such as storage and some work areas, but not in most offices or public areas.

Poured concrete walls may be furred out to allow for the passage of mechanicals so that they need not be embedded in the concrete. The most commonly used types of furring are the wetwall and the drywall systems (Fig. 18-2), but any material may be used as long as sufficient space is left between the materials for all the mechanicals which must be placed. The space required is determined by the largest mechanical passing through (usually the pipes), the direction of its run and whether it crosses any other mechanicals.

Metal raceways may be installed in a poured concrete floor (Fig. 18-3) to allow

(a) Threaded insert

(b) Loop insert

Reinforcing bar

Hanger

(c) Dovetail slot insert

6"

7"

6" inside depth tray

(d) Hanger

(e) Pipe hanger

FIGURE 18-1 / Typical inserts and hangers

Caulk

Gypsum
plaster

Plaster base

Metal
runner

Ceiling attachment

Insulating wool
(optional)

Metal
base

Base attachment

(a) Free standing furring

Min — 10 d
nail at
each lath
joint — wire
tied to
channel

Long length
plaster base

Cold rolled channels
wire tied to brackets

Adjustable
wall furring bracket

(b) Adjustable wall furring bracket and attachment of plaster base

FIGURE 18-2 / Wall furring

Standard header duct or trench duct may be used

Concrete slab

Metal deck

Trench duct

Header duct

(a)

Header duct fits in depressed slab area

(b)

Trench duct

Metal deck

Electrical cell

Dual pre-set insert

(c)

FIGURE 18-3 / Metal raceways

for the passage of electrical and telephone wires and conduit. In this manner, changes may be made and wires added with a minimum of cost and time. The raceways may be either level with or below the surface of the concrete. The manufacturers of metal decking for floors have been most resourceful in adapting their systems to electrical and even distribution systems.

18-3   PRECAST CONCRETE

Either the mechanicals are placed on top of the precast concrete and embedded in a concrete topping, or they are placed below the concrete structural member.

Electrical work below the precast concrete is usually attached to it by a clip and an insert, while pipes are suspended by hangers. Either the hangers may be fitted into the joints between the precast members, or the inserts may be cast into the members. The conduit may sometimes be placed inconspicuously although any pipes, ducts, junction boxes and terminals would be unsightly in most areas, and either a suspended ceiling or soffit is used to conceal the mechanicals similar to Fig. 18-10 (which also relates to poured concrete). The double tee may be a soffit area right in the recessed area of the tee to house mechanicals running in the direction of the span (Fig. 18-4).

Mechanicals required for the space above the precast concrete may be run in concrete topping, or an entire elevated floor area may be used. Junction boxes and conduit may be placed in the forms and precast in the concrete. When entire walls are precast, the conduit and boxes are often cast right into the wall.

Holes may be cut into the precast concrete to allow the vertical passage of mechanicals. The holes may be cast circular or rectangular or may be field cut with a diamond core drill. The sizes of the holes must be coordinated with the manufacturer's recommendations. The width of the holes in the tees cannot exceed the distance between the stems (Fig. 18-5). Hollow core slab manufacturers have steel header pieces available to allow for a variety of cutout sizes (Fig. 18-6).

When double walls (partitions) are used to allow vertical passage of mechanicals, it may be possible for each of the structural elements to bear (rest) on one of the walls, allowing the easy and economical passage of mechanicals [of course, the cost of constructing two bearing walls must be considered (Fig. 18-7)]. This approach may also be used for poured-in-place concrete.

18-4   WOOD

Laminated wood beams and arches with a wooden deck, between the pieces of laminated wood, are easily cut to allow for the passage of pipes through the roof. When conduit runs for lighting fixtures are needed on the ceiling, the decking may be routed (grooved) parallel to the edge to conceal the electrical conduit. Either the conduit is laid in one of the grooves (Fig. 18-8), left in the top of the laminated section, or a wiremold

Channel or
clip angle

Ceiling trim

Tile or gypsum board

(a)

Studs, channels,
or clip angles

Trim

Gypsum board
or plaster

(b)

Louver gypsum   Clip
board panel   angle

(c)

FIGURE 18-4 / Double tee soffit

Max. width
of cutout

FIGURE 18-5 / Double tee

Clip angles
bearing on
deck units

Continuous angles support
for deck units

FIGURE 18-6 / Hollow core plank header

FIGURE 18-7 / Double bearing walls

Steel
channels

Back to back
wall hung
water closets

Furring or fireproofing   Pipe chase

Partition

FIGURE 18-8 / Channeled beam

may be run in the corner at the juncture of the decking and the laminated section. No concealed space is available for the running of ducts or pipes.

Wooden trusses, similar to the bowstring type shown in Fig. 18-9, are very adaptable, allowing the passage of mechanicals through the decking and throughout the space. Ducts and pipes may run horizontally and only large ducts may present any problems. A ceiling is usually applied to the bottom of the trusses.

18-5   STEEL JOISTS

Steel joist assemblies offer some of the most economical solutions to the problem of placing mechanicals. The space available in the joist design offers flexibility in installing the electrical wiring and piping, and the ductwork installation is limited only by the clear space available for the ducts to pass through. Suspended ceilings are then required to conceal the mechanicals running through the space, but this system may still be economical in comparison to the cost of using precast concrete without suspended ceilings. The portion of assembly used for the ceiling structure (between the finished ceiling and the floor above) is often specified with mechanical considerations in mind. For large ductwork, a soffit may be built, or the ceiling may be suspended a sufficient amount to allow passage of the ducts. Holes for mechanicals running vertically are easily cut in the decking and sleeves placed in the concrete.

When gypsum decks are used on the steel joists, openings are left by providing supports between the purlins and the sleeves or curb.

A suspended ceiling allows freedom in the mechanical layout in terms of directions, shortest distances and diagonal runs, but the cost of suspended ceiling must be considered. Soffit areas, usually constructed of drywall or plaster, are economical if mechanicals are designed to run within confined areas; however, this will require more materials—extra lengths of pipe, extra couplings, etc.—since diagonal runs may be uneconomical. A typical soffit installation is shown in Fig. 18-10.

18-6   PIPE TUNNELS

The use of a pipe tunnel (Fig. 18-11) provides concealed space for the passage of mechanicals at ground level and from building to building. Hangers from the top or

FIGURE 18-9 / Bowstring truss

from a side attachment may be used. When a large amount of mechanicals must be moved inconspicuously, the pipe tunnel is an excellent, though relatively expensive, approach. Each tunnel should be large enough that a person can pass through to check it or to make repairs when required. Access may be from the ends, or access doors may be built in.

18-7 PARTITIONS

The partitions through which the mechanicals run horizontally and vertically must also be considered. The solution will vary depending on the type of wall.

Masonry walls can be cut out to receive vertical electrical wiring and some piping, but cutting these units is expensive. When a large amount of piping is required,

FIGURE 18-10 / Typical soffit installation

Courtesy of United States Gypsum Co.

FIGURE 18-11 / Pipe tunnel

such as for bathrooms, the most common solution is the double or furred-out wall which leaves space for the mechanicals. This solution allows great freedom in installing the mechanicals in both horizontal and vertical directions. If only a few vertical pipes are involved, such as roof drains, either the masonry may be broken or cut, or smaller units may be used to allow space. Be certain that the wall is thick enough to conceal the pipe and that an interior finish is placed over the masonry. For exposed masonry walls, an opening is left for the pipe, and thin pieces of masonry are placed around it. The core holes of two-core blocks can be lined up to allow vertical passage of the conduit and pipes; be sure to check the core's size at its smallest end to determine size limitations.

With metal stud drywall and wetwall construction, the type of stud used and the clear wall space must be considered. For mechanicals running horizontally, solid metal studs are available with knockouts 24 in. o.c. (this may vary with the manufacturer) or with prepunched holes. Truss-type studs (Fig. 18-12) are also available which offer the most flexibility and may allow installation of slightly larger sized pipe. Where horizontal mechanicals are such that they cannot pass through the studs, double or core walls are used. This type of construction is often used where there is a large concentration of mechanicals, such as for bathrooms. For vertical runs, the width of the stud may provide sufficient space for the mechanicals, or the double or core wall may be used (Fig. 18-13). Solid plaster walls have only enough space for electrical conduits.

Poured and precast concrete walls are discussed above in Secs. 18-2 and 18-3. Such walls may be furred out with wetwall or drywall construction similar to that used for masonry walls, and vertical runs may be accommodated by blocking out that portion of the form where the pipe, conduit, or duct would run.

$1\frac{5}{8}''$ to 6''

Plan

(a) Metal stud

$1\frac{5}{8}''$ to 6''

Plan

(b) Truss type stud

FIGURE 18-12 / Truss-type studs

18-8   COORDINATION REQUIREMENTS

Coordination among the various contractors (general plumbing, electrical and HVAC) is important in the understanding of: Who is responsible for What? Why? When? Listed below are the major areas of coordination required between the electrical and general contractors.

Item	*Coordination Requirements*
1. Underground Utilities	Location, size, excavation by whom, from where?
2. Equipment	Recessed depth, size of access openings, method of feed, supports, by whom, size limitations.

FIGURE 18-13 / Vertical runs

Item	Coordination Requirements
3. Distribution	Outlet locations, materials, method of feed, chases, in walls, under floor, overhead, special considerations.
4. Terminal Fixtures and Devices	Location, method of support, finish, color and material.
5. Mounting Surfaces	What is mounting surface? Can it work?
6. Specialty Equipment	Field provisions, storage.
7. Scheduling	Work to be done? When required? Job to be completed on time—who—why—when?

Listed below are the major areas of coordination required between the plumbing and general contractors.

Item	Coordination Requirements
1. Underground Utilities	Location, size, excavation by whom, from where?
2. Building Entrance	Floor sleeves, supports.
3. Mechanical Room Equipment	Supports required, location, anchors, by whom?
4. Distribution	Wall sleeves, hangers, chases, in wall, roof vents, access doors.
5. Fixtures	Method of support, feed, outlets, built-in, floor drains, vents.
6. Finishes	Factory or field.
7. Specialty Equipment	Field provisions, storage.
8. Scheduling	Work to be done, when required? Job to be completed on time—who—why—when?

Listed below are the major areas of coordination required between the HVAC and general contractors.

Item	Coordination Requirements
1. Underground utilities	Location, size, excavation by whom, from where?
2. Equipment	Method of support, location, by whom, anchors, access for receiving and installing, size limitations, flues, roof curbs.
3. Piping	Wall sleeves, size limitations, chases, in walls, under floors, floor sleeves, expansion compensators, access doors.
4. Ductwork	Sizes, support, access doors, drops, outlet sizes, chases, outside air louvers, roof curbs, lintels.
5. Terminal Equipment	Recesses for CUH, RC, FC, etc., size of radiation, method of concealing, grille fastenings.
6. Mechanical-Electrical Responsibility	Who is doing what?
7. Finishes	Field or factory?
8. Scheduling	Who? Why? When?

QUESTIONS

18-1. What are the primary considerations when determining the size of the space required to run the mechanicals?

18-2. What is the *sleeve*, as the term applies to concrete construction?

18-3. Why is coordination between the mechanical systems designer and draftsmen and the architectural designer and draftsmen so important?

18-4. Why is coordination between the mechanical contractor and the general construction contractor so important?

18-5. What limitations are there on holes when precast-concrete double tees are involved?

18-6. What limitations are there on duct sizes when steel trusses are used?

18-7. What are *pipe tunnels*, and when are they used?

18-8. What type of masonry wall construction may be used for the partition wall housing the plumbing between back-to-back bathrooms?

18-9. When might double or core walls of drywall or wetwall construction be used?

18-10. What problems may occur when mechanicals are embedded in concrete?

CHAPTER 19

SECURITY, FIRE, AND SMOKE SYSTEMS

19-1 GENERAL

Except in a relatively few instances, building security has traditionally received little consideration during the design stage. However, the increase in crimes against businesses amounts to over $12 billion a year, and the increasing threats of violence from bombings and "shoot-outs" have resulted in significantly increased interest in security.

Building security must be approached in four basic ways: selection of materials used in the building, building design, guards, and electronic alarm systems.

19-2 MATERIAL SELECTION

Carefully select doors, windows, and their hardware to be certain that they will discourage intrusion. The windows should be designed so that the glass cannot be removed from the outside, and the hardware should be such that the window cannot be opened from the outside with a plastic card or wire. The doors in question should be metal, and locks should be selected which cannot be opened with a credit card. Also be certain that the door's hinge pins cannot be taken out from the outside of the building and the door removed. Maximum security lock systems are available which have keys that cannot be duplicated on existing key cutting machines; duplicate keys must be ordered from the manufacturer and are sent only to authorized persons. Obviously, these suggestions are not foolproof, but they do provide an economical beginning to building security.

Many building codes require that all doors which lead into stairways and exits be operable from both directions in case of fire or emergency. When such a door is not to be used except in an emergency, it may be wired to an alarm system which activates when the door is opened; large signs should be placed on such doors warning of the alarm system setup.

Buildings which are more prone to security problems because of the location or the type of occupancy should be built of materials which prevent easy entrance. For example, exterior wood frame walls are much easier to "open up" than poured concrete, concrete block, or brick walls. The roof assembly should also be carefully selected. It is easier to cut or "crowbar" an opening in a plywood roof than a concrete or gypsum roof.

19-3   BUILDING DESIGN

The designers of the building should pay particular attention to the locations of doors, windows, loading docks, and money-handling rooms. These areas should all be easy to view from other surrounding areas and be well lit (as should elevators and stairways). Ledges and exterior ornamentation which might allow people to climb up the side of the building should be avoided. Probably one of the best investments in terms of security is the provision of high levels of illumination throughout the project.

19-4   GUARDS

Guards are used to provide security in many buildings. It should be noted that seldom may a guard be compared with a policeman in terms of providing such security because the guards that are hired seldom have the training that policemen receive. Such guard jobs are generally low paying; and yet one survey has shown for over $\frac{1}{3}$ of those guards interviewed that the guard job was the best job available to them and that they had been unemployed before they took the guard job. Many of the guards hired range from those too inexperienced to do the job properly (for example, students who do homework on the job) to those who are not capable of handling the job (for example, some semi-retired personnel). It is interesting that those persons hired to protect the building and materials are the lowest paid personnel in many companies, perhaps making them susceptible to stealing or taking bribes for "looking the other way."

Neither guards nor electronic devices by themselves are the complete answer. The selective use of electronics, tied into central control points, reduces the need for guards. Using this approach, adequate money should be available to hire and train qualified guards.

19-5 ELECTRONIC ALARM SYSTEMS

For most projects, an electromechanical alarm system such as described here provides economical and effective security. Such systems have been used extensively in residences and in commercial, industrial, and institutional buildings. The setup of the system is quite simple, especially when it is installed in new construction. The monitoring system consists of the power source which is connected by an electric circuit to all the doors and windows selected and to the alarm. Once the system is set, if the circuit is broken at any of the contact points (at a door or window), the alarm goes off. There are many types of installations and equipment available, depending on the equipment manufacturer and the desired security. The system may be connected to every door and window or only to a select group of doors and windows.

CONTROL UNITS

The control unit used to activate and deactivate the circuit should be powered by the regular household power (120 V) available, with a stand-by battery power source to take over in case of a power failure. Many of the units have lights which indicate when the circuit is on. In addition, they may have a test alarm button so that the entire system can be checked.

To allow the occupant to leave and re-enter without sounding the alarm, an exit/entry control kit is installed. It includes an outside key-operated switch and an inside switch at the door. This type of control kit will sound the alarm if any attempt is made to disconnect the outside wallplate. Indicator lights on the wallplate turn on when the system is activated. Some exterior control kits are simply activated and de-activated by an outside key-operated switch with none of the protective features mentioned.

When the outside control kit is used, a push-button interior alarm switch is installed. One inside alarm switch may be installed for the entire system, or several may be installed to operate individual doors and windows. The latter allows the opening of a door or window without having to de-activate the entire system.

Also available is a control kit with a time-delay exit and entry feature. This control delays the operation of the system, allowing the occupant to leave or re-enter the building without setting off the alarm. With this control kit, an outside key-operated switch is necessary.

Control kits should be mounted where they will be readily accessible to the adult occupants but not to any children or visitors—for example, in a closet, laundry area, bookcase, or cabinet.

ENTRY DETECTORS

The entry detectors usually used are either the plunger or the magnetic type.

The plunger-type detector is recessed in a hole about ¾ in. in diameter and 1¼ in. deep. It can be used on both doors and windows and is installed so that when the door or window is closed, the plunger is pushed in, and when the door or window is opened, the plunger pushes out, setting off the alarm.

The magnetic-type entry detector may also be used on both doors and windows. The two pieces of the detector are surface mounted so that when the door or window is closed, they are in contact with each other, and when the door or window is opened, the magnets are separated, setting off the alarm.

Another entry detector often used is the floor-mat detector which will activate the alarm if stepped on. Common concealed locations for the floor-mat entry detector include under the rugs inside all exterior doors and just below windows.

ALARMS

The alarm set off by the various systems may be a bell inside and/or outside the building, a bell inside and a horn outside, a horn inside and/or outside, or a horn with a light (beacon). In some locales, the alarm system can be connected directly to the police station. The type of alarm which will produce the best results should be used. When available, the best arrangement is to tie the alarm system into the police station. Generally, the next best arrangement is to have an inside bell or horn with an exterior horn and a light. The more noise the system makes, the more likely it is that neighbors will hear it and call police—and the more likely it is that whoever breaks in will leave without taking anything. To be effective, this type of system must depend on the cooperation of neighbors, so be certain that they understand what the alarm means and that they should call the police to report any attempted break-in.

Quite often these alarm systems are combined with the fire/smoke alarms discussed in Sec. 19-6.

More elaborate electronic security systems utilizing ultrasonic sound, photoelectric, and microwave devices, audio-activated devices and closed-circuit television are also available. The advantages and disadvantages of these systems are compared in Fig. 19-1. Many of the systems are used in combination to achieve maximum control. Often the integrated system is set up with a number of alarms that may warn of smoke, fire, and intruders. Obviously, the larger the building complex is, the more money that should be available for security systems.

ELECTRONIC ACCESS

Electronic access control is being used by many large companies to control employee entrance into various areas. A commonly used access control requires insertion of a coded electronic "key" into a wall-mounted receptacle that decodes the "key" and

Type	Features	Application	Limitations
Ultrasonic High frequency (ultrasonic) sound, inaudible to human ears, completely saturates and is contained within the enclosed space to be guarded. Any slight movement or sound within the space will change the echo pattern and trigger an alarm.	Three-dimensional protection. Sound is inaudible. Detects all movement. Confined to enclosed space.	Banks, stores, plants, warehouses, office buildings, storage areas.	May be of limited effectiveness when placed near sound absorbent materials (e.g. carpet).
Photoelectric Invisible beam of infrared light. An alarm sounds when the beam is broken.	Up to 1,000-foot range. Interior or exterior models available.	Large areas or small, warehouse to doorway.	
Microwave Radar device which emits inaudible, measured radio signals. When person enters the field, the signal is interrupted and an alarm is set off.	Penetrates walls. Effective range to 10,000 sq ft.	Warehouses, storage areas, offices, banks, plants.	Movement outside the area being controlled may set off alarm.
Closed circuit television Cameras available with remote scanning, tilting, and zooming controls. Many areas may be monitored by one guard watching a group of receivers.	Low light level cameras available. Guards required cut in half.	Large complexes, hotels, warehouses, apartments, elevators, stairways, banks.	Cameras are costly. Due to high value of cameras, they are sometimes stolen.
Camera A surveillance camera set to take pictures automatically or on a signal.	Takes over 3,000 pictures before cartridge must be replaced. Signal may be a switch, foot plate, or any other electrically wired item.	Pilferage, vandalism, holdups, banks, loan companies, areas where money is handled.	Automatic setting could miss all the action if set to take photos too far apart. Expensive if photos taken too often. May provide photo of person but they then must be found.
Electromechanical Systems of floor mats, buttons, tapes, photocells, and screens that sound an alarm when activated.	Flexible, inexpensive system. Will deter unskilled intruders.	Schools, homes, warehouses.	Skilled intruder will easily avoid this type of security.
Audio All noise over a set level is picked up by a two-way microphone. Noises received above the level set off the alarm.	Guard may question intruder by microphone without being in physical contact with him.	Offices, warehouses, storage areas.	Loud noises from outside the area may set off alarm.

FIGURE 19-1 / Security alarm system

activates the door lock only for the proper "key." This type of lock is much more secure than the standard cylinder lock used on most doors. Another control method requires the employee to punch a code number on a keyboard, and within several seconds, a picture of the person who is assigned that number is flashed on the screen for the guard to check. It operates by the same principle as the instant replay technique used on television and uses the same materials. A third access device requires a person to place a hand on a hand plate; the machine then measures such things as finger length, finger tip angle and skin translucency and compares this information either with an identification card which is magnetically coated or with information which has been placed in the memory of the computer.

19-6   FIRE AND SMOKE ALARM SYSTEMS

One of the greatest fears of any homeowner, businessman, or director of an institution is fire. While the prime concern is always the loss of lives in a fire, many a business has never again risen from the smoke and flames. The threat of a fire destroying lives and property can be tremendously reduced by the proper installation of smoke detectors.

First, fire and smoke alarms are *not* the same thing. A fire detector is a device which can be preset to go off at a particular temperature. For example, most fire alarms for the interior of a residence are preset to go off when the air temperature goes over 135°F; technically, they are fire-heat detectors. A smoke detector is a device which has been preset to go off when a certain percentage of smoke accumulates (usually 2% to 4%). The smoke detector does not go off if it gets hot; its photoelectric cell activates the alarm only if it senses a 2% to 4% obscuration of light per foot. Similarly, the fire-heat detector does not activate if there is smoke, only if the heat goes above the preset temperature. Since most fire fatalities are due to smoke inhalation (even before the flames are widespread), the smoke detector offers the most protection and gives the quickest alarm in most installations.

Fire and smoke detectors may either be wired into the electrical system or be battery operated.

Those detectors that are wired into the electrical system should be designed to receive supplemental power from batteries in case of power failure. Such units should also have a small light which will go on if the battery fails, or some other type of device to notify the occupants that the battery must be changed. Fire and smoke detectors are often installed as part of the overall security system, as discussed in Sec. 19-5. When used in conjunction with the security system, different types of alarm signals are used, usually a steady signal when there is fire or smoke and a pulsating signal when there is forced entry. Such a setup means that neighbors should be made aware of the different signals and of what should be done if the alarm goes off. In some areas, it is possible to have the fire alarm connected to a central emergency office or to the fire station.

Battery-operated fire and smoke detectors should have a small light or other device to indicate that the battery is still functioning properly, as with the backup battery power source discussed above. They require no connecting wiring to the electrical system of the building, and this generally makes them ideal for installation when remodeling. While they have an alarm which will warn occupants of the building of a fire or smoke, they cannot be connected to an exterior alarm which might alert neighbors who could call the fire station and they cannot be directly connected to the fire station.

In residences, the detectors are usually placed in a hallway (or other access area) leading to the bedrooms; in homes with bedrooms on the second floor, the units would be placed at the top of the stairway and near the kitchen. In other types of buildings, a careful check of the floor plan should indicate the best locations.

The installation of fire and smoke detectors is being required, especially in residences and institutions, by more and more building codes. Such codes may specify detector requirements and locations.

QUESTIONS

19-1. Why has building security become increasingly important?

19-2. What types of electronic devices are used to provide building security?

19-3. Which of the systems listed in Question 19-2 is best suited to a residence, and why?

19-4. What is the difference between a fire detector and a smoke detector?

19-5. What problems may arise in hiring security guards for buildings?

CHAPTER 20
SOUND CONTROL

20-1   SOUND

This chapter discusses the proper design and installation of the mechanicals to be certain that they will not be a source of noise in the building. The control of acoustical problems is of prime concern, and the best results are achieved by anticipating the problems before they occur. First, the principles of sound transmission will be discussed, followed by the measurement of sound levels and the architectural and construction elements which must be considered in reducing noise.

20-2   SOUND TRANSMISSION

Sound may be transmitted through the air (airborne) or through the structure (structure-borne). Planning is required to reduce the transmission of sound from the exterior to the interior and from room to room. Basically, in each space we want to keep the necessary sounds in and the unnecessary or undesirable sounds out.

510

Sound is not selective; it passes (transmits) through most building materials and any openings, no matter how small. As sound passes through building materials (walls, floors and ceilings), its intensity is reduced, with the amount of reduction dependent on the types of materials and the construction used. Sound passes more readily through lighter, more porous materials than through heavy, dense, massive materials, and assemblies of materials. The use of sound absorbent materials on walls, ceilings, and floors will increase the transmission of sound through the surface; that is, it will make the room in which the sound originates quieter, but part of the sound will travel to the surrounding rooms.

20-3   DECIBELS

The decibel (dB) is used to measure the intensity of sound levels within the frequency range of human hearing. A chart showing relative sound levels in dB is shown in Fig. 20-1. From this chart, observe that a level of 25–40 dB is reasonably quiet, while noise

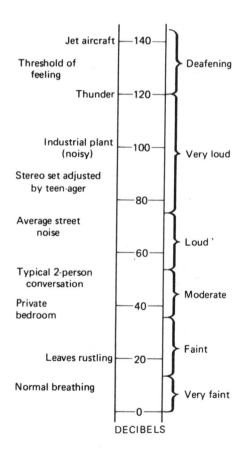

FIGURE 20-1 / Decibels

levels of 60 dB and up become increasingly noticeable. The object is to reduce the noise to a reasonable level, not to eliminate it.

The important point to remember in dealing with decibels is that the apparent change in loudness varies greatly with actual change in sound level. A change of 3 dB is just barely noticeable to the listener, while a change of 5 dB is easily noticeable and a change of 10 dB makes a significant sound difference. A change from 50 to 60 dB makes the noise seem twice as loud while a change from 50 to 40 dB makes it seem half as loud. The following table relates changes in sound level to changes in apparent loudness.

20-4   ELEMENTS

Included in this section is a discussion of the various architectural and construction elements which must be considered to effectively control sound. Some of these elements fall outside of the mechanical designer's prime areas of concern and responsibility, but he should be aware of them and be certain that they are not overlooked.

Generally, the elements would be considered by the designer in the following order:

1. Surrounding environment

2. Arrangement and layout of rooms

3. Shape of rooms

4. Reflecting surfaces

5. Isolation of vibration

6. Isolation of impact

7. Isolation of sound

SURROUNDING ENVIRONMENT

The surrounding environment should be carefully checked before a building site is actually purchased and, once purchased, before planning room arrangements and wall materials. In addition, the zoning should be carefully checked to determine what types of businesses (and accompanying noise sources) may move into the surrounding area.

The location for a building should be chosen with the use of the building in mind. For example, a nursing home should not be placed under the approach pattern to an airport.

Once a site has been selected, exterior noise problems may be reduced by orienting the building on the site to reduce direct sound transmission and reflective sound from surrounding buildings (Fig. 20-2) and equipment. Another method of sound reduction is to shield the building from major noise sources using other build-

(a) This orientation exposes maximum wall area directly to the noise source

(b) Less wall area exposed to direct noise source

(c) Use other buildings as shields from noise sources

(d) Shielding with other buildings reduces surface of building receiving sound

(e) Courtyard facing street, provides surfaces for sound reflection

 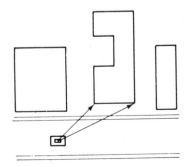

(f) Quieter arrangement but a large amount of wall area faces traffic.

(g) Use other buildings as shield, shortest wall faces noise source.

FIGURE 20-2 / Building orientation

ings, barrier walls and natural topography. Any barriers used, such as walls or other buildings, should be as close to the noise source and as high as possible.

In addition, the general layout and design must consider existing or possible future noises from surrounding areas. If there is an existing noise source—for example, noisy equipment used in an existing building—the general layout of the proposed building should place rooms which require quiet away from the existing noise and from noisy rooms. In the new building, perhaps the rooms for mechanical equipment may be placed closer to the noise source since they will not be affected by it. Figure 20-3 shows a suggested schematic solution to such a design problem.

Many times the site itself and the project being designed necessitate that the quiet areas must be located adjacent to a noise source. The noise can still be reduced by placing the solid walls on the side of the building facing the noise source and by placing the windows on the side facing quieter areas (Fig. 20-4). Still, the designer must be careful that sound doesn't enter through the windows by bouncing off an adjacent wall (Fig. 20-5).

ARRANGEMENT AND LAYOUT OF ROOMS

Noisy rooms should be separated from quiet rooms by as great a distance as possible. The building layout should be designed so that rooms which are not as susceptible to noise, such as closets and corridors, act as buffers or baffles between those areas which contain noise sources and those which require quiet (Fig. 20-6). The rooms from which the noise will originate should be located wherever noise from exterior sources may be expected. Quiet areas should be located as far as possible from exterior noise sources. As an example of separation of rooms, a conference room should not be placed next to manufacturing areas or even noisy business machine areas or secretarial pools.

The travel of sound between rooms may also be controlled by avoiding air paths in the placement and design of doors and windows (Fig. 20-7).

SHAPE OF ROOMS

The room proportions used will affect the sound reflection within the space. Room shapes to be avoided are long, narrow rooms or corridors with high ceilings and rooms

FIGURE 20-3 / Planning sound zones

FIGURE 20-4 / Sound shields   FIGURE 20-5 / Sound reflection

that are nearly cubical. Each of these conditions will cause excessive reverberation (sound reflection).

Ceilings which are domed or vaulted (or any concave surfaces) tend to focus the sound, causing it to be distorted. Large auditoriums with low ceilings also create a situation in which it is difficult for some of the audience to hear. Concave surfaces and large flat surfaces may be broken with splayed areas in order to diffuse the reflection of sound and to direct the sound as desired.

REFLECTING SURFACES

All walls, floors, ceilings, and furnishings have certain characteristics which control the amount of sound they will reflect and absorb. If the surfaces in a room tend to be highly reflective, the room will probably seem loud, and it may even have a slight echo. An example of a room with highly reflective surfaces is one with plaster ceilings and walls and a terrazzo floor. The highly reflective qualities of a room can be controlled by using materials which absorb a large amount of the sound, such as carpeting, heavy drapes, and stuffed, upholstered furniture. Acoustical tile is also commonly used when a highly absorbent material is desired. Acoustical tile is most frequently used on ceilings but it is an economical wall covering also.

ISOLATION OF VIBRATION

Since the structural elements of the building readily transmit sound throughout the building, no noisy or vibrating equipment should be attached to them. Equipment within the building, such as heating units, pumps, and motors, should be mounted on

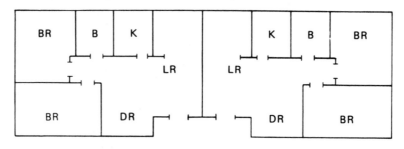

By mirroring (flopping over) the plan an approximately
equal noise level on each side of the wall for both
apartments is obtained.

(b) Closets, storage units, or
    book shelves may be used to
    act as buffers.

(c) Closet in bedroom
    acts as a noise buffer.

FIGURE 20-6 / Noise buffers

resilient machinery mounts and bases which are available. Soft, resilient subfloor
materials are often used under the wearing surface of the floors and under the equipment to reduce the transfer of vibration from the equipment to the structure.

Equipment located in the basement of a building may be placed on resilient
mounts and a "pad" of concrete which is isolated, by expansion joints, from the rest
of the floor. This is an example of discontinuous construction which is very effective
when it can be used.

Vibration noises from equipment are also transmitted through pipes, ducts, or
other similar conductors. The transmission of noise from the equipment, through these
noise conductors and into the various rooms may be reduced by providing a break
where they leave the equipment. Ducts and certain types of pipes may be "broken"
with flexible couplings and resilient connections (Fig. 20-8). Water pipes should be
provided with expansion valves, expansion tanks, and air chambers throughout the
system to reduce water hammering and knocking. Noise resulting from expansion and

(a)   Poor window placement

Corridor

(b)   Staggered doors offer more privacy than
doors opposite one another. Placing a
sound absorbing material on corridor walls
will reduce sound reflection.

FIGURE 20-7 / Doors and windows

contraction of the water pipes (usually a creaking and groaning sound) may be controlled by using expansion joints in the line.

ISOLATION OF IMPACT

Impact sound is that sound caused when one object strikes another. Typical examples of impact sound are footsteps, falling objects (such as shoes, toys, and machine parts), and hammering. When a structure is rigid and continuous, the sound easily travels through it. Impact noise may be controlled most effectively by using absorptive materials (such as carpeting), by isolating the noise sources (using discontinuous construction) (Fig. 20-9), and by reducing the possibility of flanking sounds (Fig. 20-10). The introduction of a masking or background sound (Sec. 20-5) should also be considered, but its effectiveness is limited when the sounds to be covered over are loud.

Isolation may be accomplished by separating the surface which will receive the impact from the structure supporting it. Floors may be isolated from the structure (Fig. 20-11) by using resilient subflooring and underlayment materials. Walls may be isolated from the structure by mounting the finish materials on resilient channels. The

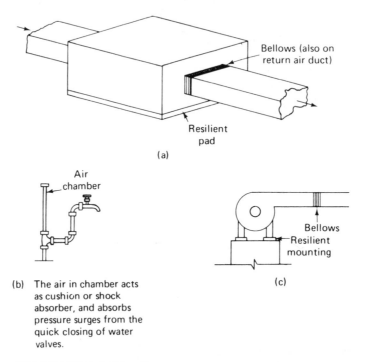

(a)

(b) The air in chamber acts as cushion or shock absorber, and absorbs pressure surges from the quick closing of water valves.

(c)

FIGURE 20-8 / Vibration

ceilings and walls in the surrounding spaces may also be mounted on resilient channels. Carpeting with a thick pad below it is one of the best absorptive materials in terms of reducing impact noises.

Flanking paths provide a channel through which the sound may easily travel. Rigidly connected electrical conduit, pipes, and air ducts are excellent examples of flanking paths. Walls which are continuous between floors, floors which are continuous from room to room, and structural elements which are continuous also provide flanking paths.

ISOLATION OF SOUND

The amount of airborne sound transmitted between rooms will depend on the materials and methods used in the construction. Sound transmission through walls depends on the mass (or unit weight) of the walls and on their inelasticity.

Massive, thick walls provide excellent sound barriers, but economically there is a point of diminishing returns. As the mass is doubled, the transmission of sound will be reduced by about 5 dB. Therefore, mass alone is not an economical solution.

The building of staggered stud walls with blanket insulation between the outer wall surfaces (Fig. 20-12) is also a method of sound control. Even slightly more

(a)

Resilient
mounting
Isolated concrete pad

Space may be filled
with expansion joint
filler

(b) Staggered wall

2 x 6
plate
Caulk

Flexible gasket

Metal curtainwall

MOTEL
ROOM

Masonry

MOTEL
ROOM

(c) Plan

MOTEL
ROOM

Walkway to
2nd floor
rooms

Railing

Precast or
poured-in-place
concrete

Resilient
pads

MOTEL
ROOM

MOTEL OR
APARTMENT

(d) Wall section

FIGURE 20-9 / Discontinuous construction

effective is the building of two separate walls with no structural connections between
them (Fig. 20-13). Another control method involves the use of resilient channels to
mount the wall covering surface, thus dissipating the sound energy in the channels.
These methods also have their practical limitations. For any given mass, as the air
space doubles, the transmission of sound is reduced about 5 dB (Fig. 20-14).

The practical, economical limit of sound reduction through walls is about 50 dB.
With the use of background masking noises, this reduction is adequate for most
conditions. At the same time, great care should be taken to eliminate as much sound
transmission as possible through flanking paths, air ducts, soffits, and items placed
back to back, such as medicine cabinets, electrical outlets and lighting fixtures. Sound
transmission through doors and door arrangements and through windows and window
arrangements must also be carefully considered in achieving noise control.

(a) Ductwork as a flanking path.
Insulation placed in the duct would
help reduce the noise.

OFFICE Air register

CORRIDOR ⊏========⊐ (Baffle)

Flanking path

Air register

Plan

Air register

Air plenum

Air register

Flanking path

OFFICE | CORRIDOR

Section

Above corridor used as air plenum

(b) Flanking path may be broken by:
1) Offset (staggered) registers and place insulation on walls of plenum.
2) Place baffle between the registers.

FIGURE 20-10 / Flanking paths

Room

Floor

Resilient pad

Supporting wood sleepers

FIGURE 20-11 / Isolated floors

FIGURE 20-12 / Staggered wall

Staggered wall with
insulation STC 50

20-5   BACKGROUND NOISES

An effective means of reducing the awareness of sound is to use background noise within the room. The illustrations in Fig. 20-15 show a typical example of the effect of background noise in masking undesirable sound. Many stores and restaurants use piped-in music to mask the noise of people working, traffic passing, and multiple conversations. Background noises are often introduced into very quiet "dead" rooms—for example, sleeping areas in nursing or rest homes or in residences on busy streets—where any noise, such as coughing, would be disturbing. They also provide a measure of privacy for speaking and telephone communications.

Acceptable levels of background noise range from 25 to 35 dB in bedrooms; 30 to 40 dB in living rooms, offices, and conference rooms; and 35 to 45 dB in large offices, reception areas, and secretarial areas. When background noises allowable to

FIGURE 20-13 / Double wall

Double wall
with insulation
STC 51

Air space	Sound transmission loss (decibels)
$\frac{3}{4}''$	30
$1\frac{1}{2}''$	35
$3''$	40
$6''$	45
$12''$	50

FIGURE 20-14 / Air space

such relatively high decibel ratings are combined with effective transmission ratings for walls and floors, it is possible to tolerate relatively high surrounding noise levels.

Background noises include piped-in music, radios, records, or even the noise made by hot air heating and air-conditioning systems in the building. The blowers on most heating and cooking units provide a background noise capable of masking many of the noises around us. While many blowers are set to automatically shut off when the thermostat does not call for heat or cooling, it is worth the small extra cost to have these blowers on all of the time to provide both background noise and air circulation.

FIGURE 20-15 / Background noise

Sound inaudible — the level of the sound must be brought at least 10 dB below the background noise to make it inaudible.

Materials and assemblies of materials are rated by a variety of different methods, each with its own meaning. The most common ratings are Sound Transmission Class (STC), Average Transmission Loss (TL), Noise Reduction Coefficient (NRC), Sound Absorption Coefficient at One Pitch (SAC), Impact Noise Rating (INR), and Impact Insulation Class (IIC).

SOUND TRANSMISSION CLASS (STC)

This rating represents the transmission loss performance of the construction over a broad range of frequencies. The results are plotted, and a standard curve based on human responses at the various measuring frequencies is used to determine the rating given. The higher the rating, the better the construction in terms of reducing the sound. This rating is considered one of the most dependable in measuring overall performance.

AVERAGE TRANSMISSION LOSS (TL)

The transmission loss performance of the construction is tested over a range of nine different frequencies. The results of these tests, at each frequency, are averaged together for a transmission loss rating. This does not take into account the fact that some people are more sensitive to noise in some of the frequency ranges than in others. It is possible that the construction does not provide the transmission loss desired at the proper frequencies.

NOISE REDUCTION COEFFICIENT (NRC)

This rating is used to measure the ability of a material to absorb sound rather than reflect it. Part of this absorbed sound is "killed" within the material, and part of it is passed through to the other side of the material. The NRC rating—which averages the absorption coefficients of the middle frequencies, rounded off to the nearest 5%—can theoretically range from 0 to 1, where a perfectly reflective material is rated at 1. If a material has an absorption rating of 0.25, the material will absorb 25% of any sound which strikes it and reflect 75% of the sound. When selecting materials, keep in mind that a difference of 0.10 in the NRC rating is seldom detectable in a completed installation.

SOUND ABSORPTION COEFFICIENT AT ONE PITCH (SAC)

This rating for sound absorption ability represents the peak performance for the material. It is not a representative rating of the material over the range of frequencies people hear. The SAC rating ranges from 0 to 1, similar to NRC.

IMPACT NOISE RATING (INR)

This system is used to rate the ability of floor-ceiling assemblies to resist the transmission of impact sound. Ratings are based on plus (+) and minus (−) ratings from a standard curve, with a plus rating indicating a better-than-standard performance and a minus rating indicating a less-than-standard performance. The standard (0) is based on average background noises that might exist in typical, moderately quiet, suburban apartments. An INR of +5 indicates that the assembly averages 5 dB better than the standard. Where louder background noises are found, as in urban areas, a minus INR (to about −5) rating may be used without any detrimental effects. In quieter areas, an INR rating of +5 to +10 would be used since not as much background noise is available to mask the sound. The disadvantages of this rating system are its lack of relationship to the STC ratings and the negative values, which tend to cause confusion in the use of INR.

IMPACT INSULATION CLASS (IIC)

This system is also used to rate the ability of floor–ceiling assemblies to resist the transmission of impact sound. IIC ratings are expressed in decibels and are more closely related to the STC ratings for airborne sound transmission than is the INR system. The IIC rating of any given assembly will be about 51 dB higher than its INR rating; therefore, an IIC rating of 61 would be comparable to an INR of +10. It should be noted that deviations can occur, and individual test data should be checked.

QUESTIONS

20-1. What is *sound transmission*?

20-2. If the sound level changes from 42 to 45 dB, how noticeable would it be to a person in the same room? What if the sound level changes from 42 to 52 dB?

20-3. How can the surrounding environment affect sound control?

20-4. What methods may be used to control and isolate vibration noises in buildings?

20-5. How can building orientation affect the sound level inside the building?

20-6. What is a *flanking sound path,* and how may this problem be avoided?

20-7. Define background noise. How is it used in controlling objectionable sound?

20-8. How can background noises be introduced into a space?

20-9. Why should the surrounding environment be checked before the building is designed?

20-10. How can the surrounding noise environment affect the design of a building?

APPENDIX A

N ←

80'-0"

2'-0"   76'-0"   2'-0"

BEDROOM   B   K   DINING   DINING   K   B   BEDROOM

11'-0"   8'-0"   5'-6"   13'-6"   15'-0"

W4   W3   W2

BEDROOM   LIVING   LIVING   BEDROOM

21'-0"   15'-0"

6'-0"   D1   D2   W1

36'-0"   40'-0"

UP   DN   5'-0"   13'-0"

DECK   DECK

2'-0"   2'-0"

EDGE OF ROOF

TYPICAL FLOOR PLAN

Design data

Apartment building, 4 story
Floor to floor height: 10'-0"
3-in. service main
Street main pressure: 50 psi
2 exterior hose bibs
Street main to riser distance: 60 ft.
Flat roof
Occupancy: 2.5 persons per apartment
Heat loss values (U)
    walls   0.13
    roof   0.71
    windows and doors   0.61
Cooling values (HTM)
    walls   3.1
    roof   2.9

SCHEDULE		
NO.	SIZE	TYPE
D1	3'-0" × 6'-8"	1¼" WOOD
D2	6'-0" × 6'-8"	ALUM.-SLIDING
W1	5'-0" × 4'-0"	WOOD-D.H.
W2	5'-0" × 3'-0"	"
W3	3'-0" × 4'-0"	"
W4	4'-0" × 4'-0"	"

SINGLE GLASS

TYPICAL FLOOR PLAN

Design data
Apartment building, 3 story
Floor to floor height: 9'-0"
3-in. service main
Street main pressure: 55 psi
3 exterior hose bibs
Street main to riser distance: 85 ft.
Flat roof
Occupancy: 1.5 persons per apartment

APPENDIX C

NORTHEAST ELEVATION

FLOOR PLAN

527

SHINGLES

SHEATHING

12

4

1/2" PLYWOOD

6" INSULATION (R-19)

1/2" GYPSUM BOARD

2'-0"

BRICK

3/4" AIR SPACE

1/2" PLYWOOD

3 1/2" INSULATION (R-11)

3/8" PLYWOOD

1/2" PLYWOOD

CARPET

3 1/2" INSULATION (R-11)

TYPICAL SECTION

SITE PLAN
1" = 20'

20 15 10 5
0 10 20 30

WINDOW SCHEDULE		
NO.	SIZE	TYPE
1	6'-0" x 5'-0"	CASEMENT
2	4'-0" x 3'-0"	"
3	3'-0" x 4'-0"	"
4	4'-0" x 4'-0"	"
5	2'-0" x 2'-0"	"

INSULATING GLASS

DOOR SCHEDULE		
NO.	SIZE	REMARKS
1,4,6	3'-0" x 6'-8"	
9,10	6'-0" x 6'-8"	
5	7'-0" x 8'-0"	
2,12	2-2'-6" x 6'-8"	
3,7,8,11 12,14,19	2'-8" x 6'-8"	
13,15,16 17,18,20	2'-4" x 6'-8"	

Design data
Occupancy: 2 adults, 4 children
Design temperature:
    heating: 10 F, 70 F
    cooling: 95 F, medium
Draperies, except kitchen
Roof, dark

APPENDIX D

FRONT ELEVATION

FLOOR PLAN

531

SHINGLES (DARK)
SHEATHING
FASCIA
SCREENED VENT
3/8" PLYWOOD
GRADE

12
4 |

RAFTER
CEILING JOIST
3½" INSULATION (R-11)
½" GYPSUM BOARD

1'-6"

2¼" INSULATION (R-7)
1" AIR SPACE
CARPETING
3/4" PLYWOOD
2" AIR SPACE
2¼" INSULATION (R-7)
FLOOR JOIST
SILL

TYPICAL WALL SECTION

100.0'

103

N

104

120.0'

120.0'

104

PROPOSED
HOUSE

103

100.0'

BELL VIEW RD.

SITE PLAN

WINDOW SCHEDULE		
NO.	SIZE	TYPE
1	2-3'-6"×4'-4"	WOOD, D.H.
2	3'-6" × 4'-4"	WOOD, D.H.

SINGLE GLASS

DOOR SCHEDULE		
NO.	SIZE	REMARKS
1,4	3'-0" × 6'-8"	WOOD & GLASS
6,9,11,13	2'-6" × 6'-8"	
2,3	2'-0" × 6'-8"	
16	1'-6" × 6'-8"	
8	5'-0" × 6'-8"	BIFOLD
5,7,10, 12,14,15	2'-4" × 6'-8"	

Design data
Location: Richmond, Va
Occupancy: 2 adults, 3 children
No window shading
Roof, dark

INDEX